# Brahmabandhab Upadhyay

## The Life and Thought of a Revolutionary

# Brahmabandhab Upadhyay
## The Life and Thought of a Revolutionary

Julius J. Lipner



DELHI
OXFORD UNIVERSITY PRESS
CALCUTTA CHENNAI MUMBAI
1999

*Oxford University Press, Great Clarendon Street, Oxford OX2 6DP*

Oxford New York
Athens Auckland Bangkok Calcutta
Cape Town Chennai Dar es Salaam Delhi
Florence Hong Kong Istanbul Karachi
Kuala Lumpur Madrid Melbourne Mexico City
Mumbai Nairobi Paris Singapore
Taipei Tokyo Toronto
*and associates in*
Berlin Ibadan



ISBN 0 19 564264 3

Typeset by Eleven Arts, Keshav Puram, Delhi 110 035
Printed in India at Pauls Press, Delhi 110 020
and published by Manzar Khan, Oxford University Press
YMCA Library Building, Jai Singh Road, New Delhi 110 001

This book is dedicated to

Sajal Bandyopadhyay

George Gispert-Sauch, s.j.

The Fathers of St Xavier's College, Calcutta,

past and present.

# Prologue

Binoy asked: 'Where is that India you speak of?'

Placing his hand on his breast, Gora said: 'There—where the compass within points to, night and day. Not in your Mr Marshman's History of India.'

Binoy said: 'Does your compass point to something real?'

Gora said with spirit: 'Of course it does! I may forget the way, I may founder, but that glorious harbour of mine does exist! Can it be that my India, perfect in every way—full of prosperity, of knowledge, of virtue—isn't real? That only the illusion we see about us exists: this city of yours—Calcutta—with its offices and lawcourts, this bubble of a few bricks and timber ...?

Can we ever find life in the midst of this mirage? We wither away in it with each passing day. There is a true India, a perfect India. Unless we take our stand there, try as we might with mind or heart, we shall never be able to draw upon the true sap of life. So I say everything else is false: the learning we get from books, the vanity of titles and degrees, the lure of craven livings! We must sail the ship towards that harbour by making light of such pulls. And if we drown in the attempt, so be it! But I can never forget that true, that perfect form of India!'

From *Gora* by Rabindranath Tagore

# Contents

# Note on Translations

Unless stated otherwise, all translations in this book are by the author. To save space, I have not always given in full the Bengali of the texts translated. Instead, somewhat arbitrarily no doubt, I have inserted the Bengali of what I have judged to be key words or phrases (as are likely to interest the reader) in the translation in parentheses.

There is no international convention for the transliteration of Bengali. I hope, however, that my use of diacriticals will enable those who know Bengali to decode the transliteration I have adopted. I have not used diacriticals for Bengali and Indian names, or for castes, scriptures, titles of works and publications in accordance with the publisher's policy. Diacriticals appear in transliterated text.

# Abbreviations

| | | |
|---|---|---|
| ABU | : | 'Āmār Bhārat Uddhār' (article by B. Upadhyay). |
| BCE | : | *Bombay Catholic Examiner.* |
| Bl. | : | *The Blade: Life and Work of Brahmabandhab Upadhyay,* by B. Animananda. |
| GLA | : | Goethal's Library Archives. |
| HA | : | 'Hindujātir Adhaḥpatan' (article by B. Upadhyay). |
| HE | : | 'Hindujātir Ekniṣṭhatā' (article by B. Upadhyay). |
| INB | : | *An Indian Nation-Builder: Brahmabandhab Upadhyay (1861–1907),* by B. Animananda (Rewachand Gyanchand). |
| K | : | Appendix *Ka* in UBBJ. |
| KC | : | *Kṛṣṇacaritra,* by Bankimcandra Chatterjee. |
| LOE | : | *Light of the East,* edited by G. Dandoy, s.j., in collaboration with P. Johanns, s.j. |
| OX9 | : | Letter by Upadhyay (April 9, 1903) to R. Tagore from Oxford. |
| *Report* | : | *Report of Native Newspapers in Bengal.* |
| RV | : | *Ṛg Veda.* |
| SK | : | *Sekele Kathā,* by Nistarini Devi. |
| SKT | : | Upadhyay's *Śrīkṛṣṇataṭtva* lecture. |
| *Sketch* | : | *Swami Upadhyay Brahmabandhav: A Sketch in Two Parts,* by B. Animananda. |

| | | |
|---|---|---|
| Sp-m | : | The monthly *Sophia*, edited by B. Upadhyay. |
| Sp-w | : | The weekly *Sophia*, edited by B. Upadhyay. |
| SWSB | : | *Speeches and Writings of Hon. Surendranath Banerjea (Selected by himself).* |
| TC | : | *The Twentieth Century*, edited by B. Upadhyay. |
| TS | : | 'Tin Śatru' (article by B. Upadhyay). |
| UBBJ | : | *Upādhyāy Brahmabāndhab o bhāratīya jātīyatābād*, by Uma and Haridas Mukhopadhyay. |

# Acknowledgements

Though it is not possible to mention everyone by name, I would like to thank all those who helped in the making of this book. In particular I would like to thank Sajal Bandyopadhyay, gifted Bengali poet and teacher of Bengali at St Xavier's School, Calcutta, with whom over the years, I have spent many hours in *āḍḍā* or friendly conversation, discussing, among other things, nuances of Upadhyay's Bengali. This book is dedicated to Sajal. I would also like to thank George Gispert-Sauch, s.j., Professor Emeritus of Indian and Systematic Theology at Vidyajyoti College of Theology, Delhi, for unstinting advice and hospitality. (George and I are co-editing a two-volume anthology of Upadhyay's writings in the Library of Indian Christian Theology series, published by The United Theological College, Bangalore.[1]) This book is also dedicated to George. Warm thanks are also due to Fr H. Rozario, Librarian of the Goethal's Library at St Xavier's, Calcutta, for allowing me the run of the Library and Archives during my regular visits;[2] Mr Roman Gomes, Chief Assistant at the Goethal's Library, who with unfailing cheerfulness and a Nelsonian eye, fostered my research (and, of late, Mr W. Brown, assistant to Mr Gomes); Swami Lokeshwarananda, gracious host during my visits to the Ramakrishna Mission and Institute of Culture, Gol Park, Calcutta; and Ms Abhaya Dasgupta, former Deputy Librarian at the Institute, for facilitating my studies so kindly and efficiently.

A special word of thanks to the managers of the Bethune-Baker and Burney Funds (Divinity Faculty, Cambridge University) for

1 Volume 1, *The Writings of Brahmabandhab Upadhyay,* with a Résumé of his Life and Thought, was published in 1991. After many delays, Volume 2 is nearing completion.

2 For a similar kindness I must mention Frs J. Erlich and Hous, former Librarians, now, alas, deceased.

generous assistance, to the Trustees of the Spalding Trusts, for their recurrent generosity in helping finance my visits to India, and to the Cambridge Committee for Christian Work in Delhi for inviting me to give the Teape Lectures under the Westcott Foundation, in India in 1981. In the intervening years numerous other commitments have come in the way, but at long last these lectures have formed the backbone for the flesh and blood of this book.

Finally, I thank the Jesuit Community of St Xavier's, Calcutta, who welcomed me as one of their own as I lived among them during my numerous research forays to Calcutta. Decades ago, many from this community, Indian and expatriate, had the dubious pleasure of educating me through school. Though most of these outstanding men have passed to their rest, I have always been inspired by the memory of their personal warmth and dedication. Their successors continue to serve the cause of education, religion and scholarship in India in exemplary fashion. Indeed, it was the Jesuits of St Xavier's, especially Fr P. Turmes, who had the sagacity and foresight (as ever) to preserve enough of Upadhyay's writings to make this study worthwhile. In gratitude and esteem then, for all that I owe, I also dedicate this work to them.

JJL<br>
Faculty of Divinity<br>
Cambridge<br>
1998

# Introduction

The cognoscenti, past and present, of various circles—historical, cultural, religious and political—all agree that Brahmabandhab Upadhyay (1861–1907) made a significant contribution to the shaping of the new India whose identity began to emerge from the first half of the nineteenth century. Rabindranath Tagore, that luminary of India's awakening as a nation and Upadhyay's contemporary (they were born in the same year), described him as 'a Roman Catholic ascetic yet a Vedāntin—spirited, fearless, self-denying, learned and uncommonly influential'.[1] Another, writing of Upadhyay's role in India's nationalist movement, declared: 'Vivekananda lit the sacrificial flame of revolution, Brahmabandhab in fuelling it, safeguarded and fanned the sacrifice'(Debsarma, B.E.1368:11).[2] Yet a third, referring to Upadhyay's pioneering attempt to Indianize Christianity, has called him a 'prophet disowned'.[3] Christian and Hindu, holy man and savant, prophet and revolutionary nationalist—Upadhyay is a figure of paradox. In writing this book I have sought not so much to resolve the paradox as to explain how it came about.

The list of notables in India who were forced to take stock of Upadhyay in one way or another is impressive. A few may be mentioned here: the 'Rev.' Kalicaran Banerji, Keshabcandra Sen and Pratapcandra Majumdar, Ramakrishna Paramahamsa and Swami

1 *Tini chilen romān kyāthlik sannyāsī apar pakṣe baidāntik—tejasvī, nirbhīk, tyāgī, bahuśruta o asāmānya prabhābśālī* —('influential' not least with respect to Tagore, as we shall see). From the Preface (*ābhās*) of the first edition of Tagore's *Car Adhyay*, p. i.

2 *Bibekānanda biplober yajñānal jvāliyāchilen, ār brahmabāndhab tāhāte habiḥ nikṣep kariyā sei agnihotrake rakṣā o barddhan kariyāchilen.*

3 See the title of C. Fonseca's article in *Vidyajyoti: Journal of Theological Reflection*, April 1980.

Vivekananda, Debendranath and Rabindranath Tagore, Annie Besant, Aurobindo Ghose and Bipincandra Pal. Not only in India but also in England, there were a number of lesser lights who had to come to terms with this formidable personality. Clearly, Upadhyay was in the thick of that complex cultural process we call India's 'freedom movement'. Yet how is it that lip-service apart, there has been so little critical, rounded study of a man one of the foremost Indians of modern times has described as 'uncommonly influential'? Several reasons come to mind.

Upadhyay resists neat pigeon-holing. It is difficult to make sense of him in terms of the disjunctive categories usually employed to interpret the social, religious and political phenomena of nineteenth century India. Was he a Hindu or a Christian? Surely he couldn't be both! Was he a reformer or a revivalist of Hinduism, of Christianity? He was tried for sedition, so was he a political extremist? One of 'us' or one of 'them'? Enigmas cloak the man.

Further, Upadhyay can be an embarrassing figure to contend with for would-be admirers. His chequered career can give rise to conflicting emotions. As we shall see, his indubitable patriotism seems to be tinged with unacceptably chauvinist sentiments, while in his at times original theological explorations, the spectre of unorthodoxy raises its head (What does it mean to be a 'Hindu-Catholic'?). Again, many Hindus do not take kindly to the claim that an important figure of India's struggle for independence kept a high profile as a Christian for a prolonged period of his life, while many Christians look askance at the prospect of a pioneer Indian Christian nationalist being referred to (not least by himself) also as a Hindu. There is an ill-concealed prickliness about Upadhyay that makes him hard to evaluate and potentially unattractive to tackle.

This prickliness is to the point in an India beset today by various crises of identity. Hindus and Christians in particular must grasp the nettle Upadhyay represents. What does it mean to be a Hindu, a Christian, an Indian today? An inquiry into the life and work of Upadhyay raises these questions in an acute form, and begins to shape answers. Christians especially need to be concerned. Culturally and religiously they have for the most part been an ambivalent minority in India. Now Upadhyay is becoming something of a cult figure among members of the Indian Christian intelligentsia. We have noted that he has been called a 'prophet disowned'. He has also been called the father of Indian (Christian) theology (see Aleaz, 1979: 77, 1994: 243). Buildings have been named after him in prestigious

Protestant and Catholic theological institutions.[4] Those interested in the process of indigenizing the Christian faith in India and elsewhere are looking to Upadhyay as a model for their purposes.

In the end this adulation may be justified. But it must rest on due discernment. Too often critical appreciation of the thinker is turned into uncritical veneration of the person, as if intellectual acumen invariably entails moral irreproachability. The problem with Upadhyay is that he tends to be held up on the basis of insufficient knowledge. Let me come clean and say that I believe he is an important man—in much, an admirable man. Yet in the course of this study I hope to present evidence—lost to sight hitherto—that may well give the cult makers pause for thought. If Christian churches are to take this remarkable man to heart, as well they might, he must be encountered face to face, 'warts and all'. That goes for his political and cultural admirers as well.[5]

Another reason why Upadhyay tends to elude scholarly attention is the inaccessible nature of his work. Upadhyay published much, but a significant part of his publications seems to be lost (especially from the Bengali journals he edited in his final years), and the bulk of what remains lies off the beaten track (mainly in the Goethal's Library at St Xavier's, Calcutta). A number of Bengali articles are scattered in various libraries in Bengal. Repressive measures by both the British government and the Catholic Church, the fact that much of Upadhyay's writings was directed at the literati and therefore had a relatively small circulation, and the fate of aging newsprint in the humid climate of West Bengal (the Goethal's Library material is in a precarious condition) account for the relative physical inaccessibility of the Upadhyay corpus.[6] Of the Bengali, sufficient remains in the

4 For example, in the United Theological College in Bangalore and in the Papal Seminary in Pune respectively.

5 Recently, Upadhyay has returned to Bengali attention. A series of letters in Bengali written by him during a visit to England and first published in the *Bangabasi* (November 1902 to September 1903) was reprinted in a well-known Calcutta newspaper, the *Bartaman* (see Sunday June 3, 1990 and following Sundays).

6 'As to *Sandhya* [a Bengali newspaper edited by Upadhyay] all our efforts at discovering a set have proved useless. The work of destruction by the police has been done ruthlessly': Turmes in his Preface to *The Blade* (Animananda:ii). Various sightings of parts or complete sets of the originals of Upadhyay's Bengali journals have been reported, but like the Loch Ness Monster, have not yet been run to ground. Sajanikanta Das (B.E.1368: 521–9) says that quite a number of editorial articles from the *Sandhya* had recently come to hand, together with many complete issues of the paper (p. 524). He continues that he would be making all of these available in due course

original or in translation for us to accurately gauge its content and influence. Most of the English writings are extant. Thus, we have the basis to undertake a considered study of Upadhyay's work.[7]

As to the inaccessibility of Upadhyay's thought, that is determined by the wide range of his concerns and is compounded by the complexity of the times in which he lived. Like so many of the prominent English-educated Bengali thinkers of his day, Upadhyay wrote substantially in two languages. These were English, the lingua franca of the Indian intelligentsia, and Bengali, his mother tongue, which was developing as a means to assert Bengali nationalist identity.[8] In addition, Upadhyay also wrote some significant Sanskrit verse. Further, he shows familiarity with neo-Thomistic and other western thinking as well as with traditional and contemporary Hindu ideas. Thus, first-hand research on Upadhyay requires a range of competences.

Upadhyay is also apt to be misunderstood. After his conversion he sought passionately to show, by pen and by deed, that by becoming Christian he had not ceased to be a patriotic Hindu. The tension inherent in this claim tended to mislead, in Upadhyay's time, and it does so today. It does not facilitate a balanced assessment of the man.

These reasons then, severally or in combination, have militated against objective, rounded studies of Upadhyay. The temptation is to deal with him selectively or by over-simplification or by silence. This leads us to inquire into some of the main studies available on our subject.[9]

---

(and reprints a few of the editorials in the article). I have not been able to ascertain how many issues of *Sandhya* he had in his possession, or how many of the editorials (if indeed they were all by Upadhyay) were finally published. Death seems to have prevented Das from completing his project.

7 As noted in the Preface, G. Gispert-Sauch and the author are preparing an anthology of Upadhyay's writings in two volumes. Though this anthology will not be exhaustive, it will be fairly comprehensive. Volume 1 has been published (with a Résumé of Upadhyay's Life and Thought by the author); volume 2 will have the Bengali content of the publication. One of the major reasons for the delay in publishing this volume has been not only the translation but the laborious (and sometimes fortuitous) collection of Upadhyay's scattered Bengali writings.

8 In spite of numerous stylistic innovations taking place at the time, to which Upadhyay contributed, this Bengali was often markedly Sanskritized.

9 With increasing frequency, Upadhyay is also being briefly mentioned or commented upon by historians, theologians and others as they focus on a variety of concerns. Though I shall use such material where relevant, I shall not make a survey of it.

In the Bengali works, Upadhyay is generally regarded primarily as a Hindu patriot from a social or political point of view, while his allegiance to the Christian faith is underplayed as an aberration or as of little account. Where his Christian commitment is not underrated, the work is largely silent about it. Prabodhcandra Simha's biography *Upādhyāy Brahmabāndhab,*[10] the first in Bengali, and Uma and Haridas Mukhopadhyay's *Upādhyāy Brahmabāndhab o bhāratīya jātīyatābād* ('Brahmabandhab Upadhyay and Indian Nationalism', 1961, hereafter UBBJ) do not come to terms with Upadhyay the Christian. They imply that his conversion to the Christian faith was not a true conversion and concentrate on other matters. Bolai Debsarma's *Brahmabāndhab Upādhyāy*[11] is a pastiche of reminiscences and scarcely nods in the direction of Upadhyay's Christian concerns. The same attitude prevails in Jogescandra Bagal's *Brahmabāndhab Upādhyāy.*[12] Significantly, it begins as follows: 'Brahmabandhab Upadhyay is very well known to the Bengali as someone who was an ascetic political leader.'[13] Manoranjan Guha's slim volume *Brahmabāndhab Upādhyāy* (1976, B.E. 1383) is more balanced; it does not belittle Upadhyay's Christian commitment but it also does not discuss the theological issues involved (nor does it take account of much relevant data).[14] However, I hope to show that any study of Upadhyay that seeks to do him justice must take his Christian concerns and commitment seriously and cannot forbear to analyse them, and that the rationale underlying his self-description as a 'Hindu-Catholic' was pivotal to his life.

[10] No date, but post-1908 and well before 1946, the dates of the two English biographies by Animananda. Its style and tone indicate that it was published not much later than the late 1920s. Besides, Turmes notes in *The Blade* (1946) that Animananda's first biography and 'Prabodh Chandra Simha [sic] have been out of print for many years' (Preface, p. i). In 1904 Simha helped Upadhyay run the Sarasvata Ayatan—Upadhyay's school for boys in Calcutta, conducted on traditional lines.

[11] See note 2. Except for some material added later by the author, this book was first published serially in the monthly journal *Prabarttak* in 1938.

[12] First published in *Śanibārer Ciṭhi* (1963, B.E. Paus 1370: 195–216), and then published as a separate booklet with minor changes and Appendices, in 1964 (B.E. 1371). References are taken from the latter.

[13] *Brahmabāndhab upādhyāy ekjan sarbbatyāgī rājnaitik netā baliyā bāṅgālīr nikaṭ samadhik prasiddha:* p. 5.

[14] He wrote in a letter to me (dated August 5, 1979), 'I wrote a small book on [Upadhyay] but without being able to look into the material lying with the Jesuit Fathers.'

The Christian source material, on the other hand, tends to show embarrassment or hostility in respect of Upadhyay's 'Hinduness' or the socio-political involvement of his last years. In any case, commentators in general, Christian or Hindu, fail to grasp the ideological thrust—nationalist in the broad sense—of Upadhyay's Christian conversion from its inception.

The first English biography we have—the first biography of any kind—is *Swami Upadhyay Brahmabandhav: A sketch in two parts* (hereafter *Sketch*, 1908[15]), by Rewachand Gyanchand (1868–1945). Rewachand, a Sindhi, wrote under the name of 'Brahmachari Animananda,' which he assumed after he became a Roman Catholic. He had been converted by Upadhyay and was his close companion from about 1891 till 1904. Animananda himself was a remarkable man.[16] Loyal to Upadhyay's memory (we are told by one who knew him well that Upadhyay was his 'guru'), he wrote the *Sketch* as much to convince himself as others that Upadhyay remained a Catholic to the end.[17] The *Sketch*, now practically unavailable, was intended by Animananda to be superseded by his later biography. However, it contains some information not published elsewhere.

In 1928, Alfons Väth s.j. published his *Im Kampfe mit der Zauberwelt des Hinduismus*,[18] much of which is concerned with Upadhyay. Väth comments that the 'apologetical intention' of the *Sketch* was too evident, Part II having been written 'to defend Upadhyay's later views and to prove that he remained Catholic to the end'. Further, Väth accuses Animananda of having been selective with the sources.[19]

15 Published by its author (under the name of 'B. Animananda' in Part II), Calcutta. Part I is entitled, 'A Story of his Life' and Part II, 'A Study of his Religious Position'.

16 There is a pamphlet on his life, *A Teacher of Genius: B. Animananda*, by P. Turmes, s.j., 1963.

17 See the *Sketch*, Part II, pp. 3–5. Turmes also admits as much: 'Part II ... 'The Character of his Faith', minutely enumerates all the signs showing Brahmabandhab's Catholic Faith' (Turmes, 1963: 46).

18 The full title is *Im Kampfe mit der Zauberwelt des Hinduismus: Upadhyay Brahmabandhav und das Problem der Überwindung des höheren Hinduismus durch das Christentum*.

19 'Die apologetische Absicht tritt zu stark hervor. Hauptzweck des zweiten Teiles der Schrift ist es, die späteren Anschauungen Upadhyayas zu verteidigen und den Beweis zu führen, dass er bis zum Ende katholisch blieb ... hat er [Animananda], so scheint es, aus seinen Quellen zu einseitig ausgewählt, was zugunsten seines Helden spricht' (p. 10).

As we have indicated, there is some truth in these charges. But Väth himself seems to have written with an ulterior motive. In a volume of data on Upadhyay in the Archives of the Goethal's Library, a note prefaces the transcript of a short but somewhat unsympathetic account of Upadhyay prepared by a Sindhi, Khemchand Amritrai Mirchandani. Khemchand had followed Upadhyay into the Catholic Church in Sind but later became disillusioned with his mentor. The note has it that Khemchand's account was written 'at the request of Rev. Fr Vath s.j., who wrote from Germany that a Catholic priest who had apostatized to Protestantism [a Dr F. Heiler], was proclaiming there that the Catholic hierarchy in India had been very intolerant and unjust to Upadhyay and that this was an illustration of the usual policy of the Church'.[20]

Reading between the lines, one concludes that it was a major aim of Väth's book to refute Heiler's accusation and defend the way Upadhyay was treated by Catholic ecclesiastical authority. Väth himself notes that in his book *Sadhu Sundar Singh, ein Apostel des Ostens und Westens,* Heiler holds 'petty fanatics' ('engherzige Zeloten' is Heiler's expression) responsible for the failure of Upadhyay's life's work[21]—a charge, he points out, Heiler repeats in his later work *Christlicher Glaube und indisches Geistesleben,* in which Upadhyay is given more attention (Väth,1928: 10–11). Väth finds it 'incomprehensible' that Heiler could make so grave an accusation without first 'having studied the sources'. From his own work, he claims, it will be clear why it was inevitable that ecclesiastical authority had to intervene against Upadhyay's journalistic endeavours.[22] In fact, in

20 See the Goethal's Library Archives (GLA), *Varia* I, pp. 118ff. In the Introduction to his book Väth describes as most valuable an article 'in which Mr Khemchand Amritrai, a disciple and longstanding co-worker of Upadhyay's, writes down his thoughts on his revered master and the changes he went through': 'Wertvoll ... ist vor allem ein längeres Schriftstück, worin Herr Khemchand Amritrai, ein Schüler und langjähriger Mitarbeiter Upadhyayas, seine Gedanken über den verehrten Meister und dessen Wandlungen niederlegt' (p. 12). Khemchand's account is given as an Appendix in Hull, n.d.: 517–21.

21 There is an abridged English translation of this work, entitled *The Gospel of Sadhu Sundar Singh* (published in a limited edition as part of the Sadhu Sundar Singh Centenary Celebrations by The ISPCK, Delhi and the Christian Institute for Sikh Studies, Batala, 1989); on p. 249 we read: '[Upadhyay's] life-work ... was ruined by the opposition of the Roman hierarchy. Narrow-minded fanatics not only condemned his ideas, but even forbade him to exercise any religious and theological activity.'

22 'Es ist unbegreiflich, wie Prof. Heiler seine schweren Vorwürfe gegen indische Oberhirten erheben konnte, ohne die Hauptquellen studiert zu haben. ... Da wird es uns klar, warum es zu einem Einschreiten seitens der kirchlichen Behörde gegen seine Zeitschriften kommen musste' (p. 11).

his book Väth concluded, after having intimated to the contrary in a letter to Animananda, that Upadhyay may well have apostatized,[23] and that in any case his ideas on indigenizing the faith were on the whole misguided. Thus, it is difficult not to draw the conclusion that Väth had his own axe to grind in writing his book.[24]

Väth's book greatly disconcerted Animananda. We are told that he was dissatisfied with Väth's 'strange interpretation...[of] the facts. On reading Vath, Animananda set to work again' (Animananda, 1946: i) to 'vindicate his guru' (Turmes,1963: 59). This labour materialized, in 1946, in the form of a more comprehensive biography of Upadhyay called *The Blade: Life and Work of Brahmabandhab Upadhyay* (hereafter Bl.).[25] In fact the research was undertaken to offset not only Väth's book but criticism of Upadhyay and his methods arising from publication of the *Sketch* and an article by Animananda on Upadhyay in November 1922 in the journal *Light of the East* (edited by G. Dandoy s.j. in collaboration with P. Johanns s.j.). Animananda was encouraged in this work by a Belgian Jesuit then teaching in

23 Turmes (1963: 71) quotes from the letter in English: 'You need not be afraid that my book will be unfavourable to the Swami. I agree in general with his ideas ... he was thirty years in advance of his times.... I firmly believe with you that he died a Catholic at heart.' This was in 1926. But in his book published two years later, Väth casts doubt as to whether Upadhyay remained a Catholic to the last. He says in the Foreword: 'And he was once a Christian.... It is therefore profoundly to be regretted that this ... richly gifted man became in his final years more and more a stranger to his Church and once again had strong leanings towards paganism, though we may have to admit that in his own conscience he felt a child of his Church till the very end.' 'Und er war einst ein Christ.... Es ist deshalb tief zu bedauern, das der. ... reich begabte Mann in seinem letzten Jahren der Kirche immer mehr ein Fremder wurde und wieder stark zum Heidentum hinneigte, wiewohl wir annehmen dürfen, dass er sich vor seinem Gewissen bis zuletzt als Kind seiner Kirche fühlte.' Turmes says that Väth's book came as a shock to Animananda (1963: 71), yet Väth finds much to praise in Upadhyay and in many ways has written a useful book.

24 In fact, in an article entitled 'Fr Vath on Upadhyay Brahmabandhav' (*Indian Theological Studies*, September 1993), Y. de Steenhault s.j. shows, under various headings, Väth's somewhat supercilious bias against Upadhyay regarding the latter's struggle against ecclesiastical authority.

25 Though the publisher gives no date, we can deduce that *The Blade* was published in 1946 from a reference to the year of publication at the end of the Preface to Turmes (1963). In GLA there is a typescript with the heading, 'An Indian Nation-Builder: Brahmabandhab Upadhyay (1861–1907) by B. Animananda (Rewachand Gyanchand)' (hereafter INB). Presumably this was the prototype of *The Blade*. Though INB contains a little extra information (and apparently no factual discrepancies), clearly *The Blade* was intended to be and must be treated as the authoritative version for general reference.

Calcutta, P. Turmes, who recognized the importance of Upadhyay. After doing most of the research Animananda died—the book still unfinished 'when the pen dropped from his hand in January 1945' (Bl. p. ii). Some weeks earlier Animananda had made over his notes and papers[26] to Turmes, who then edited, completed and published the book under Animananda's name. Notwithstanding its apologetical intention, *The Blade* remains the best biographical source we have for Upadhyay, except perhaps for the last few years of his life (for those, Bengali sources, especially UBBJ, come into their own).

But did Väth himself make use of all the sources? He did not know Bengali, so he was unable to use Upadhyay's Bengali publications directly. He writes: 'For the last four years of his life, when Upadhyay wrote mainly in Bengali, we must rely entirely on Animananda,' and continues, 'But in the year 1903 Upadhyay's transformations had in essence come to an end. He had already taken that turning which was to draw him ever further from the Church though without the link being entirely snapped' (p. 12).[27] But well before 'the last four years,' Upadhyay was writing in Bengali, nuancing his ideas in a way that had no exact parallel in his English writings. Moreover, Bengali sources about Upadhyay intimate one or two twists in his road, post-1903, which give a fuller picture of what he was about.

This brings us to Animananda. He had parted from Upadhyay in 1904, when Upadhyay was well into what we may call his 'nationalist phase', and so was no longer the latter's close companion. Though Animananda is said to have had a complete record of Upadhyay's works and no doubt knew Bengali (how proficiently is uncertain[28]),

26 See Bl., Preface, p. ii. Presumably (with additions from Turmes—and others?) these were preserved in GLA in the form of five volumes of *Varia*.

27 'Nur für die letzten vier Lebensjahre, wo Upadhyay hauptsächlich Bengali schrieb, sind wir auf Animananda allein angewiesen. Aber im Jahre 1903 waren Upadhyays Wandlungen im wesentlichen abgeschlossen. Er hatte schon den Irrweg betreten, der ihn immer weiter von der Kirche entfernte, ohne indes die Verbindung ganz abzubrechen.'

28 '[Animananda] possessed a complete collection of Upadhyay's works both in English and Bengali. When the police came to ransack his school for 'seditious literature', he made a bonfire of it all' (Turmes, 1963: 71). I have in my possession the carbon copy of an undated, single sheet of typescript (approximately A4 size) entitled 'Shri A Hazra's testimony concerning Brahmabandhab Upadhyay'. The opening paragraph reads: 'I, Shri Anthony Hazra, was known in the school of Swami Animananda as Dinabandhu Hazra.... My master was known as Brahmachari Animananda. It was in the year 1931 that one day he told me to go to the first floor of the building

his apologetical concerns and his sometimes puzzling silences about aspects of Upadhyay's Bengali writings (silences that would have been grist to the unsuspecting Väth's mill) must affect to some extent the comprehensiveness and reliability of his biographies.

This study of Upadhyay is not intended to be definitive, of course, or even exhaustive. The complexity of the man and continuing research into the no less complex nature of his times render any pretensions to 'definitive' studies in these areas hollow. Further, as I shall indicate later, there are aspects of Upadhyay's thought we shall not go into. I have but sought to inquire searchingly into someone who I believe is richly deserving of study and of whom various reasons have conspired to make a shadowy figure in the world of scholarship. To this end I have quoted extensively, not least from Upadhyay. Let the man speak for himself.

In time and place, Upadhyay stands at the crossroads of the new India. He has been hailed as a signpost for the way forward by disparate, sometimes opposing groups: nationalists, reformers, revivalists, indigenizers of the Christian faith. Perhaps this study will bring to life someone who by his life and work illuminates not only the different concerns to which he was dedicated, but also the ways in which we ourselves may come to terms with the diverse forces that confront us in this increasingly cross-cultural world.

---

where his room was, to open his almirah [cupboard] and find a bundle of papers of deep orange colour called Sandhya.... He ordered me to burn them, as they were the papers edited by the famous nationalist Upadhyaya BrahmaBandhab [sic] written against the British.... My master had a secret information that a C.I.D. of the govt. [sic] would come in search of the papers the next day and arrest him.' At the bottom the typescript has (in type), 'Anthony Hazra (Anthony Dinabandhu Hazra), an ex-student of 'Boys' Own Home' and a retired teacher of St. Lawrence High School, Ballygunge, Calcutta.' Animananda would have needed Bengali for his teaching career in Bengal, but whether he commanded the Bengali styles in which Upadhyay wrote (Sanskritized and highly colloquial, depending on context) is another question.

# Chapter 1

# The Crucible: Setting the Scene

Bhabanicaran Bandyopadhyay, known to posterity as Brahmabandhab Upadhyay, was born in 1861 in a village not far from Calcutta. Calcutta was then the capital not only of the Province of Bengal but of the whole of British India. With hindsight one could see that it was becoming the focus of Indian nationalism. Around 1861, however, the nationalist process, such as it was, was still pupate. There were scant signs politically of the India coming to birth.[1] In this chapter we consider some of the main influences—economic, social, political and religious—that shaped the Calcutta-centred Bengal of Upadhyay's birth and prepared the ground for his formative years.

In actuality forces like those we have mentioned are intertwined and are expressed in composite ways. It was no different in nineteenth-century Bengal. However, if distinguish we must, before the middle of the century tension was mounting between the Bengali and the Britisher more on social and religious than on other fronts. This is not to say that there was no political confrontation between them. We shall see that there was. But there was lacking among a truly representative swathe of Bengalis that sense of a common history and destiny, the recognition of an inalienable right to self-rule, which characterize a modern 'nationalist' consciousness.[2] Instead, regroupings

1 Thus the Bengal Indigo riots of 1859–62 were devoid of nationalist overtones: they were peasant protests against oppression from British and Indian vested interests (see Kling, 1966).

2 I realize that this notion of nationalism is itself problematical. On the kind of construction of individual and collective self-identity that it entails, see, e.g., A. Nandy, 1994.

of different kinds were taking place among socially leading Bengalis. These eventually developed, in the late nineteenth century, into an intricate linkage of ideas and events that became the vanguard of Indian nationalism. Let us inquire into some of the main conditions that allowed, or perhaps prompted, these regroupings to come about, before we go on to consider those that concern us most.

The Permanent Settlement in Bengal of 1793 under Lord Cornwallis, the governor-general, had a permanent effect on the upper-class[3] Bengali. It resulted in the fragmentation of the land, the break-up of most of the large, traditional zamindari or landholding houses, a complicated and multi-tiered revenue-collecting process, and (by the early 1800s) in the creation of some large nouveau-riche zamindars or landholders but of many middling and small ones.[4] It is doubtful whether the grim lot of the ryot or cultivator at the bottom of the heap improved in any appreciable way, but to survive the zamindars themselves now had to function in what was effectively a new milieu. The division, subdivision and inheritance of land, in the context of the British assumptions about landed rights and the dispensation of justice that underlay the Settlement,[5] gave them a litigious mentality. In pursuing this bent they realized that it was useful to learn English.

In this context let us take note of an important development in the Bengal of the time. This was the growing social and political divide among upper-class Bengalis—religiously there had always been a gap—between Hindus and Muslims.[6] The Muslims did not take kindly to the prospect of accommodating to British ways, whereas the Hindus increasingly did. The Hindus had nothing to lose. New rulers were being substituted for old: in the process the Hindus could

3 'Upper-class' and 'upper-caste' are to be understood as largely but not entirely co-extensive expressions. 'Upper-caste', used loosely here, refers exclusively to Hindus (especially Brahmins, Baidyas and Kayasthas). 'Upper-class' includes some Muslims and those Hindus (e.g. wealthy but technically lower-caste) who, unlike the groups mentioned above, had only social or economic claims.

4 On the Permanent Settlement, see Marshall (1987: 119ff and chapter 5). On the rise of a landholder in the Settlement's aftermath, see N. Mukherjee, 1975.

5 For a good analysis of these assumptions, see Stokes, 1959.

6 Muslims formed about a third of the Province's population and about half of the population of Bengal proper, which included 'the districts of Burdwan, Birbhum, Bankura, Midnapore, Hooghly, Howrah, Twenty-Four Parganas, Nadia, Murshidabad, Jessore and Khulna, as well as those comprised by the Divisions of Dacca, Chittagong and Rajshahi (except Darjeeling), the district of Malda and the State of Hill Tippera' (H. and U. Mukherjee, 1958: 3).

gain. The Muslims, however, were losing the ascendancy they had had over Hindus under effective Mughal and Nawab rule. So long as Persian and Urdu, which were culturally more congenial to them, continued as languages of administration under British rule, they could make a go of it. But they were psychologically unprepared for the encroachment of English education, the more so when the British made English the language of preferment in the mid-1830s. After this, upper-class Muslim fortunes, already on the wane, declined rapidly in the Presidency.[7]

The Hindus for their part were throwing off a familiar and irksome yoke with no future, apparently for a future of promise. And if it meant accommodating to one alien regime instead of another, they were prepared to do it. This is why, to put it rather simplistically, Hindu and Muslim grew apart in the circumstances. As we shall see, it was the Hindus who capitalized on English education. In general, they would now make the running for representative government and then self-rule, for the social and religious reform that would characterize the new India. In time this gave them a privileged place in the echelons of power. We are all too familiar with the latter-day consequences of this rift. High-caste Bengali converts to Christianity who were active in the birth of nationalism generally threw in their lot with the Hindus (Lipner in Coward, 1987). Upadhyay, born and brought up a Brahmin, was no exception. We have good reason then for focusing on relevant (upper-class) Hindu activity in this chapter.

Many of the newly formed Hindu zamindars became absentee landlords. Not given traditionally to working or improving the land, and in many instances needing to supplement the meagre income from their holdings, they looked for jobs in the British orbit—as clerks, pleaders, doctors, lawyers, teachers, journalists, relatively junior civil servants and police personnel (the top posts were reserved for the British), and so on. The demand for these jobs took time, of course, to build up. It was exacerbated by the fact that with few exceptions, the Bengali was slowly being squeezed out of opportunities for commercial enterprise. External trade was largely in European hands,

7 As indicated in the *Report of the Council of Education, Bengal Presidency, for 1851–52*, which notes: 'The important subject of the continued failure of all our efforts to impart a high order of English education to the Moohummudan community, still occupies the anxious attention of the Council', and 'During the past year there were in the Government Institutions of Bengal, including the Vernacular Schools, upwards of 11,000 pupils, of whom 103 were Christians, 791 Moohummudans, 189 Arakanese, Mugs, Bhaugulpore Hill boys, and Coles, and the rest Hindus'; p. xlii.

while Bengalis faced stiff competition from other Indians where internal trade was concerned. Further, in the advanced sector of the economy, the crash of 1847 was a blow from which the Bengali businessman never recovered (Kling in R. Van M. Baumer, 1975). From the early 1800s, then, upper-class Bengalis felt an increasing need to come to terms culturally with the British to earn a living. The pressure to learn English and understand English ways was mounting.

The stimulus to anglicize the Bengali came from two sources: the missionary and the administrator. Among the missionaries, pre-eminent in this regard from the beginning of the century were the British Baptist trio, William Carey (1761–1834), Joshua Marshman (1768–1837) and William Ward (1769–1823). They were based in Serampore, a Danish enclave some 14 miles from Calcutta.[8] From there they plunged into an extraordinary ministry of service whose effect was felt well beyond Serampore in space and time. With the help of pundits they translated the whole or parts of the Bible into numerous Indian and other oriental languages. They undertook research not only on the customs, beliefs and language of the Bengalis (helping standardize Bengali as written prose), but also on other aspects of their environment (e.g. Carey was an expert botanist). They pioneered and perfected printing techniques for the dissemination of their translations, books and tracts, publishing among other things the first Bengali newspaper. They preached to non-Christians and to Christians. They opened schools run on English lines, and taught in various institutions of higher learning.[9] They championed the cause of the poorest of the ryots vis-à-vis the government and the zamindar. In short, they generally made their missionary, scholarly, literary, educational, political and socially concerned presence felt. It is incumbent on one to acknowledge this for their contribution to the making of modern Bengal has often been underrated.[10]

In the opening decades of the nineteenth century it was the Seramporists in particular among the missionaries who took the

8 A residence of convenience, since it was not till 1813 that the East India Company permitted missionaries to practise their calling in the territories it administered.

9 Thus Carey became Professor of Sanskrit and Bengali at the College of Fort William in Calcutta, which was sponsored by the East India Company.

10 For a detailed account of the work of the Serampore trio, see E. Daniel Potts, 1967. For a more general treatment of the Serampore mission, see Stephen Neill, 1985: ch. 9, and Brian Stanley, 1992: ch. 2.

leading role in establishing English education in Bengal from primary school upwards. Here 'English education' means not only the teaching of English but also the infusion of western ideas along English lines. They saw good reason for this. As evangelical Protestants they found it theologically more difficult than Roman Catholics, for example,[11] to countenance non-Christian, especially 'heathen' religions. As the religion of the majority in the land, Hinduism was their chief target. They deplored Hinduism and its cultural expressions. They subscribed to the view that contemporary Hinduism was socially, morally and theologically irredeemable.[12] Socially, Hindus were prey to casteism, ritualism and 'beastly practices' such as infanticide and suttee; morally, Hindus had a predilection for lying, laziness and debauchery, and theologically Hindus were either polytheistic idolators or arrogant monists. In short, these missionaries lived and preached a puritanical faith in whose eyes Hinduism was a tissue of falsehood and spiritually debilitating, whereas Christianity was spiritually uplifting and in accord with the emergent truths of western scientific inquiry. The missionaries believed that it was through the medium of English that they could disseminate western ideas of history, physics, geography and ethics, as well as Bible knowledge and Christian doctrine. Scientific and religious knowledge would go hand in hand. In the process they would counter the invidious influence, as they saw it, of the *tol* or native seminary in which Sanskrit and its fantastic religion-orientated notions of astrology, law, metaphysics and morals were inculcated, the very basis of the Hinduism they sought to discredit.[13]

The Seramporists realized that Bengali could not be dispensed with as a medium of instruction: the level of English attained by those who studied it in their schools was on the whole low. But their concern for the vernacular was largely as a vehicle for the communication

[11] Later we shall elaborate on the theological implications of this distinction.

[12] In this they shared the stance of a prominent member of the Clapham Sect, Charles Grant (senior), as expressed in his influential work, *Observations on the State of Society among the Asiatic Subjects of Great Britain, particularly with respect to Morals, and on the means of Improving It; written chiefly in the Year 1792*, but published in 1797. Grant played a major role in setting the terms of the East India Company's renewed Charter of 1813, especially as to the de-restriction of missionary activity in the territories the Company administered. For a review of Grant's *Observations* and the extent of its influence see Trautmann, 1997: 101f.

[13] This policy included the Muslims. Before very long, however, Christian missionaries would have to contend with rationalist agnosticism and atheism that would also influence young Indian minds through the English medium.

of western ideas and their faith. Hence their labours, especially Carey's, to make Bengali a suitable means for the job. And English education was to be the medium for dispelling false Hindu notions about reality so that ideally their charges would be receptive to 'true' Christian teaching about God.[14] To preside at the apex of their educational work the Baptists in 1818 founded Serampore College which still stands, 'as an institution where Indians could be thoroughly trained for missionary service and thus enabled to work alone' (Potts, 1967: 33).[15] In one way or another, Upadhyay was much influenced by or involved in Catholic and Protestant missionary activity both educationally and religiously.

British administrators and policy-makers of influence too had economic, political and, in some cases, religious reasons for anglicizing the upper-class Bengali. For Charles Grant (the elder)[16] and W. Wilberforce, influential in framing Company policy in the early nineteenth century, the interests of duty and British commerce happily converged in their call for anglicization. With familiar logic they argued that Hinduism in particular was degenerate. Hindus needed to be civilized by British law, British ideas and hopefully British religion through the medium of English. This process should produce a population appreciative of British tastes and goods, and trade, greatly to Britain's advantage, would thrive.[17] But this argument was opposed by those among the British who valued traditional oriental learning and education in India. This anglicist-orientalist debate came to a head when Thomas Babington Macaulay, recently arrived in India, was made President of the Committee formed to decide future government policy for higher education in the country.[18]

[14] 'In common with almost all evangelicals of their day, the Serampore missionaries possessed an unshakable belief that the dissemination of useful knowledge must in itself promote the ultimate advance of the gospel' (Stanley, 1992: 51).

[15] It took many years for the College to realize its aims.

[16] See note 12 and S. Neill, 1985: 146–8 for relevant comments on Grant.

[17] Stokes, ch. 1, analyses the argument.

[18] The Committee of Public Instruction, 'which was divided, five against five, on either side of [the] controversy.... Half of the members were for maintaining and extending the old scheme of encouraging Oriental learning by stipends paid to students in Sanscrit, Persian, and Arabic; and by liberal grants for the publication of works in those languages. The other half were in favour of teaching the elements of knowledge in the vernacular tongues, and the higher branches in English' (Trevelyan, 1901:290). There is an account of Macaulay's role in this debate, pp. 290–2. On the controversy see also ch. 2 of *British Paramountcy and Indian Renaissance*, Part II: vol. X of R.C. Majumdar (ed.), 1965, and Kopf in Cannon and Brine, 1995: 146ff.

Macaulay, anglicist spokesman *par excellence*, noted in his classic Education Minute of 1835:

> It seems to be admitted on all sides that the intellectual improvement of those classes of the people who have the means of pursuing higher studies can at present be effected only by means of some language not vernacular amongst them. What then shall that language be? One half of the Commitee maintain that it should be English. The other half strongly recommend Arabic and Sanskrit. The whole question seems to me to be which language is the best worth knowing.[19]

Much was at stake: for the British, the expenditure of appreciable sums of money and, as will become clearer presently, the prospects and security of British rule in India. For the Bengali intelligentsia, who took an active part on both sides of the debate, such things as the meaning of Bengali and Indian identity and progress.

With Lord Bentinck as governor-general (1829–35), the decision went in favour of the anglicists. Neither Bentinck nor Macaulay had approached the issue with an open mind. Both had made up their minds already as to what the decision should be. Macaulay's masterly Minute only clinched the argument, yet it is significant that he claimed that 'the natives are desirous to be taught English, and are not desirous to be taught Sanskrit or Arabic'. This seems to have been the case. Alexander Duff, that redoubtable Scottish educationist and missionary, reported that at the time in Calcutta the 'excitement [for English education] continued unabated. They pursued us along the streets. They threw open the very doors of our palankeen; and poured in their supplications with a pitiful earnestness of countenance that might have softened a heart of stone' (Duff, 1839: 526–7).[20] Already in 1817, as an earnest of their intentions, leading Bengalis successfully sought government cooperation in establishing Hindu College in Calcutta. It was to be run on English lines and soon became the premier establishment among a growing number of similar institutions dotting greater Bengal. The anglicist victory seemed to be the answer to Bengali prayer.

[19] For Macaulay's Minute, see Majumdar, 1965: 81–5.

[20] This was the response to a particular project Duff was helping organize, but it shows graphically the demand for English education among aspiring Bengalis.

Though the anglicists won, that does not mean that the government refused to support either vernacular education at lower levels[21] or even traditional oriental learning. Bentinck's departure in 1835 and a sense of realism on the part of the British (in response to continued pressure by the orientalists) resulted in a compromise. Orientalist education, including Sanskrit College (founded in Calcutta in 1823 to promote Sanskritic learning), continued to receive some government patronage.[22] But the die was cast. English education, with enthusiastic support from Bengalis of standing in society, was henceforth to be crucially favoured. By the time he started school in the mid-1860s, Upadhyay was heir to a well-established tradition.

In his Minute, Macaulay revealed the agenda of the anglicist administrators: 'We must at present do our best to form a class who may be interpreters between us and the millions whom we govern; a class of persons, Indian in blood and colour, but English in taste, in opinions, in morals and in intellect.' This would secure British rule in India and, at the same time, increasingly advantageous trading partners.[23] The reality did not turn out quite as envisaged. What was formed by English education in Bengal was a new kind of Bengali

[21] The standard of such education, even in the middle of the century, was a source of concern to the government. The 1851–52 *Report of the Council of Education for Greater Bengal* notes: 'The great existing difficulty experienced by the Council is in procuring good teachers for the lower classes, well acquainted with their own vernacular languages. It is scarcely possible to imagine the great amount of ignorance of their own tongue, which prevails even among educated Natives. The system of teaching Bengali by the old class of Pundits has failed so entirely, as to induce the Council to suppress these useless offices as they gradually fall vacant, and to insist upon all Native masters possessing such a knowledge of their mother tongue, as to enable them to teach the very moderate acquaintance with it, which is required in Zillah Schools'; p. xlii.

[22] 'By his famous Minute of 24 November 1839, [Lord] Auckland [governor-general, 1836–1842] effected a compromise solution of the education problem. He attributed the whole controversy to the paucity of funds, and by allocating additional funds he allowed Oriental learning its due share of patronage. The existing institutions of Oriental learning were continued, stipends were substituted by adequate scholarships, and the preparation and publication of useful books in Oriental languages were also assured. At the same time he granted more than a lakh of rupees for the promotion of European learning through English schools' (Ali, 1965: 62).

[23] Of this Minute, Stokes (p. 46) opines: 'Never was the doctrine of assimilation so baldly and crudely stated.' However, Macaulay envisaged that one day India would be politically free, though bound to the British in the way described.

usually referred to as the 'bhadralok'.[24] In essence, bhadralok-mindedness consisted of cultural adaptability and migrational flexibility on the part of mainly the upper-caste Bengali.

As English education took hold, the Bengali developed a taste not only for the writings of Shakespeare, Cowper, Wordsworth and so on, but also for the ideas of thinkers such as Voltaire, Hume, Kant, Paine, Bentham, the Mills, and T. Parker. Western notions of law, freedom, patriotism, citizenship, equality, personhood, rights, happiness, literature, science, history and reason mingled with or supplanted their traditional Indian counterparts (if there were such). This led the Bengali to reassess his relationship with the British. He was no longer satisfied with being the docile interpreter between his political masters and 'the millions they governed'. The new ideas of freedom, equality and patriotism he was assimilating led him to demand greater Indian representation in government, and eventually independence. In effect, English education sowed the seeds for what was to become the nationalist movement and then freedom from British rule.

The synthetic (often syncretic) mentality that resulted from English education was the hallmark of the bhadralok. A new kind of identity was being forged. In trying to make sense of two worlds where it really mattered, in his personal life, the bhadralok was sometimes more, sometimes less successful. No doubt there were many inconsistencies and unworthy compromises. This was inevitable. Many parodies exist of the bhadralok,[25] some written by Bengalis themselves. But there were plenty of instances of great creativity, boundless energy

24 Literally, the 'gentility, cultured folk' with special reference to men. Bhadralokness was essentially a male preserve. It was only later in the century that the bhadralok systematically allowed their womenfolk (bhadramahilā) to be exposed to the same westernizing influences, and that too for opposing reasons. Some believed that women thus educated would uphold traditional values, others hoped that such women would support reform (see Borthwick, 1984). David Kopf (1969) points out that already in 1823, another 'Bhabanicharan Bannerji' uses the term 'bhadralok' (in a sense close to that noted by us) in his book *Kalikata Kamalalay*. 'Bhabanicharan does not always clearly distinguish between the new Babu class of professional intellectuals and the absentee land-owning gentry of Calcutta, which he calls bhadralok, or class of cultivated gentlemen' (note to p. 209). Soon 'bhadralok' covered both groups and was opposed, not so much to those who were *'abhadra'* or 'uncouth' (as J. H. Broomfield suggests, 1968: 6) but rather to the *'chotolok'*, i.e. the low-born, and by implication, ill-bred. See also Anil Seal, 1970, under 'bhadralok' in Index.

25 As the 'baboo/babu' in the pejorative sense. Cf. the 'bandarlog' (to be construed as 'bhadralok'?) of Kipling's *Jungle Book*.

and, in the context of a puritan ethic, dedication to selfless causes. The bhadralok revolutionized India. Contrary to Kipling's much-quoted line, East did meet West in the bhadralok, and Upadhyay is one fascinating example of this confusing but richly instructive encounter.

But bhadralok-mindedness also consisted in a readiness to migrate, to move home temporarily or permanently. Seeking jobs under British patronage (inside and outside the Presidency) required this. The great lure, however, was Calcutta, astride the Hooghly in the Gangetic delta, the hub of British influence and power. This is where so many of the absentee landlords absented themselves to in the wake of the Permanent Settlement. Calcutta had the jobs and the educational and other facilities the bhadralok needed. Throughout the nineteenth century it was in every way the focus of the bhadralok experience.

As the century progressed the British were laying the infrastructure to consolidate their rule. They gradually built up a communications network of roads, bridges, postal and telegraph services, riverine and coastal steamships, and the railway (from the early 1850s). With the annexation of land, more and more of the subcontinent fell under their cultural and military sway, including the 'independent' princely kingdoms. This allowed for the spread of English education. In the process a country only attenuatedly united hitherto by a 'great tradition' of Sanskritic religion and the (waning) influence of Mughal culture became something of a political unit. The bhadralok made full use of this for their own ends. In pursuit of suitable opportunities for their talents, they fanned out across the land from Calcutta as their notional centre, carrying with them a reputation as purveyors of English and harbingers of change. This explains, to some extent at any rate, why Upadhyay could leave Bengal and sojourn for a considerable time in Sind in north-western India.

We must now consider one more important influence of the period: the work of western Indologists such as W. Jones, H. Colebrooke, E. Burnouf and H. H. Wilson. From early in the century the researches of these scholars transformed the way bhadralok college students, the intelligentsia of the future, assessed Hinduism. Not content with seeking to merely understand the cultures they studied, the orientalists[26] also often evaluated them according to the religious and other criteria of their circumstances. In becoming susceptible to the

[26] For a passionate if overstated analysis of this term, see E. Said's *Orientalism*, Penguin edition, 1985. For a more recent study, see Breckenridge and van der Veer (eds), 1993, and Trautmann, 1997.

use of the historical-critical method, i.e. to the use of a particular rationality in the study of Hinduism, the students also became susceptible to western notions of what Hinduism *should be.*

The western Indologists, almost to a man, distinguished between Hinduism past and present: between a golden age, usually of Vedic India, and the religion that had cumulatively taken its place, subject to the various evils, as they saw it, of casteism, priestcraft, idolatry, suttee and so on. A modern scholar describes the favoured contrast thus:

> The Jones-Colebrooke portrayal of the Vedic age to which a Müller would add the finishing touches, and which today is widely accepted, depicted a people believed to have behaved very differently from present-day Hindus. It was the first reconstructed golden age of the Indian renaissance. The new view romanticized the virtues of the Aryan inhabitants of north India in the second millenium B.C. Instead of being introspective and other-worldly, the Aryans were thought to have been outgoing and non-mystical. They were pictured as a robust, beef-eating, socially equalitarian society. Instead of oriental despotism, scholars discerned tribal republics. There were apparently no laws or customs to compel a widow to commit sati. There were no temples, and there was not the slightest evidence to suggest that Aryans concretized idolatrous images of their gods. And to round out the picture, also absent were the fertility goddesses, the evil personification of Kali, and the rites and rituals of later Tantrism' (Kopf, 1969: 41).

In fact, the noble savage in his western image! Summing up, Sir William Jones (1746–94), one of the earliest and most influential of the orientalists,[27] whose greatest legacy, perhaps, to oriental studies was the founding of the Asiatic(k) Society in Calcutta in 1784, declared: 'Nor can we reasonably doubt, how degenerate and abased so ever the Hindus may now appear, that in some early age they were splendid in arts and arms, happy in government, wise in legislation, and eminent in various knowledge' (Marshall, 1970: 251).

Throughout the nineteenth century the bhadralok accepted the orientalist contrast between Hinduism past and present. This encouraged them to look at the workings of Hinduism in their lives and society with a critical eye in the light of the value judgements inculcated by English education. They found contemporary Hinduism

[27] On Jones, see S.N. Mukherjee, 1968, Cannon and Brine, 1995, and Trautmann, 1997.

wanting in many respects. This was to their credit, for whatever may be said about the manner in which they arrived at this conclusion, there can be no doubt that the Hinduism of the day showed widespread decadence.[28]

In fact the bhadralok responded to Hinduism largely on the westerners' terms. They acquiesced in the classic colonial psychology that distinguishes between a superior 'us' and an inferior 'them' to the advantage of those who rule. Made aware in a hundred ways that the westerner regarded many aspects of their living culture with contempt and ridicule, at first they grasped at the opportunity to salvage some pride from a bygone age, though the periods or characters singled out by them for praise varied circumstantially.[29] But in due course the bhadralok made the distinction serve their own purposes. The ideal past—Vedic India or idyllic Vrndaban, Krishna Vasudeva or Shivaji the liberator—became a rallying symbol to challenge western religion, western ways and western rule. Such self-assertion is a distinguishing feature of many bhadralok movements, social, political or religious, of the later nineteenth century. When in due course Max Müller would reinforce the distinction with racist overtones by appealing to the pristine racial and cultural qualities of the Vedic Aryans, many upper-caste bhadralok eagerly identified themselves as 'Aryan' in some way (*ārya* means 'noble' in Sanskrit), with fateful consequences for their interpretation of caste Hinduism and Indian unity. And all this in an age totally ignorant of the great achievements of the indigenous Harappan civilization which peaked well before supposedly Aryan culture dominated.

Their classicist concerns prompted the orientalists to make much of Sanskrit (the word comes from *saṃskṛta* meaning 'polished, perfected'), the traditional pan-Hindu language of high culture. This had its effect on the bhadralok, though they had always retained a residual respect for their scriptural tongue. Now cultivating Sanskrit

28 *Pace* C. A. Bayly's comment, 'The proper context for the Christian and rationalistic impact of the early nineteenth century was ... the vitality and not the decadence of Hindu (and Muslim) religion in India' (1988: 162). Not so, at least with regard to Hinduism in Bengal. We must ask, of course, what exactly is meant by 'vitality' and 'decadence' here, but in the generally accepted sense of a falling away from the norm, Hinduism in Bengal at the time was largely decadent. 'Vitality' there was, in caste and sex discrimination, priestcraft and ritualism, and so on.

29 Generally, however, they followed the orientalists and focused on Vedic India.

gave further scope for winning self-respect.[30] But there was much more to it than that. For the bhadralok, the Sanskritic tradition, of which Sanskrit was the vehicle and bond, acted as a great uniting feature of Hindu India. Many believed that if it was suitably publicized, critical study of this tradition would not only affirm the great achievements and cultural heritage of Hindus, but also give respectability and guidance for attempts at socio-religious reform. Further, it would counter the tendency to deracination, about which many were becoming increasingly alarmed.[31]

There was something very myopic about all this, of course. In seeking to affirm their 'Aryan' roots, upper-caste bhadralok generally failed to ask themselves how the vast majority of Hindus—the low-caste ryots, the untouchables, even upper-caste women—would react to this concerted attempt at Sanskritization, at reconstructing a tradition that had always bestowed crucial social and religious privileges on upper-caste, especially Brahmin, males. No doubt in the process a number of traditional divisions between the bhadralok themselves were breaking down: between Brahmin and Brahmin, Brahmins and other upper castes, and even upper and lower castes. The rise of the bhadralok as a plural body was evidence of this. Further, the rising self-confidence of the bhadralok and the growth of urbanization resulted in the blossoming of the Bengali language (still appreciably Sanskritized in its literary forms), which influenced a widening cross-section of the population. But what the bhadralok

30 For an analysis as to how the orientalists stressed Sanskrit as a defining norm of an essentialized construct called 'Hindu literature'—a construct the bhadralok generally accepted—in the relationships of power between colonizer and colonized, and how this generated the asymmetrical 'past-present' cultural divide noted above, see Vinay Dharwadker, 'Orientalism and the Study of Indian Literatures', in Breckenridge and van der Veer, 1993. Dharwadker, however, fails to note that the Sanskritic tradition (rather than a constructed 'Sanskrit literature') already occupied a privileged position in the minds of the intelligentsia, thus lending itself to the totalizing process implemented by the colonial regime and accepted by the bhadralok. As S. Pollock says in his fine article, 'Deep Orientalism? Notes on Sanskrit and Power Beyond the Raj' in the same work, 'Sanskrit knowledge presents itself to us as a major vehicle of the ideological form of social power *in traditional India*' (p. 77, emphasis added). On the other hand, the bhadralok (including Upadhyay) used the potential of this totalizing process to turn the orientalists' constructs against the colonizers in the ways I discuss here and elsewhere in the book.

31 In due course, this would lead to Hindu revivalism as a potent factor of Hindu nationalism at the turn of the century in Bengal, and by implication as a divisive element where relations with Muslims were concerned. See chapters 14 and 15.

were about as a whole was hardly calculated to effect a radical egalitarian change in the new society they envisaged (except perhaps in some cases for their womenfolk). By and large,[32] they unwittingly assimilated to their understanding of Hinduism whatever the westerner regarded as of value, and dismissed the rest as expendable. Thus, in the nineteenth and early twentieth centuries, the bhadralok contribution to change, powerful and effective though it was, was an elitist one, by default, no doubt, but elitist all the same. It was the likes of M.K. Gandhi who gave the freedom movement a populist dimension throughout India.

During the early stages of British rule, British administrators, high and low, were quite tolerant of Hindus—if not for what they were then at least for what they had been. The conclusions of scholars like Jones fostered this attitude. In any case most of the British still believed that they were in India to trade. Novelty and diplomacy prevailed: why ruffle the peahen that laid the golden egg? But by the 1830s, as Liberal, evangelical and imperialist attitudes in policy-making began to take hold, and a growing number of the middle class entered administrative service, British warmth towards Hindus and Indians in general began to cool.[33] The British became irreversibly imperialistic. They fostered an image of themselves as disciplined, manly accomplishers of difficult tasks in contrast especially to the effeminate, feckless Bengali male.[34] And Upadhyay? As both Hindu and Christian he would play a wondrously chequered part in the scenario: in the bhadralok attempt both to reform and to revive various aspects of Hinduism, to Sanskritize Hinduism anew (though he fell headlong into the 'Aryan trap'), to vitalize Bengali culture, and to bring about Indian independence. As for unflattering images of Bengali prowess, he derived a grim satisfaction, as we shall see, from being an iconoclast.

We now have the background to consider some of the most important groupings among the bhadralok that set the scene for

[32] There were exceptions of sorts; see Tapan Raychaudhuri, 1988.

[33] 'By 1835 one detects a certain smugness among the islanders, and this superior tone of voice came not as it would later come, from an arrogant Right, but from a highly moralistic Left. The middle classes, newly enfranchised, were emerging into power: and it was the middle classes who would eventually prove, later in Victoria's reign, the most passionate imperialists of all' (Morris, 1973: 38, quoted in A. Nandy, 1983, ftnt. 4, pp. 4–5. Morris' remark, however, is not made with particular reference to India as stated by Nandy).

[34] Nandy (1983) elaborates this point.

Upadhyay's formative years. Two of the most influential in the first half of the century were the Brahmo Sabha (Assembly of Brahman, that is, of the Supreme Being, later renamed the Brahmo Samaj or Society of Brahman), and Young Bengal. The first was founded by a Bengali Brahmin, Rammohan Roy (1774?–1833?), the second by Henry Louis Vivian Derozio (1809–31), a youth of Indo-Portuguese extraction.

The Brahmo Samaj became probably the most potent instrument for social and religious reform in nineteenth century Bengal. To appreciate its far-reaching influence among the bhadralok, we must first consider the ideas of its founder, who has with justification been called 'the father of modern India'. Rammohan played a seminal role in the rise of the bhadralok, and in shaping their activities and thinking.[35] He was born in rural Bengal, in a home where Vaishnava and Sakta influences prevailed. After the usual village kindergarten, he was schooled in Persian, Arabic and Sanskrit.[36] By the early 1820s he was well settled in Calcutta as a gentleman of means, one of the nouveau riche produced in the wake of the Permanent Settlement. His financial success enabled him to devote time to disseminating and implementing his ideas for wide-ranging reform of his milieu. He had acquired a good knowledge of English and of western thought, and a reputation as an independent thinker in Bengal, England and America.[37]

As the foundation of his programme for reform, Rammohan had begun a campaign to interpret Hinduism in terms of a Vedantic monotheism. If he could convince both the foreigner and his Hindu peers that the Vedic scriptures (he concentrated on their contemplative portion, the Vedanta) inculcated a strict monotheism and a high morality, important consequences would follow. First, Hindu prestige would rise (the public relations element was an important part of Rammohan's project). Second, by the enactment of appropriate laws and other means, the British would help create the right atmosphere for bringing about sweeping reform in a now admittedly decadent Hindu culture. Hindus, for their part, would be encouraged to abandon what Rammohan regarded as misguided practices of polytheism, idolatry, discrimination based on sex, caste and creed, and all that

[35] See, e.g., Crawford, 1987.

[36] For a critical résumé of Rammohan's life see Killingley, 1977, especially chapters 1 and 2.

[37] For the American scene, see Jackson, 1981: 32–5.

stemmed from them, such as suttee, polygamy and animal sacrifice. No doubt this would be a slow process. But a vital beginning would be made in Hindu society from its top layers, and its healing influence would radiate down. In this way, Hindus could throw off the yoke of rapacious pundits and priests in whose interests it was to perpetuate such evils.

This was a bold project and the verdict of history must be that in the long term it met with remarkable success. Rammohan pursued it indefatigably, sometimes with little or no support. Besides producing a considerable output of theological writing, the groundplan of his campaign, he was variously active in trying to initiate wide-ranging cultural reform. In the anglicist-orientalist controversy he supported the anglicists. He was convinced that English education would sweep away the cobwebs of a stultifying conservatism from the Indian mind. He fought hard, by means of tract and petition, for the suppression of suttee and his efforts helped bring about its abolition under Bentinck in 1829. In a range of ways Rammohan took an enlightened hand in improving the lot of many of his compatriots.

The inspiration for Rammohan's programme came from various sources: from his earlier study of Islam, from a unitarian reading of the Bible, especially the New Testament, from western ideas about human equality, worth and freedom, and from a historical-critical inquiry into scripture and human history. The life and place of Christ occupied a pivotal position in his understanding of reform. Some doubt has been cast as to whether Rammohan was motivated by genuine religious zeal or by purely utilitarian considerations—as early as 1845 he was assessed as a 'religious Benthamite'—but we need not be too cynical on this score. Being genuinely religious ought not to preclude one from disinterestedly appreciating the utility of one's faith. With regard to his motives for reform let us give him the benefit of any doubt here. There seems to be no hard evidence that his personal religious protestations were simply a front of some kind.

Rammohan wrote chiefly in English and Bengali, nuancing his thought differently in each language.[38] His religious position remained basically the same, however, though it was in the English writings that his grand design came out most clearly. According to this design the major historical religions possess sound scriptural testimony about the nature of deity and human fulfillment. The vagaries of time and human nature, however, have distorted this testimony by doctrinal

[38] Killingley (1977) has done valuable work in analysing this contrast.

and other accretions and have led humanity astray. Thus, miracle-mongering is now rampant. People believe in mediatorship of one kind or another in their relationship with the deity. Superstition, bigotry and persecution in religion are the order of the day. In short, religion has long become a gullible and damaging way of life, enslaving rather than liberating the mind.

But reason, intuition and divine grace jointly enable us to form a sound idea of the 'one, true God'—author, governor and judge of the universe—and of our duties to God and one another. Rammohan saw these duties as the expression of a humanitarian ethic ideally exemplified in the life of Jesus. They are based on the principle that all human beings are to be treated as fundamentally equal, irrespective of sex, birth or creed, are entitled to personal fulfillment in this life, and are capable of the same ultimate destiny. There is no such thing as intrinsic inferiority on grounds of sex, caste or race. Theologically it is invidious to talk of a 'chosen' people. All human beings are entitled to walk the same effectual path to salvation with the help of divine grace.

Rammohan articulated his views by concentrating on two religious traditions: the Hindu and the Judaeo-Christian. In Hinduism he regarded the Upanishads (especially as encoded in the Vedanta—or *Brahma-Sutras*), and to some extent the *Bhagavadgita,* as best encapsulating right understanding about divine and human nature. Claiming that he was but following the vision of the ancients, he interpreted these texts monotheistically, though in his Bengali writings he sometimes gave them a monistic or Advaitic slant. The Advaitic tradition was well regarded, in theory at any rate, by the intelligentsia of the day, and it may well be that Rammohan accommodated Advaita as a ploy to win his (Bengali) readers' good will. Till the final decade of his life and in a number of his important works, the thought of Shankara (eighth century C.E.), the champion of Advaita, exerted great influence, but on the whole more as a foil than as a model for his own thinking. Nevertheless, this emphasis on Shankara played its part in bringing Advaita to the fore as the basis of subsequent attempts by bhadralok intellectuals to rehabilitate Hinduism. Upadhyay later became a prominent exponent of this trend.

In his English works Rammohan generally dismissed the *smṛtis* (secondary scriptural texts), especially the folkloric Puranas—the inspiration for the Hinduism of the time—as the chief reason for Hinduism's downfall. His Bengali writings, however, indicate that he was prepared to tolerate practices advocated by Puranic Hinduism till such time as their adherents were ready to follow the strictures of

Vedantic monotheism. A case in point was the worship of the deity under manifold forms (including the iconic). This was tolerable in so far as it was propaedeutic to the realization that the one, true God, as formless Spirit, must be worshipped solely in a way appropriate to this mode of being.

One of Rammohan's outstanding contributions to the making of modern Hinduism was his attempt to universalize the concept of *dharma* or righteous living. This concept traditionally applied to what one's caste, sex and circumstances of life required one to do or avoid. Rammohan enlarged it to refer to the fundamental principles of a humanitarian ethic. It is significant that all or nearly all of these elements—the focusing on Advaita, the provisional tolerance of aspects of Puranic Hinduism, the enlarging of the concept of *dharma*, as well as the stress on monotheism and a universal ethic, of course—reappear as directly or indirectly deriving from Rammohan in the reconstruction of Hinduism of influential bhadralok thinkers of the century. Upadhyay integrated all these elements into the development of his thought.

Where Christianity was concerned, Rammohan located its scriptural heart in the synoptic Gospels, especially the Sermon on the Mount. In 1820 he published *The Precepts of Jesus: the Guide to Peace and Happiness,* a collection of Gospel teachings that he believed give clearest expression to 'all that is necessary to salvation'. 'These precepts,' he says, 'separated from the mysterious dogmas and historical records, appear ... to the Compiler to contain not only the essence of all that is necessary to instruct mankind in their civil duties, but also the best and only means of obtaining the forgiveness of our sins, the favour of God, and strength to overcome our passions, and to keep his commandments.'[39] Rammohan may well have modelled *The Precepts* on the *Bhagavadgita* in so far as the *Gita* is supposed to contain a body of universal, ahistorical teachings about human fulfillment deriving from a divine source. By 'mysterious dogmas and historical records' Rammohan meant such missionary favourites as the doctrines of the Trinity, Incarnation and Atonement, and the alleged historicity of Christ's miracles, all of which he rejected as man-made distortions of the true meaning of Christ's life.[40]

39 *Precepts*, 1834: 105–6.

40 The doctrines made of Christianity a divisive and partisan faith, obscuring the effectiveness of Christ's universal teachings. Further, whose version of these dogmas, among the many vying for allegiance, was one to accept? The miracles tended to sensationalize faith in God. In any case, miracle for miracle, the Hindu scriptures came out on top, said Rammohan.

Rammohan regarded Jesus as humanity's moral exemplar, appointed specially by divine providence to show us how to orientate ourselves to God. There is nothing distinctively divine about Jesus' being that sets him apart from the rest of us. Thus, in one stroke, Rammohan did away with such traditional Christian doctrines as those of the Trinity, Incarnation and Atonement, according to which God the Son, as distinct from God the Father and God the Holy Spirit, became truly human without abandoning his divinity, and by his life and death on the Cross atoned once and for all for the sins of humankind.

> It was characteristic of the office of Christ to teach men, that forms and ceremonies were useless tokens of respect for God, compared with the essential proof of obedience and love towards him evinced by the practice of beneficence towards their fellow creatures [*Precepts*, p. 104].... Let us give up such an unscriptural and irrational idea, as attributing to Jesus, or to any human being, a double nature of God and man, and restrain ourselves from bringing Christianity to a level with the doctrines of heathenish polytheism [*Precepts*, p. 443].

This entry into the world of Christian apologetics incurred the vigorous opposition of missionary zeal. To Rammohan's lasting disappointment, instead of receiving ecumenical support for his programme of reform, he now had to contend with indignant missionary opposition. Assuming the role of the representative of the missionaries, the Seramporist and Trinitarian Joshua Marshman (editor of the *Friend of India*, the organ of the Baptist Missionary Society) rounded on Rammohan for eviscerating Christianity of its doctrinal and historicist foundations. But as his response was to show, Rammohan was no pushover for a muscular Christian attack. In the protracted debate that followed, Rammohan defended his position with erudition and not a little wit.[41] This much-publicized debate was important for subsequent bhadralok activity. It showed how a determined and competent 'native' could stand up to the British on their own terms

41 He says with fine sarcasm: 'For having relinquished the notion of the triune, quadrune, and decimune gods, which I once professed when immersed in the grosser polytheism prevailing among modern Hindus, I cannot reconcile it to my understanding to find plausibility in one case [the Trinitarian], while the same notion is of acknowledged absurdity in another [the Hindu]'; *Precepts*, p. 391. A careful summary of the debate is given in Crawford (1987), ch. 5, pp. 48ff.

and emerge with credibility.[42] It also encouraged many reform-minded bhadralok admirers of Rammohan to regard Jesus, usually divested of traditional Christological doctrine, as the ideal type of a humanitarian ethic. Upadhyay's own devotion to Christ goes back to these roots.

In 1815, Rammohan had founded the Atmiya Sabha (the Assembly 'of and for our Own'), the point of the name being that, as in all his endeavours, it was his aim to reform Hinduism from the inside, not attack it from the outside. A number of leading Calcutta Bengalis attended its meetings, to which the local press gave due attention. But the society was short-lived. In 1828 or 1829 Rammohan's socio-religious concerns received a more enduring framework when he started the Brahmo Sabha.

The aim of the Sabha was to propagate his Vedānta-based monotheism and to foster the egalitarian social changes this would engender. This was envisaged as taking time. For when it began, the Sabha had little or no organization (it had no formal membership) and retained some traditional taboos (e.g. only Brahmins were allowed to read the Vedas). Clearly Rammohan intended not to offend his more orthodox Hindu peers if he could help it. But a number looked askance at this project. This resulted, at the beginning of the 1830s, in the founding of the Dharma Sabha (the Assembly for the Preservation of Dharma) by Radhakanta Deb, the doyen of the so-called bhadralok conservatives.

Its aim was to counter the influence of the 'progressives' and to defend orthodoxy, not so much against western influence, but against western influence *on its own terms*. Radhakanta, in his own way, was bhadralok-minded. He was a founder-governor of Hindu College and in favour of educating Bengali women on western lines. The Dharma Sabha, moreover, functioned western-style by committee and democratic vote. But Radhakanta believed that Rammohan was going about meeting the challenge of the times in a manner that was irreparably culturally alienating. It is in this light that we must see Radhakanta as also a defender of the right to practise suttee and

42 Characteristically robust when trading words, Rammohan was always courteous (unlike some of his opponents, e.g., Marshman himself). Rammohan was much praised in the Anglo-Indian press both for his arguments and his conduct in the debate. As for Marshman, Carey himself admitted in a letter of August 2, 1811, that Marshman's regard for the feelings of others was 'very little, when the cause of God is in question'' (see B. Stanley, 1992: 42).

polygamy, which he regarded as integral to the continuity of Hindu dharma. The moral is that the 'conservatives' and 'progressives' among the bhadralok may be described as such relative to particular issues. 'Progressives' under one hat could become 'conservatives' under another. It is important to realize this for assessing the various activities of the bhadralok, Upadhyay included.

Rammohan was the vital centre of the Brahmo Sabha, and when he died the Sabha's prospects seemed bleak, until Debendranath Tagore (1817–1905) took a hand. Debendranath (father of Rabindranath) came from a wealthy family that had also done well out of the Permanent Settlement. Dwaraknath, his prestigious father, had been well known to Rammohan as a member of both the Atmiya and Brahmo Sabhas. In 1839, from the Tagore home at Jorasanko in Calcutta, Debendranath, who had studied in Hindu College, established a society called the Tattvabodhini Sabha. The declared aim of this society, which purported to 'awaken one to Reality' (*tattvabodhinī*), was the propagation of the Brahmo way of life, in effect, more or less the ideology that Rammohan had worked out.

There was one important difference at least in so far as Debendranath and his closest colleagues were concerned. Far from showing particular admiration for Jesus' personality or for Christianity as embodying a universal ethic, they vigorously opposed the spread of Christian influence and missionary attacks on their Vedānta-based interpretation of Hinduism. This they did through English and Bengali publications, in particular the monthly Bengali journal, the *Tattvabodhinī Patrika* (started in 1843).

Their chief missionary opponents were Alexander Duff and his associates. This is significant for the image of Christianity implanted in the minds of the leading Bengali intellectuals of the day. The faith of Duff and Co., like that of the Seramporists, was Protestant with strong Evangelical ingredients.[43] As such it differed in tone and in approach to Hindu belief and practice from that advocated by Roman Catholic theology. Catholic faith was adaptable to non-Christian religion in a way that Evangelical faith was not. Later we shall consider the theological basis for this distinction and examine how Upadhyay sought to exploit it to the full. For the present suffice it to say that since it was in an Evangelical form that the Christian presence in Calcutta mounted its most vociferous challenge on Hinduism, many westernized Bengalis viewed Christianity as an all-or-nothing affair,

43 Duff (1806–78) was Calvinist.

uncompromising towards their religion whether reformed or not. For all practical purposes any consequential distinction between Protestant and Roman Catholic versions of Christianity as regards their approach to Hinduism was lost on these bhadralok. Indeed, the leading upper-caste converts to Christianity in Calcutta were all Protestants,[44] mostly protégés of Duff and his associates.

In effect the Tattvabodhini Sabhaists were confronted with a religious foil whose inflexibility allowed them to hammer out their own understanding of both Hinduism and their cultural identity. It was a laborious process, carried out through the ensuing debate with the missionaries.[45] Eventually the Sabhaists abandoned their original claim that the Vedas were infallible and settled for 'the purified heart, illumined by knowledge perfected by Self-realisation'[46] as the source of religious truth. This rationalist-intuitionist stance was reached by about the middle of the century. But the Vedic scriptures were not entirely discarded. In August 1850, Debendranath published a manual, the *Brahmodharma Grantha*, comprising mainly Upanishadic extracts supplemented by a universal ethical code, which was to act as the religious handbook of his followers.[47]

In the process of articulating their self-understanding, the Sabhaists adopted the prevailing western view of the nature of religion: that religion is a personal faith-response, no doubt, but equally if not more important, it comprises a definite credal system of belief. This view underlay the researches of the orientalists who assumed that their approach was 'objective', that is, concerned with what 'Hindoos'

44 These converts did distinguish between Protestant and Catholic Christianity, of course, but even they tended to sit lightly to Protestant denominational differences; see Lipner in Coward, 1987. However, there is a further nuance to be considered here. Some Hindu converts (and even Hindu sympathizers of Christian teaching) were more taken with Evangelical Protestant Christianity precisely because of its uncompromising nature. It gave them the basis for a more trenchant critique of their ancestral faith, which they perceived as decadent, than the more accommodating principles of Catholic theology. As Ashis Nandy points out, 'This made Catholicism less attractive to the social critics and reformists among the babus who were searching for new bases for social criticism and for new uses of aspects of western culture in India' (1994: 56).

45 'It was only in 1844–5 that the controversy between Brahmo and Christian missionaries began in earnest' (Amiya Sen, 1993: 52).

46 *Ātmapratyayasiddhajñānojjalitaviśuddhahṛday*; as quoted in Ali, 1965: 30.

47 See Kopf, 1979: 106–7 Chapter 7 of Kopf's book is largely devoted to Upadhyay in a rather negative light and has a number of factual errors.

(a collective term) believed and practised, rather than 'subjective', or evaluative in terms of their own (in fact largely unquestioned) cultural and religious preconceptions. Thus was attenuated in bhadralok minds the age-old Hindu understanding of religion as a way of life comprising firm if inclusivist beliefs that were a function of an established *orthopraxy*, in favour of the western predilection for determining religious allegiance on the basis of doctrinal *orthodoxy*. Earlier, Rammohan had been smitten by this tendency. This explains his attempt, and the efforts of later bhadralok thinkers, to reconstruct Hinduism largely in terms of an identifiable system of beliefs, whether this could be called a Vedantic monotheism or something else.

Linguistically, the debate between the Sabhaists and the missionaries resulted, as the century gathered momentum, in the development of the Bengali language. In the attempt to articulate their ideology as Bengalis, especially through the *Patrika*, members of the Tattvabodhini Sabha (notwithstanding the fact that the days of the Sabha as such were numbered) played a prominent part in shaping Bengali into an apt medium for communicating modern ideas. By the time Upadhyay was growing up, the bhadralok were acquiring a new confidence and pride in the use of their mother-tongue. This allowed westernized Bengalis not only to think genuinely bilingually, but also to counteract the tendency to cultural alienation by strengthening their indigenous roots. In due course this contributed to the formation of a nationalist consciousness in which bhadralok novelists writing in Bengali (e.g., Bankimcandra Chatterji) were closely involved. In time Upadhyay was also to make a significant contribution to the nationalist cause by his use of Bengali.

After an initial stand-off period of a few years (no doubt because the Brahmo Sabha was under suspicion for its allegedly pro-Christian leanings), Debendranath took his Tattvabodhini Sabha into the closest possible alliance with the Brahmo Sabha. By 1843 the ideologies of the two Sabhas were practically identical. It was in that year that Debendranath and some of his Sabhaists declared themselves Brahmo, and he became the leader of the Brahmo Sabha, which he promptly renamed the Brahmo Samaj. His leadership was of momentous import for the Samaj.

> He changed the Samaj from a loose society into an organization whose members were formally initiated. He drew up a declaration of faith, created a new liturgy with non-idolatrous rites, and provided for both Brahmo schooling and propagation. [Debendranath] Tagore

> himself was inclined towards the contemplative and the devotional aspect of Hinduism, and was preoccupied almost exclusively with religious reform.[48] Under his leadership, the Brahmo Samaj moved closer to the mainstream of Hinduism, with a stress on devotional and ethical duties. While strengthening its organization and propagation, it also grew quickly in numbers (Damen, 1983: 4).

The Tattvabodhini Sabha and *Patrika* became propaganda instruments for Brahmo ideology. The Sabha provided preachers to champion the Brahmo cause. By the 1870s Brahmo missionaries and sympathizers had made their way along the railway and other routes not only into greater Bengal but also into the more distant regions of the country.[49] Brahmo ideas were gaining currency among the (English-)educated of the land.

Meanwhile, during the 1850s, the Tattvabodhini Sabha became dominated by a humanist faction that was more interested in socio-cultural reform than in Debendranath's programme for religio-ethical change. Disillusioned, the Brahmo leader wound up the Sabha in 1859. Debendranath was not to know that the Samaj was about to enter one of its most turbulent phases under the influence of his brilliant protégé, Keshabcandra Sen, who had joined in 1857. It was in a Samaj under Keshab's sway that Upadhyay became a Brahmo and embarked on a career that was to transform his devotion to a purely human Christ into the substance of orthodox Christian commitment. This story we leave to another chapter. By 1861, however, the year of Upadhyay's birth, the Brahmo Samaj had become a quintessentially bhadralok movement. It was run on western lines with a membership of westernized, mainly upper-caste Bengalis who nevertheless were on the whole not unmindful of their Bengali heritage.

If the Brahmo Samaj functioned as the Trojan horse of change within Hinduism, Young Bengal acted as a battering ram against the citadel of Hindu orthodoxy. The movement started under the presiding genius of Henry Louis Vivian Derozio, who was born in 1809. Derozio went to an English-teaching school in Calcutta run by a Scotsman named David Drummond (1787–1843). 'Drummond was a scholar-poet, and as a notorious free-thinker an exile from his native land. It may safely be conjectured that Derozio derived from Drummond his

48 On the other hand, some of his closest associates stressed social reform.

49 In time, as regional identity outside Bengal formed, these emigrant bhadralok became ghettoized.

taste in literature and philosophy, his love of Burns, his faith in the French Revolution and English Radicalism' (S.C. Sarkar, in A. Gupta, 1958: 17). Derozio's brilliance led to his appointment, before he was twenty, as lecturer in 'European literature and history, both classical and modern, and also [in] the history of modern Europe' to the senior students of Hindu College (P.K. Mitra, 1988: 38). There he became the centre of an adoring band of pupils (some of whom were not taught by him in College[50]) who, under his guidance, proceeded to question the traditional practices of their ancestral religion. These radicals were called Young Bengal. Inspired by their mentor's free-thinking spirit, they started journals and debating societies where they discussed without inhibition such topics as the existence of God, the status of women in society, virtue and free-will, patriotism and various features of Hindu culture, past and present. The approach they employed was a scientific-rationalist one, and their gurus were the likes of Voltaire, Bacon, Hume and Paine. Of Derozio and his disciples it has been said that:

> He used to impress upon them the sacred duty of thinking for themselves—to be in no way influenced by any of the idols mentioned by Bacon—to live and die for truth—to cultivate all the virtues, shunning vice in every shape. He often read examples from ancient history of the love of justice, patriotism, philanthropy and self-abnegation; and the way in which he set forth the points stirred up the minds of his pupils. Some were impressed with the excellence of justice, some with the paramount importance of truth, some with patriotism, some with philanthropy' [R.C. Majumdar, 1965: 39].[51]

The iconoclasm of Young Bengal alarmed their elders and Derozio was forced to resign from Hindu College in April 1831. He died of cholera on Christmas Eve of that year, only 22 years old.

It is true that in defiance of tradition many Derozians outraged Hindu sensibilities. As one newspaper report put it, they showed their contempt for conventional Hinduism by 'cutting their way through ham and beef and wading to liberalism through tumblers of beer'. By the mid-1840s Young Bengal was petering out as a recognizable movement.[52] However, the seeds of reform sowed by Derozio were

[50] One of these was Krishnamohan Banerjea, who later became one of the most illustrious converts to Christianity of his times; see Lipner in Coward, 1987.

[51] Quoting from Pearychand Mitra's *Life of David Hare*, p. 82.

[52] Mitra (1988) identifies four targets of Derozian criticism: traditional Hinduism, Christianity, the Brahmo Samaj and, in a later phase, the British administration.

to bear fruit. A goodly number of the Derozians were joining Debendranath's Tattvabodhini Sabha, where before long as constituents of the 'humanist faction', they assumed a dominant role. It was through this filter that Derozio's influence lived on.

Thus far we have concentrated on focuses of social and/or religious reform. But in the first half of the nineteenth century, moves to politicize the bhadralok mind were by no means absent. These were integrated into the bhadralok-inspired forces of change as a whole, and involved a number of by now familiar dramatis personae. Rammohan Roy, for one, had political goals (see Crawford, 1987, especially chapter 8). Indeed, a unitive political consciousness among the bhadralok was being formed by dribs and drabs.

Two of the earliest organizations that heightened such awareness, but still mainly on a partisan or provincial level, were the Landholders' Society (or Zamindars' Association as it was first called, formed in 1838) and the Bengal British India Society (formed in 1843). The purpose of the one was 'to represent the landed interest. By this it understood the interests of landlords rather than of the tenants or actual cultivators ... there is nothing to show that the Society tried to promote the interests of the raiyats or of the people in general.'[53] The purpose of the other, which had a tiny membership from among the Bengali intelligentsia, spoke vaguely of the welfare of 'all classes' and tended to generate more debate than action. Yet in their limited way both societies envisaged and sought political reform.[54]

The two societies in effect banded together in 1851 to form the British Indian Association. The Association's antecedents reveal its vested interests. It was hardly representative of either Indian or even Bengali public opinion. Yet it marked what may be called the period

53 Nilmani Mukherjee (1975: 59). In fact the members of this Society were also concerned to rebut charges made by missionaries that they neglected the basic human rights of the ryots under their charge.

54 There were other kinds of politicizing instruments. According to Ali (1965), one of the most important of such stimuli was the so-called Liberty of Conscience Act (Act XXI of 1850). This Act was intended to protect the rights of inheritance of converts to Christianity against the view that the Hindu laws of inheritance were essentially religious and therefore could not be tampered with by government even if they adversely affected those leaving the Hindu fold. 'The Act spread among Hindus a belief that the Government had abandoned the policy of neutrality in religious affairs and had allied themselves with the missionaries in their work of evangelisation' (Ali, 1965: 136). See the whole of chapter 6. P.K. Mitra (1988: 48ff.) summarizes evidence that the Derozians attacked the 'British Colonial Administration' in their publications mainly in the decade 1833–43.

of proto-nationalism in the Presidency. It represented a serious and concerted attempt on the part of upper-class Bengalis, mainly bhadralok, to put aside caste and other differences and to agitate for short-term political changes in the context of a larger political vision. As to short-term changes, the Association was formed in view of the renewal of the East India Company's Charter in 1853. In 1852 the Association sent directly to the British Parliament a petition which:

> dwelt at great length upon the evils of the union of political or executive power with the legislative, and prayed for the establishment of a separate Legislature, possessing a popular character. Among other prayers in the petition may be mentioned ... separation of the functions of magistrates and judges, abolition of salt duty ... and the stamp duties; and discontinuance of the payment for ecclesiastical establishment [R.C. Majumdar, 1965: 450].

Though this petition produced scant results, it was made with long-term political reform in mind, including, notably, Indian representation in government. In 1852 similar societies were formed in Bombay (the Bombay Association) and Madras (the Madras Native Association). The Calcutta Association, however, took the leading and often the coordinating role. By and large, the luminaries of the British Indian Association pursued their objectives with implicit faith in the benevolence of British rule. So far as they were concerned, British rule was a providential dispensation instituted to help India shake off the stagnation of the past. Far from opposing it, they wanted to cooperate with it—at most, to reform it. Throughout the nineteenth century, this attitude to British rule prevailed among many of the influential bhadralok despite an escalation of political and social tension between the British and Indians following the Uprising (or 'Mutiny') of 1857. As we shall see, Upadhyay's own attitude to British paramountcy in India underwent a number of changes—from hostility at first, to the accredited view that it was a benevolent rule, once more to a virulent antagonism. In due course we shall review these changes. For the present we note that the British Indian Association helped substantially to politicize the bhadralok mind in preparation for a more inclusivist nationalist consciousness of the kind inspired by Surendranath Banerjea in the 1870s. It was this consciousness that took the young Upadhyay by storm.

One final point. The climate of change heralded by Rammohan's westernizing outlook together with the various revivalist reactions to it discussed in this chapter—in short, the emergence of bhadralok-mindedness—is generally referred to as the 'Bengal Renaissance'. This is something of a misnomer. Renaissance of some kind there was, no doubt. There was the attempt to bring to birth again an ideal social, ethical or religious past that would purify the dross of the present, to revitalize aspects of the Sanskritic tradition and to reconstruct the vernacular.[55] The Renaissance slogan, *Vetera optima sunt* ('old is gold'), captured in important measure the spirit of the times.

However, no less apt was the motto of the Enlightenment, *sapere aude* ('Dare to think for yourself'). The currents of liberalism, patriotism and rationalism that surged in on the tide of English education were much in evidence, as we have seen. The rise of the bhadralok represented an amalgam of both Renaissance and Enlightenment trends. It is in this light of the dialectic between past and present that we must view bhadralok activity at the time—the British Indian Association, Young Bengal and the Brahmo Samaj, no less than the Dharma Sabha. As we have intimated already, these groupings and regroupings represented the fashioning of a new identity among Bengal's elite. Another dialectic was at work here: that between one's individual and one's collective identity. The interacting complexities of these two sides—traditional and modern forms of individuating consciousness on the one hand (e.g. the self-affirmation of bhakti-spirituality no less than the new notions of citizenship and 'privacy'), and traditional and modern forms of collectivizing consciousness on the other, such as those arising from caste and the new socio-economic and political groupings—created a dynamic and (psychologically) unpredictable environment for the bhadralok. This had its personal repercussions, and we will have occasion to recall it from time to time in this book.

In a dense but fascinating work,[56] Sudipta Kaviraj writes:

> It is a commonplace in the history of ideas that the past, at least the past which lives in popular imagination and acts upon history through popular behaviour, is a construct of the present, the past that the present would have liked to have had, which it considers appropriate for itself, its self-created lineage [1995: 72].

There is a deep and well-expressed insight here, the insight that *the* past (whatever that might be) is irrecoverable, that, in fact, the past

55 Conspicuous by its absence at the time was a comparable resurgence of the aesthetic as represented by the fine arts, especially drama, painting, sculpture and architecture.

56 *The Unhappy Consciousness: Bankimchandra Chattopadhyay and the Formation of Nationalist Discourse in India*, OUP, Delhi, 1995.

is in some sense amorphous and is re-created anew in the present or in *a* present (whether yours or mine or some community's). Yet in Kaviraj's way of putting it, one forms the impression that it is only the past that is thus amorphous, and that the reconstructed past is a ready-made child of a ready-made present. But the 'present' too is in the process of being shaped, *not least by its own past*. The relationship between these two is symbiotic. So it was in the Bengal of this book, and indeed, in the Bengal of that time that you, and I, now perceive.

I am not arguing for a past and present that can be deconstructed away. I do not believe that history is that amorphous; history as narrative of a series of experienced events resists a total hermeneutic dissolution. I am pointing out that perspective is a necessary structural component of historiography. This structural component underdetermines interpretation; it also gives the past and the present a contingency, a fluidity, that we must take seriously in our grasp of things. What I have written here of Upadhyay's formative context I believe to be accurate and hence informative, but also, by definition, open to ongoing interpretation. There is a further consequence of our analysis in the light of this methodology, namely, that it was in a Bengal pregnant with possibilities and anticipation that Upadhyay, or—to give him his family name—Bhabanicaran Bandyopadhyay, was born in 1861.

# Chapter 2

# Firebrand:
## Adolescence

Though with hindsight events and changes seem to have occurred with bewildering speed in Upadhyay's short life of 46 or so years, it is a major aim of this book to show that they form a unified whole. It will be helpful, however, to divide his life into four phases, though these are of unequal length. (1) *The Path to Manhood (1861–1881/82):* this period takes account of the formative influences of Upadhyay's life and ends with his introduction to Keshabcandra Sen and the Brahmo way of life. (2) *The Brahmo Years (1882–1891):* this period saw Upadhyay working as a Brahmo in Sind and terminates with his conversion to the Christian faith. (3) *The Hindu-Catholic Comes of Age (1891–1903):* this period begins with an uncompromising commitment on Upadhyay's part to Catholic doctrine and ends with a muscular appreciation of Advaitic Hinduism. Upadhyay sets off for the West to test and ratify his commitment as a 'Hindu-Catholic'. (4) *The Nationalist Phase (1903–1907)*: the shortest period, during which Upadhyay, increasingly disillusioned with his Church, plunged into the vortex of Bengal politics. This phase ends with his death.

Bhabanicaran Bandyopadhyay (the surname is anglicized as Banerji), or Bhabani, as we shall call him now, was born on February 11, 1861[1] in the village of Khannyan in the Hooghly district. It was an undistinguished village, except perhaps for the fact that it lay on the

1 There is some confusion about the exact date. The *Sketch* gives Bhabani's date of birth as February 2 (p. 1), but *The Blade* has February 11 (p. 8) with the note, 'According to the horoscope presented by the family.' Simha (p. 1) gives, 'on the first of Phalgun', i.e. February 14–15, but with no supporting evidence. UBBJ settles for February 11 with a note to the effect that this date was derived from Bhabani's horoscope, which was in Fr Turmes' possession. I have found no trace of the horoscope.

railway between Burdwan to the north-east and Howrah (due south-west), which bordered Calcutta. One can see significance in this: the Banerji house, we are told, in which Bhabani was born and spent his early years, overlooked the railway track. Bhabani was born at the crossroads of change so to speak, between the pulls of traditional Bengal and the lures of the fast-changing capital city, some 35 miles away. The tension between village and city—continuity and change—was always to lie at the centre of Bhabani's life.

By orthodox Bengali standards, the Banerji family had a respectable pedigree. It is not clear where their ancestral home was. Simha (p. 1) says that it was in Khanakul-Krishnanagar. But the family had had a long association with Khannyan.[2] Bhabani's paternal great-grandfather, Madanmohan, was noted for his orthodoxy.[3] As a Kulin Brahmin he entered into numerous marriage contracts, as was often done by his peers at the time—in his case, no less than 50.[4] Eventually he settled down with a girl called Jagadamba.[5] It was his son, Haracaran,

2 This we get from *Sekele Katha* (SK), 'Bygone times', which is an autobiography by Nistarini Devi, Bhabani's paternal aunt. This short work contains a fascinating account of her times by the author, who enjoyed a long life, and is especially rich in data about Kalicaran Banerji, Bhabani's famous paternal uncle. SK records that Chatterji 'Mahasay', the father of Bhabani's father's father's wife (!) was well-known in Khannyan, having established the local village deity (p. 1).

3 Traditional upper-caste Bengali society being patriarchal, ancestral records stress the father's side in determining lineage, pedigree, socio-religious status etc.

4 'Kulin' signifies the ritually purest and socially most elevated stratum of the caste. This attribute made (male) Brahmins the most desirable of marriage partners in a caste-conscious society, and gave rise to 'Kulinism', the practice of formally marrying many eligible girls so as to produce, in particular, Kulin sons. The husband spent his time visiting his (often far-flung) wives in their parents' homes, to fulfill his marital obligations and collect the husband's 'fee'. As can be imagined, this practice was open to much abuse and criticism (not least with regard to the dowry system, which was in force); for an early indictment see Krishnamohan Banerjea's essay, 'The Kulin Brahmins of Bengal' (1844). Madanmohan's polygamy is confirmed by two other sources: B. R. Barber (1912) and S.K. Barber writes, 'Kali Charan's father had two wives, and his grandfather, Madan Mohun Banurji ... had fifty-four' (p. 3; Simha (p. 1) gives the number as 50). SK avers that in his notebook, Madanmohan had the addresses of his '56 marriages' (p. 6).

5 Simha implies that this was in Hoera, a village some two miles from Khannyan. But SK is clear that Jagadamba was living in her father, Chatterji Mahasay's, hut in Khannyan when Madanmohan stayed on with her. Simha indicates that Madanmohan himself broke his Kulin status (*svakṛtabhaṅga han*) by this marriage. This only means that Madanmohan ceased to practise the Kulin way of life, not that he had lost his Brahmin respectability or been outcasted in any way. There is an interesting if somewhat garbled account in GLA, *Varia* 5, as to how Madanmohan came to live with Jagadamba. SK gives a similar account.

from this marriage, who had the house built in which Bhabani was born.[6]

Haracaran had but two wives. His junior wife, Candramani, bore him eight children, including three sons (all of whom survived): Debicaran (Bhabani's father), Kalicaran (who became a leading Christian convert and nationalist) and the youngest, Tarinicaran.[7]

Haracaran was bhadralok-minded. He seems to have had some exposure to a westernized education, and the traditional form of Kulin polygamy was not to his liking.[8] He served the British in the police force, helping Major (later, Sir William) Sleeman in his successful drive against thuggee. Haracaran's field of operations was the rugged terrain of much of what is modern Madhya Pradesh. As a base, he built a house in Jabalpur.[9] The town lies not far from the bank of the Narmada river as it begins to dip southwards, and was conveniently located for Sleeman's purposes. Many of the thugs who surrendered to him were confined there. The Jabalpur connection is not without significance. Bhabani visited the town on more than one occasion later in life, not least when in search of a suitable site to establish his experimental Hindu-Catholic monastery. It became a kind of retreat for him. A little over a decade after coming to Jabalpur, and while still based there himself, Haracaran despatched most of the family to live in Khannyan[10]; it would be more convenient to marry off some of the children from there. At first the family lived in Khannyan in a hut. This proving unsatisfactory, Haracaran gave instructions that a proper brick house be built. A comfortable two-storey house was constructed in which a shrine was erected to Kali,

6 According to SK, Haracaran (Simha, 'Harachandra', p. 1) was away working in Jabalpur when he gave instructions that a proper brick house was to be built. Till then the family were living in a hut.

7 Nistarini notes that except for her (and possibly another sister) the other girls died; we have no names for three who died consecutively. Nistarini was born third, after Debicaran. Barber (p. 2) says that Kalicaran was 'the eighth son. To be the eighth son is considered a very good omen'. 'Eighth child' is correct. Haracaran had children also by his other wife, Khetramani.

8 Both these facts emerge from a handwritten note in the GLA copy of Simha (p. 1); see also GLA *Varia* 5, pp. 55–6.

9 His work took him first to Gorakhpur where Debicaran and Nistarini were born. Kalicaran was born in Jabalpur.

10 Khetramani and her children seem to have stayed on with Haracaran. Haracaran and Khetramani would visit the home in Khannyan for the celebration of Durga Puja, the great autumnal festival of Hindu Bengal.

and Durga Puja celebrated in style.[11] It was in this house that Bhabani was born.[12]

Like his father, Debicaran was an officer in the police force and distinguished himself in running dacoits (bandits) and thugs to ground. He is said to have been a disciplinarian with an iron will and violent temper.[13] He had three (surviving) sons by his wife, Radhakumari[14]: the eldest was Haricaran, who became a doctor in Calcutta; then came Parbaticaran who in due course practised as 'a pleader in the moffussil' (*Sketch*, pt. I, p. 4); the youngest was Bhabanicaran, the subject of our narrative. It is clear then that Bhabani grew up in a home firmly open to western influences. That's as may be. The household was also subject to traditional Hindu and Bengali culture: this stemmed from Candramani, Haracaran's junior wife and Bhabani's grandmother, who, with help from Nistarini for a while, ran the household in Khannyan.

Bhabani's mother died when he was about a year old. It fell to Candramani to bring the boys up, the more so since Debicaran's work often took him away from home. This she did with zest, being especially fond of Bhabani, the baby of the family. Though Candramani had no frog-in-the-well mentality—she had lived away from her native environment in Gorakhpur and Jabalpur—she was steeped in the religious culture of Bengal. By all accounts she was a formidable person, fiercely conscious of her role as a Brahmin woman. There is an archival note that later Upadhyay 'used to tell ... how once his grandmother being challenged by her husband about her courage to die as a 'sati' held her finger to the flame without even flinching until she had to be dragged away' (*Varia*, vol. 4, p. 137).

It was Candramani who instilled in Bhabani a deep knowledge and love of traditional rural Bengal. This is important, as we shall see, since rural Bengal was the familiar environment not only for the ryot but also for many of the (urban) bhadralok, who had ancestral homes in the villages that they regularly visited. 'Continuously in his grandmother's company during childhood, Upadhyay learnt

11 Apparently the house was built under Debicaran's supervision. Debicaran was married after the move to Khannyan and had got a good job in the region; he was acting *in loco parentis*. Nistarini waxes strong on the size of the house and the family's consequent fame in the village. But its building incurred considerable debt.

12 It no longer stands (Bl., p. 9).

13 Nistarini gives some examples of this temper.

14 According to *Varia* 5 (p. 86) their first son, Bhagabati, died at an early age.

unadulterated Bengali (*khā̃ṭi bāṅgālā*) as well as a great deal of the chit-chat of a Bengali household and many of the village rhymes and riddles of the time. Later all this household chit-chat and the village rhymes and riddles learnt in childhood, appeared in many places in [his Bengali daily] the *Sandhya*.'[15] The *Sandhya*, which appeared a few years before Upadhyay's death, became a very popular newspaper (especially among the urban bhadralok) and played an important role not only in innovating Bengali journalistic style, but in forming Bengali nationalistic consciousness. Notably in the *Sandhya*, Upadhyay was adept at getting across his socio-political message by freely lacing it with ingredients from his homespun knowledge of Bengali culture.

Candramani ruled the household with a firm hand. The following tale recounted in the *Sketch* (pt. I, p. 4) shows well the tensions between tradition and modernity at work in the Banerji home during the boys' upbringing. Parbaticaran, the second of the three, had developed a taste for bread and butter. This was not the traditional unleavened bread, of course (known, in its various forms, as paratha, chapatti, luchi, puri etc.), but *pāu ruṭi*, the white leavened bread of our modern bakeries. The making and selling of such bread was usually in Muslim hands at the time, and this put it beyond the pale of orthodox Bengali diet. Parbati would despatch his younger brother to fetch the bread, which Bhabani did willingly enough. But then rather than 'run the risk of being caught red-handed by the

15 Simha, p. 2. Guha (pp. 2–3) writes that since Upadhyay was very fond of children, he was 'forever reciting nursery-rhymes'. He quotes an example (here freely translated) that Aruncandra Datta (then the President of the Prabartak Sangha) remembered hearing as a child from Upadhyay himself: The hungry jackal (to the crab in its hole).

> Tis I, your servant, goddess sublime,
> Come out of your hole, accept homage of mine.
> The wary crab—
> I've eaten so well, I'm racked with ague,
> If worship you must, then from afar will do.

*śiśurā tā̃r priyo chilo bale brahmabāndhabke ciradin chaḍār karbār karte hayeche. śaiśabe śrī aruṇcandra datta.... brahmabāndhaber mukhe śune je-sab chaḍā śikhechilen tār du-ekṭi ekhano smaraṇ karte pāren. jathā—śiyāl (garter bhitare kākḍār prati):*

> *kiṃkari kiṃkari parameśvarī*
> *garte theke beriye eso, namaskār kari.*
> *kākḍā: kheyechi deyechi gāye eseche jvar*
> *bhakti thāke dūr thekei namaskār kar.*

grandmother' while entering the house, Bhabani would throw the bread wrapped in paper to his brother, who would be waiting on the terraced roof, there to indulge his forbidden craving.

There can be no doubt that Candramani had a lasting impact on Bhabani.[16] In the permanent absence of the growing boy's mother and the regular absences of his father, she influenced him not only culturally as we have seen, but also psychologically. The penetrating influence of Bengali women on their menfolk is well known—in the role of Parvati or Uma, bride and mother; of Sita and Savitri, devoted wives; of Durga and Kali, fierce and exacting protectors; of Lakshmi, the bringer of prosperity.[17] Later in life Upadhyay on occasion referred to his grandmother, usually with tenderness, sometimes with awe. Who can doubt but that her forceful personality, firm but protective towards him—Candramani often stayed the retributive hand of his stern father—played a large part in moulding Upadhyay's tendency to idealize women. Upadhyay never married; he lived in the shadow of various mother figures. In due course we shall see how he placed woman on a pedestal, rather than affirm her in the earthy relationship of marriage. It must have been Candramani too who inculcated in Bhabani a pride in his caste status, which had fateful consequences in later life.

It is important to consider the varied religious influences at work in the Banerji household. We have already noted that special provision was made for the worship of Kali in the house, and that the family regularly celebrated the Durga Puja, Hindu Bengal's main religious festival. These facts indicate that the dominant religious tradition of the house was Sakta, whereby the goddess, especially in her forms associated with Siva, is worshipped as the personification of the power (*śakti*) of the deity. The Sakta orientation of the family can also be deduced from the names of the three boys—all namesakes of the goddess.[18] In any case, high-caste Bengalis like the Banerjis often had strong Sakta leanings. It was fitting that Kali was worshipped in

[16] For a time Nistarini also must have exerted some influence; she too was a strong-minded woman. But before long, being widowed, she was sent from pillar to post among various members of the extended family. Upadhyay seems never to mention her.

[17] See, e.g., Ashis Nandy, 1980, and Manisha Roy, 1975. Also see Hawley and Wulff, 1984, especially pp. 129–209.

[18] And, not least from Candramani, whom Nistarini characterizes as a dyed-in-the-wool Sakta (*ghor śākter meye*; SK, p. 16).

a household in which the male heads of two generations (Haracaran and Debicaran) earned their livelihood by apprehending those dreaded and perverse devotees of Kali, the thugs. Only Kali the orthodox could quell Kali the unorthodox, though the dividing line between the two was often blurred. Even in the mid-nineteenth century, the worship of Kali as a respectable cult was not of very long standing.[19] And in this tradition, the image that seemed to weigh with Bhabani was not the Goddess's softened, sensual aspect, which especially the sage Ramakrishna was to popularize later,[20] but rather Kali the terrible, the black, naked mother goddess, garlanded with a necklace of severed heads, with scimitared hand upraised to strike the enemies of her devotees. It was this Kali that Upadhyay was to portray in graphic Bengali towards the end of his life, as the avenging symbol for the liberation of his motherland from foreign domination.

But the mollifying influence of Vaishnavism must also have been present: Aspects of Vaishnavism, which in cult form tended to be followed mainly by the lower castes in Bengal, were deeply embedded in the Bengali psyche. These included not only the passionate love relationship between Krishna and Radha as depicted in Gaudiya Vaishnavism,[21] but also the characters and incidents of some Puranas and the well-known epics, the *Ramayana* and *Mahabharata*. Itinerant bands of minstrels would regale folk of all social strata in rural Bengal by enacting episodes from these sources. *The Blade* notes an instance when 'Bhedo' (Bhabani's nickname as a child) was enthralled at the prospect of such a display.[22] Bankimcandra Chatterjee, who by his novels and essays greatly inspired the nationalist movement in Bengal, described the Krishna consciousness of the region thus:

> In the Bengal region devotion to Krishna [*kṛṣṇer upāsanā*] is well-nigh all-pervasive. Village after village has a Krishna temple, in house after house there's Krishna worship [*kṛṣṇer pūjā*]. Almost every

19 'It was not until the poetry of Ramprasad Sen [circa 1718–75] that Kali's character gained a well-developed compassionate and maternal side, which made her a fitting receptacle for the heart's devotion' (McDermott in Lopez, 1995: 55).

20 For a good account of an early representation of this ambiguous image, see McDermott (in Lopez, 1995).

21 Note that Bhabani's mother's name was 'Radhakumari', and that Haracaran's senior wife, Khetramani, had some Vaishnava affiliation (so Nistarini: *'āmār bimātār baiṣṇab mantra'*, p. 16).

22 pp. 11–12; the source seemed to be the *Ramayana*. Such enactments also had an influence on the young Ramakrishna. See *Life of Sri Ramakrishna*, Advaita Ashrama, 1971: 26.

> month has a Krishna festival [*kṛṣṇotsab*], in almost every festival scenes from Krishna's life are enacted [*kṛṣṇajātrā*]. A song about Krishna [*kṛṣṇagīti*] is in nearly every throat, Krishna's name is on every tongue. One person has a list of Krishna's names on the clothes he wears all day, another the imprint of Krishna's name on his body. Some won't make a journey without uttering Krishna's name, others won't study or write a letter without first writing it. The beggar will accept no alms without first crying, 'Victory to Radha and Krishna!' When we hear something we don't like we express our disgust with the words, 'Radha-Krishna!' When looking after some captured bird we teach it to say, 'Radha-Krishna'. Krishna is all-pervasive in our region.[23]

A somewhat exaggerated claim in the introduction to a book on Krishna, no doubt, but it makes a valid point: Krishna consciousness was an integral part of the local culture. In his final years, Upadhyay held Krishna up to Bengalis as the rallying focus of his call to national unity. The rationale of this exaltation contained an appreciation of the pervasiveness of Krishna consciousness in Bengal. In addition, Upadhyay wrote a number of fine articles in Bengali describing Krishna as a devotional ideal. We shall discuss his stance on Krishna in the appropriate place.

Finally, we must consider another influence that doubtless had an important bearing on the young Bhabani. This was his uncle Kalicaran's regular contact with the Banerji home after his conversion to Christianity. Notwithstanding strong family opposition, Kalicaran was baptized in 1864, when he was a seventeen-year-old student in the Free Church Institution in Calcutta. Bhabani was then not much older than three. Somewhat surprisingly, Kalicaran was allowed to visit the family home in Khannyan regularly. This bears eloquent testimony not so much to the tolerance of the Banerji household as to Kalicaran's mature grasp of his new-found faith, which he did not allow unduly to subvert his former life-style. *The Blade* (p. 10) notes: 'But of a Saturday, from Calcutta, would come the uncle Kali Charan Banerjee. He was working in Calcutta as a busy student. He had become a Christian, but his habits in no wise differed from the homely customs of Khanyan. He would settle down in the parlour and teach Bhabani his first lessons.'[24]

[23] From the 'Upakramaṇikā' of the *Krsnacaritra* in *Bankimcandrer Granthabali*, Part II, B.E. 1316: 403a.

[24] Barber (1912:22) says: 'Mr Banurji continued to visit his old home, and though no other members of the family ever became Christians they welcomed him among

Kalicaran went on to become not only a leading Churchman but also a prominent nationalist. He and Bhabani remained on friendly terms throughout their subsequent careers and died within a few months of each other. One of the main aims of Kalicaran's life was to show that one could be a Christian and remain a patriot. In this attempt he was something of a pioneer. The Banerji family, the growing Bhabani included, must have followed his career with interest. The important thing was that by becoming a Christian without being abrasively unHindu, Kalicaran had broken an important psychological barrier vis-à-vis his family. If he hadn't exactly legitimized conversion to the Christian faith, he had at least made the prospect conceivable. Perhaps a seed had been sown in the impressionable Bhabani's mind that was to come to fruition years later.

Like other little boys of five or so, Bhabani first went to the local village school or *pāṭhśālā*. The village schoolmaster, who was nicknamed 'Pitambar the Lame' (*khōḍā pītāmbar*), seemed to fit the classic image of his kind. A martinet, he was wont to 'exorcise the spirit of inattentiveness among the boys by dint of a blow or two'.[25] We are told that Bhabani, though highly intelligent, was also an 'independent little fellow' (Bl., p. 10) and often felt the brunt of his wrath. Later, Upadhyay the teacher, was reluctant to vent corporal

them.' Then in a Note he adds: 'Two nephews did become Christians, one of them a Roman Catholic; but he was no ornament to the Christian faith, for in his enthusiasm for the national movement, he again became a Hindu and remained one till his death'. Thus in a word does he dismiss the complex commitments of Upadhyay's life. A statement of Nistarini's on Kalicaran the Christian is worth noting (p. 39): 'No one in the family disregarded him because he was a Christian; rather, when formal respect was to be shown this fact would be ignored. Kalicaran laid to rest the view that by becoming a Christian one separates from one's Hindu kin so decisively that later the missionaries found it very easy to make Christians. He would observe the customs of Bhai-phota and Jamai-sasthi; during Sarasvati Puja he would do worship to his books; he regarded his mother as a deity.' *Khṛṣṭān bale paribārer kehai tāke amānya kare nāi; baraṅ praṇām karbār samay se kathā bhulei jeto. khṛṣṭān hale je hindu bhāider saṅge taphāt haye jāy, e bhābṭi kālīcaraṇ eman mere- diyechilo je, pare pādrīder khṛṣṭān karār anek subidhā hayechilo. se bhāiphōṭā nito, jāmāi-ṣaṣṭhī katto. sarasvatī pūjāy bai pūjā katto. māke debatār mata dekhto.)*

25 *Cheleder madhye ekṭu kichu edik odik dekhilei prahārer coṭe bhūt bhāgāiya den*; Simha, p. 3. A classic description of the irascible Bengali village schoolmaster—lameness and all—can be found in Lal Behari Day's *Govinda Samanta or the History of a Bengal Raiyat*, vol. I, 1874: ch. xii, 'The Village Schoolmaster'. We may ask whether a folkloric memory is at work in narrative of this kind, making stereotypes of individuals, or indeed whether these individuals feel that they have to live up to expectations!

punishment on his charges; he sought to win them over by camaraderie and by earning their respect.

Before long Bhabani was launched on what seems, to all intents and purposes, a rather unsettling westernized school career. First he attended the Chinsura Hindu School nearby. Then Debicaran was transferred to the adjacent town of Hooghly. The whole family moved, and Bhabani joined the Hooghly Branch School there (the 'branch' of the government-run Hooghly Collegiate School at Chinsura). Then, apparently, his guardian(s) moved to Calcutta, for Bhabani 'was admitted to the General Assembly Institution where he attracted the attention of the principal, Mr Jardin' (Bl., p. 12).[26] By this time Bhabani was about 9 or 10 years old. He 'secured a prize for general proficiency almost every year. Although in the fifth class, he competed with the boys of the first class in English Reading and carried off the prize to the astonishment of all' (*Sketch*, pt. I, p. 4).[27] Clearly Bhabani was able to cope with the chopping and changing of schools. *The Blade* avers (p. 31) that it was in the General Assembly Institution that he first learnt about and became attracted to the person of Christ. Established by the Scottish General Missionary Board in the 1830s, the school would have insisted on Bible study as a necessary component of the curriculum. The nurturing of another important seed had begun. When Bhabani was 13 or so, the family returned to the Chinsura area and he was admitted to the Hooghly Collegiate School. From here, at 15, he passed the Entrance Examination, which gave him access to higher education.[28]

26 The *Sketch* (pt. I, p. 10) mistakenly implies that it was at this point that Bhabani met and befriended Naren Dutta, the future Swami Vivekananda. Väth (p. 72) follows the *Sketch* on this. *The Blade* (p. 26) puts things right by noting that it was 'in 1880 or thereabouts that [Bhabani] met Naren Dutt'. At the time Bhabani was teaching in the General Assembly's Institution, while Naren was a College student elsewhere. We shall take note of their meeting in chapter 3. *The Life of Swami Vivekananda*, Vivekananda's 'official' biography (Advaita Ashrama, 1960:24), agrees with *The Blade*'s chronology.

27 In the school system of the time, there were eight or nine classes in all, starting from the higher class-number (when students began the study of English) and terminating at the first or entrance class, during which students were prepared for the 'Entrance Examination', i.e. the University Matriculation Examination.

28 On the Entrance Examination, see previous note. The Hooghly Collegiate School occupied rooms on the ground floor of the building also housing Hooghly College. The building was erected in 1810 and in 1837 was purchased by the Committee of Public Instruction for what was known as Mohamed Mohsin's College. A ground floor plan of the building can be consulted in Government of India (Occasional Reports No. 6): *Educational Buildings in India*, Calcutta, 1911; see p. 28 and facing page.

It was between the ages of 13 and 15 that Bhabani began to make decisions that had an important bearing on his life. At 13, he was invested with the sacred thread. This is the ceremony that marks the coming of age of male, upper-caste Hindus. It affirms their twice-born (*dvija*) status, and the worldly and spiritual responsibilities it entails. Upadhyay claimed later that by then he had read the two epics, the *Ramayana* and the *Mahabharata,* 13 and 7 times respectively. Both are Vaishnava texts, in their traditional Sanskrit versions compiled in the centuries around the beginning of the Christian era.[29] They are peopled with male and female characters larger than life—celestial and demonic, virtuous and dastardly, human and animal—and abound with tales of wonder and derring-do. Their main characters and events are known to most Hindus, and their story-lines act as the basis of devotion in particular to Rama and Krishna respectively, the avatars or human 'descents' of the deity Vishnu.

Upadhyay's boast would have referred not to the reading of the Sanskrit versions of the *Ramayana* and *Mahabharata,* but to their shorter Bengali forms attributed respectively to Krittivas (early fifteenth century) and Kashiram (early seventeenth century).[30] In essence both epics treat of the tensions between *dharma* (righteousness) and *adharma* (unrighteousness) in our relationships, and about the costly

29 Traditionally the *Mahabharata* was reckoned to be a hundred thousand verses, the *Ramayana* about a quarter of that length.

30 Far from being translations of the Sanskrit, the vernacular texts substantially modified the latter, while retaining basic themes and characters. 'Their interest is ethical, not literary, and the world they reproduce is not the ancient India of Valmiki and Vyasa [the reputed authors of the Sanskrit *Ramayana* and *Mahabharata* respectively], but the Bengal of their own day' (Ghosh, 1948: 76). They were extremely popular among Bengalis, and in whole or in part were often committed to memory from an early age, a task made easier by the fact that they used the *payār* metre, the standard rhyming couplet of Bengali poetry. In his *The Bengali Ramayanas* (1920: 170), Dineshchandra Sen states that, 'at 7 years of age I had committed almost the whole of Krittivas's Ramayana to memory without any conscious effort'. See chapter 3 of Sen's work for a comparison between Valmiki's *Rāmāyana* and Krittivas' version. This custom of memorizing the text has persisted into more recent times. Tarapada Mukherjee (1928–90), who lectured in Bengali at the School of Oriental and African Studies, University of London, wrote: 'What I say ... is based on my personal experience. I was born and brought up (until I was 16) in a village which is now in Bangladesh. What I say is ... true in respect of that part of the country during that period.

Bengali children learn the stories of the epics from their mothers or grandmothers or aunts before they can read or write. When they are in their teens they begin to recite or chant the metrical adaptations of the Ramayana by Krttivasa and the Mahabharata by Kasiramdasa. Before becoming an adult the child recites the two

triumph, in human terms, of *dharma* over *adharma*. Most of their chief male characters, including Rama and Krishna, belong to the Kshatriya or warrior caste, and the dominant themes, usually set in a martial context, are concerned largely with just conflict in a righteous cause. In similar vein, Bhabani read novels by Bankimcandra Chatterjee, Rameshcandra Dutt and Sir Walter Scott. Future events suggest that all this stirred the imagination of the increasingly restive youth, as he became aware of the political situation of his country.

It was at about this time that Bhabani did a remarkable thing. While still at Chinsura, after school hours he would regularly cross the Hooghly by boat to study the Sanskritic tradition at a famous *ṭol* or native seminary at Bhatpara, on the other side. And, 'when he was free at home it would be a real pleasure for him to read Sanskrit and to try his skill with the knotty riders of Euclid' (Bl., p. 12). There is something remarkable in one so young having the vision and commitment, on his own initiative and against the trend, to pursue the study of his native tradition apace with his successful career in the westernized schools. Among his peers at the time there was increasing pressure to rely on a westernized education to get on in life. Native learning would lead nowhere. Bhabani did not swallow this piece of conventional wisdom. Indeed, Sanskrit was to remain a central concern for life. About a year after being invested with the sacred thread, he resolved never to eat fish or meat (a truly mind-boggling decision for a Bengali youth of Bhabani's background); he kept this resolution for the rest of his life with one exception in each case, as we shall see. The reason for his vegetarianism is not given, but it fits in with his decision to attend the *ṭol*, and no doubt was meant to develop his self-image as a Hindu and a Brahmin.

In school he fell in, as *The Blade* quaintly puts it, with 'a set of tipsies'. It was almost *de rigueur* for the more defiant among the adolescents of the age to cock a snook at traditional taboos. Though he would hand 'cups of wine to others' in a spirit of camaraderie, Bhabani himself never touched a drop and would often have to tend

texts several times either for his own pleasure or for the benefit of his elders for whom it is a pious act to listen to these scriptures. For months I have recited the Mahabharata to a group of old women, some of whom could not read the texts themselves.... Girls of 11 or 12 must know the stories of the two sacred books. They must demonstrate their knowledge of the Ramayana and the Mahabharata before they are accepted as brides in a respectable family' (private communication). So Bhabani's boast was nothing too wonderful.

to drunken friends (*Sketch*, pt. I, p.5). Their plight increased his opposition to alcohol, and years later (under the influence of Keshab Sen, who had himself been impressed by the Salvation Army in this regard) he joined a temperance pressure group, the Band of Hope, and inveighed against the demon drink.

Bhabani was also an accomplished sportsman. He particularly enjoyed swimming, football, cricket and Indian-style wrestling. We are told that he believed that mental health depended on the health of the body. To this end he encouraged his friends to exercise regularly. At play, and as we are about to see, at war, he was the leader of the local youths, with even his two older brothers, Haricaran and Parbaticaran, following his lead. Thus, at about 15 or 16, having passed the Entrance Examination and joined the First Arts course[31] at Hooghly College in Chinsura, Bhabani is presented to us as no ordinary youth: vigorous in mind and body, with the vision to respect tradition without being enslaved by it, he was on the lookout for a cause in life. He found it through the Armenian incidents.

At the time in Chinsura there lived the remnant of a once flourishing Armenian community that had settled there to trade since the mid-seventeenth century, soon after the Dutch had established the port as a commercial centre.[32] Some Armenian youths had taken to amusing themselves by throwing stones at the earthen pitchers of the local Hindu women who came to the river bank to draw water. Repeated requests by Bhabani and his band to desist fell on deaf ears. On the contrary, their appeals were regarded by the Armenians as a challenge to continue. There was a pitched battle between the rival gangs. The upshot was that the foreigners[33] 'saw no other recourse but to flee in all directions. With coats and trousers torn, hats lost, and bearing the marks of the recent battle on their backs

[31] Writing in 1912, Barber comments (Note, p. 8) on the First Arts or F.A. course as follows: 'The F.A. examination now called the Intermediate Arts, which is held at the end of the second college year, might be termed the halfway house in the collegiate career. Many stop here, because they are anxious to get into service, or from lack of means to prosecute their studies further. A man's ability and salary are often gauged by the letters he puts after his name. Some are even proud to possess F.F.A. (Failed First Arts) to show that they have at least read up to that standard and taken the examination.'

[32] The Dutch ceded Chinsura to Britain in 1826 in exchange for Sumatra. On the presence of the Armenians, see M.J. Seth, 1937: ch. xxvi, 'Armenians in Chinsurah'.

[33] Simha, who gives the most detailed account of the episode (which shows that his book contains original material), uses the term *phiriṅgi*—not a sympathetic word.

and cheeks, they returned each to his own home' (Simha, p. 5). The altercation lasted on and off for a couple of days. Eventually the law was called in; the elders of both communities, however, managed to resolve the matter out of court. The account given in *Varia* 5 intimates that Bhabani had been spoiling for a fight in the first place. If he had meekly requested the Armenians to desist on the grounds that they were in breach of their own (Christian) scriptures (which he had studied in school), he would have been taken for a coward. Battle was the only solution. Antagonism between the two groups had been building up for some time. Another melée is recorded over the alleged assault by the Armenians on an old Bengali woman.

There was a humane side to Bhabani. In the manner of cock-fights, there was a popular practice at the time of organizing 'duels' between bulbuls caught for the purpose. The bulbul is the Indian nightingale (family *Pycnonotidae*). Once, when a large crowd had gathered to witness such a spectacle, Bhabani turned up with his band and demanded that the show be abandoned. He got his way since no one wanted to take on the youths. This happened several times so that the number of bulbul fights in the area soon declined.[34] In what he regarded as a just cause, Bhabani was not afraid to use or threaten violence.

The Armenian business rankled in Bhabani's mind. Soon after, probably in 1876, the nationalist leader Surendranath Banerjea visited the area to lecture. Surendranath had returned from England in 1875 after having unsuccessfully pleaded against his dismissal from the Indian Civil Service, and been unjustly 'shut out', as he saw it, from the Bar. He was then appointed Professor of English in the Metropolitan Institution in Calcutta. From here he embarked on a series of lectures in the region 'upon such subjects as Indian Unity, the study of History, the Life of Mazzini' with a view to stirring up patriotic sentiment among the youth of Bengal (S. Banerjea, 1963: 32–3). Surendranath was a constitutionalist, believing that under British rule Indians could come of age politically through constitutional agitation, not violence. Bhabani managed to meet Surendranath during his visit and related his grievance against the Armenians, seeking redress. He received a promise that Surendranath would personally petition the authorities in the matter.

Years later, in an address in Calcutta's Beadon Square, Upadhyay referred to this meeting with the nationalist and to the effect it had

34 This information is derived from *Varia* 5.

on him. He recalled that even then, young as he was, he was dissatisfied with Surendranath's policy of appeasement (see Simha, p. 6). In an important autobiographical article entitled 'My Deliverance of India' (*Āmār Bhārat Uddhār*, hereafter ABU), Upadhyay describes his reaction as a youth to Surendranath's lecture campaign. 'When I was 14 or 15, Suren Babu started a new movement.... Bengal was roused by his lectures. I could neither eat nor sleep. Just as the milkmaids were intoxicated at hearing Krishna's flute, so was I.... If I couldn't hear a lecture my heart sank; but when I did hear one, and had finished applauding and was returning home, my heart felt empty—it seemed there was a void inside' (ABU: 1–2).[35]

Simha continues (pp. 6–7) that it was after the meeting with Surendranath that Bhabani became convinced that only force would drive out the foreigner. They've come to our country, he thought, they've waxed fat on what it has to offer, and then they want to quarrel with us! The arrogance! This can't go on. He'd become a soldier; he'd learn warfare and drive the foreigner out by force! This thought possessed him completely. He could no longer concentrate on his studies, and cast about for an opportunity to become a soldier. At 16 or so, he applied to enlist as a soldier for the mounting Zulu campaign in southern Africa (not to help the British presumably, but to learn warfare). His application was detected and turned down by an official who was a relative, 'on the ground of his being a minor' (Bl., p. 14).[36] On another occasion, he took it into his head to jump on a train heading west in the hope of becoming a soldier in some princely state in the Raja's army. Parbaticaran, his older brother, suspecting that something was afoot, caught up with him at a nearby station and brought him home (Simha, p. 7). With some success, efforts were made to convince him to continue his studies.[37]

Bhabani was now about 17. He was still in the First Arts class in Hooghly College, and still brooding about studying war and somehow driving out the foreigner.[38] Surendranath's policy of constitutional

35 This piece was first published on May 26 and June 2, 1907 in *Svaraj*, a Bengali weekly edited by Upadhyay.

36 Bhabani was probably closer to 17. For an account of the Zulu campaign, see Donald Morris, 1965.

37 Simha seems to have mixed up subsequent events. There is some confusion about the train of events in the sources, and I have tried to establish a chronology.

38 This was a not uncommon objective among young militant patriots of the time. See Peter Heehs, 1993, especially chapters 2–3.

agitation became increasingly galling. In desperation Bhabani decided to beard the lion, or at least one of his chief lieutenants, in his den. He would discuss his position with Anandamohan Bose, one of Surendranath's chief collaborators. Presumably Anandamohan was chosen because he was a friend of Bhabani's uncle Kalicaran, another leading figure in their camp, and Bhabani could exploit the family connection to secure an interview. The plan worked. He was granted an interview with Anandamohan in the latter's Calcutta home.

At the meeting, Bhabani, to Anandamohan's amusement, blurted out: 'Not through pen but through sword!' and was then treated to a discourse on the virtues of constitutional agitation, especially under political masters as civilized as the British, whom Anandamohan called the 'apostles of freedom' (ABU). Bhabani returned home unconvinced. There was nothing for it but to take the matter into his own hands. He decided to run away to Gwalior, some 700 miles north-west of Calcutta, there 'to learn the art of war and drive away the *phiriṅgī*.'[39] Gwalior was the capital of the territory ruled by the Maharaja Scindia. Bhabani could have been under no illusions about Gwalior's lack of true independence under British paramountcy. Nevertheless, it was a symbol of the great Maratha power of old, and allegedly still a centre of Maratha military prowess.

So it was that one day in 1878, with Rs. 10 in hand (his unpaid college fees for two months), Bhabani stealthily started off on the long journey to Gwalior. With him went three like-minded colleagues. Bhabani was a born leader. In one enterprise or other during his chequered career, he was wont to gather about him a company of loyal friends who were prepared to stick by him, come what may. The reader will often have occasion to note this. It says much for Bhabani's personal qualities and force of character.

Since cash was in short supply, they could afford tickets by train only as far as Etawah, a town about 70 miles north-east of Gwalior; the rest of the journey would have to be made on foot. The band spent the night at Etawah, and set off at dawn for their destination. It was a gruelling journey. The travellers had little or no food; it was summer and blazing hot by day. The terrain was rugged and sparsely

39 *Juddhabidyā śikhiba—phiriṅgī tāḍāiba* (ABU, p. 4.) *Varia* 5 mentions an added reason for Bhabani's wanting to abandon his studies. Parbati, a poor scholar, had failed his First Arts examination and was embarrassed at the prospect of having to repeat the year in the company of his younger brother. Bhabani wanted to spare him this embarrassment.

vegetated, the more so since the rains had not come. The way was perilous too, since this was bandit territory. For most of the journey the freedom fighters tagged along with a small group of men who claimed to be the Maharaja's soldiers returning to duty after home leave. Our adventurers had a nagging fear that their guides might be bandits in disguise, luring them to their doom. But as they neared their destination and nothing untoward happened, their spirits rose. With flagging limbs but rising hopes they approached Gwalior. Upadhyay describes how, on the last night of their march, their spirits soared as one of the band, who had a fine voice, burst into a patriotic Bengali song: 'Tell me, India, how long will it be before we swim across this ocean of misery?'[40]

They reached Gwalior in four days—penniless, ravenous, exhausted but nothing daunted. In the words of the *Sketch*, 'On their arrival ... copious showers of rain refreshed the land and little currents of water began to flow. The citizens hailed them as mahatmas [great souls] and the rivulet brought them forth a fish which they caught, boiled and swallowed with a pinch of salt, they were so hungry. It was on this occasion only ... that Bhabanicharan tasted fish'.[41] The escapade proved abortive. Within a week of their arrival in Gwalior, before they could make any headway towards achieving their objective, the father of one of the four, a high official in the police, arrived to shepherd them home.[42]

Not long after his return, Bhabani's family had him transferred to the Metropolitan Institution in Calcutta, where the well-known educationist and champion of women's rights, Isvarcandra Vidyasagar, was Principal. Bhabani stayed with his eldest brother, Haricaran, who was a medical student in the city. It was hoped that Haricaran would have a calming effect on the restless youth and that under his watchful eye Bhabani would be more amenable to pursuing his studies. Not a

40 *Kata kāl pare, bala, bhārat, re, duḥkha sāgar sā̃tāri pār habe* (ABU, p. 10).

41 Pt. I, p. 6. Presumably Animananda means that this was the only time Bhabani tasted fish *after* he had resolved to be a vegetarian.

42 They had written back to a friend, revealing their whereabouts (ABU, p. 11). There is a note in the GLA copy of Simha which says that it was the father of Saratcandra Shome, one of the band, who brought them home. The note describes Mr Shome as an official in the 'E.I.Ry' = Eastern Indian Railway(?). Perhaps he was in the railway police if this information is to be squared with the ABU description that 'he was a high offical in the police-department' (*tini ekjan puliś bibhāger ucca karmmacārī chilen*; p. 11). The note also intimates that only three (including Bhabani), not four, set off for Gwalior.

bit of it. The Metropolitan Institution harboured at least one important influence that could only fan the flames of revolutionary ardour. Bhabani was now 18, in the second and final year of the First Arts course. Surendranath Banerjea, who taught English Literature in the College, would rouse his students (Bhabani included) to patriotic fervour by stirring references to contemporary Italian nationalists. 'Who among you will be a Mazzini, a Garibaldi?' he would cry, and his hearers, clapping enthusiastically, would respond, 'All! All!'[43]

But this was not enough for the young firebrand. He grew more and more disheartened by Surendranath's uncompromising repudiation of Mazzini's call to violence. The Italian nationalist's revolutionary teachings, averred Surendranath, were 'unsuited to the circumstances of India and ... fatal to its normal development, along the lines of peaceful and orderly progress' (S. Banerjea, 1963: 40). 'Peaceful and orderly progress' towards India's freedom from foreign domination was hardly what Bhabani had in mind. In frustration, he turned to 'siddhi', a crude and easily available narcotic prepared from hemp leaves. This had an unnerving effect. 'Once he got so intoxicated that he kept on screaming the whole night' (*Sketch*, pt. I, p. 5).

But it was an incident involving Surendranath that decided Bhabani to leave off the drug. He was attending one of the nationalist's English classes, still under the lingering influence of siddhi, and fell asleep at his desk behind a pile of books. During the course of the class, Surendranath had need of a volume in Bhabani's possession. When told that Bhabani was asleep, he is reported to have said: 'I have no need of the man; I am in need of his book.'[44] This summary dismissal, almost of his manhood, by someone who advocated a virile patriotism for the youth of the day,[45] stung Bhabani to the quick. He declares that he resolved then to give up siddhi, and that he never touched it again (ABU, p. 13).

There is strength of mind here. While the drug had not become an

[43] ABU, p. 15. Giuseppe Mazzini (1805–1872), who had died not long before, had a great impact on Surendranath. See S. Banerjea, 1963: 40, and Surendranath's lecture, 'Joseph Mazzini' (1876) in *Speeches and Writings of Hon. Surendranath Banerjea (Selected by himself)*, Natesan & Co., Madras, n.d. (hereafter SWSB).

[44] *Āmi mānuṣṭike cāhi nā—mānuṣṭir baikhāni cāi* (ABU, p. 13).

[45] 'I sought by every possible means in my power to kindle in the young [men] the beginnings of public spirit, and to inspire them with a patriotic ardour, fruitful of good to them and to the motherland' (S. Banerjea, 1963: 32).

addiction,[46] the firmness of Bhabani's resolve, its uncompromising nature, was absolute. He went further. He determined not to complete his college studies, and not to marry: he would devote his life single-mindedly to the struggle for India's freedom. But in his own way—by force. He resolved to try his luck in Gwalior again. This time he would go alone.

The way Bhabani's mind worked was no doubt unusual in comparison with the more pragmatic goal-setting of his peers, but it was not particularly mysterious. His own personal background (we have seen that he was mindful of his Brahmin status, according to which he was meant to uphold disinterestedly the autonomy of Hindu *dharma*), the beleaguered state of his motherland (here was a mother figure he could serve in the absence of his human mother), the virile and selfless patriotism inculcated by Surendranath, and a macho ideal, deriving partly from the image the British were projecting of themselves and partly, by reaction, from their caricature of the Bengali male as effeminate (see chapter 1), all combined to produce Bhabani's bent of mind.

There was a strong romantic strain to all this. It arose in large measure from such writings as Bankimcandra's first novel, *Durgesnandini* (The Chieftain's Daughter), published in 1865. Bhabani was familiar with this work, and as we shall see, it affected him not a little. *Durgesnandini* is a story about patriotism and knightly chivalry, and tells of the recapture of Bengal from Pathan usurpers by a Rajput emissary of the Moghul emperor in Delhi. The following extract, which comes early in the book, is significant not only for the tone it sets, but for obvious correspondences with British rule:

> When first the waves of Muslim soldiers, in the fervour of their new faith [*nabadharmānurāge*], poured into India from the encircling Himalayan peaks in the pride of their strength, the Rajput heroes, Prithviraj and the rest, checked that flood with extraordinary valour. But it was the wish of Providence [*bidhātā*] that India decline. So the Rajput rulers being disunited at the time, began to quarrel with one another. The Muslims systematically conquered the Hindu rulers one by one, and established the Delhi regime.[47]

46 Its influence was short-lived. Animananda, without saying why Bhabani gave up the drug, informs us that 'After some 8 days, he had had enough of it and did not touch it the rest of his life' (*Sketch*, pt. I, p. 5).

47 Bankimcandra's most famous patriotic novel, *Anandamath* (The Abbey of Bliss), which is about celibate ('Hindu') warrior-monks rising up against non-Hindu oppressive rule, could not have been an influencing factor at this time, for it started publication serially in March-April (Bengali month, Caitra) 1880, in *Bangadarsan*, the journal Bankim himself edited. Bhabani never mentions the novel in this connection. But, as we shall see, *Anandamath* was to play a significant role in Bhabani's thinking at a later date.

Bhabani was approaching 19 when he made off for the second time to Gwalior, this time with something of a heavy heart.[48] Since he had more money (Rs 30) on this occasion, he was able to travel by train to Agra, and thence to Dholpur. At Dholpur he stayed with a family acquaintance who was the Rana of Dholpur's tutor. Though his host was taken aback at his plans, he made him welcome for the night. Mutton was cooked for the evening meal. This put Bhabani in a quandary, for his resolve not to eat meat had been in force for about five years. He tells how, as a soldier-to-be, he felt embarrassed to say that he was a vegetarian, so he tucked into the meat, and asked for more! This was the last time he broke his resolution. That evening there was to be a nautch display at the Rana's house, and Bhabani's host invited him along. 'But I did not go. I thought that someone who had taken up the burden of rescuing India does not attend nautch shows.'[49]

The last leg of the journey, the 36 miles or so from Dholpur to Gwalior, had no rail link. Those who had the means could hire a horse or travel less grandly in a two-tiered camel-drawn carriage. Bhabani's finances dictated the latter course. The carriage set off at about 10 p.m. He describes how, from his vantage point in the upper storey, after he had come to terms with the jolts, he fantasized about the battles he would lead against the enemy.

> Thus I travelled in the camel-cart, delighting in the creations of my mind. I couldn't sleep a wink. My mind was filled with the stories of *Durgesnandini* and *Bangabijeta*. It seemed that in the dark, in the wind and rain, I gave my horse his head and roamed freely. How many perils I encountered! How many enemies I despatched! So many fantasies came to mind, yet I came across no Tilottama, nor did I moor my boat to visit some Sarala. This much toughness there was to my deliverance of India, and this intransigence hasn't left me, even in my mature years (ABU, pp. 21–2).[50]

They arrived in Gwalior, or rather in Laskar, the city's residential part, early in the morning. Bhabani had nowhere to stay; he had decided to avoid Bengalis for fear of detection. As he was walking down the main street, somewhat at a loss, a man came up to him

48 The following account is taken from ABU, pp. 16ff.

49 *Āmi jāilām nā. mane karitām, je bhārat uddhārer bhār laiyāche, se nāc tāmāsā dekhe nā* (ABU, p. 18).

50 *Bangabijeta* is a novel by Rameshcandra Dutt. Tilottama and Sarala are heroines in *Durgesnandini* and *Bangabijeta* respectively.

and invited him to act as tutor to a Sikh gentleman's young son. Indeed, Bhabani would have been clearly recognizable as a Bengali. As noted in chapter 1, it was not uncommon for Bengalis to travel far from home, and they had a reputation for knowing English. As English teachers they were in demand. Bhabani accepted the invitation. Thus began the first of a series of teaching jobs in his life. Bhabani found that his conditions of employment restricted his movements too much, so he left after a week and, through the good offices of the person who first accosted him in the street, put up in the house of a young man who worked as a *munshi* or clerk in the Maharaja's employ. Soon news got round that a good English teacher was in town, and without formalities Bhabani ran a small school for Brahmin boys. But he accepted no fees: as a Brahmin he would not sell knowledge to Brahmins. He subsisted by giving tuition to a non-Brahmin boy. Some time passed in this way, but as he himself says (ABU, p. 26), he was no nearer to accomplishing the purpose for which he had come to Gwalior.

Clearly Bhabani's sense of caste and its obligations was strong. Was it not incongruous then, we may ask, even reprehensible, for one so self-consciously a Brahmin to seek to follow the *dharma* of a Kshatriya or warrior? Surely Bhabani, with his background of Sanskritic education, was aware of this? Hindu tradition is clear on the matter. 'Better one's own caste duty, though lacking in merit' says the ancient and influential *Bhagavadgita*, 'than the caste duty of others, though well performed. Better to die in one's own caste duty; that of others is fraught with peril' (3.35). Bhabani makes no mention of this apparent violation of the dharmic code. Perhaps, in the ardour of youth, he justified it by the exigencies of the time, tried to offset it by a more rigid adherence to his Brahmin status in other ways. Later in life, new ideas would emerge on the Bengal scene that would articulate the ideal of the warrior-ascetic, reconciling, in a new synthesis, the goals of the Brahmin and the Kshatriya. But for now this remained a hazy conception in Bhabani's agitated mind. In any case, before many days were to pass, he would have to come to terms with the reality of the situation.

About a fortnight after his arrival in Gwalior, he obtained an interview with the Commander of the Maharaja's army. He tells how, when he expressed his wish to enlist as a soldier, the old man answered that he was Commander in name only; he had no real authority. He could do nothing for Bhabani. The reason was soon given. Some time before, a mock-battle had been staged between sides led by the then Maharaja, Jayaji Rao, and the Commander. The occasion was a grand one; high-ranking British army officers had been invited to watch the spectacle. At the height of the manoeuvres, when the Commander had the upper hand, the Maharaja requested a break for the passage of his midday meal. The Commander agreed, on condition that his adversary surrender—which the Maharaja did! From then on, the Commander fell into disfavour and was in effect relieved of his authority, the mantle of command falling on one Shamser Khan, a self-indulgent young man (ABU, p. 29).

It wasn't long before the truth sank in. Bhabani realized that in the present state of affairs, India had neither the will nor the wherewithal to drive the foreigner out by force. If Maratha military prowess had fallen so low—its authority emasculated, the flower of its army disgraced before the enemy himself—he might as well abandon his plan to become a soldier. In fact, Bhabani was finally growing up. The time for mad-cap schemes was over; he would have to decide more soberly what to do with his life. Easier said than done! Bhabani's mind was in a turmoil; the future remained uncertain. He would return home, but beyond that he was unsure what to do, for other factors in the equation had not changed. He was still determined not to marry, not to pursue a college career, to devote his life to reinstating India's self-respect, to liberating India from foreign domination. As he left Gwalior, how could he know that in giving up the sword he was to train his pen to become a more effective weapon in India's cause than any sword he might wield?

# Chapter 3

## Like an Ember Smouldering: Under Keshab's Influence

Bhabani returned to his long-suffering family, disillusioned. He had given up the ideal of the celibate warrior, but not that of the celibate. His commitment as an ascetic to the struggle for India's autonomy took on a larger, more far-reaching vision by his embrace of a new ideal, that of the celibate teacher. We must try and understand what lay behind this. The sexual psychology of the times has been analysed, plausibly in the context of contemporary perceptions I believe, in terms of the interplay between three poles: *puṃstva* or masculinity, *strītva* or femininity and *klibatva* or effeminacy (Nandy, 1983: 7–8).[1] As indicated previously, the Victorian contrast between the masculine and the feminine was total, and reflected and reinforced in important respects the traditional Hindu understanding of the cultural opposition between man and woman.[2] For Bhabani as a man, the established man-woman contrast held out no conscious threat to his masculinity as such. Women were women and men were men and never the twain could meet, at least not psychologically. What he made of this, in terms of his personal circumstances, we shall consider in its proper place. But the situation was different in the case of the 'masculine-effeminate' polarity. The British projection of their own masculinity, in contrast to the depiction of the effeminate Bengali male that was gaining ground, threatened the equilibrium of this polarity vis-à-vis Bengali males. As Nandy

1 Nandy speaks of '*purusatva* (the essence of masculinity), *naritva* (the essence of femininity) and *klibatva* (the essence of hermaphroditism)' (pp. 7–8). While acknowledging his distinctions, I prefer my own terminology.

2 To appreciate the Hindu view see, e.g., Leslie, 1989.

says, 'The polarity defined by the antonymous *purusatva* [masculinity] and *naritva* [femininity] was gradually supplanted, in the colonial culture of politics, by the antonyms of *purusatva* and *klibatva* [effeminacy]; femininity-in-masculinity was now perceived as the final negation of a man's political identity, a pathology more dangerous than femininity itself.... Now there was an attempt to lump together all forms of androgyny and counterpoise them against undifferentiated masculinity' (Nandy, 1983: 7–8). The ideal of the celibate teacher, once the more obvious ideal of the celibate warrior proved unworkable, was meant to affirm Bhabani's 'undiluted' masculinity. How so?

Given Bhabani's overall political aim in life—'political' in the broad sense of seeking India's autonomy in the face of foreign political (in the narrow sense) and cultural aggression—he tried first to affirm his masculinity by embracing the ideal of the celibate warrior. In the context of the polarity we are considering, the role of the warrior acted as the 'masculine' pole, that of the constitutional reformer represented the 'effeminate' pole. The effeminacy of the constitutionalist, or appeaser in Bhabani's eyes, lay in his inability to accomplish his political ends. So the way of the constitutionalist had to be eschewed.

But literally realizing the warrior ideal proved impracticable. The polarity then appeared in another form. Masculinity would be preserved by adopting the ideal of the celibate teacher, effeminacy guarded against by rejecting the life-style of the worldling. The worldling was the householder (*grhastha*), traditionally concerned with such worldly ends as marriage, the acquisition of wealth and so on. How was the householder effeminate from our point of view? Not in the purely physical sense, of course, for in the normal course of events by definition he exercises his masculinity by begetting offspring. The householder was effeminate in the spiritual sense, for he affirmed his masculinity by gratifying himself in the pursuit of worldly ends, not by ascesis. According to traditional Hindu spirituality this meant that he was unable to build up spiritual power or *tapas*. The celibate, on the other hand, by the ascesis of celibacy, was able to accumulate *tapas*, which could then be released in various ways to transform the world. Hindu folklore is full of tendentious tales about yogis (celibate ascetics) who are either storehouses of *tapas* which they then use to devastating effect for their own ends, or who have been emasculated spiritually (i.e. they have lost the *tapas* they have accumulated) by falling for the sexual charms of beautiful temptresses. By affirming his masculinity physically, the householder so to speak lost his masculinity spiritually, with its potentially transforming powers. The celibate, by foregoing the exercise of his masculinity physically had the capacity to assert it spiritually, in more far-reaching ways. This view has its counterpart in the spiritualities of other religious traditions. Celibacy, therefore, was a crucial factor in the 'masculine' psychology of a Hindu youth in tune with the traditional spirituality of his faith and pursuing a visionary goal in life.

Further, the *tapas*-acquiring yogi could be one of two kinds: either the ascetic activist (*karmayogī*) or the ascetic contemplative (*jñānī*). The contemplative withdrew from the world, seeking liberation from it through the path of meditative absorption (*jñāna*) on the true nature of the self (*ātman, puruṣa*). Action (*karman*), which should be entirely disinterested (*nishkāma*), as to both its bodily and mental aspects, was to be kept to a minimum. The *tapas* thus acquired would purify the *jñānī*'s being, consume the karma he had accumulated hitherto and enable the liberating knowledge to break through. The *karmayogī*, on the other hand, remained *in* the world without being *of* it. He was an activist, gaining liberation by pursuing the path of disinterested action. The self-purifying *tapas* built up through this ascesis could also act for the welfare of all (*lokasaṃgraha*). The *Bhagavadgita* is the locus classicus for teaching that recommends the way of the *karmayogī* in a theistic context, i.e. where the *karmayogī* is counselled to act altruistically out of love for the Lord alone. Such action is efficacious and brings about the salvation of the yogi. Significantly, the instruction is imparted by Krishna, the embodied Lord, to his warrior-friend, Arjuna. Clearly, if Bhabani was to follow the ideal of the yogi, it would be for the life of the *karmayogī* that he was temperamentally suited. The ideal of the *karmayogī* became the binding force of Bhabani's life. We shall have many an opportunity to observe this ideal taking progressively clearer shape in the course of his career.[3]

But why the celibate teacher? Teaching in traditional Hinduism was more than just a form of livelihood—it was a vocation. Puritan Victorian morality tended to endorse this point of view. The teacher

3 The idea of the patriotic *tapas*-accumulating *karmayogī*, in the guise of the celibate warrior-monk, is central to the plot of Bankimcandra's novel, *Anandamath* (see chapter 2, note 47). From the time the novel appeared on the scene serially (early 1880), Bhabani would have followed it avidly, and no doubt it would have reinforced much of the thinking analysed here. It helps to explain Bhabani's and Narendra Nath's behaviour as friends (see further).

did not merely feed mundane information to his charges, but nurtured their moral and spiritual development. He was their friend, philosopher and guide, they were his spiritual children, so to speak. Here was the occasion for one's masculinity, in the spiritual sense, to be exercised. Besides, according to Hinduism, teaching in this sense was the special responsibility of Brahmins. We have seen how naturally Bhabani turned to teaching when forced to make ends meet in Gwalior. He was sensitive to his Brahmin status, refusing to charge Brahmins for his service. But there was a further, overarching consideration. As a teacher concerned with building up the moral and spiritual qualities of his 'children', he would be contributing to his overall political objective of emancipating India.

It was commonly believed among the bhadralok at the time that a close connection existed between moral and spiritual growth on the one hand, and political maturity on the other. Thus the nationalist Surendranath Banerjea, who, we have seen, influenced Bhabani not a little, voiced this common belief when he declared, 'We find from a broad survey of history that moral and spiritual regeneration is the precursor of political regeneration' and again, 'moral regeneration, which in most cases is synonymous with spiritual regeneration, must precede political regeneration, and must precede the accomplishment of national greatness ... this is a proposition which receives confirmation from the facts of universal history' (S. Banerjea, SWSB: 400, 401–2). Thus by his teaching career, Bhabani would help build up the moral and spiritual potential of the country's youth, and in the process contribute to the nationalist cause. The *tapas* accumulated by his celibacy would increase his influence and charge his career with a far-reaching power. As a *karmayogī* this is how he could work for *lokasaṃgraha* or the welfare of all. I am not suggesting that Bhabani worked all this out clearly in his mind, of course. That would be unrealistic. He returned from Gwalior confused and disillusioned. But his personal background, the ideas to which he would have been exposed, his study of and commitment to his Hindu religion, and the sensitivities to his faith and caste status that he displayed, all combine, as I hope to show, to make our analysis more than plausible. The underlying rationale of his new vocation at its various levels—physical, psychological, political, moral and religious—no doubt took only nebulous form in his mind but it could have been a strong motivating force for all that.

It wasn't long before these ideas began to gel, even if only inarticulately, and their motivation to take effect. Bhabani returned to Calcutta towards the end of 1879. *The Blade* describes what followed as 'a period of blind groping'. We have tried to show that though these times may have been dark, they embodied a rationale that was of a piece with what went before. Bhabani, rather than changing direction in life, had now, more or less unwittingly in the gloom, expanded his horizon. Though the exact chronology is uncertain, it seems that soon after his return from Gwalior he took a teaching post in Memari, a small town some miles north-east of Khannyan, not far from Burdwan. There he fell ill with malaria; to recover his health he stayed for some time in the more salubrious climate of Jabalpur. When his health improved he travelled about to hermitages and monasteries in north-eastern and central India, including Hardwar and Allahabad. Bhabani was casting about for a new path in life, it is true—the process of sublimating his masculinity had begun—yet at the same time he had the opportunity to learn more about the cultural unity-in-diversity of his people. Such experiences would be pieced together in the course of his life and would result in important conclusions.

Bhabani returned to Calcutta, and on a salary of Rs 25–30 per month became a teacher in the Free Church Institution, a well-known missionary college founded in 1843 after the split in the Church of Scotland. We are not told exactly what he taught. He was now about 20, and augmented his income by taking private tuitions. One of his private students was a youth named Kartikcandra Nan. After teaching Kartik for a term, Bhabani announced to the boy's father that since he regarded Kartik 'as his own brother' he would accept no tuition fee (Bl., p. 24). This heralded a life-long friendship between Bhabani and Kartik. Kartik was to be a close friend and helper of Bhabani in the latter's final years—another example of unwavering loyalty to Bhabani through the vagaries of life. In his spare time Bhabani deepened his knowledge of Bengali and Sanskrit literature and tried to learn French and Hindi. Doubtless his travels in north India impressed upon him how widespread the influence of Hindi was. Later in life he was to recommend the adoption of Hindi as a national language, a remarkable thing for a Bengali to do in the linguistically sectarian climate of the times.

Bhabani taught in the Free Church Institution for about a year. *Varia* 5 gives some information that endorses the thrust of the analysis with which we started this chapter. We are told that Bhabani paid special attention to his backward pupils: he believed that more was to be gained for the nation by encouraging them than his more gifted students. His concern for exercise, or 'physical culture' remained unabated; this was an obvious dimension of masculinity that could be cultivated. He would rebuke those who took no interest in exercise, saying that British might had conquered India and Indian might would regain the motherland.

It was during this time (around 1880) that Bhabani befriended Narendranath Dutta, who would be known to the world as Swami Vivekananda. Naren, who was two years younger than Bhabani, was in the final year of his First Arts course at the General Assembly Institution. The two young men would have met as habitués of the Sadharan Brahmo Samaj, the group that had broken away in 1878 from their parent body, the Brahmo Samaj of India. In its first flush, their friendship was warm. Both had muscular frames and both enjoyed combative sports, Naren specializing in wielding the quarter-staff (*lāṭhi*), while Bhabani expressed a preference for wrestling. But both had other, more refined interests. 'The two friends would often get up picnics and festivals in a suburban garden called the "Hermitage". Here they would have musical fiestas and animated discussions on ... things religious and social, political and philosophical' (Bl., p. 26). In the course of time Bhabani and Naren Dutta would drift apart, each to follow his own path in life. But Bhabani, at least, followed Naren's career with interest if not always with approval. Towards the end of both men's lives they re-established fairly close contact, with important repercussions for Bhabani. Now, however, in their salad days, it would have been ideas current mainly in the circles of the Sadharan and other Brahmo Samajes that they discussed so animatedly. We must inquire into what these Samajes were about, for Bhabani was about to be sucked into their world, from which he would emerge as a committed Brahmo.

As we have seen in chapter 1, it was Debendranath Tagore who gave the Brahmo Samaj its unstoppable momentum for reform in nineteenth century Bengal. Nevertheless, in the quarter century or so after Debendranath took a hand, the Samaj underwent two major divisions that progressively weakened it. At the centre of these splits was the charismatic figure of Keshabcandra Sen (1838–84).[4]

Keshab began his Brahmo career as Debendranath's protégé. Keshab had joined the Samaj in 1857, but came into prominence in Samaj affairs a year later, after his first meeting with Debendranath.

4 On Samaj history and Keshab's role, see Damen, 1983, Kopf, 1979 and the 'Biographical Sketch' in Scott, 1979.

This meeting galvanized the two men and the Samaj with them. At the time, to Debendranath's consternation, Samaj policy was being taken over by the Young Bengal faction with their westernizing, rationalist tendencies. These ran counter to Debendranath's own more spiritual, theistic, Hindu cast of mind. Debendranath hoped that Keshab, who showed dynamic leadership potential and with whom he experienced a deep rapport, would reorientate and rejuvenate the Samaj. The charismatic Keshab did not disappoint his mentor. By 1862, when Keshab was publicly appointed Acharya or chief (religious) minister of the Samaj, his pre-eminence was established. The Debendranath-Keshab partnership turned Samaj policy round towards the kind of theism Debendranath had in mind and was reorganizing Samaj life. But soon important differences of emphasis appeared in the thinking of the two men.

Keshab, always of a questing, moralistic disposition that sat lightly to authority, started pressing for changes. He soon built up a following from among the more liberal, socially oriented, westernized Brahmos. Keshab, who was not a Brahmin, advocated an egalitarian life-style for Samaj members. Brahmin privilege and the display of caste difference, as symbolized by the wearing of the sacred thread, for example, should be discouraged and the dismantling of traditional social barriers between men and women encouraged. As to doctrine, Keshab advocated the individualistic practice of a puritan ethic informed by intuition into God's will for us, rather than relying on a scriptural revelation of saving truths. Social transformation for the better could be brought about only by the individual's living an upright life as exemplified by those he called Great Men, not by some process of political revolution. Like Surendranath, Keshab believed that British rule was a providential dispensation for India; it would enable the civilizing influence of Christian values to regenerate his compatriots. In his seminal lecture 'Great Men' (in which Great Women are conspicuous by their absence), given in September 1866, he analysed the Great Man as being distinctively selfless, sincere, prophetic (i.e. challenging to the social and moral order in which he found himself), and efficacious. By his life and message, the Great Man acts as an exemplar not only for his own historical context, but universally, for all humankind (see Scott, 1979: 73f). There was more than a touch of Thomas Carlyle in this notion.

Keshab, who preached a Unitarian-style social gospel, regarded Christ as the Great Man *par excellence*. He never ceased to display a deep, personal devotion to Christ, but he was quick to distinguish between Christ and Christianity. Christ, he pointed out, was an Asiatic with universal appeal. He had no special divine status, but, himself sinless, preached forgiveness of sins for all through his selfless life. Christianity, at least the Christianity offered to India, was a different matter, in its doctrines and dress a western import, tending to 'denationalize' the Indian who adopted it. The alienating character of Christianity as deplored by Keshab (and resisted by such eminent Christians as Kalicaran Banerji, Bhabani's uncle) was to loom large in Bhabani's own understanding of his Christian commitment in due course.

At the time, however, Keshab's religious outlook also took on a distinctively Vaishnava cast. This emerged in his endorsement of the practice of *saṃkīrtan*, the collective, sometimes frenzied singing of devotional hymns to the deity. By this he hoped to build up religious fervour (*bhakti*) in the Samaj. In all these particulars, that is, by his advocacy of egalitarian reform among Brahmos, of devotion to the person of Christ, and of extrovert religious behaviour, Keshab was out of tune with the socially more conservative, undemonstrative, Upanishad-based religiousness of Debendranath. Increasingly, the two were unable to see eye to eye. It came as no surprise then when Keshab and his followers broke away to form the Brahmo Samaj of India. Those who remained with Debendranath called their organization the Adi Brahmo Samaj.

Keshab became the life and soul of his Brahmo Samaj—too much so in fact. It seems that in his own eyes he took on the role of a Great Man: one ordained by God to implement, at the right time and place, a new, efficacious idea for the spiritual progress of humankind. Events had led up to this self-perception. In 1870 Keshab had visited England. Although well received, he was disappointed by the gap he perceived between Christian theory and its practice in the body politic. Christian England preached one thing, especially to her colonies, and practised something different. (How many other Indians who visited the mother country of the Empire were similarly disillusioned, including Upadhyay many years later!) Keshab returned convinced that the Christian vision needed completion by a distinctively Indian contribution, and then implementation by an Indian. The new conception would regenerate the English-speaking world—the most progressive bloc of humankind—of which England, at the centre of her empire, was the symbol. Delusions of grandeur? Perhaps, but Keshab was in earnest. Thus was born the idea that was to develop into the New Dispensation ('Naba Bidhān' in Bengali), an amalgam of ideas and practices culled from different religions, especially Hinduism and Christianity, with Keshab, its Great Man, at the head.

In 1872, the Brahmo Marriage Act was passed, for which Keshab fought ardently. The Act recognized the Brahmo rites of marriage, non-orthodox from the traditional Hindu point of view, as legal, in effect rendering the Brahmo Samaj of India, at any rate, a non-Hindu sect in the public eye. Keshab was now free to fashion his new religious synthesis. This consisted of various ingredients, mainly Hindu and Christian. The Vaishnava practice of devotional singing and processions was firmly endorsed. Calcutta was regaled, and not a little touched at times, by these noisy and fervent outpourings of devotion. Traditional, non-sectarian, Hindu practices were also encouraged among the Keshabites, such as the taking of personal vows (*vrata*) in pursuit of an ascetic goal of spiritual perfection (*vairāgya*). Yet Keshab never abandoned, nor made any secret of, his personal devotion to Christ as humankind's purely human moral and spiritual exemplar, and he continued to display a keen sense of sinfulness and God's forgiving mercy.[5]

In 1872, Keshab formed a Missionary Conference, consisting of a select band of unquestioning Brahmos, with himself as its head. The 'missionaries' would live under Keshab's direct guidance and propagate his ideas. The Missionary Conference became Keshab's inner circle, by which he hoped to establish his undisputed leadership of the Brahmo Samaj of India. By 1875 it was his view that the divine will was expressed to chosen individuals by direct inspirational command (*ādeś*), and that he, Keshab, was God's chief instrument in this regard. By then he had also started calling his new religion—God's chosen means for the regeneration of humankind—the 'New Dispensation'.

But Keshab did not go unchallenged. In fact, the Brahmo Samaj of India was becoming increasingly polarized. On one side stood Keshab and his Missionary Conference, on the other, a liberal faction (a number of whom had supported Keshab when he broke away from the original Samaj) that had become alarmed at the way their leader was turning his back on the reform package that led to the 1866 split. This faction consisted of 'constitutionalists'; in other words, they wanted the Samaj to be run on democratic lines, according to an agreed constitution. They did not like Keshab's increasing authoritarianism, his formation of the Missionary Conference with

5 For details see Kopf, 1979, and Damen, 1983.

its special status, his notion of divine inspirational command directed especially through himself, or his attempts to synthesize a new religion. A number were not particularly religiously inclined at all. They wanted to get on with their original programme of social reform. In passing we note that a leading member of this group was Anandamohan Bose, the very same to whom the anguished Bhabani had blurted out some years earlier: 'Not through pen, but through sword' (see chapter 2). Anandamohan's stress on constitutionalist reform in politics was of a piece with his preference for constitutionalism in the administration of the Samaj.

In short, the Brahmo Samaj of India was heading for a rift. This happened in ironic circumstances. The 1866 split was occasioned by rival attitudes to the emancipation of women in the Samaj. Keshab and his group wanted social barriers to be dismantled apace; for Debendranath it was a case of *festina lente.* This time round, it was Keshab who seemed to be anything but progressive in his attitude to women—to his own daughter, in fact. In violation of Samaj policy concerning the minimum age for the marriage of daughters of Samaj members,[6] Keshab married his eldest daughter to the ruler of Cooch Behar. What seemed a cynical coup to the advantage of Keshab's family (if not to the 'child bride' involved) understandably scandalized many, inside and outside the Samaj. Much ink flowed for and against Keshab's decision. In defence of Keshab *The Theistic Quarterly Review,* edited by P.C. Majumdar, one of Keshab's chief supporters at the time, published the following statement:

> The marriage has its advantages which no social reformer could overlook. One of the foremost Native Chiefs of Bengal, a ruler of many thousands of men, a young man of theistic views, educable and susceptible, has been associated in marriage with the daughter of a man who admittedly leads the most important social and religious movement in the land. The moral influence of such a measure cannot but reach the masses of the Cooch-Behar State, though it may take time to do so [March 1, 1879; p. 26].[7]

This kind of argument did not convince many in the Brahmo movement led by Keshab. The Cooch Behar marriage was the last straw for many who had become disenchanted, for reasons already

6 And indeed, in contravention of the Brahmo Marriage Act of 1872, which Keshab had championed.

7 For relevant information on the expansion of the Samaj and the aftermath of the marriage, see Kopf, 1979: 324–9.

given, with Keshab's leadership. In 1878, the dissident faction broke away from the Brahmo Samaj of India, to form the Sadharan Brahmo Samaj—the leading lights of which were liberal bhadralok dedicated mainly to the social reform of their country. It was not so much their ideas as their enthusiasm for action that would have encouraged both Bhabani and Naren to frequent their company two years or so after the rift. But where the Brahmo Samaj and Bhabani were concerned Keshab would have the last word. So let us stay with Keshab for the time being and review the development of his career.

An important consequence of the break of 1878 was that from then on, remaining in the Brahmo Samaj of India would entail personal allegiance to Keshab. Keshab had succeeded in making something of a personality cult of the movement. There were no constraints now on his attempts to synthesize a new religion. To this end he continued to experiment both conceptually and ritually. His aim was not to make a compilation of elements from different religious traditions (in effect mainly from Hinduism and Christianity as we have noted) but to harmonize these elements into a new synthesis that would transcend and supplant the old faiths. The birth of the 'Church' of the New Dispensation was formally announced on January 25, 1880. Keshab was to be its Great Man, though he did not announce it so baldly.

It is not to our purpose to summarize the main features of the New Dispensation (for this see Damen, 1983). But one or two examples of the way Keshab went about fashioning his new synthesis are worth considering, all the more so since in due course they seem to have influenced Bhabani's own religious development in important ways. Thus, the Keshab who earlier had decried 'idolatry' entirely now began to look for an 'inner meaning' to forms of mainly Bengali icon worship. Apparently he did so for two reasons: one, to make his brand of Brahmoism more acceptable to the Hindu public (this had begun to weigh with him now), and two, to use ingrained and traditional forms of worship to intensify Brahmo devotionalism. An important focus of this concern was the validation of the worship of God as mother, especially through the Bengali festival of Durga Puja. Thus, early in the programme, in 1878, the following Keshabite sentiments were expressed:

> The great national festival of the Hindus is just over. Thousands and tens of thousands in all Bengal have offered their homage to the goddess Durga. Are we to fold our arms and remain indifferent

> to the spectacle?... Is there nothing good in the Durga Puja?... is there anything in it that we should love and honour, even we who are opposed to idolatry? The Brahmo may hate the falsehood which idol-worship involves, and the vices which generally accompany it, but he must humbly sit at the feet of the true Durga-worshipper and learn the truth and devotion which Durga Puja inspires.... The whole picture there is the picture of human redemption wrought by the motherly tenderness of the Lord, who comes with wisdom, happiness, beauty and welfare into the devotee's heart and subdues sin with his almighty grace [quoted in Damen, 1983: 225].

And in an article entitled, 'The Philosophy of Idol-Worship', written in 1880, Keshab himself said:

> Hindu idolatry is not to be altogether overlooked or rejected ... it represents millions of broken fragments of God. Collect them together, and you get the indivisible Divinity ... [Hindu] idolatry is nothing but the worship of a Divine attribute materialized. If the material shape is given up, what remains is a beautiful allegory or picture of Heaven's dispensations.... Never were we so struck with the divinity of the eclectic method as when we explored the gloomy regions of mythological India. The sermons now delivered in the Brahma Mandir [Church] are solely occupied with the precious truths discovered therein, and our own occupation is merely to gather the jewels as we go on. We have found out that every idol worshipped by the Hindus represents an attribute of God, and that each attribute is called by a particular name. The believer in the New Dispensation is required to worship God as the possessor of all those attributes [quoted in Damen, 1983: 228–9].

We have quoted at some length from the Keshabite thinking of the time as regards "idol worship" reinterpreted and the motherly nature of the deity because both these ideas played a significant role in the later Upadhyay's rehabilitated Hinduism. They were to lie dormant for many years, but it was Keshab who first made Bhabani alive to the part they could play in a reconstructed Hinduism.

It is not clear when Bhabani entered Keshab's orbit.[8] The fact

[8] The *Sketch* is confused in this regard. 'About [the] time when the great Keshub was away in England, Bhabanicharan came across a young Brahmo gentleman in whose lodgings Keshub's family stayed. After the return of Keshub from Europe, he became one of his most ardent admirers' (pp. 7–8). But Keshab returned from England in 1870, when Bhabani was but 9! Perhaps what is meant is, 'Some years after the return of Keshub from Europe....'

that he, along with Naren Dutta, sought the company of Sadharan Samajists at about this time must not be misconstrued. The conceptual boundaries and physical restraints between the different Brahmo Samajes of the time were fairly fluid, and those who were not dyed-in-the-wool followers of any Samaj, like Bhabani, felt free to move about more or less as they pleased between meetings and members of the various Samajes.[9] In any case, there would not have been much in the intellectual life of the Sadharan Samaj—under the sway of Mill's Utilitarianism and the idealism of Hegel and Kant and to some extent of Comtean positivism—nor in the Samaj ideology of constitutional political change, to have held Bhabani for long (the leopard was lying low, not trying to change his spots). What attracted him would have been the intellectual ferment and youthful ardour for social and moral change characteristic of life in the Sadharan Samaj.

But perhaps it was under the iconoclastic influence of the Sadharanists that Bhabani gave up wearing the sacred thread. It is recorded that he 'threw off the sacred thread long before he became a Brahmo. Rev. Promoth Lal Sen [a missionary of the New Dispensation Church] never saw him with the thread.'[10] Now Bhabani was soon to fall in with Keshab, and it is unlikely that it would have been under Keshab's influence that Bhabani gave up the thread. By that time Keshab, who was rehabilitating aspects of traditional Hinduism, had developed a markedly more conciliatory attitude to caste.[11] Bhabani *formally* became a Brahmo of the New Dispensation some six years after becoming Keshab's disciple. As Upadhyay, Bhabani was to take up the sacred thread again dramatically, towards the end of his life.

Though we do not know exactly when he was first drawn in, we

9 In connection with Naren and his association with the Samaj we have the following comment: 'Narendra Nath Dutt ... was a member of the Sadharan Brahmo Samaj even in 1882. He also used to go to Brahmananda Keshab Chandra very often and also used to visit the Adi Brahmo Samaj occasionally' (see G. C. Banerji, 1931: 126).

10 See under 'Talk with Nalu Babu', p. 135 of *Varia* 3, GLA.

11 Thus his spokesman, P.C. Majumdar, writes in *The Theistic Review and Interpreter* (August, 1881): 'The Brahmo Samaj is not an institution to break caste. We believe that caste restrictions have on the whole produced much good to the Hindu ruin which will surely overtake it in these days of materialistic rage and positivistic recklessness. Caste has often prevented drunkenness and debauchery, dishonesty and vice.... The attitude of the Brahmo Samaj is therefore one of great caution and moderation.'

do know that by September 1881 Bhabani was in Keshab's orbit, for when Keshab staged his play *Naba Brindaban Natak* on the 15th of that month, Naren 'played the part of the Yogi while Bhabani busied himself by selling the tickets for the performance'.[12] We also know who introduced Bhabani and Naren to Keshab. This was Priyanath Mallik, at first an habitué of the Sadharan Samaj but subsequently a close follower of Keshab. Mallik once testified, 'My age is now 73 years and of the men that I brought within the fold of Navavidhan, Bhabani (Upadhyay Brahmabandhab) and Naren (Vivekananda) became famous.... I can bear witness boldly that both these men, specially Vivekananda, owed the beginnings of their spiritual culture to the pattern set by Keshab Chandra.'[13]

What held Bhabani to Keshab? We have noted that there was not much intellectually or otherwise to Bhabani's taste in the Sadharan Samaj. On the other hand, Keshab's puritan ethic, his attempts to rehabilitate Hindu modes of thought and practice, and his vibrant personality would have appealed to the idealistic youth. Perhaps Bhabani found in the demonstrative Keshab the father figure his own disciplinarian and often absent father could not provide. In time he was to become a favourite of Keshab's, and his loyalty to Keshab's person never diminished.

One other important personality of the times rivalled Keshab for

12 Bl., p. 27. Other sources give Naren's role, more correctly, as the *ṛtvik* or priest; see, e.g., note 13. On what the play was about, see Damen, 1983: 236–7.

13 Quoted (in translation from the Bengali) in G. C. Banerji, 1931: 345. Mallik's claim is corroborated by *Varia* 3, p. 135 (under 'Talk with Nalu Babu, 12th Oct., 1928'): 'It was Rev. Priyanath Mullick of the Nava Vidhan, who too then frequented the [Sadharan] Brahmo Samaj that brought [Bhabani] to Keshab. P. Mullick introduced Vivekananda to [Ramakrishna] Paramahansa.' In fact Mallik also claimed to have introduced Naren to his future guru. This testimony (in translation from the Bengali) is also found in Banerji: 'Everyone knows that the first part of Vivekananda's life was formed in the Brahmo Samaj. At the very first he made acquaintance of the Sadharan Brahmo Samaj, then after he came to know me [i.e. Mallik] he began to have leanings towards Navavidhan. It was I who took him and introduced him to Keshab and he came to be selected to act as ritwik and do some singing in the staging of the Navavrindaban.... In those days I would conduct divine service and he used to sing hymns. One day while we were at worship thus, the late Ramchandra Dutt brought [Ramakrishna] Paramhansa there. Paramhansadeb listened to the... hymns and at the end started an ecstatic kirtan himself. Then he told Naren (Vivekananda) ... "I am very pleased with [your] song, do visit me."... So far Naren was an intellectual, rationalist ... Brahmo. From now he came under the influence of Paramhansa and the course of his life was changed' (pp. 343–4). But cf. *The Life of Swami Vivekananda*, Advaita Ashrama, pp. 30–31.

Bhabani's affections. This was the sage Ramakrishna Paramahamsa. Bhabani was introduced to Ramakrishna in Keshab's company. In 1882 (four years before his death), Ramakrishna was beginning to be well known. Though he had heard Keshab speak some years earlier, Ramakrishna first met Keshab in March 1875. Thereupon the two men met frequently, each growing in regard for the other. Much polemical ink has flowed under the bridge of their friendship, mainly as to who was the dominant influence in the relationship.[14] In fact, the views of each, especially as to the motherhood of God and the underlying unity of religions, developed through the influence of the other with repercussions for their followers.

For a time Bhabani sought Ramakrishna's company. Once 'in the dress of a wrestler with only a loin cloth tied around his waist, Bhabani ... walked all the way to Dakshineshwar. When Ramakrishna saw him, he exclaimed, "Ah, I see you are a hero"' (Jitatmananda, 1981: 224). So Ramakrishna was also impressed by him! The sage invited Bhabani to visit him often, and would show the youth special marks of favour, such as throwing himself upon him during a trance (*samādhi*); 'this was regarded by the disciples as special favour on Bhabani Charan' (*Varia* 4, p. 140). Guha also records a particular incident, related by Gaurgobind Gupta, sometime student of the later Upadhyay, that shows Ramakrishna's childlike nature. Upadhyay himself told Gaurgobind that once when as a young man he visited Ramakrishna, the sage told him: 'Play the horse, I'll climb on your back and ride you,' which he did.[15] Note that Bhabani must have been regarded as a strong fellow for the request to have been made in the first place. Though Bhabani revered Ramakrishna and always cherished his memory, he did not stay to become his disciple in the

14 See G.C. Banerji, 1931 for the Keshabite side. In his weekly journal *Sophia* (July 14, 1900), Upadhyay wrote: 'It should be pointed out that the Paramahamsa too benefited considerably by his association with Keshav.... It was Keshav who brought into prominence the personality of the Paramahamsa. Keshav's influence, too, tended to broaden the mental and spiritual horizon of his friend, though this broadening could not find full and proper scope owing to the long settled ideas and habits of the Paramahamsa and his want of touch with the thought and life of the world at large.... In the name of truth and fairness, let not Keshav's indebtedness to Ramakrishna be unnecessarily exaggerated.' Upadhyay was a loyal friend.

15 *Gaur gobind gupta ... brahmabāndhaber nija mukh theke śunechen—paramahaṃsadeb ekdin brahmabāndhabke—takhan tini nabajubak bhabānīcaraṇ—balechilen, 'tui ghoḍā ha, āmi tor piṭhe caḍe ghoḍā ghoḍā khelba' ebaṃ tai karechilen* (Guha, 1976: 52). Gaurgobind went on to teach Philosophy at Rangpur College (the town is in present-day northern Bangladesh).

way Naren Dutta did. It seems that he found Ramakrishna too mystical, and, for all the sage's open-mindedness, religiously and socially too unsophisticated and parochial for his taste.[16] It is all the more surprising then to read what Upadhyay had to say in a Bengali article towards the end of his life about the significance of Ramakrishna. We shall assess this in its place.

So Bhabani chose to walk Keshab's way. As he drew nearer to Keshab, he was especially struck by two of his mentor's main concerns: Keshab's attachment to the person of Christ and his attempts to synthesize aspects of the Hindu and Christian religions in particular. Keshab's stance in respect of these two concerns is made clear in *The New Dispensation,* an English weekly started in 1881.[17] Both these concerns were to develop as central features of Bhabani's own religious commitment. Bhabani became more and more involved in Keshab's religious and social activities. When the latter formed a Band of Hope to march in protest against the consumption of alcohol, Bhabani joined; when Keshab started a Bible study class, Bhabani enrolled. He became a close and much-loved disciple and often visited Lily Cottage—Keshab's residence and the spiritual centre of the New Dispensation movement. We can only assume—we have no firm information—that after he left off teaching at the Free Church Institution, Bhabani earned a living through private tuitions and that he may well have continued to stay with his brother, Haricaran.

In July 1883, some six months before Keshab's death, five undergraduates, followers of the New Dispensation, would meet in the house of Krishnabihari Sen, Keshab's brother, for a few hours of common study. About a month later, the group moved to 29/2 Madan Mitter Lane and called their club 'The Eagle's Nest'.[18] The aim of the club was self-improvement in the context of New Dispensation thought. The members circulated (among friends only) a hand-written pamphlet which they named *The Journal.* In it they revealed 'their deepest thoughts, inner experiences and small faults'.[19] Bhabani,

16 See note 14.

17 'The first instalment was published on March 24, 1881. Rather than being an official publication of the Apostolic Darbar [i.e. the Missionary Conference], it appeared to be Keshab's personal review for some time' (Damen, 1983: 202, ftnt.13).

18 The *Sketch* (pt. I, p. 9) and Bl., p. 28 are at variance here. The latter gives the number of undergraduates involved as 7, and the year as 1885. The *Sketch* seems to give the more reliable information, at any rate as to the year, since one of the founding members of the club, Hiranand Shaukiram, a Sindhi, returned to Sind in 1884.

19 'In einem 'Journal' schrieben sie ihre tiefsten Gedanken, inneren Erfahrungen und Fehler nieder' (Väth, p. 75).

though at first not a member, often visited the Eagle's Nest. Soon he joined 'in the capacity of Sanskrit teacher' (Bl., p. 28). From the middle of the 1870s, Sanskrit had begun to play an increasingly important rôle in Keshab's Samaj, not least in connection with his interest in ritual. The names of three of the club's founding members are known: Kalicaran Palit, Nandalal Sen, and Hiranand Shaukiram Navalrai. Nandalal ('Nalu') and Hiranand ('Hira') became close friends of Bhabani and were to play important parts in his life.

After some of the club's members had graduated, the Nest moved, probably in 1885, to 17 Bhavani Charan Dutt Lane and acquired a press from which was issued a fortnightly review, the *Young Man*, successor to *The Journal*. Nandalal was its editor and Bhabani his close collaborator. In 1886, the *Young Man* was succeeded by the weekly *Concord*, which became the publication of the Concord Club, itself successor to the Eagle's Nest. The Concord Club was established at what was then 18 Krishna Singhee's Lane (later to be known as 18 Bethune Row; Kartikcandra Nan, to whom Bhabani had given private tuition after returning from Gwalior, lived here. Years later his house was to be the first office of Upadhyay's politically controversial Bengali newspaper, the *Sandhya*). No copies of *The Journal*, the *Young Man* or the weekly *Concord* seem to have survived.

Bhabani and Nandalal were the leading lights of the Concord Club.

> Its object was 'the moral, social, intellectual and physical advancement of young men'. Its programme comprised classes for the study of Philosophy, History, Political Economy, and opportunities for meetings, lectures, discussion, musical entertainments and indoor and outdoor games.[20] The monthly subscription was Rs. 1 and the entrance fee was Rs 2. The Maharaja of Cooch Behar was the patron, W. W. Hunter the president, and Nandalal Sen the honorary secretary. Among the members we find the cream of European and Indian society—five judges of the High Court, the president of the Bengal Chamber of Commerce, members of the Legislative Council, professors, lawyers, doctors and zamindars. The premises at 18 Bethune Row soon proved to be cramped and the Club proceeded to 298 Upper Circular Road [Bl., p. 29].

Three study groups were started in the club: two were conducted in English, for the study of Shakespeare and the Bible; the aim of the

[20] Here Bhabani took a special interest.

third, which was run in Bengali, was the acquisition of general knowledge. The club was thus quintessentially a bhadralok organization so far as its Bengali clientele was concerned, with its members open to influences indigenous and western, trying more or less successfully to work out a synthesis in their lives. Bhabani sought to balance both sides: the Sanskritic tradition on the one hand, and the western on the other.

The club seemed to be a success. The weekly *Concord* was converted into a monthly, and articles were solicited from scholars and litterateurs. Probably at Bhabani's request, his well-known uncle, Kalicaran, agreed to act as editor. The first issue of the journal appeared in January 1887. The title page notes that the editor is 'Kali Charan Banurji' and that the journal is published by 'B.C. Banerji from The Concord Club, 18, Krishna Singhee's Lane'. There is a note by the editor, quoting from the prospectus of the club: 'The Review ... will "serve as an organ for a fair, free and full discussion of questions of public utility, ... seek to educate, influence and direct public opinion on subjects social, political, intellectual, moral and religious ... [and] concentrate into a focus the thoughts of great thinkers and writers in every department of human affairs."' Each issue was about 40 pages long. Some idea of the journal's range of content and contributors can be had from a sample of the contributions of the first six months:

January

Justice to Journalists: Their Social and Literary Recognition, by S.C. Mookerjea

The Indian Press, by G.A. Stack, M.R.A.S

Adopt but Adapt—or Thoroughness in Education, by Krishna Behari Sen, M.A. Calcutta

February

Worship of the Dead, by Jogendra Chandra Ghosh

Morality and Religion—Shall they be taught in our Schools? by J.P. Jones, Madura

March

The Land of the Midnight Sun, by R.C. Dutt, C.S

The Soil and the Seed, by P.C. Mozoomdar

May

Hindus and Mahomedans: The present Tension between them, by Kunja Behari Thapar (Lahore)

June

Sanskrit versus Science, by J.C. Dutt

Some well-known names will be recognized even in this shortened list of contributors. It is doubtful whether Kalicaran, busy as he was in so many other matters, acted as much more than honorary editor of the *Concord.* Most of the work of running the journal must have devolved on Bhabani, who, as publisher, forbore to contribute articles to it. But insufficient experience on the part of the club's young administrators resulted in insufficient funds, not least because some of the contributors to the journal were paid for their services. By the end of 1887, the Concord Club and its journal were wound up owing to a lack of money.[21]

Keshab had died in January 1884. His 'Church' was then subject to bitter infighting as to who should take his place. For many of the New Dispensationists it was a case of 'The King is dead. Long live the King!' In the row over whether some successor should occupy Keshab's marble pulpit or whether the pulpit should remain vacant out of reverence for the dead leader, Bhabani 'saw that [P.C. Majumdar] occupied the Vedi (pulpit) of Keshub ... [he] believed that Mozoomdar was the successor and representative of Keshub and as such had a right to take his place in the Mandir [church-building].'[22] Bhabani became an ardent supporter of Majumdar and regularly visited Peace Cottage, where Majumdar lived.

Majumdar's own personal regard for Christ no doubt continued to strengthen Bhabani's devotion in this regard. In 1883, Majumdar had published *The Oriental Christ*; though he stressed Christ's orientalness here in an essentially Unitarian context, he accorded Christ a more central and comprehensive role in human affairs as the type of the perfect human being, than Keshab ever did. Bhabani joined the Bible study class at the Concord Club, and to this end even learnt some New Testament Greek. His teacher was a Reverend Townsend of the high-church Oxford Brotherhood of St Paul (i.e. the Oxford Mission), which was established in Calcutta in 1881. It is not without significance for our story that Townsend later became a Catholic priest. By this time Bhabani's personal regard for Christ was such that when Nandalal Sen put up a picture of the boy Krishna in the club, Bhabani installed one of the 'Ecce Homo,' which depicts Christ humiliated and maltreated by Pilate's soldiers before he was sentenced to death

21 '*The Concord* was finally amalgamated with *The Interpreter* edited by Bhai Pratap Chandra Mazumdar' (*Varia* 4, p. 148). Majumdar had started *The Interpreter* in 1884.

22 *Sketch*, pt. I, pp 8–9; *The Blade* (p. 31) follows this passage almost verbatim.

by crucifixion. Nearly a decade later Bhabani was to write with deep emotion of his devotion to the 'Man of Sorrows'.

By his involvement with the publications of the Concord Club Bhabani had entered a new phase of his enlarged nationalist aspirations as discussed at the beginning of this chapter, a phase very much propelled by the same momentum that had prompted him to turn to teaching after his disappointment at Gwalior. This concerned the work of the journalist in its broadest sense, which at the time, like teaching, was at its best also considered (by earnest bhadralok at any rate) a responsible, soul-building 'vocation' in life. Thus when Bhabani wrote to his friend Hiranand (who had returned to Sind and taken up journalism) on July 7, 1884, he asked: 'How fares our Hira in his editorial dignity? Is Journalism an edifying and a sacred task to him?'[23]

Further, journalism had some advantages for Bhabani that teaching did not: its field of operations could more readily be considered a battleground—here the pen becomes a sword, publications targets to be defended or attacked, arguments and counter-arguments the cut and thrust of combat, Truth the cause, and India the prize. In this light, truly the journalist was a man of action, well suited for the way of the *karmayogī*. Besides, larger armies of souls could be influenced and won over.

By this analysis, we do not seek to indulge in idle fantasy or some literary fancy. Evidence will be given to show that Bhabani did indeed regard his growing involvement with journalism as a theatre of war. In fact, the ideal of the warrior had been transmuted into the ideal of the combative journalist. The cause was the same. And though Bhabani continued to teach off and on for the rest of his life for the reasons given, it would be through journalism that his nationalist aspirations would find their fullest realization. The celibate state would continue to act as the residual power-source for the whole enterprise. Finally, journalism had this inestimable advantage that because it purported to instruct and edify, and to seek and safeguard the truth, it was an occupation in accord with Bhabani's status as a Brahmin. As a journalist Bhabani could kill two birds with one stone: he could fight more effectively than the soldier (and teacher) in India's cause, and he could do so as a Brahmin. Paradoxically, the journalist could be viewed as the Brahmin warrior *par excellence*; further, the ideal of the *karmayogī* would be more effectively implemented. It was not long, then, before the pen became Bhabani's sword.

23 *Sketch*, pt. I, p. 9.

# Chapter 4

# Faith's Brave Spark: The Brahmo Years and Conversion to Christian Faith

In January 1887,[1] some six years after living under the Brahmo umbrella, Bhabani took an important step. In the sanctuary of Lily Cottage,[2] where his mentor Keshab had lived, he was formally initiated into the Church of the New Dispensation by one of its foremost missionaries and scholars, Gaurgobind Ray (Roy). Clearly this was not an impulsive decision by a callow youth. Bhabani was now 26; the decision was six years in the making. Nor was it inconsequential, both in wider and in narrower context. On the one hand it was a conscious step away from orthodox Hinduism and all it stood for. On the other, it was a deliberate choice for a particular form of Brahmo commitment and leader, namely P.C. Majumdar, in a movement riven by factionalism and conflicting leadership loyalties.

But our budding *karmayogī* needed some inspiring *karman* or action to sink his teeth into. For the time being the Concord Club and its activities supplied the need, but it was beginning to wind down. By the end of the year it had folded. Nor was there much inspiration within his 'Church'. It had become a sea of agitation. 'The history of the New Dispensation during the next decade [i.e. after Keshab's death in 1884] is a sad story of bitter conflicts, misunderstandings, distrust and striving for leadership' (Damen,

1 The date is uncertain. *The Blade* has 'Sunday 6th January' (p. 31). *Sketch* is mistaken about the year: 'One Sunday morning, on the 4th of Magh 1808 of the Saka era, i.e. in 1886' (pt. I, p. 11). 'The sixteenth of January' is the date given in an article entitled 'Swami Upadhyay Brahmabandhav' by B. Animananda, 1935: 469.

2 More a 'palatial mansion', as some of Keshab's critics called it, than a cottage.

1983:322). Hardly the environment in which a young idealist, committed to regenerating India, could thrive. Bhabani was at a loose end. So it came as a great relief when he received a letter in July 1888 from Hiranand Shaukiram Advani, the Sindhi he had befriended in the 'Eagle's Nest' (see chapter 3). Hiranand wrote from Hyderabad in Sind, requesting Bhabani to join him and help found a school for boys.

Hiranand (1863–1893) in his short life went on to become a notable person in his own right. By the time he died he was called 'Sadhu', i.e. 'holy man'. He belonged to the Amil caste. His elder brother, Dewan Navalrai, was a propertied Senior Deputy Collector in Hyderabad. During a visit to Calcutta he had become a follower of Keshab and upon his return established a Brahmo mandir in Hyderabad in 1870. He sent his younger brother to Calcutta to study for a degree in Keshab's sphere of influence. Hiranand came to Calcutta in 1879 as a youth of sixteen, and joined the Church of the New Dispensation. In 1883 he was one of the founder-members of the Eagle's Nest, which eventually became the Concord Club.

Hiranand was also a devotee of Ramakrishna. In the *Life of Sri Ramakrishna* we are told that he used to visit the sage often during his college days in Calcutta (Advaita Ashrama, 1971: 494). So in the close-knit worlds of the disciples of Keshab and Ramakrishna and of the members of the Eagle's Nest, all three of which Bhabani inhabited, he would have had plenty of opportunity to get to know Bhabani well. Bhabani and he became firm friends. After graduating Hiranand returned to Sind in 1884 and became the editor of two newspapers in Karachi, the *Sind Times* (English) and the *Sind Sudhar* (Sindhi).[3] When he heard that Ramakrishna was seriously ill, he journeyed the 2000 or so miles to Calcutta to visit him.[4] No doubt he met Bhabani too.

The school was to be established in Hyderabad, the 'recognized centre of education, culture and social transformation'[5] in Sind. In it 'emphasis would be placed on the formation of character and the study of Sanskrit' (Väth: 77).[6] Why the special emphasis on Sanskrit?

3 He wrote to Bhabani in the first half of 1884 requesting him to ask his uncle, Kalicaran Banerji, to contribute to his (English?) newspaper. In a warm letter, Bhabani wrote back declining: 'I am not the man to influence my uncle to make him your correspondent.' He closes with the poignant words, 'Our Church is being torn into shreds.' This is the same letter quoted in chapter 3, note 23.

4 An account of this meeting is given in *Life of Sri Ramakrishna*, p. 494ff. and in vol. 2, ch. 27, sec. 3–5 of the *Śrī Śrī Rāmkṛṣṇakathāmṛta* (by 'M').

5 Hull, vol. 2, pt. VI, 'The Sind Mission' by F. Parmanand, p. 504.

6 'In der auf die Bildung des Charakters und das Studium des Sanskrit das Hauptgewicht gelegt werden sollte.'

We have seen that in Keshab's build-up to his religion of the New Dispensation (which was meant to have firm roots in Hindu tradition), a special place was given to Sanskrit. But there may well have been another, more strategic reason in connection with the school's image. The Arya Samaj, a new movement begun by Swami Dayananda Sarasvati (1824–83)—the first successful Samaj was established in Bombay in 1875—had become a force to contend with in the north-west. Was the Arya Samaj 'reformist' or 'revivalist'? These terms are applied so loosely in general that it is difficult to say with precision. It was both. Reformist, in that Dayananda sought to do away with what he decried as the current Hindu religion of polytheism, idolatry, excessive ritualism, priestcraft, and caste and sex discrimination. Revivalist, in that he sought to bring about change by reviving the religion of the Vedas as he saw it, among other things a monotheist, non-icon-worshipping, egalitarian faith. The Arya Samaj and Dayananda's views will figure elsewhere in this book. Suffice it to say for the present that the Aryas laid great store by the study of Sanskrit in the schools they were establishing.[7] For a Brahmo school to be competitive in the circumstances, an emphasis on the study of Sanskrit was particularly desirable.

We can understand now why Hiranand chose Bhabani to help him establish the school. Not only did they have much in common as friends, but Bhabani had a reputation for being a Sanskritist. And we have explained too why Bhabani was nothing loath to leave Bengal for Sind in aid of a worthwhile, pioneering cause. Besides, ideologically Bhabani was not journeying to virgin territory. Brahmo influence was quite strong at least in the main urban areas of Sind. So in 1888, accompanied by his friend Nandalal Sen (another co-founder of the Eagle's Nest, and close collaborator in the running of the now defunct Concord Club; see chapter 3), Bhabani arrived in Hyderabad. The city had a reasonably large population (assessed at about 70,000 in 1901) and was situated on the bank of the Fuleli river. It is approximately 90 miles north-east of Karachi and 550 miles south-west of Lahore.

The Union Academy, the school the three friends established, 'began its useful career on 28th October 1888 with but half a dozen pupils' (Bl., p. 32). Between the two brothers, Navalrai and Hiranand, it had been decided that the former would put up much of the capital

7 On this and the influence of the Arya Samaj in northern India at the time, see K.W. Jones, 1976.

whereas the latter would be headmaster. Nandalal was put in charge of administration, and Bhabani became Sanskrit teacher and games master.

The school flourished. In due course it acquired more staff; understandably these were also Sindhis. Two of the earliest who joined were Khemchand Amritrai Mirchandani and Parmanand Mewaram, both of the Amil caste like Hiranand. In time Khemchand and Parmanand were to regard Bhabani as something of a guru, with important consequences. The Union Academy 'was soon considered by Mr Jacob, the Inspector of Schools, the best school in Sind' (Bl., p. 32). After Hiranand died it was called the Navalrai Hiranand Academy and eventually became the centre of a network of affiliated schools. By 1910 it had about 2000 students on its rolls.[8]

Its success was based on the secure foundations laid by the school's earliest teachers, among whom Bhabani played a prominent role. From the beginning he established a close relationship with the students, especially where outdoor activities were concerned. He became

> the idol of the boys. He would fly kites with them, play cricket, teach them gymnastics or football and swimming. The boys would fetch plaintain-tree trunks from a garden on the banks of the Fuleli, and with them as crude craft and Bhavani as skilful pilot, would venture to the middle of the canal and safely back. It was Bhavani who lifted the ban against swimming, once the privilege of loafer and truant.... During the mango season they would buy a big jar of mangoes, bury them in the sand below the cool water and do justice to them after the exercise had sharpened their appetites (Bl., pp. 32–3).

This is not a picture of the cold ascetic. We have in Bhabani here a warm, virile, disciplined young man, friend, philosopher and guide to his 'children', whom by word and example he sought to build into full-blooded servants of their country. There can be little doubt that all the relevant ingredients of his make-up analysed earlier were hard at work: masculinity versus effeminacy; the importance of physical exercise and discipline; the building-up of *tapas* for patriotic ends;

8 There is a photograph of 'The Navalrai Hiranand Academy, Hyderabad, Sind' together with a plan of the ground floor, facing p. 65, in Government of India Department of Education, Occasional Reports No. 6, *Educational Buildings in India* (Calcutta, 1911). The foundation stone of the Academy was officially laid by Lord Sandhurst in 1895, seven years after the school was opened.

and the patriotic rationale of the educational process no less than the sublimated patriotic ideal of the warrior.

This becomes doubly clear from an article he wrote in that period of his life on the occasion of the Dasahra festival (the counterpart in the north of the Bengali Durga Puja). There are different aspects to Dasahra, but at its heart lies the celebration of Rama's conquest, in a great battle, of Ravana, the ogre-king of Lanka. 'But how will it be celebrated?' demands Bhabani rhetorically:

> Our people, dressed in their effeminate finery, will go in the cool of the evening to enact the pillage of Lanka with a few mumbled mantras.... Think of the modern Greeks celebrating the anniversary of Alexander's conquest of India by sipping tea and munching biscuits.... Come, let us reason together before you proceed to take part in the womanish display. Where is your chivalry, your valour? Does your blood course through your veins ... when you hear of Haldighat, the Thermopylae of India where thousands of Rajputs died to a man in defence of their hearth and home? Do you ever pay homage ... to the memory of the great Shivaji or the lion-hearted Ranjit Singh?... India's whole head is sick and her heart is sad.... Awake, arise, learn self-respect; be inspired with patriotic chivalry and then celebrate your national festivals.[9]

What did he have in mind? Wrestling displays? Mock battles with blood-curdling cries, bows, arrows and muskets? Probably.

During his long sojourn in Sind, Bhabani's was anything but a parochial mentality. He encompassed India in his thinking. He took Sind to heart. He learned Sindhi and studied the variegated culture of the region. He acquired a lasting admiration for Guru Nanak, the gentle founder of the Sikh faith. And though he practised broadly as a Brahmo missionary, even officiating once at a Brahmo marriage,[10]

9 Quoted in Bl., p. 34; neither source nor date is given. In the battle of Haldighat (June 1576), Man Singh, on behalf of the Mughal emperor Akbar, defeated the insurgent Rajputs under Rana Partab Singh of Udaipur. The Maratha Shivaji (17th century) and the Sikh Ranjit Singh (18th-19th century) challenged Mughal and British power respectively.

10 The concept of 'the Brahmo missionary' was indeterminate. 'It is not easy to define a Brahmo missionary. No Brahmo missionary was ever ordained or appointed. No Brahmo missionary receives any pecuniary remuneration.... He is simply fed and clothed by the Samaj, and his family, if he has any, is looked after. He is nominally subordinate to the authorities ... but practically independent. He does any work which he thinks is calculated to answer the vocation of his life. He does secular work, such, for instance, as editing a newspaper, or teaching in a school-room, and he preaches and conducts services' *The Theistic Quarterly Review,* ed. P.C. Majumdar (March 1, 1879).

he did not allow his Brahmo commitment to erect barriers between him and the communities among whom he lived. This was no mean achievement, for the Brahmos of the region had acquired, with some justification it must be said, a reputation for taking to alien, i.e. anglicized, ways. This charge of being 'denationalized' was levelled repeatedly against the Brahmos by the Arya Samaj, waxing ever stronger in the area. For example, in May 1882, the *Arya Magazine* described the Brahmo way of life thus:

> Some [Brahmos] took unhesitatingly to coats, hats and pants without any censure from their co-labourers. Thus indirectly encouraged they went further, and began to indulge freely in the habit of resorting to hotels and eating with forks and knives on tables. In a word they commenced to imitate the customs and manners of Europeans.... They ... began to exchange presents in Christmas, to which they saw no objection. They thus saw all evil in everything national, and all good in everything European (quoted in Jones, 1976: 42–3).[11]

Bhabani, the patriot, sympathized with the charge. Brahmo notwithstanding, he wore nothing but 'simple svadeshi [indigenous] dress' (Bl., p. 32) and being a strict 'vegetarian and a teetotaller, could mix with Sindhi Brahmins, and won their admiration by his knowledge of Sanskrit literature' (Bl., p. 33). He was particular not to alienate himself gratuitously from the local people. He was proud to be Indian. It was here, in the context of being a Brahmo 'missionary' in Sind, that he realized the full implications of and developed his earlier patriotic inclinations towards indigenous dress and manners. This was a lesson he took to heart, as we shall see.

But under the surface of this seemingly self-assured and popular young man a storm was brewing. His quest for religious truth was as intense as ever. In 1888, the year he arrived in Sind, he had to hasten to Multan (a town some 400 miles north-east of Hyderabad), where his father, Debicaran, lay dangerously ill. Debicaran, having married again and changed his job,[12] had fallen ill and come to Multan for

[11] The Aryas were pressing one of the chief objections made by their founder, Dayananda, against the Brahmo movement in his magnum opus, *Satyartha Prakas*. See *Light of Truth or An English Translation of the Satyarth Prakash*, by Dr Chiranjiva Bharadwaja, 1975: ch. 11, p. 467. Dayananda says: 'The people belonging to [the Brahmo Samaj] are very much wanting in patriotism, having imitated the Christians in many things (p. 467).... They eat and drink most indiscriminately (p. 468).'

[12] Exactly what he was now doing is not clear. A marginal note in the GLA copy of Simha (p. 24) says that Debicaran worked in the 'Engineer-in-Chief's Office at Lahore'.

respite. He was now on his deathbed. During a night of vigil, Bhabani came upon a copy of Joseph Faa di Bruno's *Catholic Belief or A Short and Simple Exposition of Catholic Doctrine* on a bookshelf and read deep into the night. We do not know how or why Debicaran acquired this book. It would not have been a surprising addition to the library of someone with Debicaran's bhadralok background. In any case, it was a standard work running to many editions. The fifth edition, endorsed by Cardinal Manning and published in 1884, was over 400 pages long and divided into three parts.

Part I (222 pages) gave a comprehensive treatment of Catholic teaching; part II (81 pages), entitled 'Practical directions to a Protestant before and after being received into the Catholic Church', was less doctrinal in nature. Part III (112 pages) was entitled 'Miscellaneous' and contained such headings as 'The Transmission of the Sin of Adam to his Children considered', '"Justification by Faith Alone" considered', 'Chief Heresies', 'Census of Catholics in the World', 'List of 180 Protestant Sects in England and Wales' and 'Parting words to one who feels convinced of the Truth of the Roman Catholic Religion, and who does not join the Church'. As can be imagined, in keeping with the spirit of the times, this book was not ecumenical in tone. And equally in keeping with his martial spirit, it was a tone Bhabani was to adopt in due course when he entered his phase of muscular Christian conviction. But we anticipate.

Debicaran did not recover. His eldest son, Haricaran, arrived from Calcutta the day after his death and returned with the widow. Bhabani was free to make his way back to Hyderabad and resume his duties. He took Faa di Bruno's book back with him.[13] No doubt this book had a significant if hidden influence on subsequent events.

In the months that followed, the single religious question that dominated Bhabani's mind concerned the nature of Christ. This was not an upstart thought. It had been nurtured, more or less explicitly, for years, ever since Bhabani had been introduced to study of the Gospels as a boy in the General Assembly Institution. Under Keshab's and P.C. Majumdar's tutelage Christ had become a living friend to

13 *Varia* 2, pp. 95–111 has a section entitled 'History of the Catholic Mission in Sind' by Parmanand, in which the author notes, 'While still in the Academy [Bhabani] had found a copy of Bruno's "Catholic Belief" in his dying Hindu father's library at Multan which he had brought to Hyderabad. He read it and showed it to us' (p. 99). See also Hull, vol. 2, p. 507. UBBJ, p. 21, has, mistakenly, 'Bruno's *Catholic Faith*', and so does Guha, p. 15, apparently following UBBJ. Simha makes no mention of the book.

him, the Bible more familiar territory. Faa di Bruno's book stimulated, or should we say crystallized, his inquiries into the theological status of Jesus. He now studied the question closely.

Bhabani grew in the conviction that Jesus was not a mere man. Jesus alone of all religious leaders of the world claimed to be sinless, to forgive sin. This claim could not be dismissed lightly since Jesus was obviously a man of outstanding goodness. And if indeed Jesus were sinless and realized the implications of what he was saying as reported in the New Testament, then in some fundamental respect he must be more than merely human. He must be truly divine as well as truly human. In a light different from that cast on it by Keshab and Majumdar, Bhabani pored over the traditional Christian claim that Jesus was God the Son incarnate as a human being.

On Christmas day, 1889, in the CMS (Church Missionary Society) Mission Hall at Hyderabad, this well-known Brahmo gave the first of a number of public lectures on Christ.[14] In the lecture, entitled 'Christ's claim to attention', Bhabani declared that Jesus was the Sadguru, that is, the true sinless teacher of the world. The other religious leaders of India and the world implicitly pointed to Christ; in him alone would all Hindu spiritual hopes be fulfilled. The lecture created a stir, not least in the Union Academy, for it was hardly Brahmo talk! About that time a Rev. Joseph Redman, a CMS missionary,[15] 'sent letters to thirty young men of Hyderabad, inviting them to accept Jesus as their Saviour' (Bl., p. 36). Several agreed, in the spirit of this challenge, to attend a weekly Bible study class. Bhabani joined this class. He was also in touch with a Mr R. Heaton, an Anglican clergyman, who convinced him that Jesus was indeed raised from the dead. This belief is of fundamental import for traditional Christian faith. No doubt Bhabani would have realized its implications well. 'If Christ has not been raised,' says St Paul 'then our preaching is in vain and your faith is in vain' (I Cor.15.12ff, New Testament). It wasn't long before Bhabani accepted the traditional Christian doctrine of the Trinity.

But being Bhabani, he did not leave it at that. He was outspoken in his religious views to the discomfort of all concerned in the Union Academy. In the circumstances, a budding Christian was not good publicity for the school. To save embarrassment all round he handed

[14] Subsequent lectures were given in the CMS Hall and in the Victoria General Library.

[15] He went on to work in the Simla hills and baptized the well-known convert, Sadhu Sundar Singh.

in his resignation towards the end of May 1890. This event is recorded as follows by Hiranand's biographer: 'Mr. Banerji, beloved for his many virtues by his pupils and his colleagues and believed to be a Bhakt [devotee of God] by the Brahmins of Hyderabad, announced ... that he had become a convert to Christianity and wanted to give up secular work in order to work for that religion' (Hull, op. cit., vol. 2, p. 506).

This statement was somewhat precipitate. Mr Banerji hadn't exactly become a convert to Christianity. He was not even baptized; he did not belong to a particular Christian denomination. Further, he was nowhere near converting to Christianity if by 'Christianity' is meant the way European Christians dressed, ate, worshipped and behaved socially. In other words, he was far from converting to Christianity as a western cultural phenomenon. It was the Christian faith and its perception of Jesus to which he was being drawn inexorably. Nevertheless, these distinctions were lost not only on the public at large but also on his next of kin. At the alarming prospect of Bhabani's imminent conversion to the Christian faith (and all that this seemingly implied, namely, expulsion from Hindu society, 'denationalization'—though on this score Hiranand should have known better—and so on), Hiranand felt obliged to telegraph the news to Haricaran. Perhaps the new head of the family could take appropriate action. The telegram brought a poignant reply:

> 81–82, Durga Charan Mitter's Street,
> Calcutta
> 27th May, 1890
>
> My dear Sir,
>
> Your telegram reached me like a thunderbolt. I could not decide for two days what I should do; hence the delay in replying. Where is Bhavani now? Kindly tell him not to make an unhappy brother more unhappy. Sir, kindly ask him to remember his poor old grandmother who has been shedding tears unremittingly since the death of his father.
>
> I cannot leave Calcutta at present. My daughter's marriage takes place very soon.... I entreat you to do whatever is necessary on my behalf. Ask him not to become a convert to the Christian faith at least for some time. He should give an opportunity to me for an interview. What more can I write to you? Though I do not know

you personally, I cannot conclude my letter without expressing my sincere thanks and heartfelt gratitude to you for the interest you have taken on my behalf.

Yours faithfully,
Haricharan Banerji[16]

Where was Bhabani? In new accommodation, braving the storm of public protest that ensued. He seems to have acceded at least to Haricaran's request to postpone baptism; he needed six months, he said, to continue his study of Christian teaching and to finally make up his mind. What exacerbated matters was that he held prayer meetings and discussions in his residence that former colleagues from the Union Academy, among others, attended. Openly declaring one's Christian predilections (after vaunting one's Sanskritic heritage) and then apparently proselytizing young men from respectable (Hindu) families were hardly popular moves. At this stage the names of three young men who attended Bhabani's meetings regularly, all Sindhis, are noteworthy. They are those of Khemchand and Parmanand (both of the Union Academy; see earlier) and Lekhraj Tilokchand.

Khemchand and Lekhraj had started a school in the area, the Proprietary School, in 1886. Parmanand joined the staff in 1887. In due course the school was closed,[17] the boys were sent to the Union Academy and Khemchand and Parmanand became teachers at the Academy. It seems that this happened after all three had got to know Bhabani and regard him as their mentor. Lekhraj did not join the Academy's staff but remained in Bhabani's circle of influence.

With teaching temporarily barred to him as a vocation, Bhabani naturally gravitated to journalism. In accordance with our analysis at the end of chapter 3, this would now assume importance as the framework within which he would attempt to realize his life's aspirations. In August 1890, he started a monthly journal called *The Harmony*. '*The Harmony* (Royal, 16 pages) will, for the present, be published for five months from August to December 1890. But earnest efforts will be made to make it a permanent monthly journal....'[18] Apparently these efforts did not bear their intended fruit. For apart from some quotations from the journal, we hear no more of it, nor have any issues come to hand.

16 Bl., p. 37.

17 On the Proprietary School, see the journal *Light of the East* (abbr. LOE), edited by G. Dandoy s.j., Calcutta, June 1942, pp. 93–4.

18 See *Varia* 3, Animananda's 'Life of B. Upadhyay', p. 83.

Some of the journal's aims were as follows: to expound Hindu and Christian doctrines; to reconcile and harmonize 'pure' Hinduism and 'pure' Christianity; to preach Christ as the eternal Son of God, as the Logos or divine Word implicitly or otherwise pointed to by all prophets and saints before and after his incarnation; to preach Nanak as a teacher of bhakti or religious devotionalism and as the founder of an 'eclectic theism' that exalts purity and religious faith above doctrine and ritualism (*Varia* 3, pp. 83–5).

The dominant line of Bhabani's thinking at the time is clear from a long quotation taken from the editorial, 'Ourselves', of the first issue of *The Harmony.*[19] Here Bhabani attempts to clear up the confusion as to whether he is Brahmo or Christian, for he had never formally repudiated Brahmoism. He claims that his attempt to reconcile Hindu and Christian doctrine stems directly from the theology of 'that great man' Keshab Chandra Sen whom 'God raised up ... to preach "The New Dispensation" which inculcates harmony of all religions in spirit and in truth'. Thus, the reason for naming the journal *The Harmony* is plain. So is his continuing loyalty to Keshab's memory. It is his 'humble' mission, he says, to continue Keshab's work of attempting to harmonize religions. Is he a Christian then? 'What a sweet name! What a noble thing it is to be a Christian and believe in a loving father that desireth not the death of a sinner. What a consolation it is to be a Christian and believe in Jesus, the Redeemer of fallen humanity and the Source of all Righteousness! What a blessedness it is to be a Christian and believe in the Holy Spirit who sanctifies the human soul.' But this is orthodox Trinitarian belief, far beyond what Keshab, and P.C. Majumdar for that matter, ever maintained. Nor on this basis is it easy to understand how Bhabani was to 'harmonize' all religions, even if he had only Hinduism, Christianity and, perhaps, Sikhism in mind.

Later, with hindsight, Bhabani himself realized how fundamentally his own position on the Trinity differed from that of Keshab. Keshab's (and Majumdar's) stance was essentially Unitarian, Bhabani's was properly Trinitarian. The fulcrum of this difference was Bhabani's and Keshab's views on the theological status of Christ. Later Bhabani would make this clear in an article entitled 'Why did not Keshub Chandra Sen accept Christ?' published in his monthly journal, *Sophia* (February 1895). 'When we say that he did not accept Christ we

[19] Ibid., pp. 85–7; Cf. Bl., pp. 38–9, where the year is wrongly given as 1889.

mean that he did not accept him as an eternal *Person* co-equal and one with the Father,' he wrote. For Keshab, Christ was a morally superior human being, perhaps the ideal Great Man, but different from other human beings, not qualitatively, but in degree only. Keshab's was a 'degree-Christology'.

For Bhabani, however, Jesus was fully human, no doubt, but he was also truly divine, the incarnate Son of God. This status no other human being could replicate. This was orthodox Christology, integral to which was the doctrine of consubstantiality. According to this doctrine, there is one personhood in Christ but two natures, divine and human. From the point of view of person, i.e. the agent to whom responsibility and actions are attributed, Jesus is divine, the second person of the Trinity. He is 'Son' in that as person he is 'generated', i.e. he is the perfect spiritual 'image' of the self-knowledge of the first divine person, the 'Father'. The bond of perfect love between 'Father' and 'Son' in this scheme is a person in 'his' own right, the Holy Spirit.[20] But all three persons share the one, indivisible divine nature. Hence there is but one God. However, the Son (and only the Son, according to traditional Christian teaching) has also taken on human nature by incarnating as a human being for the salvation of the world. Thus, the one divine person of the Son has two natures, divine and human.

In due course, Bhabani, who understood this doctrine well, would write eloquently, both theologically and devotionally, of its implications in a number of ways. We shall deal with aspects of his developing, and in some respects original, Christology in the appropriate place. Here we point out that already in December 1890, in *The Harmony*, Bhabani reaffirmed traditional Christian teaching not only concerning Christ's divine Sonship in the scheme of the Trinity, but also to the effect that the claim to this Sonship was integral to the original Gospel message. 'To say that the idea of Sonship is a later invention or interpolation is as improbable as to say that the character of Hamlet is a later invention or interpolation in the play,' continues the article.

Thus already by mid-1890, by his conviction that Jesus was 'the Son of God', 'the Redeemer of fallen humanity' and 'the Source of all Righteousness', and that he was raised from the dead, within the context of traditional doctrine about the Trinity, Bhabani had stepped

20 These designations are placed in quotation marks because, according to Christian theology, they represent human ways of speaking. Essentially God is pure spirit, and is neither male nor female. We can now dispense with the quotation marks.

over the threshold of Brahmoism into orthodox Christian commitment—had he but realized it. Here the authorities of the Union Academy were more perceptive than he.

But though the excerpt from *The Harmony* of August 1890 intimates that Bhabani's belief in the Trinity was orthodox, it also makes it clear that this was no ordinary Christian commitment. 'People here understand by the term ... "Christian", a man who drinks liquor and eats beef, who hates the scriptures of India as lies and her inspired men as impostors. If we are called Christian in this sense of the term we are not Christian,' the article continues. Indigenizing his Christian commitment was to be a unifying theme of Bhabani's life and thought. Though the elements of this theme are first intimated here verbally, we recall Bhabani's habit, from the beginning of his arrival in Sind, of always wearing *svadeshi* clothes. Further, he hints that he has not repudiated Hinduism; *he* does not 'hate the [Hindu] scriptures of India as lies and her inspired men as impostors'. On the contrary, as the aims of *The Harmony* record, it was his intention in the journal to harmonize what he referred to as pure Hinduism and pure Christianity. What he might have meant by these designations we will inquire into later.

So had Bhabani abjured Brahmoism? 'Never!' thunders the excerpt. 'We still belong to the fold of the Catholic Church of the New Dispensation ... [but] many think that the New Dispensation of Keshava is incompatible with the belief in Christ as the Redeemer of fallen humanity and the Source of all righteousness. If this be the New Dispensation, we are not of the New Dispensation'. In fact, to coin an expression, Bhabani wanted to have his cake and eat it. Loyal to Keshab, he wanted to continue Keshab's work as he saw it, and as a Brahmo. After all, he had come to Sind on the Brahmo ticket. Christian at heart, he was not yet ready psychologically to declare himself a Christian. Much remained to be sorted out, and he was still in a confused state of mind. He admits as much by the way the excerpt concludes. 'This is, in short, our position. Let us be called by any name. We mean to preach the reconciliation of all religions in Christ whom we believe to be perfectly divine and perfectly human.' Bhabani was proceeding one step at a time, as the mists cleared before him.

Towards the end of 1890 he made a visit to Calcutta. One presumes that he met his apprehensive family and stated his position. Whether he succeeded in calming their anxieties we do not know. He soon returned to Sind, the struggle to articulate his religious commitment a driving force. He continued to study the Christian tradition, with special reference to Roman Catholicism. 'Ever since he read Bruno's work,' says *The Blade*, 'he had made good use of the Catholic priest's library at Hyderabad' (p. 43). The prayer and study meetings at his home continued too. He was very close to taking the next step.

On February 25 or 26,[21] 1891, Bhabani was formally baptized a Christian by the Rev. Heaton, the Anglican clergyman who had helped him believe that Christ was raised from the dead. Clearly Bhabani had established some rapport with Heaton. But this did not mean that he had become an Anglican. He made that very clear. He was a believer in the Gospel, a Christian. He was convinced of Christ's divinity and followed the Gospel injunction to be baptized of water and the Holy Spirit. He was not convinced of which Church to follow, indeed whether he should belong to any denomination at all. At the time, 'Like his uncle Kali Charan Banerji he used to say that Indian followers of Christ should not mix in the controversies of the [foreign] Churches. They should form a national, indigenous Church of their own and maintain good relations with all' (Bl., p. 43). So it was that that same evening, when asked by a census official whether he was a Roman Catholic or a Protestant, he replied, 'Neither. Put me down as an Indian Catholic.'[22] One step at a time.

Nevertheless, the die was cast. He was now formally a Christian. He had declared his hand publicly. Let us pause here to consider the nature of his conversion. Bhabani has been accused, not least by Hindu biographers, of embracing the Christian faith for reasons that were less than wholly commendable. This ties in with our remarks in the Introduction of this book, that Hindus tend to look askance at his conversion, dismissing it as a kind of aberration.

Simha declares that it was superficial knowledge of the Hindu tradition and a certain precipitate restlessness that led Bhabani to become a Christian, to embrace 'this alien way of thinking' (*ei mlecchabhāb*). He writes:

> In adolescence, when the religious sense awoke in him, he first of all sought refuge in Keshab-babu. Keshab-babu then was the sole

[21] February 25 is the date given in Hull (vol. 2, p. 507) for Bhabani's baptism. *Sketch*, pt. I, p. 13 and Bl., p. 44 give February 26, while in his article on Upadhyay in LOE (August 1942), Animananda records the date as February 20 (1891).

[22] Bl., p. 44. Cf. Hull, vol. 2, p. 507. Still it is significant that he used the term 'Catholic'.

> hope of modern youth. At the time, though [Bhabani] made some inquiries into the Hindu religion, it was all done through coloured spectacles. In fact, his learning was superficial, and it was because of this that he was unable to enter deep into Hindu religion. The little that he did grasp, he mistook for the whole. On the other hand, he found no peace by remaining within the Brahmo fold. His spirit became restless in the search for truth and, thus confused, in a short time he embraced the Christian religion.[23]

The mind boggles. Bhabani's knowledge of the Hindu tradition is supposed to have been skin-deep. There is a sense in which we can say that even the lifelong learning of a scholar of any discipline is partial, not deep enough. There is also a sense in which we can say that even a youth's grasp of something goes to the heart of the matter. It is a question of the quality of one's knowledge, rather than the quantity; a question of commitment and scholastic pedigree, rather than the parroting and display of factual information.

On the matter of commitment and pedigree, where knowledge of the Hindu tradition is concerned, Bhabani cannot be faulted. Even Simha admits that from infancy Bhabani was reared, on his grandmother's knee, in traditional Hindu lore. He prized this knowledge, nurtured it and put it to good effect in his Bengali writings towards the end of his life. When barely a teenager, he had already read the Bengali *Ramayana* and *Mahabharata* umpteen times.

He had a lifelong commitment to Sanskritic learning, the very matrix of orthodox Hindu religion. While his schoolboy peers, many with an eye to the main chance, were busy absorbing western ideas (and ways) in westernized schools, Bhabani did not forget his ancestral faith. Of his own initiative, the reader will recall, he would cross the Hooghly to the *ṭol* at Bhatpara to immerse himself in Sanskritic learning. He joined the Eagle's Nest on the strength of his knowledge of Sanskrit. His unwavering abstinence from meat and fish, from early adolescence, with one lapse in each case as we have recorded, is eloquent testimony to the depth of his commitment to Hindu tradition.

23 'At the time ... he embraced the Christian religion': *sei samay jadi-o tini hindudharmer kichu kichu ālocanā karilen kintu se samasta-i raṅgin caśmār madhya diyā. uparibhāger kichu śikṣā karilen baṭe kintu ei ek kāraṇe hindudharmer antare prabeś karite samartha hailen nā. jataṭuku pārilen, seiṭuku sarbasva baliyā dhāraṇā kariyā lailen. parantu brāhmodharmer āśraye thākiyā-o tā̃hār śāntilābh haila nā. satyer anusandhāne prāṇ asthir haiyā uṭhila; ebaṃ ei byākulatāy kichudin pare khṛṣṭīya dharma grahaṇ karilen.* (p. 30).

And as for abstaining from alcohol, there was no lapse. Indeed, it was his adherence to strict Brahminical codes of behaviour, no less than his knowledge of Sanskrit, that endeared him, even as a Brahmo, to the Brahmins of the north. To brand such commitment to Hinduism as superficial, as mistaking the whole for the part, is to make a travesty of the facts.

Bhabani was not precipitate in his adoption of the Christian faith, nor did his faith represent an alien way of thinking.[24] He was a man of restless energies, presumptuous on occasion perhaps, but in decisions concerning the course of his life neither fickle nor overly hasty. He waited seven years in the Brahmo orbit before being initiated formally as a Brahmo. His bhadralok background exposed him to western and Christian thought from early youth. He built on this by attending Bible study classes and by prolonged personal research into Christianity. His English was excellent, somewhat florid perhaps to suit the times, but an apt medium for imbibing western ideas. In a real sense he was mentally bicultural and hardly alien to Christian thought. It was because he understood its contemporary structures so well that he realized both the incongruity and the expendability of so many of its expressions when transplanted into Hindu soil. He did not seek baptism overnight nor jump precipitately into a Church. The decision to become a Christian took many a year to mature, and was still to develop as we shall see.

Another kind of explanation given of Bhabani's conversion is that it was utilitarian in motive, that it had a kind of 'instrumentalist' rationale. It is tendered by Haridas Mukhopadhyay, co-author of UBBJ. 'Patriotism was with [Upadhyay] the first instinct and passion, religion the second. Religion was harnessed by him as an instrument of national regeneration. He changed that instrument several times—Hinduism, Brahmoism, Anglican Christianity or Protestantism, Roman Catholicism and Vedantism—according to the exigencies of the situation in order to serve the supreme ends of Indian Nationalism.'[25]

This explanation, if it is not to be an accusation—and many would deem it an accusation since religion is supposed to be a matter of conviction, not of 'the exigency of the situation'—is based on a certain view about religion, that is, that religious faith is expendable in a

[24] *Mlecchabhâb* can also mean 'uncouth way of thinking', but perhaps Simha does not mean that.

[25] Quoted from a letter to me dated September 15, 1987. In any event, 'Anglican Christianity' should not figure here.

'higher' cause (be it nationalism or whatever). It does scant justice to Bhabani. It neglects entirely the evidence available and the heartfelt sacrifices he made out of the courage of his conviction. Bhabani was a man of action; he was also an idealist. He was certainly no instrumentalist in matters of faith and morals. To follow his religious lights, he gave up the security of his job at the Union Academy, and apparently the close friendship of Hiranand. He incurred the disappointment, not to say shared the anguish, of his family, including his beloved grandmother. He suffered the opprobrium and wrath of the Sindhi community among whom he lived, whereas before he was the centre of their admiration. Having given up his living quarters at the Academy, he eventually found new accommodation, 'sweeping the rooms and preparing his scanty meals himself while a deluded and infuriated mob hurled mud and stones into his house' (Bl., p. 45). Though the Protestant missionaries offered him accommodation on generous terms to help him out, he steadfastly declined (Bl., p. 44). He lived entirely on his own resources. Nor did he for the sake of convenience take refuge under the umbrella of a particular Christian denomination after baptism. He was prepared to go it alone till he could see clearly what he must do. These are not the actions of a religious instrumentalist.

Further, Mukhopadhyay's explanation entirely neglects other kinds of evidence. Bhabani continued to draw friends and even strangers to the prayer meetings and discussions in his residence. What attracted them was his fervour. As mentioned before, Khemchand, Parmanand and Lekhraj attended frequently. Good Friday of 1891, some weeks after Heaton had baptized him, was celebrated with great devotion. About 50 young men, including Rewachand—the future Animananda —were present. Rewachand was so impressed that he told Bhabani the next day that he resolved to become a Christian. Years later, in an article entitled 'How I found Christ' in *Light of the East* (June 1935), Animananda describes the occasion thus: 'It was on Good Friday, after his baptism on 26th February 1891, that Brahmabandhav organised a meeting and his earnest pleading about the divine character of Our Lord influenced me so much that I desired to renounce the world and be a Christian missionary.' It was nearly two years later that Rewachand, maintaining close contact with Bhabani throughout, finally took the plunge and became a Christian. Khemchand and Parmanand too, following Bhabani as their leader, in due course became Christians, at considerable personal cost.[26] Would it be possible for Bhabani to inspire and encourage such faith over a protracted length of time if his own religious commitment were not genuine?

Finally, Mukhopadhyay's interpretation entirely neglects the testimony of Bhabani's devotional Christian writings and activities, abundantly in evidence till a couple of years before his death. It also overlooks some decisive evidence of his religious commitment at death's door. The reader will have ample opportunity to assess the authenticity of this devotion as the book progresses. We must dismiss then, without more ado, any attempt to make sense of Bhabani's religious affiliations on the grounds of expediency in the service of some higher cause. Bhabani's religious career was of a piece with, not opposed or subservient to, his patriotism. True, he wished ardently to regenerate India, but not at the cost of his integrity. Rather, his religion, his patriotism, his nationalism, were but expressions, at different but interpenetrative levels, of the integrity that on the whole illuminates his life. I say 'on the whole' for I do not wish to suggest that his life's lights, which he pursued so assiduously and zealously, were not on occasion dimmed, even misguided. The presiding genius of Bhabani's life was at times flawed. To stumble is the lot of human beings. But even the stumblings of this man of fire can give flashes of insight along paths that we may not traverse. For such instruction, let us wait and see.

Khemchand's and Parmanand's standing in the Union Academy declined in direct proportion as their friendship with Bhabani and their leanings towards the Christian faith increased. Some parents of boys at the Academy protested at these Christian associations. Accordingly, both Khemchand and Parmanand felt obliged to resign

[26] Khemchand became a Catholic on December 21, 1891, according to Hull, vol. 2, p. 508; Animananda, however, in LOE, September 1942, p. 140, gives April 7, 1892, as the date. There are articles on Khemchand by Animananda in LOE, June 1942 to February 1943. It was Khemchand who wrote the somewhat unsympathetic account on Upadhyay mentioned in the Introduction to this book. Parmanand was received into the Catholic Church on October 27, 1891. Animananda has written on Parmanand in LOE, June–December 1939 (see also January 1940). Bhabani acted as godfather at both Khemchand's and Parmanand's baptisms. Before Bhabani himself was baptized according to Catholic rites, Khemchand and Parmanand felt obliged to resign from the Union Academy on account of their Christian leanings. In his account Khemchand writes, 'We could not pass the streets without being jeered at and pelted' (p. 507). *The Blade* implies (pp. 48–9) that Lekhraj left the group once public hostility mounted.

from the school.[27] Bhabani felt a sense of responsibility. Mainly to help Khemchand support his brother through College, he first taught as assistant master in the CMS High School in Hyderabad. But before long he went to Karachi to become the editor of a biweekly, the *Sindh Times.* 'His monthly salary was to be as many rupees as the number of subscribers he managed to add that month' (Bl., p. 46). But in about a month Bhabani resigned. He had written an article accusing one of the three civil surgeons in Sind—the name had been withheld—of issuing certificates in exchange for bribes. The three civil surgeons jointly threatened to sue the paper if the accusation was not retracted. Bhabani refused to retract and resigned; the paper's proprietors retracted.

By this time he had decided to join the Roman Catholic Church. This may come as something of a surprise, but from Bhabani's point of view the decision made good sense. Let us inquire into why someone who only a few months before had considered himself an 'Indian Catholic' was now prepared to be called a Roman Catholic. The reasons seem to have been personal, theological and what we may call 'political' in the broad sense of this term.

Representatives of the Catholic Church were not unknown to Bhabani. He seems to have been well known at the 'Catholic priest's library at Hyderabad' as we have noted earlier. Besides, Faa di Bruno's work had had ample opportunity to make a deep impression; he had acquired it about three years earlier. It is true that personally he seems to have been more influenced by Protestant pastors along the way; however, his personal involvement with representatives of the Christian Church was not confined exclusively to Protestants. In any case, such personal considerations were not decisive with Bhabani when it came to choosing a Christian denomination to belong to. There is another consideration here. This is the individualistic nature of his spiritual development hitherto. For all the personality cults at its centre, both Keshab's and Majumdar's religious organization fostered an individualistic spirituality. The spirituality of the Church of the New Dispensation was experimental and exploratory. As such it was doctrinally unsure. Administratively too, this 'Church' lacked direction and firm and tested structures of management. It had no history to speak of; and withal it was disintegrating before Bhabani's eyes. Against this background, it is plausible to reason that Bhabani felt attracted by a religious organization, such as the Roman Church,

[27] See previous note.

which was different in all these respects: regimented in spirituality and administration, of ancient pedigree, and with a future and sense of direction that, for all practical purposes, were more or less assured. So far as their public image was concerned, the Protestant Churches could not compete in these respects.

But perhaps more important in helping him choose his Church were reasons of other kinds. Let us start with the theological. These had to do with Christian teaching about the relationship between divine grace and human nature in the aftermath of the 'Fall' of Adam and Eve, the first human beings. According to Roman Catholic doctrine of the time, it was by an act of disobedience that our first parents lost the supernatural state and its fruits that God had originally bestowed upon them, the state that enabled them to live forever in the divine presence. By their free, sinful act they incurred and then transmitted to the rest of humanity our familiar natural condition, which is susceptible to harmful ignorance, disordered passions, suffering, death and the final loss of God's fulfilling presence (namely 'hell'). This is what it means to be born in 'original sin'. Catholic doctrine teaches that the Fall, however, did not corrupt human nature entirely; it only vitiated it, giving human beings a propensity to sin, to transgress God's law impressed on their hearts. But God's sanctifying or saving grace, offered freely to all—through baptism, this grace is made available to the Christian in plenary form—can justify, purify, strengthen, heal and build on human nature and so enable it to participate once more in the supernatural life of God. Sanctifying grace freely given and humbly received transforms human beings into 'children of God'.

God's chosen means for bestowing this grace in the first instance is the life and death of Jesus, the incarnate Son. Christ's resurrection from the death of the Cross and his return to the Father ratifies and consummates this saving act, especially through the continuing presence and action of the third Person of the Trinity, the Holy Spirit, in the world. Even non-Christians are eligible for saving grace. So long as they strive to live according to their best lights (which is only possible by God's enabling grace in the first place) they will attain their ultimate destiny—not in so far as they live misguided lives as non-Christians, of course, but through the saving grace won for them by Jesus' life and death, did they but realize it! Indeed the divine largesse is disposed to inspire in the lives and faith of all peoples particular insights, doctrines and teachings that can act as the stepping stones for saving grace to do its work.

On the whole, for Catholic doctrine the language of the economy of saving grace, i.e. of the sanctification of human nature, was the language of restoration. In and through Christ, saving grace restored fallen human nature to its supernaturally elevated state before the Fall.[28] Figuratively speaking, human nature was restorable since the Fall had only damaged it, not destroyed it beyond repair. The Catholic slogan in this respect was *Gratia perficit naturam*, namely, 'Grace perfects nature'—implying that human nature is not entirely spiritual quicksand; it contains firm ground on which grace can build.

As intimated, such a doctrine had implications for religious activity outside the formally constituted body of Christian believers. Since, as a consequence of original sin, human nature is only flawed and not utterly depraved, 'natural' religious activity, that is, the attempts of non-Christian peoples to reach God, through their philosophies, theologies and worship, without explicitly affirming the truths of Christian revelation, are not necessarily in vain. By God's enabling grace, they are likely to contain a basis on which saving grace may take effect. This means, among other things, that they are likely to contain natural truths or insights that dispose those who are sincere, all things being equal, to acknowledge either in this life or in some future reckoning the saving/supernatural truths of Christian revelation (namely, the truths of the Trinity, Incarnation, Resurrection, Atonement, the abiding and guiding presence of Christ's Spirit in the Church, and so on). Or, to use another image, natural reason can bring to light natural truth in such a way that it tends to find its culmination in supernatural truth, that is, the truths of Christian revelation as interpreted by the Catholic Church. In this way, natural truth(s) and supernatural truth(s) can be mutually complementary, the one level acting as a stepping stone to the other.

The implications of this Catholic view for one sympathetically disposed to Hindu religion in the first place—for someone like Bhabani, that is—are evident. The history of Hindu religious striving need not be written off. In theory at least, there is every possibility of finding within this history the natural building blocks of the supernatural edifice of faith, of finding natural truths that clamour for their supernatural consummation. And in practice, who could doubt that this possibility would be realized? Had not western scholars, some of them professing Christians, themselves acclaimed the glorious

28 Though the effects of the Fall—sin, suffering and eventually death—will be finally done away with for the redeemed only in the post-mortem life lived in God.

achievements of ancient India, achievements religious no less than secular? Thus, a Hindu convert to Roman Catholicism had scope for *rehabilitating* Hindu religion in some way. For Bhabani, patriot that he was and ardent student of the Sanskritic tradition, this was all to the good.

This scope barely existed in Protestant, especially non-Conformist, teaching concerning the Fall. Aspects of Anglican Christianity in particular could make such scope, it is true, but the Protestant attempt to do so gathered momentum only from about the turn of the century. Till then it was the voice of Evangelicalism that overwhelmingly dominated Christian teaching among the Protestant camps in India. According to this teaching by and large, the Fall completely vitiated the original goodness of human nature. Human beings, heirs to the consequences of the Fall, were naturally incapable of making any headway to speak of, towards salvation. All natural religious striving, however grand it might appear to human eyes, was void—generally shot through with pride and depravity. Salvation was possible only through new life by conversion in Christ. The old ways—ancestral non-Christian religious ideas and practices—had to be extirpated, to allow God's saving grace to take effect through Christ's atoning death on the Cross. There was no complementarity here between natural and supernatural. On the contrary, the language of the economy of grace in the context of Evangelical Protestantism was the language not of restoration (as in Catholic doctrine) but of re-creation, the re-creation of a new humanity in Christ.

The consequences of such an exclusivist attitude towards non-Christian religions were clear, especially as regards Hinduism, which, we have noted in chapter 1, was obviously singled out for attack by Protestant missionary zeal. There was nothing redeemable in Hinduism on the natural level for the new life in Christ. The convert was to be deracinated where Hindu religion was concerned. The following two extracts, both products of the age, may be regarded as representative of these two ways of thinking, the first of the Evangelical Protestant, the second of the Roman Catholic:

> Nothing ... can be more opposite than the Spirit of the Gospel and the spirit of Hinduism whether manifested in the grossest idolatry or in the highest refinement of the Vedanta. That Gospel which is founded on the doctrine that 'every imagination of man's heart is evil, is *only* evil continually'—that among men, 'there is none that doeth good, no not one' ... that 'no fountain can set forth both salt

> water and fresh'—and that 'an evil tree cannot bring forth good fruit'—must be death to the spirit of Hinduism, to the pride of man in every false religion ... [for] 'without *shedding of blood*' there is no remission.... [Christ] maketh intercession for none but those who renouncing all their righteous deeds, yea their repentance and counting them 'loss and dung' trust in his blood for the forgiveness of sins.[29]
>
> There are men so narrow as to say, that no soul among the heathen can be saved. The perfections of God, the attributes of mercy, love, tenderness, justice, equity—all rise up in array against so dark a theology.... Every soul created to the likeness of God is illuminated by the light of God even in his creation.... Every living soul therefore has an illumination of God in the order of nature, by the light of conscience, and by the light of reason, and by the working of the Spirit of God in his head and in his heart, leading him to believe in God, and to obey him.[30] ... From the beginning, the Holy Spirit of God ... has dwelt in every created soul and wrought in every man born into this world.... God casts no one away.... Even throughout the heathen world the Spirit of God is present working in the hearts of men. If they fail of eternal life, the failure is in their own will, and not in the will of God.[31]

Bhabani would have been mindful of this contrast, especially with regard to its bearing on Hindu religion, and, for the reasons given, it is clear to which side he would be drawn. He was up-to-date in Catholic thinking on this and other matters.[32] Moreover, the potential

[29] From the Baptist Joshua Marshman's, 'Reply to Rammohun Roy's final appeal against the atonement and the Deity of Christ' in *The Friend of India*, Serampore, 1824.

[30] From Cardinal H.E. Manning, 1875: 6–8

[31] Ibid., p. 67. Before his entry into the Roman Church Bhabani read this work and quotes from it later.

[32] 'Mr. Banerji used to bring from the Father's library [at Hyderabad] Manning, Newman and Bishop Meurin's writings' (Hull, vol. 2, p. 507). John Gabriel Leo Meurin (1825–1895) was born in Berlin, from his father's side of remote French extraction. He was ordained into the secular clergy but joined the Society of Jesus in 1853. He arrived in India in 1858 and became Bishop of Bombay in 1867. In 1887 he was appointed Bishop of Mauritius where he died in 1895. He was buried in the Catholic Cathedral at Port Louis. For further information, see Hull, vol. 2, pp. 136ff. Bhabani would probably have read *Select Writings of the Most Reverend Dr Leo Meurin, s.j. with a Biographical Sketch of His Life*, by P.A. Colaco, Bombay, printed at the Examiner Press, 1891. There are chapters here entitled 'God and Brahm', 'The Use of Holy Images', 'On the existence of God', 'On the idea of the Infinite' etc. One can see how Bhabani could have made use of this work in his later writings on philosophical theology, Christian doctrine, and the relationship between Hindu and Catholic thought. With respect to the last category, Bhabani subsequently rejected Meurin's combative conclusions.

complementarity of the natural/supernatural divide in Catholic thinking permitted a tolerance of those 'natural customs' that did not seem to militate directly against the exigencies of one's (supernatural) faith. This would have been of crucial importance for Bhabani, who was both proud of his ancestral culture and sensitive to the charge that conversion to Christianity tended to 'denationalize' the Hindu. In an article entitled 'Dogma and Theology', which appeared in the first year of publication of his monthly journal, the *Sophia* (September 1894), Bhabani wrote in connection with a view expressed by his former mentor, P.C. Majumdar: 'He is ... right in deprecating the denationalizing of converts. It matters very little whether the follower of Christ wears a turban or a topi. The Catholic Church has never taught her converts to give up national customs and habits which are not expressive of superstition.' More on this point later.

There seem to have been other theological and/or ecclesiastical attractions in the Roman tradition for one of Bhabani's Hindu background. We may single out here amid such things as Catholic predilection for liturgical ritual and the Church's requirement that its clergy be celibate (see earlier for our discussion on celibacy),[33] the Catholic teaching on devotion to the saints, especially the Virgin Mary. From early in his conversion Bhabani developed a deep devotion to Mary. He claimed that someone from a Hindu background could appreciate the rationale of Catholic devotion to Mary and the saints. In a letter dated July 21, 1893, intended to encourage Khemchand, who had written from Karachi indicating that he had become dispirited by Protestant attacks, he writes (in the combative spirit of the times):

> [The Protestants] have ridiculed the doctrine of the invocation of saints and our devotion to the Blessed Virgin. Woe be to them! We ask the prayers of saints, not because God is not infinitely more inclined than they are, to hear our prayers, but because we follow the universal order established by God.... The law is that the remote is drawn nearer by means of the intermediate. Are not saints and angels nearer to God than we are?... God dispenses grace but through the intercessions of saints, and above all, the Blessed Virgin....
>
> Protestants think that they will expose us by telling people that the Catholics are so superstitious as to believe that God, even God, obeys Mary. Every Hindu will at once understand the transcendent

33 Also see chapter 5.

> meaning of this devotional language. Hindu shastras are full of such sayings. Nay, more than these, God is not only obedient to bhaktas [his devotees] but [is] the servant of their servants ... [Mary's] arms of clemency enfold this globe.... Angels and saints are ministers of God and she is the Queen of ministers.... We shall now show to the people of Sindh that our religion and not theirs [the Protestants'] can satisfy the national cravings of piety [INB: 196–7].

The key lies in the phrase 'the universal order established by God'. For Bhabani, in spite of its name, the 'Roman' Church was the universal Church that revealed, ratified and fulfilled that order. In apologetical vein, Faa di Bruno's work had contrasted the universality and orthodoxy of the Catholic Church with the alleged divisiveness and unorthodoxy of Protestantism, under such headings as 'Infallibility of the Church and of the Pope', 'Only one True Church', 'First Mark of the True Church: Oneness of Faith, of Worship, of Sacraments, and of a Supreme Ruler', 'Third Mark: Catholicity' (in Part I), and (in Part III), 'Chief Heresies', 'Difficulties of Private Interpretation [of Scripture]' and 'List of 180 Protestant Sects in England and Wales'. Barely twenty years earlier, in 1870, the first Vatican Council had affirmed the infallibility of the Pope. For Bhabani this would have put a seal on the rightness of Catholic claims to theological and ecclesiastical orthodoxy. In later writings, Bhabani frequently referred to Protestant activity as 'sectarian'. We have a window into his thinking at the time of his conversion from a none-too-ecumenical letter he wrote a little over a year later to Rewachand, who was still deliberating about joining the Catholic Church. We are told that this letter decided him; he became a Catholic not many weeks later. The letter is dated February 7, 1893, and was sent from Karachi.

> I wish you could have at first examined some of the Anglican Thirty Nine Articles. I am sure you would have been shocked at their utter unreasonableness, unscripturalness and contrariness to the testimony of the entire body of the Fathers.... How to know that this man and not that one is a true believer? The reply is, by the standard of the Written Word of God. Read it with prayerfulness and you will know what true Christianity is. Here is the rub—plunged again into the abyss of uncertitude! Strange to say, such is the conscious or unconscious perversity of man that ceaseless contention and unendable confusion in the Protestant camp does not open their eyes to the necessity of a living Church. Mr Redman reads the Gospel with prayerfulness and is guided by the Holy Spirit that the consecrated bread and wine are nothing but symbols of

> the body and the blood of Christ, and Mr Shepherd reads the same with prayerfulness and is guided by the Holy Spirit to understand that it is a blasphemy to believe as Mr Redman believes....
>
> There can be no certitude outside the true Church of Christ [the Roman Catholic Church].... The Church is imperishable. Let enemies roar and howl without, she stands unruffled on an immovable Rock, the faith of the Holy Apostolic See, founded by the glorious apostles Peter and Paul. Believe in her and confound all heretics. If Christ has left us without his living voice, our faith is vain.
>
> I am glad you have been given Littledale.[34] Read it carefully point by point.... You read one point and jot down your difficulties about it if you have any. Send them to me and I am confident I shall be able to solve them and show the unsoundness of the charges.... And also do not hear Mr Redman....
>
> In the heat of the controversy do not forget your devotions. Remember him, love him who died a bitter death for our salvation, and to die for whom is a privilege given only to a select few [INB: 194–6].

In spite of close contact with Anglican pastors earlier in his religious development—contact that one hopes Bhabani appreciated—there seemed little if any prospect that he would join the established Church of his country's foreign rulers. This brings us to the 'political' considerations of his conversion. His attitude here was plain and deep-rooted. There is no evidence that he ever held a view different from that expressed in his journal, the weekly *Sophia,* that the Church of England was 'an instrument of the State' (October 20, 1900), just 'a national institution established by law' and 'presided over by a Protestant Sovereign' (August 25, 1900). His patriotism made him constitutionally incapable of expressing allegiance, albeit in an implicit way, to the Sovereign of his colonial rulers, or of joining the 'national' Church (supposedly established not by God but by human law) of the same regime. So, all told, Bhabani decided to become a Roman Catholic, but the overriding reason for his conversion was, as is clear from the last sentence of the letter quoted above, his faith in Jesus Christ.

34 This and the next sentence are omitted from INB but they occur in excerpts of this letter printed in Turmes, 1963: 17. No doubt Turmes had the original. 'Littledale' is a reference to *Plain Reasons against Joining the Church of Rome,* by R.F. Littledale, 1881–2, which the Rev. Redman had lent Rewachand.

It seems to have been in July-August of 1891 that Bhabani was prepared for reception into the Catholic Church by a Jesuit priest named Theophilus Perrig. Though Perrig was posted in Sukkur, a very old town on the banks of the Indus some 250 miles north-east of Karachi, he was staying briefly in Karachi at the time.[35] And on September 1 Bhabani was formally received into the Catholic Church by another Jesuit named Bruder.[36]

Bhabani chose 'Theophilus' for his baptismal name apparently for two reasons (Bl., p. 46): loyalty to the priest who prepared him for his Catholic baptism, and as a mark of his devotion to the Christian Trinity, since 'St. Theophilus is believed to have been the first writer to use the word "Trinity".'[37] It may well be that these two reasons converged to prompt Bhabani to be baptized as Theophilus. Otherwise it is difficult to see why he chose this rather unusual name. Bhabani was the sort of person for whom such signs of appreciation for a teacher would have meant something; and, subsequently, he gave much attention in his writings to the Christian doctrine of the Trinity. This culminated in his magnificent Sanskrit hymn to the Trinity, which we shall comment upon in due course. So far as I am aware, Bhabani was hardly, if ever, referred to by the name 'Theophilus'. Rather, it was a Sanskrit equivalent that stuck. 'Theophilus' means 'friend of God' in Greek, so does 'Brahmabandhab' in Sanskrit. We now know from where 'Brahmabandhab' was derived. But it would be some time before Bhabani would assume this Sanskritic designation. For the time being he continued to be known by his Bengali name.

[35] Perrig (1850–1910) was one of four brothers, all of whom became Jesuits. After a ministry in Bombay (1884–1886), Perrig spent 14 years in Karachi, Sukkur and Bhusawal. He returned to Bombay in 1900 and remained there till his death. I am grateful to his nephew, Fr Felix Clausen, s.j. of De Nobili College, Pune, for this information. Note that in 1858 the Catholic missionary apostolate of the whole area was placed in Jesuit hands.

[36] Since he had already been baptized but not as a Catholic, he was conditionally re-baptized according to the custom of the Catholic Church. *Varia* 3 (p. 135) records an interesting piece of information, though it is not clear to which phase of Bhabani's conversion it refers: 'When Bhavani became a Christian in Sindh, [P.C.] Mozoomdar wrote to him a very affectionate letter asking him to come and stay in his old home which was ever welcome [sic] to him. He gave this letter to Nalu babu [Nandalal Sen] to preserve lest it be lost.' The letter is lost.

[37] This is a reference to Theophilus, Bishop of Antioch, who in the latter half of the second century makes mention of the Blessed Trinity in his *Apologia ad Autolycum*, II.15.

This brings us to the end of our second division of his life ('the Brahmo years'), a life that had already seen remarkable and rapid, but in the light of discussion hitherto, I hope not bewildering, change. Bhabani was now 30. Already, during his few years in Sind, he had made a considerable impact for one so young. His impact was to grow and expand, but not before faith's brave spark had burst into flame.

# Chapter 5

# Faith Inflamed:
## Early Concerns and Clearing the Ground for His Christian Faith

In this and the following seven chapters we shall examine Bhabani's activities and work in the next decade of his life, till 1902 in fact, when he departed for a visit to England. That decade saw momentous changes in his life, giving the impression of a film speeded up. Just as well perhaps, for the end was in sight, though he was not to glimpse it yet. In these ten years he moved from a muscular Christian commitment towards constructing an apologia for what he regarded as representative features of Hinduism, and began to give shape to a 'Hindu-Catholic' faith in terms of Advaitic philosophical theology and an idealized understanding of the caste system. These years too saw Bhabani mature as a journalist and suffer disappointment as an indigenizer of his faith. He was not the first to come up against an adamantine wall of ecclesiastical authority. In his case, it sowed the seeds of bitterness against his Church as an institution and set the stage for the last, explicitly political phase of his life. For this was a decade in which he glimpsed that his great experiment of indigenization was doomed.

Soon after Bhabani converted to the Roman Catholic faith, two of his friends, Khemchand and Parmanand, followed his example.[1] The going was not easy. We have already seen how unpopular he and his friends became. In fact, 'Bhavani was ejected from his house by the Hindu house-owner and with difficulty secured a house belonging to a Muslim, and later on, one belonging to a Jew. Khemchand's father threatened to kill himself; Parmanand's mother refused to eat.' (Bl., p. 48).

1 See chapter 4, note 26.

Gradually this kind of opposition subsided, not least from the close families of Bhabani's convert friends because the latter did not give up their traditional dress and eating habits; they showed that becoming Catholics was not synonymous with adopting outlandish ways. And it was Bhabani who gave guidance in this matter. But the conversions caused a stir in the area. Various religious organizations—*soi-disant* anti-Christian or pro-Hindu—mobilized to counter Bhabani's influence. These included the Arya Samaj and the Radha Soami movement.

Bhabani made Hyderabad his headquarters but divided his activities between Hyderabad and Karachi. For a short period he taught mathematics for two hours a day in St Patrick's High School in Karachi[2] to help procure a dowry for his eldest brother's daughter, Sarojini, to whom he was very attached.[3] So as to initiate discussion on philosophical and religious questions, he started a debating society in Karachi, which interested a number of Arya Samajists; he also gave lectures and organized prayer meetings in both Karachi and Hyderabad, which Hindus and Brahmos alike attended. All in all he made something of a splash and was taken seriously. His intention was clear—'to bring India to the Faith' (Bl., p. 50).

But his Christian apologetic had no particular focus. It was targeted on any opponent that came in his sights, including Protestant Christianity and its missionaries. Indeed, Bhabani's most virulent opposition to Protestantism was evident in the years immediately following his conversion. He waged war not only by pen but also by deed. Skirmishes of the latter kind could be quite dramatic, as the following incident reveals.

Sometime in 1892, the Rev. W. J. Abigail, Principal of the CMS High School in Karachi, delivered a lecture on Luther. *The Blade* assures us that Abigail had been 'thoroughly Protestant, Anti-Catholic', that 'plenty of abuse had been hurled against the Church' (p. 50). Bhabani felt called upon to defend his Church with equal vigour. He gave an uncompromising, apologetical reply, also concentrating on

2 This school was opened in 1861 by a Fr J.A. Willy s.j. 'Originally called St Patrick's English School, it was officially registered as a High School in 1867, and in 1868 as a European and Eurasian High School' (Hull, vol. 2, p. 365). Begun with only 3 pupils on its rolls, by 1886 the boys' school had 200 students (by then a girls' wing had also been opened).

3 When Sarojini was a little girl, Bhabani and she treated each other as favourites. We do not know if Sarojini actually married, but she seems to have died young (see Bl., pp. 24–6).

Luther. The goaded Abigail gave a counter-lecture, during which he asked, 'Is Mr Banerji here?' Mr Banerji was in Hyderabad. He was informed by telegram that the Rev. Abigail had publicly challenged him. Bhabani was in Karachi the very next day, eager to take up the gauntlet.

Abigail gave another lecture in Luther's defence (with Bhabani and a priest friend in the audience) during which he made a rather rash statement implying that Bhabani had unduly influenced a youth minded to become a Protestant, to convert to Catholicism.[4] In a flash Bhabani rose to his feet and declared: 'This is a lie!' In confusion, the lecturer replied that he had heard the news from the Chairman, who said in turn that *he* had heard it from someone else. Eventually the charge was retracted, to the cheers of the packed hall. Clearly a good time was being had by all.[5] That was the combative atmosphere that prevailed at the time, not only between Catholics and Protestants, but in general between Christians and various Hindu groups such as the Arya Samaj. It will help us to understand the tone of much of Bhabani's initial assessment of other faiths.

Bhabani spoke on Luther again, and his lectures on this subject were published in two pamphlets (which have not come to hand). However, there seems to be no doubt that it was the substance of these lectures that appeared in the form of a serial in four parts in Bhabani's monthly journal, the *Sophia* (January, February, July and September, 1895), under the heading 'Was Luther a Reformer?' It would be as well to inquire into what Bhabani wrote here, for this serial contains the gist of his understanding of and opposition to Protestant teaching. His views in this respect underwent no substantial change subsequently.[6] We shall also be able to discern at this early

4 The actual words Abigail is reported to have said are: 'I know a young man who has sold his body and soul to Mr Banerjee,' with reference to 'a young Sindhi Amil who was on the way to Protestantism but eventually became a Catholic' (Bl., p. 51).

5 In fact the lecture broke up in disorder. Bhabani's companion, a Fr Misquetta, no doubt encouraged by Bhabani's intervention, himself got up in due course and challenged the speaker to substantiate his statements on Luther to further cheers from the audience.

6 The *Bombay Catholic Examiner* (BCE: a weekly journal and perhaps the premier publication officially endorsed by the Roman Church in India at the time) notes with editorial approval in its issue of June 19, 1896, that a 'small *brochure*' entitled 'Was Luther a Reformer?' had been 'lately issued from the *Sophia* office at Hyderabad, Sindh'. The *brochure* could not have been that small and may well have duplicated the *Sophia* serial which runs cumulatively to a substantial article. As we shall show later, it is significant that the BCE should thus editorially approve a piece of intricate theological writing by Bhabani.

stage of his Catholic commitment certain lines of thought, concerns and options which materialize in important ways later.

Luther's position for Bhabani represented the essence of the mainstream Protestant stance, irrespective of denominational groupings. The first part (January 1895) considers three points: (1) whether the Church made the scriptures available to the faithful, contrary to the claim that Luther 'discovered' a Latin Bible 'in the Library of his monastery', which opened his eyes to the doctrinal and other corruptions of the Church and led him to urge that the scriptures be translated and made freely accessible to all; (2) whether Luther's teaching that 'man's nature is utterly corrupt, that he has lost the freedom of will, that he cannot do anything good' is true, and (3) whether man can be saved by faith and works (according to the teaching of the Catholic Church), or by faith alone (as Luther taught).

On the first point, Bhabani is at pains to show that translations of the Bible in various languages were available to the faithful, under the aegis of the Church, before Luther's alleged discovery, before in fact Luther was born. The Anglican ecclesiastical historian S.R. Maitland (1792–1866) is quoted in support,[7] and reference is made to the list of Bibles in the Caxton Exhibition in South Kensington of 1877, which according to a quotation from *The Church Times* (a standard Church of England publication) disproved 'the popular lie' of Luther finding the Bible, or of its earlier unavailability (even in German editions). 'One is at a loss to understand, writes the editor of the *Sophia,* how 'Protestant historians venture to repeat this lie notwithstanding its having been exposed the hundreth time.' But Bhabani does not discuss whether the Church at the time actually encouraged the faithful to take recourse to the Bible privately, especially in the vernacular (as Luther did); that is what was at issue in the debate about the availability of the scriptures. Bhabani is keen to show that the Church countenanced the printing and dissemination of the Bible, and in support he does no more than trot out a few statistics.

On the next point Bhabani asserts that 'man's will, though weakened by sin, has not lost its freedom, that he can, in the order of nature, perform good works which rise as memorials to heaven for mercy and grace.' One can see a reference here to the New Testament story of the unbaptized Roman centurion, Cornelius (see Acts, ch. 10), a man whose good works found favour with God. The

7 The excerpt is taken from *The Dark Ages*, 3rd edition, p. 469.

implication here is that the will even of non-Christians is not necessarily corrupt 'in the order of nature', and that in cooperation with God they can work towards their salvation. Rather than directly trying to vindicate Hindu religion in the order of nature, Bhabani here seems to be more keen to affirm the distinction between nature and grace (see chapter 4) in such a way as to show that they can work together, under God's providence, in saving harmony. But the argument, if one can call it such, is very condensed; by not realizing its implications, though, and by teaching that 'man's nature is utterly corrupt ... that he cannot do anything good', that in fact human beings are in no way responsible for their own ultimate destiny, Luther 'upset by this hideous doctrine the entire scheme of redemption'.

The third point continues the second. In essence Bhabani quotes the Epistle of St James (2.19, 20, 24) in defence of his view that the 'Catholic Church teaches that man is justified by faith and works.' The wider implications are the same as for the second point. And Bhabani concludes: 'The Protestants, the offspring of Luther, do not reject the Epistle of St James, but cannot forsake the sweet and convenient doctrine of justification by faith alone.' The point is that this doctrine is *convenient,* for it is based on a felt assurance of salvation rather than on striving to cooperate with divine grace. 'Luther was the inventor of this presumption, a sin against the Holy Ghost.' Note how in the phrase 'the Protestants, the offspring of Luther', Luther is seen to represent Protestants and Protestantism.

The second part of the serial (February 1895) is devoted entirely to answering the charge made by Luther and 'our Protestant brethren' that 'the bishops and priests of the Catholic Church, notoriously the Popes, sell forgiveness of sins on cash payment': in short, to the vexed question of the use of Indulgences. There follows a knowledgeable and careful analysis of the Catholic understanding of Indulgence at the time, namely, how Indulgence is (1) 'the remission of temporal punishment due to forgiven sins' (2) 'through the merits of Jesus Christ and his saints', (3) 'by the performance of good deeds'. All this is supposed to be in accordance with scripture (Matt. 16.19 is quoted). Luther defied scripture and preached a felt assurance of salvation as sufficient for salvation. 'By this novel doctrine [Luther] gave to all a full Indulgence,' says the editor of *Sophia* caustically, adding 'Corrupt man accepted this easy condition of salvation with great glee.' On the other hand, 'the Catholic doctrine of Indulgence 'teaches us to fear the justice of God, shows us that we are members of one body [the whole Church with its earthly and heavenly complement, with Christ as its Head], gives us the privilege of receiving from others to make up our deficiencies, [and] encourages us to the performance of good works.' We noted in an earlier chapter how the Hindu ideal of the *karmayogī* attracted Bhabani in the context of the sublimation of his political aspirations. It is not difficult to appreciate, then, Bhabani's sympathy for the contemporary Catholic doctrine of action as a means to salvation; this doctrine could be viewed as theologically complementing the *karmayogī* ideal.

The third part of the serial (July 1895) deals at length with Luther's 'assertion of the right of private judgement in matters of religion', an assertion for which Bhabani had a peculiar horror. 'Peculiar' because his own background rendered him susceptible to its charms. He himself had emerged from a tradition—Brahmoism, especially the Church of the New Dispensation—that had no authority structures except loyalty to a chosen leader, and that by implication had always encouraged individualism. Yet he now belonged to a Church noted for its regimentation in matters of belief and for its ecclesiastical authoritarianism. So, with a fierceness that is not all that surprising, he attacked Luther's (and all Protestantism's) supposed wilful and arbitrary claim to the right of private judgement in interpreting the Bible and deciding matters of faith. 'The great distinctive principle of the Reformation was the assertion of the right of private judgement in matters of religion,' he declares. 'This was the means adopted by Martin Luther for the emancipation of the human mind.'

Bhabani's treatment of the topic first considers the effect, as he sees it, of implementing this 'means'. 'Anarchy, confusion, division, and dissension were the immediate outcome of this principle of liberty,' he says sweepingly. 'The reformers who deserted the Catholic unity were very soon hopelessly split into sects.... Intolerance and bigotry were at their height and still it is said that liberty of thought was the basis of the new system founded by Luther.' No doubt Bhabani had a point. But the shrillness of his charge stemmed from his desire for security and unity in the institution to which he now belonged. This is the man who had bewailed the state of his former Church with the words, 'Our Church is being torn into shreds.'[8] For him—for a period at least—there must be no return to that unnerving condition. So Bhabani quotes Luther with the aim of showing how disastrous his policy of private judgement turned out to be: how Luther himself

8 See chapter 4, note 3.

'hurled anathemas of perdition on those who ventured to differ from him,' being 'untrue to his professed principle', and how those who followed his 'seductive bait' realized, too late, 'to their bitter grief and disappointment', the predicament they were in.

Bhabani next examines 'the intrinsic nature of the principle of private judgement'. For this he takes recourse to his distinction between natural truths and supernatural truths of religion, a distinction we broached in the preceding chapter. We must give it more attention, for it was a cornerstone in a number of different contexts in Bhabani's thinking. Here it helps him make short work of the Protestant approach (under Luther's name) to religious authority and Biblical interpretation.

Natural religious truths, contends Bhabani, fall within the sphere of reason. These truths 'human reason can find out by deductive or inductive inference'. Bhabani does not give examples here. Supernatural truths 'are above reason but not contrary to reason'; they cannot be discovered by reason but can be seen to be reasonable. They fall within the sphere of revelation and are apprehended by faith, 'and we believe them to be true on the authority of God who can neither deceive nor be deceived'.

Now, asks Bhabani, on what grounds do the Protestants believe the revealed truths of Christian doctrine? On 'the authority of God or of their reason', i.e. private rational judgement? Hardly on grounds of the latter since in that case the revealed truths of the Bible would cease to be such; they would be accessible to 'the natural process of reasoning' and there would be no need for revelation. Thus Protestants must rely for revelation on the authority of God and 'the oft-repeated Protestant vaunt "no authority but reason and private judgement", is like the roaring of autumnal clouds which bring no rain.'

But how does one know what God intends by revealed truths? How to interpret the Bible correctly? Private judgement is of no avail, for if 'two contradictory meanings of a certain doctrinal passage be presented to the faithful by two opposing parties, how can the faithful decide by private judgement which is the true God-given sense, for the doctrine is supernatural and beyond the sphere of reason?' The only way one can understand the Bible correctly and arrive at a correct doctrinal formulation of the Christian faith, is to submit to the authority of God's representative on earth, the Roman Catholic Church, for 'she alone knows the mind of God as revealed to the Apostles'. Such submission is not the abrogation of reason but its vindication, for 'it is the highest, the noblest and the most rational act of finite reason to submit to God, the supreme Reason'. On the other hand, to rely on private judgement to discern the supernatural truths of the Christian faith is to 'deny the supernatural character of the religion established by Christ'. In this way, reason realizes its limits and is properly disposed to appreciate the reasonableness of supernatural Christian doctrines.

All this stress on reason as the ultimate tribunal of truth in the Protestant use of 'private judgement' is selective in regard to the Protestant approach. In fact, it concentrates on rationalist tendencies in Anglican thinking towards the end of the nineteenth century and discounts more Evangelical trends according to which the powers of reason were distrusted. After all, Bhabani himself accuses Luther, the 'Father' of Protestantism, of relying on a *felt* (i.e. non-rational) assurance of salvation as a sufficient condition for salvation.

For his part, Bhabani could rest secure on the authority of the Catholic Church to provide certitude in matters of faith and morals on the basis of the natural/supernatural distinction. There is much scope for the vigorous use of reason within the framework of this distinction, for 'rationally' defending Catholic doctrine against opposing views, for 'rationally' explicating the natural truths on which the supernatural rest, for showing the reasonableness of the latter and the way they harmonize with the former. Hitherto, this use of reason had been attempted only within guidelines laid down in terms of *western* philosophical and theological categories. There was no substantial precedent for anything else. And, so far, Bhabani was content to remain within those cultural guidelines. But in time he would seek to articulate a Catholic understanding of the natural/supernatural distinction by making use of ostensibly *Hindu* practices and concepts. This was uncharted terrain; and politically and theologically, it raised unprecedented problems. In the event, his former individualistic tendencies would reassert themselves in the face of ecclesiastical intransigence and conflict would result.

There is another matter we must advert to in this part of the serial. It is Bhabani's propositionalist understanding of religious truth, faith, revelation and the proper function of reason. For Bhabani it is the indicative statement, understood more or less literally, that conveys, *par excellence,* what is true in general and religiously true in particular. Reason operates best when it yields truth in this form, and truth is best expressed propositionally (as the outcome of 'deductive and inductive inference'—see earlier). These emphases were the mark, of course, of Catholic thinking of the day. But such thinking had an atomizing effect on one's understanding of human nature and human relationships. Intellect (whose proper function is to reason) is demarcated from the will, which is demarcated from the affective life and so on. The individual is composed of a number of separate functions and levels that are ideally meant to act in harmony. Religious faith, rather than being the orientation of the whole individual, an organic stance for living, is largely a matter of mentally assenting to a ratified body of propositions (faith consists in knowing 'the mind of God as revealed to the Apostles'[9]). Further, this atomistic understanding of the individual is translated into an atomistic understanding of society. Society, rather than being a kind of open-ended matrix of persons in relationship, becomes a conglomeration of individuals related only externally. The human person is not an interpersonal, social reality (whatever else he/she may be), but is a sort of monad, inherently an island-fortress with all channels of communication strictly regulated. Bhabani later tempered this perspective on life—fairly pervasive in Catholic intellectual circles at the time—when formulating his understanding of the nature of Hindu society through Advaitic insights.

Finally, the fourth part of the serial (September 1895) is devoted to attacking Luther's moral stance on celibacy, to showing 'how he lowered the ideal of perfection by violating the evangelical counsel of celibacy and destroyed the very principle of social purity by breaking the unity of the marriage tie'. 'Social purity' is an interesting phrase and sits oddly here. But when one realizes that in a few years Bhabani would argue vigorously in defence of an idealized form of the institution of caste and against interracial commensality and marriage (partly on the grounds that Hindu practice in this respect conforms with nature in a way that does not militate against the supernatural order as understood by Catholic faith), one glimpses what lay, unconsciously at this point, at the back of Bhabani's mind. In this article he is directly concerned to attack Luther's personal sexual morals and his advice regarding marriage to those who turned to him. Personally, Luther 'committed a two-fold sacrilege by breaking his vow of celibacy and marrying a virgin consecrated to the service of God.' Publicly, he is quoted as counselling 'the knights of the Teutonic order' as follows: 'The precept of multiplying is older than that of continence.... It would be better to live in concubinage than in chastity. Chastity is an unpardonable sin, whereas concubinage,

9 Bhabani also talks of faith in terms of finding which of 'two contradictory meanings of a certain doctrinal passage' has the 'true God-given sense' (see earlier).

with God's assistance, should not make us despair of salvation.'[10] But this is to violate Christ's own teaching that celibacy is 'a very high virtue' (Matt: 19.12 is quoted in support). Thus Luther 'reformed Christ. Blasphemy!' How could he be a reformer of morals?

There is an unspoken assumption underlying this part of the serial that it is distinctive of Protestantism to compromise on the sanctity of marriage. The Catholic Church, on the other hand, which enjoined celibacy on its priests and nuns, is praised for upholding a very high ideal of marriage, in keeping with the mind of Christ of course, an ideal that saw religious celibacy as intrinsically morally superior to conjugality. On a number of occasions Bhabani sees it as a Protestant trait to lower the marriage ideal, and as a consequence to endanger the moral life of society. In *Sophia*, in an article entitled 'The unity and indissolubility of the marriage bond' (June 1894), he compares the Protestant ideal of marriage unfavourably with the Catholic. The reason for this disparity is the acceptance of divorce and remarriage among Protestants in express violation of the scriptures. Henry VIII, 'that monster of lust', is attacked for having divorced his lawful wife. 'Since the perpetration of that unlawful act, the inviolable matrimonial bond has been broken loose in England.'[11]

In fact, the perceived Protestant stance on marriage threatened Bhabani's own masculinist ideal of the *karmayogī* in which a polarity had been set up, as we have seen in chapter 3, between the celibate ascetic on the one hand, and the worldly, sensual individual on the other. Through his celibacy, that is, the accumulation of *tapas* or spiritual energy, the ascetic could raise the moral tone of those who came under his influence, however this influence was then exerted. Whether he realized it or not, that was the ideal that governed Bhabani from early adolescence (see chapter 3). The worldling could not exercise such power. The professed Catholic ideal of marriage, which put a premium on chastity within the indissolubility of the marriage bond and pointed to the moral superiority of celibacy, reinforced

10 This quotation somewhat misrepresents Luther's view. Bhabani gives other examples.

11 Again in *Sophia* (April 1898), he writes: '[Divorce] is in violation of the law of Christ and the teaching of the Catholic Church. It is only in Protestant communities that such laxity is permitted and practised. And that is but natural. Protestantism is essentially individualising in principle and disintegrating in its influence. Divorce, which is the disruption of the family, was originated by Protestantism and Protestantism was originated, to a large extent at least, by divorce.' Luther and Henry VIII are then cited as supporters of divorce.

Bhabani's thinking on that point. It was another reason for his continuing attraction to the Catholic Church. And all this is linked to the place of women in his thinking, a topic we shall consider elsewhere.

Though Bhabani periodically criticized Protestants and Protestantism, usually in general terms, till the end of his writing career in English (circa 1903), there is no further attack as sustained as the Luther tracts. We may conjecture that Bhabani had shot his bolt where 'Protestantism' was concerned. He believed that he had got its measure, that there was nothing substantially new to say. More important, to continue to attack the Protestants in a sustained way would appear as an in-house quarrel—Christian versus Christian. Hindus would be ill equipped to make sense of the theological jargon and issues of this domestic debate. It would leave them cold. But, in the fervour of his new-found faith and in the service of his national aspirations, Bhabani wanted to confront the Hindu, 'to bring India to the Faith'—this is where the real battle, indeed his heart, lay. After the Luther lectures of his debate with Abigail in 1892, which not only got the adrenalin going but also had the effect of showing his credentials as a committed, combative Catholic to all and sundry (including the ecclesiastics of his own Church), Bhabani turned his attention to what was his chief objective—winning the minds and hearts of Hindus.

At the time a campaign was only half-forming in his mind. He published, apparently at random, a pamphlet entitled 'A short treatise on the existence of God' (1893; 29 pages). Its immediate aim was to counter the atheistic rationalism of a growing number of young Sindhi intellectuals. But the underlying motivation was also beginning to take shape: to convince educated Hindus, by rational argument without recourse to scriptural evidence of any kind, of the existence of a God possessing properties that traditional western philosophy of religion, or 'natural theology' as it was sometimes called, associated with monotheistic belief; that is, a personal creator-God who is omniscient, omnipotent, essentially blissful, righteous and so on. This was the framework of what Bhabani would later call 'rationalist theism'. The truths of this theism could be arrived at by the natural light of reason; upon them the supernatural truths of Catholic teaching could be harmoniously superadded. Both kinds of truth were thus compatible because both stemmed from the same provident source, the one God worshipped by the Catholic Church. In short, rationalist theism would be a *preparatio evangelica*, i.e. a preparation for the reception of the Gospel of Christ.

Let us review the treatise briefly to appreciate Bhabani's theistic approach. Bhabani's aim is nothing less than to demonstrate rationally that God exists, i.e. that there is an omniscient, omnipotent, spiritual First Cause, infinite in the sense that it has '*no* parts'; it is that 'to which *nothing* can be added, from which *nothing* can be subtracted'. Anything that has real parts in any way or is susceptible to being divided in some sense can never be actually infinite. Bhabani's God, in other words, is essentially utterly self-contained, indivisible and immutable. It is crucial to be apprised of this conception of the deity, for it underlay the whole of Bhabani's theology and was the theological cornerstone of his subsequent attempt, as we shall show, to equate Catholic, that is, Thomistic natural theology, with rational theism in a Hindu context. It was the cornerstone of his strategy of a *preparatio evangelica*. This tract, though he may not have realized it, is the beginning of his lengthy campaign to win the educated Hindu to the Catholic faith.

The tract contains five pieces of reasoning designated 'Proofs' purporting to show that such an infinite Being exists. To some extent these Proofs overlap with Thomas Aquinas' 'five ways' of trying to establish rationally the existence of God. We need not go into a detailed exposition of Bhabani's thesis. It will be sufficient to indicate the tenor of his approach and the line of his argumentation. The first Proof argues that because matter and human souls are subject to change, they are not eternal. Further, the nature of that change is such that 'it must have been caused to exist by some other being which is immutable, eternal and self-evident.' Since an infinite series of changes or of mutable beings is impossible, 'right reason compels us to fall back upon an immutable, self-existent being which is the First Cause of all mutable beings. This being is God the Creator.' A number of things are assumed in this Proof, including an atomistic understanding of matter, the existence of spiritual souls in human beings, the impossibility of there being an infinite series of changes or mutable beings and particular definitions of time and eternity.

Philosophically, the second Proof is an extension if not the basis of the first. Its starting point is our experience of the mutability of being. In so far as something changes in some respect it passes from potentiality to actuality in that respect, and in the process depends ultimately on 'a being which is immutable itself but causes mutations in others. This being is actuality itself. There is no potentiality in it.... This being is God who is distinct from all other beings subject to modification. He is the Creator and the Preserver and it is he who causes his creatures to pass from one state to another and makes them grow from perfection to perfection.' These two Proofs resemble in important points St Thomas' 'Way from Motion' (*ex motu*), which argues from motion in the world to a Prime Mover that is itself not susceptible to motion or change in any way.[12]

The third Proof argues from order in the universe to a supreme Orderer, a First Cause that is 'an intelligent Mind who presides over nature's work and adapts means to ends with foreknowledge of ultimate results'. For the order—the adaptation of means to ends—that we see about us cannot spring from chance. Explaining order in the universe by recourse to chance is 'most unphilosophical and unscientific.... For what is chance but an uncaused phenomenon?' And an uncaused phenomenon is 'intrinsically absurd'. Nor is the order of the universe an eternal innate property of matter. If 'this first disposition is eternal and essential to matter, then it would have ever remained unchangeable and could not have resulted in another disposition and the formation of the present cosmic system would have been impossible.' Hence the conclusion that there is an intelligent First Cause.

Again, a number of things are taken for granted in this Proof, and a number of alternatives are not considered. For example, it is assumed that an uncaused phenomenon is 'intrinsically absurd' and that an *infinite* Final Cause is required to account for the *finite* order of the universe, however complex this order may be. As to the second point, Bhabani would have been well advised to consider the view of the classical Vedāntins, who contended that it is not warranted logically to jump in this way from a *finite* effect, or a complex of finite effects—granted that the phenomenon or phenomena in question were known to be an effect in the first place—to an *infinite* cause. Further, Bhabani has also not considered the alternative that if the 'orderly march of successive phenomena' were an eternal property of matter, it could be a property manifesting itself eternally but repetitively, perhaps cyclically, precisely in the way people are experiencing the world to be. In short, his concept of 'eternal' is arbitrary and unclear. It is not necessary to continue our critique. Clearly the idea for this Proof comes from Aquinas' fifth way, that is

12 See, e.g., Aquinas' *Summa Theologiae*, I.2.3.c., and the *Summa Contra Gentiles*, I.13.

'from the governance of things' (*ex gubernatione rerum*), which argues for the existence of a God whose providence governs the world.[13]

In the fourth Proof, which is very briefly laid out, Bhabani contends that 'the origin of organic life must be attributed to a Being who is infinite Life and who first put into matter the germ of life' because 'the theory of an infinite series of living organisms in eternal succession is self-contradictory'. How this is so is not clear. Our earlier comments about the possibility of an infinite series, about the logical jump from finite to infinite, and about Bhabani's concept of 'eternal' apply here. In any case, we have here more an assertion than a 'proof', reminiscent of some rhetorical questions Augustine asks in his *Confessions*.[14]

In the fifth and final Proof, also very brief, Bhabani maintains that the human attributes of free will and intellection, being spiritual, imply the existence of a cause that is similar, 'and he is God, a spirit and a free agent, who is the First Cause of the human race'. There is something here of Aquinas' proof from the grades of perfection in beings (the fourth way).

What concerns us is not so much the cogency or otherwise of these Proofs; we note, rather, their rationalist bias, their alleged appeal to pure reason: a legacy of the Enlightenment. We have commented on the reason for this insistence. Also noteworthy in this context is Bhabani's recourse to what scientists were saying. Throughout the treatise Bhabani quotes western scientific sources to support his views. Under the first Proof T.H. Huxley is quoted to the effect that 'the scientific investigator is wholly incompetent to say anything at all about the first origin of the material universe', while under the third

13 See *Summa Theologiae*, I.2.3.

14 'I know that I was a living person even [as a baby].... Where could such a living creature come from if not from you, O Lord? Can it be that any man has skill to fabricate himself? Or can there be some channel by which we derive our life and our very existence from some other source than you?' (Penguin Classics, p. 26). Bhabani was probably familiar with the *Confessions*. He would have come across it as a visitor to the Eagle's Nest a decade earlier when he was still a College student (see chapter 3). Väth informs us that the *Confessions* was Hiranand's favourite reading while he was a member of this group, and implies that it was through Hiranand in particular that Bhabani was drawn to the Eagle's Nest. 'Die 'Bekenntnisse' des hl. Augustin mögen ihnen vorgeschwebt haben; denn wir wissen, das ... Hiranand aus Sindh ... Augustins Bekenntnisse sich zur Lieblingslesung gewählt hatte. Bhawani, obgleich kein Mitglied, fühlte sich zum Adlerhorst hingezogen und schloss Freundschaft mit Hiranand' (pp. 75–6).

Proof Newton is quoted as saying: 'This most elegant contrivance, consisting of the suns, planets and comets, could not originate but by the design and power of an intelligent Being.' St George Jackson Mivart (1827–1900), a biologist who converted to Catholicism,[15] is adduced, under the fourth Proof, in support of the view that life cannot arise from inorganic matter. The point Bhabani wants to make, in other words, is that his thesis is in accord with modern scientific thinking; this was calculated, no doubt, to strengthen its cogency.

But perhaps of greatest interest is the Thomistic slant of the whole treatise. This comes out not only through its structure (e.g. Five Proofs), but in the way Bhabani quotes St Thomas explicitly on the nature of time, and in his use of Thomistic terminology (e.g., 'actuality', 'potentiality' in the context of change and creation), and its western neo-Thomistic articulation. We have seen that in the process leading up to his conversion Bhabani familiarized himself with Catholic thinking. His philosophical bent was especially shaped by the neo-Thomism of the Manuals of Catholic Philosophy published by the Jesuits in the Stonyhurst Series, which was well under way. The reader will recall that the influence of the Jesuits was strong in north-western India, and the Stonyhurst Series was an important English contribution to the resurgence of Thomism at the time.

In the aftermath of the Enlightenment, there was, in Catholic intellectual circles towards the middle of the nineteenth century, especially on the Continent, a return to the principles of the Scholasticism of the Middle Ages with special reference to the philosophical thought of Thomas Aquinas. This neo-Scholasticism was not an uncritical rehash of the old ideas, but an attempt to rethink them critically in order to meet the challenges raised against the Christian world view by current positivistic and idealist thinking. According to this thinking, it was only the natural sciences and mathematics that could yield truth in any acceptable sense. For only these disciplines provided the evidence—the evidence of the senses or of logic— that enables us to arrive at verifiable conclusions. It was not rational to accept any other kind of evidence as genuine, and 'truths' derived from such evidence were not really truths since they were not properly verifiable. This reasoning rendered irrational the 'truths' of a natural theology, not least the kinds of conclusions that Christian thinkers down the ages claimed are derivable from the

15 But he was considered to have died an apostate and was denied a Catholic burial by English ecclesiastical authority.

natural light of reason, the truths, for example, that there is an infinitely perfect, personal, spiritual being called 'God', that God has created the world, that humans have spiritual, substantival souls that are immortal, that after death God punishes the wicked and rewards the good, that the destiny of human beings is to enjoy the divine presence, and so on. Hume and Kant, each in his own way, were the main thinkers appealed to in support of this stance. The Catholic Church and its philosophers wished to combat this empiricist challenge and to justify the conclusions of their natural theology, and they turned to a revised Scholasticism (in the main to a reconstructed Thomism) as their most effective weapon. Bhabani, mainly through the Stonyhurst philosophers, was heir to this attempt.

The very idea that the existence of the God who is described above can be proved through reason was affirmed by the First Vatican Council (only about a quarter of a century before, in 1869–70) in its constitution, *Dei Filius*. This declares:

> Holy Mother Church holds and teaches that God, the beginning and end of all things, can be known with certainty from the things that were created, through the natural light of human reason ... but that it pleased His wisdom and bounty to reveal Himself and His eternal decrees in another and a supernatural way.... It is to be ascribed to this divine revelation that such truths among things divine as of themselves are not beyond human reason can, even in the present condition of mankind, be known by everyone with facility, with firm certitude and with no admixture of error (Quoted in Neuner and Dupuis, 1983: 40–1).

That it would be to Thomism that the Church would look with special hope in its efforts to work out a natural theology for the modern world was ratified by Pope Leo XIII, the 'Pope of St Thomas', in his encyclical *Aeterni Patris* of 1879. Leo XIII's predilection resulted in a resurgence of Thomistic studies in Catholicdom.[16] In the vanguard of this movement in the English speaking world were the contributors to the Stonyhurst Series, among whom the Rickaby brothers (John and Joseph) and Bernard Boedder were well known. We can thus understand the antecedents and sources for Bhabani's recourse to Thomism in his rational approach as a Catholic convert to the educated Hindu. Moreover, it is important to realize that the *starting point* of Bhabani's *preparatio evangelica,* of his intellectual attempt to bring

[16] For a useful if somewhat biased account, see Watzlawik, 1966.

educated Hindus to Christ, relied heavily on a Thomistic framework for the distinction between the natural and the supernatural. This reliance he never really abandoned, even after he began to formulate a 'Hindu-Catholic' interpretation of that distinction.[17]

We can see how the groundwork for this approach was being laid from a correspondence Bhabani initiated with the Jesuit thinker Bernard Boedder (of St Mary's Hall, Stonyhurst). Boedder's *Natural Theology* had been published in the Series in 1891. On December 7, 1892, Bhabani wrote to Boedder requesting clarification on what was to become a central concern of his theology, namely, how an utterly perfect, self-contained Absolute is also a creator God, that is, produces finite being, with the saga of cosmic imperfection, human sin and fallibility this implies.[18]

Boedder's reply was dated January 5, 1893.[19] 'You have done a real service to me by your candid and clear exposition of some of the

[17] Some three years after the publication of 'A short treatise on the existence of God', Bhabani delivered a lecture entitled 'The Infinite and the Finite' to non-Christian audiences, first in the Framji-Cowasji Hall, Bombay, and soon after in the Town Hall, Trichinopoly. This was published in pamphlet form under Catholic auspices, reaching a third edition in 1918 ('price one anna'). The Prefatory Note informs the reader that this lecture 'was not intended to be a proof of the existence of God. The lecturer took that for granted and intended solely to explain the nature of God and His relations to creatures.' This is indeed the case, yet the lecture resonates to themes and concerns of the treatise we have analysed. There is the same appeal to reason 'which is the common heritage of us all', rather than to any doctrinal or scriptural authority. The exposition turns on the statement that 'the Infinite is the Being which transcends negation; which is all-inclusive; and contains all perfections which you see in finite creatures' and that this Being is 'the primary cause of the finite', not by dividing itself into parts, nor by some process of emanation or evolution or projection, but by 'omnipotent decree', that is by 'the transference of the ideality [of the finite] into reality' (Bhabani's paraphrase for creation out of nothing). Thus can the Infinite be understood to be entirely independent and self-contained, immutable and indivisible. Bhabani's philosophical understanding of God remains essentially intact. But in contrast to the earlier treatise, one notices a significant change in presentation. Though the underlying linguistic framework is still Thomistic ('He is not potentiality'), the lecture is interspersed with one or two Hindu expressions, e.g. '*ātmārām*', self-contented, to indicate the divine perfection, and a tailored reference apparently to *Kena Upanisad* II.2, the idea being that 'we can *apprehend* Him; but we cannot *comprehend* Him.' The lecture is well put together. Bhabani had a commanding presence and we are told that as a lecturer he invariably impressed his hearers favourably; also, the lecture must have sold well to have run to a third edition.

[18] Bhabani's side of the correspondence is not extant. Inquiry has shown that there is no trace of it in the archives of St Mary's Hall, Stonyhurst College.

[19] The letter is copied in INB, pp. 57–8.

greatest difficulties in *Natural Theology*' he writes. So, according to an acknowledged authority in Thomism, Bhabani's grasp of the system was highly proficient. We shall remember this testimony for future reference.

Boedder continues: 'Your first difficulty concerns the harmony between God's immutability and Creation in time. It culminates in this statement: "If, according to you, the causal virtue of his essence is exercised only temporally, then the essence of God is not an actuality in its entirety, for under one aspect at least it undergoes change by the transit from a potential to an actual relationship. If the essence of God possesses an intrinsic virtue of causality, it must needs act, it must enter into a relationship. Does this necessary act consist in creating finite things? That cannot be. Then what is the necessary act?"'

To this 'able exposition' Boedder responds that God's causal power is not really distinct from his free will and that though God wills freely from eternity to create, the effects of his creative act come into being only at the particular moments decreed by his wisdom. On the part of God, the creative act, a free exercise of the divine will, is eternal; on the part of the creature, this act is realized temporally. Consequently, there is no actual relational change in God; it is the creature that undergoes such change in the transit from non-being to being.

Boedder then goes on to answer 'the other aspect of your difficulty proposed in the following words: "God's essence is infinite love and therefore infinitely communicative. As infinitely communicative he needs must communicate. If not, he is essentially non-communicative and becomes only temporally communicative."' Boedder writes that God's creativity is not necessitated *ad extra,* that is, outside his being, and that therefore it need not 'actually produce creatures before the moment predefined'. He then makes reference to the mystery of the Blessed Trinity (apparently mentioned by Bhabani in this context in his letter), as throwing 'a great light upon the truth that God necessarily loves himself'. By itself reason can arrive at a more or less adequate monotheism that can then be enriched by a reason enlightened by the revealed truth of the Trinity. In other words, reason enlightened by faith points to the reasonableness of the mystery of the Trinity, namely, that God's creative love is necessarily communicated internally in the form of the tri-personal but single divine being.

Towards the end of his letter Boedder writes, 'I was very glad to see from the whole of your letter that the great apostle of India, St Francis Xavier, has obtained for you a share of that tender devotion to the Blessed Trinity which filled his heart with heavenly delight.' Bhabani followed up with a letter seeking further clarification on the issues with which his first letter was concerned. The reply he received was substantially the same, once more touching on how unaided reason can only hint at a plurality of persons within one divine being. 'True, it is impossible for us to explain on grounds of any experience positively how a Being not actually productive [in the contingent act of creation] can be as perfect as a Being actually productive. Therefore we are inclined to assume that in God too there must be some sort of actual productiveness [in the form of a plurality of persons]. Reason cannot find any basis whereupon to justify satisfactorily such an assumption' (INB: 59).

The whole correspondence is conducted in Thomistic terms. It is important not only because it shows the formative influence of Thomism in the shaping of Bhabani's theology, but also because it reinforced the distinction between the religious truths of natural reason and the religious truths of revelation. Of particular importance too is the way this distinction is illustrated—by reference to a theological concern of Bhabani's that would endure, the relationship between God's creative act and inner life, an inner life that revelation pronounces is trinitarian. Later, in his persistent effort to explore how far into the divine essence the natural light of reason can penetrate, Bhabani expounds this relationship in the context of his most sustained intellectual contribution to an indigenous Christian theology: an interpretation of the Vedantic conception of the nature of the Absolute as *saccidānanda* (Being, Consciousness, Bliss), and of the production of the world as *māyā*.[20]

But the Boedder correspondence highlights another aspect of Bhabani's life: his religious devotion. His intellectual concerns did not exist in a vacuum; they were inspired by a personal faith that gave them meaning and purpose. *The Blade*, no doubt on the testimony of Animananda, who was a close companion of Bhabani in Sind, records that every morning Bhabani would meditate and attend Mass. He went to confession weekly 'and when doing so his sense of sin was so keen that he considered himself a handcuffed prisoner before

[20] It is significant that Bhabani retained Boedder's letters till the end of his life, though they seem now to have been lost.

the Court of Heaven, asking forgiveness of sins.... He received Holy Communion every Sunday with due preparation and spent a quarter of an hour in thanksgiving' (pp. 53–4). Clearly his was not an instrumentalist faith. Legalistic perhaps, as so much of Catholic devotion then was, but genuine and deep. His disciples Parmanand, Khemchand and a third, Bulchand, were impressed by his example. On May 29, 1893, Animananda (or Rewachand as he was called then) was finally baptized and became the fifth member of the little band.

Bhabani the *karmayogī*, the ascetic warrior fighting India's nationalist cause on the moral and religious fronts, muscular Christian with a vengeance, lacked a suitable war chariot for his intellectual campaign. No stranger to journalism, he soon began to fashion one in the form of a Catholic monthly he proposed to edit. He mooted the idea in 1893 to a Fr A. Bruder s.j., parish priest in Karachi, who had baptized him. Bruder was doubtful about a convert, and a recent one at that, taking on the task of expounding Catholic doctrine without any special training. Bhabani then followed a course of action deeply revealing of the man, and one he was to adopt as and when he saw fit on future occasions. Where ecclesiastical authority was concerned, when one route was barred to some objective of his, he immediately sought an alternative route presided over by an equal if not higher authority. In theory he was prepared to submit to such authority in the spirit of 'holy obedience', but for Bhabani, whatever other dimension it might have, ecclesiastical authority was also a manipulable mechanism. If he pulled the right levers, he could work it to his advantage. Not only did he have a shrewd understanding of his Church's tendencies to legalism, but the individualism of his pre-Christian religious formation led him to view Catholic ecclesiastical authority in a legalistic light. As we shall see, this attitude proved to be his undoing. But that came much later, when rising disenchantment with his Church as institution matched his failure to work the system.

So, finding that his Jesuit parish priest in Karachi balked at the course of action he proposed, Bhabani went over his head, travelled to Bombay and 'submitted his plan to the Superior of the Jesuits in the Bombay Mission. Fr Jurgens listened sympathetically and did all the needful' (Bl., p. 54).[21] That Bhabani was of forceful personality there can be no doubt. He had already acquired a band of admirers

[21] Sind was under the Bombay (Jesuit) Mission at the time. J. Jurgens s.j. (1847–1916) was Superior of the Mission from 1888 to 1894 (and became Archbishop of Bombay in 1907).

so devoted that they had been led to renounce their ancestral beliefs at great personal cost and follow his example in embracing the Christian faith. And now the Superior of the Bombay Jesuit mission, doubtless a cautious man, had been convinced by his earnestness and persuasiveness (not to mention his Catholic record in Sind) to sanction what in the cold light of day must have seemed a great risk: the editing of a Catholic journal by a recent convert with no accredited theological training, in an arena of hawkish interreligious rivalry and scrutiny. Some personality! It was adequately housed. Bhabani was of muscular build with an intelligent, sensitive face to which the requisite *gravitas* was endowed by a generous beard and bridging moustache. He dressed only in Indian-style attire.

The journal saw the light of day in January 1894, entitled '*Sophia*. A Monthly Catholic Journal'. The reader was informed that it was 'edited by B.C. Banerji'. The monthly *Sophia* survived for about five years and acts as a comprehensive index of Bhabani's intellectual development and concerns. Each issue was about 16 pages long (about A4 in size), carried inside the front cover a quotation from the book of Wisdom (7. 7b–8, 7.10, 9.11, 13, 17–18, with the word 'Sophia' substituted for 'wisdom'), and consisted in the main of four or five articles by the editor and other contributors.[22] The journal generally ended with items of information, and short extracts or quotations that, if they were of a religious nature, invariably showed Catholicism in a favourable light.

[22] Notable among these contributors was the Swiss Jesuit, Alois Hegglin (b. 1850, arrived in India in 1884), who had been sent to Sind in 1893 by his superiors to foster and consolidate the conversions to the Catholic faith led by Bhabani. 'Fr Hegglin arrived in Karachi on December 30th, 1893 and remained here till the beginning of February, whence he moved to Hyderabad. He had already befriended Banerji in Karachi and by turns gave lectures with him and contributed articles for the journal 'Sophia' which had been set up.... In Hyderabad Hegglin took part in Banerji's social evenings and was often his companion on his walks through the city and its surroundings.' 'P. Hegglin traf am 30. Dezember 1893 in Karachi ein und verblieb hier bis Anfang Februar, worauf er nach Haiderabad übersiedelte. Schon in Karachi scholss er mit Banerji Freundschaft, hielt abwechselnd mit ihm Vorträge und lieferte Beiträge für die damals gegründete Zeitschrift 'Sophia'.... In Haiderabad nahm Hegglin an Banerjis Gesellschaftsabenden teil und war oft sein Begleiter auf seinen Gängen durch die Stadt und die Umgebung' (Väth, 86). Later Hegglin and Bhabani drifted apart. Hegglin went on to specialize in Hindu thought and taught Sanskrit at St Xavier's College, Bombay (from 1895 to 1912), whence he engaged in controversy with the then Upadhyay over the latter's attempt to Christianize the Vedantic concept of *māyā*. More on this later.

Under 'Objects' on page 1 of the first issue there appeared the following points:

1. To solve the fundamental problem—What is the end of man and how to attain it?

2. To represent faithfully to the Indian public the essential teachings of the Vedas, Upanishads, Darsanas, Samhitas and Puranas.

3. To expound the doctrines of the Catholic Church founded by Jesus Christ.

4. To facilitate the comparative study of different religions—especially, the ancient religious systems of India, modern Theism, and the Christian and Catholic Religion—by setting forth their distinctive features in a popular way, and thus to help the seekers after truth to arrive at the true knowledge of the True Religion.

5. To discuss social and moral questions affecting the well-being of Indians.

Under the heading 'Ourselves', the editor had written:

> The scope of our undertaking may naturally create apprehension. It may be suspected that those religious systems to which we do not profess allegiance will be presented in a distorted form to subserve an aggressive end. It may also be apprehended that the stern realities of the Catholic religion will be softened down to easy acceptability. But we assure the public that we will staunchly follow the strictest rule of verity. We will try our utmost to represent faithfully the distinctive features of different religions.... Our chief object is to facilitate the comparative study of different religious systems with philosophic sobriety but without compromising laxity.

On the next page the editor declares, 'We will also discuss social and moral questions but will not dabble in politics.'

All very well. But in fact the tone of the journal was apologetical in favour of Catholic teaching, sometimes militantly so. After all, as we have seen, the articles on Luther (published in the journal) hardly avoided presenting the reformer's position 'in a distorted form to subserve an aggressive end'. And what of the editor's desire to help 'seekers after truth to arrive at the true knowledge of the True Religion' by applying 'the strictest rule of verity' with 'philosophic sobriety'? In the context of the partisan religious journalism of the age, readers could be in no doubt as to which the 'True Religion' would be.

At the same time, the *Sophia*'s declared aims are catholic in another sense. The journal was intended to be read not exclusively by Catholics or even Christians, but also by educated Hindus. Hence Bhabani's avowal (to which he faithfully adhered) of giving preference to the exposition of Hindu thought. Moreover, he remarks in the editorial ('The New Year') of the issue dated January 1898: 'So far as we know *Sophia* is the first Catholic attempt in India as a journal meant for Hindu readers.'

How successful was it in reaching Hindu readers, and how large was its circulation? No figures exist to provide exact answers, but there is no doubt that the *Sophia* made its mark among educated Indians. On occasion it was alluded to by non-Christian papers, notably the *Arya Messenger* (in polemical vein). It regularly carried correspondence from Hindus. It also had a Catholic readership, especially in the South. Later, when ecclesiastical authority saw fit to forbid Catholics from reading its successor, the weekly *Sophia,* which presumably sought to trade on the monthly's established readership, the official proclamation denouncing the paper was addressed to the Archbishop of Madras. Khemchand, in his Note (already mentioned) appended to vol. 2 of Hull's work (pp. 517–21), notes that with his headquarters in Hyderabad, Bhabani 'carried on his propaganda in right earnest in Sind; and his philosophical monthly *Sophia* had by this time achieved a high reputation' (p. 517).

Other sources speak approvingly of the monthly journal. In its issue of February 15, 1895, the *Bombay Catholic Examiner* (BCE), the flagship weekly of the Catholic Church in the subcontinent, asks 'material and moral support' of its readers for the *Sophia*. 'The enterprise is new,' it remarks, 'there exists no Catholic paper in India conducted on the same principle, or that applies so directly to the educated portion of the natives; it deserves to be encouraged in its modest beginnings by a benevolent assistance.'[23] The *Ceylon Messenger* was warmer in its praise. It is quoted in the BCE (under 'Indian Intelligence', issue of October 1, 1897) as saying: 'That excellent journal, *Sophia,* edited by a Brahmin convert ... shows ... admirable grasp of Catholic philosophy and theology.... It deserves to be ranked among the best philosophical Magazines of the day.' In 1896, till mid-August that year, the BCE carried an advertisement for the *Sophia* towards the end of each issue. 'Sophia. A Monthly Catholic Journal,' reads the advertisement, 'Edited by a Brahmin Convert.' Its object

[23] Under the heading 'Review' in a one-column article on *Sophia* and its editor

was 'to show to the Indian educated public the excellence of the Christian and Catholic religion by contrasting it with other religions, especially Hinduism' (not much impartiality here!) and, still as part of the advertisement, under the caption 'Opinion', a blurb from the *Illustrated Catholic Missions* (November 1895) refers to 'that able and zealous Catholic writer (Editor of *Sophia*) ... and his venture [which] deserves the highest praise and encouragement.'

The Church supported the journal, both as to its aims and financially. The BCE article mentioned earlier (February 15, 1895) notes that 'His Grace the Archbishop of Bombay [Theodore Dalhoff s.j.] has given the paper his full sanction and grants a considerable pecuniary assistance towards its maintenance ... several Archbishops and Bishops favour it with their subscription.... To bring the journal more effectively to the notice of non-Christians, the editor sends copies free of charge to a number of native reading-rooms, whose managers have agreed to admit the paper.' The annual subscription was Rs 3. So the programme and contents of the monthly *Sophia* were officially approved and supported by ecclesiastical authority; the paper was influential, had an appreciable readership among educated Hindus and Catholics and was well received by the Church. This redounded to the editor's credit. Why and how ecclesiastical authority rounded on him in later years will prove all the more intriguing.

But the *Sophia* was continually short of funds. Commercially, its readership was still too small. This is not surprising. To begin with, its catchment was limited. Only a tiny minority of the population could cope intellectually with the level, and we may add, alienness, of its philosophizing. There was also a limited interest-factor. The journal was entirely devoted to religious issues, especially to analysis of Catholic doctrine vis-à-vis Hinduism. Finally, there was hardly any light relief. The journal maintained a more or less serious tone throughout. In the editorial of January 1898, the paper's lack of development is lamented: 'Starting four years ago [the *Sophia*] has not grown in bulk, which is a matter of regret to its Editor and to not a few of its well-wishers; still it has widened the circle of its readers and the sphere of its influence.'

Note that in the journal's charter, Bhabani promises not to 'dabble in politics'. Perhaps from the viewpoint of ecclesiastical authority this was more significant than it appears. We shall consider this matter later. Certainly the overtly non-political rationale, discussed earlier, that guided Bhabani's career at the time prevailed. But the *Sophia* was still implicitly political in the sense that it was intended to purge its Hindu readership of moral and religious error and to establish a 'rational theism', in keeping with Catholic natural theology, on which could be grounded the revealed truths of Catholic faith. This was a political objective in that Bhabani believed that true patriotism was a natural consequence of a sound religious and moral perspective. It was not that the end, namely, patriotism and greater national autonomy, justified any means, so that if becoming a Catholic or moving in this direction helped, it should be encouraged. Rather, the Catholic way was intrinsically right and good, and as such engendered true patriotism in its wake.

Thus, especially in the context of an analysis of Hindu and Christian (i.e. Catholic) beliefs, Bhabani set out in the pages of *Sophia* to instil the natural religious truths of right reason, as a *preparatio evangelica*. The implied distinction here between the natural truths of reason and revealed truths of faith was an established Catholic principle, also ratified by the First Vatican Council in its constitution, *Dei Filius:*

> The perpetual common belief of the Catholic Church has held and holds also this: there is a twofold order of knowledge, distinct not only in its principle but also in its object; in its principle, because in the one we know by natural reason, in the other by divine faith; in its object, because apart from what natural reason can attain, there are proposed to our belief mysteries that are hidden in God, which can never be known unless they are revealed by God.... Nevertheless, if reason illumined by faith inquires in an earnest, pious and sober manner, it attains by God's grace a certain understanding of the mysteries, which is most fruitful.... But it never becomes capable of understanding them in the way it does truths which constitute its proper object.... However, though faith is above reason, there can never be a real discrepancy between faith and reason, since the same God who reveals mysteries and infuses faith has bestowed the light of reason on the human mind.... Not only can there be no conflict between faith and reason, they also support each other since right reason demonstrates the foundations of faith.... It is therefore far remote from the truth to say that the Church opposes the study of human arts and sciences; on the contrary, she supports and promotes them in many ways ... if rightly pursued, they lead to God with His grace' [Neuner and Dupuis, 1983: 45–6].

Here, elaborated, is the official Catholic view on the relationship between reason and faith and between natural religious truths and revealed truths, and on how the study of human arts and sciences can 'if rightly pursued' lead to God. Here is the rationale, in other words, for a Catholic convert, residually sympathetic towards his ancestral religion, to approach the philosophical-theological study of this religion as enshrining 'the foundations' of the revealed truths of his new-found faith. The application of this rationale to Bhabani is plain to see. Hinduism, properly interpreted, 'leads to God'. Further, there was no doubt that Hinduism had this capacity. Did not the western orientalists speak highly of the tradition's golden Vedic past (see chapter 1)?

At the beginning of his campaign, it was broadly to Vedic Hinduism that Bhabani looked for elements of that rational 'theism' on which the Christian message to Hindus could be built. The earliest sustained expression by Bhabani of the natural/supernatural distinction in this context occurs in an article in *Sophia* (Sp-m) entitled, 'Our attitude towards Hinduism' (January 1895). It is the burden of the article to distinguish, in by now familiar terms, between the Roman Catholic and 'Protestant' (or 'sectarian') approaches to evangelization. We quote rather fully since this article launches Bhabani, as it were, on his campaign of evangelization. Sectarian missionaries, he writes, 'prepossessed as they are by a ... theology which teaches that man's nature is *utterly* corrupt, are incapable of finding anything true and good in India[24] and in her scriptures ... for nearly half a century, since the commencement of their evangelical crusade, [they] have been labouring under the delusion that the more it can be shown that the Hindu scriptures are so many lies, the more rapid will be the propagation of Christianity in India.... What has been the result? Educated India has been thoroughly estranged and she looks upon Christianity as a destroyer and not a fulfiller and perfecter of what is true and good in the country.' For Bhabani, Christian faith must fulfil, not destroy 'what is true and good' in Hinduism. That Hinduism can be fulfilled in this way is assumed on historical grounds ('the glory that was India') and *a priori* (theological) grounds.

To the 'Protestant' approach the Catholic attitude is contrasted: 'The Catholic Church does not believe in the utter corruption of man. Man, fallen man, can reason rightly and choose what is good, though he is much hampered in his rational acts by the violence of his lower

24 Bhabani regularly identifies India with 'Hindu India'. His nationalist aspirations, like those of the majority of nationalist Hindu leaders in the first stages of the freedom movement, tended to marginalize non-Hindu minorities, especially the tribals and the Muslims.

appetites.' Cardinal Manning, Pope Clement XI and St Paul (Rom. 1.20) are adduced in support of the view that 'every man is a born Theist. At the first dawn of his reason, in spite of passions and prejudices, man partakes of the universal light of Theism which reveals to him that he is an imperfect image of a Perfect Reason, Holiness and Goodness. A careful student of the religious history of mankind will find that the doctrine of universal Theism held by the Catholic Church is verified even in the most corrupt faiths of the lowest race.'

Now follows a revealing opinion. With the possible exception of ancient Greece, avers Bhabani, it is in Hindu thought that 'human philosophy', or insight into the 'invisible things of God', has reached its acme. What aspect of Hindu thought is this? Bhabani quotes from the Upanishads to support his contention (e.g. Isa 5, 6, 8; Kena I.5, 6, 4) and from the *Bhagavadgita* (11.18), that is, later Vedic religion, though, as we shall see, in subsequent discussions Bhabani also appeals to early Vedic thought. We then come to the nub of the article. These sublime Hindu insights express natural religious truths (i.e. that the Supreme Being is unique, spiritual, all-pervasive, omniscient, omnipotent, imperishable etc.), whereas

> the religion of Christ is *supernatural.* All the doctrines of Christ, the Holy Trinity, the Atonement, the Resurrection, from beginning to end, are beyond the domain of reason.... The truths in Hinduism are of pure reason illuminated in the order of nature by the light of the Holy Spirit. They do not overstep reason.... But though the religion of Christ is beyond the grasp of nature and reason, still its foundation rests upon the truths of nature and reason. Destroy the religion of nature and reason, you destroy the supernatural religion of Christ. Hence a true missionary of Christ, instead of vilifying Hinduism, should find out truths from it by study and research. It is on account of the close connection between the natural and the supernatural that we have taken upon ourselves the task ... to form, as it were, a natural platform upon which the Hindus taking their stand may have a view of the glorious supernatural edifice of the Catholic religion of Christ.

Bhabani's rationale for evangelization, in terms of the thinking already discussed, could not be stated more clearly. By this device Bhabani could pursue and endorse Hindu behaviour, so far as this was possible, on the natural level, while affirming allegiance to Catholic faith (the essence of which was supernatural). In fact, this was the only way to proceed. The Protestant way of denigrating Hinduism was by implication destroying 'the supernatural religion of Christ'. Bhabani could be a patriot and a Christian simultaneously (and so could all his Indian readers), a far from uncontentious combination at the time.[25]

Bhabani suited the action to the thought. This article and an important event in his life coincided. In the issue of December 1894, the following declaration appeared in the *Sophia:*

> I have adopted the life of Bhikshu (mendicant) Sannyasi. The practice prevalent in our country is to adopt a new name along with the adoption of a religious life. Accordingly I have adopted a new name. My family surname is Vandya (praised) Upadhyay (teacher, lit. sub-teacher), and my baptismal name is Brahmabandhu (Theophilus). I have abandoned the first portion of my family surname, because I am a disciple of Jesus Christ, the Man of Sorrows, the Despised Man. So my new name is Upadhyaya Brahmabandhu. I hereby declare that, henceforward, I shall be known and addressed as Upadhyaya Brahmabandhu, or, in short, Upadhyayji, and not Banerji, which is an English corruption of the first portion of my family surname, Vandya-ji.

Some of Upadhyay's etymology here is dubious. From the Sanskrit form—'Vandyopadhyaya'—of his Bengali name, 'Bandyopadhyay', he derives the meaning 'Praised sub-teacher'. This seems acceptable. But that 'Banerji' is an English corruption of 'Vandya-ji' is disputable. In any case, the change of name is an important, self-determining act. It seems not to have been ratified legally (e.g. by deed-poll). But it was a public declaration of intent, the outward form of an inner frame of mind to live and act in a certain way. He declares publicly that henceforth he will live a religious life; by this his celibate status is affirmed. Further, his approach will be Hindu, so far as this is consonant with his Catholic faith. The new Sanskritic name signifies this. Who will determine the Hindu form of his Catholic faith? He will.

25 In an article entitled, 'Why did not Keshub Chandra Sen accept Christ?' (Sp-m, February 1895), Bhabani expatiates on 'the Protestant view' about the relationship between nature and grace. 'With the Protestants generally, supernatural life means the power to conform the human will to the will of God received by man through faith in Christ. According to them, it is naturally impossible for man, he being utterly corrupt owing to original sin, to choose what is good. Even his good works done before the life of faith are sinful in their nature and ... deserve the wrath of God. Therefore they call the corrupt old life natural life and the new life supernatural life.' For the reasons described, however Bhabani's Catholic allegiance set him against this line of thinking entirely.

On the front cover of the same issue, the usual 'Edited by B.C. Banerji' was replaced by 'Edited by Upadhyaya Brahmabandhu'. In the issue of November 1895, however, without adverting to it, the name was changed to 'Brahmabandhav' (pronounced 'Brahmabandhab' in Bengali[26]). It is this form that has stuck. There seems to be good reason for the change. As the declaration above makes clear, 'Brahmabandhu' was intended as the Sanskrit equivalent of Theophilus, meaning 'God's friend'. However, in traditional Sanskrit literature, *brahmabandhu* is usually used sarcastically to refer to a Brahmin who has failed to live up to the expectations of his caste.[27] This would hardly do! Upadhyay must have twigged, or someone must have pointed it out to him.[28] Brahmin status was still to mean much to him, as we shall see. So the name was changed to Brahmabandhab (which means the same, but without the negative resonance).[29]

26 Bengali has no 'v' sound.

27 Here are some examples, spanning about two thousand years of usage. In *Chandogya Upanisad* VI.1.1 (circa 7th century B.C.E.), the sage Uddalaka Aruni gives his son the following advice: 'Svetaketu, live the life of a celibate student, for, my son, there is no one in our family unlearned (in the Vedas) like some *brahmabandhu*' (*śvetaketo vasa brahmacaryaṃ na vai saumya asmatkulino'nanūcya brahmabandhur iva bhavatīti*; cf. the *rājanyabandhu* of Brhadaranyaka Upanishad VI.2.3). Shankara, in his commentary, says that the *brahmabandhu*, 'not being himself a committed Brahmin, exploits Brahmin connections' (*brāhmaṇān bandhūn vyapadiśati na svayaṃ brāhmaṇavṛtta iti*). In his *Prakasika*, Rangaramanuja (15th–16th century) glosses: 'Someone who is himself unBrahminic but who exploits his connection with Brahmins is said to be a *brahmabandhu*' (*yaḥ svayam abrāhmaṇa eva san brāhmaṇān bandhutvena vyapadiśati sa brahmabandhur ity ucyate* Anandasrama ed., vol. 63). We have another example in the *Bhagavata Purana* (10th century?) in I.7.35. Asvatthama, the son of the Brahmin archery teacher, Drona, has been captured by Arjuna, the Lord Krishna's close friend. Asvatthama has committed a heinous crime; he has murdered some young boys, children of Arjuna and his brothers, in their sleep. To test Arjuna, Krishna advises him to kill Asvatthama: 'Slay this *brahmabandhu*, this fellow who has killed innocent sleeping boys at night' (*brahmabandhum imam jahi yo'sav anāgasaḥ suptān avadhīn niśi balakān*); that is, 'Slay this false Brahmin who violates the code of *dharma*.' See also I.7.57 (cf. the *dvijabandhu* of I.4.25).

28 This does not necessarily reflect on his competence as a Sanskritist, but it does raise interesting questions about the focus of his studies in the *ṭol* and subsequently.

29 Rewachand, whom Upadhyay had inspired to become a Catholic, followed suit and adopted the title 'Animananda'. Zacharias (1933) translates this as 'Bliss-in-Littleness' (p. 28, note), a translation probably derived from Animananda himself, since Zacharias met and interviewed Animananda.

In keeping with the change of name, Upadhyay underwent a change of appearance. The muscular frame and bearded face remained. But from towards the end of 1894 Upadhyay went barefoot and his *svadeshi* clothes were exchanged for the traditional saffron robe of the Hindu renouncer.[30] Most Christians (not least the clergy) and Hindus would have been bewildered by this, if not suspicious. Hindus might read it as a trap for the unwary! For Christians it might signify that Upadhyay was perhaps still consorting with the enemy, or a convert in name only. The first time Upadhyay attended Church in Hyderabad dressed thus, the scandalized priest, who had not been forewarned, turned him out. 'Quietly he repaired to the Presbytery and changed his dress' (Bl., p. 59). Then Upadhyay's strategy in dealing with Church authority came into play. 'He appealed ... to the Archbishop of Bombay who was not inclined to give way. But Upadhyay urged saying that the opinion of the Bishop of Lahore ought to count more than the decision of a simple parish-priest. But in Lahore he had been allowed to wear the saffron garb. The permission was granted' (Bl., p. 59).[31] To allay qualms and distinguish his Christian allegiance he wore an ebony cross hung from the neck. And thus be-crossed, saffron-clad and barefoot, this doughty pioneer set off on a journey to indigenize his faith, to synthesize East and West in a new spirituality. There was a long way to go, and the road would be hard and full of disappointing twists. He lived off alms[32]: 'often he would shut himself up in a small room and there discipline his body, the ass, as he called it, with a whip' (*Sketch*, pt. I, p. 18). But no ass he; mind, soul and body dedicated to his Cause, heart aflame, he strove to forge ahead.

30 What prompted this is not clear: perhaps a combination of different stimuli stemming from the life-style of Hiranand, some Arya Samajists and even Vivekananda (who, as a Hindu monk, had made a sensational and much-publicized impact on the World Parliament of Religions at Chicago in late 1893 dressed in saffron robe and yellow turban).

31 He was last in Lahore apparently in early November to lecture.

32 Probably in the form of donations for lectures given and living expenses for editing *Sophia*.

# Chapter 6

## Fire-eater Part I: Upadhyay's Opposition to 'Traditional Targets'

In the next few chapters we embark on a study mainly of Upadhyay's thought till about the time of his preparations for departure to England. During this time Upadhyay wrote almost exclusively in English, chiefly as the editor of *Sophia.* For most of this period he laboured successfully to remain in good standing with his Church in accordance with his stated aim to bring educated India to Christ—really, educated Hindus to the Catholic faith. But as his thinking developed it did not turn out to be as simple as that. Within the framework of the natural/supernatural distinction discussed earlier, he sought to reconstruct Catholic commitment in terms of a Hindu basis for the reception of the Gospel. This is where problems with ecclesiastical authority arose. Till that reconstruction took shape he basked in his Church's benign tolerance of the novelty of his approach. But as the Hindu features of his approach went deeper and became more insistent—intrusive, in the eyes of relevant authority—opposition mounted, and disenchantment set in on both sides. This led to Upadhyay's confusing, if not confused, desire to visit England.

What concerns us, in the analysis of his thought, is what was foremost in Upadhyay's mind during this period: articulating a preparatory base for the reception of Catholic teaching by Hindus. To this end we shall not consider those aspects of his position that simply repeated or expounded, in a western context, the Catholic, especially the Thomistic, thinking of the day. As suggested in the preceding chapter, there was nothing particularly innovative or interesting here, though we should point out perhaps that these discussions (e.g. on the nature of sin, death, miracles, God, divine action, scriptural prophecy, time, eternity) were invariably able and faithful to tradition, and could rise to heights of the requisite subtlety. Our focus is more to the point. Perhaps it is also worth noting in anticipation that Upadhyay's stance during this time was not overtly political. It was political only in the broad sense defined hitherto, namely, in the sense that the pursuit of sound morals and religion laid the basis, personally and collectively, for a responsible use of political freedom and as such, was patriotic.

For our purposes, Upadhyay's thought can be distinguished under two headings: repudiatory and affirmative, that is, pertaining to what he judged militated against his agenda, and to what he thought was supportive of it. The targets he attacked can be divided into traditional and contemporary. We shall deal with his treatment of the traditional targets first.

## Traditional Targets

### *Advaita Vedānta*

By the last decade of the nineteenth century—the process had begun much earlier—the Advaitic system as championed by Shankara, the great eighth century philosophical-theologian, had been established among western orientalists and westernized Hindus alike as the acme of religious Hinduism. So in singling out Advaita Upadhyay was not doing anything very surprising. Here is how G. Thibaut, whose early English translation of Shankara's commentary on the *Vedanta-* or *Brahma-Sutras*[1] in the authoritative *Sacred Books of the East* series has also become an enduring one, assesses Shankara Advaita (in his Introduction to Part I). Upadhyay knew the translation well and, as we shall see, quoted from it extensively. Thibaut says:

> The commentary here selected for translation ... is the one composed by the celebrated theologian Sankara.... There are obvious reasons for this selection. In the first place, the Sankara-bhashya [commentary] represents the so-called orthodox side of Brahmanical theology which strictly upholds the Brahman or highest Self of the Upanishads.... In the second place, the doctrine advocated by Sankara is, from a purely philosophical point of view ... the most important and interesting one which has arisen on Indian soil.... In the third place, Sankara's bhashya is, as far as we know, the oldest of the extant commentaries.... [It] is the authority most generally deferred to in India as to the right understanding of the Vedanta-Sutras, and

1 A seminal, aphoristic treatment of the nature of Brahman, the ultimate reality, and of our relationship to it, based on Upanishadic insights.

> ever since Sankara's time the majority of the best thinkers of India have been men belonging to this school [Thibaut, 1890: xiv–xv].

Thibaut's appraisal is contentious in various ways, of course. But we have quoted it to show traditional Advaita's standing generally in educated opinion of the time. Among the westernized Bengalis, this opinion was a long time in the making. Its chief instigator in the early part of the century was Rammohan Roy. Though Rammohan himself differed from Shankara in important respects, it was mainly in his Bengali writings that he made of Shankara the outstanding authority in traditional Hindu theology (on this see Killingley, 1977). Subsequently, Shankara never lost this status among the Bengali intelligentsia.[2] Indeed, Upadhyay's contemporary and former close friend, now Swami Vivekananda, was busy publicizing Shankara Advaita as the quintessence not only of Hindu thought but of a universal religion.

It will be helpful at this point to quote fairly extensively from Thibaut's interpretation of Shankara, not only because his formulation may be regarded as representative of the current westernized understanding of Advaita but because it seems to have been the basis first of Upadhyay's rejection of Advaita in this early phase of his Christian commitment and later of his attempt to reconstruct a central dialogue-partner for the Christian faith. After citing two other western sources as 'trustworthy' aids for understanding 'Sankara's system' (Deussen, 1883 and Gough, 1891), Thibaut writes:

> What in Sankara's opinion the Upanishads teach, is shortly as follows. Whatever is, is in reality one; there truly exists only one universal being called Brahman or Paramatman, the highest Self.... It is pure 'Being', or, which comes to the same, pure intelligence or thought (caitanya, jnana).... Whatever qualities or attributes are conceivable, can only be denied of it.... Brahman is associated with a certain power called Maya or avidya to which the appearance of this entire world is due. This power cannot be called 'being' (sat), for 'being' is only Brahman; nor can it be called 'non-being' (asat) in the strict sense, for it at any rate produces the appearance of this world. It is in fact a principle of *illusion* [emphasis added]: the undefinable cause owing to which there seems to exist a material

2 Traditionally Bengal was not noted as a stronghold of Advaitic thought. Bengal's traditional intellectual forte was logic, and the region's religious focuses in the 'high' tradition were devotion to Krishna (especially in the form of Caitanyaism) and the Goddess.

> world comprehending distinct individual existences.... We may say that the material cause of the world is Brahman in so far as it is associated with Maya. In this latter quality Brahman is more properly called Isvara, the Lord....
>
> The phenomenal world or world of ordinary experience (vyavahara) thus consists of a number of individual souls engaged in specific cognitions, volitions, and so on, and of the external material objects with which those cognitions and volitions are concerned.... External things, although not real in the strict sense of the word, enjoy at any rate as much reality as the specific cognitional acts whose objects they are.
>
> The non-enlightened soul is unable to look through and beyond Maya, which, like a veil, hides from it its true nature. Instead of recognizing itself to be Brahman, it blindly identifies itself with its adjuncts (upadhi), the fictitious offspring of Maya, and thus looks for its true Self in the body, the sense organs, and ... the organ of specific cognition. The soul, which in reality is pure intelligence, non-active, infinite, thus becomes limited in extent, as it were, limited in knowledge and power, an agent and enjoyer. Through its actions it burdens itself with merit and demerit, the consequences of which it has to bear or enjoy in series of future embodied existences, the Lord—as a retributor and dispenser—allotting to each soul that form of embodiment to which it is entitled by its previous actions....
>
> The means of escaping from this endless saṃsara [round of rebirth], the way out of which can never be found by the non-enlightened soul, are furnished by the Veda.... That student of the Veda ... whose soul has been enlightened by the texts embodying the higher knowledge of Brahman ... obtains at the moment of death immediate final release, i.e. he withdraws altogether from the influence of Maya, and asserts himself in his true nature, which is nothing else but the absolute highest Brahman [Thibaut, 1890: xxiv–xxvii].

This is a fairly comprehensive summary of the contemporary westernized understanding of the basics of Advaita metaphysics and soteriology. Certain features of this exposition are particularly relevant: (1) the non-personal nature of the absolute Brahman; (2) the ultimately 'illusory' nature of the personal Lord, empirical reality and individual selves (i.e. the perspective of *māyā*); (3) the universal applicability of the law of karma and rebirth, and (4) the pantheistic nature of the relationship between the absolute Brahman and the phenomenal world. Thibaut does not use the term 'pantheistic', but the word was commonly used in this connection among the western and Hindu intelligentsia.[3] Upadhyay, in the first flush of his new-found dualist, theistic, realist and non-transmigrationist faith, set to work with a vengeance to warn his educated compatriots of the dangerous pitfalls of Advaita in terms of this understanding. He refers to Advaita sometimes as 'pantheism' and sometimes simply as 'Vedanta' or 'Vedantism' (in keeping with the view that Advaita, as the quintessence of religious Hinduism, was the accredited interpretation of the religion of the Upanishads or Vedanta, though in fact there were a number of other schools of Vedantic thought).[4]

First we must show what Upadhyay understood by Vedantic thought so-called. The first brief exposition occurs in Sp-m, July 1894 ('What does Hinduism teach?'). Hinduism teaches, we are told,

> that there is one undivided Essence, that this Essence *apparently* becomes many, that the state of its being many is this creation. The cause of the unity being transformed into multiplicity is, according to Hindu philosophy, the mixture of Being (sat) with non-being (asat).... The first product of the union of the absolute Being with non-Being is Isvara (Personal God)... [The Hindu] migrates into different scales of life according to the fruits of his deeds till he attains to the knowledge that he is himself the absolute Being conditioned by non-being [viz. Maya].

In the next issue of *Sophia* Upadhyay proceeds to explain, not on the basis of faith but of 'pure reason', why all this will not do ('What does Pure Reason teach?'). 'Pure reason' teaches that a Supreme Being that produces the world by the multiplication of self-transformation, real or apparent, through some inherent principle of non-being is no Supreme Being at all, for 'this would be to destroy the very essence of the Supreme Being'. Reason teaches that the Supreme Being is the Creator and First Cause of all being. Itself immutable—else there would

3 In his well-known *Dialogues on the Hindu Philosophy* (written in 1861), Krishnamohan Banerjea, the eminent Bengali scholar and Christian convert, devotes a whole chapter (Dialogue VIII) to showing how Shankara's thought is 'pantheistic'.

4 In *The Twentieth Century*, the last journal he edited in English, Upadhyay writes in an article entitled 'A brief outline of Hinduism': 'It is difficult to define Hinduism comprehensively. For the purpose of this article let it be defined as a body of doctrines inculcated explicitly or implicitly in the Vedanta and developed by Sankara and other theologians of the Advaita (monistic) School' (April 1901). And in the weekly *Sophia* we have, 'What is Vedantism? It is the religion of the Upanishads as taught by Vyasa and expounded by Sankara. The schools of Ramanuja and Madhva are called Vedantic by sufferance' (August 11, 1900).

be infinite regress in the chain of mutable being—and 'actuality itself', this Being 'causes mutations in others' that are a mixture of actuality and potentiality. In fact, pure reason 'breaks the backbone of the Advaita theory' about the Supreme Being or God. 'A God subject to [some principle of mayic] limitation is not the true God, but a creature of speculation run to extravagance.' Here the teaching of pure reason coincides neatly with traditional Thomistic teaching.

The August, October and November issues of *Sophia* that year contain a serial entitled 'Vedanta Philosophy' in which Upadhyay purports to expound, without critique, the first two Parts of the *Brahma Sutras* according to the 'most learned and lucid commentary' of the 'great Sankaracarya'. The primacy of the Advaitic position for educated Hindus is described as follows: 'The doctrine of the one eternal Being without a second, from whom proceeds this universe and in whom it is ultimately absorbed, is the cornerstone of Hinduism. Hinduism repudiates the doctrine of creation and teaches that Nature is Brahman and Brahman is Nature' (August). At the end of the third article, Upadhyay gives a summary of Advaita:

> We may now give a summary of the Vedanta philosophy. There exists one Being only without a second. The apparent multiplicity is only a projection of him. He is periodically enveloped by maya (illusion) and produces dreams like the human mind in sleep. Those dreams constitute the multiplicity of beings. He becomes many by ideating and not dividing his substance. There is no such reality as dualism. The sense of dualism is an illusion. A being subject to the illusion of dualism must pass through the misery of repeated births and deaths till he arrives at the supreme consciousness of ego and ego only. That state of consciousness in which ego is the subject and ego is the object, that state of spiritual elevation where all relationship is eliminated, where the onlyness of self reigns supreme, is mukti (salvation).

It is not difficult to discern the main ingredients of the standard westernized interpretation of Advaita in these and preceding comments by Upadhyay: 'pantheism' ('Nature is Brahman and Brahman is Nature'), illusionism, the ultimate repudiation of dualism and a personal God, and of creation *ex nihilo,* and so on. Indeed a gaping chasm appears between this formulation of Advaita as a monistic system and traditional dualist Thomistic philosophical theology. And yet, before very long, Advaita will be rehabilitated as the Hindu vehicle *par excellence* of an indigenous Catholic faith.

Meanwhile, the columns of *Sophia* resound to enfilades against the perniciousness of Advaita. Here he rails against 'the utter falsity of the prevailing Hindu error of Advaitavad (Pantheism)' ('Our attitude towards Hinduism', January 1895), there he declares that 'our one great object in life is to banish Advaitavad from India' ('*The Light of the East* and Ourselves', August 1895). In 'Our new Programme' (January 1896) we are told that it is *Sophia*'s aim 'to show that Pantheism ... is utterly false', while in 'The Supreme Being under Delusion!' (January 1896) we are advised that 'careful consideration will show that Advaitavad is the old, old spirit of pride which wriggles itself into newer and newer forms as the ages run on.... This Pantheism is the cause of all the dirt and filth that befoul [the characters of India's] gods, her heaven and her worship.' Christian teaching is opposed, we are assured, because it 'commands the Vedantists to give up their Sphinx-like, repellent, lonely, impersonal Deity' (September 1896). Quite. Till about 1897 or thereabouts, that is, when this traditional target will start metamorphosing into a key weapon of Upadhyay's revisionary campaign.

Advaita was attacked as particularly invidious because it had this tendency to 'wriggle itself into newer and newer forms in guises old and new.' The old guises were the classical formulations attributed to Shankara and his traditional successors, the new were the contemporary expressions (some claiming Shankara's authority) put forward by Swami Vivekananda and others. We shall come to these in due course.

### *The doctrine of karma and rebirth*

In 'Conversion of India: an Appeal' (*Sophia*, October 1894), Upadhyay writes: 'The first step to be taken ... to effect [India's] conversion, is to eradicate from the minds of the Indian people certain erroneous and mischievous doctrines. They are the following: (1) God is all, all is God; (2) God, man and matter, all three are eternal; (3) the doctrine of transmigration. These three doctrines are eating into the very vitals of the Hindu race.' The first error was identified as that of Advaita, the second as the teaching of Swami Dayananda (to be considered later), and the third was traditional and, at least in the upper-caste psyche, deep-rooted belief in karma and rebirth.

In fact, there are many variants in Hindu tradition of the teaching on karma and rebirth, and Upadhyay doesn't help matters by assuming that his readers and he understand the same thing by his references to the 'doctrine of transmigration'. The mainspring of the doctrine is the teaching that action (*karman* in Sanskrit) performed in accordance with or against the code of *dharma* or righteousness normally generates a metaphysical deposit (anglicized as 'karma') that, unless countermanding forces apply, the agent of that action must experience in some way. There are different views about what exactly *dharma* means in this context and whether this action must necessarily be deliberate. Various kinds of exception to the karmic law are recognized, for example, enlightened, or ethically disinterested, agency, the transference of karma, and divine intervention. Nevertheless, in general, righteous action generates karma, which 'matures' as desirable experiences (or good 'fruit'/*phala*), while unrighteous action produces undesirable experiences or bad fruit. In the normal course of events the agent of action must experience the good or bad fruit his or her action produces. But such retributive experience need not and does not take place in one life. Thus it is that the innocent may suffer and the wicked prosper (the fruit of bad and good karma respectively).

In fact, the traditional belief is that the karmic process is beginningless (though it need not be endless, of course). Each individual is the apt vehicle to experience the maturing karmic fruit of the beginningless linear series of lives (generally believed to include animal reincarnations) of which he or she is the present expression and potential perpetuator. It is in this sense that an individual may say that he or she is experiencing the karma perpetrated by him or her in previous lives. This is a highly simplified account of the belief in reincarnation that the *Sophia*'s Hindu readers would generally have held.[5] Upadhyay was opposed to this teaching because he believed that it implied an erroneous conception of natural and moral evil (or sin), which in turn militated against acceptance of what he regarded was a key feature of sound social order: vicarious suffering.

As to the nature of evil, Upadhyay was a Thomist. That is, he considered evil, not as something negative or positive, but as a 'privation of being'. The burden of an article entitled 'What is evil?' (*Sophia,* March 1894)[6] is to show that evil is 'the deficiency of some

5 Nevertheless, such belief raises a number of critical questions, e.g. about epistemological identity and moral accountability between individuals across the hiatus of rebirth in a series of lives, and the moral and epistemological nexus of animal and human reincarnations. Upadhyay will raise some of these questions. For a more detailed account of Hindu belief in karma and rebirth, see ch. 9 of Lipner, 1994; for a critical inquiry, see Reichenbach, 1990.

6 Based probably on a lecture Upadhyay gave in response to a statement by Hiranand 'early in 1893 ... in the Brahmo Mandir at Hyderabad that Christianity gave to the principle of evil a positive existence' (Bl., p. 53).

good *which ought to be present*'. In support Aquinas is quoted.[7] In this article Upadhyay seems to have in mind only natural evil—that 'evil' which is not a moral perversion of the will (moral evil). 'It is no evil that a rose-plant is *not* as tall as a palm; it is no evil that a butterfly is *not* as huge as an elephant,' he instructs. This is because the absence of magnitude in the smaller creatures mentioned is not an absence that is *due*[8]; rose plants and butterflies are not supposed to be as large as palm trees and elephants. This is where the transmigrationist, and the pantheist for that matter, go wrong. For them natural evil is a negative rather than a privative feature of being. The transmigrationist bases his understanding of karmic retribution on the belief that it is an evil to exist on a scale of being lower than the human. It is Upadhyay's argument that we must distinguish here. From the human point of view rebirth as a lower form of life may well be undesirable. But existing as sub-human, per se, is not necessarily an evil. 'A little thought will show that inequality [in grades of being], as such, which is the necessary outcome of the absence in a thing of perfections not due to its being, is no evil. Each creature has a measure of fullness of being peculiar to its nature and it is perfect in itself if there is nothing wanting to its fullness.'

For Upadhyay it was important to gain a correct understanding of what good and evil, perfection and imperfection, are. This understanding ramified with a sound grasp—so far as that is possible for the limited human intellect—of the nature of God as absolute perfection and of our proper relationship to God above us, to one another as equals, and to animals below us, in the scale of being. Thus right living, and indeed, right faith, is made possible. To believe, as the transmigrationist did, that evil karmic retribution resulted in a sub-human form of life is to work, in part, with a wrong understanding of good and evil and of our status as humans and how we should relate to one another. We shall expatiate on the last point with reference to Upadhyay's view of vicarious suffering presently, but perhaps it should be pointed out that vis-à-vis the traditional doctrine of karma and rebirth Upadhyay seems to be pleading something of a special case. For according to this teaching it was not so much rebirth as a lower form of life that was undesirable, as the unpleasant

7 Apparently from Ia, IIae, 18.1, Response of the *Summa*; see Blackfriars ed., vol. 18.

8 But, we may add—to illumine Upadhyay's point—an absence of health would be; a blighted rose plant or a butterfly with a damaged wing would exemplify natural evil.

experiences compatible with this form of life. To take a larger perspective, according to this doctrine it is the whole process of *saṃsāra*—repeated birth and death as the result of karma—that is undesirable, and blissful liberation from that process that is the desired goal.

For reasons given above, it is not surprising that the Advaitin equally falls foul of Upadhyay's critique. The 'pantheist' doctrine 'of the final emancipation of man by being absorbed in the divine essence,' he says, has its 'source in the false notion of the negativeness of evil.' Since for the pantheist evil is *asat* or non-being, finite existence in any form, even in heaven, is evil in so far as it lacks absolute perfection. According to this view, 'every creature ... is engulfed in negation, and there is no emancipation ... from this limitless negation ... unless one be absorbed ... in the infinite divine Essence, which alone is above all negation and therefore beyond the reach of evil'. So the Advaitic view of evil will also not do, for it does not respect the inviolate distinction between creator and created, infinite and finite. If, however, the Advaitin were to accept that evil is privative, then, ceasing to be a 'pantheist', he would accept that heavenly bliss, or the state of communion with God, although still a created condition, is the destiny of man. For in so far as this state is free from any imperfection due to man as man,[9] it is also totally free from evil and becomes an acceptable goal to strive for. In later years, even after he had started to reinterpret Advaita in a positive vein, Upadhyay did not alter his understanding of the nature of evil as privative[10]; rather, he reformulated the Advaitic view of evil in Thomistic vein.

But Upadhyay's main objection to the doctrine of transmigration was that, by virtue of its theory of karma, it did not allow the concept of vicarious suffering to be viewed in a positive light. Upadhyay maintained that acknowledgement of vicarious suffering was essential to right living. There were, in fact, other kinds of assault by him on the theory of rebirth. There was the serial, 'The Theory of Transmigration Refuted' (Sp-m, July, August, October, November, 1894), in which Upadhyay levels mainly epistemological arguments against the teaching. Here he argues that the repeated rupture of the thread of self-awareness across births in a particular series of

9 Understandably for the time, Upadhyay's language was not gender-egalitarian.

10 In the weekly *Sophia* (September 29, 1900) he writes with approval: 'The scholastic doctrine is 'being is good', and 'evil is the privative absence of being and not a positive existence'.

reincarnations is inconsistent with the transmigrationist's other claim that the soul is immaterial, for it must be essential to immaterial souls to retain self-consciousness amid changing bodily circumstances (July); that experience of memory lapses, however extensive, in this life is not analogous to the loss of self-awareness mentioned above, on the grounds that this self-awareness is radical to our being whereas memory lapse occurs at a different level; and that the doctrine of transmigration cannot be supported by such empirical arguments as that it explains (by the process of pre-natal learning) such dispositions as the fear of death or the ability of the young to suckle. Such dispositions are 'purely involuntary acts natural to [one's] organic constitution ... Put a quinine pill [into an infant's mouth] and it will suck it and make a wry face. Should we therefore conclude that it must have tasted in a previous life a quinine pill—perhaps manufactured by a transmigrationist ... and then learned how to make a wry face?' (August).

In the October issue Upadhyay returns to this point. The argument suffers from the logical fallacy of *anavasthā* or infinite regress, he says. The transmigrationist maintains that the rebirth process is beginningless. When then could these dispositions have really been *learnt*? Never. It is simpler to say that they are innate. In the final article, Upadhyay comes closer to his real objection against the doctrine. He considers the transmigrationist's claim that innocent suffering can be explained only on the basis of the law of karma. This explanation is unsatisfactory, avers Upadhyay, because it offends our moral sense of a just and provident God. He gives the example of a child suffering from fever, supposed, on the transmigrationist's view, to be the fruit of bad karma, and asks rhetorically:

> Dost thou metamorphose an infidel into an innocent pretty little child ... who does not know what is good or what is evil, and then punish him for his infidelity? Never! ... Almighty just God! To what a low level hast thou been degraded by false prophets and false philosophy? The transmigrationist has simply upset, by his foolish theory, the entire moral economy of Providence.

In sum, Upadhyay goes on to argue that innocent suffering of natural evil (e.g. fever)—the only kind of evil considered in the article—can best be explained as part of the economy of nature. God cannot reasonably be expected to play fast and loose with natural law, ordained by him. If he did, there would be no such thing as natural law and we would be plunged into chaos.

But so far as Upadhyay is concerned, we have not really reached the heart of the matter. In fact this serial and its arguments can be regarded as merely propaedeutic, a clearing of the ground. Upadhyay really gets down to business against the 'transmigrationist' over the bearing he believed the karma theory has on the possibility of vicarious suffering. Why this doctrine agitated Upadhyay, as a Christian, is expressed in a nutshell in item 6 of a 'New Programme' announced by *Sophia* in January 1896: 'To show that the theory of transmigration is a philosophical blunder and is destructive of the principle of the brotherhood of man.' We have glimpsed how Upadhyay sought to show up the doctrine's *philosophical* inadequacy; his real objection lay in the statement that the theory 'is destructive of the principle of the brotherhood of man'. In fact, for Upadhyay this revolves on the notion of vicarious suffering—a favourite and longstanding theme.

Vicarious suffering is discussed as early as April 1984 in *Sophia* in a dialogue between 'Believer' and 'Enquirer'. Says Believer: 'Nature not only sanctions but enforces vicarious suffering. For one single fault of a common officer during a battle, the greatest power in the world may be doomed to slavery for centuries. For one single immoral act of a man, his descendants for generations ... may be afflicted most seriously. It is only selfish men who say that they do not hold themselves liable for others. Suffering for one another is one of the most sacred laws of God.'

In the next issue, Enquirer is convinced. 'I am ashamed of myself,' he confesses. 'Without this principle of vicarious suffering, of bearing one another's burden, where would be the virtue of self-sacrifice, the sanctifying sense of responsibility? What a terrible thing is sin!' True, the immediate context of this dialogue is the nature of original sin (the article, which began serially in March, is entitled, 'The Fall of Man'), yet a hidden agenda—attacking the implications of belief in karma—is not difficult to detect. Certain code words, as we shall see, provide a clue: 'vicarious suffering', 'bearing one another's burden', 'selfish', 'responsibility'. Things come out into the open in other contexts. In July 1897 ('Degeneracy of India'), in answer to the question why India is fallen, we are told: 'One of the most potent reasons ... is her doctrine of *karma* ... What is the law of karma? In its essence it is: As a man sows, so he reaps.' But this rule has been misapplied in India.

> Indian philosophers have jumped from the premiss of karmic law to the unwarrantable conclusion that there can be no vicarious

> suffering, that each individual bears his own burden.... The sense of responsibility, the virtue of self-sacrifice, have jumped out of the window of India's heart, because the monstrous doctrine that the range of suffering does not go beyond one's own self entered the door of her reason.... She cannot be regenerated unless she believes that vicarious suffering ... is the foundation of the brotherhood of man which is being consummated by the present order of nature and grace.

Why does 'grace' appear—rather oddly—here? Another clue, to be returned to in due course. But the argument against karma in short is this: belief in the karmic law entails belief that whatever I undergo in life is entirely the consequence of my own doing (whether from a previous life or otherwise), that, from the perspective of rebirth, there is no such thing as innocent suffering or the responsibility for it, that we do not and cannot 'bear one another's burdens' by effectively putting ourselves out for one another or taking to heart the sufferings we have imposed on others, that each person is a moral island. This belief militates against divine justice, mercy, and providence and the teaching of the 'brotherhood of man', which is founded on the notion of vicarious suffering.

The most extended treatment of the theme of vicarious suffering occurs in *Sophia*, June 1898 under the title 'Bear ye one another's burdens' (a quotation taken from St Paul's Letter to the Galatians 6.2). Since the gist of Upadhyay's argument is known, we need note here only two features: (1) The article was written in response to a piece in a rival journal, the *Arya Messenger,* which attacked the 'Christian doctrine of vicarious atonement'. Significantly, Upadhyay launches into a defence of vicarious suffering for 'the whole framework of society is raised upon the principle of vicarious suffering'. (2) Key examples of vicarious suffering are as follows: 'born idiots for life ... because their parents led a life of intemperance and wickedness', 'good parents ... the prey of lifelong sorrow because their children walk the path of sin' and so on.

Compare these comments from the weekly *Sophia,* June 1900 (Under 'Questions and Answers'): 'Vicarious suffering is the very central principle governing the present economy of nature, and one of the most powerful means employed by Providence in correcting the aberrations of man', exemplified negatively by 'a chaste, youthful wife made wretched by the faithlessness of her husband', and positively by a now repentant drunkard who has seen his 'hoary mother and beloved wife, ragged and wretched like himself' as a result of his indulgence, and so on.

The various examples we have mentioned point to some confusion or at least unclarity in Upadhyay's understanding of vicarious suffering. Can it at all be suffering voluntarily *for the sake of* another, on behalf of another, that is, bearing the guilt of another (is this what 'bearing one another's burdens' means?), or does it mean suffering, voluntarily or involuntarily, *as a result of* another's action and bearing another's burden consequentially in this way? Though the examples given appear to be weighted in favour of the second interpretation, the first, it seems, is also intended. Upadhyay says, 'In this consists the solidarity of the human family that the members bear one another's burdens. The believers in the perverted law of *karma* ignore the patent fact of innocent suffering. In their heartlessness they destroy the privilege of suffering for the guilt of another. It is innocent suffering that binds the warring elements of the world in harmony.... Responsibility will be but a word in a lexicon if there be no possibility of one reaping what another sows' (Sp-m, 'Notes', August 1898).

Enough has been said for us now to uncover the underlying motive of Upadhyay's sustained hostility to the doctrine of karma and rebirth. In fact, apart from some clues in other contexts (e.g. the 'grace' noted earlier, the expression 'Bear ye one another's burdens'), Upadhyay doesn't mince words in an article referred to earlier (the response to the *Arya Messenger*'s attack on the Christian doctrine of vicarious atonement). Under the heading, 'Application to Christ', Upadhyay declares that it is God's will to pardon the guilt of collective and individual human transgression through the atoning life and death of Christ, provided that we 'believe in Christ the Godman, are sorry for [our] sins and obey his law'. *So the doctrine of karma is ultimately reprehensible because by its teaching of a highly individualistic morality it prevents us from accepting the fact that Christ's death atoned vicariously for our sins*—a central tenet of Christian belief. And, as Upadhyay suggests in various places, the more clearly one acknowledges this fact, the more ethically disposed we become to accept Christ's teaching.

We have called the doctrine of karma and rebirth a 'traditional' target of his polemic. This is true in so far as the basic teaching Upadhyay attacked is of ancient pedigree in Hindu religion. But, as intimated earlier, Upadhyay's attacks were exacerbated and appreciably shaped by modern variants of the belief, such as those argued by the Arya Samajists, and the so-called neo-Vedāntins whose champion was Vivekananda, and particularly by the Theosophists, as represented by Annie Besant. This is the background for his polemic against rebirth with respect to arguments concerning the pre-natal learning of physical and moral dispositions etc.[11] He was also goaded by Besant's claim that the New Testament and other Christian sources at least implicitly advocated belief in karma and reincarnation.[12]

By about 1900, when Upadhyay's rehabilitation of Advaita in particular was well under way, we notice a significant, if subtle, change in his treatment of karma and rebirth. In the English writings, allusions to belief in transmigration, now comparatively rare, tend to become non-judgemental. Talk of *karman* (action) as a facet of the belief is sparse, while, mostly in the Bengali writings now, the role of *karman*, invariably understood in its general sense of 'action', in the context of a reconstructed Advaitic work ethic, assumes a high profile.[13] But these changes will be dealt with later, in the appropriate place.

### *Hindu 'polytheism'*

Let us begin with a somewhat artificial distinction: that between 'Vedic' and 'Hindu'. There are some grounds for it in Upadhyay's own usage. In effect, 'Vedic' refers mainly to the content of the early part of the Vedas, the Sanskritic canonical scriptures, 'Hindu' to the various

[11] See, e.g. 'An Examination of Mrs Besant's Lecture on "Man the Master of his own Destiny (Concluded)"' (Sp-m, September 1895). Besant's contention is misconceived, argues Upadhyay, that diversity stemming from natural talents, environment, and moral dispositions, if attributed to God, presupposes divine favouritism and a lack of justice and order in this world, and that the most reasonable explanation is that 'Man is the source of this diversity.... As he sows in his previous lives so he reaps in the present life.' Upadhyay's criticism is not unfamiliar: 'diversity in nature', he avers, rather than implying want of justice and order *is implied* by justice and order. 'Perfect identity destroys relationship. Man can exercise justice only when there is diversity. In diversity then is divine justice clearly manifest. And what is order but unity in diversity?' Diversity in itself casts no aspersions on God, for the goal of human living is neither endless spiritual progress nor identity with the Godhead but doing the divine will in one's everyday circumstances and attaining to one's merited perfection in God's company after death. Here the finite/infinite divide is sought to be preserved. Moral diversity is the result of free choice, often cumulatively reinforced, in this life, and not of inherited dispositions from previous lives. Thus karmic individualism as opposed to personal responsibility is repudiated.

[12] See, e.g., 'Hinduism and Christianity as compared by Mrs Besant' (Sp-m, June 1897). Here, by means of a counter-exegesis, Upadhyay attempts to show that Besant's interpretation of scriptural texts (e.g. Matt.17.10–12, Jn.9.2–3) in favour of rebirth is wrong.

[13] These aspects of Upadhyay's thought are given little or no attention by Animananda, Väth and others.

popular theistic sects and cults, Sanskritic and non-Sanskritic, that started to spread across the land by about the beginning of the Common Era. We shall see in a later chapter that Upadhyay did not interpret the early Vedic religion of a plurality of gods *(devas)* as strictly polytheistic. In attacking the traditional polytheism of his compatriots he had in mind chiefly the objects of worship of later Hinduism, and here he singled out the figure of Krishna.

Where this 'polytheism' was concerned, Upadhyay was opposed to its supposedly degrading and idolatrous nature. Understandably at the time, he was innocent of the highly sophisticated analyses of myth and symbol that characterize scholarship today, but he was not unaware that these tropes could be interpreted variously. Yet he appeared unsympathetic to such attempts. In 'Our Attitude Towards Hindu Reformers' (Sp-m, February 1896), one of three kinds of 'reformers' he considers are the 'Hindu Revivalists'. These, he declares, seek to 'preserve intact each and every iota of the doctrines and practices that go by the name of Hinduism'. Among other things, 'the idolatry and the gross superstitions of the Puranas, the most unholy and obscene legends about gods and goddesses and *avatars* (incarnations) are advocated by them as wholly true and conducive to the eternal welfare of man.' Yet, somewhat inconsistently it would seem, when challenged about certain beliefs, e.g. that Krishna, 'God incarnate', was 'so voluptuous as to take away the clothes of the milkmaids and compel them to appear before him entirely naked', they resort to allegory as an explanation of the 'esoteric meaning' of the story.[14] Such people are misguided according to Upadhyay. 'They are not reformers but deformers. They are not friends but foes to their fatherland. They are blinded by national pride.... they take advantage of the almost invincible ignorance of the masses and flatter their vanity. They should be exposed right and left.' Ironical, then, that not many years hence, the later Upadhyay, in the full flood of his reclamation of Hindu religion, should single out Krishna, in terms of the hidden symbolism of this and similar episodes, as *the* inspirational figure for the national unity of Mother India (cf. the 'fatherland' in the quotation above). But we anticipate.

Meanwhile, Upadhyay sought 'right and left' to continue his exposé of Hindu deity worship, with special reference to the

[14] This is a favourite story about the youthful Krishna for those devotees who look to the *Bhagavata Purana* (circa 9th–11th century), where the details are given, as a central text of their faith.

voluptuous Krishna. Why especially Krishna? Because Krishna, with his pervasive popularity and accoutrements of avataric (so-called incarnational) doctrine, appeared, in the guise of a saviour figure, as the chief potential rival to Christ. In the description of his new programme for the monthly *Sophia* (January 1896), Upadhyay states that it is one of his aims 'to show that Jesus Christ is the only God-man and that the life of Krishna, the most prominent of Hindu incarnations ... as depicted in the Bhagavat ... deserves to be blotted out of the memory of man, and that the sooner it is blotted out, the better for the spiritual and moral welfare of India.' Upadhyay distinguished, as this excerpt intimates, between the Krishna of the *Bhagavadgita* and the Krishna of the *Bhagavata Purana* (= the 'Bhagavat').[15]

In 'Krishna of Bhagavat' (Sp-m, January 1895), the latter is taken severely to task. 'For the moral safety of India', no less, 'Krishna of Bhagavat should be denounced and abjured by all right-minded patriots. Bhagavat itself warns us of the danger of imitating Krishna.[16]... Bhagavat is full of bhakti (loving devotion) but no amount of sophistry can explain away the stern fact that it is sullied by the immoral life of Krishna.' Incidentally, note the appeal to all 'right-

[15] The *Bhagavadgita* (or *Gita* as it is usually called), appears as chs. 23–40 of Book 6 of the Sanskrit epic, the *Mahabharata*. The epic itself is thought to have evolved from about 400 B.C.E. to 400 C.E., while the *Gita* may be assigned to about the beginning of the Common Era. The *Gita* text, which is in the form of a dialogue traditionally 700 stanzas long, purports to be the teaching of Krishna, the embodied deity, to his friend, Arjuna. Besides describing himself as the source, mainstay and end of the universe, Krishna, who appears as a majestic and loving figure solicitous for the well-being of the whole world, instructs Arjuna about various matters, including the immortality of the soul and the means to salvation. Krishna teaches that the highest path is that of selfless devotion to himself—to be not *of* the world while yet in it—and the highest goal, unity with him. The *Bhagavata Purana*, circa 9–11th century, is a much larger and more diffuse text, running to 12 books in its received form; its central message, nevertheless, is single-minded devotion to Krishna. In contrast to the Krishna of the *Gita*, who is often regarded as a full-blown personality in a self-contained scripture, the Krishna of the *Bhagavata* is a far more rounded character, especially in the stories about his childhood and youth. It is in this latter context that he is sometimes seen to be 'voluptuous'. Though in theory both Krishnas are supposed to be the same person, not infrequently Hindus dichotomize them, disregarding the one and worshipping the other. Many, however, do establish some form of synthesis between the two in their religious lives.

[16] A reference to a well-known exchange in the *Purana* (Bk. 10, ch. 34), where the sage Suka tells king Parikshit that ordinary mortals cannot always follow the example of the exalted beings: one should do what they say and not what they do.

minded patriots'. As indicated in other places, signs of the underlying rationale for *Sophia*'s existence regularly come in and out of view. Upadhyay's over-arching motive for publishing *Sophia* is patriotic, and hence 'political' in the broad sense. But it is also essentially religious. By morally and spiritually educating his (non-Christian) compatriots, he is helping forge a nation ready to control its own destiny; but he is also preparing the ground for faith in Christ so that ideally there will be a complementarity between political and religious fulfillment.

So India has to be saved first, especially from the Krishna of the *Bhagavata*. This 'incarnation' of Vishnu, the editor of *Sophia* declares, 'stands unrivalled amongst the sons of man in his voluptuousness' ('The Supreme Being under Delusion', January 1896). This Krishna 'is represented as having seduced hundreds of virgins and married women and insisted on examining all parts of the naked bodies of some of them' ('An Aspect of the Hindu Revival', June 1897). Upadhyay is being rather harsh on Krishna here. Both 'seduced' and 'insisted on examining' are contentious expressions in the context of the Puranic passages Upadhyay seems to have in mind, and he overlooks the serious concern and careful arguments and interpretations expressed by later Hindu theologians precisely in this connection. But Upadhyay was not troubled by such niceties; he was more concerned to make a point.

The Krishna of the *Bhagavadgita*, or rather, the *Gita* itself, is given easier passage. True, the *Gita* imparts erroneous doctrine in that it teaches '(1) the identity of the supreme Soul with human souls, (2) transmigration, and (3) the divinity of Krishna'; nevertheless it is a 'treasure-house of Hindu wisdom and piety', especially in so far as it encourages the performance of one's duty without selfish motives ('Gita', Sp-ṃ, June 1895). Again, here statement 1 is highly debatable. And we note in passing that it is only later, in the Bengali writings, that Upadhyay shows at length his appreciation especially for the *Gita*'s teaching on action.

It may not have escaped attention that in denouncing Puranic religion, characterized, among other things, by image worship, Upadhyay seems preoccupied with its alleged libidinous nature. In the article cited earlier ('Our Attitude Towards Hindu Reformers'), all four examples given to illustrate the unwholesomeness of this religion are sexual: (1) Krishna stealing the milkmaids' clothes and compelling them 'to appear before him entirely naked'; (2) the god Indra violating the bed of the sage Gotama; (3) Siva, 'the third person of the Hindu triad', acting obscenely before his wife and the heavenly court, and (4) 'chaste matrons and innocent virgins' defiling 'their hearts and hands by making of clay most obscene emblems (*linga*)' of Siva. The linga, of course, is Siva's phallic emblem.[17] No doubt there is much sexual content, often in violation of traditional dharmic laws, in Puranic religion. This would focus the attention of any commentator, not to mention someone with Upadhyay's background, an unsophisticate in the interpretation of mythological folklore, who had internalized so many of the sexual taboos of Victorian Catholic morality.[18] Upadhyay's censoriousness was heightened, however, by his status as a celibate ascetic. We shall return to his view on sex when dealing with his attitude to women.

The other prong of Upadhyay's objection to Hindu image worship was that it was idolatrous. This too is expressed in contrast to Catholic veneration of images. The burden of 'Hindu Idolatry and Catholic Image-Worship' (Sp-m, July 1897) is to show that Hindu image worship and Catholic image worship are entirely different things. Catholics *honour* images of Christ and the saints, just as loyal subjects honour images of the Queen. There is only a difference of degree, not of kind, between the two forms of veneration. Can Hindu image worship be placed in this category? No. 'Do Hindus commit the heinous sin of idolatry, which, in its essence, is to serve the creature rather than the Creator, in worshipping gods and goddesses and their images?' Yes. For example, do they not personify the Ganges, pray to it and believe that it can wash away sin? 'If this be not idolatry, let the word 'idolatry' be erased from all lexicons.'

The same distinction is drawn, in the weekly *Sophia* (July 7, 1900), under 'Questions and Answers': 'He who elevates the finite to

[17] For a similar sexual emphasis see, e.g., 'The Supreme Being under Delusion' (Sp-m, January 1896), which refers to 'Brahma ... the first emanation from the impersonal Supreme Being' being 'defiled with a woman', to Siva as 'notorious for his shameless and unclean behaviour', to the Hindu heaven as 'peopled with infamous women ... whose business is to dance in the court of heaven and defile religious ascetics', and so on.

[18] 'There are plenty of contradictory and obscene stories of the wildest description regarding Brahma, Vishnu and Siva who make up the Hindu Triad.... The unholy character of the Trimurti [= Triad] is notorious.... Compare with this medley of fancies the clear and definite teaching of Christianity regarding the Holy Trinity, blessed for ever and ever.... To identify the Holy Trinity with the fanciful Trimurti is to identify light with darkness' ('Hinduism and Christianity as compared by Mrs Besant', under the heading 'Trinity and Trimurti', Sp-m, February 1897).

the infinite or vice versa is an idolator. There is no harm in making images, but it is sinful and carnal to make the images so many means to belittle God or magnify puny creatures. The Catholics do not *worship* images of saints, but *honour* them as one would honour the image of the Queen Empress.' Yet a few years later Upadhyay and his friend and closest disciple Animananda would go separate ways over Upadhyay's permission to Hindu youths in their school to perform traditional ritual image worship in honour of the goddess Sarasvati. There was more to this incident than meets the eye, as we hope to show. The point here is the dramatic change of attitude in Upadhyay to things traditionally Hindu within a relatively short space of time.

It would be a mistake to suppose, however, that during the period under review Upadhyay was confined to his editorial desk.[19] On the contrary, he was busy travelling and lecturing across the land, often by invitation, in general pursuit of his missionary goal to lead educated Hindus to the Catholic faith. (A number of these lectures appeared, suitably revised, in subsequent issues of the *Sophia*). So let us pause awhile to consider these activities. First though, how did Upadhyay support himself and manage to finance these tours? In a variety of ways. He lived off alms, which he was not averse to receiving or cadging. In the Sp-m, May 1898, we read that during a prolonged stay in Calcutta in March that year, Upadhyay and Animananda went about, in imitation of the Bauls (itinerant Bengali religious minstrels), 'singing hymns in Bengali and Sanskrit and receiving alms'. Again, in a letter to the Bishop of Nagpur on Shrove Tuesday, 1899, he writes, 'May I expect something from your Lordship as Lenten charity?' Probably his main source of income was a salary deriving from subscriptions to his journal(s). Also, his hosts during his lecture tours

[19] Notwithstanding the 'New Programme' he gave to the *Sophia* in the issue of January 1896. This 11-point agenda can be summarized as follows: to show that 'theism' is the 'primitive religion of man', and that the Hindu mind has 'stirred' in this direction especially in the Vedantic period (points 1, 2); that there are grave flaws in Hinduism nevertheless, especially the doctrines of 'Pantheism', transmigration, and worship of Krishna whose life 'deserves to be blotted out of the memory of man' (points 3, 4, 5, 6, 8); that the goal of human existence is God as described by Catholic philosophy, that 'Jesus Christ is the only God-man' who alone has redeemed humans from sin, that the Catholic Church is the true Church of salvation ('N.B. One who is *externally* separated from the Catholic Church but is in good faith united with it *internally* by the conformity of his will to the Divine will'), that a mark of this true Church is the pre-eminent sanctity of its saints, and that the 'truths of Hindu philosophy' can be 'stepping stones to the Catholic faith' (points 3, 4, 7, 8, 9, 10, 11). We have already examined how Upadhyay deals with a number of these points.

must often have offered hospitality and expenses. There can be no doubt, however, that his was a straitened existence; he was invariably short of money. He lived an austere life with no eye to the main chance financially. (Though he lived, as we shall see later, in more or less abject poverty during his visit to England in 1902–3, he refused to sanction the selling of tickets to hear his lectures for his pecuniary benefit.[20]) Upadhyay took his commitment as a sannyasi—a man who had renounced the spirit of acquisitiveness—with impressive seriousness and often to his cost. Besides, it was traditionally fitting for a sannyasi to request and receive alms, sometimes interpreted as religious fees (*dakṣiṇā*) for services rendered.

During this period, Upadhyay became fairly well known among educated circles in the land. He travelled quite extensively. In September 1895, the secretary of the 'miniature' Parliament of Religions convened at Ajmere invited him to lecture on the Catholic faith. He gave two lectures, which were well received, and was put up in the Franciscan house in the city (Bl., p. 60). From Ajmere he left for Agra, with financial assistance from the Friars, and then headed north-west to visit the Golden Temple at Amritsar. Attired as a mendicant, he was not allowed at first to board the up-market mail train for Amritsar. In fact, 'the policeman actually whipped him off when he attempted to get into the train' (Bl., p. 60). But 'he bore it patiently saying that it was not right to get his poor countryman into trouble.' An influential Punjabi, however, saw to it that he did board and discovered later, much to his chagrin, that he had helped a Christian![21] Upadhyay reached the temple on the festival of Diwali. His adventures were not over. In the crowded temple he saved an old woman from being 'crushed to death' by loudly berating the heedless throng.

Towards the end of 1895, Upadhyay had embarked on a campaign to counter the influence of Annie Besant, whose pronouncements on theosophy—with their implied message that Hinduism was a fountainhead of spiritual wisdom—were being warmly received among educated Hindus. In the next chapter we shall see that theosophy was one of the chief contemporary targets of Upadhyay's missionary

20 This is reported in connection with lectures he gave in Cambridge, but there is nothing to suggest that it was not his general practice.

21 But where was the crucifix mentioned earlier, suspended from his neck? It seems that on occasion Upadhyay did not wear it. *The Blade's* account of this episode and subsequent events in the Temple is based on that of the *Sketch*, I, pp. 19–20.

strategy. In 1896 Upadhyay toured widely, lecturing against Besant's theosophical views but also taking the opportunity to speak on other topics. His itinerary included Madras, Trichinopoly (Tiruchirappalli), Bombay, Karachi, Lahore, Sukkur and Hyderabad (in Sind). The tour made him well known to Catholics and others. Though on occasion he spoke to small, select audiences (e.g. in the Hall of the Arya Samaj in Bombay, towards the end of March, on the Necessity of Prayer), he also addressed very large gatherings. On March 25 and April 1, in the Framji-Cowasji Hall in Bombay, he spoke to '600-800 educated Hindus' (see Bl., pp. 62–3) on 'The Primitive Parabrahma and Mrs Besant's God' and 'The Infinite and the Finite' respectively. His lectures were invariably well received, even by those who had earlier thrilled to Besant's blandishments. We are told by *The Blade* that the famous savant Justice M.G. Ranade, who chaired the April 1 lecture, publicly remarked after its conclusion that 'if Catholicism is what the lecturer places before us, I would not mind putting myself down as a Catholic' (ibid.).

*The Bombay Catholic Examiner* of Friday, April 17 had a major feature-editorial on Upadhyay consisting of a full page of two columns, and almost a full column on the next page. 'Bombay has enjoyed of late,' the article informs its readers, 'the unique sight of a Brahmin convert to the Catholic faith delivering lectures as a Christian Sanyasi.... Dressed in a floating garment of yellow colour, he goes his way bareheaded even in the heat of the summer and barefooted even in the cold of winter, his food is purely vegetable, and his drink water.... Never within the memory of the present generation had a Catholic in Bombay delivered a speech in the oriental garb of a Sanyasi, and though the cross which he bears over his dress ought to have removed every doubt, still many asked the anxious question, "Is he a Christian? What, he is a Catholic!"'

In fact, there are no less than three separate significant references to Upadhyay's activities in this issue: the editorial just cited, a long summary of the lecture 'The Infinite and the Finite', and, under the heading 'Indian Intelligence', a brief account of a lecture visit Upadhyay made to Trichinopoly immediately after Bombay. Upadhyay's standing with his Church had never been higher; his experimental approach oozes ecclesiastical approval and reassurance. Yes, he is different, comes the message, but don't worry he's a Catholic, he's on our side. He's targeting the educated Hindus—opinion formers and leaders—for the faith, and undermining the views of some of our chief rivals; he's a Brahmin convert, remember. And he's doing it in a way that might work. His views are orthodox enough, so we'll back the experiment for the time being. (The BCE is reassuring: on departing for Sind, Upadhyay 'received the good wishes of the Bishop of Trichinopoly'; further, 'Last year he appeared as the representative of the Catholic faith at the miniature parliament of religions.' 'This seems to us ... a suitable opportunity ... to recommend to [our readers] again the spreading of the tracts from Trichinopoly, and of the *Sophia.*' Upadhyay is described as the 'zealous and learned editor of *Sophia.*')

This was heady stuff. Doubtless the publicity and adulation increased Upadhyay's confidence and commitment to his cause. In the *Sophia,* June 1896, he is careful to quote, for the benefit of his readers, most of the BCE's descriptive editorial of his work. Catholics are thereby reassured of his orthodoxy, and Hindus of his representativeness. Both groups must take him seriously. So when his Church officially repudiated his approach and turned its back on him, barely five years later, Upadhyay's disenchantment was all the more bitter.

After Bombay he headed for Trichinopoly at the invitation of the Rector of St Joseph's College there. He spoke to the present and former students, Catholic and non-Christian, to loud acclaim, and on April 9 delivered the Bombay lecture on the finite and the Infinite in the Town Hall.[22] But his visit was brief. Armed with the 'good wishes of the Bishop of Trichinopoly' he returned to Sind. By July 5 he was in Karachi. He wrote that day to Animananda back at base in Hyderabad, urging him to join him. 'We have decided to begin our missionary operations in Karachi.... I will deliver a lecture on "National Greatness" on Wednesday next [the lecture was delivered in the Max-Denso Hall on the 8th as scheduled].... Make haste [and] come to Karachi. We will preach here and then go to Tatta. If the weather is very oppressive then we may not prolong our tour.... We must not sit idle. We must be up and doing.... Without you we cannot begin our work.' The letter intimates that in Hyderabad their landlord was a Jew; as Christian converts they would have been hard put to it to find suitable accommodation owned by Hindus. Further details of this tour are wanting, but can there be any doubt—from the use of such expressions as 'missionary' and 'preach' (their main target was Besant and her

22 See note 17, chapter 5.

views)—that we have correctly analysed Upadhyay's guiding motives during this period as basically religious within the framework of the natural/supernatural distinction rather than narrowly and tendentiously political? On November 21 and 22, Upadhyay gave two lectures at Lahore to crowded halls, attacking Besant's theosophical views. His anti-theosophical campaign that year came to a dramatic climax shortly after; the details are given in chapter 7.

Another important undertaking of Upadhyay's in 1896 was his collaboration in the founding of the journal *Jote*. It was a fortnightly, and appeared for the first time on October 1. There is some information about it in the Jesuit publication *Light of the East*. In the November 1939 issue of this publication, in an article on Paramanand (one of Upadhyay's early Sindhi convert-disciples), we are told that the *Jote* was 'the first pice paper in Sindh', i.e. the first low-cost paper aimed at a mass readership.[23] 'During the first years of its existence, it was an Anglo-Sindhi journal. The Sindhi portion was written by Paramanand and Rewachand, the English by Mr Banerji and Khemchand. In September 1897 when Paramanand's career as a teacher came to an end, he took charge of the *Jote*, and from 1900 became its sole editor till his death on November 29, 1938. It treats of Religious, Social, Moral and Educational subjects' (p. 210).[24]

None of the early issues of *Jote* have come to hand but a copy of the Special Golden Jubilee Number, marked 1896–1946, exists in the archives of the Goethal's Library. It was published from Hyderabad in Sind under the editorship of N.F. Kotwani, O.F.M. There is a Dedication on the first page (after the cover) 'To the Memory of Four Great Men': 'Upadhyay: the Philosopher', 'Khemchand: the Journalist', 'Paramanand: the Scholar' and 'Animananda: the Educator'. This description of Upadhyay indicates that he was the driving force behind the *Jote*'s founding and the inspiration of its tone and ideas, at least during the early days. As we have shown, the attitude here was hostile to aspects of Hinduism. LOE (article cited) notes: 'As regards controversies Paramanand belonged to the old school of missionaries

[23] Four pice made up one anna, and sixteen annas a rupee.

[24] The *Jote* became a popular and influential paper. LOE says later that in 1925 a 200-page book called the *Gul-Phul* or Flowers, and consisting of articles culled from '30 files of the *Jote*', was published. 'It was prescribed by the Bombay University for the Matriculation examination for 1925–6, and has been sanctioned by the Vernacular Text-Book Committee of Sind for use in schools. The second part of *Gul-Phul* appeared in 1936' (pp. 212–3). These articles would all have been in Sindhi, of course, under the editorship of Parmanand; it is doubtful if Upadhyay would have authored any.

who wanted to build Catholicism on the ruins of Hinduism.... His prejudice against Hinduism grew with age when he came in contact with Upadhyayji, who during the first period of his missionary enterprise employed the destructive method, then very much in vogue, for the conversion of India' (p. 212).

In fact, in the Golden Jubilee number there is an article on Upadhyay (pp. 12–5) by Turmes, under the title, 'The Founder of Jote'. This article says nothing about how *Jote* was conceived or launched; it dwells on controversies surrounding Upadhyay's last years and we shall refer to it again later. But on p. 4 we have the statement, 'My founder, that great genius Swami Upadhyay Brahmabandhav (alias Babu Charan Banerji) gave me a very nice name when he called me The Jote derived from the Sanskrit word, Jyoti, meaning Light.' The stark contrast between light and darkness in Upadhyay's religious vision of the time is highlighted by the names of the journals, *Sophia* and *Jote*: the Light of Truth versus the Darkness of Falsehood. Though we have not seen any early numbers of *Jote,* there can be no doubt that his (English) contributions would have reflected the contents of *Sophia*; it was *Sophia* that was the main vehicle of his ideas and aspirations.

By early 1897 the Bombay plague had spread to the North West. Upadhyay played a heroic part in combating its baleful effects, but we shall come to that in a later chapter. From mid-March to mid-April, he undertook a second lecture tour of the South 'at the invitation of the Bishop of Trichinopoly and with the permission of the Archbishop of Bombay' (Bl., p. 66). Evidently his first visit had gone down well. He gave two lectures in Madras, the first on 'Hindu Pantheism and Man's Relation to God' which drew over 500 people, and the second on 'Religion, Natural and Supernatural' which had an audience of more than a thousand. Before going on to Trichinopoly, he lectured at Srirangam, city of the famous temple presided over by the great Srivaishnava theologian, Ramanuja, in the twelfth century; appropriately perhaps, the title of his lecture was 'The Highest Motive of Action'. At Trichinopoly he spoke on 'The Supernatural End of Man', and then continued further south to 'Palamcottah' (thus Bl., i.e. Palayancottai) and Tuticorin. Easter week was approaching so he returned to Trichinopoly and the spiritual base of St Joseph's College. 'He followed the exercises of the Three Days' Retreat [a common practice in Catholic schools at the time] and on Easter Sunday addressed the Annual Gathering of Past and Present Pupils of St

Joseph's College on the "Apostleship of the Christians". The same day he left for Sindh to resume his usual work.'

With hindsight, this second southern tour with its focus on Trichinopoly was something of a watershed in Upadhyay's conceptual development. To him, after two apparently successful southern visits, the South seemed a more congenial field of operations for his approach. During his stay at Trichinopoly during the second tour, he discussed his germinating views with a Fr John Castets s.j., who taught philosophy at St Joseph's and who had taken the Chair during the lecture on 'The Supernatural End of Man'.[25] In a letter (dated December 10, 1928, excerpted in Bl.) Castets writes about his meeting with Upadhyay: 'We had very subtle discussions on the possibility of converting the apparent (?) [sic] Pantheism of Sankara into a Theism palatable to Catholics.... He [Upadhyay] meant to settle down in the South. He had understood that he was distrusted in the North. He had an eye on our Catholic Brahmans hoping to find disciples among them. I presided at one of his lectures in the Trichinopoly Town Hall: all his expressions were perfectly correct.'

Distrusted in the North by whom, one wonders. By ecclesiastical authority or by Catholics; perhaps by Hindus? From the rave reviews in the BCE, it seems that he was not particularly distrusted by officialdom at this stage. It is interesting that Upadhyay actually mooted the idea of settling down in the South. No doubt de Nobili and his successors had established a tradition of Brahmin converts who were allowed to continue their caste-based life-style. Increasingly Upadhyay was coming to approve of this. During his first visit to Trichinopoly Upadhyay 'was received with open arms by the little Catholic Brahmin colony and put up with the senior member of the community, Mahadeva Iyer' (Bl., p. 63).[26] But again with hindsight, it is unlikely that Upadhyay, a Bengali rooted in his own culture, could have settled easily away from home for long. As we shall see,

25 Castets (born in 1858 in France) joined the Jesuit Noviciate at Toulouse in 1879. He offered himself for the Madura Mission and arrived in August 1881; he remained subsequently in India for the next 55 years till his death in 1936, never once returning to Europe. He was ordained priest in 1893. Somewhat outspoken and unbending, he was nevertheless regarded as a person of great integrity. He was perfectly competent then to evaluate Upadhyay's views, and his testimony is worth recording.

26 In the second half of 1896, *Sophia* ran three articles about the de Nobili experiment. Two were in the form of a narrative entitled 'Fr de Nobili's Converts', while the third was headed 'The Old Madura Mission'. The tone of all three articles is approbatory.

Bengal, or rather the metropolis of Calcutta, was drawing him slowly but surely into its embrace for his last years.

But the discussion with Castets may well have clarified or at least catalysed a significant new slant in his thinking. Tiny clues appear earlier, as in the 1896 lecture, 'The Infinite and the Finite', namely, the interweaving, as a matter of course, of Hindu references as expository aids.[27] But in my view, the watershed article justifying a fresh appraisal of Hindu thought in Upadhyay's methodology appeared in the July issue that year (1897) of *Sophia*, under the title 'Hindu Philosophy and Christianity'. This matter is considered in a later chapter. Towards the end of 1897, Upadhyay returned to Calcutta for a period of some months. By that time he had already made a number of crucial changes in his approach: he had entered the last phase of aspiring dialogue before disillusionment with his Church began to creep in. We shall deal with this later. But first we must consider Upadhyay's opposition to contemporary targets as part of his combative programme to prepare his educated compatriots for the reception of the Gospel.

27 More of this detective work in the next chapter.

# Chapter 7

# Fire-eater Part II: Upadhyay's Opposition to 'Contemporary Targets'

In this Part, we shall deal with the contemporary targets of Upadhyay's campaign to prepare educated (Hindu) India to receive the Gospel.

## Contemporary Targets

### *Theosophy*

Theosophy was the form of 'Neo-Hinduism' that Upadhyay loved to hate. Nowhere are his remarks more caustic, perhaps, than in his diatribes against theosophy. Theosophy, after all, was going down well among educated circles in the subcontinent, with the charismatic Annie Besant as its mouthpiece.[1] Her eclectic message of occultist, mystical and rationalist tendencies—largely informed by Hindu terminology and beliefs—as the fulfilling wisdom for the human race was music to the ears of an elite smarting under the colonial domination of the very tribe to which Besant herself belonged. Besides, she was a magnetic speaker, all the more so in her image cultivated for the Indian crowds. 'The graceful folds of her white sari blended with the silver hair and softened the contours of her grave, sweet face.'[2] Here then was a formidable challenge for our gladiatorial hero, and he responded to it enthusiastically.

1 Besant (1847–1933) had become a Theosophist in 1889 and visited India for the first time in 1893.

2 Quoted in Bl., p. 2; source unknown.

Upadhyay had scant respect for theosophy's intellectual content. One notices in his early critique a tendency to describe various aspects of theosophical teaching (with special reference to Besant's views) in terms of the epithet 'zero', and thus to nullify it. In 'The Hindu Revival' (*Sophia,* June 1894), commenting on theosophy (a 'neo-Hindu' movement for Upadhyay), he writes: 'The Theosophists ... teach that there is no extracosmic God, that God is ... non-being, zero, an undifferentiated algebraic something.'[3] Again, 'The Theosophists believe in a God who is subject to cyclic evolutions; ... pack up ... all beings ... with all their phenomenal relations, differentiations and manifestations, within the compass of the eternal minimum being, unrelated, undifferentiated and unmanifested, you will have some idea of the God of the Theosophists, a God known by such grand titles as "non-being", "zero", 'cosmic space' etc.'[4] Here 'zero' refers directly to the nature of God. Elsewhere it refers rather to the socio-moral effect of such pantheistic theology, with particular reference to Besant's consistent call to Universal Brotherhood. 'The long and short of the Theosophic teaching is that we are all brothers *because each one of us is the identical God.* What a nice brotherhood!... The theory that man is God kills all relationship.... The basis of brotherhood is intercommunion, and intercommunion will mean zero if all relationship be eliminated. True brotherhood consists in adjusting our relationship with our fellow-brethren by loving them as ourselves for the sake of the love of God, and not in imagining that there is only one ego and nothing else.'[5]

Upadhyay was opposed to theosophy because it taught a form of what we might call 'process pantheism'—the doctrine of an encompassing, evolving principle that acts as the basis for a life of altruistic service.[6] Such teaching militated against his notion of a self-fulfilled, immutable God, who is nevertheless a community of persons (a Trinity) providing both the model and the rationale for the love of neighbour in our lives. But this was not the whole story. Besant's theosophy also did a disservice to 'Hinduism', i.e. Advaita as the so-called quintessence of Hindu thought. For Advaita's Supreme

3 See also 'The Mysterious Being' (Sp-m, July 1894): 'The holy doctrine of the Blessed Trinity [= the Mysterious Being of the title] will drive away Theosophy, whose God is something like zero.'

4 'An Examination of Mrs Besant's Lecture on "Man the Master of his own Destiny"', (Sp-m, July 1895).

5 'Theosophy and Universal Brotherhood' (Sp-m, November 1894).

6 For an analysis of Besant's thought (and an integrated résumé of her life) see Wessinger, 1988.

Being was also not an evolving *je-ne-sais-quoi* substrate of the mass of being; rather it was traditionally characterized as unchanging Sac-Cid-Ānanda: pure Being-Consciousness-Bliss. Perhaps it was significant that before very long Upadhyay would begin to rework Advaita's *saccidānanda* as *the* Hindu conceptual basis for an understanding of the Trinity.

So Upadhyay, targeting Besant and breathing fire, challenged her to a public theological debate, dogging her steps, as *The Blade* informs us, in Bombay, Trichinopoly and Lahore (see also ch. 6). 'Wherever she had lectured, he too had by lectures refuted her claim' (p. 2). In November 1895, the *Sophia* published an 'Open Letter to Mrs Annie Besant' (dated November 6, and addressed from Hyderabad, Sind), under Upadhyay's name. It contains various points of interest and is worth quoting at length:

> I am a Kanauj Brahman by birth. My original name is Bhavani Charan Vandya Upadhyaya (Banerji), but I am now known as Upadhyaya Brahmabandhav (Theophilus). As a genuine Brahman I was, while very young, agitated by the desire to know God (Brahmajijnasa).... God Almighty, the Author of my being, in His inscrutable ways, has, at last, brought me to His true fold, the One, Holy, Catholic and Apostolic Church, which teaches that the destiny of man is to see Him whose Being is Knowledge and Love, for whom to be is to act—to see the Infinite, self-satisfied Act, having no need of a finite term as Its resultant.... I yearn to make known to my countrymen this glorious privilege which has been conferred upon them by Almighty God and make them accept the Christian and Catholic faith....
>
> In short, dear madam, I am a Brahman by birth and a Christian and Catholic by faith. Circumstances have brought me to Sindh, and I am working now for the dissemination of the Catholic faith in this province. The conversion of a few respectable Hindus and the apprehended conversion of a few others have greatly agitated the Hindu community of Hyderabad (Sindh). In their anxiety the Hindus have invited you here to deliver lectures for the purpose of arresting the progress of the Christian and Catholic religion....
>
> Now, dear madam, is it not desirable that an opportunity should be given to the Hindus for contrasting the Theosophic or Hindu and the Catholic conceptions of the Infinite and His relation to the finite? I, therefore, invite you to a public discussion with me on the above subject.... I am a Brahman by my present and first birth, and you profess to have been a Brahman in your last birth. It is a Brahman's duty and a Brahman's privilege to hold religious discussions (Dharmavichara)....

> You may consider me too insignificant to measure swords with... for your satisfaction that I am worth powder and shot, I am sending you by today's post one or two specimens of the journal 'Sophia', edited by me, and the printed substance of a lecture of mine....
>
> In conclusion, I adjure you in the name of the living God, in the name of all that is dear and near to you, in the name of my beloved country, to meet me in public at any place, at any time, and in any way you choose, for the purpose of giving my countrymen a grand opportunity to judge by contrast the Theosophic or Hindu and the Christian and Catholic faiths....

Let us pause to digest this dramatic statement. It is no less than a (somewhat pompous) challenge to a duel! The prospect of a close-cropped, saffron-clad, be-crossed Indian male preaching Christian belief, exchanging 'powder and shot' with a silver-haired and silver-tongued, sari-clad Englishwoman defending Hindu ideas, 'in public, at any place, at any time' boggles the mind. In the event, the clash was to be somewhat less clear-cut than Upadhyay would have liked, and the OK Corrall more like a boxing-ring with seconds in than out. But we shall describe what happened in good time.

First, let us return to the open letter. There can be little doubt that Upadhyay continued to take pride in his caste status, a status he was prepared to vaunt to his advantage. We shall have occasion to appreciate the significance of this pride later through complex if changing contexts of his life. In the folklore of the time, a 'Kanauj' Brahmin was a Brahmin of unquestionable pedigree, whose ancestors were invited from the North (Kanauj etc.) to Bengal in the eleventh century by the ruler Ballal Sen to purify the orthodoxy and lineage of the local Brahmins, who were considered degenerate. The status of 'kulin' supposedly arose from this small influx of Brahmin families.

Note too the description of Upadhyay's God: 'self-satisfied Act', essentially Being, Knowledge and Love. Exit Besant's 'zero' God, which Upadhyay hopes to supplant by his own deity (to which in Upadhyay's estimation the Advaitic Absolute approximates far more closely than Besant's ultimate being).[7] Recall from the last chapter that Upadhyay was already beginning to reappraise Advaita as quintessentially representative of Hinduism; as such it would be the most appropriate basis on which to build an appreciation of the Roman Catholic

7 Hence by 'Theosophic *or* Hindu' in the extract quoted Upadhyay means 'Theosophic *as* (supposedly) Hindu', i.e. as 'Neo-Hindu'.

understanding of the divine reality, first as a metaphysical being (in accordance with the light of natural reason), and then as Trinity (as taught by Revelation).[8] Upadhyay's missionary intentions are clearly signalled as religious and as patriotic. Nothing has changed here as to motivation and goal. Upadhyay actually claims that the success of his missionary efforts is the cause for Besant's being invited by local Hindus to deliver countervailing lectures. The reality may not have been as straightforward as this, but at least we may conclude that Upadhyay had a high profile in the area and had caused quite a stir religiously in educated circles. In support of this conclusion we shall see that *Sophia* was taken seriously by rival publications. Finally, an important if implicit distinction—one Upadhyay exploits more and more explicitly—is discernible, namely, the distinction that one can remain a Brahmin 'by birth' and a Catholic 'by faith', in other words that, as Upadhyay will maintain, given the appropriate circumstances, one is entitled to be labelled a 'Hindu-Catholic'. This distinction is a derivative of the more basic natural-supernatural divide discussed earlier; what is of particular interest here is that it is a tradition-specific derivation, relevant to Upadhyay's own situation. It intimates that Upadhyay is refining strategy for a particular missionary campaign.

Now to the 'powder and shot' of the battle at hand. Nothing much, except presumably the already described dogging of steps happened after the publication of the letter. However, towards the end of 1896, it was announced that Besant would (finally) give two lectures in Karachi, not far from Upadhyay's headquarters in Hyderabad. Here, perhaps, was the chance Upadhyay was waiting for. When 'large posters in big blue letters' (Bl., p. 1) went up on Karachi walls proclaiming that Annie Besant would speak on December 10 and 12 in the Max-Denso Hall on the underlying unity of Hindu, Christian and Theosophic teaching, even larger posters in 'red letters' were put up inviting the public to the same venue, on December 11 and 13, to hear two counter-lectures by Upadhyay. Naturally the Hall was packed on each occasion.

The gist of Besant's lectures and Upadhyay's critique is given in four articles published serially in *Sophia* (January, February, May, June, 1897) under the title, 'Hinduism and Christianity as compared

8 The chronological order of this progressive understanding is the inverse of the logical order, of course, for it is the Catholic doctrine of the Trinity that would shape the 'natural' theological understanding of God leading up to it.

by Mrs Besant'.[9] In the first article Upadhyay discusses Besant's view that both Hinduism and Christianity, like theosophy, have a secret and a public teaching; while the esoteric wisdom 'is only to be imparted to the worthy', the public teaching is open to all. Upadhyay scorned this idea, reviewing and countering on each score Besant's tendentious interpretation of the Christian tradition in particular—the New Testament, the Church Fathers and the Roman Catholic Church. He concludes:

> The Catholic Church repudiates such spiritual duplicity. She has no hidden doctrines opposed to open doctrines. She cannot keep any doctrine as secret.... Has she not been commanded by her divine Master to teach all things whatsoever she has learnt from him, to preach on the housetops what she has heard in the ear? Every Catholic, be he ignorant or learned, must believe in the entire deposit of doctrine given by Christ to his Apostles, neither more nor less, and on the wholeness of his faith depends his salvation ... the philosopher understands the doctrines in their different bearings, and the monk applies them to the realisation of greater perfection in life, while the peasant apprehends the doctrines in a simple way and the busy man of the world realises them as much as is possible in his state of life. But they believe in the same articles of faith.

This teaching of Besant's was particularly repugnant to Upadhyay for he regarded it as imperilling the unity of belief of his Church, both as to content of belief and the believers themselves (actual and prospective); it set up invidious distinctions of various kinds. Besides, the principle of secret and public teaching was open to abuse in that changes of opinion, for whatever reason, among those in control could be conveniently passed off as yet further revelations of the esoteric wisdom in the appropriate circumstances. Indeed, there is no doubt that Upadhyay thought that this is what Besant and others did rather unscrupulously on occasion (with regard to their teaching on reincarnation, for example). As late as 1900—towards the end of Upadhyay's public critique of theosophy—in referring to a recent meeting at which Besant upheld the teaching, he writes: 'The Universal Religion must be one and the same for everybody.... The higher stage in religious life does not consist in the knowledge of a larger number of spiritual truths but in the deeper appreciation of the old, unchangeable and un-addible articles of faith' (the weekly *Sophia,*

9 The first article reverses the order of 'Hinduism' and 'Christianity' in the title.

October 20, under 'Notes'). That rather atomic view of faith as entailing a fixed deposit of propositions for belief, which may nevertheless continue to be unpacked, clarified and made relevant for life's changing circumstances, persists.

In the second article we come to the nub of Upadhyay's quarrel with Besant, namely, Besant's 'unknowable God'. Besant, says Upadhyay, claims that both Hinduism and Christianity ('the Christian scriptures, the early Fathers, and the more learned theologians of the Catholic Church of the present day') agree with theosophy in proclaiming an essentially unknowable Supreme Being. 'Sixteen long winters of atheism have benumbed the memory of Mrs Besant,' concludes her opponent, referring to an earlier period of her life. She has forgotten that the Christian scriptures declare a God with such attributes as knowledge, love, power and holiness. The Hindu sacred texts also teach that the Absolute is consciousness and bliss. No doubt we cannot *comprehend* the Supreme Being which is infinite, but we can *apprehend* its various attributes. 'The concept which we have of God is not merely negative but both negative and positive, or as the theologians call it, negativo-positive.'

Based on the argument, then, that God is knowable by us, the rest of the article goes on to challenge 'some vague and superficial items of analogy' between Christianity and Hinduism that Besant put forward, to wit, a similarity between Trinity and Trimurti, the Bull of Siva and the Lamb of God, and the Cross and various Hindu symbols. Each alleged analogy is spurned by Upadhyay. 'To identify the Holy Trinity with the fanciful Trimurti is to identify light with darkness'; 'Siva is one thing and the bull another', whereas 'the lamb of God is not a particular animal that has some peculiar relation to the Son of God ... but the idea that Christ suffered Himself to be led to death, like an innocent lamb to the slaughter-house, to atone for the sins of the world, is symbolised by a lamb bearing a cross'; finally, 'the Christian cross is a *historical* symbol and expresses the fact that Christ died on the cross', while cross-like signs such as the Hindu swȧstika have a completely different meaning. Here we have further evidence of Upadhyay's subtle, distinguishing mind.

The third article deals with 'the subject of Pantheism'. Mrs Besant, who wishes to identify herself with God(!), 'wants to prove that Christianity as well as Hinduism teaches the oneness of man with the Supreme Being'. Well, she can't. For one, it is only partly true to say that Hinduism is pantheistic. In a rare (and convenient) appreciation of other traditions of Hinduism, Upadhyay points out that millions of Vaishnavas find pantheism repugnant. Further, it is 'totally and entirely untrue to represent Christianity as teaching the gross error of God being all and all being God'. Mrs Besant's efforts to construe a few biblical texts as pantheistic (I.Cor. 3.16; Gal. 4.19; Eph. 4.13, 4.15; I.Cor. 15.28), Upadhyay argues, are entirely misconceived.

The fourth and last article takes up Besant's claim that 'the Jews, the Apostles, the early Fathers of the Church, nay, Jesus Christ Himself believed in the doctrine of re-incarnation.' Each of Besant's exegeses of scripture to this end is given a contrary explanation. Upadhyay concludes his overall critique by saying: 'Mrs Besant assumes the air of one that is qualified to teach the Hindus the essence of the Christian religion as well as their own; but the foregoing, we think, will show every thoughtful reader that she has studied little, that she is exceedingly shallow, that she knows neither the Hindu nor the Christian religion, and that it would be very profitable both for her and for her hearers, if she were to spend more time and care upon her own instruction.' In short, theosophy, the darling of Annie Besant, has nothing to offer educated and aspiring Hindus (rather, let them turn to the Catholic faith for fulfillment).

Thus blast and counter-blast; but echoing volleys and ricochets notwithstanding, the two protagonists still had not met face to face. A showdown between Upadhyay and Besant, flanked by their followers, did follow soon after the lectures. 'The opening was courteous.' Upadhyay asked Besant to substantiate three claims she had made: first, that the Bible declared an unknowable God. 'A Protestant Concordance was at hand. She eventually turned to Romans 11.33.' Upadhyay pointed out that the text spoke not of the nature but of the ways of God as unfathomable. 'She agreed.' Second, Upadhyay asked Besant to back her claim that the Upanishads taught an unknown God. Besant replied that no isolated text need be quoted; the whole context bore her out. On the contrary, countered her relentless adversary, 'everywhere God is qualified as Being, Awareness, Bliss.' Finally, 'a copy of Father Rickaby's book ... was offered her to prove her statement that the Stonyhurst Jesuit theologian held God to be unknowable. This was too much for her friends. She fumbled about the pages.... The assembly waxed rowdy. The sannyasi [Upadhyay] and his friends quitted the room, satisfied with what they considered a moral victory' (Bl., pp. 3–4).

Powder and shot in this case had produced more of a smoke-screen than a moral victory, it would appear. The duel was something of a mismatch, based on incompatible premises. Besant was no philosopher; the content of her message was governed by tonalities, moods, images. Upadhyay, on the other hand, strove for analytic rigour, precision of thought. The two protagonists were on different wavelengths. But there is a postscript. A letter dated Karachi, December 14, and signed by Annie Besant, was sent to Upadhyay: 'Dear Sir.... I trust that some day you also may feel that God is an object of adoration rather than a subject for debate, and that He is better served by truth and good-will than by the stirring up of strife.'[10]

Point taken. Upadhyay was still the militant sannyasi engaged in sublimated combat for his cause. In Upadhyay's case this martial aspect was reinforced by his intransigent and somewhat legalistic faith, something hardly exceptional in the circumstances. Upadhyay's consistent critique of theosophy, of which we have given the main points, tails off by the turn of the century when he starts to write less in English and more in Bengali with different ends in view.

But in one matter Annie Besant had misjudged her adversary. So far as Upadhyay was concerned, his God was not only a God worth fighting for, but also a God worth living for, 'an object of adoration'. From time to time we catch glimpses of Upadhyay's lively faith in the pages of *Sophia*. Without apology we quote at length from an Easter homily by Upadhyay published in the journal in May 1895:

> Greatest of days, day thrice blessed, day blessed for ever, that was chosen to behold the Saviour's triumph! Death, the grim tyrant, boasted to hold his victim fast. Had he not millions laid low before?... What, then, was the poor Galilean to him—the stern leveller of all that breathe the breath of flesh?
>
> But lo! When scarce the dawn of the third day reddened the mount of disgrace—the sacred Mount of Calvary—the soul of the Galilean drew near the silent captive of the sepulchre, the bruised and mangled frame that had been torn with a thousand wounds, and bursting the fetters of death, clad with imperishable life and vigour, uprose in the glory of transfiguration—a heaven of beauty—the Saviour's body. The earth trembled with fear and awe at this majestic deed—and well might she tremble, for since Abel, first of all mortals, had closed his eyes in death she had not witnessed the like event....
>
> And ever since that first Easter Day a stream of hope and consolation, of joy and bliss has gone forth from the sepulchre hallowed by the

[10] I have been unable to trace this letter.

> best of all victories—bringing gladness into fainting hearts, refreshing sufferers in their trials, relieving the sadness of those mourning over the bier of dear departed, and quickening the precious seeds deposited in the dreary abodes of mortality for the day of resurrection....
>
> O blessed day of Easter! Day of hope and of joy! How sweet is thy memory to the weary pilgrim!... Thou but changest the house of the grave into a transitory mansion over which it will once be said: 'Why seek ye the living with the dead? He is not here. He is risen.'
>
> Pause, then, a moment, my soul, from the turmoil of the world and reflect; drink in the thrilling sounds of the Easter Alleluja! Behold the wondrous contest, in which Death and Life have battled together! See, the seals are broken, the stone is rolled away, the sepulchre is untenanted, the burial garments are laid aside, the guards are fleeing, and the earth is quaking with fear! Lo, thy Saviour is risen, the Conqueror of Death, and will lead thee to victory! Alleluja!

Theologically this is quite unoriginal; as a literary composition it shows a command of the language and some flair, though it is written in the florid style of the day. Nevertheless, that there is a deep personal faith here—a touching anguish of heart—cannot be gainsaid.

## *Brahmoism*

On the whole, Upadhyay looked back on this movement, now irredeemably splintered in membership and doctrine, more in sorrow than in anger. For had not Brahmoism in the past 'done good work'? 'It has combated idolatry and superstition and prepared the way of the Lord.'[11] But its commitment to theism had been diluted, and it was beset with sectarianism. Further, with one or two notable exceptions, the Brahmo movement was losing its respect for Christ on which so much of its theistic and human ideals had been built.[12]

11 'A Survey of the Religious Movements of New India. I. The Brahma Samaj' (hereafter 'Survey', Sp-m, August 1898). In the literature of the times both 'Brahma' and 'Brahmo' were used of the Samaj.

12 Keshab, here, was the model for Upadhyay. For though his views were never orthodox by traditional Christian standards, he had continued to profess Christ as 'the prince of prophets', the 'ideal man', the 'culmination of humanity' ('Why the Brahmas do not accept Christ', Sp-m, August 1897). In 'Survey' Upadhyay writes: 'The spirit of individualism which is the characteristic of the Brahma cult, was in [Keshab's] case greatly sobered and steadied by the luminous ideal he found in the personality of Christ. This, we maintain, was the chief source of the moral strength of the Brahma

In an early *Sophia* article,[13] Upadhyay analysed the Samaj's doctrinal divisions as follows: 'Now the Brahmo Samaj ... is lapsing into old errors. One section of it is a medley of neo-Hegelians, Vaishnavites and Rationalists. Another section is slowly drifting towards Pantheism. Their chief organs boast of their synthetic doctrine that man is of the same substance with God. This doctrine is the deadliest enemy of Theism. If the Brahmos hold to this doctrine seriously the hour of the reign of Theism in their Samaj will be struck ere long.' In particular it was the Sadharan Samaj that he consistently associated with pantheism.[14] Too many Samajists also succumbed, unfortunately, to a kind of theosophic malaise, the doctrine of eternal progressivism. 'To aspire and to aspire, to struggle and to struggle, for ever and ever to aspire and to struggle to become but never to be an infinite God, is the creed of the progressive school.'[15] Upadhyay argues, as he does in another context noted earlier, that this aspiration is based on the misapprehension that it is an evil to be finite. On this understanding, since human nature will always be characterized by finitude, humans are doomed to a perpetuity of being subject to an evil state. The right view, as taught by the Catholic Church, is that finitude, namely, our created state, is not an evil in itself, and that it is the human destiny to experience eternal and heavenly communion with God where one will enjoy perfection in full measure in accordance with our created condition. In sum, Upadhyay deplores the way Brahmos are losing direction on the whole, and his final word seems to be that Brahmoism has outlived its usefulness and is a spent force—in contrast to his next target.

---

movement.... From the living spiritual and elevating religion of Christ the movement acquired a sustaining power, a cohesive principle and a moral backbone which counteracted the disintegrating influence of Rationalism. All this is now lost.' P.C. Majumdar, as Upadhyay's mentor who succeeded Keshab, is also singled out as an honourable exception. 'Is Mr Mozoomdar a Christian? We know him very intimately and can say with certainty that he is not. But he has certain views in regard to Christ which are not shared by the majority of his fellow believers in the Brahmo Samaj. He does not differ, even by an inch, from his great master, Keshav Ch. Sen, in his conception of Christ', (Sp-w, July 7, 1900, under 'Notes').

13 'Conversion of India—an Appeal' (October 1894).

14 'There is a pretty large number of Brahmos in the Sadharan Samaj who are downright Pantheists and believe in metempsychosis'; 'Divisions in the Brahma Samaj' (Sp-w, December 8, 1900). See also 'Survey', August 1898.

15 'Eternal Progress of the Soul' (Sp-m, September 1894).

### *Vivekananda's Neo-Vedanta*

Upadhyay attacked the views of this friend of earlier days with greater seriousness and, it must be said, relish. For one, he sought to underplay Vivekananda's sensational debut at the Chicago Parliament of Religions in 1893: 'It is no exaggeration to say that, barring Swami Vivekananda's picturesque appearance, a certain dash with which he spoke, and the novelty of his doctrine, there was stronger and more general sympathy felt and expressed in America for Mr P.C. Mozoomdar of the Brahmo Samaj.'[16]

Doctrinal novelty for the American public, that is, not for his compatriots. For, according to Upadhyay, Vivekananda was merely reinterpreting traditional Advaitic teaching or 'pantheism', which was full of 'the old, old spirit of pride which wriggles itself into newer and newer forms as the ages run on' and which 'has held India under the bondage of error and unholiness for such a long, long period'.[17] The bane of Advaita was, according to Upadhyay, that it was founded on spiritual pride, hubris, conflating the human and the divine states, demolishing the humility due to the creaturely condition in the presence of the Creator.[18] Thus, at this stage of his critique, Upadhyay rather dramatically denounces the 'lie' of pantheism (with special reference to the teaching of Vivekananda) supposedly spreading like wildfire throughout India.[19]

At the Chicago Parliament of Religions Vivekananda had dared to say, reports Upadhyay, that 'it is a libel to call man a sinner'. For were not human beings, indeed, the whole world, in reality the

[16] 'Dr Barrows in India' (Sp-m, February 1897). This title alludes to Dr J. H. Barrows, chairman of the General Committee of the Chicago Parliament of Religions, who visited India to lecture in December 1896. Kopf assesses Majumdar's address at Chicago as follows: 'It was an intellectual's lecture: formal in structure, precise in vocabulary, and deliberately elevated in tone and style to attract the cultivated mind' (1979: 21).

[17] 'The Supreme Being under Delusion' (Sp-m, January 1896).

[18] A common and, indeed, misconceived Christian objection at least against traditional Advaita, to the present day. Protestant and Catholic theologians (e.g. H. Kraemer and K. Rahner) have persisted in making this objection in contemporary times. But this is not based on a knowledge of the original texts, which are uncompromising in their insistence on systematic ego-stripping in the process of Self-realization so that it is eventually impossible to think that 'I' (some personal ego) am 'God' (some separate personal deity). In the authentic tradition of Advaita there is no room for spiritual pride. Upadhyay appreciates this in due course.

[19] 'Three Capital Lies' (Sp-m, September 1897).

Absolute shrouded by the veil of ignorance and illusion? As such, human beings could not be intrinsically sinful. This teaching was anathema to Upadhyay: it militated against the doctrine of human creatureliness before one supreme Creator God—the foundation of all forms of theism, not least the 'Vedic theism' of the early Hindu scriptures that Upadhyay had made much of, and his understanding of which we shall examine in the next chapter. In short, Vivekananda's brand of pantheism undermined the propaedeutic truths of Vedic theism.

Upadhyay's most characteristic attack on Vivekananda's position occurs in the article 'Neo-Hinduism run wild' (Sp-m, October 1896). Here Upadhyay first quotes extensively from a recent lecture by Vivekananda, whom he describes as one of neo-Hinduism's 'champions'. The lecture had been published in the *Brahmavadin*, a recently established journal (edited by a Perumal Alasingha) that was to act as the vehicle of Vivekananda's thought and work. 'It is the greatest of all lies,' Vivekananda is quoted as saying, 'that we are men: we are the gods of the universe.... The worst lie that you ever told yourself was that you were a sinner.' In fact, deluded by ignorance about the divinity of our 'true selves', we think of ourselves as mere mortals, as intrinsically different from one another and the world in which we live. In truth, 'everything that you see or feel or hear, the whole universe is ... the Lord Himself.... He is the man who is talking. He is the audience that is here, He is the platform on which I stand.... It is all He.' Upon realizing this inner identity we shall be able to relate to one another in true perspective: the wife will love her husband as she ought, as God himself, and vice versa. 'That mother will love the children more who thinks that these children are God himself,' and so on.

Not for Upadhyay a benign interpretation of these words! On the contrary, he saw them as militating against everything he so staunchly championed—the uncompromisingly theistic, sin-affirming, contrition-demanding, pardon-offering, obedience-exacting, hierarchical and legalistic world of the official Roman Catholic theology of the time. So he attacked them with gusto. For Vivekananda creation is no other than the dream-like projection of the supreme Reality; sin, nothing but the self-delusion of this perfect being; redemption, but the banishment of divine ignorance. 'Cease to think that you are anything but God and all sins will be washed away,' writes Upadhyay sarcastically. 'Believe that you are he, the one infinite existence, and in a moment all selfishness will disappear.' And he continues with elephantine humour:

> Concord will reign everywhere for then one team of eleven gods will play cricket matches with another team of eleven gods without the help of umpire-gods, and one set of tipsy gods will drink the health of another set ... with the greatest cordiality ... without requiring the divine intervention of police-gods. Know that you, he, she, and it are the self-same god and ... you will see the vegetarian god munching the vegetable-god ... the lecturer-god stamping his foot on the platform-god, the youth-god walking with a fashionable stick-god.... Identity everywhere!... O tempora! O mores! This is the mystery of creation and redemption revealed to man by neo-Hinduism!

Only a concerted attack based on the truths of 'primitive theism' supported by the 'invincible arguments of St Thomas and other Catholic philosophers' will be able to drive 'this monster of neo-Hindu error' to take refuge 'in dark holes and caves'. Before long, however, Shankarite (if not Shankara's) Advaita would be rehabilitated by Upadhyay and Vivekananda viewed in a very different light indeed.

### *Swami Dayananda and the Arya Samaj*

Last but certainly not least, we consider Upadhyay's robust opposition to the teachings of Swami Dayananda Sarasvati (1824–83) and of the organization he founded, the Arya Samaj.[20] The Samaj, militantly anti-Christian and pro-Hindu, and enthusiastically 'reformist' and 'revivalist' depending on context, was especially active in north-western India with Lahore as its centre of operations. Regular clashes between Upadhyay and the Samaj were inevitable, both having acquired a high profile and bases in the same area with social, religious and implicit political objectives in view. Both were also involved in vigorous publishing ventures.

Under 'The Hindu Revival' (*Sophia*, June 1894), Upadhyay provides a neat summary of the Arya teachings that particularly agitated him: 'The Arya Samajists are boldly preaching that the Almighty is unable to create, that man and matter are co-eternal with God, that man's destiny is to pass through endless series of transmigrations, that the state of salvation is temporary, that the attainment of heavenly bliss does not once for all emancipate man

20 On Dayananda and the early activities of the Arya Samaj, see Jordens, 1978, and Jones, 1976, respectively.

from the painful cycle of birth and death; and they assert, not apologetically, but with unbounded dogmatism, that all these doctrines are explicitly taught in the Vedas.'

It was not all negative. In so far as the Samaj, and Dayananda, (1) sympathized with theism, that is, preached one Supreme Being who cared for the salvation of the world and individual souls, and (2) repudiated pantheism and idolatry, they were to be welcomed as allies in the battle for India's soul.[21] In so far as he perceived this theism to be clothed in an anti-Christian polemic, Upadhyay was vigorously opposed to it. As intimated in the quotation, there was another consideration. Following Dayananda, Aryas claimed that their views were Vedic, based essentially on the Vedic canon. Here the earliest texts or Samhitas were especially relevant, for, in articulating his views, Dayananda had paid special attention to their interpretation. But before he turned to Advaita as encapsulating *par excellence* Hindu insights into the nature of God and God's relationship with the world, it was in the Vedas, not least the Samhitas, that Upadhyay found the Hindu theism that would best serve his evangelistic purposes. It was thus incumbent on him to show that Dayananda's brand of Vedic theism, in contrast to his own, had no standing in the sacred texts.

Upadhyay launches into his attack on Dayananda's exegeses of Vedic hymns in the opening numbers of the *Sophia*. In the very first issue, under the title 'Theism in the Vedas' (January 1894), he mentions two conflicting 'theories' about the meaning of the canonical texts. The first is in the tradition of Sayana, 'the ancient expounder of the Vedas' (actually circa fourteenth century C.E., but very much in the classical tradition), according to which the earlier part of the Vedas inculcate 'physiolatry, that is, the [ritual, sacrificial] worship of fire, air, water etc.' as beneficent manifestations of the supreme formless being taught in the later part of the Vedas. 'The worship of

21 In a Note (Sp-m, June 1897) commenting on the murder of the provocative Arya preacher, Pandit Lekhram (1858–97) at the hands of a fanatical Muslim, Upadhyay writes: 'A strong indigenous body of theists however defective their religion, and however hostile to Christianity, can do some good in these days when Pantheism and Idolatry stalk unblushing across the country'. And under 'Survey', (Part 2, September 1898), he applauds Dayananda's 'zeal for the cause of Theism, and his advocacy of the inalienable right of every human being to worship the One God in spirit and in truth. The chief cause of India's degeneration has been the grave injustice of her teeming masses being deprived of the glorious privilege of paying homage to their Maker. Against this injustice Dayananda fought with all his might and, so fighting, he helped the regeneration of the country.'

gods is only a stepping-stone to higher knowledge. The Vedas themselves profess that sacrifices and oblations can only give wealth, prosperity, long life, or at best, a higher stage of existence, but cannot give final bliss. It is only the knowledge of God that can emancipate souls from the miseries of ceaseless birth and death, and that knowledge is found in the latter part of the Vedas.... Such is the argument of the Hindus in defence of the Vedas which they hold to be the breath of God.'

Then there is the new interpretation of Dayananda Sarasvati—'a man of remarkable genius'—'which repudiates with scorn the idea that the Vedas inculcate nature-worship.' In fact, according to Dayananda, the Vedas are monotheistic through and through. 'How could they be the pure word of God if they taught physiolatry?' How can physiolatry/nature-worship—'error', 'sin' and (theological) 'treason'—be a stepping stone to right understanding and spiritual emancipation? Now which interpretation is correct, the traditional one or Dayananda's? In forthcoming issues Upadhyay proposes to put both to the test of 'grammar and common sense'. In effect, the sum of his efforts will be the thesis that neither of the rival views mentioned is quite correct; that in the Vedas 'amidst physiolatry and idolatry, anthropomorphism and pantheism, amidst the darkest aberrations of the Indian intellect, irrepressibly flashes out the sublime idea of the One True God'[22]; in short, that the Vedas contain the germs of a sounder theism than that proposed by Dayananda.

From February to April inclusive (1894), in Parts II–IV of the article entitled 'Vedic Theism', Upadhyay carefully analyses some of Dayananda's exegeses of the early Vedic texts. We need not give a detailed account of this analysis; an example or two will suffice. Upadhyay starts with Dayananda's interpretation of the opening line of the Ṛg Veda: *agnim iḍe purohitam* (RV.1.1.1). According to Sayana, that is, according to the traditional interpretation, says Upadhyay, this means: 'I praise (*iḍe*) fire (*agnim*), the priest (*purohitam*), i.e. one who offers oblations.' Dayananda, on the other hand, offers an alternative explanation in two parts, depending on whether *agni* is understood legitimately either as 'God' or as 'fire'. In both cases, however, *purohita* is to be glossed as *dadhāti,* meaning 'that which holds before or previously'. In other words, according to Dayananda, when *agni* is understood as 'fire', the text means, 'I praise fire which has the power to transform things', i.e. I praise fire the *purohita* =

22 'Theism in the Vedas. III,' (Sp-m, March 1894).

*dadhāti* = which holds previously, that is, is inherently (= previously) able to transform things by its burning action. In other words, 'I praise fire which has inherent transforming power by its burning action.' Upadhyay says that this interpretation is quite unjustifiable. 'Evidently the ordinary meaning of the word 'purohita' (priest) has been discarded because it cannot be applied to inanimate fire.'

Continuing Dayananda's exegesis, when *agni* is understood as 'God', the text would read: 'I praise God the *purohita,* viz. the one who holds (the primordial atoms or the universe in its ethereal state) previous to (creation).' God in this understanding is not a creator, bringing the constituents of the world into existence out of nothing by his power alone, but a maker or fashioner of the world from constituent material that coexists with him. God, and only God, has the power to constitute the world out of its coexisting 'primordial atoms'. Thus, 'before' the universe was fashioned, God 'holds' the primordial atoms in his power. This is what *purohita* = *dadhāti* means in this second interpretation of *agni* according to Dayananda, concludes Upadhyay.

But, of course, this 'theistic' interpretation will not do for Upadhyay. True, it posits a pre-existing God who is uniquely powerful—so far so good. But the God of Dayananda's interpretation is not powerful enough. Only a *creator* God, a God who could start the world off from nothing, by fiat alone, would have the omnipotence requisite for an acceptable theism according to Upadhyay. So Upadhyay's underlying *theological* objection to Dayananda's exegesis is fronted, it must be said, by a perfectly plausible grammatical critique.

The rival interpretation, in both its parts, turns on the word *dadhāti,* the gloss for *purohita.* Dayananda, notes Upadhyay, quotes the ancient authority Yaska in support of this gloss. But, Upadhyay argues, Yaska cannot be adduced in support here. In his famous work, the *Nirukta,* Yaska glosses *purohita* as *pura enaṃ dadhati,* 'one *whom*—kings or men—hold before' and not, continues Upadhyay, 'as Dayananda explains, '*pura enaṃ dadhāti*' (one *who* holds *something* before).' In other words, Dayananda's interpretation is guilty of a number of fatal exegetical flaws. He misquotes an authority; he turns a passive sense into an active; his interpretation is counter-intuitive.

Yaska glosses *purohita* as 'one whom others hold before' where *dadhaṭi* is third person plural, present indicative (*others* hold before). This sense is arrived at by correctly understanding the *hita* of *puro-hita* as the passive past participle of the root *dhā* (of which *dadhati* is the third person plural, present tense). Thus, according to Yaska's gloss of *purohita,* the god *agni* is to be revered as one who is held or placed before as a priest by others, to offer oblations etc. on their behalf. Dayananda, however, glosses *purohita* as 'one *who holds* something/someone before...', where *dadhāti* is third person singular, present indicative. In this event, *dadhāti* cannot give the correct sense of the passive *hita.* According to the correct passive sense, if, as Dayananda suggests, *agni* is understood as 'God', the text *agnim iḍe purohitam* should read, says Upadhyay, 'I praise God who is held (by the primordial atoms) previous to (creation).' 'Held by the atoms! Almighty indeed!' is the scathing conclusion. Here Upadhyay's theological objection to Dayananda's theistic interpretation surfaces. So Dayananda's exegesis is to be rejected 'because of its evident opposition to authority, grammar and common sense' (February 1894). We note Upadhyay's confident Sanskrit critique.

A final example. In the same verse of the Ṛg Veda, *agni,* besides being described as *purohita,* is also called *ṛtvik.* Sayana, notes Upadhyay, understands *ṛtvik* as 'a kind of priest', as an extension of *agni*'s priestly function first intimated by *purohita.* But according to Dayananda, *ṛtvik* is to be glossed as *ṛtau ṛtau yajati saṅgīkaroti,* i.e. as 'one who combines in due time'. When *agni* is understood as 'fire', the text means that one should revere fire as that which by its action effects different kinds of combination in things, whereas when *agni* is taken as 'God', the text means that one should revere God as the one who 'combines the primordial atoms in the time of creation'.

This 'novel meaning' of *ṛtvik* is not wrong grammatically as in the case of *purohita,* concedes Upadhyay, 'but we find no trace of this meaning in the ancient authorities.... Dayananda has invented this far-fetched meaning to thrust into the Vedas his pet theory of the eternity of matter. If the Vedas can be made to say that God combines primordial atoms in the time of creation, then the theory of the eternity of matter will be authoritatively established. Hence this ingenious interpretation' (March 1894). Ingenious but quite untenable. What Upadhyay intends in these articles is not to challenge Dayananda's claim that the Samhitas teach monotheism, but to show that Dayananda's brand of monotheism, Vedic or otherwise, is seriously defective. 'Is it not a mockery to say that God is infinite but He cannot create, that He is, like a potter, in need of some external agency [the primordial atoms] to carry out His design?' (March 1894).

Elsewhere (Sp-m, November 1894), Upadhyay devotes a substantial article to repudiating the concept of a 'Potter' God. Dayananda is explicitly mentioned as teaching this idea, in the tradition of the Hindu Logicians or Naiyāyikas, who proposed the 'very curious piece of reasoning' that 'as a potter cannot make a pot without having recourse to earth or clay, so God cannot make this material universe without having recourse to existing matter.' Upadhyay condemns this conception as 'childish', and its God as 'anthropomorphic'. He goes on to distinguish between 'finite' and 'infinite' in such a way that God's infinitude transcends our finitude not only in degree but also in kind so that 'God is God because he is a full being and does not require any object to help him to live or act.' God is *sui generis*; the divine love, knowledge, power etc. are unconditioned, unlike ours. It is only this God, not the potter-God, who is worthy of our worship.[23]

Upadhyay was also strongly opposed to Samaj teaching about the ultimate human destiny. According to Dayananda the bliss of salvation is temporary; those in the heavenly state, after enjoying the rewards of their good karma, must return to the cycle of birth and death. This is a 'godless, cheerless error' opposed to a right understanding of the divine plan for human salvation (See 'The true doctrine of the end of man as opposed to the teachings of Svami Dayananda Sarasvati', Sp-m, December 1894[24]). This article represents an attempt by Upadhyay to give a detailed refutation of Dayananda's understanding of the end-state. The crux of Upadhyay's rebuttal is his belief that 'in the beatific contemplation of God, in the possession of the universal good, consists the everlasting happiness of man.' We cannot fall away from this experience; the blessed are held eternally by and in the self-sufficing divine goodness and love. 'Once we possess [God] we possess him for ever'.[25] Note, in passing, the Thomistic bias of Upadhyay's understanding of final beatitude. It is essentially a *contemplation* of God, rather than, as traditional Augustinians, say, would describe it, a loving union of wills. We may add that Upadhyay could not abide too Dayananda's proposal that the ancient custom of *niyoga* or levirate—according to which a widow was permitted, in

23 See also 'The teachings of Nature regarding Creation', (Sp-m, April 1898), for a similar treatment in places.

24 We are told that this article was based on a lecture delivered by Upadhyay at Lahore on November 1 that year.

25 In 'Is the state of salvation everlasting' (Sp-m, October 1895), Upadhyay attempts to show, by an analysis of Hindu texts (including texts Dayananda adduces in support of his view), that his opponent's 'new-fangled theory of temporary salvation is like the catching at a straw by a drowning man'.

certain circumstances, to be impregnated for the sake of bearing children in the name of the dead husband—be revived by his followers. As can be expected this proposal came in for some scathing comment.

We can now sum up the main points of Upadhyay's critique of Arya doctrine especially as it derived from Dayananda's teaching. All in all, it held out a deficient and uninspiring form of theism: it proposed a God who was unable to create, who was co-eternal with souls and primordial matter, and to whom penitent prayer was out of place; it taught salvation as a temporary end, superseded by the law of karma and rebirth; it was morally suspect (e.g. with regard to the recommendation to practise *niyoga*, and the factional quarrels among Aryas after Dayananda's death as to whether meat eating was sinful); and last but certainly not least, its handling of the Vedas was highly dubious, in effect based on a private ('Protestant') interpretation of the scriptures in defiance of the traditional, authoritative exegetical practices.[26] Arya religion was both regional and devotionally off-putting; Upadhyay saw no future for it.[27] Nevertheless, as we have seen, the Arya Samaj preached monotheism of a sort. This was a useful beginning, for though, contrary to Arya teaching, the earlier part of the Vedas preponderantly inculcated 'physiolatry' (see earlier), there were sections in the Vedas, in both the earlier and later parts, which were well on the way to indicating that 'man is by nature a pure Theist' in the acceptable sense of this term ('Theism in the Vedas. IV', Sp-m, April 1894). This facet of Vedic theism, as understood by Upadhyay, we shall discuss in the next chapter.

We have often referred to Upadhyay and his activities in martial terms. This is by design and is meant to reflect Upadhyay's implicit and explicit self-image. As we have pointed out before, Upadhyay the sannayasi did not withdraw from the world—a traditional ideal. On the contrary, various cultural features of the times combined to mould his ascetic lifestyle in the role of the *karmayogī*, the selfless activist dedicated to fighting for his patriotic and religious ends. It was thus that he could begin to reconcile the expectations of his Brahmin status

[26] This point is made clearly in 'Survey' (Part 2) where Upadhyay condemns the Arya doctrine of the infallibility of the Vedas, which are to be interpreted by private judgement.

[27] Here he was wrong. The Arya Samaj continues to be an influential movement—especially in northern India—not so much through its doctrinal views as by the way it is associated politically with the on-going attempt to champion chauvinist Hindu ideals.

with his long-felt inner urge to fight Kshatriya-like for his cause. So Upadhyay's *Sophia* writings are not lacking in martial terminology. There was his desire to 'measure swords' with Annie Besant, to exchange 'powder and shot' with her. Again, in 'The Penal Code of Transmigration' (Sp-m, June 1894), he writes, 'We purpose to carry on the crusade against the doctrine of transmigration till it is driven out of India.' With respect to Advaita, he avers: 'We declare war against such a soul-killing system' ('The *Light of the East* and Ourselves', Sp-m, August 1895); again, 'We will wage war—a war to the knife—against this monstrous doctrine and will not retire from the field until we hew it asunder' ('The Supreme Being under Delusion', Sp-m, January 1896).

Upadhyay's strident views were noted by a number of *Sophia*'s peers, and on occasion led to sharp exchanges in print. Both Upadhyay and *Sophia* were big guns on the scene. For instance, the *Arya Messenger* of December, 5 1894, took Upadhyay to task for defending the doctrine of creation out of nothing[28]; the following month in *Sophia* there was a robust reply. *Sophia* and the *Arya Messenger* crossed swords on more than one occasion.[29] Indeed it was largely in polemical vein that Upadhyay either adverted to or received attention from other local publications.[30] In one way or another he was in the limelight till the end of his days.

But the glare of publicity was soon to prove increasingly uncomfortable under scrutiny from his own Church, in connection with his developing views on the nature of Hinduism and its relationship with his own faith. It is this development that we must now consider.

[28] 'I am sorry that a gentleman of the type and abilities of Mr Upadhyayji should have advanced arguments which are quite absurd.'

[29] In the weekly *Sophia* (August 1900), Upadhyay describes the *Messenger* as 'the organ of the 'cultured' party of the Lahore Arya Samaj'.

[30] But not always. In 'The *Light of the East* and Ourselves' (Sp-m, August 1895), Upadhyay gives a quotation from *Light of the East* (an apologetical Hindu paper) which quotes from the *Epiphany*, which approvingly quotes a passage from *Sophia* criticizing Advaita! Needless to say, the *Light* mentions the *Sophia* extract only to rubbish it, and *Sophia* mentions the *Light* for the same reason. But there was also more unqualified praise for Upadhyay in Hindu publications. *The Blade* quotes the *Subodh Patrika*, 'the organ of the Prarthana Samaj' as saying, after Upadhyay had given a lecture opposing Annie Besant's views: 'We may console ourselves with the fact that Mrs Annie Besant has had a very powerful opponent in Upadhyay. We hope he will deliver similar lectures all round India, and thereby do a signal service to his mother country' (p. 62).

# Chapter 8

# Light from the East? Constructing a Hindu 'Platform' of Belief and Practice

Upadhyay the Christian had never, of course, repudiated Hinduism in its entirety. On the contrary, as we have shown, his ancestral faith was intended to act as the 'platform' for the supernatural edifice of Christ (in its Catholic form). But to begin with, this platform was envisaged as being constructed largely out of the planks of 'Vedic theism': largely, but not entirely. Let us first examine what exactly Vedic theism meant, before we go on to inquire into how the 'largely' of this conception developed into a new basis for underpinning the Catholic teaching that was to bring Upadhyay's compatriots to Christ.

Vedic theism was a species of natural theism, the Vedic contextualization of the 'naturally attained' insight into the nature of the divine being—the 'general revelation' made available by God to the human mind—that the Catholic theology of the time sanctioned. As such, it is the product of 'natural reason', of the human intellect functioning properly, in the current Catholic theological jargon, with only ordinary, not extraordinary, divine assistance. Further, it can be gleaned from the earliest part of the Sanskritic scriptures, especially the Rk Samhita.[1] It consists of 'the idea of a Supreme Being, who knows all things, who is a personal God, who is father, friend, nay, even brother to his worshippers, who rewards the virtuous, punishes the wicked, who controls the destinies of man, who teaches the Rishis [ancient seers], who watches over the welfare of his creatures,

1 Also called the Rg Veda ('g' becoming 'k' before the 'S' of Samhita).

temporal as well as spiritual' (Sp-m, April 1896: 'The Primitive Parabrahma and Mrs Besant's God'). There were earlier, more condensed descriptions of what Upadhyay understood by theism, Vedic or otherwise, though the above is perhaps the most comprehensive summary available.

The theme of Vedic theism, as the original basis for Upadhyay's continuing appreciation of his ancestral faith after his induction into the Catholic Church, is the subject of a serial in four parts from the very first issue of *Sophia* (Sp-m, January–April 1894). The aim of these articles is to show first, that in religion the human heart is naturally inclined to theism ('the belief in (1) the existence of [one] God, (2) the moral sense in man, (3) the law of retribution according to individual merit or demerit'; January 1894), notwithstanding positions taken, e.g. by Comte and Spencer, to the contrary, and second, that the Vedic Samhitas enshrine theism, albeit somewhat obscurely. As we have indicated in chapter 7, in this series Upadhyay also elaborates his view that of two alternative interpretations of Samhita religion available, that proposed by Sayana (the traditional fourteenth century authority) and that argued by Swami Dayananda, Sayana's is the more wrong-headed.

Sayana in fact maintains that the Samhitas teach 'physiolatry'—'the worship of fire, air, water, etc.'—as the propaedeutic, for the spiritually less advanced, to Upanishadic religion, which deals with 'the One without a second'. No doubt there is much physiolatry and polytheism in the Vedas, says Upadhyay, but there are also noble expressions of pure theism. This is where Dayananda scores over Sayana. Dayananda has both overstated his case by contending that the religion of the Rk Samhita is in no wise polytheistic,[2] and pleaded a very special one, often on an exegetically unsound basis, by arguing that the God of the Veda is not a creator God, coexisting as He does eternally with souls and the material constituents of the universe (see chapter 7). Nevertheless, unlike Sayana, Dayananda is right when he says that Samhita religion is *fundamentally* monotheistic.

On various occasions in *Sophia*, Upadhyay elaborates in defence of Vedic theism, even after he had adopted the view later on that the culmination of Hindu religion as a basis for the reception of the Gospel was not Vedic theism but what we may call 'Vedantic theism'. At that point it was not that he had come to denigrate Vedic theism but

2 Dayananda's attempt to make the Veda 'thoroughly theistic' is 'more ingenious than correct' (Sp-m, April 1894: 'Theism in the Vedas, IV').

rather that he thought so much more highly of Vedantic theism. Before the transition, however, it was Vedic theism that he concentrated on. Was there a specific reason for this? It appears that there was. We may identify it with the belief among Christians at the time, including influential converts, that ancient peoples had been in receipt of a 'primitive natural revelation' from God, presaging in various ways the supernatural and final revelation in Christ that was to come.

This was not contrary to Roman Catholic teaching. Some Indian Christian converts went on to draw the implication that since the Vedas were among the most ancient of available scriptures—as western Orientalists, in particular Max Müller, assured them—they were a prime candidate for discerning the lineaments of this primitive divine revelation.[3] In fact, for these Indian theologians the Vedic revelation was second in quality or promise only to the revelation of the Old Testament. Thus Upadhyay could write:

> The primitive form of man's religious belief was Theism as opposed to fetishism, polytheism, nature-worship and other corrupt forms of religion. The reason of our assertion is that we cannot conceive without violating our nature and common sense that He who made man hid himself from him.... How can such an act be compatible with infinite Goodness?... A man is a born Theist' (Sp-m, January 1894: 'Theism in the Vedas, I').

> We hold that the substratum of all religions is Theism which is the primitive revelation of God. Hindu scriptures abound with Theistic conceptions though they are encrusted with the hard layers of pantheism and idolatry. The more ancient its [Hinduism's] scriptures, the purer they are. In the Vedas we do not find any trace of the immoral legends of the Puranas. Indra and Agni, Varuna and Vayu,

3 It would have been surprising if Upadhyay was not familiar with the views of the Bengali Brahmin, Krishnamohan Banerjea (1813–85), illustrious nationalist and convert to the Anglican Church, who wrote that 'the fundamental principles of Christian doctrine in relation to the salvation of the world find a remarkable counterpart in the Vedic principles of primitive Hinduism in relation to the destruction of sin, and the redemption of the sinner by the efficacy of Sacrifice, itself a figure of *Prajapati*, the Lord and Saviour of the Creation, who had given himself up as an offering for that purpose [p. 181].... Christ is the true *Prajapati*—the true Purusha begotten in the beginning before all worlds, and Himself both God and man. The doctrines of saving sacrifice, the "primary religious rites" of the Rig Veda—of the double character of priest and victim, variously called *Prajapati*, *Purusha*, and *Viswakarma*—of the Ark by which we escape the waves of this sinful world—these doctrines, I say, which had appeared in our Vedas ... may be viewed as fragments of diamonds sparkling amid dust and mud [p. 196]' (see Banerjea's 'The Relation between Christianity and Hinduism' in Philip, 1982).

> are each addressed as the Supreme God. There are mantras which plainly teach that Indra and Agni, Varuna and Vayu, are but different names of the one Deity. Even if physiolatry in the Vedas cannot be explained away, still we find them full of sublime conceptions of the Supreme Being, the Creator and Ruler of heaven and earth.... Hindus must become Theists before they can ... adopt the means appointed by God [viz. the Catholic faith] to raise man above his created nature to the rank of being heir to the same eternal felicity of which the infinite God is the sole possessor' (Sp-m, February 1896: 'Our Attitude towards Hindu Reformers').

Here we see the rationale for Upadhyay's early preoccupation with Vedic theism. If (educated) Hindus can be convinced of their own distinctive heritage of theism, they will on that basis be receptive to Catholic teaching. In his appreciation of Vedic theism, Upadhyay singles out the Vedic understanding of God and of human sinfulness and its divine forgiveness. His analysis of the Rg Vedic hymn 10.121 (Sp-m, February 1896: 'The Hymn "Ka"')[4] is a good example of how he tackled the first point.

He entitles the hymn 'Ka', because, as he points out, 'each *mantra* (verse) of this [hymn] ends with the query: *Who* [*ka*] is that *deva* whom we should worship with oblation?' The exegesis in fact turns on the first mantra of the hymn which Upadhyay first gives in Sanskrit and then translates, 'Hiranyagarbha was begotten before all. The begotten became the sole lord of creatures. He holds heaven and earth. Who is that *deva* whom we should worship with oblation?' The translation is more or less accurate. The interpretation is revealing.

At the outset Upadhyay skews the interpretation by stating that *hiraṇyagarbha* would commonly mean 'begotten of gold'. In fact, this compound is commonly translated as 'golden germ/egg', though Upadhyay's translation does not do violence to the Sanskrit. His next step is more contentious. Appealing to a 'famous commentary' entitled the *Rijvartha* (more precisely, the *Ṛjvartha,* the commentator Durga's well-known work (circa thirteenth century C.E.), on the ancient authority Yaska's Vedic gloss, the *Nirukta*), he contends that here *hiraṇya* means, not 'gold' but 'wisdom'.[5] So *hiraṇyagarbha* becomes 'begotten of wisdom'.

4 Which, perhaps because of the corrupt edition used, he mistakenly refers to as 10.120.

5 Durga does gloss Yaska's *hiraṇyamaya* (for *hiraṇya*) by *vijñānamaya,* viz. 'consisting of knowledge'. See under *Nirukta* 10.23.

A more or less faithful translation follows of the next two verses of the hymn in which Hiranyagarbha is celebrated for his pervasive grandeur and sovereignty. 'We are Christians,' declares Upadhyay, 'Still we can chant the sukta [hymn] "Ka" in unison with the *rishis* of old. In this hymn we see how the Word of God fills the whole world and enlightens all persons, whatever time or place they may belong to. It is man, man alone who corrupts this universal light of God and deludes himself into errors and falsehoods.' He makes no bones about stating that these errors and falsehoods comprise the accepted interpretation of the hymn by 'later Pantheistic philosophy', namely Advaita, according to which Hiranyagarbha is 'the first product of the illusory self-limitation of Brahman'.

So, Upadhyay has solved the riddle of 'Ka'! For *ka* refers to the 'Word of God'. Further along, he shows only marginally more interpretive restraint. 'Who is this first-begotten?' he asks somewhat rhetorically. 'Is he the same of whom David sang: "The Lord said to me, 'Thou art my son, this day have I begotten Thee"? [Psalm 2.7].... Is he the same who was in the beginning with God, by whom all things were made, and without whom was made nothing that was made? [Jn 1.1–3].' The allusion is clearly to Christ. Upadhyay then goes on to strengthen this allusion by noting 'another very striking thing' about the hymn, namely, that it declares that the world and scripture were produced by sacrificing the first-begotten. What does all this point to? 'We do not want to dogmatise on the matter. At any rate it can be safely concluded from what has been stated above that in the Vedas are found a very sublime conception of one supreme Being, the idea of divine generation somewhat resembling the Christian doctrine of divine Sonship, and an account of the sacrifice of the first-begotten of God the virtue of which supreme act is far-reaching.'

We can see how, then, the Samhitas can become a *preparatio evangelica*. If only his Hindu compatriots would acknowledge these crypto-Christian meanings and take the necessary steps!

As to Upadhyay's preoccupation with Vedic teaching on human sinfulness and divine forgiveness, we may consider his analysis of two Rg Vedic texts, the part-hymn 7.86.3–5 and the whole hymn 1.25,[6] as representative. Both texts invoke Varuna, the deity in Vedic religion most closely associated with the presiding over of order, both moral and natural, out of chaos. Again the first text, ascribed to the

6 Under the titles 'Vedic Idea of Sin' (Sp-m, July 1896), and 'A Hymn to Varuna' (Sp-m, November 1896), respectively.

sage Vasistha, is translated acceptably enough.[7] And again, Upadhyay is keen to stress its universal applicability. 'It should be observed that Vasishtha does not give here his individual belief about sin but the unanimous opinion of all wise men. He feels that he has, on account of sin, incurred the wrath of Varuna and been separated from him' for, as Upadhyay has declared earlier, 'Sin is essentially an offence against God who is our sovereign and father.... By it man incurs the wrath of God. This is the plain verdict of reason and common sense'. Thus Vasistha is echoing the 'primitive belief of man about sin' in sharp contrast to arrogant 'theosophic wiseacres' and 'pantheists' who have perverted this natural insight by regarding sin as the 'outcome of pure and simple ignorance'. This godless doctrine only leads to moral ruin and to misery.

But the more elaborate treatment is of RV 1.25, a hymn of 21 verses that is translated in full. In analysing its content, Upadhyay divides the hymn into two parts: the first deals with the nature of Varuna as representative of deity, the second concerns Varuna's gracious relationship with the human being as repentant sinner. Upadhyay concludes his analysis as follows:

> Varuna is derived from the root *var*, which means to envelope, to cover. It is no unfit name for God whose immensity surpasses the whole universe.... [Varuna] belongs to a time when the belief in one supreme God ... was not yet obliterated by the fantastic plurality of divine beings that made up the later religion of India, and the character ascribed to him is just what a naturally uncorrupted mind ought to think of God ... ruler ... all-powerful, all-wise, the avenger of evil and hater of sin ... forgiving. Man honours him as father, lord ... and judge; he has no excuses for his sins but asks for mercy; he feels sin to be the ... ruin of the life of the body and of the soul ... he implores God to free him, and he will gladly enjoy this life ... for he is still a stranger to the strange doctrine that life is an evil followed by lakhs [hundreds of thousands] of transmigrations.

These analyses were published in 1896. Remarkably, by 1897, the religion of the Rk Samhita as enshrining the high point of Hindu belief, as the natural basis for the reception of the Christian revelation, was supplanted by a reinterpretation of the Vedanta; in short, Vedic theism gave way to Vedantic theism. Let us inquire into this transformation.

[7] The translations may have been Upadhyay's own, but a close comparison with the words and phrases of P. Peterson's translation of both 7.86 and 1.25 in Peterson, 1888, indicates that Upadhyay must have consulted the latter work closely.

It must not be thought that even from the very beginning of his conversion to the Catholic faith, Vedantic religion was unrelievedly condemned. We must be precise about the meaning of 'Vedanta' here. 'Vedanta' as used by Upadhyay and his contemporaries can be understood in two senses: (1) as the Upanishads, the final phase of the Vedic scriptures (hence *vedānta* = the end (*anta*) of the Veda), and (2) as the philosophical-theological school that based its teaching on the Upanishads. In Upadhyay's day, by common consent this was the school of Advaita, as established by the eighth century theologian Shankara. Advaita, as we have mentioned earlier, was generally regarded among the Hindu (and western Orientalist) intelligentsia as the apex of Hindu philosophical and theological thought.[8]

From the very beginning of his conversion, Upadhyay had good things to say about Vedanta in its first meaning and expressed a hesitant admiration for Vedanta in its second meaning, though not, of course, without qualification.[9] We have already reviewed in chapter 6 the reasons for Advaita's high standing in the educated mind at the time, reasons that Upadhyay shared. Let us now indicate the early signs of Upadhyay's appreciation of Vedanta especially in the first sense specified.

In the very first issue of *Sophia* (January 1894), in the article on theism in the Vedas, Upadhyay writes:

> The Vedas themselves profess that sacrifices and oblations can only give wealth, prosperity, long life, or at best a higher state of existence, but cannot give final bliss. It is only the knowledge of God that can emancipate souls from the miseries of ceaseless birth and death, and that knowledge is found in the latter part of the Vedas. (Vide Sankara's Introduction to the Chandogya Upanishad).

8 Today, more properly, 'Vedanta' in its second sense is commonly understood as that philosphical-theological tradition, comprising a number of rival schools, which bases its religious outlook on an interpretation chiefly of the Upanishads. In this understanding Shankarite Advaita is but one school, albeit a very important one, of Vedanta.

9 A 'hesitant' admiration because on the one hand Advaita as 'pantheism' was drawing the Hindu intelligentsia, the leaders of the Hindu masses, away from their spiritual destiny in Christ, while on the other hand, its greatest teacher Shankara was commonly acknowledged as a mind of the highest order. Upadhyay thrills to this estimation when he comments, 'The great Sankaracharya has written a most learned and lucid commentary on [the Brahma] Sutras' ('Vedanta Philosophy I', Sp-m, August 1894).

The article cited earlier, 'Our attitude towards Hinduism' (Sp-m, January 1895), is more to the point. It is in this article, it will be recalled, that Upadhyay draws his important distinction between 'the [religious] truths in Hinduism' as truths of pure reason or 'natural' truths, and those in the Christian (i.e. Catholic) faith as supernatural revelation. But he also claims that nowhere, except perhaps in ancient Greece, has the true light of natural religion 'shone forth so brilliantly as ... in India.... A few verses which we quote below from the Upanishads, the repository of Indian spiritual wisdom, and from [the] Gita, the treasure of the Hindus, will show what a sublime conception the primitive Hindu had of the divine Being.' He then quotes passages from the Isa Upanishad (5, 6), the Kena Upanishad (1.4–6, 2.2) and the *Bhagavadgita* (11.18) in support. These quotations purport to speak of an ineffable, omnipresent, omniscient, imperishable, provident, sovereign, spiritual, personal Supreme Being.

In spite of this fulsome praise for the spiritual insights of the Upanishads, in subsequent analyses of Hindu theism Upadhyay does not consistently develop this appreciation (similarly for the *Gita*); he reverts, as we have seen, to the theism of the Vedic Samhitas as encapsulating the highest Hindu natural religious truths. After all, the Samhitas are the earlier part of the Vedas and as such closer in time to the 'primitive divine revelation', and hence are 'spiritually purer' than the Upanishads or the *Gita*.[10] In time, for reasons we shall consider, this distinction will dissolve away for Upadhyay. But we must also note that in the same article he makes it a point to say that he will not forget to show 'the utter falsity of the prevailing Hindu error of Advaitavad (Pantheism)'. And we have seen what short shrift he gave to Swami Vivekananda's neo-Advaitic interpretation of the Upanishads and of Shankara.

We have recorded towards the end of chapter 6 that during his second lecture-tour of the South in early 1897, Upadhyay had a conversation with Fr John Castets s.j. of St Joseph's College,

[10] There were other sporadic instances of appreciation of Upanishadic religion. For example, in Sp-m, March 1896, he interprets 'A Parable from the Kena Upanishad' as teaching, among other things, 'a strong allegorical protest against polytheism', that 'without the power of God even the gods are helpless' and that 'no being can know God if not enlightened by *Vidya*, the word of God'. Likewise for the *Gita*. Under 'Gita' (Sp-m, June 1895) Upadhyay declares, 'Gita is a treasure-house of Hindu wisdom and piety.... It is the quintessence of the Upanishads.' Nevertheless, he continues, it contains the erroneous doctrines of identifying the supreme soul with individual souls, of transmigration, and of the divinity of Krishna.

Trichinopoly. A letter by Castets quoted in that chapter speaks of 'very subtle discussions' between him and Upadhyay about Upadhyay's desire to investigate 'the possibility of converting the apparent (?) Pantheism of Sankara into a Theism palatable to Catholics'. Clearly, the phrase 'apparent (?) Pantheism' here is significant. Hitherto, as our analysis of Upadhyay's understanding of Shankara has shown (chapter 6), Upadhyay was in little doubt that the received tradition of Advaita, Shankara's or otherwise, was pantheistic. By the time of his conversation with Castets there has been a sea change in his estimation of Advaita. It is now the potential source of a theism palatable to Catholics; Vedantic theism is supplanting Vedic theism. The key text in which this is indicated is the article 'Hindu Philosophy and Christianity' (Sp-m, July 1897).

Though Upadhyay doesn't say so in so many words, from the article it is crystal clear that by 'Hindu philosophy' he means the philosophical-theology of traditional Vedanta, while 'Christianity' is assimilated to Catholic thought. The task of philosophy, says Upadhyay, is not to challenge or change Christian revelation but to support, defend, clarify, expound and develop it and to show its relevance for life. In the past the philosophy of Aristotle, adapted 'of course *minus* its errors' by 'the sovereign intellect of St Thomas Aquinas', has performed this service for the 'Christianity of the Catholic Church'. But though in 'substance' it is everywhere the same, in *form* the Catholic Christianity we have is a western phenomenon and therefore alien to Hindu minds.

The Catholic faith has now finally encountered another brand of philosophy that, though it may contain more errors 'because the Hindu mind is synthetic and speculative, and not analytic and practical', is unquestionably superior to the Aristotelian-Thomistic synthesis. This is the Vedantic philosophical system. Just because the 'neo-Hindus' have used it against the Christian faith is no reason to discard it; rather it should be won over in the service of 'Christianity as Greek philosophy was won over in the middle ages'. Vedanta should be made to 'hew wood and draw water' for the Catholic Church. The Vedantic desire, again assimilated to Hindu religious aspirations *tout court,* has sought, from early [post-Samhita] times, to penetrate to the heart of the divine mystery, affirms Upadhyay. In trying to attain this impossibly exalted end without the divine sanction of supernatural revelation, it has overreached itself and come to some erroneous conclusions. Yet as an expression of the 'natural desire' to know God in himself and as a cumulative attempt to understand the divine mystery in the light of reason it has been unequalled in the annals of philosophical-theological inquiry. Even the errors themselves, the 'heroic struggle to harmonise unity with diversity', the 'desperate attempt to preserve the absolute nature of God by the elimination of the necessary relation between subject and object', that is, the potential Hindu contribution to a doctrine of creation and the interior life of God, are illuminative.[11] The Vedantic heritage must now be put to the service of the Catholic Church in India. Nowhere is the word 'pantheism' even mentioned in this short piece.

This is a remarkable re-evaluation of Vedanta, and various points in it, both explicit and implicit, are worthy of note. It is based on a virtually absolute compartmentalization between the insights of the 'natural' light of reason and supernatural revelation. These two levels literally function like physical building blocks. Aquinas took the insights of 'Greek, viz. mainly Aristotelian, philosophy', purged them of errors, and fashioned them into an intellectual platform on which the grid of supernatural truths (as formulated by the Church of Rome) could be superimposed. The task now facing Indian Catholic theologians (including Upadhyay) is the fairly straightforward one of replacing the Greek platform by a Vedantic one, only in this case, if the construction is done efficiently, the revelational edifice will stand on a sounder footing and be shown to better advantage.

It is significant that Upadhyay is not clear as to whether both western *and* Indian observers will be in a position to appreciate the improved structure or only indigenous Catholics. In other words, he has left unconsidered, perhaps understandably for the time, the questions so central to intellectual deliberations today about interreligious and intercultural commensurability, namely, does truth or religion have an 'essence' or 'substance' detachable from an outward form, can truth in religion arise or be perceived independently of culture-specific or culture-conditioning factors, does it make sense to speak of 'natural' truths and 'supernatural' truths in value-neutral or culture-neutral terms? (and so on). Till the very end Upadhyay leaves such issues undebated, nor does he elaborate in this article, beyond

11 This stress on the long-standing and noble Hindu aspiration to penetrate the divine mystery was a favourite one; it is suggested as the principal reason for the rise of Advaita in the first place. See the article, 'Whence arose Advaitavad in India?' (Sp-m, February 1896). 'The principal cause [for Advaita's arising in India] appears to be the attempt of the Hindu mind to penetrate into the inner life of God, to know him as he is, unrelated and absolute, by means of speculative thought.'

mooting a suggestion or two, on how Vedanta can be made 'the handmaid of Christianity'.[12]

Without wishing to anticipate too much, we can mention here how Upadhyay later attempts to articulate the relationship in certain areas between Vedanta and Catholic belief. He does it not by seeking to implant Christian concepts in Vedantic soil so as to arrive at a genuine first-order indigenization of the Christian faith, but rather by constructing more or less exact correspondences between Vedantic ideas and Thomistic ones so that Vedanta in some respects may be seen as a form of crypto-(neo-)Thomism and Shankara as St Thomas in disguise. This is a mode of transplantation, not of implantation; it also tends to assume that language is made up of more or less complex combinations of word units, each with a specific semantic content (the 'building-block' theory of words), rather than of words whose meaning is derived from context. Further, henceforth when Upadhyay criticizes Vedanta as 'pantheistic', he largely has in mind the 'neo-Vedanta' or 'neo-Hinduism', as he calls it, of Vivekananda.[13] For him, Vivekananda's version is a distortion of the real thing. Yet it was Vivekananda who was the catalyst for Upadhyay's reappraisal of Advaita.

Notwithstanding an ongoing if qualified appreciation by Upadhyay of Upanishadic insights as an expression of natural knowledge about God, his reappraisal of the traditional Advaitic interpretation of the

12 The suggestions comprise (a) the distinction between *ātman* or spirit and *manas*, translated as 'mind', as clearing away to some extent 'the mist which envelops the doctrine of the union of the divine nature with the human in one personality', (b) the Vedantic doctrine of God 'realising himself in spiritual heroes and *avatars*' as illumining the Christian belief that the human destiny is to 'become perfect like God by union with him who is *real* God and *real* Man', and (c) the division of all material objects into the three Samkhya categories of *sattva*, *rajas* and *tamas*, which may give 'a new complexion to the Ascetic Theology which shows the way to perfection'. None of these three suggestions is subsequently developed.

13 That 'neo-Hindu' for Upadhyay generally designates Advaita as interpreted especially by Vivekananda and the like is clear from numerous references; see, e.g. Sp-m, August 1896: 'The *Prabuddha Bharata* or *Awakened India*, a neo-Hindu monthly, published in Madras, has been sent to us for review. Its object is to popularise Vedantism'. Towards the end of the article Upadhyay writes, 'The kernel of Vedanta is, as expounded in the Chicago Parliament of Religions [a clear reference to Vivekananda], that God Almighty somehow or other gets himself tied down to matter and thinks himself as matter.... We are sorry to see that our new contemporary has taken to the advocacy of such a horrid doctrine.' Under 'Notes' in Sp-m, June 1897, Upadhyay refers to the *Brahmavadin*, 'another neo-Hindu journal', as advocating a reprehensible form of Vedanta.

classical Upanishads—in other words, the transition from advocacy of Vedic theism to that of Vedantic theism as the most promising basis for embracing the Catholic faith—seems relatively abrupt. I have yet to come across a satisfactory explanation for it. Yet the reason for Upadhyay's change of mind lies, I believe, in Vivekananda's (unwitting) influence on him. Many years after they parted company to follow different mentors, Upadhyay did not lose track of his increasingly illustrious contemporary. He makes regular references to Vivekananda's activities and ideas in the pages of *Sophia*. In chapter 7, we have noted how he referred somewhat deprecatingly to Vivekananda's participation in the Chicago Parliament of Religions of 1893. But from the time of this sensational debut on the world stage, Vivekananda was a marked man, not only for the educated Indian public, but also for the editor of *Sophia*, who painted him as *the* champion of a new interpretation of Advaita and as such a Pied Piper of a particularly destructive form of pantheism. By his teachings, Vivekananda was leading educated India (Hindus really) astray; he was a chief rival of the work of *Sophia*, whose objective was to lead educated Hindus to Christ (really, the Catholic Church). But Vivekananda's public success was the very reason for Upadhyay's change of strategy.

In January 1897, when Vivekananda returned to India, he was welcomed in the role of conquering hero. He had taken the Chicago conference by storm, and by his teachings that Advaitic social, ethical and religious insights—his 'practical Vedanta'—lay at the heart of all true religion, begun the process of restoring self-esteem to an educated Indian public smarting increasingly under colonial rule. In short, he had enlivened the patriotic cause under the banner of Advaita.

By early 1897 then, Upadhyay was faced with the *fait accompli* of Advaita being regarded as a chief, if not the chief, religious instrument of personal and collective *svarāj*. In effect, Vivekananda was successfully telling the Hindu elite that if they adopted a lifestyle based on fundamental Advaitic insights (as interpreted by him, of course), they would be equipping themselves spiritually, ethically and psychologically for eventual self-rule. This, I believe, is why Upadhyay reassessed the potential of Advaita as a religious propaedeutic for the reception of the Catholic faith. The more his compatriots grew in spiritual and political maturity on the basis of their ancestral tradition, the better they would be prepared to become 'Hindu-Catholics' and achieve fulfillment as human beings. For obvious reasons it would be counter-productive to eulogize Vivekaṅanda's own interpretation of Advaita; that must continue to be derided. It would have to be classical Advaita, which bore the stamp of traditional authority, that was reappraised.

In 'An Exposition of Catholic belief as compared with the Vedanta' (*Sophia,* January 1898), Upadhyay sets to work in earnest to implement his new strategy. Here he announces his intention of showing 'systematically' the extent of the agreement and disagreement between the Catholic religion and Vedanta about 'the principal doctrines that concern the eternal welfare of man, viz. (1) the nature of *Parabrahman* (Supreme Being), (2) His relation with finite beings, (3) the destiny of man, (4) sin, and (5) salvation.' The 'great Sankara' will be his authority for understanding Vedanta. The article concentrates on 'the nature of *Parabrahman*' and declares that Upanishadic descriptions of the ultimate reality as *sat,* 'positive being', *cit,* 'intelligence', and *ānanda,* 'bliss', correspond to the teaching of 'Catholic philosophers [who] arrive by reasoning at the knowledge of God ... [as] ... eternal, one, purely positive, intelligent and supremely happy.'

In fact in this article Upadhyay does little more than offer an interpretation of the Upanishadic passage, 'In the beginning, the Self, indeed, was this; nothing else whatsoever blinked. He thought, "Let me produce worlds"' (Aitareya Up. 1.1.1).[14] This is taken to mean that the ancient sages taught that there is only one supreme, eternal Being, the first creative and intelligent Cause of all beings. 'It is certain that the Vedantic Rishis had a very clear conception of the universe existing ideally in the intelligence of God from eternity.... He ... created that which was beheld. Nothing was created that was not beheld.... We cannot be sufficiently thankful to God Almighty for having imparted this transcendent knowledge of himself to our ancient ancestors.' Nowhere in this article does Upadhyay seek to show where Catholic thought and Vedanta disagree in their understandings of the Supreme Being, and in subsequent analyses Upadhyay focuses almost exclusively on only the first two items on his comparative agenda, i.e. (1) the nature of the Supreme Being as (a) *sat,* (b) *cit* and (c) *ānanda,* and (2) the Supreme Being's relationship to finite reality, which is discussed in terms of the doctrine of *māyā.* We can now consider his analysis of each item in turn.

14 *Ātmā vā idam eka evāgra asīt; nānyat kiṃcana miṣat. sa aikṣata lokān nu sṛja iti.* Upadhyay translates this as follows: 'In the beginning there was only one being; nothing else existed. He beheld: Shall I create the *lokas*?'

(1a) *Parabrahman* or the Supreme Being of the Vedanta as essentially *sat-cit-ānanda* forms the subject of more than one explicitly or implicitly comparative discussion in the *Sophia,* in its monthly and weekly versions. The fullest analysis, however, which may be treated as representative of Upadhyay's views on the matter, occurs in the weekly *Sophia,* and spans five issues (June-July 1900), under the title 'Being'.[15] It is important to note at the outset that Upadhyay was not being innovative in using these three terms to describe the Supreme Being of the Vedanta (in both senses). In the classical Sanskritic tradition, later, post-Shankara Advaita not infrequently used this formula to designate the Absolute[16]; it was based on various Upanishadic and other scriptural descriptions of ultimate reality. In Upadhyay's own time, his former mentor Keshabcandra Sen, expressly referred to the Christian Trinity as *'Sat, Chit, Ananda'*.[17] Upadhyay's originality lay in his attempt to show that the *sat, cit* and *ānanda* of classical Vedanta as a description of ultimate reality corresponded more or less exactly to the understanding of the nature of God of Catholic *natural* theology, that is, neo-Thomistic reasoning about the essence of the divine being.

By now some of this will be familiar, but it is perhaps worth repeating, to show the consistency and tenacity of some of Upadhyay's theological ideas. *Parabrahman* (literally, 'the supreme *Brahman*'), says Upadhyay, is first and foremost *sat* or being. *Sat* here means necessary being, that is, being whose nature it is to exist in and for itself. With the force of 'mathematical proof' it can be shown that such being must be immutable, one, eternal, infinite, conscious and blissful; it is also free, and as such, is the sustaining First Cause of all other, created being. We note in passing that in fact this 'mathematical proof' accords neatly with the neo-Thomistic ideas of logical certainty of the day.

[15] See also, e.g., 'Sat' (Sp-m, October 1898), 'Cit' (Sp-m, March 1899).

[16] See, e.g. the *Atmabodha,* traditionally but probably erroneously attributed to Shankara, vrs. 23, 49, 56 and 64, and the later, well-known *Pancadasi* (in Swahananda, 1980), e.g., vrs. ix.18; xiii.62, 63, 80.

[17] In a lecture, given on January, 21, 1882, entitled, 'That marvellous mystery—the Trinity': 'The Father, the Son, the Holy Ghost; the Creator, the Exemplar, the Sanctifier ... Force, Wisdom, Holiness; the True, the Good, the Beautiful; *Sat, Chit, Ananda;* "Truth, Intelligence and Joy".... Thus the Trinity of Christian theology corresponds strikingly with the *Sacchidananda* of Hinduism.' Keshab's doctrine of the Trinity is not elaborated, however, in orthodox Christian terminology. When the Sanskrit words *sat, cit* and *ānanda* are combined, the compound is written *saccidānanda.*

How can we tell, continues Upadhyay, that *Parabrahman* is immutable? *Parabrahman* must be so, for as absolute *sat* it is self-subsisting: 'it has the reason of its existence within itself' ('Sat', Sp-m, October 1898).[18] Such a being, as necessarily existentially independent of any external being, is not susceptible to change by the agency of an outside force, nor does it change internally, for 'it must be always in a state of actuality.... A being whose essence and existence coalesce, that is, whose essence is an unmodifiable existence, whose duration cannot be divided into stages of a by-gone potentiality and a future actuality, is immutable' ('Being.III', Sp-w, July 1900). We cannot ask for a more neo-Thomistic rationale and vocabulary than that!

Similarly, this Being (= *Parabrahman* as understood by the Vedantic sages, and the God of the neo-Thomist philosophers) is one, infinite and eternal. There cannot be two; if there were two, a distinguishing characteristic would give one 'something which the other has not, thus reducing it to want and destroying its infinity.... Hence infinity is unity; a self-existent being cannot but be one' ('Being. IV', July 1900). Infinity, in fact, is 'fullness of being', which is another way of saying absolute self-subsistence. 'Plenitude is the necessary content of existence *per se* and plenitude is infinitude' (ibid). Again, neo-Thomistic language.

There is little if any reference to Vedantic texts in the serial 'Being' article. There is a half-hearted attempt at supporting exegesis in the earlier 'Sat' article (Sp-m, October 1898). There we are assured at the end that 'the Vedanta calls the eternal Being, *Parabrahman,* the only *Sat, Om Tat Sat.*' *Om* is the mystic syllable of the Sanskritic tradition, referring in Vedantic exegesis to the Supreme Being; *tat* means 'that'. Thus the cryptic formula *Oṃ tat sat* can be translated 'Om, That is Being'. In ancient scripture, it occurs in the *Bhagavadgita* (17.23–26). No doubt the *Gita* is an important source text for classical Vedantic exegesis, including for Shankara. But thus far Upadhyay is taking a great deal for granted in assuming what 'the Vedanta' means by the expression *Oṃ tat sat* as referring to *Parabrahman,* for in his interpretation it virtually means what the neo-Thomists mean in their philosophizings about the nature of God!

(1b) 'The radical meaning of *Cit,*' declares Upadhyay, 'is "increasing", "growing", "becoming more"' ('Cit', Sp-m, March 1899).

18 The same sentence occurs under the heading 'Immutability' in the third part of the serial article mentioned (see July 1900).

This etymology is dubious, but it serves Upadhyay's purposes marvellously, for his whole (implicitly comparative) interpretation of *Parabrahman* as *cit* is built upon the idea of *cit* or consciousness in the form of self-awareness as being self-reproductive, that is, intrinsically propagative. *Parabrahman* is essentially *cit*, says Upadhyay: 'for him to be is to know. It is written in the Upanishads that he grows by brooding (*tapas*)[19] and his brooding is knowledge. He reproduces his self as *Sabdabrahman* (Logos) by *ikshana* (beholding)' (ibid.) The allusion here to the 'procession' or 'generation' of the Son from the Father within the Trinity is clear. Thus the Upanishads dimly prefigure Christian revelation. In the act of self-awareness the Supreme Being, as *Parabrahman* or God, reproduces (i) internally in a necessary way, and (ii) externally, purely contingently.

(1b.i) This feature of the divine knowledge is spelled out in the 'Being' serial as the 'rational' basis for the Christian extrapolation hinted at in the earlier 'Cit' article. 'To be is to act' says Upadhyay, 'and to be related, internally and externally' ('Being.V', Sp-w, July 1900). But he has also said that for the Supreme Being, to be is to know; it follows then that to know entails internal and external relatedness. 'The self-existent Being acts upon itself by intelligence. Its act is self-knowledge.... It is related within the term of its own being as subject and object.... The result of its self-act is an eternal distinction between its knowing self and known self without any division in the substance.' Again, this is a Thomistic concept, the so-called rational basis, of the revealed truth of the existence of the Trinity. According to this basis the generation of the second Person of the Trinity, the Son, occurs as the Image, the self-reflection, of the first Person, the Father, that is, as the known Self begotten of the knowing Self. This is not spelled out, of course, but the implications are latent in the language. So far as we, finite knowers, are concerned, our act of self-awareness requires consciousness of a non-self for its actualization.

> I know that I am, on the condition of bringing the *me* into contact with the *not-me*.... [But] the Infinite cannot go out of itself, for there is no horizon which bounds or limits its being.... Who can understand how the eternal Being mirrors in the ocean of knowledge its infinite Image?.... The Infinite begets itself in thought, is self-knowing and self-known, but what distinguishes the generating self

[19] See, e.g., Taittiriya Upanishad, 2.6.1

> from the eternally generated self cannot be known by any rational process of thinking. Man can only know this mystery of the inner life of the self-existent One if it be revealed to him.

For the knowledgeable Catholic reader (and potential ecclesiastical censor!) the theological implications of this passage are clear—and acceptable. Thomism beckons educated Hindu India, via the Vedanta, to the Catholic Church.

(1b. ii) The Supreme Being's contingent, external relatedness will be dealt with under Upadhyay's treatment of the doctrine of *māyā*.

(1c) But *Parabrahman* (or God) is also essentially *ānanda* or bliss. This aspect of the divine being is not given much comparative attention by Upadhyay. It is treated as a sort of entailment of the other two attributes. For in knowing itself, the 'Infinite ... naturally and necessarily takes delight in the objective self projected by thought.' In traditional Thomistic terminology, this is how the generation of the third Person of the Trinity, the Spirit, is explained. 'The self-existent Being is Bliss,' avers Upadhyay. Here then we have an explanation of the *Parabrahman* of the Vedanta as *Saccidānanda* in terms that are unmistakably neo-Thomistic and as such, it was no doubt hoped, doctrinally orthodox to the increasingly narrowing gaze of ecclesiastical authority.[20]

(2) Nowhere, perhaps, in implementing his agenda does Upadhyay introduce the comparative element more explicitly than in his treatment of the Supreme Being's relationship with finite reality in terms of the doctrine of *māyā*. The analysis starts in a substantial article, 'The true doctrine of Maya' (Sp-m, February–March 1899).[21] Upadhyay begins by hailing 'St Thomas [as] the most accredited representative of the philosophy of the western world, as well as the greatest master of Catholic theology.' Indeed, Thomism synthesizes in an unrivalled way the truths of the various Vedantic schools, being itself 'far more unitary ... in its world-view, than the pure Vedanta school itself [viz. Advaita].' Commensurability, if not synthesis, can go no further when he announces that he will now discuss 'the Thomistic and *Catholic doctrine of maya* [emphasis added]'. In the analysis that follows, Shankara and Aquinas, as representatives of their traditions, perform a *pas de deux*, now openly quoted, now

[20] Upadhyay's personal life in association with the development of his thought is dealt with in the next chapter.

[21] This was a joint issue of *Sophia*. The reason is given in the next chapter.

implicitly interpreted. We are given the impression that their ideas on the subject of the Supreme Being's relationship with the world are interchangeable, separated only by the historical accidents of time and language.

*Māyā,* Upadhyay assures us, is what St Thomas calls *creatio passiva* or 'passive creation', which is 'a quality of all that is not Brahman'; in other words, it is total existential dependence, the continuous receiving of being, not in any self-generating manner, but from the Supreme Being who is the source of all being. Upadhyay then switches to another sense of the word, i.e., 'abundance', which he derives from Shankara's commentary on the *Vedanta Sutras* 1.1.13–14. However, here he is confusing the Sanskrit feminine noun *māyā* with the suffix *-maya* (the latter signifying abundance). In this sense, we are told, created being as *māyā* 'is, as it were, the overflow of the divine being, knowledge and bliss, and results from the desire of Brahman to manifest and impart his own perfections'. Aquinas' work, the *Summa Contra Gentiles,* 2.14, is adduced in support.

We are then given a third, supposedly shared meaning: 'illusion' in the sense of 'wonderful power'. Since created being has no right to existence in itself, since of itself it is 'darkness, falsity and nothingness' (or *tenebrae, falsitas et nihil,* says Upadhyay, quoting St Thomas), it is an illusion to regard finite being as existing in any way apart from the divine being. Creatures 'exist by *maya,* i.e., by the habit of participating in the divine being and springing from the divine act.' Here Vedantic and Thomistic language are fused. Whereas in his early writings the alleged illusionism of traditional Advaita was dismissed as a religiously corrupting form of pantheism (see chapter 6), here the term 'illusion' is rehabilitated by an appeal to Thomistic metaphysics. By extension, *māyā* designates a mysterious form of divine activity, 'neither real nor unreal' (a traditional Advaitic expression), whereby 'the phenomenal multiplicity results from the immutable Unity', and 'being is communicated to the finite'. The conclusion of this point is put in a mixture of Advaitic-Thomistic terminology. '*Maya* is neither real nor necessary, nor unreal, but contingent.'

Finally, we are given yet another, related, meaning of *māyā*. It is 'the fecund divine power (*sakti*) which gives birth to multiplicity.' This last sense is a far cry from the meaning with which Upadhyay began his analysis—that of *creatio passiva.* In Upadhyay's analysis *māyā* becomes a comprehensive comparative term, accommodating diverse aspects, both active and passive, of the Thomistic and Advaitic doctrines of originative causality. So much so that 'from the ontological point of view the Vedanta [i.e. traditional Advaita] is in perfect accord with the Thomistic philosophy.' Truly, this is rehabilitation of Advaita writ large. Yet at the same time, Advaita is made to say nothing really distinctive about originative causality or the relationship between the Supreme Being as creative, and finite reality.

One difference is recorded though—not a difference of view, but a difference of completeness. In one important respect, Advaita stops short of the whole philosophical truth. For Advaita maintains that 'the existence of creatures [including human beings] is like a dream in as much as it is fleeting and phenomenal' (here the dream analogy of Advaita is also rehabilitated), yet 'Catholic theologians hold that man, as man, will live for ever'. How to explain this difference? Upadhyay answers that Advaita is right so far as it goes. Both Advaita and Thomism agree that of themselves creatures 'should and actually they do tend, every moment, to dwindle into nothingness.' Divine revelation, however, has come to the rescue of Catholic theologians by teaching that 'individual souls have been blessed by God to live forever.' This is a perfectly free decision of the divine will that can be known only if God reveals it.

In this article then, not only do we have a fine example of Upadhyay's method in his attempt to rehabilitate traditional Advaita, but we are also told how the natural wisdom of the Advaita is related to the supernatural wisdom of Catholic thought, of the way, in fact, Catholic theology *completes* Advaitic theology. The relationship is not one of reconstruction, least of all of rejection; rather, it is one of completion by a process of addition. Revelational truths in their existing western-Catholic formulation simply need to be superadded to a receptive corpus pre-interpreted as crypto-Thomistic. This leaves very little room indeed for an original formulation of Catholic faith in terms of indigenous tradition.[22] In the process what has been produced, however, is a new, if tendentious, interpretation of traditional Advaita, the very charge Upadhyay indignantly laid at Vivekananda's door! We shall take up this matter later, when we

22 Aleaz, 1994: 214–5, then, confuses the issue when he says that 'Upadhyaya does not reinterpret either of the Vedanta concepts *Saccidananda* and *Maya* to serve as the explanation of a ready made Christian theology. Rather he shows that *Saccidananda* is Trinity and that *Maya* expresses the meaning of the doctrine of creation in a far better way than the Latin root *creare*'. But we have shown that the vehicle of this 'expression' is neo-Thomistic in the first place and therefore not particularly indigenous or original, and that it will not do to say simply that Upadhyay

examine the way Upadhyay's reconstruction of Advaita (especially of *māyā*) was challenged by an Indologist from within the confines of the Catholic Church.

We must now make explicit one further feature of Upadhyay's comparative observations, namely, that the Supreme Being in both the Catholic and Advaitic philosophical-theological traditions is in itself utterly self-sufficient; as such it is not necessarily related to finite reality. In other words, creation or the originative production of being is a completely free, contingent divine act. One could almost say that for Upadhyay this is *the* distinguishing feature of (a correct understanding of) the Supreme Being. The reader will recall how years earlier, even shortly after his entry into the Catholic Church, this was one of the main matters he raised in seeking to clarify his mind in his correspondence with the Stonyhurst theologian B. Boedder (see chapter 5).

Why was this characteristic of the divine being so important? Theologically, because it was seen as bearing on one of the central mysteries of the traditional Christian understanding of God: Does God *need* to create? If so, then God is not self-sufficient and hence is imperfect, especially since the product of his creative act is so manifestly flawed. Conclusion: then there can be no God. But if God does not need to create, why has he done so, and why such an imperfect product? Indeed, a glance at the effects of an alleged creative act raises acute questions about the divine omnipotence, goodness and wisdom, about the very essence of deity itself. A whirlpool of theological inquiry bubbles around the fundamental issue of the nature of the divine being, especially as a potential and actual Creator, and Upadhyay felt the need to plunge in. But more significantly perhaps, psychologically and spiritually, the dynamic immutability of God, the absence of a divine intrinsic and extrinsic necessity to create and the affirmation of God's absolute blissful self-sufficiency acted as a lodestar in a world of shifting identities, cultural uncertainties and personal insecurity. If this patriarchal God was in heaven, all could be right in his world!

---

*shows* (as if this were plain) that *Saccidānanda is* Trinity. For Upadhyay, *Saccidānanda* prefigures on the level of natural reason the fuller, clearer revealed (Christian) truth of the Trinity, a truth which Christian natural theologians (in particular Thomists) have sought to understand with the hindsight of revelation, and whose (Thomistic) vocabulary Upadhyay has unabashedly borrowed to interpret the meaning of '*saccidānanda*'! Does this make him the 'Father of Indian Christian theology', one wonders.

It is perhaps no accident that the classical feminine nouns and principles of traditional Hindu conceptions of originative production—*prakṛti* (or the principle of space and time), *śakti* (the principle of creative power) and *māyā*—were consistently not only de-feminized, but also firmly subordinated to the masculine deity that both Catholic theology and Advaita shared in Upadhyay's understanding.[23] So it is that repeatedly in various observations on the deity, whether in the Hindu or Christian context, Upadhyay harps on the theme of the divine self-sufficiency, on there being no intrinsic need for the Supreme Being to create, to be related outside itself. In the Hindu context this is the meaning he gives to various well-known descriptions of *Brahman*, both scriptural and commentarial.[24] Put another way, Upadhyay's God (whether in neo-Thomistic or reconstructed Advaitic context) was a 'hard-centred' reality: metaphysically self-sufficient, monolithic, apart. Indeed, a very western God. The Hindu deity, on the other hand (at least in the Sanskritic tradition), tends to be 'soft-centred': a polycentric being whose nature spills into the realms of its multifarious outreach, where centres and boundaries are fluid both metaphysically and experientially.[25] Was Upadhyay's reconstructed

23 For example, in the article 'The true doctrine of Maya', no mention is made of the fact that in much traditional Hindu thought (though hardly in classical Advaita) *prakṛti*, *śakti* and *māyā* are generally symbols or forms of the Goddess. Thus mention of *prakṛti* towards the beginning of the article is made simply in terms of 'matter', while both *māyā* and *śakti*, as 'passive' and 'contingent', and 'fecund divine power' respectively, are uncompromisingly marginal and subordinate attributes of the divine nature.

24 For example, 'God is Love. His love can only be and is fully satisfied by loving himself, his own perfections.... His relationship with other beings is not necessary to him, it is contingent. He is equally happy whether he is related or not.... He is *atmarama*, happy in himself' ('The Arya Samajists and Ourselves', (Sp-m, January 1895). For *ātmārāma*, 'resting/rejoicing in the Self' and parallels in Hindu religious literature, see, e.g., the *Narada Bhakti Sutra*, vr. 6, Chandogya Upanishad, 7.25.2 and Mundaka Upanishad, 3.1.4); *Brahman* 'is *asanga*, not in need of any companionship; he is *atmarama*, self-satisfied. He does not require to come out of himself to appease the cravings of his nature.... The whole Hindu tradition is full of the aspiration to arrive at the knowledge of God abstracted from all notions of relationship' ('Whence arose Advaitavad in India?', Sp-m, February 1896; on the use of *asaṅga*, see Brhadaranyaka Upanishad, 3.8.8, 3.9.26, 4.2.4 etc.). 'The supreme Being is called *Nirguna* in Vedanta. The word literally means "having no attribute".... *Nirguna* means that the attributes which relate the Infinite to the finite are not necessary to his being. For example, Creator-hood is not an intrinsic attribute of the divine Nature' (an untitled Note, Sp-w, July 7, 1900).

25 For more on this idea in larger context, see Lipner, 1996.

God likely to penetrate Hindu hearts and minds and draw them to an alien faith?

We are now in a position to appreciate a remarkable hymn composed by Upadhyay in Sanskrit during this phase of his life. The hymn appears in the monthly *Sophia* (October 1898) under the title 'A Canticle'. It is described immediately after, in the Devanagari script, as a *stotra*. Traditionally, *stotras* tend to be sung or chanted, not recited; they consist of eulogistic descriptions or names of their subjects. By and large, this is what we get in Upadhyay's short canticle. Before we consider the hymn, it is worth pointing out that after many years in obscurity it has made an impression in Christian circles in India. In an important article analysing the hymn, G. Gispert-Sauch s.j. notes that the 'hymn was put to music about twenty years ago by Fr R. Antoine s.j., of Calcutta, and was sung in public worship during the International Eucharistic Congress of Bombay in 1964' (Gispert-Sauch, 1972: 60f).[26] This Congress, an extended act of public Catholic worship and solidarity, drew great crowds and publicity, and was attended by Pope Paul VI.[27]

So that even the non-Sanskritist may appreciate the tonal resonance and potential liturgical solemnity of the hymn, a transliteration from the original, which appeared in Devanagari, follows:

*Vande Sac-cid-ānandam.*
*Bhogi-lāñchita-yogi-vāñchita-caramapadam. [Refrain]*

*Parama-purāṇa-parātparam,*
*Pūrṇam akhaṇḍa-parāvaram,*
*Trisaṅga-śuddham asaṅga-buddhaṃ durvedam. [1]*

*Pitṛ-savitṛ-parameśam ajam,*
*Bhava-vṛkṣa-bījam abījam,*
*Akhila-kāraṇam īkṣaṇa-sṛjana-govindam. [2]*

26 Gispert-Sauch adds in a note that the hymn 'is printed in the *Prayer Book and Hymnal*, published for the 38th International Eucharistic Congress of Bombay, 1964 (hymn no. 2). It is also printed with Indian musical notation in *Vandana*, edited by G.M. Dhalla, Bombay, 1968' (p. 60). I have myself sung it or heard it sung on various occasions in India. We shall come to the other, lesser-known Sanskrit hymn of Upadhyay in due course.

27 As we shall see, Antoine made two significant changes to the text of the hymn, presumably to render it more orthodox to Christian ears.

*Anāhata-śabdam anantam,*
*Prasūta-puruṣa-sumahāntam,*
*Pitṛ-svarūpa-cinmaya-rūpa-sumukundam.* [3]

*Sac-cidor melana-saraṇam,*
*Śubha-svasitānanda-ghanam,*
*Pāvana-javana-vāṇīvadana-jīvanadam.* [4]

A reading will reveal the humming resonance of this hymn, emphasized by the rhyming expressions at the end of each verse and the refrain; this gives the *stotra* its singing quality in the context of a rhythm that varies in terms of beat rather than syllable. There has been no attempt to reproduce classical Sanskrit metres.

Further, I detect the influence of well-known invocations in Bankimcandra's famous patriotic novel, *Anandamath,* first published serially in March–April 1880,[28] on this hymn. The novel contains an acclaimed paean to 'The Mother', that is, Mother India, in mixed Sanskrit and Bengali, sung by a senior warrior-monk or *santān,* a 'child' of this mother. This song soon became famous in the nationalist movement, and was first sung at the assembly of the Indian National Congress in 1896. The song, which begins *Vande mātaram,* 'I worship/salute the Mother', contains numerous epithets describing the beauty, fertility and boon-bestowing qualities of the land, not to mention Mother India as the apotheosis of such attributes as wisdom, righteousness and valour etc. The short first stanza, which is in Sanskrit, now follows with a translation: *Vande mātaram. sujalāṃ suphalāṃ malayajaśītalāṃ, śasyaśyāmalāṃ mātaram.* 'I worship/salute the Mother, well-watered, fruitful, cooled by pleasant breezes, the Mother, dark with corn.' Perhaps this is enough to indicate the similarity between the descriptive styles of the two hymns, inclusive of the mode of address, *Vande....* We shall point to another instance of an invocation in *Anandamath* apparently influencing Upadhyay's hymn.

What did Upadhyay have in mind, we may ask, in composing and publishing his canticle? Celebrating as it does the *Saccidānanda,* the one existing, conscious, blissful Being, was it meant to appeal chiefly to Hindu readers? Or was it intended to be an ecumenical, sectarian-free eulogy of the supreme reality? This is how Upadhyay himself explains its rationale: 'The Sanskrit canticle is an adoration of that ancient *Parabrahman* ... according to Catholic faith.... [It] sings of the Father-God (*Parabrahman*), the Logos-God (*Sabda-Brahman*) and the Spirit-God (*Svasita-Brahman*), One in Three, Three

28 See chapter 2, note 47.

in One.' Thus the hymn is unambiguously sectarian. It is meant to express Catholic teaching about the nature of the Blessed Trinity. But this is only part of the picture. The hymn is composed in Sanskrit, traditionally not a linguistic matrix of the official teaching of Christian doctrine, yet no attempt has been made to create or import neologisms from a non-Sanskritic source. The hymn is a Sanskritic articulation of Catholic doctrine. It is here that we can speak significantly of a different kind of resonance and even originality in Upadhyay's hymn. These pertain to the way Sanskrit expressions with traditional Hindu resonances are made to yield Christian meanings. Once it is accepted that the traffic is all one way, that it is Upadhyay's intention to put Sanskritic Hinduism to the service of Catholic teaching rather than to *reconstruct* Christian insights in the indigenous fires of a Sanskritic crucible so as to re-form Christian doctrine, then one has to acknowledge how masterfully Upadhyay has achieved his purposes. This is straightforward fulfillment theology at its most brilliant.

Upadhyay's own English rendering of the hymn errs generously on the side of Christian terminology.[29] Our own annotated translation follows:

> I worship [the One who is] Being, Knowledge, Bliss,
>
> The Highest Goal, whom ascetics yearn for but the worldly dismiss. [*Refrain*]
>
> The Supreme, Ancient, Higher than the high,
> [Who is] Fullness, Wholeness, Beyond yet nigh.
> The Pure Threesome, unrelated Wisdom, Hard to comprehend. [1]
>
> The Father, Impeller, Highest Lord, Unborn,
> The Seedless Seed of the tree of being,
> The universal Cause, who a watched-over creation doth tend. [2]
>
> The Word unsounded, Infinite,
> The Person begotten, supremely Great,
> The Substance of the Father, Form of knowledge, our saving Friend. [3]
>
> The One who from the union of Being and Knowledge doth flow,
> The Sacred Breath and Cloud of Joy,
> Who Cleanses, Moves swiftly, Speaks the Message and life intends. [4]

It will be noticed that while the refrain and first verse celebrate the Trinity as absolute being, consciousness/knowledge and bliss, the

[29] Gispert-Sauch's translation (1972) is much stricter.

succeeding verses eulogize the Father, the Son and the Spirit respectively. Though expressed in Sanskrit, the hymn is quite orthodox in that there is no obvious attempt to reformulate an understanding of the Trinity in reconstructive indigenous terminology. The first person is still referred to as the 'Father' (*pitṛ*) who is the unbegotten (*aja*), impelling (*savitṛ*), universal, intelligent cause of being. There is possibly one interesting potential innovation in the first verse. The last term describing the Father is *govinda,* an appellation in Hindu tradition used most distinctively of Krishna, hailed in the Vaishnava tradition and more universally in Upadhyay's day through the increasingly non-sectarian popularity of the *Bhagavadgita,* as one of the two most important descents in human form of the deity (Rama being the other). There might be scope for elaborating a theology in which the Father is likened in familiar accessibility, if not in character, to Krishna. But this idea was far from Upadhyay's mind, for he was fully aware that traditional Christian doctrine precluded the first person of the Trinity, the 'Father', from being regarded as incarnate or descending into the world in any real sense. This act of solidarity with the world was reserved for the second person, the 'Son'. Thus, to play safe, Upadhyay translates *govinda* as 'the preserver of the world', an orthodox if anodyne phrase, though he might have been a little bolder and settled for the linguistically acceptable 'Cowherd'.[30]

The next verse, dedicated to the second person of the Trinity, refers to the Son as the 'Word' (*śabda*), begotten (*prasūta*) of the Father, the image or substance of the Father (*pitṛsvarūpa*), of the form of consciousness (*cinmayarūpa*), and our Saviour (*sumukunda*). All these epithets follow the official teaching of the Church.[31] Finally,

30 Gispert-Sauch opts for the more Biblical 'Shepherd'. Once more, I detect the influence of *Anandamath* on Upadhyay's use of *govinda.* Early in the novel, a young woman with babe in arms is being pursued by ghoulish marauders in a forest. As she collapses, exhausted and on the point of discovery, she hears the refrain: *Hare murāre madhukaiṭabhāre, gopāl gobinda mukunda śaure, hare murāre madhukaiṭabhāre.* This is an invocation to the Lord Krishna; it was uttered by her rescuer, one of the warrior-monks. Two of the epithets of Krishna here are *govinda* and *mukunda,* both well-known Vaishnava terms. It may be that Upadhyay derived these descriptions of the Supreme Being (see further for *mukunda*) from this source. In Antoine's edition, *govinda* was discarded—no doubt to expunge its Hindu resonance as Gispert-Sauch notes—and replaced by *viśveśam* (Lord of all); this was an unfortunate substitution, since reasons of censorship apart, it destroys the rhyming ending of the original and overlaps semantically with 'Highest Lord' (*parameśam*) in the first line of the verse.

31 *Mukunda,* which literally has the sense of 'Giver of salvation/liberation', is also a name of Vishnu (and sometimes of Siva). This is the second term Antoine replaced in his edition; his substitute was *Jiśu-Kriṣṭam.* Once more the rhyme is lost. For a comment on the provenance of *mukunda* for Upadhyay, see previous note.

the last verse speaks of the 'holy Breath/Spirit' (*śubha-svasita*), who proceeds from the union of Being and Knowledge, Father and Son, whose essence is bliss, and who purifies, quickens and inspires—this being the very soul of orthodox description of the Spirit. So we are not talking about radical theological reinterpretation here. And it is no surprise that the cold glare of ecclesiastical officialdom, which kept his activities firmly in its sights, let the hymn pass without comment. For the relevant authority, if it cared to evaluate the hymn, must instinctively appreciate that, far from being theologically subversive, it eulogized, almost word for word in the Sanskritic tongue, an entirely neo-Thomistic and orthodox divine being.[32]

But this does not mean that Upadhyay did not achieve something significant in the composition of the canticle. To begin with, it was quite something for a Catholic, in the context of a doctrinally and, as we shall see, at the highest levels administratively repressive hierarchy, to publicly 'dialogue' with a traditionally non-Christian language in this way and to demonstrate its malleability for his purposes. This was a pioneering beginning. Nor was any attempt made to divorce the terminology of the hymn from its cultural roots. On the contrary as we have noted, Hindu resonances abound (it is just that their undeniable Hindu potential is kept firmly suppressed). Gispert-Sauch (1972: 60f) has shown how steeped the hymn's vocabulary is especially in the language of the classical Upanishads and the *Gita*. Upadhyay's faith, he concludes, has been 'proclaimed in such a way as not to appear completely extraneous to the religious history of India' (a significant use of 'completely'). In Upadhyay's day and circumstances, this was a marked and influential achievement, the model for a number of subsequent rich, cross-cultural meditations—by Christians it must be said—on the nature of the Trinity as *Sac-cid-ānanda*.[33] And here lies the rub. The 'dialogue', in this respect, has

32 In an interesting article in *The Church Times* (November 4th, 1910), praising Upadhyay's attempts to culturally root his faith, the well-known later associate of Gandhi, C.F. Andrews, says, before giving the translation of both of Upadhyay's Sanskrit hymns, 'He published and used constantly in his own devotions the following two canticles of praise. His disciples used them also, and carried copies about with them wherever they went' (p. 618). Earlier Andrews had said intriguingly, 'Some day I must tell [Upadhyay's story] in full, for I have lived in close contact with one of his most intimate disciples.' I have not been able to detect who this might have been.

33 Of which Gispert-Sauch's (1972) is one, and the well-known Swami Abhishiktananda's book, *Saccidananda: a Christian Approach to Advaitic Experience* (1974), another.

been one-sided, initiated and sustained by Christians—in fact, it has been something of a monologue. Hindus seem not to have been drawn in, perhaps because they still perceive the invitation to dialogue as being intended, in the manner expressed by the hymn, to 'fulfill' Hindu insights in a triumphant Christian conclusion.

There is a further problem, one that did not register with Upadhyay, and that is only beginning to be grasped by Christian dialogists in India today: the problem of holding up *Sanskritic* paradigms, which the hymn clearly does, as the models for an ideal Hindu-Christian dialogue and/or synthesis. Where does this leave the non-Sanskritic or counter-Sanskritic paradigms of so many Hindu castes and communities, a large number of which are beginning to perceive themselves as long-standing victims of religious, social, economic and political oppression by Sanskritic norms and practices? On the Hindu side, Upadhyay's dialogic poles were exclusively and unabashedly Sanskritic. In a later chapter we shall comment on the prospects of such encounter, but Upadhyay's experiments in this regard have contributed richly to the shaping and focus of the ongoing discussions of today, at the very least by creating anew an atmosphere of the *felt possibility* of prospective dialogue.[34]

Upadhyay's ideas were not developing in a vacuum, of course. They were being formulated in the context of vigorous activity on a number of fronts, not least a looming confrontation with ecclesiastical officialdom. It is to these aspects of his life that we now turn.

34 Upadhyay is mentioned in a more or less positive dialogic light by various Christian thinkers, e.g. C.F. Andrews (in the article cited above), Dom Henri le Saux o.s.b. (alias Swami Abhishiktananda) 1964, Jarrett-Kerr, 1972: ch. 16, Boyd, 1974, Aleaz, 1979, 1994, 1995. See also the earlier Bibliography under Appendix II of Gispert-Sauch, 1972.

It is interesting to note that between the Sanskrit text of the canticle and its comment and translation, Upadhyay interposed in Devanagari script, but without a translation, his version of the Lord's prayer. A faithful English translation would read: 'Our Father, who lives in the heavenly realm (*dyuloka*), holy is your (*tava*) name to us. May your kingdom (*sāmrājya*) extend (*virājatām*) to earth (*iha*), may your decree (*śāsita*) be obeyed on earth as in heaven. Give us (*dehi dehi naḥ*) this day our daily sustenance (*ājīvana*), and free us from our sins (*pāpān*) as we free those who do us harm (*aśubhakṛt*). Do not lead us into temptation (*pralobhana*), but protect us (*trāhi*) from evil (*asat*). Amen.'

# Chapter 9

## The Flames of Recrimination: A Hindu-Catholic Monastery

On the feast of St Benedict (March 21) 1950, a small hermitage called Saccidananda Ashram was formally established on the banks of the Kaveri by the village of Tannirpali and only about a mile and a half from the larger village of Kulittalai in Tamil Nadu, under the guiding presence of two remarkable men, the Abbé Jules Monchanin (Swami Parama Arubi Anandam, 1895–1957) and the Benedictine monk Henri le Saux (Swami Abhishiktananda, 1910–1973). The ashram nestled in a mango grove, which the founders named 'Shantivanam' (wood of peace). The ashram in Shantivanam is now well known and has grown considerably in size and influence in the ongoing if patchy Christian experiment to indigenize the faith in India. As the two Swamis themselves indicate,[1] they were, in the words of one authoritative chronicler, 'responding to the call of Brahmabandhav Upadhyaya to the Church in India to be truly Indian and to abandon its western "clothing".'[2] That call had been voiced, in the context of similar aspirations, over 50 years earlier. Let us examine Upadhyay's efforts towards establishing his experimental ashram.[3]

It was not enough for Upadhyay, as we have seen, to be a thinker of thoughts, to disseminate ideas; he was essentially a *karmayogī*, a

1. See Monchanin and le Saux, 1964: 17, 28, 32, 66.

2. Stuart, 1989: 43. See also Abhishiktananda, 1959: first frontispiece, pp. xvii–xix, 14, 23, 37–8, 79 etc. The book consists of three main parts: a Memoir about Monchanin, a 'Garland of Memories' by several authors, and excerpts from Monchanin's writings. Though the name of the author/editor is not given, it was Abhishiktananda who wrote the Memoir and compiled the work (see Stuart, 1989: 127f.).

3. In the ensuing discussion we follow Upadhyay's example and use 'ashram', 'monastery' and *maṭha* interchangeably.

man of action. In the first year of *Sophia*'s publication, in an article entitled 'Conversion of India—an appeal' (October 1894), he proposed that 'the Indian Bishops should combine together and establish a central mission.' This mission would 'engage the services of itinerant missionaries who should travel all over the country and confront the principal teachers of Pantheism, Theosophy and other anti-theistic religions and hold public discussions with them.' Earlier in the article he had declared that the three doctrines that 'God is all, all is God; God, man and matter, all three are eternal; [and] the doctrine of transmigration'—views that morally and theologically represented anti-theistic positions in his understanding of this expression—were mainly responsible for preventing Hindu India from fashioning a firm base of 'true theism', that is, 'the religion of natural reason' and 'the preamble of faith', upon which 'the structure of the supernatural religion of Christ' could confidently be laid. The central mission would school the itinerant missionaries—the Catholic Church's elite corps of shock troops—in the knowledge and ability to overcome their anti-theistic rivals. After all, Upadhyay pointed out, the Arya Samaj, which had its headquarters in Lahore, operated on similar principles.

Upadhyay then describes the life-style of the members of the proposed central mission.

> People have a strong aversion against Christian preachers because they are considered to be destroyers of everything national. Therefore, the itinerant missionaries should be thoroughly Hindu in their mode of living. They should, if necessary, be strict vegetarians and teetotalers, and put on the yellow *sannyasi* garb. In India a *sannyasi* preacher commands the greatest respect. The central mission should, in short, adopt the policy of the glorious old Fathers of the South. The missionaries should be well-versed in Sanskrit, for one ignorant of Sanskrit will hardly be able to vanquish Hindu preachers.

The mission should also have a journal, supported by the Bishops which would further its cause. There are several points of interest in this extract. Upadhyay stresses the importance of the yellow sannyasi garb for his itinerant preachers. A couple of months later, as we have noted, he himself donned the saffron robes. Among other things perhaps by this he intended to signal his desire to head the mission. Further, he was shrewd enough to indicate that he was not proposing something entirely new. A similar experiment had won ecclesiastical approval in the past. The 'glorious old Fathers of the South' was a reference to the endeavours of de Nobili, Beschi and others of the seventeenth and eighteenth centuries. Note too that it was taken for granted that the missionaries would conform to traditional Sanskritic rules and practices. This was to be the image of the Catholic Church as it sought to indigenize the faith in the face of 'a deep-rooted impression [created by 'Protestantism'] that Christianity is synonymous with denationalisation.' For Upadhyay Sanskritization was synonymous with a national Church and an indigenous faith.

It is only in February 1897 that a fresh appeal is launched in *Sophia*. Religiously, India is in a desperate situation, we are told. The 'infernal errors' propagated especially by 'Annie Besant's as well as Vivekanand's propaganda' are seducing educated people from their original, sublime belief in a personal God who has created the world and rewards the just and punishes the wicked.

> A score of learned and zealous missionaries, holy men, of ascetic habits, and a metaphysical turn of mind issuing from a common centre of operations established in India, subject to a common central authority, travelling all over India, giving lectures and holding public disputations with learned Pundits—can, we feel sure, transform the face of educated India within a few years.... It is not to be supposed that we wish to limit the aim of the proposed itinerant mission to the establishing of fundamental principles of religion. No, we desire at the same time that the preaching of the whole doctrine of Christ should form an important part of its programme. We appeal to the noble dignitaries of the Church to give this matter their serious consideration ('The Impending Crisis—An Appeal').

The noble dignitaries of the Church were taking their time. To be fair, it was a revolutionary proposal. Though Upadhyay had been careful to stress the centralizing character of the mission in both appeals (he knew his Church), he was asking for money and backing for an experiment that hadn't exactly been a glowing success when tried by 'the glorious old Fathers of the South'. He himself was a recent convert to the faith, something of an *agent provocateur*, long on new schemes and short on reticence (his dignitaries knew *him*). His central mission could lead to misunderstanding and conflict, not only among Catholics and non-Catholics, but also in the sensitive political atmosphere of the Church's relationship with its colonial rulers. So the Church's authorities were in no particular hurry to respond.

In the intervening years Upadhyay had not been idle in trying to give substance to his scheme, both behind the scenes and in the public forum. We have already discussed his eye-catching appearance, his first successful tour of the South (in 1896), his showdown with Annie Besant in Karachi in December of the same year. This itinerant sannyasi, at any rate, was making an impact in the desired manner. Was he not the right person to support on a venture that would result in more of his kind? After publishing the appeal quoted above, he undertook in March-April his second lecture-tour of the South. It was also at about this time, as already noted, that he seriously considered the rehabilitation of (classical) Advaita as the most fitting expression of the indigenous natural religion required to act as receptor for the supernatural faith of his Church. The watershed article, 'Hindu Philosophy and Christianity', mentioned in chapter 8, appeared that July. In short, Upadhyay was shaping the intellectual content of the proposed ashram's programme.

*The Blade* informs us that towards the end of 1897 Upadhyay travelled from Bombay to Calcutta, where he made a prolonged stay before returning to Sind. In Calcutta, in keeping with traditional sannyasi practices, he declined to live with his family. He stayed with a former Brahmo acquaintance, 'cooked his own food and maintained himself on alms.... On the 28th February 1898, he was joined by a Sannyasi fellow-worker [Animananda] from Sindh. Cymbals in hand, the two went about singing hymns in Bengali and Sanskrit and receiving alms' [Bl., pp. 69–70]. What an extrovert Upadhyay was![4] Yet the wandering sannyasi life, mooted in the earlier appeals, was obviously exerting an increasing hold on him, both practically and as a dream in terms of the ashram, for the future.[5]

The record shows that for the rest of 1898, seeking to establish the ashram and define its image and programme dominated Upadhyay's activities. Under 'A Catholic Monastery in India' (Sp-m, May 1898), Upadhyay declares that it was the ancient monastic system of the west that consolidated the influence of the Catholic Church.

4 *The Sketch* (pt. 1, p. 75) records two of these Bengali hymns. As a sample, here is one, with the Bengali and our translation: *āji ānande gāo sabe naraharinām, narahari narahari naraharinām. kumārī-dulāl bāla jagatpāl, darśan kari hay pūrṇa manaskām. kāler svāmī prabhu antarjāmī, kālbaśe āsi tini dilen paritrāṇ.* 'Today, all sing with joy Narahari's name, Narahari, Narahari, Narahari's name. When I see the Virgin's infant child, Saviour of the world, my heart's desire is sated. The master of time, the Lord, the inner Ruler, he came bound to time and saved us.'

5 *The Sketch* notes that at this time 'Upadhyayji's mind was now occupied with but one thought—to establish a *Matha* [monastery]. He went about from place to place, seeking advice and guidance' (pt. I, p. 23).

And 'monastic life is exceedingly congenial to the soil of India'. In fact, he continues, perhaps a trifle wishfully, there are plenty of ashrams 'presided over by famous *sannyasis*' in India, whose itinerant ascetic disciples continue to spiritualize the Hindu. Their 'Hindu Catholic' counterparts, trained in the ashram he proposes, are the best hope of the Catholic Church for the conversion of India. This challenging expression, 'Hindu-Catholic', appears again, in similarly defining circumstances, in an important article published in *Sophia* that July. The article is entitled, 'Are we Hindus?' Where religious faith is concerned, answers Upadhyay editorially, we are Catholic. This is a universal faith, proclaiming universal truths, transcending the particularities of country and race. But 'by birth we are Hindu and shall remain Hindu till death.' To be Hindu in this sense prescinds from the content of belief. Hindus have always believed different things, from monism to various forms of theism, without ceasing to be Hindus. To be Hindu is to be prone to a certain way of thinking and living; it is an orientation in the world. 'We are more speculative than practical, more given to synthesis than analysis, more contemplative than active.' Further, in our life-style, affirms Upadhyay, 'in observing caste ... in eating and drinking ... we are genuine Hindus'.

Upadhyay then makes a crucial nexus for his purposes. The more committed one is to the Catholic faith, the more one follows the 'genial inspiration of the perfect *Narahari* (God-man), our pattern and guide', he declares, the better 'Hindu' does a Hindu become, 'the more we love our country.' This link between Catholic devotion to Christ and patriotism is neither explicated nor justified. But clearly it serves his cause well to state it. We have seen earlier that elsewhere Upadhyay attempted to justify it on the grounds of his Cartesian-like distinction between natural and supernatural: Catholic teaching proclaimed that the natural could act as a suitable receptor for the supernatural. Hence Hindu 'naturalism', living and thinking as a Hindu, was compatible with Catholic supernaturalism or faith. But the leap from potential to actual compatibility here is a crucial one and requires justification, not to mention the statement that Catholic faith actually enhances patriotism. Upadhyay never actually sought to argue this stance. It was taken for granted.

Upadhyay concludes this short article with another Cartesian statement: 'We are Hindus so far as our physical and mental constitution is concerned, but in regard to our immortal souls we are Catholic. We are *Hindu* Catholic.' By implication, the human being is split in two: on one side there is an immortal soul, detached from context, space and time, the inhabitant of a world of universal and timeless revealed truths; on the other side there is a body and mind embroiled in the empirical reality of thinking and behaving. On the basis of this division, it is all the more easy to affirm and follow one's 'Hinduness'.

With respect to the proposed *maṭha*, however, was Upadhyay somewhat grandly envisioning himself as a famous sannyasi of the Catholic Church, presiding over conquering armies of theological combatants in the battle for India's soul? He was given to dreaming dreams, as we have seen, and the heady fantasies of martial victory that filled his thoughts during the youthful escapades to Gwalior—about which he writes so nostalgically towards the end of his life—were now replaced by dreams of a different kind. These dreams would fade in the glow of rising flames of recrimination.

The ashram should train two kinds of renouncers, continues Upadhyay: the contemplative and the itinerant. The first would remain in the ashram, working the land in an effort to make the community self-sufficient and bringing down God's blessings on the world by their life of meditative ascesis. The second would endeavour to penetrate 'the darkest nooks and corners of India' in their campaign to evangelize the land. 'The proposed institution ... should be conducted on strictly Hindu lines. There should not be the least trace of Europeanism in the mode of life and living of the Hindu Catholic monks. The *parivrajakas* (itinerants) should be well versed in the Vedanta philosophy as well as in the philosophy of St Thomas.'

In the article Upadhyay makes a significant observation. He declares: 'Several Bishops and missionary priests do not only share with us this conviction but have promised encouragement and help in the undertaking of starting a *Matha* (monastery) in India.' The next article on the monastery ('Our New Scheme', Sp-m, July 1898) is devoted to showing how much support he is getting for his plan. He has received encouragement from many quarters, he says. He quotes 'a learned and venerable priest' who observes approvingly that his 'starting point is the principle of *accommodation* to the genius of the Indian people. This principle is quite in accordance with the mind of the Holy Church....' The readers are told that another 'who holds a very high position and is responsible in a large measure for moulding the character of the coming generation of the Indian priesthood' believes that the idea of the monastery will, if submitted to the authorities in Rome, win immediate approval. A bishop, we are informed, 'has been gracious enough to offer his apostolic protection and patronage to the monastery if it be lodged within his diocese', while an enthusiastic 'European gentleman ... has actually selected a site for the monastery' and has promised to help in securing it. Finally Upadhyay quotes from an 'appreciative leader' in the *Catholic Watchman* (published in Madras): 'When Catholic exponents of the truth appear before [Hindus] with all the dignity and sacredness of their own Sannyasis, and with no trace of Europeanism about them, the Hindus are sure to give them a respectful hearing, as we see in the case of Upadhyayji himself.' Encouraging no doubt, but one cannot but remark on the conditional and somewhat nebulous nature of the cooperation offered. It is as if the salient anonymity of the people concerned were an indication that each was prepared to cooperate provided the others broke cover first.

In August that year ('The Clothes of Catholic Faith', Sp-m), a new twist was given to the shaping of the monastery's image. A note of desperation seems to enter Upadhyay's anxious efforts to legitimate his unconventional scheme. He must show to the satisfaction of the authorities that, on the one hand, the Catholic faith is universal, and on the other, it can be most effective in India only in indigenous garb. He begins with a bold move. 'The Sanskrit words *ka* and *sthala* mean "time" and "land" respectively. If we join the two words and form an adjective we get the compound *kāsthalika*, which means 'pertaining to all times and lands'. Hence *kāsthalika* or Catholic faith is a faith which extends to all ages and climes.' Even the name of the faith (and by extension of the monastery) lends itself to a Sanskrit equivalent!

This very same faith, supernatural at source, ancient in origin ('The Catholic religion was revealed to man as soon as he was created,' but declined in time owing to human frailty so that a new revelation was needed), essentially one though intended for all, must adapt to circumstances if it is to fulfill its destiny and evangelize the world. In India it must come across as indigenous, preferably Vedantic (as understood by Upadhyay). 'In our humble opinion it is the foreign clothes of Catholic faith that have chiefly prevented our countrymen from perceiving its universal nature.... Our Hindu brethren cannot see the sublimity and sanctity of our divine religion because of its hard coating of Europeanism.' Upadhyay, perhaps unwisely, goes on to give examples of this unseemly carapace. He mentions the 'supernatural virtue of poverty' as generally practised by the Catholic clergy. Such practice makes little impact on Hindus. 'They cannot understand how poverty can be compatible with boots, trousers and hats, with spoon and fork, meat and wine.' These are 'objects of luxury' to the Hindu. Rather, in the way of de Nobili and others, to make an impression poverty must be practised 'in *Hindu* clothing, poverty synonymous with abstinence from meat and drink, living as mendicants in humble dwellings'.

One may well wonder how Upadhyay's Catholic episcopal readers, European to a man, and on the whole not averse to a little meat and wine, would have taken to criticism that in effect discredited their way of life. Perhaps in a manner reminiscent of John's Gospel 9.34. Upadhyay then moves on to criticizing the current mode of teaching the Catholic message. 'Our missionary experiences have shown us how unintelligible the Catholic doctrines appear to the Hindus when presented in the Scholastic garb. The Hindu mind ... is opposed to the Graeco-Scholastic method of thinking. We must fall back upon the Vedantic method in formulating the Catholic religion to our countrymen.' The Vedanta must be purged of its errors, no doubt, but this can be done. 'Were not Plato and Aristotle also guilty of monumental errors?' Another sweeping criticism of current practice is implied here. And would the authorities, we may ask, be expected to appoint Upadhyay, a fairly recent convert himself, to lead this theologically complex reversal of a well-established trend? By this time, the reader will recall, Upadhyay's rehabilitation of 'Vedantic theism' in the pages of *Sophia* (e.g. 'An Exposition of Catholic belief as compared with the Vedanta', January 1898) was well under way (see our analysis of this theme in chapter 8). Perhaps he would have been better advised to formulate the problem more sensitively and his proposed scheme as no more than a cautious experiment in the first instance.

Indeed, his impetuousness in the matter had begun to ring alarm bells in the corridors of ecclesiastical authority, among those wearers of 'boots, trousers and hats' and partakers of 'meat and wine' and exponents of the uncongenial 'Graeco-Scholastic method of thinking' whom he so openly called to account as purveyors of the Catholic faith in India. Probably unknown to him, on June 12, 1898, Archbishop Theodore Dalhoff s.j. of Bombay had written to Monsignor Ladislaus-Michael Zaleski, the Apostolic (Papal) Delegate to India, and the highest Catholic ecclesiastical dignitary in the land, drawing his attention to Upadhyay's project and requesting advice.[6] Why had Dalhoff initiated this action? Sind, the base of Upadhyay's activities,

6 The sequence of correspondence on this matter is given in Bl., pp. 81–2. None of the letters have come to hand.

had been assigned to the Archdiocese of Bombay, which was under Dalhoff's jurisdiction. As a Catholic activist Upadhyay was, in a manner of speaking, Dalhoff's responsibility. Dalhoff was anxious to know what his Church's Papal representative thought of this unconventional and increasingly publicized project.

It would be as well at this point to make Zaleski's acquaintance. Zaleski, a Lithuanian, was Papal Delegate to the subcontinent from 1892 to 1916 and resided in Kandy (in the north of Ceylon, today Sri Lanka but at the time part of the subcontinental Raj). LOE describes him as 'a great nobleman by birth and education'[7]; nevertheless, he was totally unsympathetic to non-western cultures and religions. We quote in support excerpts from his *Epistolae ad Missionarios* [Letters to Missionaries], Part II.[8]

> Christianity alone can bring civilisation. Heathenism, whatever form it assumes, may sometimes take an exterior appearance of civilisation, but it always leaves the soul of the people plunged in barbarity and superstition. There is no civilisation outside Christianity. Christianity made Europe the leading continent of the world, and Christianity alone has in itself the power to civilise other countries. Therefore, I say, the progress of the Catholic Faith in India, is the progress of India' [Letter 23.II, November 22, 1904; pp. 123–4).

> Heathenism in India, under whatever form it appears: Hinduism, Buddhism, or the indefinite worship of the aborigenous tribes, is nothing but demonolatry mixed with fetishism' [Letter 11, p. 57].

These extracts assimilate Christian religion at its best to the Catholic faith, and identify Christianity with western civilization. Western civilization is civilization proper; Indian civilization and Indian religions (lumped together as 'heathenism', one of Zaleski's favourite expressions) are on the whole an expression of barbarism (not to mention demonolatry). It is hard to see how such an attitude of utter contempt for and horror of Hindu practice and thought could, even from the outset, generate the least sympathy for Upadhyay's project.

But Zaleski was also a high authoritarian in an ecclesiastical tradition not noted for its latitudinarianism. Hear him again:

7 September 1928, in a review of Väth; see p. 6. The BCE, in a leading article on Zaleski (February 24, 1900), says that he was born 'from parents connected by birth and alliance with the highest and most ancient aristocracy'.

8 Mangalore, 1915.

> In the Catholic Church, the duties towards God are so strictly bound with the duties of a good citizen that one could not consider as a good Catholic a man who is not loyal and faithful to his Sovereign, because all authority comes from God and he who rebels against authority does not fulfil the political programme which our Lord Jesus Christ imposed on the Catholic Church when he said: Reddite ergo quae sunt Caesaris Caesari et quae sunt Dei Deo [Return to Caesar the things that are Caesar's and to God the things that are God's] [Letter 23.II, op. cit., p. 125].

> Loyalty, submission and reverence to their legitimate rulers should be the distinctive badge of every Catholic [Speech on March 21, 1901; p. 426].

> I dislike very much and emphatically disapprove the so-called intercollegiate matches and sports between catholic and non-catholic schools [Letter 71, p. 366].

> Needless to say that a Catholic daily paper should always be rather of a conservative shade; rather support Government than join the opposition [Letter 24, Oct. 2, 1905, p. 142].

> Ask yourselves if you are not sinking slowly into the pit, allowing yourselves sometimes to treat lightly the laws, the discipline, the customs of the Church; criticising the orders of your superiors, principally of your Bishops, or tacitly agreeing with those who do so, nourishing in your hearts too lenient feelings towards heretics and other enemies of God, and excusing them on the plea of good faith [Apostolic Message to the Clergy of India, November 26, 1908; p. 497].

Some of this may be interpreted as an expeditious expression of prudence in the face of British rule allied to an established Church that was not Roman Catholic, or as paternalistic concern for a relatively little band of indigenous clergy only recently established and struggling to find their feet in overwhelmingly non-Christian surroundings. After all, it was Zaleski who played a significant role in the founding of the Pontifical Seminary at Kandy (which formed part of his jurisdiction) in 1893 for 'the training of native clergy' in greater India.[9] Nevertheless, the underlying intolerance of the man for the ancient

9 'In 1884 Leo XIII sent the first Apostolic Delegate to India, Mons. Achile Gagliardi. The Delegate was accompanied by a Polish Monsignore as his Secretary, Ladislas M. Zaleski. In addition to his office as Secretary, the latter was charged by Rome with a secret mission. He had to study the possibilities of establishing a general Seminary

cultures and religions of the subcontinent rasps through his words.[10] We now have an idea of the formidable opponent Upadhyay faced in his bid to win ecclesiastical approval for his scheme. The stance each brought to the potential role of Hindu tradition in evangelizing India could not be further apart.

Not unexpectedly then, 'Zaleski strongly opposed the project, asking Mgr Dalhoff to inform Upadhyay accordingly' (Bl., p. 81). Dalhoff, no doubt, did so. From subsequent events we can assume that Upadhyay now followed a familiar course of action: when one ecclesiastical superior proved uncooperative, he tried to get his way with another. To appreciate this strategy it is important to realize how the Catholic Church operated in such matters. Whether Zaleski could override the jurisdictional authority of the various Catholic episcopal heads in their dioceses is a moot point. As Papal Delegate he represented the political status and authority of the Roman Pontiff in India, and as such certainly exercised a strong moral authority in overseeing the running and reputation of his Church. But whether he could, beyond expressing approval or disapproval in the context of his enhanced status, attempt directly to control events in a particular diocese over the head of its own episcopal authority is open to question. No doubt Dalhoff, after seeking his advice, was hardly minded to flout it. In the matter of granting approval to Upadhyay's scheme then, he must have said no, or at least put it on hold till the situation clarified further. Without ecclesiastical approval Upadhyay could not proceed.

This is where the strategy mentioned earlier came into play. Upadhyay withdrew from Dalhoff, whose jurisdiction was the

---

for the whole of India. Zaleski gave himself enthusiastically to the mission confided to him.... The general Seminary of Kandy was the result of ... the reports he sent to Rome. In spite of opposition and difficulties the Seminary was started in 1893, by order of Leo XIII' (de Melo, 1955: 318–9).

10 It was all the more ironical then that he could adopt as his own the motto given to the Pontifical Seminary (which moved to Pune in India in May 1955) by Leo XIII: 'In 1894 the Pope had a special medal coined to commemorate the opening of the Seminary. The medal bore the following inscription: *Filii tui, India, administri tibi salutis* [viz. Your own sons, India, shall administer salvation to you]. On July 16, 1894, the Delegate, commissioned by the Holy See, sent the medal to all the Ordinaries of the Delegation' (de Melo, 1955: 319). LOE (ibid.) is constrained to say: '[Zaleski] had kept much of the self-assurance of a medieval autocrat. Rather a ruler than a diplomat or a theologian, he would easily consider views different from his own as heresies and any criticism of ecclesiastical authority as schism ... he was ... entirely out of touch with India's mind and thought.'

Archdiocese of Bombay, and approached Mgr Charles Pelvat, the Bishop of the adjacent diocese of Nagpur. Perhaps Pelvat was sounded out as part of a wider trawl, or possibly because the town of Jabalpur, a feature of the Bandyopadhyay family's collective memory as the scene of earlier residence and derring-do (see chapter 2), was located in his diocese; after the family had moved to Bengal, the youthful Upadhyay, as we have seen, had visited the town on one or two occasions. Pelvat agreed to support the project, holding out, it seems, under mounting pressure in the face of Zaleski's hostility. For Zaleski, after he had replied to Dalhoff expressing his opposition to Upadhyay's scheme, wrote to the Sacred Congregation for the Propagation of the Faith (the relevant body) in Rome on August 16 that year seeking Rome's approval for his stance. Perhaps surprisingly, in the absence of a case for the defence, Rome replied granting it (letter dated September 13). Surely Pelvat must have been aware of the situation. Yet, courageously one assumes, he held firm on behalf of Upadhyay.

This impression is reinforced by an article, entitled 'The Casthalic [sic] Matha', published in the January 1899 issue of *Sophia*. 'The *Kasthalik* or Catholic *Matha* (monastery),' we are told, 'will be located on the Narmada profanely called "Nerbudda", just where this ancient stream encounters the Marble Rocks.... The spot is romantically situated in the very heart of India and commands almost equally the three great cities of Calcutta, Bombay and Madras. The *Matha* will be placed under the protection and guidance of the venerable Bishop of Nagpur. He has very kindly undertaken to nurture the infant institution. He has most generously placed at our disposal a commodious dwelling house near the locality till the monastery be erected.'

The article gives a somewhat florid description of the aims of the *matha*: 'Here ... will be reared up true *yogis* to whom the contemplation of the triune *Sachchidanandam* will be food and drink.... Here will grow up ascetics who will ... do penance for their own sins as well as for the sins of their countrymen by constant bewailing and mortification.' It then deplores the barren record of the Catholic Church in India: 'We have not brought forth a single saint to adorn the Holy Altar.' Obviously this is because of the alien way in which the faith has been preached and lived in India. The Kasthalik monastery will change all that. Here 'will the transcendent Catholic devotions be clothed in Hindu garb' and by a study of both the western Catholic tradition and a rehabilitated Advaita, the indigenizing of the faith will take place.

Once again, it seems, Upadhyay was jumping the gun. There is record of a series of five letters written by him to Pelvat (dated February 14, 15, 16, 17 and 19, 1899, that is, five months after Zaleski had heard from Rome), charting his progress, or rather the lack of it, in establishing the monastery under Pelvat's patronage. All the letters are written from Jabalpur. Jabalpur is some 23 km from the Marble Rocks, a well-known scenic spot.[11] Upadhyay had arrived in the city two days before he wrote the first letter, on the Monday before Ash Wednesday. A 'companion from Madras' was with him. 'Two or three more from Calcutta are expected very soon' (letter, February 14). These were all to be the first novices of the proposed monastery.

The first letter expresses concern that a bungalow apparently singled out by Pelvat as the place to start their monastic experiment (that 'commodious dwelling place near the locality') was being occupied by nuns, the illness of one of whom meant that the others could not vacate. So, for the time being, Upadhyay has to make alternative arrangements. The letter also mentions that Upadhyay had visited 'Bhera Ghat' or the Marble Rocks that morning. He expresses the desire to rent a house at the site so that he and his companions can spend Lent 'in solitude and silence, in prayer and penance.... We can easily come on Saturdays to Jubbulpore and stay overnight, make our confession, hear Mass and receive the Blessed Sacrament and return by the morning train.' He awaits the Bishop's view on this, but in any case he intends to spend two or three days at the Rocks with his companion. The letter closes with a revealing paragraph. 'I have not written to His Excellency the Delegate Apostolic as yet. Is it not advisable that we should be given a trial of knowing ourselves and feeling our strength under your pastoral care before applying for ecclesiastical sanction? The monastery should exist for some time *permissively* before it can be *formally* launched'. This is a shrewd

[11] Captain J. Forsyth, who seemed to spend much of his time indiscriminately shooting the wildlife around him, was moved to write (see Forsyth, 1919): 'What visitor to Jubbulpur can ever forget the Marble Rocks!... the charm of coolness and quiet belonging to these pure cold rocks, and deep and blue and yet pellucid waters, is almost entrancing. The eye never wearies of the infinite variety of effect produced by the broken and reflected sunlight, now glancing from a pinnacle of snow-white marble reared against the deep-blue of the sky as from a point of silver.... Here and there the white saccharine limestone is seamed by veins of dark green or black volcanic rock; a contrast which only enhances, like a setting of jet, the purity of the surrounding marble.' The Madhya Pradesh State Tourist Office continues to advertise the Marble Rocks as a site worth visiting.

attempt—the italicized distinction is a masterly use of Catholic legal-speak—to reassure Pelvat and to buy time. No doubt Pelvat wanted Upadhyay to argue his case directly with Zaleski. Upadhyay probably thought that it would be harder to order the termination of a controversial experiment that was, to all intents and purposes, working successfully, than to scotch the scheme before it got off the ground.

In the second letter Upadhyay proposes to reconnoitre the site in order to find the most suitable place to locate the monastery. He is still in need of interim accommodation, and is residing temporarily in a nearby bungalow owned by the diocese and already used by members of the clergy. The situation is clarified in the next, short, note. 'Father Servage advised me to rent a house temporarily and stay there till the bungalow be vacant, as it would not be ... convenient to lodge us ... in the parochial house for many days.' In the letter of February 17 Upadhyay reports some progress. He has rented a 'good and commodious' house close to the hospital in the city for ten rupees a month. He wishes he could spend his Lent 'in solitude in Bhera Ghat' but since he cannot find suitable accommodation there, he proposes to visit the place 'from time to time'. Then follows another revealing statement. 'In "Sophia" I shall no more write anything about the monastery without consulting your Lordship. Now everything concerning it will be attributed to your Lordship, therefore nothing should be published without your approval.' Clearly the January article in *Sophia* had been too ostentatious for so sensitive a project. It had put Pelvat in a very difficult position. By attributing 'everything concerning' the *maṭha* to Pelvat, Upadhyay was shielding himself and indeed exposing Pelvat. Even Upadhyay could see that it would not be wise to subject Pelvat to further exposure without consultation.

The last letter of the series begins by thanking Pelvat warmly for his 'paternal generosity'. Pelvat had responded to Upadhyay's earlier request (letter of February 14) for 'something ... as Lenten charity'. *The Blade* informs us (p. 80) that early that year Upadhyay, his friend Animananda and a third companion, all with their heads shaved, 'were seen going barefoot through the streets of Jubbulpore', begging for their food 'by order of the Bishop' (surely a convenient exaggeration). Each cooked his own meal in accordance with caste custom. One is alerted to the fact that Upadhyay (and his companions) were eking out a rather precarious existence. His letter continues: 'We are now lodged in our house in the city—five of us, two from Bengal, one from Sindh and one from Tinnevelly and myself. One of the Bengalis is a young Brahman of about 15 years of age. He was with the Jesuit fathers of Calcutta. They have sent him to us to be educated and trained in religious life.'

The person from Sind was Animananda, of course. The 'one from Tinnevelly' was a youth named Shankerji (no doubt the earlier 'companion from Madras' ), while the two Bengalis, both Brahmins, belonged to communities whose traditional occupation was to work as cooks. The implication is that though they did not come from well-to-do backgrounds they had maintained caste and, like the others, were ritually pure. The little community, from the point of view of their founder at any rate, were going to start off on the right foot.[12]

The extent of Upadhyay's zeal for maintaining caste (even in Jabalpur) becomes clear from an incident of the time recounted by Prabodhcandra Simha. Simha, who gives no source, reports that the head of a local missionary institute (*miśanarī bidyālay*) who knew Upadhyay required a competent mathematics teacher. Upadhyay sent him one of his 'disciples' (*śiṣya*—probably Animananda in view of his subsequent career as a teacher). The head proposed that the teacher receive a salary and be given refreshment of milk and bananas. When Upadhyay was informed of this, he said to the disciple, 'Whatever the foreigner gives is tainted; nothing is to be touched or eaten' (*mleççher dātabya jā kichu khāsta sakal-i asprṛśya o akhādya*). The word used for 'foreigner' is the derogatory *mleccha*. When the missionary heard why Upadhyay would not accede to his proposal he was deeply offended and did not pursue his request for a teacher (Simha: 35–6).

Upadhyay had devised a spartan life-style for the members of the fledgling *maṭha*. Image was important. The Bengali youths, the two youngest of the group, wore their sacred thread and the traditional tuft of hair on the crown of the head (signifying the ritual purity of the twice-born). They possessed but one shawl (*cādar*) and covering garment (*dhuti*) each. It seems that each member was still required to beg regularly, and to cook his food separately in accordance with strict caste practice. Each slept on the floor and used a single blanket, rising at 4 in the morning and retiring to sleep at 10 p.m. The day was passed 'in study, prayer and meditation' (see the *Sketch*,

12 It is also interesting to note that Upadhyay seems to have won the confidence of at least some influential Jesuits in Calcutta for them to send him a prospective novice for his ashram. This significant fact will be adverted to again in due course.

pt. I, p. 25).[13] A dramatic statement from the *Sketch* (pt. I, p. 25) gives us a glimpse of the romantic idealism of it all. 'Each novice, after completing his course of studies, was to make a retreat and then had to roam about in the cities of India, all by himself, for six months, begging his way from place to place, and if he returned alive to the central *matha* he was to get the *garic* [renouncer's saffron] garb'.

By all accounts that Lent was an important one for Upadhyay. *The Blade* tells us that during that period Upadhyay 'retired to a hill and fasted for forty days in imitation of his Master [i.e. Christ]' (p. 80). He ate sparingly but once a day at dusk, cooking a little rice by himself. The details are unclear; one wonders what part he played in the life of the little community. As was to happen on more than one future occasion during joint ventures, it was probably Animananda who saw to the daily running of the project. 'The whole night from Maundy Thursday to Good Friday [Upadhyay] spent in adoration, kneeling before the Blessed Sacrament. Later on he would with great feeling refer to these happy days.' In fact, shortly before his death, steeped in the vortex of political activity and well known for his scathing denunciation of the British and western cultural norms, he is reported to have said: 'Why do I accentuate the differences between the Bengalis and the English? I often laugh at myself for the Supreme is in all. I shall give up all this one day and go away. My present joy is nothing in comparison with my bliss when I was on retreat ... in Jubbalpore' (*Varia* 3, p. 109). Those who denigrate Upadhyay's commitment to the spiritual life as a form of political expediency have an impossible case to sustain.

*The Blade* surmises that 'it was on the banks of the Nerbudda, as far as we can judge, that his long wandering mind finally crystallised an interpretation of the Vedanta which to him appeared conclusive and destined to be the Indian foundation of the Catholic Religion' (p. 82). It seems to agree with Väth that it was as a result of reflection at Jabalpur that 'Advaitavada and Sankara' were rehabilitated as the basis of a Vedantic theism, and that *māyā* was identified with contingent being. *The Blade* refers to the article 'The True Doctrine of Maya' as the seminal source for this 'new', latter insight.

13 A reference to the *maṭha* in Turmes, 1963, gives the impression that this regime of begging etc. was applicable to all: 'The remembrance of these months never faded from Animananda's mind. He would often tell ... of those happy days ... [spent] in fasting, begging, contemplation, vigils and study. They slept on the floor, on a mat, with one sheet, without a pillow.... Rising at 4 a.m. Meditation on the way to Church. Night Meditation from 9 to 10.... Rewachand [Animananda] was to be the Acharya [the Teacher-in-charge]' (p. 21).

But we think this analysis mistaken. The process of reconstructing Advaita in Shankara's name as a Vedantic basis for the reception of Catholic teaching was well under way by the time of the Jabalpur venture. We have suggested earlier that the reason for this was Vivekananda's continuing stress on Advaita upon his triumphant return to India. One recalls Upadhyay's 'subtle' discussions concerning a rehabilitated Advaita with Fr Castets during his southern tour of 1897 as also the article 'Hindu Philosophy and Christianity' published in the July issue of *Sophia* that year. We have seen further that in the important article, 'An Exposition of Catholic belief as compared with the Vedanta' (Sp-m, January 1898) in which Upadhyay seeks to demonstrate traditional Advaita's compatability with the Catholic philosophical theology of the day, Shankara is cited as his authority for interpreting the 'Vedanta'. The Sanskrit Canticle *Vande Saccidànandam* was published already in October 1898. Last but not least, we note that 'The true doctrine of Maya' was published in the joint February-March issue of *Sophia* in 1899. Since there is a separate number entitled March 1899, it is reasonable to assume that the joint issue appeared late (i.e. in March). But Upadhyay arrived in Jabalpur on February 12, two days before the beginning of Lent. His Lenten retreat could have got under way only after he had arranged accommodation etc. for his little group, that is, in the last week or so of February. Holy Week that year fell towards the end of March. If the article on *māyā* was conceived during the Lenten retreat, it must have been written and despatched for publication well before the end of that reflective period. In other words, things seem to have been pretty rushed for a whole new direction to have crystallized. This is hardly likely. In short, Upadhyay's thoughts on Advaita, and specifically on *māyā* as they are articulated in the article referred to, were part of a process that, *māyā,* we have argued, began much earlier.

Contrary to *The Blade*'s implication, there is no clearly discernible focus to the *māyā* article. As we have seen in chapter 8, the article puts forward several interpretations of the meaning of *māyā*, of which *māyā* as contingent being is just one. The purpose of the article is to show, with reference to the concept of *māyā* and from the viewpoint of natural theology, compatibility between Thomistic and traditional Advaitic teachings about the production of contingent being, from both divine and finite perspectives. This can be seen as the extending of a process of interpretation begun some years earlier. It is not right then to speak of a new *orientation* discernible in the *māyā* article in an attempt to salvage something from the Jabalpur experience. It may well be, however, that the space afforded Upadhyay for reflection during that Lenten retreat deepened his conviction and understanding in regard to Advaita's susceptibility as a basis for Catholic evangelization, and encouraged him to proceed further along that path.

So far as the Kāsthalika *maṭha* was concerned, things didn't work out. Dalhoff had already withdrawn his support, as noted, 'remarking that Mr Banerji was unsteady'.[14] Pelvat, who was then prevailed upon to take over, was unable to sustain the adverse (official) pressure upon him. Khemchand, in *his* deposition after Parmanand's piece in Hull, says that after Zaleski wrote to Pelvat opposing the scheme, Pelvat advised Upadhyay to submit his proposal to Rome for approval (op. cit., p. 518). Whether upon advice or not, Upadhyay resolved to do so in person. With Pelvat's letter of introduction in hand and the passage money provided by a benefactor in Mysore (he had travelled to the South en route), he arrived at Bombay, his port of departure. 'But at Bombay, he got something like erysipelas, and he could not proceed' (Hull, p. 518).

When he became fit enough to travel again, Upadhyay apparently did not return to Jabalpur to wind up the project; instead he went to Karachi to edit a 'Congress newspaper with the double object of relieving financial embarrassment and of equipping me [Khemchand] better for journalistic work in connection with his future plans' (ibid.). The community in Jabalpur was left leaderless. After a couple of months Upadhyay visited the doomed *maṭha* to terminate the experiment. It seems that the Jabalpur venture was a watershed in Upadhyay's life. In the light of Dalhoff's alleged judgement that Upadhyay was 'unsteady', it is interesting to note Khemchand's assessment of his former mentor's character. 'He was a most noble soul—very self-sacrificing, devoted, selfless and burning with zeal for the salvation of India. But he was very impatient and impulsive in forming judgements and plans, and in carrying them out, or giving them up. His very zeal made him restless and unsteady. He understood and appreciated the Catholic principle of obedience to authority; but being brought up in the traditions of the Brahmo Samaj and modern religious thinking, it was often with difficulty that he submitted to superiors, and sometimes he secured his object by pressing too much, or by going from one diocese to another' (op. cit., p. 517).

There is much shrewd insight here; impatience, impulsiveness and restlessness were abiding, at times almost compulsive, passions

14 Thus Parmanand in his excursus, 'The Sind Mission', Part VI of Hull vol. II; see p. 511.

in Upadhyay's ceaseless struggle to find himself. These sharpened the cutting edge of an individuality that had been fashioned from its earliest years by a regimen of self-reliance, first in a home bereft of parental role playing (the reader will recall that in the absence of his mother, who died a year or so after he was born, and his disciplinarian father, who was often away in the line of duty, Upadhyay was brought up under the stern if traditionalist eye of his paternal grandmother), and later in an environment—the Brahmo movement—noted for its personality cults and improvised rules of practice. But another factor played its part in this regard: that of Upadhyay's celibate life-style. In a society where one was generally socialized in and through domestic, especially marital, relationships, the celibate could plough a very lonely and individual furrow. It was Upadhyay's celibate way of life in this context that enhanced his impetuous individualism, that made it difficult for him to walk any path of patient and watchful resignation. Upadhyay was not 'unsteady', he was tumultuous; he was not disloyal but importunate. These traits were far from virtues in a Church in which the wheels of unquestioning obedience ground very slowly indeed.

Perhaps it was just as well that the *maṭha*-experiment failed, for, we may ask, how indigenous would it really have been? Was it not in crucial respects destined to be a very western phenomenon? Administratively it was conceived as highly centralized; the meticulous routine of its discipline was nothing if not imitative of that of western monasteries.[15] More important, perhaps, as we have argued thus far, the thought patterns underlying its 'Hindu-Catholic' theology as formulated by Upadhyay were heavily Thomistic, that is, westernized. Indeed, towards the beginning of the *māyā* article cited, its author assures us that he proposes to 'study the Thomistic and Catholic doctrine of *maya*'! And this, as we have tried to show (see chapter 8), was not an expedient attempt to infiltrate truly Hindu ideas in western linguistic guise. At the level of deep structure, I submit, Upadhyay's Hindu-Catholic theology thus far is more western Catholic than native Hindu. If Zaleski had understood this and withdrawn his objection to the establishing of the *maṭha,* the course of the history of Catholic witness in India might have been very different! Paradoxically, it seems that the ashram that Upadhyay's abortive experiment inspired fifty years later at Kulittalai was closer to the original intention, notwithstanding

[15] For a sustained plea that the Hindu ashram is/should be at best only minimally structured, see Vandana, 1978.

the fact that neither of its founders was of Indian extraction. Moreover, in an important aspect of its envisaged life-style, Upadhyay's scheme would have run counter to Christian precept (if not practice), namely, that of the rigid maintenance of caste and racial divides. Even here a good case can be made for saying that Upadhyay's stance was not consonant with traditional Hindu teaching for, according to this teaching, the true sannyasi or renouncer has transcended the social and racial barriers of the human condition and is not bound by them. For important reasons, then, it is perhaps just as well that the Kāsthalika *maṭha* was not a success.

Not surprisingly, the *Sophia* suffered during the period of Upadhyay's attempts to establish the *maṭha.* Its editor himself laments this. Under 'New Year Greetings' (January 1899, published from Calcutta), Upadhyay writes: 'We crave the indulgence of our subscribers to be patient with our shortcomings. Of late we have not been able to devote much attention to our dear little Sophia. We were obliged last year to wander from place to place, homeless, friendless, following the guidance of our ideal which has taken hold of our entire being—the ideal of founding a Catholic monastery in India.' We have seen that following this there was a joint issue for February–March (published from Karachi). After this, the monthly *Sophia* ceased publication. Upadhyay had fallen ill on his way to set sail for Europe. But more important, he was sick at heart, disillusioned with his Church, apprehensive of implacable opposition from the highest Catholic ecclesiastic in the land. He took a job, as we have noted, probably the only situation open to him at the time, editing a political newspaper in Karachi, not least to escape 'financial embarrassment'.

The whole experience, including this editorship, which rode high on his disillusionment, was a turning point in his life. For what may well have started as a coincidence, a more narrow politicizing of his journalistic skills, led more and more to its own self-justification. Upadhyay now became minded to add overt politicization to his patriotic campaign to evangelize India. In other words, thanks in good measure to the unwitting Zaleski, evangelization for Upadhyay would now need to be expressed more explicitly through the political liberation of his compatriots. Having, so to speak, journalistically sniffed the blood of the Englishman and his foreign ways at Karachi, he soon realized that he could wage a more effective campaign at the heart of it all, in Calcutta, the political and cultural capital of British India. Moreover, Calcutta had the advantage of being the city in which he felt most at home. So, some time 'in the early part of 1900' (Bl., p. 86)—in the fateful words of Khemchand (Hull, op. cit., p. 518)—'having conceived the idea of carrying on a powerful propaganda of press and platform from the metropolis of India, he ... shifted to Calcutta'. The story of this most consequential move is continued in the next chapter.

# Chapter 10

# In the Glow of the Dark Crystal:
## Return to Calcutta—Hindu 'One-centredness' as a Way of Life

Upadhyay was to live for only seven more years. Uncannily, it seems, fate had led him back for this final period of his life to the city of his formative days, a city that lay at the heart of the new India and new era now taking shape, a city about to enter one of the most turbulent cultural and political phases of its chequered history. Calcutta in 1900—with a population of about 850,000[1]—was a multifaceted phenomenon, a metropolis of complex contrasts: of white sahebs, brown bhadralok and a vast array of migrant and shifting unskilled and artisan labour; of a western, urban culture and its bhadralok synthesis (increasingly distanced from the popular culture of the city and its rural roots, yet romanticizing village life in some circles); of mansions and palaces for a tiny minority and of humble dwellings and hovels for the majority; of a Black Town mainly in the north and a White Town towards the centre—a city of joy for the few but of dreadful nights for many.[2]

On the political front, there existed at the time, in Sumit Sarkar's words, a hiatus between two dominant myths, 'when the dream of progress under British tutelage was fading away, yet the alternative myth of a patriotism that solved all problems simply by driving out the foreign rulers had not yet gathered force' (Sarkar in S. Chaudhuri,

1 According to the census of 1901; see *Census of India, 1901, vol. VII, Calcutta, Town and Suburbs, Part III*, pp. 2–3. The precise figure for the Town of Calcutta is 847,796.

2 For an idea of the structure and culture of Calcutta by 1900, see S. Gupta, 1993: 29ff., S. Banerjee, 1989, S. Chaudhuri, 1990.

1990: 104). In 1900 this hiatus was banking up on its revolutionary side, and we shall see how Upadhyay played an important role in this mythic construction. Towards the end of November that year in the *Sophia*, now a weekly (see further), Upadhyay was to depict this ambivalent situation in his own manner:

> We look upon the English in the same way as a delicate, helpless, chaste woman looks upon her husband who is an alien by race and has won her more by force than by goodness—though the memory of the violent rupture may have been much sweetened by subsequent treatment. She does not love him but clings to him all the same because if deserted by him, she will be a captive of some other gallant bully worse than her present spouse. She would rather woo death than remarry any other stranger.[3]

The Russian bear loomed on the horizon! It was not long however before India was to be transformed in Upadhyay's constructions from the helpless wife of the analogy into the bloodthirsty, puissant Kali, wreaking judgement on her children's oppressors through her dance of destruction. But the time of this transformation had not yet come.

When Upadhyay first arrived in Calcutta in 1900, he rented a small house in Beadon Street, situated, as was to be expected, in the Black Town or northern sector of the city. 'He lived [there] for some time with his Brahmacaris' (Bl., p. 86). These may have been (at least some of) the inmates of his ill-fated ashram, though we are not sure. In any case, we hear no more of these companions (except for Animananda, of course). When Khemchand and his little daughter, Agnes, joined them in April, they moved to a larger residence at 1, Gour Mohan Mukerjee Street. But the journalistic bug was itching to find expression; now journalism became Upadhyay's chief vocation. He was at the heart of Empire in the subcontinent, at the centre of bhadralok sentiment and activity. In short, he was at last potentially in the thick of things, and it was up to him to convert this potentiality into actuality.

June 19 saw the first issue of the weekly *Sophia*, edited from this address. The journal is introduced as follows: 'We have great pleasure in presenting "Sophia" ... in a new garb. During the five years of its existence as a monthly it has met with a considerable measure of success. This encourages us to widen its scope and develop it into a weekly review of general politics, literature, sociology and comparative

3 'Do we love the English?' (Sp-w, November 24, 1900); reprinted in TC, December 31, 1901.

theology—Upadhyaya Brahmabandhav, Editor.' Khemchand acted as the journal's Manager. The paper, in folio format, is twelve pages long with two columns to each page. Though no statement of aims is spelled out in this issue, a significant difference from its predecessor is the declared intention to include 'general politics' in its scope; comparative theology remains an objective. In both these respects, Upadhyay was playing with fire where his Church was concerned, and Zaleski, it seems, had no shortage of informants.

In fact, besides continuing his deliberations on religion, during the weekly journal's short life Upadhyay wrote provocatively on two additional topics: politics and caste. We shall consider his developing views on religion and politics in due course; it is time now to discuss his stance on caste.

There can be no doubt that after the Jabalpur fiasco, Upadhyay's writings on caste increased both quantitatively and defensively. This is evident in the weekly *Sophia.* Though caste, at least in his personal life, had always been a major concern (recall, for example his teetotaller, vegetarian and celibate life-style to signal his high 'Hindu' identity, his open letter to Annie Besant claiming to be a 'Kanauj Brahman' by birth, the strict code of practice devised for the Jabalpur ashramites), Upadhyay's views on caste had been sporadic and ambivalent. In the eleven-point agenda described as 'Our New Programme' in the January 1896 issue of the monthly *Sophia,* there is no mention of caste as a major focus.[4] On the contrary, point 6 declares that it is the editor's intention 'to show that the theory of transmigration is a philosophical blunder and is destructive of the principle of the brotherhood of man'.[5] We have seen how keen he was to discredit the belief in karma and rebirth.

As for caste, in February 1897, under 'Notes' (p. 1) in the same journal, commenting on a recent issue of the *Arya Patrika* (a publication of the Arya Samaj), he writes: 'The caste system is the strongest bulwark of popular Hinduism, and unless that is broken down, reformers, whether religious or social, will be able to achieve no permanent success.' Yet under 'National Greatness', the transcript

4 See chapter 6, note 19.

5 What may be described as two other important 'practical' concerns of this period were the desire to abolish 'Hindu polytheism' including the image-worship and 'obscene' myths associated with it (see chapter 6), and, though this received less attention, instilling respect for women in Hindu culture (we shall deal with this matter later).

of a recent lecture, he had referred earlier (August 1896) to 'the growth of that grand system of caste which was once the strength of India and is now its bane.' Is there inconsistency here? Not if we make the requisite distinctions.[6]

The basic distinction one must keep in mind is that between *varṇa* and *jāti*. *Varṇa* in the classical Hindu tradition is a very old concept and occurs in its most significant ancient context in a hymn of the Rk Samhita which belongs to the oldest strata (circa 1200 B.C.E.) of the canonical scriptures or Vedas. In the *Puruṣa Sūkta* or hymn celebrating the primeval sacrifice of the cosmic person from which various constituents of the universe arose, we read: 'His mouth became the Brahmins, his arms became the warriors [*rājanya*[7]], his thighs became the traders [*vaiśya*], from his feet the servants [*śūdra*] were born' (10.90.12[8]).

This apportioning underlay the *varṇa* system or system of four caste orders. Note that it derives from an image that is hierarchical and organic—two of the abiding features of the *varṇa* system. At the top of this natural hierarchy are the Brahmins or priests and religious teachers, regarded as ritually the most pure; at the bottom are the Sudras, who, as ritual purity progressively declines down the hierarchy, are actually ritually impure. The first three strata were known collectively as the *dvija* or twice-born, i.e. besides their natural physical birth they were reborn spiritually by formal initiation (*upanayana*) into Hindu society. The Sudras were denied this privilege. With some qualifications, the system soon became hereditary, though early historical details remain unclear.[9] In the course of time strict rules were formulated governing commensality and intermarriage between the four caste orders. Severe penalties could be incurred if these rules, based on degrees of ritual purity and impurity, were transgressed; the severest penalties were reserved for transgression with and by the Sudras. It was this kind of separatist thinking that eventually gave rise to the phenomenon of untouchability as part of the caste

6 Upadhyay himself did not do so; when writing in English, he generally uses the word 'caste' indiscriminately.

7 From ancient times equated by Hindu commentators with the Kshatriyas.

8 Though this verse is sometimes regarded as an interpolation, it is still very old and has traditionally been perceived as part of the hymn.

9 A counter-view to the effect that caste-placement was or ought to be a function of behaviour rather than birth runs through Sanskritic tradition, but this was always a subordinate strand.

system when transgressions by sexual and commensal intercourse inevitably occurred.

Who were the Sudras and untouchables? In time the Sudras' designated occupation of serving the *dvija* changed into other kinds of (usually menial) work, yet both Sudras and untouchables retained their status of ritual impurity. Their number included certain mixed castes, aboriginals and eventually foreigners, but we do not have a full picture of their ancestry since the gap in our knowledge between the ideals of the normative texts and what actually happened in Hindu society is still too great. But we have clues. One of the original meanings of *varṇa* is 'appearance' or 'colour'. *Varṇa* distinctions could well have arisen, then, on the basis of a racial, indeed racist, component. Subsequently, colour and to some extent ethnicity became integral features of the concept of *varṇa* in the Sanskritic tradition. In this connection, the twice-born referred to themselves as *ārya* or 'noble', that is, they were of noble stock, speech and mores, in distinction from Sudras and other 'barbarians' who in some basic way were regarded as un-Aryan. Sanskrit, the language of high culture and of the sacrificial ritual (which lay originally at the centre of Vedic religion), was the symbol of Aryanness; consequently its use was traditionally carefully controlled. As we have seen in chapter 1, elements of this symbolism played an important part in shaping Hindu bhadralok identity in the nineteenth century, hence Upadhyay's continuing preoccupation with Sanskrit and its symbolic implications, especially at a time when alien rule was being perceived in his circles as increasingly irksome.

If *varṇa* provided the framework for the theoretical construct of caste, *jāti* or 'birth group' was a reflection of social reality. While there were only four *varṇas*, there have been and remain thousands of *jātis*. How these *jātis* arose is, on the whole, shrouded in the obscurity of the past. Numerous myths exist to explain the origin of various *jātis* within the *varṇas*. In reality it is not always easy to slot a particular *jāti* into a particular *varṇa* without controversy; not infrequently this *varṇa* allocation is irrelevant for practical purposes (though in theory it must be possible to relate every *jāti* to a caste order or *varṇa*). Further, owing to migration, change of occupation and the invoking of various ideological norms (often expressed by convenient myths), there has been constant jostling among the *jātis* of a particular context for positions of relative superiority in terms of ritual purity and other socio-religious advantages. When it is realized that even among the Brahmins of a particular locale (not to mention other *varṇas*), there is often a jealously guarded *jāti* hierarchy of degrees of ritual purity in terms of non-reversible practices concerning occupational roles, the exchange of food and marriage partners, the daunting complexity of the Hindu caste system becomes more apparent.[10]

Ideologically and socially, then, this was the situation that confronted Upadhyay in his deliberations about caste, a phenomenon that remained a central and ineradicable feature of Hindu society and religion, with all its hierarchical, naturalistic, organic, racial, occupational, regulatory and purity-conscious implications. Upadhyay's writings on caste, in English and Bengali, draw on all these implications, though it is only in the Bengali texts that Upadhyay's underlying agenda for caste (in terms of the distinction between *varṇa* and *jāti*) is more clearly revealed. No analysis of his views on caste, then, can be complete without reference to the Bengali texts; these important works were all written in this final period. First, however, we shall have to put Upadhyay's views into context.

In an article entitled 'Hindu modernisers and the public arena: Indigenous critiques of caste in colonial India" (in Radice: 1998), S. Bayly has identified three schools of thought among these critiques in the late nineteenth century. These schools of thought respectively viewed:

> '1. Caste in all its forms as a divisive and pernicious force, and a negation of nationhood.
>
> 2. Caste as *varṇa*—to be seen as an ideology of spiritual orders and moral affinities, and a potential basis for national regeneration.
>
> 3. Caste as *jāti*—to be seen as a concrete ethnographic fact of Indian life, a source of historic national strengths and organized self-improvement or 'uplift.' (pp. 96–7)

On the basis of these distinctions, Upadhyay's views on caste fall mainly into the second category. It was caste interpreted in an ideal form as *varṇa* that he sought to endorse; by implication the plethora of *jātis* that characterized contemporary Hindu society was a sorry distortion of the ideal.

We have noted that the failure of the Jabalpur *maṭha* seemed to exacerbate his sense of alienation from his Church. This alienation was invested in his increasingly defensive perception of caste as the

[10] For further discussion on *varṇa* and *jāti*, see Lipner, 1994, especially ch. 5.

bulwark of a reconstructed Hindu identity that separated and safeguarded Hindus from all things alien, especially their colonial rulers. In short, this was one way Upadhyay, largely unwittingly perhaps, could hit back at what Zaleski stood for.

In happier times, when the flush of conversion had not yet worn off and he seemed to enjoy the less ambivalent support of his Church, even as a self-conscious Brahmin it seemed easier to him to allow egalitarian Catholic precepts to breach traditional caste boundaries. He worked tirelessly and selflessly for the stricken when the Bombay plague of 1896 reached Karachi in early 1897. At the time Upadhyay was based in Hyderabad, but he left the city to nurse the plague-afflicted in Karachi. *The Blade* tells us that he informed his 'disciples' of his intentions by letter, once he had left Hyderabad. He did not want them to try to persuade him not to go and risk his life. When some of his Catholic followers tried to dissuade him anyway, 'he severely rebuked them. Their Master had given His life on the Cross for suffering mankind. How could a disciple of Jesus refuse to risk his life?' (p. 5).

The same source notes that it was the poor whom Upadhyay sought to help. The 'rich' and 'middle-classes', presumably those of the higher castes, had already left the infected areas. 'Upadhyay went about looking for the deserted men and women in the hidden lanes and by-lanes of the town. He would sweep their houses, cook for them, console them and bring medical aid' (Bl., p. 5). It was only when the authorities enforced hospitalization for the stricken and enlisted the help of four nuns to tend them in hospital that Upadhyay ceased his ministrations.

The tenor of his thinking at the time is also apparent from a eulogy to a young Sindhi, Daulatsingh, whom he had led to the Catholic faith and who, following his example of tending the plague-stricken, had died of the disease in Sukkur, and from a letter to Rewachand (Animananda).

'Daulatsingh!' writes Upadhyay in memory of his friend, 'You are the weak and tender transformed into strength and beauty. You are the pupil illuminated by the light inaccessible; I am the teacher groping in darkness.... I will sing your praise and stop the mouth of your slanderers that your Saviour and my Saviour may be glorified. They call you foolish. Your heroic self-sacrifice is foolishness to them. I will speak to them of your divine wisdom. I will show them the depth of your faith and hope and above all your charity.'[11]

[11] Quoted from the *Jote*, 3.6.1897 in Bl., p. 6.

In the letter to Animananda (Bl., p. 7), Upadhyay asks with passion, 'Why can't we touch men's hearts? Because we are not Christ-like.... We have not learnt as yet to suffer for those who repel us, at least, who have no attraction for us. Let us be eager to sacrifice our lives for persons with whom we have no blood-tie, towards whom our hearts naturally do not flow; and then only the Holy Spirit will fill us with power and grace. Jesus is our ideal and nothing short of Him should satisfy us.'

I am not suggesting that Upadhyay would have acted differently had he been confronted with a similar situation in later life after his more strident views on caste had been articulated. We shall see that this interpretation of caste/*varna* permitted the breaching of established caste barriers in times of need. It was just that after Jabalpur, the caste framework was viewed with increasing passion as a more salient and wide-ranging means of Hindu socio-cultural defensiveness and solidarity.

The basis for Upadhyay's understanding of caste is laid out in the weekly *Sophia* (August 25, under 'Questions and Answers'). Upadhyay is giving an editorial response to 'a Brahmin' (invented?) who asks if 'there is any natural basis on which the caste-system was framed' but who suspects that it was invented by his Brahmin ancestors for 'purposes of self-aggrandisement'. Consequently, Upadhyay's interlocutor is considering whether to abjure caste 'by throwing away my sacred thread'. Upadhyay answers:

> You will commit a great mistake in throwing away your sacred thread.... The caste-system has not a bad origin as you suppose. It was framed on the basis of the human constitution. According to Hindu psychology man is composed of four divisions—first, the organs of work...; second, the organs of sense; third, *manas* or mind which governs these organs; and the fourth is *buddhi* or intellect which deals with supra-sensuous things. Society too has four parts, corresponding to the four divisions of the nature of man. The working class represents the organs of work; the trading or the artisan class represents the senses, inasmuch as they minister to their comforts; the ruling class corresponds to the mind which governs the senses; and the sacerdotal class, whose function is to learn and teach the scriptures and make others worship, is a manifestation of *buddhi*. The psychological division of man and society is the natural basis on which this ancient system of social polity was framed.

Though this is supposed to be a 'psychological' rather than a morphological division (as in the Vedic analogy)—actually it is a functional division—there are still marked similarities between the two constructions. Both are natural and organic (patterned on the human constitution)[12]; both are hierarchical (there is talk of governing, ministering and different levels of being), tied in with a division of labour. Clearly, Upadhyay is giving a rationale for the traditional, four-tiered *varṇa* division. What we have described as *jāti*, the profusion of actual birth groups in Hindu society, is dismissed as an aberration. 'Social reformers should, if they wish to establish a vigorous national unity, turn their attention first to the abolition of unnecessary, whimsical divisions and sub-divisions of caste' (Sp-w, October 27).[13] Note that this system, described in the language of the various race theories being bandied about at the time by social theorists, is defended as the preserver of the unity or 'integrity' of the Hindu 'race'—in particular the 'Aryan race'—in the face of the culturally and racially disintegrative forces of westernization. 'It was caste that preserved the Hindus from being transformed into hybrids of the Semitic stock. It is this social polity which still checks mammon-worship on the European scale' ('Questions and Answers', Sp-w, September 15); 'The caste system which diversifies the principle of Hindu unity should be restored to its original salutary order of divisions' (Sp-w, October 27). Again:

> In ancient days India was one. The gulf between the conquered aborigines [i.e. the Sudras] and the Aryan conquerors was gradually bridged over by the process of social assimilation. But now such unification with the alien races which have taken possession of the country will make low hybrids of the Hindu. There may exist unity and utmost cordiality in matters political and even religious, but social connexions with foreign residents and settlers can now in no way be tolerated. The most dangerous factors which are threatening to create serious breaches in our society are English civilisation, English education, English refinement, English ideas.... Not that we should repudiate English civilisation altogether; what is good in it should be received but not before we encounter it half

[12] 'Hindu society is an organism', in its basic structure the result of 'the process of natural evolution' (under 'Notes', Sp-w, October 27, 1900).

[13] 'Caste is an evolution of Hindu nature. Its accidents, accretions, stereotyping excrescences may be removed but the essential constitution of the system cannot, we think, disappear' (ibid.).

> way and divest it of its aggrandising character ['Social Penance', TC, July 31, 1901].

In an earlier article he had proposed that two conditions must be observed if someone wished to remain a 'faithful Hindu': (1) abstention from interdining and intermarrying with non-Hindu races 'such as Europeans, Mahommedans etc.'; and (2) abstention from the consumption of beef since beef-eating was abominable to Hindu sensibilities ('Integrity of Hindu Society', Sp-w, November 10). Intermarriage among Hindus *could* be a good thing; in any case 'they should never be made occasions for expulsion from the society itself'. After all, the Vaidyas and Kayasthas of Bengal 'are the products of intermarriage' and represent 'some of the most advanced classes of Hindu society'. The Vaidyas and Kayasthas are thus let off the hook; they were (and are), with the Brahmins, at the forefront of bhadralok society. Thus, observing basic caste rules and distinctions (in terms of the *varṇas*) preserves racial and moral integrity. It is proof against 'mammon-worship' to which Europe has succumbed and also safeguards social and cultural unity. It is the bastion of Hindu identity and potential progress in a difficult situation.

But what are the marks of a desirable social system with reference to 'Hindu identity', in terms of which 'true progress', that is, the regeneration of a fallen India, can be judged? For this we turn to an important and substantial Bengali article that may be regarded as summing up Upadhyay's views on caste and the good life. The article, entitled *Varṇāśrama dharma* ('The code of caste-status and the stages of life'), was published in February–March 1902 (Bengali Era: Phālgun, 1308) in the well-known journal *Baṅgadarśan* (pp. 534–47) in its new format under the editorship of Rabindranath Tagore.[14]

According to Upadhyay, in the context of a currently fallen (*bhraṣṭa*) India, even further imperilled by colonial rule, 'progress' (*unnati*) or national regeneration can best be understood in terms of

[14] Bankimcandra Chatterjee was the editor of the original series. In the first issue (January 31, 1901) of Upadhyay's last publishing venture in journalism in English, the short-lived monthly review, *The Twentieth Century*, which he co-edited with N. Gupta, there is an anonymous article entitled 'Varna Ashram or the Aryan Social Divisions'. In a table of contents with other articles against Upadhyay's name (and pseudonym), its unassigned status is perhaps surprising. On the basis of style and content, however, it is clearly the work of Upadhyay, being a less developed version of the Bengali *Varṇāśramadharma*. The Bengali article is reprinted in an (incomplete) anthology of Upadhyay's Bengali writings entitled *Samaj*. It has been reprinted again in B. Ghosh, 1987: 30ff., from which references are quoted.

a consolidation of present, and so far as possible, reclamation of lost, 'Aryanness' (*āryatva*). It is remarkable how salient the term 'Aryan' is in this essay. The distinguishing characteristic of Hindu Aryanness, we are told, is 'one-centredness' (*ekniṣṭhatā*). 'One-centredness', essentially a religious concept, has an intellectual and a social dimension. In due course we shall discuss the former (the subject of another article); here we shall examine the latter, since, according to Upadhyay, the traditional code of caste status and the stages of life (*varṇāśrama dharma*) is no more than Hindu one-centredness in its lived form.

'One-centredness' is the directing of all energies, personal and collective, to experiencing the ultimate oneness—or rather non-twoness (*advaita*)—underlying all the multiplicity and differentiation of worldly existence. In this reckoning, everyday multiplicity has an ambivalent and deceptive quality. If not approached in an enlightened way it tends to divisiveness and disintegration, to strife and a deep-felt sense of unease, both individually and socially. But if tackled aright, with the insight of 'one-centredness', it leads to cooperation and a sense of community, and to ultimate well-being. More than any other people, the ancient Hindus developed and fostered the one-centred outlook.

> The basis of being a Hindu (*hindutva*) is one-centredness. The Hindu's way of thinking, Hindu philosophy, the Veda ... the Codes, the Puranas—all converge on the One. For reality is one, not two. The One manifests in many forms—this is the Hindus' supreme realisation. In the corpus of Vedic hymns, it is the greatness of the One that is described.... The knower, the thing known and the knowing act; the causal agent, the action and its instrument; the giver, the recipient and the gift—the ultimate oneness of these triads was first declared in the Vedic chants. Then, dissolved in the shining bliss of the Vedanta [the Upanishads], the empirical triadic aggregates of which we speak were finally subsumed into the oneness deriving from the Real.[15]

How is this unitive mentality, the mark of Hindu 'Aryanness', achieved socially? In two ways, answers Upadhyay: externally by racial

15 *Hindutver bhitti ekniṣṭhatā. hindur cintā-praṇālī, hindur darśan, bed, ... saṃhitā, purāṇ—samastai ekmukhīn. bastu eki, dui nahe. Eki bahurūpe pratibhāta hay—ihāi hindudiger carama siddhānta. samagra bedgāthāy ekeri mahimā barṇita āche.... Karttāi kārjyarūpe pratibimbita, sraṣṭāi sṛṣṭirūpe pratiphalita. Jñātā, jñeya o jñān, karttā, karma o karaṇ, dātā, grahītā o dān—ei tiner pāramārthik ekatva bedmantre ābhāṣita haiyāchila, ār bedānter ānandajyotiḥte bilīn haiyā byabahārik tritvya-samūha bastughaṭita ekatve parjyabasita haiyāche* (p. 36).

separatism, and internally by the implementation of the *varṇa* structure and by conformity to *āśrama* practice (which we shall deal with presently). As will become clear, the whole argument harks back to the supposedly halcyon past of Vedic India reconstructed on the basis of an idealized interpretation of various texts.

In the ancient subcontinental past, we are told, the Aryans[16]—whom Upadhyay blithely equates with the 'true' forebears of contemporary Hindu culture at its best—were confronted by a 'dark-skinned' (*kṛṣṇakāy*) race, who were worshippers of wood, stone, ghosts, ghouls and so forth. Religiously, then, the latter were certainly not one-centred. Further, religiously they were bitter opponents of the Aryan cult (*āryatantra*). It was necessary to keep them 'at arms's length lest by mingling with them Aryan blood become contaminated, mixed castes arise and Vedic religion be obstructed'.[17] These non-Aryans, or perhaps un-Aryan people (*anārjya*), were called Sudras.

If the Aryans, a superior race (*uccajāti*) and naturally a magnanimous people,[18] had consorted with an inferior race (*nicajāti*) with a religion hostile to their own, racial and cultural confusion would have ensued, and one-centredness been lost. 'It is because the force of this ancient magnanimity (*suhṛdayatā*) was checked by injunctions and prohibitions that the Aryan race's caste (*varṇa*), religion (*dharma*) and purity (*śuddhatā*) were preserved' (p. 32).

> If the far-seeing authors of our sacred texts had not strictly regulated our interaction (*ācār byābahār*) with the Sudras, then even the little

[16] Upadhyay uses 'Aryan' as essentially a racial term. According to modern scholarship, however, it more appropriately describes the language(s) spoken by the ancient people(s) of whom Upadhyay speaks. Whether these people(s) were also ethnically different from those in their midst who used different, so-called Dravidian, languages is a separate issue, and one much debated today. See, e.g., Trautmann, 1997.

[17] *Tāhāder sahit saṃmiśraṇe pāche ārjyarakta dūṣita hay o saṃkarjātir utpatti hay o beddharmer bighna hay, ei āśaṅkāy tāhādigake dūre dūre rākhite haiyāchila* (p. 31).

[18] In another, shorter Bengali article of the period, entitled *Tin śatru* ('Three Enemies', hereafter TS) and also published in *Bangadarsan* (śrābaṇ B.E. 1308, i.e. July–August 1901, reprinted in *Samaj* and B. Ghosh, 1987), Upadhyay expatiates comparatively on this magnanimity or open-mindedness (*udāratā*). The ancient Greeks were adept at uniting similars; the ancient Romans specialized in uniting dissimilars, whereas the Aryans 'taking their stand on a fundamental truth that transcends place and time (*maulik deśkālātīta satya*), receive(ed) another's essential teaching by pouring it into the crucible of their own core (truth)' (see Ghosh, 1987: 17–18). This assimilative method was the most superior, for it allowed the Hindus to develop their civilization without violating their cultural integrity.

> Aryanness left to us would have been lost. Rajputana, begetter of heroes, would today be full of snub-noses and yellowed eyes; instead of lotus-faced Hindu beauties, females with low brows and grotesque faces would adorn our literary groves [ibid.].

One could hardly encounter more crudely racist language than that.[19] Originally then, racial apartheid was necessary not only to counter physical decline, but on aesthetic grounds! Cultural apartheid was necessary, continues Upadhyay, to preserve 'our' highest good (*paramārtha*), 'since the non-Aryans were followers of a way that was both worldly and ritually deficient'.[20]

Nor are those westerners in closest cultural contact with contemporary Indians, argues Upadhyay with passion, in a position to assume the moral high ground and criticize this Aryan separatism. Are not blacks in present-day America treated by their white compatriots in similar fashion? Indeed, 'it is doubtful whether the ancient separation between Aryan and non-Aryan can compare with the rigid barrier that even now exists between whites and blacks in the egalitarian and civilized country of America.' And the British, as everyone knows, are no less conscious and protective of their racial otherness. 'This kind of social separation is usually beneficial,' concludes Upadhyay. 'If the English were to countenance [interracial] marriages, would they not suffer national debilitation (*jātīya hīnatā*) and corruption (*bikṛti*)?' (p. 32).

On the internal front, the ancient Hindu lawgivers in their wisdom devised the system of *varṇa* and *āśrama* to bind the Aryans into a single community and to effect their social and religious well-being by developing their one-centred mentality. The beauty and strength of the *varṇa* system, avers Upadhyay, is that it is patterned on the way the human organism works. The human organism is an integrated whole made up of various parts with their own modes of functioning; it is one yet many. Aryan society too, thanks to the ancient Hindu sages, had a similar structure. In elaborating this idea, Upadhyay refers to a famous Upanishadic teaching (see e.g. Taittiriya Up. 2.2.1ff) that the underlying Spirit manifests in the human being through five experiential sheaths: the bodily, the breath, sensation, the mind, and ecstasy or bliss.

> The non-dual Spirit [*advayātmā*] having entered the five sheaths ... by its wondrous power [*māyāprab̄hābe*], has manifested in the form

19 Such raw prejudice is not found in Upadhyay's English writings.

20 *Anārjyerā saṃskārhīn prabṛttipraṇodita mārger upāsak chila* (p. 33).

> of the self-conscious individual [*ahaṃpratyāyī jībātmā*]. Just as there are five sheaths to every person, so too society has five sheaths. The bodily sheath or the organs of action [*karmendriya*] of the individual correspond to those in society who earn their living by labour and service [the Sudras]. The sheath of breath is analogous to those who work as merchants because society survives by the transactions of buying and selling [in the way breathing represents a transaction between the organism and its environment]. Those who govern and protect society [the Kshatriyas] are like the sheath of sensation; just as the faculty of sensation [*manas*] controls the sense organs so the Kshatriyas control the citizenry. The Brahmins are similar to the sheath consisting of consciousness, for mental acts [*buddhibṛtti*], consisting of consciousness, are directed within [*antarmukhī*]. The Brahmins' specific duty is ... [to] draw their disciples' minds [*antaḥkaraṇa*] from the gross towards the subtle, to uncover the inner vision, and to direct the mind's various constructs [*saṃkalpabikalpa*] towards the One [*ekmukhīn karen*]. The renouncers [*sannyāsīrā*] are like the sheath of bliss. They transcend the stages of life [*āśrama*], and are beyond the various injunctions and prohibitions, wandering where they will. The main burden of following life's highest goal has been placed on them. From bliss comes creation; in bliss there is permanence [*sthiti*], the culmination of all worldly flux [*biśva saṃsārer parjyabasān*]. So those who enjoy the bliss of renunciation are lords over all, the gurus of the world [p. 41].

The reader will not have failed to notice the Hindu context and resonances of this passage. This is one way in which Upadhyay has developed the English version of his conception of *varṇa*. He is able to communicate thus more familiarly and effectively to the Bengali literati. He has also added a fifth layer to the hierarchy, that of the renouncers or sannyasis (who are mentioned in this context in the anonymous 'Varna Ashram' article of the TC). These represent the highest aspect of human experience, an underlying and integrative bliss of fulfillment; as such they are, spiritually and symbolically, 'lords over all, the gurus of the world.' This, incidentally, was a useful affirmation of Upadhyay's own renouncer life-style; it lends authority to what he is saying. If Hindu society were to conform to this ancient functional, natural, organic stratification, it would be well on its way to national reintegration, self-control and spiritual and physical well-being.

The argument continues, as we shall see, but we may pause to ask some questions: did it not dawn on Upadhyay, as he launched forth, that this model of national regeneration may have been deeply alienating to perhaps the largest section of the society whose reconstruction he was proposing, that is, the 'Sudras', whose ancestry had been depicted racially and religiously in the most offensive terms, and who had been humiliatingly consigned as a group to the bottom of the heap in perpetuity? Could the Sudras be expected willingly to share this self-glorifying, patronizing vision of a Brahmin sannyasi? Yet Upadhyay was not alone, as Bayly's distinctions intimate, in formulating such schemes.[21] The crass unrealism and insensitivity of it all are breathtaking. Note too that whereas a few years earlier belief in the law of karma (supposedly obstructing society's ability to bear one another's burdens) was one of the main reasons given for India's decline (see chapter 6), now it is deviation from the ancient dharma of caste and stage-of-life that is responsible for India's sorry condition. In fact the concept of action/work (*karman*) is constructively reinterpreted in Hindu context as we are about to see.

We must now consider the other half of Upadhyay's socio-religious model, that of the *āśramas* or stages of life. This too is an ancient conception, of central concern to the lawgivers of the pre-Common Era. Though in the early texts the *āśrama* system has different forms, the synthetic 'classical' version has four successive stages: that of (1) the celibate student (*brahmacarya*), (2) the householder (*gārhasthya*), (3) the forest-dweller (*vānaprasthya*) and (4) the wandering renouncer (*saṃnyāsa*). These four stages, from youth to old age, ideally chart the human development through life of a twice-born male (see Olivelle, 1993).

According to Upadhyay, this system too was geared to fostering social and individual one-centredness in the Hindu body politic. The *āśrama* system achieved this by making the individual selfless, not a seeker of power and wealth (*aiśvarya*), but a doer of properly assigned work for duty's sake, so that the whole of society could benefit.

> The four stages of life were created for the practice of selfless [*niṣkām*] action. By the severe discipline of celibacy [*brahmacarya*], concupiscence [*bhogbāsanā*] was brought well under control, and notwithstanding the burden of poverty, the spirit of competitiveness [*jigīṣāprabṛtti*] in particular was properly quelled by adhering to one's lineal duties; and in old age, once wife and offspring were left behind and one's hard-earned wealth and power forsaken, by

21 With respect to the distinctions between the 'Aryans' and the 'aboriginals' the former encountered in ancient times, Upadhyay was taking his cue from orientalist race theories of the day. See Trautmann, 1997, especially chapter 7.

> departing to the forest the knots of desire were loosened, the pleasures of [karmic] heavens were disdained and one prepared to be immersed in the highest bliss.
>
> When one contemplates the stage of life of the forest-recluse [*vānaprasthya*] ... the mind is filled with amazement.... Irked by the final enjoyment accruing from a lifetime's labour ... and bruised in the struggle of [life's] victories and defeats, the Aryan householders then departed to the forest! They had rights over the work, not over its fruit.... Every Aryaṇ life was reconciled to this ideal laid down in the Gita [pp. 37–8].

We have already noted the status and role accorded to the renouncers; they are the symbols and purveyors of the highest bliss, showing by their presence that a foretaste of the human ideal can be achieved in this life as the apogee of the *varṇāśrama* code.

The last extract brings out another central concern of this essay: the ideal relationship between the Aryan and his work/action. Whereas hitherto, mainly in the monthly *Sophia,* when Upadhyay discussed *karma* or action it was chiefly to refer to the self-interested action that in the traditional Hindu view engendered rebirth, now, writing for Hindus in Bengali, he idealizes *karma* as the disinterested action (*niṣkāma karma*) that does *not* lead to rebirth. It is the selfless work assigned to one by the *varṇāśrama* code that brings about one's own ultimate well-being through seeking the integrity and well-being of society. In the behavioural sphere, it is the action that consummates Aryan one-centredness; it is a form of activity that is really of the nature of inactivity for by it one remains *in* the world without being *of* it, one engages with the world for *its* best interests, not one's own. This is how Upadhyay interprets the ideal of *nivṛtti* or 'active withdrawal', in contrast to *pravṛtti* or 'selfish involvement'. It is a universal ideal taught in the *Bhagavadgita.*

> When the Aryan householder at the time of his departure to the forest made over the wealth he had acquired by work to his successor [his son or sons], then his glowing, living example of renunciation made it abundantly clear that standing and honour were established through work [*karma*], not by the enjoyment of the fruit of work. A wholesome pride arose towards one's work through this renunciation of wealth laid down by the forest-dweller stage of life. But pride does not arise in connection with any kind of work. I must revere that work [*karma*] by which my male ancestors became renowned, that action [*karma*] by the cultivation of which they

> were prepared to forsake all their wealth. Let us give up wealth, even our life—but not our ancestral duty [*kaulik karma*]. If the work were not given priority through pride in one's lineage once the fault of adhering to the desire for its fruit had been abandoned, then it would not have been possible to focus the whole of society on disinterested work [*niṣkām karma*]. It is on the basis of self-respect that one must be led slowly to the supreme goal [*paramārtha*]. If there is no self-respect [*ātmamarjādā*] there can be no vision of the Ultimate [p. 38].

Similarly, the various strata of Hindu society should work selflessly for the common good and thereby for their own self-fulfillment in the line of their ancestral duty: the Brahmin by giving instruction, the Kshatriya by governing and protecting, the Vaisya through business, and the Sudra by labour. In this way racial, lineal and *varṇa* pride will be fostered and society will hang together as one unit. There is an attempt here, though it is still hierarchical and elitist, to overcome his earlier more atomistic view of society.

Several questions arise. First, in the light of this ideal what must be done to cope with the reality of the situation—the long history of inter-*varṇa* marriages that have occurred, not least the 'interracial' marriages, that is, those between the Aryans and the Sudras? Upadhyay answers that in the past, as the barbaric Sudras were gradually civilized through contact with the Aryans, they were assimilated up to a point both culturally and racially. However, this assimilation was kept in check by means of stringent controls, especially where commensality and further intermarriage were concerned, particularly in respect of the mixed castes (to the disadvantage of those castes, called *pratiloma,* arising especially through hypergamous intermarriage, i.e. unions in which the males were of a lower caste status than their wives). Because such assimilation was strictly monitored, Hindu civilization retained some measure of its Aryan character.

Nevertheless, there was flexibility in the system, and exceptions were permitted for the public weal in difficult times. Upadhyay quotes a number of the ancient authoritative law codes to this effect. He says nothing about the way the current 'degenerate' system might be purified so as to approximate to the ancient ideals. Since, however, in contemporary times the challenge to Aryan norms from European civilization and presence is greater than ever before, interdining and intermarriage with Europeans, as the main gateway to loss of Aryan values, must be strictly prohibited, though cordial relations with them in other ways may well be sought. 'Because the Europeans are a very proud race, they don't make too much fuss of us. If they were as attracted to us as our cultured folk are to them, then by now how many hundreds of our Misses Hemalata and Mrnalini would have become Mrs Fox and Mrs Hogg, and the country would be full of unseemly offspring of mixed breed (*deśṭā jabarjaṅgī jātphiriṅgite bhariyā jāita*)' (p. 34).[22]

Would not adhering to lineal work and caste duty enfeeble society by reducing motivation and stifling talent? No, answers Upadhyay. On the contrary, it gives security and direction in life. The system has always accommodated special talent: was not Drona, though a Brahmin by caste, still an expert in warfare, and Janaka, though a Kshatriya, a teacher of Brahmins? The more ordinary individual, on the other hand, instead of being pushed through a mediocre education and then into a mediocre, uninspiring job as in the present western system, would, according to the traditional way, know the vocation expected of him and follow it without anxiety.

In fact, the great advantage of the *varṇāśrama* code, continues the argument, is that it minimizes those great and truly divisive banes of modern western society, competitiveness and ambition. Real divisiveness, real social chaos and human strife, arise not from the caste distinctions, but from ambition and competitiveness. This Europe has in large measure. Europe seeks to dominate nature, both socially and environmentally.

> In [Europe] competition [*jigīṣā*], rivalry [*pratijogitā*] and lust for power wax strong. To conquer the elements, to tame nature, to win mastery over a cruel and intractable environment—this is Europe's ideal. No doubt this is a great and laudable ideal.... But this is not what Jesus sought. It fits in with the European mentality, but it does not derive from Jesus. It is only a prerequisite [*kāryabhūmi*] of Jesus' ideal. And many a time have the two ideals come into grave opposition; sometimes Europe has won, and sometimes Jesus.
>
> India's ideal is victory over work [*karmajay*], not the acquisition of power [*aiśvarjyalābh*]. So here there is such pride in work [rather than desiring its fruit], such love for the *varṇa* code, repudiation of competition, and fostering of equanimity [*śāntabhāb*]. But because

[22] One may note that the offensive but unusual phrase *jabarjaṅgī jātphiriṅgi* seems punningly to refer here 'to a famous composition by the popular songster Bhola Moira in a [religious] musical duel with the Eurasian Anthony Phiringi'. I owe this observation to the anonymous reader of this book in its ms. form.

> Europe's ideal is conquest, there is such a lack of equanimity there, and such an excess of competition. The one-centredness of the Hindu race, having destroyed the divisive seeds of work, has relied on the discipline of the *varṇāśrama* code to attain the bliss of undividedness, and it is this one-centredness which underlies the structure of the *varṇa* divisions [p. 40].

So Europe stands condemned by Jesus himself, the religious teacher it professes to follow, whereas Hindu India, through its one-centred *varṇāśrama* code taught by the *Bhagavadgita,* which seeks to eliminate strife and discord, has a tradition more in keeping with Jesus' own ideal of oneness and peace. This leads us to the next question we may ask of Upadhyay's socio-religious model: could it be proposed by a Christian? Was it in accord with Christian principles?

Certainly Upadhyay thought it could and was. There is no clue in the Bengali essay that a Christian is writing; yet Upadhyay would argue that its content is not un-Christian. This is where the natural-supernatural distinction, so central to his theological reasoning, again comes into play. As has been emphasized, the *varṇāśrama* system conforms, for Upadhyay, with the human constitution; it is a *natural* human institution. As such it does not militate against Christian principles. It is a distinctive Hindu way of patterning human relationships, all the more commendable for being in conformity with human development. In 'spiritual' matters the ancient Aryans were all on the same level; it was only in 'temporal' matters that distinctions were observed—a necessary and understandable measure to preserve the 'vitality' and 'integrity' of the Hindu race. 'Formerly the Aryans ... of all classes and ranks possessed equal rights in the sight of God. All were initiated into the Vedas and all aspired after the attainment of the Infinite. There was difference only as regards vocations, ranks and other temporal matters' ('India's Downfall', TC, October 30, 1901). Thus, so long as social rulings do not violate legitimate spiritual aspirations, they are acceptable—and how could the *varṇāśrama* system, so in accord with human nature, be in the least unacceptable?

In this light, Upadhyay concludes, the *varṇāśrama* system can—indeed, should—be commended and so far as possible followed by Hindu converts to the Christian faith.

> As to whether the attitude of the Catholic Church towards caste distinctions is compatible with her great principle of the universal brotherhood of man ... the Church does *not* attach any sort of

> sanctity to any person because of his or her birth, nor make any distinction between the Brahmin and Shudra converts in regard to spiritual privileges. The latter are taught just the same truths and partake of just the same ministrations as the former.... The Church does, however, allow converts from different castes to observe their distinctions as to inter-dining, inter-marrying and the like. At the same time she does not *prevent* them from dining together or contracting blood relations.... The question now is: Is it the duty of the Church to *enforce* interdining and intermarriage as a *sine qua non* of universal brotherhood? And should she interfere when a man is deprived by his castemen of the right of social intercourse with them? (Sp-w, June 30, 1900).

Indian Christian faith has become enervated because it has become 'denationalized', that is, too westernized. 'So long as the Christians of India do not practise their faith on the platform of Hindu life and living and Hindu thought and thinking, and elevate the national genius to the supernatural plane, they will never thrive. The Indian Christian community are devoid of vigour because they have been alienated from national life and thought' (Sp-w, October 27, 1900).

Besides, as Upadhyay is not tired of repeating, the racial and social separatisms of the traditional caste system may be regarded as endorsed by God himself. Was not the ancient Mosaic law, which enforced even more stringent apartheid between Jew and Gentile, divinely sanctioned? How can a Christian who acknowledges this Biblical fact object to similar practices by the Hindus? Such practices are no more than a conformity between divine law and the natural law, for 'the supernatural is co-natural and not anti-natural' (Sp-w, November 17, 1900), and the caste system is an instance of 'the process of natural evolution' (Sp-w, October 27, 1900).

To sum up Upadhyay's stance then: By a recovery of the traditional *varṇāśrama* system, not only will India be able to keep the disintegrative forces of westernization at bay, it will have the strength to receive and integrate what it adjudges beneficial for its development from western influences.[23] Thus firmly established in self-respect and its own history and culture, and free from the European disease

[23] 'By the varnashramic way of life I certainly don't mean the prevailing social system, occupationally corrupt (*karmabhraṣṭa*) as it is and riddled with hundreds of divisions. By all means let us accept independence, amity (*maitrī*), equality etc. as from Europe, but without letting the varnashramic way of life be destroyed. If these European ways are established on the varnashramic way of life, they will bear fruit, otherwise they will only harm us' (TS, p. 19).

of lust for power and unrestrained ambition, India will be in a position to acquire material prosperity—perhaps even eventual political sovereignty—without damaging the prospects of its own spiritual fulfillment. And ideally, what would these prospects be? Embracing the Catholic faith, which could, if Upadhyay's model were implemented, be achieved without the need for self-alienating transformations. In this way, true to its best heritage of 'Aryan one-centredness', India will 'progress' into the future.[24]

24 While on a visit to England, Upadhyay published two articles in *The Tablet* (January 3 and 31, 1903). At the time, *The Tablet* was more or less the British equivalent of *The Bombay Catholic Examiner* in Catholic circles. The first article, on Hindu theism, is dealt with in the next chapter; the second article was on caste and the traditional Hindu attitude to work. In the latter, Upadhyay, after affirming that Christianity requires doctrinal conformity, whereas Hinduism, while doctrinally plural, demands social conformity, rehearses some of the main points of his general argument, that in antiquity 'the Aryans, a white and a civilised people' gradually absorbed the 'natives of the soil, who were dark-skinned savages' racially and socially; that Hindu society was divided into 'four communities', who followed hereditary occupations (though exceptions were allowed for individual talent) and who were encouraged to foster a selfless ideal of love for work itself, not for its fruits. This engendered self-respect and the unity of society without its being corrupted by competitiveness and greed. But first godless Buddhism—'a socialistic revolt led by the non-Aryan Shaka race'—and now English education and rampant 'Westernism' have weakened the original Hindu principles of social polity, and indeed, alienated Christianity in the land. Only educating 'high-caste [Catholic] Hindus without un-Hinduising them', that is, respecting the ancient social ideals, will regenerate India and bring India [educated Hindu India] to Christ and the Catholic Church. Noteworthy are Upadhyay's placatory tone, and the absence in his argument of any sustained reference to the *āśrama* system and to the view that caste is a natural, organic ordering of society.

His former collaborator in Sind, the Jesuit A. Hegglin, now 'Professor of Sanscrit at St Xavier's College, Bombay', delivered a stinging attack against this article in the BCE, February 28, 1903. He charges that Upadhyay's views are an 'extremely novel' interpretation of caste and at odds with received critical opinion both Indian and western. Hegglin's thesis is that according to Hindu tradition itself caste originated, not, as Upadhyay claims, out of disinterested love for work and for the unifying of society, but because of the deterioration of an ideal society. This decline was prompted by covetous and idle Brahmins. There is insufficient historical evidence to back Upadhyay's claims, continues Hegglin, and he derides Upadhyay's assertion that traditional caste practice was conducive to engendering self-respect and social unity. On the contrary, 'the selfish motive of gain is the very soul of the caste system and rules it from top to bottom—a prolific mother of a progeny of evils.' Therefore, concludes Hegglin, the Catholic Church is right to condemn the principle of caste, and she prudently acts to break it down, especially within Catholic circles, at every turn. This tendentious article, for all the learning it undeniably evinces (we shall have more to say about Hegglin's opposition in the next chaper), is undermined by a fundamental oversight, namely, neglecting the distinction between *varṇa* and *jāti* and its consequences, which, as we have indicated, Upadhyay himself implies in his writings on caste. Hegglin seems to have been oblivious of Upadhyay's Bengali articles.

We need not dwell too long on a critique of Upadhyay's view. We have already adverted to its insensitivity towards those who would form a large section of the communities expected to adopt this scheme—the existing low castes and untouchables, or Sudras. Surely this alienating feature alone would render the scheme impracticable from the start. As a condition of their willing, or worse, forced, participation, the Sudras would be required to acknowledge debatable but humiliating cultural and racial origins. In Pollock's poignant words, 'they would have the obligations of humanity without its privileges' (Pollock in Breckenridge and van der Veer, 1993: 108).[25] Again, for the model to work on the grand scale, who would identify the Brahmin, Kshatriya, Vaisya and Sudra *varṇas* as existing starting categories amid the plethora of disputed *jāti* systems that were (and are) so endemic a feature of the subcontinent? And so many aspects of Upadhyay's interpretation of the ancient code, e.g. its alleged flexibility under certain conditions, its putative correspondence to the human organism, its supposed universal practice in ancient times, were themselves highly contentious.

Further, extremely important in Upadhyay's own circumstances was the question of the model's supposed compatibility with Christian values. There is no doubt that the Catholic Church to some extent countenanced traditional caste observances on the basis of the natural-supernatural distinction, during its long history in the subcontinent. But this did not render such practice uncontroversial throughout the course of this history. For many, both Catholic and non-Catholic, found it hard to reconcile the Church's teaching on 'universal brotherhood' with the sometimes appalling discriminations of traditional caste practice. For those opposed to caste, the so-called Biblical endorsement of apartheid between Jew and Gentile was a red herring—no more than a human invention instituted by the Jews for self-preservation, in God's name. It needed to be acknowledged as such and acted upon accordingly; it was not a shibboleth for

[25] In 'Brahmabandhav Upadhyaya: A Hindu-Christian' (1987: 331), Jose Vetticatil writes, 'Brahmabandhav could not see how a Christian could stand unconcerned when the whole nation was on the move for freedom. The Christian faith itself had its foundations in the history of Israel's struggle for freedom and deliverance from slavery. The God of the Bible was a God who continuously sided with the poor and the oppressed against the powerful and the oppressor. Faith in the Christian God necessarily should lead to an active participation in the national struggle for deliverance from foreign rule.' This anachronistic argument is far removed from Upadhyay's elitist view.

continuing racial and cultural discrimination. One cannot but reiterate how totally insensitive and extraordinarily out of touch in this regard Upadhyay must have been—himself a privileged Brahmin—to describe the discriminatory excesses of the *jāti* system as 'lesser evils', 'certain annoying accidents' that society must 'suffer ... to remain unmolested for the time being' lest the 'integrity of the social fabric' be destroyed (Sp-w, October 27, 1900), a social fabric *in fact* far removed from the ideal picture he had so blithely painted.

There is a final objection to this view: its Hindu voraciousness. India's future is assimilated to a 'Hindu' future, India's ideals to 'Hindu' ideals. In terms of Upadhyay's ideal of a reconstructed nation, where does this leave other long-standing components of the Indian population: the Buddhists, Jains, Muslims, even Christians, one might add? In the article under examination and elsewhere, the Buddhists and Muslims in particular come in for savage criticism as historically un-Hindu, i.e. un-Aryan. Note that the Buddhists seem to be un-Hindu not on ethnic grounds, but because they were deemed to have held beliefs destructive of Aryanness. The Sudras 'brought discord into the Aryan system and corrupted its way of withdrawal from the world, by worldliness' declares Upadhyay. 'Through the fault of discord, Aryan society declined. And because this decline gave scope to the Buddhist nihilists (*baināśik*), India, bereft of the Aryan ideal, collapsed' (p. 46).[26] The Muslims, on the other hand, seem to be un-Aryan, like the Sudras, not least on ethnic grounds. 'If there were no

[26] Upadhyay writes at greater length on the Buddhist role in ancient India's decline in another Bengali article entitled *Hindujātir adhaḥpatan* (hereafter: HA, 'The Downfall of the Hindu Race', *Bangadarsan*, B.E. Māgh 1308; C.E. Jan.–Feb.1901; reprinted in *Samaj* and Ghosh). There is an English version of this entitled 'India's Downfall', in TC, October 30,1901. This is also heavily critical of Buddhist influence on ancient 'Brahminism', but in a truncated and less robust form. In HA, Upadhyay declares: 'It was when the Hindu race, worn out by the conflicts of life, and, weakened by the mingling of dissimilars and disoriented, was being spun round in the wheel of karma, that the Buddha made his appearance.... We must acknowledge that the Buddhists' protest against unenlightened rituals was reasonable. But in seeking to crack the shell they smashed the core. In trying to do away with divisiveness they axed at its very root the Hindu's essential treasure of religious belief and practice [*āstikyabuddhi o barṇadharma*].... There is yet another specific reason for the spread of the Buddhist way of life. The Buddhists' destructiveness [*baināśikatā*] appeared in the garb of religion [*dharma*]. The Buddha assumed God's place [*īśvarer sthān*] and began to be worshipped himself.... The doctrine of the Void [*śūnyabād*], dressed up in ochre robes and accompanied by conch-shell, bell, incense and lamps, shrouded India. Hindus are religious-minded; seeing the form of religion, they were taken in.... Though Buddhism is irreligion [*nāstikatā*], it was found acceptable because it came in the

strict rules to the effect that one must not even touch water at the hands of a Muslim, there would have been racial chaos (*jātibibhrāṭ*) ... [for] the Muslims would have used drinking water as a pretext to sate their lust for wedding Hindu maidens.... Thus our leaders safeguarded us by striking at the very root. We took everything from the Muslim—his dress, behaviour, learning, customs—but taking water was prohibited. This intransigence has saved us' (p. 34).

Besides their being depicted in offensive terms, it is not clear what role these two Indian minorities are envisaged as playing in Upadhyay's regenerated India. If they are to find a rightful place, must they first become Hindu? If so, how? By embracing the *varṇāśrama* system as Sudras? And if they chose to adhere to their ancestral ways, must they be consigned forever to second-class status, unequal members of the new, 'progressive' India? The prospect repels. We shall have occasion again to marvel at Upadhyay's apparently unfeeling endorsement of such a hugely flawed model in theory on the one hand, while exhibiting, on the other, a far more humane personal code of conduct in practice. To a large extent, these essays—in English and Bengali—were clarion calls, somewhat skewed exhortations by Upadhyay to his (educated) Hindu compatriots to take stock of themselves; they were not intended to set out practicable proposals for change, notwithstanding their publication in the influential *Bangadarsan*. Nevertheless, they may well have influenced opinion.[27]

Indeed, we may conclude this discussion on an extenuating note. Perhaps by formulating this scheme for a reconstructed nation in

---

form of religion' (Ghosh, pp. 25–6.). But after a period of forced and false show, Buddhism *naturally* declined and was virtually expelled from India by a Hindu awakening initiated by Shankara. Nevertheless, 'Buddhism so vitiated the Hindu character that the discipline of disinterestedness [*kāmanābibarjita sādhan*] became utterly savourless.... Hundreds of worldly sects shattered the country. Hindu rule was re-established, but no longer was there unity.' (ibid., p. 28). In this essay, once more Upadhyay presses his theme that Hindus are not apathetic, they 'are not averse to action; they are averse to the fruits of action'. They love the work; they eschew the power that accrues from it. He concludes that there are three reasons for India's decline: (1) the natural weariness that arises from performing action without ulterior motive; (2) the excessively liberal mingling of Aryan and non-Aryan; and (3) the Buddhist rebellion. It is time again to try and recover the Aryan ideal, he concludes.

27 It may be of interest to note that this kind of exclusivist definition of *hindutva* or 'Hinduness' is in important respects directly antecedent, both historically and logically, to the subsequent far right ideology of *hindutva* in contemporary India; for a critique of this ideology, see Basu et al., 1993.

terms of Hindu paradigms, Upadhyay, largely unconsciously, was seeking to exorcise powerful tensions within himself. In the public eye, he was a Brahmin convert to the religion of an alien minority increasingly being perceived as hostile to India's best interests as a nation, yet he burned to show that he was not a traitor but a patriot, in a sense more Hindu than conventional Hindus. People in Upadhyay's position often err on the side of conservatism. 'See', Upadhyay may have been saying to himself and to everyone else, 'though Christian by faith I am still Hindu to the core, steeped in my ancestors' ways, and a lover of my country. Far from being incompatible, Catholic faith and Hindu identity may coexist in a complementarity that can fulfill India's highest aspirations as a nation.'

There was another tension, with personal ramifications, which Upadhyay may have sought to allay by delineating his social paradigm. This is the complex tension arising from the interaction between traditional Kshatriya aims (the preservation of dharma, of social polity in the form of the *varṇāśrama* system), the duty of the Brahmin to instruct in the ways of dharma, and the goals of the sannyasi or renouncer who is supposed to transcend the claims of *varṇa* and *āśrama*. How could Upadhyay, who was not loath to trade on his Brahmin status and who yet presented himself as a sannyasi, fight the good fight, Kshatriya-like, in defence of *varṇāśarma dharma* for his compatriots?

He could do this by interpreting the role of the sannyasi as the culmination of the *varṇāśrama* system. The sannyasi is the sign and catalyst of the blissful unity (*ekatva*) of society that the *varṇāśrama* system had been calculated to engender. In other words, he is the walking embodiment of Aryan ideals. And how does he achieve this? By performing appropriate action (*karman*) disinterestedly for the common good (*lokasaṃgraha*). In this the sannyasi is the exemplar of Aryan society in which the ideal is to pursue *svadharma*—one's traditionally prescribed way of life in accordance with *varṇa* and *āśrama*—selflessly for the welfare of the whole. This ideal, we are told, is laid down in the *Gita*. Upadhyay is fulfilling his teaching duty as a Brahmin in part as a journalist, by suggesting how traditional ideals that worked in the past may be adapted to modern times. But at the same time he can be a patriotic sannyasi *karmayogī*, fighting selflessly to implement these ideals. This latter role was given shape and reinforced in particular, we have seen, by the renouncer-heroes of Bankim's *Anandamath*.

The androcentrism of Upadhyay's thinking cannot fail to have been noted. It is nothing remarkable for the time and context, of course. Hindu Sanskritic religious tradition has been strongly androcentric (see Lipner in Smart and Thakur, 1993). Though there was no real challenge to this basic feature in the bhadralok society of Upadhyay's time, the traditional status of women in this society had begun to be influenced by corresponding Victorian prejudices. There were opposing views among bhadralok 'conservatives' and 'progressives' about the way their womenfolk should adapt to changing times. Women, traditionally regarded as the field (*kṣetra*) in which men planted the seed for an ongoing crop of desired offspring, continued to be viewed in this passive role, but now as the field over which (no doubt well-intentioned) males fought their ideological battles. They generally were cast in Victorian moulds as helpmeets of the men, as preferably (western-) educated but always chaste and supportive mothers and wives. They had a limited life of independence as persons in their own right (see Borthwick, 1984).

Not surprisingly, Upadhyay accepted this social stereotype. Recall his striking image of India (vis-à-vis Britain) in the role of a 'delicate, helpless chaste woman' clinging to her husband lest she become captive by some other 'gallant bully'.[28] The gist of Upadhyay's views on women is given in the address mentioned earlier in this chapter, entitled 'National Greatness', delivered on July 8, 1896, at the Max-Denso Hall, Karachi (the scene, the reader will recall, of the 'cut and thrust' of Upadhyay's lectures against Annie Besant later that year; see chapter 7). A crowded hall heard Upadhyay say that 'Greatness consists in a passionate love for some idea.' 'Idea' here was not some fancy or whim, but 'an eternal verity ... which manifests or symbolises itself through particular objects.' It was this that governed the destiny of a nation, not brute force. England was great because her regulating Idea was a passion for order. 'John Bull always adheres to order at any cost; and this passion has made him and his country great.'

Ancient India was great because 'she was enamoured of an idea, the idea of the Infinite and Absolute.... It is no exaggeration to say that in ancient India the natural reason of man reached its culmination

[28] In this context, Upadhyay is traditional-minded in at least one respect: the land of India, notwithstanding its chequered career as a geographical and political entity, has usually been imaged as female in Sanskritic tradition, especially in its relationship to the king. On occasion, however, (the earlier) Upadhyay referred to India as the 'fatherland'; as he identified himself more and more with his ancestral country, he referred to it as the 'motherland'.

in regard to the speculation about the Infinite.' But this great Idea has now dimmed in the Indian (= Hindu) mind, and the nation is no longer great. Before it can again become great, three fundamental conditions must be fulfilled: India's 'sons' should 'learn to respect themselves, to respect their women and to bear one another's burdens.' On self-respect and vicariousness in Upadhyay's thought enough has been said already. Here we shall focus on the second condition: respect for women.

'Woman,' declares Upadhyay, 'is not an attendant of man ... not an undeveloped man.... If she were only a defective man, where would be love?' But he should like to go a step further: woman has *special* claims to respect. In 'the consummation [i.e. heaven]' he avers, 'love and beauty will rule.... And woman is the concrete manifestation of love and beauty. Her character is noted for tenderness, devotion and piety.' The Greek dramas, Shakespeare, Sanskrit literature—all concur in depicting woman thus. Indeed, 'the most beautiful flower that adorns the ambrosial bower of heaven, is a virgin', namely, the Virgin Mary.

Today we would be inclined to say that these sentiments patronize women (in keeping with traditional 'civilized' androcentrism more or less everywhere). Women are still somewhat unreal for Upadhyay, to be kept apart on a pedestal. He seemed unable to relate to one with any degree of comfort in the earthy context of marriage. Note that the acme of womankind, for Upadhyay, is a virgin. The celibate state, for both men and women in fact, is the most perfect. And it is women who best symbolize this safe, even rarefied condition.

In other words, women are well advised to live like saintly paragons, or they run the risk of becoming the most appalling sinners—and leading men astray. This seems consistently to have been Upadhyay's underlying assessment of women (one perfectly in conformity with the classical Hindu tradition). Thus even as a young man he would say of Sarojini, his eldest brother Haricaran's little daughter, to whom he was especially close: 'I shall make a Brahmacharini [celibate] of this girl.... She will live the life of a flower and bring up other girls in the same manner. As long as girls of that type are not seen in this country, their misery will not be eased. The holy life led by widows is excellent, but the girl who would voluntarily set aside all pleasure and follow the road of renunciation would do a nobler thing.'[29]

29 Bl., p. 24. In the event, Sarojini's fate was to be married off, and Upadhyay helped earn the money for her dowry. But she seems to have died early (see Bl., p. 25).

The 'sinners' part of the evaluation is implied in another article written by Upadhyay, entitled 'The Axe Laid to the Root' (Sp-w, September 29, 1900). This substantial piece is an uncompromising attack against women working as barmaids. Upadhyay in fact writes protectively about the women doing this job, and decries the way they tend to be exploited not only by their employers but also by their unprincipled male customers. The bottom line, however, of the article is that 'the buxom female who serves liquor at a hotel bar ... serves for a decoy to lure people to their doom through the gay and well-decorated and festive-looking door-way of intemperance and debauchery, and as such the institution of bar-maids must be denounced as a damnable device of the Devil.'

Woman, therefore, for Upadhyay was ideally a 'flower'—to be protected, admired and idolized. She was man's helpmeet and support. It was a very role-oriented view. He himself had been dominated in his formative years by women—his grandmother Candramani, his aunt Nistarini—with whom sexual relations would have been strictly taboo, of course. Even the memory of his mother, who died when he was still an infant, had been romanticized.[30] It is perhaps not surprising then, granted the compounding impact of Victorian mores and the Sanskritic tradition, that Upadhyay reacted to women as he did. As far as he was concerned, ideally she was either delicate and helpless, to be protected, or a mother figure in full control of the situation, the protectress (modelled in his early years by Candramani)—a rather traditional Kshatriya view.[31] Either way, woman was not overtly the object of an erotic relationship; by implication, sex was tolerable strictly within the marriage bond, and any depiction of sexual activity outside this, as in so many Hindu myths, was likely to be regarded as 'obscene'. Finally, the sexual divide between male and female remained impassable. Thus it was that Upadhyay could turn in the

[30] During his work among the plague-afflicted in Karachi (see earlier), he had occasion to come to the aid of a sick young woman who was apparently being sexually harrassed. After he had seen off the miscreant, 'Upadhyay remarked: I lost my mother at a very early age. I have heard it said that she was famous for her beauty. When I see a fair girl I think that perhaps my mother was like that' (Bl., p. 7).

[31] Two influential male figures of Upadhyay's early years—his father Debicaran and the lame school-teacher, Pitambar—seem to have played a formative role here by default. Ashis Nandy remarks that 'between them ... [one is left with the impression that they] succeeded in shaping for Bhavani the concept of a terrorizing male authority' (1994: 53).

final years so naturally to Kali as the divine, avenging, protective mother—a liberating symbol of his 'motherland'.

However, to revert to the 'National Greatness' article, Upadhyay ends on a stronger note. He is all in favour of the education of women. It is this that will help make India great.

> Let us educate our women, develop their susceptibilities, give free scope to their aptitudes ... and then only we shall be fit to achieve greatness.... Man is being educated and enlightened, and woman is left to pine in the dark. The discrepancy has become almost critical and a great calamity will overtake India if it be not soon remedied.

Thus Upadhyay was certainly no obscurantist in this matter. Indeed, he was a 'progressive' in the context of the times, though it was a rather patronizing and role-directed context.[32]

But in his new environment of Calcutta, Upadhyay was being embroiled in further conflict with his Church, which influenced the development of his religious and political views and changed the course of his life.

32 In Sp-w, July 21, 1900, he notes that the Arya Samajists in the Punjab had lately invested a girl with the sacred thread, traditionally a male privilege. Though this is an ineffectually extravagant gesture that cannot really be sanctioned by the normative texts, he comments, still, 'We have the fullest sympathy with the motive and the spirit which have inspired the action.' So where women were concerned, he was not afraid to flout tradition on occasion.

# Chapter 11

# A Flickering Hope: Zaleski Again and *Māyā*

In UBBJ the Mukhopadhyays write, 'The Upadhyay that we see at the beginning of the twentieth century is an ardent protagonist [*pratinidhi*] of Indian nationalism. Outwardly, he was still a Roman Catholic, but in his heart of hearts [*hrdayer gabhīre sūkṣma anubhūtite*] he was a nationalist.... Even stronger than his passion (*neśā*) to draw India into the fold of the Christian religion ... was the dream of self-reliance [*ātmapratiṣṭhā*] for Hindu society' (pp. 68, 70). The oppositions mentioned here do scant justice to the complexity of the admittedly shifting balances in this period of Upadhyay's life. No doubt Upadhyay's political ambitions were becoming more overt and strident, but this was because of rather than in spite of his heartfelt commitment to his Christian faith, and his 'nationalism', such as it was, continued to be fired by the zeal to draw his country into the Christian fold. Thus, from the August 25 issue of the weekly *Sophia* till the journal's final edition, pages 5 to 8 (inclusive) dealt with religious and social topics and were printed as a pull-out section for wider dissemination to students.[1] It is not the editorial policy of someone with secondary religious concerns to devote the central pages—the heart, one could argue—of his publication to the significant inclusion of religious discussion, expressly with wider publicity in view.

A sample of article headings found in this section follows: 'The Decennial Passion Play at Ober Ammergau' (August 25); 'The Doctrine of the Supernatural' (September 8); 'Vedic Worship' (September 15);

[1] There were 12 pages in all, pages 10 onwards usually consisting of advertisements (except in the final issue or two), including an advertisement for the *Sophia* (see further).

'Maya', and 'Humility' (An extract from the writings of St Alphonsus Rodrigues) (October 20); 'Caste' (November 3); plus articles on the nature of Hindu society and its difference from 'Anglo-Saxon/ European' social behaviour, and regular discussion on correspondence largely about Catholic policy concerning caste practices. In this pull-out section, Upadhyay consistently defends the observance of (his idealized understanding of) caste on the grounds that it is a natural expression of the Hindu genius; as such, it does not militate against the supernatural religion of Christ, which is confined to beliefs that transcend but do not contradict reason.

The same old line; nothing has changed. This continues to be the underlying rationale of Upadhyay's more strident 'nationalism' and 'dream of self-reliance for Hindu society' (to use the words of UBBJ). Upadhyay writes:

> The religion of Christ is fixed.... But its influence, so far as society, politics, literature, science and art are concerned, varies with racial differences.... No mistake could be more fatal to progress than to make the Indian Christian community conform to European social ideals because Europeans happen to be prominent in the Christian world. So long as the Christians of India do not practise their faith on the platform of Hindu life and living and Hindu thought and thinking, and elevate the national genius to the supernatural plane, they will never thrive [October 27].

A more direct rebuttal of Zaleski's stance would be hard to find. But it shows us that Upadhyay was not only outwardly a Christian, he was still committed to his faith in his 'heart of hearts'. Indeed, a full two years after he wrote this, would he have bothered to summon up the energy and courage to travel to Rome and England in the hope of convincing the relevant authorities to support his inculturating vision, if he now embraced a newfangled 'nationalism' that had begun to marginalize his Christian faith?

But there is no doubt that his political sentiments, as recorded in the weekly *Sophia*, expressed a growing disillusionment and antipathy: disillusionment with a Church hierarchy obdurately unsympathetic to his vision of an indigenized faith, and in consequence, antipathy towards the devouring westernization that that Church, and by extension his country's political masters, seemed to embody. On the negative side, Upadhyay was slowly being consumed by these two fires, and a lively Christian faith was beginning to suffer the withering effects of their blasts.

Thus, on the political front, he made caustic attacks, in the weekly *Sophia*, on two key issues of British foreign involvement in 1900: the Boer war in South Africa, and the so-called Boxer rebellion in north-eastern China. There was not much on British policy concerning India—though Lord Curzon, the viceroy, came in for some mildly unsympathetic treatment[2]—and still less on native Indian political activities, such as those of the Indian National Congress. In his more overt (English) political writings at this time, Upadhyay was largely defensive and recriminatory.

Here are some examples. On the Boxer uprising, Upadhyay comments in an article entitled 'The War in China' (June 30):

> The European Powers have combined their forces and before the serried phalanx of their united hordes, China will have to succumb as surely as the corn does to the scythe. But her bravery and heroism in the sacred cause of her national independence will ever live in the world's history.... One's sympathies in such a case cannot but tend to the side of China.

By this time, as Upadhyay was well aware, attacks on and even massacres of foreigners, and indeed native Christians in China, were recurrent. Note too his tendentious description of the rather uncoordinated uprising as 'the sacred cause of national independence' and his contrast between the 'united hordes' of the foreign powers and the 'corn' that symbolizes China. Upadhyay's bitterness against 'the West' becomes even more apparent in his remarks on the conflict (July 21). Under 'Topics of the Day', he writes:

> The Chinese imbroglio is essentially a missionary broil. There are missionaries and missionaries. There are those who ... penetrate deep into the interior of the country adopted by them, become all things to all men, and teach the people to observe the supernatural without violating what is natural and national. But there are not a few whose landing is announced by booming gunboats.... These ... present their sectarian creeds in such crystallised, outlandish forms as do violence to native instincts. They are consequently looked upon by children of the soil as so many emissaries of foreign aggression. And they are really so.... They do believe in the heart of their hearts that ... Christianity is ... synonymous with Europeanising ... Reverends Jones and Cones drive in the thin edge of the wedge and then Tommy is sent for to hammer in the thick end.

2 Mildly to begin with, and then as time went on, a little less mildly. Perhaps Upadhyay's early criticism of Curzon was on the whole muted because the viceroy was a Catholic.

This kind of writing would hardly allay the fears of an unsympathetic Papal representative for whom Christianity *was* synonymous with Europeanization and who was keen not to antagonize not only the Tommies who policed the land, but also all those Joneses and Coneses.

The editor of the weekly *Sophia* pulled no punches either in his comments about the Boer war, a bitter, attritional conflict not least for the British. President Kruger of the Transvaal, implacable foe of the British and by all accounts a jingoist to the marrow, was hailed as a noble patriot when he reckoned discretion the better part of valour and finally fled his country. 'Go Kruger go!' laments the *Sophia,* 'And as long as the word patriotism retains its meaning in the ears of men, and the slightest spark of liberty smoulders in the remotest recesses of the human heart, thy name shall be cherished and thy memory endure' (October 27). We shall have occasion to note again this journalistic tendency of Upadhyay's to oversimplify an issue for ideological ends, seemingly to the point of editorial irresponsibility.

But perhaps the more sensitive could detect even more ominous undertones creeping into the *Sophia* editorials here and there. In an article dealing with a nation prevented by an alien power ('a hard task-master') from standing on its own feet economically (obviously in reference to the British and rather oddly entitled 'The Bread Problem in India', July 14), we read: 'Sooner or later, the growing manhood of the nation is sure to revolt and rise in arms against such a shameful state of stagnancy and indolence'. 'The people of India', comments another testy editorial, 'are a gentle and law-abiding people, and even when scourged by plague and famine which entail sufferings such as would goad into desperation and lash into fury and rebellion their brethren all the wide world over, they calmly bow to the inevitable' (August 4, 'The Indian Budget in Parliament'). The suggestion that the country's calamitous state was not unconnected with British policy towards India in the first place simmers below the surface. Was Upadhyay toying with incitement to revolt in these remarks?

Whatever his real motives, the tone of the weekly *Sophia* in general caused disaffection in Church circles. It was mainly his rather high-handed defence of caste on the one hand, and his bitter denunciation of the foreign approach, whether of missionaries or of the British administration, on the other—sensitive topics that surely required a more sensitive treatment—that began to alienate those he should have set out patiently to win over.

In *The Blade* (p. 107), a letter, written many years after Upadhyay's death, from a 'Fr Lacombe' working in the South and dated May 26,

1925, is quoted as follows: '[Upadhyay's] activities against European missionaries have been very baneful; they have greatly contributed to initiate the spirit of discontent against us among the High Caste. Owing to it we have had the terrible revolt here in Trichinopoly which has done incalculable evil. Intensifying the rivalry between High and Low Caste people it has postponed for many years the possibility of appointing an Indian bishop accepted by all.'[3] This is a serious charge, and the charge of editorial irresponsibility noted earlier is not diminished by it.

The letter also indicates that the weekly *Sophia,* although published from Calcutta, was particularly influential in the South. Indeed, on the last page of the first issue, there is the caption: 'SOPHIA. Largely circulated in Southern and Western India. Formerly published at Karachi, now in Calcutta'. This is why Zaleski's open letter forbidding the reading of *Sophia* to Catholics was addressed (see further) to the Archbishop of Madras. Khemchand was the journal's manager and attended to the financial and administrative side. Both he and the editor lived at the same address: 1 Gour Mohan Mukerjee's Street, in Simla, a locality in northern Calcutta. (Khemchand returned to Sind after about a year.)

The political tone too was noticed by observers and collaborators. Parmanand, in his article on the Sind Mission appended to Hull's work mentioned earlier in this book, describes the new *Sophia* as a 'politico-theological weekly' (p. 511). In his deposition written originally at Väth's request and printed after Parmanand's article in Hull, Khemchand writes: '[The *Sophia*'s] entry into politics ... caused an unpleasant impression in Calcutta circles.' After all, Upadhyay was a prominent Catholic by this time, writing in Calcutta, the capital of the Raj. He could hardly expect, nor did he desire, to go unnoticed. We know that he was in close touch with some of the influential clerics of his Church in the city. Perhaps they and the general sense of unease at the tone of the *Sophia* prompted him to publish a kind of disclaimer, under the title 'Our Personality', in the issue of September 8. Here Upadhyay says, quite unconvincingly, that the editorial 'we' is 'really and not ornamentally plural. It is not a *personal*

3 Louis Marie Joseph Lacombe (1866–1929) was a Frenchman who joined the Society of Jesus, came to India in 1888, and was ordained priest in 1893. Most of his ministry was in the South centring around St Joseph's College, Trichinopoly. He acquired a good reputation as a missionary, having started the Catholic Truth Society of India and worked among the Brahmins. See further, *Father Louis Lacombe, S.J.*, The Catholic Truth Society of India, Trichinopoly, 1930.

pronoun....' But personal pronoun it was understood to be, and, not to mince matters, quite reasonably so. All concerned knew their Upadhyay. It is significant, however, that the disaffection caused by Upadhyay's political tone in the *Sophia* was among co-religionists and ecclesiastics, not among political circles proper, whether British or Indian. These still regarded Upadhyay's activities as basically religious. Thus, Zaleski's opposition was by way of a pre-emptive strike, rather than a response to actual political pressure.

*The Blade* informs us that since the Archbishop of Calcutta at the time had gone to Rome for one of his statutory visits, Fr V. Marchal, s.j., the Vicar General, had taken responsibility for the diocese in his absence. Zaleski wrote to him requesting that Upadhyay be asked to resign from the editorship of the *Sophia*. We are told that both Marchal, and in turn Upadhyay, complied (p. 90).

Probably the disclaimer noted above appeared after this—as if it were enough! For the journal continued to appear in exactly the same form and with precisely the same tone as before. No one was fooling anyone. Yet Zaleski now played his trump card, keeping up the charade. A letter went out from him to the Archbishop of Madras, dated September 20 (and published in full in *The Bombay Catholic Examiner* on October 6), which stated, with characteristic insensitivity, that:

> The owner of the present weekly 'Sophia' is a heathen; all collaborators are heathens. The paper has no connection whatever with the Catholic ecclesiastical authorities, and the Catholic collaborators have a few weeks ago severed their connection with it.... [There follows a quotation of the journal's aim to compare Vedantic Hinduism with basic Christian teaching].
>
> In the thirteen numbers which have already appeared, the *new Sophia* handles *ex professo* [authoritatively] the most difficult questions of philosophy and theology, in a manner which shows, to say the least, that the writer has but an imperfect knowledge of Christian philosophy and theology.... Your Grace will easily understand the danger of ... the Christian Creed itself being misrepresented when it is done by unqualified persons, and more so, when writers who are not Catholics, treat these questions *ex professo* and presume to 'supply a new garb to the religion of Christ' [a quotation from the *Sophia*].
>
> I deem it therefore necessary to warn the Catholics of my Delegation against associating and reading the said periodical Sophia....

In the autocratic atmosphere of the time, this was a devastating blow. No 'good' Catholic, ecclesiastic or layperson, would henceforth readily associate with or support in any way either the journal or its producers. Zaleski left nothing to chance. On October 27, again in the BCE, he issued a fresh declaration from his official residence in Kandy.

> In order to avoid any misunderstanding with regard to Our letter to His Grace the Archbishop of Madras, of the 20th September last, which has been published in the Catholic papers, we declare that no Catholic of our Delegation is allowed to subscribe to or read the periodical 'Sophia' without a special permission of his Bishop or Ordinary.

In the first declaration, Zaleski, though trying to maintain the charade that the *Sophia* was no longer a Catholic publication (presumably because he had been informed that Upadhyay had 'resigned' from the editorship), gave the game away as to who his real target was by including all thirteen previous issues in his condemnation (when, one assumes, all those 'heathens' were *not* in charge), and by referring to the writer of the offending articles in the singular. Even then, he didn't bother to ascertain the facts. Khemchand, a Catholic convert, and likewise Upadhyay, were still active, indeed essential, collaborators. Neither had repudiated his faith.

Upadhyay had played one last card. He had requested that an ecclesiastical censor or 'Bureau of censors' be appointed to vet every article of his for any heterodox content before it was published, so that nothing might appear that was doctrinally suspect. This request was refused by Zaleski. Khemchand opines that this was possibly because Zaleski feared that Upadhyay might succeed in convincing the censors that his views, though pioneering, were not really unorthodox. Khemchand notes that 'the ecclesiastical authorities in Calcutta ... had more or less general sympathy with Upadhyayaji's ideas of expounding Christianity in a new garb' (Hull, p. 519). It is not clear whether the request for a censor was made before Zaleski's first declaration (as Khemchand indicates) or after it.[4] Certainly the whole process was a protracted one, and during it Upadhyay continued to publish, as we have noted, exactly as before. There was no apparent

4 As indicated by *The Blade* (see p. 92, which refers to a letter from Upadhyay dated October 7, 'explaining that he was resuming the editorship and asking [for] a censor to be appointed').

attempt in the journal to soften the tone or make amends (e.g. see editorial mentioned above of October 27). The irresistible force had finally met the immovable object, and something had to give. What gave was the weekly *Sophia*. This ceased publication with its last issue on December 8.

One may wonder at Upadhyay's naivety in all this. Did he really believe that the deciding reason for Zaleski's opposition was theological? Did he not realize how disruptive, even subversive, of 'proper order, authority and image'—characteristics so beloved of autocratic ecclesiasticism—his persistent socio-political comments might appear? But the theological reasons were not far behind. Zaleski knew his name and objectives well by now. There was that small matter of the 'Kāsthalik' monastery in Jabalpur. We know how deeply unsympathetic Zaleski was to what we now call 'indigenization' of the Christian religion. In this light, Upadhyay's experiments or explorations—undertaken with such strident certainty!—must have appeared alarming to a dyed-in-the-wool conservative. Certainly Upadhyay's tone about indigenizing the Catholic faith was far more assertive in the weekly *Sophia*. It was in this publication, after all (June–July), that those assured articles (under the title of 'Being') on the nature of the supreme reality as *Sat, Cit,* and *Ananda*, appeared (see chapter 8). So there is no doubt that theological alarm bells were sounding in Zaleski's mind. All in all, Upadhyay was becoming a serious nuisance, and Zaleski acted accordingly.

But the charge that Upadhyay was theologically incompetent, that he had 'but an imperfect knowledge of Christian philosophy and theology', must have hurt keenly, especially after all the testimony we have adduced, both public (newspaper and other reports) and private (Boedder's responses etc.), to the contrary.[5] Upadhyay should have tried harder to give a more sustained *argument* for his views, rather than simply insisting that they were timely. But the die was cast.

Yet Upadhyay seems to have been unaware that this was so. He continued to be as importunate as ever. In the November 17 issue of the weekly *Sophia* a new challenge is issued—clearly by Upadhyay—in an unsigned article entitled 'The Twentieth Century'. The new century, we are told, will be blessed, especially for Catholics, by the Eucharistic Congress at Goa about to take place. Nevertheless, two things must be done to consolidate these blessings. First, 'an

5 Zaleski's lack of perceptiveness is surprising if our argument stands that Upadhyay's indigenizing theology was in effect an attempt to give Neo-Thomism, rather than directly 'the religion of Christ', a new (Indian) garb.

indigenous organisation which will undertake to establish a central educational institute for the higher training of our young men on *national lines'* must be established. By 'our' Upadhyay is referring to Catholic youths. We are not given an indication as to what this programme should be, though it is not difficult to guess what the writer has in mind. 'What is the state of affairs now? There is scarcely any Catholic whose guidance and counsel are solicited in matters concerning the political and social welfare of India.'

No doubt patriotic sentiments in the broad sense of this expression—'the political and social welfare of India'—remained central to Upadhyay's concerns, but equally central, indeed, the motivating element, was a *Catholic* patriotic response. The Jesuits were making a valiant attempt to educate the youth of the land, the article continues, but 'it cannot ... be denied that, though beneficial in many ways, the education given to our boys by the Jesuit Fathers does not tend to national development. The paucity of Indian Jesuits is one of the chief reasons why'. A good point, but would this sustain the sympathies of his Jesuit friends?[6]

'The second thing necessary,' continues the article, 'is to have a well-equipped, well-edited journal which will discuss and *agitate all questions* involving the welfare of India' (emphasis added). Such a publication will 'infuse' public-spiritedness and relevance into the Catholic presence in the country. It will also make known to Catholics in western countries the 'grievances and aspirations' of Indian Catholics. 'The Journal may be named *The Twentieth Century*', concludes Upadhyay.

The journal *was* named *The Twentieth Century*. The first issue appeared under Upadhyay's direction in January 1901. But of course the recurrent problem remained: Zaleski remained antagonistic. Upadhyay's persistence continues to amaze. Was he oblivious of the fact—with increasingly dire consequences for his own standing—that

6 In the next issue of the journal, November 24, the last but one before the end, Upadhyay criticizes a major achievement of Zaleski's tenure as Papal Delegate, namely, the Papal Seminary at Kandy that Zaleski helped establish. 'There is the Papal Seminary in Ceylon for the better training of indigenous priests' remarks Upadhyay, but 'Sanskrit is not to be found inside it. It is through this want of knowledge of Hindu philosophy on the part of missionaries that the religion of Christ has not been presented intelligently to the educated Hindu'. Following hard on the heels of Zaleski's denunciation this could only provoke rather than persuade. For the last 30 years or so (from the writing of this book), however, distinguished scholars have taught Sanskrit and Indian thought in this Institution, which was translated to Poona in 1955 and is now called Jnana Deepa Vidyapeeth.

the most powerful dignitary of his Church was immovably opposed to his attempts to 'agitate all questions' (including the political), supposedly concerning the welfare of India, *especially* with reference to the country's Catholics in mind? That his desire to act as *agent provocateur* in these matters was counter-productive? This calls for a comment about his journalistic strategy. It appeared to be lacking at least in that it consistently alienated the opposition rather than persuading it to think along his lines. This consequence was repeated a few years later when he relentlessly criticized (almost exclusively in Bengali now) what he perceived to be the depredations of British rule and western influence in India; it culminated not only in his trial for sedition but also tragically in his death. So far, then, as its proper targets of influence for a desired reconstruction or reappraisal were concerned, Upadhyay's journalism generated a failure of communication. As such it was ineffective. It was sensational, entertaining, knowledgeable, and relevant for the mass of its readers, but it was also highly confrontational and misdirected arguably where it mattered most.

*The Twentieth Century* appeared at the end of each month, beginning with the issue of January 31, 1901. It boldly stated that the editors were N. Gupta and B. Upadhyay, and that K.C. Nan was the publisher.[7] In fact, as *The Blade* points out, 'the orientation betrays Upadhyay as the soul of the journal' (p. 98). Each issue comprised 24 pages. Inside the front cover, under 'Features', we have, in a vertical column: '1. Representation of different systems of religion and philosophy. 2. Study of Hindu thought. 3. Discussion of general politics and social questions. 4. Critical notices of literature, polite and serious [sic]. 5. Review of current affairs'. Indeed, the same brief as the weekly *Sophia*. 'General politics and social questions' are clearly included. Under this list there is a statement that there will be no 'editorial' articles on theology, and that every article on religious matters 'will go forth with the imprimatur of the writer's name'.

This is curious for two reasons. First, Upadhyay will write editorially on theological topics. Second, the intended force of the term 'imprimatur' is obscure. Who was issuing this imprimatur? Certainly not Zaleski! Did it just mean that the author was assuming

7 Upadhyay's friendship with Kartik Nan was long-standing. As we have seen (chapter 3), the relationship began by Upadhyay's acting as Nan's private tutor in 1880. Now, over 20 years later, Nan returned the compliment as a sort of patron of *The Twentieth Century*. The collaboration was to continue in the forthcoming years in important ways.

responsibility for what appeared against his or her name? But then this was only to be expected. Why the use of 'imprimatur'? To compound matters, Upadhyay introduced a personal journalistic innovation. For, for the first time, he started writing under a nom-de-plume, Narahari Das, which, he explained to Agnes, Khemchand's daughter, meant 'Servant of God-made-Man' (literally, it means 'servant of the God-man'), that is, Christ. It was not always clear to readers that 'Narahari Das' was Upadhyay or indeed a Christian; both names appeared regularly against titles of articles appearing in the journal.[8] This arrangement was complicated further by the fact that Upadhyay also contributed articles anonymously, i.e. articles whose authorship remained unattributed (a blank against the title appearing in the list of contents).[9] This means that about half to two-thirds of the content of every issue of the TC was written by Upadhyay.[10] He was trying to perform a difficult balancing act: writing on 'theological' topics (topics with specifically Christian content) in his own name but in a non-editorial capacity (notwithstanding his declaration that he, B. Upadhyay, was an editor of the journal), and writing on non-'theological', but still clearly religious, topics under an assumed name (or under no name at all). This convoluted distinction simply broke down or proved misleading in the public eye.

Under the heading 'Contents', each issue generally adopted the following format: there was an item entitled 'The Month' (which focused on current, broadly political matters), and then about five to nine articles. The scope and tone of Upadhyay's political comments were similar to those of the weekly *Sophia*.[11] No respite for Zaleski

8 Cf. 'Once it so happened that a young brahman who had chanced to read the articles [by 'Narahari Das'] on the Vedanta published in *The Twentieth Century*, entered into an argumentation with [Upadhyay] and severely reprimanding him for renouncing the religion of his ancestors by becoming a Christian, recommended the said articles ... for enlightenment. Imagine the dismay of the assailant when he found out that he had been attacking the writer of the articles in question!' *Sketch*, pt. I, p. 27.

9 We can identify Upadhyay's contributions here with certainty not only because of style and content, but also because much of this material appears in revised form under his name in Bengali publications.

10 Other contributors were N. Gupta (most frequently), and on one or more occasions, Mohitchandra Sen, M. Winternitz, Romeshchandra Dutt and Merwin-Marie Snell. Some of these latter contributions appear to be reprints of talks or articles published elsewhere.

11 The China situation and the Boer war continue to be discussed. The behaviour of the European forces in China generally receives unfavourable attention. In the first issue of the TC, the Russian troops are said to 'have shown themselves to be perfect fiends'. With respect to the Boer war, we have, e.g. (No. 5, May 1901): 'However much Mr Chamberlain or Lord Salisbury may justify the war and its course, and

here. Nor did Upadhyay mitigate his remorseless attack on the destructive effects, as he saw them, of Europeanism in both social and religious matters (i.e. on political life in the *broad* sense of this expression) on, especially, Hindu India.

Thus, on the social front, the TC expresses, albeit in a truncated and somewhat restrained form, Upadhyay's idealized view of the ancient caste system, its virtues as compared to the social mores of 'the West', and the desirability for its re-implementation in current times. The very first issue summarizes this position in an anonymous article entitled 'Varna Asram or the Aryan Social Divisions'. The article is clearly by Upadhyay and condenses what he was to say later (in early 1902), more elaborately and uninhibitedly, in the Bengali article *Varṇāśrama Dharma,* published in *Bangadarsan.* We have discussed this at length in chapter 10.[12] Aspects of this view are repeated at various places in the TC. We need not discuss this further.

In the field of religious politics, Upadhyay's strategy is, as of old, twofold. On the one hand he contends that the Hindu tradition—in particular the early Veda and Vedanta—provides suitable data on the natural plane for the reception of supernatural Christian (= Roman Catholic) truths. On the other hand he maintains that the Christian faith is not to be identified with its European garb, which is uncongenial for Hindus, and that it should be propagated among Hindus in Hindu, particularly Vedantic, form. What is perhaps innovative in the TC is Upadhyay's claim that this putative Vedantic form is *superior* to its European counterpart and is better able to convey Christian truths. What continues to fascinate, however, is that this superior Vedantic expression of the Christian understanding—from the standpoint of the natural light of reason—of the (implicitly trinitarian) nature of God and the divine attributes of creatorhood,

---

apply the salve of satisfaction to the conscience of the English people, the Boers will rank among the Greeks and Romans of modern history, which will record in glowing colours the passionate and faithful patriotism of this people, their glorious and heroic struggle to retain their liberty, their unparalleled achievements on the field, and the high honour and forbearance of their leaders.' And on the Viceroy: 'Lord Curzon is a statesman of the school of compromise. He deals justly but his justice is a little mixed up with the spirit of compromise between the oppressor and the oppressed.... Justice for the sake of justice is not in his line.... Whenever he has to deal with measures affecting the vital interests of the country at large, he acts like the man in the fable who pleased nobody by pleasing everybody' (No. 7, July).

12 See note 14 of chapter 10.

omniscience etc. is once again neo-Thomism wrapped up in mainly Advaitic terminology.

The first couple of issues herald the tone and content of the publication. On the religious front, in volume 1, there is an article by Narahari Das entitled 'Sankara's Introduction to the Vedanta'. There are two articles, 'The Incarnate Logos' and 'The Madonna', by B. Upadhyay' (not to mention the anonymous 'Varna Ashram or the Aryan Social Divisions', also by Upadhyay).

In volume 2 (February), Narahari Das contributes the first article of three (the serial ends in volume 4), entitled 'M. Thibaut's Introduction to the Vedanta—A Critique'. As we shall see, the intended contrast is clear. *Shankara's* Introduction, which the author says he proposes to 'expound not criticise', is the acceptable one, whereas Thibaut's Introduction, the subject of a critique, is to be rejected. The terms of the contrast are familiar to us by now. For those who know their neo-Thomism, 'Sankara's Introduction' turns out to be a a fairly clear-cut baptism of the great Advaitin by Upadhyay. Thibaut, on the other hand, deluded by philosophies of the West, has perpetrated only misunderstanding and misrepresentation.

We need not labour the point. In the first article, Brahman, the Supreme Being, is described as pure being, and therefore pure act ('To be is to act', p. 5), and therefore, intrinsically self-contained and unrelated. The old preoccupation with God's utter metaphysical self-sufficiency, which emerged in Upadhyay's correspondence with Boedder all those years ago, remains unabated. Brilliantly, one could even say creatively, using the structure and terminology of Shankara's own thought, Upadhyay interprets this theologian for his own ends, viz. as providing intellectually the metaphysical foundation for a Christian understanding of the divine nature and its relationship with the world.

> Even a great many among those who believe in God and the next world are subject to a very subtle error. They look upon the Supreme Being as a *yushmad* [literally, a 'Thou'], a separate individual.... The All ... which is the substratum of being ... is placed on a pedestal high above the skies, no doubt, but limited and circumscribed by *separate* individualities. But there is a subtler deception played upon man by avidya [= spiritual ignorance]. God is apprehended only as a related being. His absolute nature which transcends His creatorhood is not discerned by many theists (p. 6).

In this way, the distinction between natural and supernatural, so central to Upadhyay's and current Catholic thought, is maintained.

God in his supernatural, i.e. intrinsic, being is philosophically and theologically separate from his creation. If we understand this distinction aright in all its ramifications, we can live appropriate natural existences (which include caste and other cultural practices) ready to add on theologically, liturgically etc. practices and beliefs deriving from supernatural Christian truths. Shankara, apparently, has not been deceived by the subtle errors of *avidyā* in his commentary. (How? one may ask. Through some form of divine dispensation granted especially to the Vedantic tradition and its most outstanding Hindu commentator?) Thibaut, however, the most outstanding Western interpreter of Vedanta of the day, has not been so subtle. He has misunderstood, and hence misrepresented, the teaching of the Vedanta.

This is because his very starting point is flawed. 'Indoctrinated' by a European philosophy that is essentially pantheistic and relativistic, he has interpreted 'Vedantic theism' accordingly, 'with a bent of mind ... perfectly alien to Vedantic thought'. This is nowhere more evident than in his (mis)translation of three Vedantic terms: *nirguṇa, abheda,* and *avidyā*. 'Nothing can be more unjust' declares Upadhyay, 'than to translate "nirguna" as "impersonal"'. *Nirguṇa* actually means 'tie-less' and also attributeless, since *guṇa* can mean both 'rope' and 'attribute'. Brahman is attributeless in that knowledge, goodness, bliss, and being are not divine *attributes,* they coalesce as the divine essence itself. As such, they do 'not make the supreme Being impersonal or non-personal.... The supreme Being looked at from the transcendent standpoint is *nirgunam* (supra-personal). And when considered from the related plane of creation he is *sagunam,* one having attributes'. Further, says Upadhyay, according to Shankara, Brahman is not unknowable. Shankara explicitly teaches that the Upanishads declare that Brahman is knowable as bliss, intelligence etc., though when predicated of the Supreme Being these terms have to be purified of their finite connotations.

Next Upadhyay considers the term *abheda* (non-difference). 'Shankara teaches that the individual soul is different from the highest Self (Paramatman) as well as non-different from it. If *abheda* means '*absolute* identity' as M. Thibaut supposes, then the individual soul can never be said to be distinct from the supreme Being in the face of their declared non-difference. Was Shankara so hopelessly blind as not to perceive this gross, palpable contradiction? Surely not'. What Shankara really means, says Upadhyay, is that the individual soul is a reflection (*adhyāsa*) of Brahman. 'According to Shankara, creation is a kind of communication by the supreme Being. Created things partake of his being. But this act of communicating as well as of partaking (*vivarta*) is very mysterious. No visible analogy can represent it perfectly'. Nevertheless, Shankara does very well in this respect by comparing 'the communication of being in creation ... to the sun's reflection in water'. Just as the sun remains untouched *per se* in spite of numerous and varied reflections, which have a sort of being totally dependent on their source, so 'God communicates being but is not affected in the least'. He does this by an 'inscrutable power which is called *maya*'. 'The conditions of *maya* affect the communicated beings, but [Brahman] abides unconditioned for ever and ever. The bold imageries of the East are generally misunderstood by Europeans'. According to Shankara then, the individual soul is *different* from Brahman in that it is a 'reflection' of Brahman, the result of a mysterious communication of being; it is *non-different* from Brahman 'inasmuch as [Brahman] is the substratum of the [individual soul], as the real sun is that of the reflected one. What is reflection if divorced from the original? Nothing, falsity, darkness'. *Avidyā* or *māyā*, then, is not 'illusion', it is the principle of creation. ('M. Thibaut's Introduction to the Vedanta—A Critique I', TC, February 1901).

We need not rehearse at length the Thomistic interpretation of Shankara in Upadhyay's exposition. *Māyā* is simply made out to be the principle of divine creation, which itself is 'the communication of being'. And being, 'divorced' from its 'substratum', is, to use Thomas' own phrase in Latin, *nihil* (nothing), *falsitas* (falsity), *tenebrae* (darkness). Thus, Shankara becomes a crypto-Thomist; indeed, he is the Indian precursor of St Thomas (since he lived centuries before the latter), had he but known it!

Upadhyay continues his Critique of Thibaut in the next two issues in like vein. In Part II of the Critique (March 1901), he concentrates on the meaning of the terms *māyā* and *avidyā*. 'Vedantists make a distinction between *maya* and *avidya*. The creative power, as referring to the Creator, is called *maya*, and the same power, as affecting creatures, is designated *avidya*. It should be observed that the distinction is only technical and not essential'. According to Shankara, says Upadhyay, there is no 'essential manifoldness in the Infinite'. The divine essence is one and changeless. How then does it act causally? 'Shankaracharya, the greatest apostle of Vedantism, teaches that the cause of the universe does not reside in the necessity of Being ... [which is the] foundation [of the cosmos whose] cause is in the superfluity of the eternal I AM, and not in the internal, necessary economy of divine Life. This superfluity, this munificence is called MAYA. It is divine creativeness'.

So, from the 'ontological' point of view, *māyā* is neither real nor unreal. 'It resides in God but it does not belong to the constitution of divine Life.... It has no title to being because it is a mere contingent superfluity'.

From the 'cognitional' point of view, *māyā* veils the inner nature of Brahman. Creatures, which are 'products of *māyā*', cannot rise above *māyā* 'perceive the Lord of *maya* in his absolute nature'. This gives rise to a higher and a lower knowledge with respect to Brahman. The former, which is beyond the reach of creaturehood, would know Brahman in himself, 'as transcending all relations with effected things'; the latter, which is accessible to creatures, is knowledge of Brahman 'circumscribed by duality', as abiding in relatedness. The veil of *māyā* can be pierced only in this respect, that we can apprehend (though not comprehend) *that* Brahman exists essentially as absolutely unrelated, and only contingently as related by his mysterious communication of being. This true teaching is inculcated by (Shankara-)Vedanta.

Finally, from the 'moral' point of view, *māyā* or *avidyā* is 'an occasion for sin and evil'. *Māyā*, which is hard to understand, gives scope for distorting the nature of reality, for looking upon God as necessarily related, and for bestowing upon the world, 'which is *nothing*', a reality and a desirability that it does not deserve. This is the root of all evil. 'Had creatures been endowed with the vision of the Absolute [as essentially pure and unrelated], there would be no sin, no *karma*, no *samsara* (the world of birth and death)'.

Here again, the interpretation is entirely compatible with traditional Thomistic thought. In terms of this innovative analysis of *māyā* and *avidyā* along Thomistic lines, Shankara's Vedanta becomes potentially philosophically receptive of Catholic doctrine, though this is not said explicitly. Shankara has not been interpreted as providing an indigenous context for receiving and moulding the Christian message in an unprecedented form, but as a crypto-Thomist, speaking in one-to-one Sanskritic conceptual correspondences (*nirguṇa* = supra-personal, non-related; *abheda* = non-difference, reflection; *māyā/avidyā* = divine creativeness, divine inscrutability as the occasion for ignorance and evil) vis-à-vis Thomistic discourse.

In Part III of his Critique of Thibaut (TC, April 1901), Upadhyay, alias Narahari Das, returns to Thibaut's interpretation of Shankara Vedanta as characterizing 'this world ... [as] but a dream, an illusion'. Nothing could be further from the truth, avers Upadhyay. Indeed, it would be no exaggeration to say that 'there is scarcely any human philosophy on the face of the earth which has combated so effectively the doctrine of cosmic unreality' as that of Shankara, in particular through his refutation of Buddhist idealism. 'The Vedanta [of Shankara] is founded on the rock of the veracity of sense-information'. Thibaut has completely misunderstood Shankara here. 'The real Vedantic doctrine of cosmic unreality is not that the world is an *illusory appearance*, but that it has no *necessary* reality'. It exists by virtue of a borrowed existence; it is the result of a free act of creation by Brahman. The Creatorhood of Brahman is not essential to his being. 'It is a superabundance whose presence is equivalent to its absence so far as the fulness of Brahman is concerned.... The vision that Brahman is all in all, that the world is a huge nothingness, a mere contingency, is *mukti* (liberation). This is the essential teaching of the Vedanta as expounded by the great Shankara.' Upadhyay closes his Critique with a warning to his compatriots. 'Yield yourself once to the European influence and you lose your balance. You will have no stability, no profundity.' You will be unable to appreciate that 'the Vedanta [as interpreted by Shankara] is one of the grandest achievements of man—nay, the strongest rational bulwark of Theism.'

It is ironic that Upadhyay failed to appreciate the fact that his own understanding of Shankara was so pervaded by neo-Thomistic thought. Shankara could well have been making the 'rational, theistic' points claimed by Upadhyay, but it is not helpful for appreciating the putative originality of Shankara's view to be apprised of it in Thomistic terms! All the more so if it is claimed that Shankara-Vedanta is 'the strongest rational bulwark of Theism', the best natural platform (to use earlier words of Upadhyay) for the superimposition of Catholic doctrine. In any case, the strength of Upadhyay's religious mission continues undiminished—well into 1901.

But even analytically, Upadhyay did not remain unchallenged. We may note here sustained and informed opposition to his interpretation from an internal quarter, so to speak, i.e. from within his own Church. This came from another Sanskritist and former collaborator, the Jesuit Indologist A. Hegglin.[13] Hegglin was now teaching Sanskrit at St Xavier's College, Bombay. He attacked the heart of Upadhyay's attempted rehabilitation of Advaita as a natural philosophical receptor of Catholic teaching—Upadhyay's reinterpretation of the term *māyā*. Already, in late 1900, he had written a substantial letter challenging this

13 See chapter 5, note 22.

reinterpretation; Upadhyay published this letter in the joint 15th–16th issue of the weekly *Sophia,* September 29. It appeared well after Upadhyay's important article, 'The true doctrine of Maya', published in the February–March issue of *Sophia,* 1899 (and analysed in chapter 8). In his letter, Hegglin lists thirteen meanings given to the term *māyā* recorded in the Sanskrit dictionary of V.S. Apte, well known at the time. 'From this list', contends Hegglin, 'it is clear that Maya was used in Sanskrit mostly to denote something deceitful or false, or illusory'. Even if one or two senses could potentially be redeemed to suit Upadhyay's purposes (e.g., meaning 10, the Vedic 'extraordinary power, wisdom'), these senses were too vague when compared with the Christian sense of *creare,* to create. For *creare* was used by the Christians to refer to 'the fact that God has called the world into existence out of nothing', whereas a rehabilitation of *māyā* in the Vedic sense, if one were to be true to its original meaning, could only indicate 'the wisdom and the power with which God has made the world'.

Besides, in the sense used in Vedanta philosophy (meaning 5), argues Hegglin, *māyā* stands for 'unreality, the illusion by virtue of which one considers the unreal universe as really existent, and as distinct from the Supreme Spirit'. This is 'totally at variance with' Upadhyay's attributed meaning of 'God's will to create which is to us something like an enigma, an enchantment', or, from the supposed Vedantic point of view, of the world itself as illusion in so far as it is perceived to be a reality independent of God. Even before Europeanized minds came on the scene, continues Hegglin inexorably, Shankara was understood by his indigenous adversaries (e.g. Ramanuja) to teach illusionism, that is, the final unreality of the world. Thus, concludes Hegglin, *māyā* 'primarily denoted in classical Sanskrit fraud, trickery, deceit, illusion; with this notion *maya* is known to the Hindu mind; to attempt to restore it to its original meaning is an unwise and useless enterprise doomed to failure.'

In the same issue, Upadhyay responded by saying that he was glad to have been thus challenged, for 'the idea of re-stating Christianity in the terms of the Vedanta can only grow in strength by being thoroughly sifted and analysed'. He then states that creation implies three things: (1) that God does not necessarily create; (2) that created things come into existence from prior non-existence; and (3) that 'the finite perfections are contained in the infinite in a pre-eminent way'. The western term 'creation', he continues, expresses only the second significance (that stressed by Hegglin), whereas *māyā* expresses all three. Upadhyay promises to argue this subsequently, and makes special reference to a late Vedantic text, the *Pancadasi*, which he claims defines 'the precise theological meaning of the term *maya*'. We shall return to this.

However, it seems that the closest Upadhyay comes to defending his position at length, though without specific reference to Hegglin's attack and his initial response to it in terms of the three characteristics of creation mentioned, is in the four articles of *The Twentieth Century* discussed above. This is because in these articles his stated opponent is Thibaut and not Hegglin. The articles, in fact, consider at some length the first two characteristics of 'creation' mentioned and not the third.

In 1902, Upadhyay finally started his study of the *Pancadasi*. His efforts were published in the form of a small booklet entitled *Panchadasi: A Literal English Translation with Original Texts and a Commentary in English, by B. Upadhyay* printed by R.C. Ghosh, at the Kaiser Machine Press, 48 Grey Street, 1902 Calcutta. The *Pancadasi*, circa fourteenth century, is a well-known and substantial Advaitic text showing the influence of Samkhya thought. Attributed to a certain Madhava (and composed probably in part by one Bharatatirtha Vidyaranya as well), the *Pancadasi* has been divided into fifteen chapters, comprising some 1571 verses in all. In his 'Apologia' to his study, Upadhyay declares that 'Vedantic (i.e. Advaitic) philosophy ... unfolds a peculiar aspect of the ancient Theism which is the rational basis of the revelation of God's being as above the plane of nature (*maya*)'. Scholastic thought did a fine job of providing this basis in its time. But now 'a newer and bolder method' is needed. It is 'Vedantic thought that will ... supply materials for such a system as will combat the seductive influence of current agnosticism and pseudo-idealism by elevating the human mind to the apprehension of a God whose being is above the necessity of time-relations.' To this end he will undertake a translation and commentary of the *Pancadasi*. This will also rehabilitate and rejuvenate the best in Hindu thought, and protect it from the onslaughts of a denationalizing Europeanization. In the event, Upadhyay's booklet translates and comments upon only the first fourteen verses, less than one per cent of the original; the project was not continued.[14]

Upadhyay's commentary on these verses is concerned mostly with explaining, ostensibly in an Advaitic setting, but with Thomistic

[14] By the time Upadhyay's booklet was published, at least two English translations of the *Pancadasi* were in existence. An English translation with Sanskrit text current today is Swami Swahananda, 1980.

undertones, how individual consciousness (*saṃvid*) is an unreal 'mode' of the absolute consciousness. ('The modal existence of the Absolute is called unreal to distinguish it from those modes which create modifications in causes passing into effects.... Pure and perfect [cognitive] self-initiation can only be found in a being whose act of [ontological] endurance has its source as well as its term or boundary entirely within itself ... [and] which is ... self-sufficient, independent of any conditions.') The Scholastic terminology in this explanatory passage is evident. There is brief reference to *māyā* which contains nothing new. As we have indicated before, Upadhyay sometimes lacked the staying power—or was it the patience?—to abide with what he had started and seek to bring it, notwithstanding attendant difficulties, to a conclusion. In fact, where the *Pancadasi* project was concerned, by 1902 he had other things on his mind.

But Hegglin did not let his opposition to Upadhyay's interpretation of *māyā* rest there. To conclude this topic, we may mention that once more in 1903 he challenged Upadhyay's position. We have noted (chapter 10, note 24) that, while on a visit to England, Upadhyay had contributed two articles to *The Tablet* (entitled 'Christianity in India' in two Parts, January 3 and 31, 1903). The second article concentrated on caste; the first was on Hindu (Advaitic) metaphysics as the appropriate rational theistic basis for the reception of the Gospel among his (westernized) compatriots and the banishment of current 'naturalistic' and 'evolutionist' philosophical trends among them. In this article, Upadhyay promoted *māyā* as 'a principle of illusion' by which 'God manifests himself to be the cause of the world without being essentially a Creator'. This leads to Vedanta being 'in exact keeping with Catholic philosophy', though expressed in language 'full of Oriental imagery'.

Hegglin found this unacceptable. He attacked Upadhyay's interpretation head-on in an article entitled 'Vedantism and Maya' in the BCE (January 31, 1903), and then through three further articles (BCE, April 18 and 25, and May 23, 1903) directed explicitly against a defence of Vedantic theism (in two articles, BCE March 28 and May 2) by a 'Hindu Theist'. Hindu Theist, whose identity excites curiosity, not least for his ready quotation of the Bible, Catholic teaching and Scholastic Latin terminology, had openly referred to Upadhyay with approval ('that brilliant Brahmin convert, Swami Brahmabandhav Upadhyay'). (Was Hindu Theist the pseudonym of a Jesuit sympathizer of Upadhyay's?)

In fact, Hegglin's role in the controversy in the pages of the BCE is interesting. Earlier, in a 'Leading Article' in this publication on January 24, the editor of the BCE refers to Upadhyay's contribution to *The Tablet* of January 3, querying its central claims. His main doubt centres around his last query: 'Does the Hindu thought contained in the Vedanta really coincide with Christian philosophy?' He professes not to be competent to answer this question and invites 'the attention of those versed in Sanscrit lore to the subject'. Almost on cue, Hegglin answers with 'Vedantism and Maya' in the next issue.

Indeed, Hegglin's responses in general are so antagonistic to Advaita and so superciliously certain of its unsuitability for Upadhyay's ends, that one wonders at his motivation. It is difficult to explain it alone by a scholarly desire to expound the truth or guard against error. Nor is his tone explicable by the tendency of the times—that continuing legacy of the Enlightenment—to dispute as if arriving at the truth were a simple process of sifting the 'objective' evidence. So very many intellectuals of the nineteenth century had truth in their pocket! On the contrary, Hegglin's purposes seem as tendentious as his opponent's. If Upadhyay's interpretation of Advaita was a *benigna interpretatio* (benign interpretation) for ideological reasons, Hegglin's was a *maligna interpretatio* with a vengeance. Was he acting on his own, or was he put up to it by local ecclesiastical authority?

We need not dwell on Hegglin's critique. Its main lines, devastatingly dismissive, are known: that Upadhyay's interpretation is 'novel', unsupported by western and traditional Hindu exegesis alike, that Advaita is 'Pantheism pure and simple', and that in this light, the principle of *māyā* is a logical absurdity, compromising both the perfection of God and the processes of rational thinking. Hegglin concluded: 'With the exception of Buddhism, there is no system ... in the world so iredeemably hostile to Theism as the philosophy of the Vedanta.... The Vedanta system, which Brahmabandhav offers us as a medium for the conversion of the Hindu, is one of the saddest if not absolutely the saddest aberration ever perpetrated by the human mind.' Upadhyay did not have much chance of a sympathetic hearing with so intractable a foe.

He had no chance with the latter's superior either. Two years earlier, Zaleski had pounced on *The Twentieth Century* as ruthlessly as ever. *The Blade* informs us that Zaleski was apprised of the existence of the journal while on a visit to Rome.[15] Back came the response post haste:

[15] Väth suggests (1928: 163) that Upadhyay's writings in the TC imperilled efforts made, under the aegis of British rule, by the Indian hierarchy to ensure inheritance rights

> The late periodical *Sophia* having reappeared under the name of *The Twentieth Century,* we hereby notify that prohibition regarding the periodical *Sophia* is extended to *The Twentieth Century,* and therefore all Catholics residing in the limits of our Delegation are forbidden to read, to subscribe to, and have any connection with the above said monthly review, *The Twentieth Century.*
>
> Given in Rome, outside the Flaminian Gate, the 20th of June 1901.
>
> Ladislas Michael,
> Archbishop of Thebes,
> Delegate Apostolic (Bl., p. 103).[16]

*The Twentieth Century* folded with the twelfth and last issue, December 31, 1901, but not before Upadhyay had made one last deposition, to any who would hear in the BCE (August 17, 1901). The occasion was correspondence in this publication about his connection with *The Twentieth Century.* Upadhyay's statement consists of 14 points (explicitly enumerated) to the effect that: he has always been honest about his position to the public and to his ecclesiastical superiors; the aim of *The Twentieth Century* is open debate about, not evaluation of, the various religions; he has never been convicted of perpetrating theological error—he has been condemned for trying to present Christian teaching 'in Hindu garb' (nevertheless, this is an attempt supported by 'experienced missionaries' and 'high placed ecclesiastics'); he will submit ultimately to the judgement of his Church, though he reserves the right to appeal to Rome; finally, he is a patriot, and his love for his faith and for his country go hand in hand. This last point (no. 9 in the list) is worth quoting in full: 'Next to my faith I hold my country dearest to my heart. I cannot give up my attitude of a constitutional oppositionist to the British Government which must be moved to give us the right of self-government, consistent, of course, with the integrity and supremacy of the British Empire in India. I shall deeply resent any interference in this matter on the part of the ecclesiastical authorities, provided the interference

of Christian converts in the southern states of Mysore, Travancore and Cochin, and also that a protest was lodged to Zaleski by 'Bishop Hürth of Dhaka'. So Upadhyay's activities were being monitored around the country, and Zaleski, already hostile, may have felt it necessary to respond to such promptings.

16 Väth passes a legalistic comment but without making a case for it: 'This ban too is not to be queried from the canonical point of view (*kirchenrechtlichen Standpunkt*)' (163).

be not on the grounds of faith'. Thus, politically, Upadhyay is not a radical; he will settle for British rule in India provided India is permitted a mode of *svarāj* or self-government. If only the whole affair had been handled differently, both by Upadhyay and by his ecclesiastical authorities, the course of the history of the Catholic Church in India might have been very different.

Besides what we have already discussed, *The Twentieth Century* had one or two other items of interest. We may mention first another Sanskrit hymn composed by Upadhyay that appeared in an article he wrote entitled, 'The Incarnate Logos' (January issue). The hymn is given in Devanagari script and followed by a translation. This brief article first gives, as 'a fore-glimpse of the inner life of God', a description of the inner relationships of the three persons of the divine Trinity, in classical Catholic terminology. As such it is a model of its kind. But then Upadhyay offers something new: a description of the incarnation, that is, how God the Son, the second person of the Trinity, 'united himself to a human nature' without ceasing to be divine, in terms that a Hindu might more easily understand.

To this end, Upadhyay brings into play a teaching taken from chapter 2 of the Taittiriya Upanishad according to which human nature is made up of five sheaths: the 'physical (*annamaya*) which grows by assimilation', the 'vital (*pranamaya*)', the 'mental (*manomaya*), through which is perceived relations of things', the 'intellectual (*vijnanamaya*), through which is apprehended the origin of being', and the 'spiritual (*anandamaya*), through which is felt the delight of the supreme Reality. These five sheaths are presided over by a personality (*ahampratyayi*) which knows itself'.

This interpretation calls for justification, which Upadhyay does not offer. He continues, however, that in Christ (or God incarnate), these five sheaths are present, making him human, but they are 'presided over by the Person of the Logos himself [the second Person of the Trinity] and not by any created personality (*aham*).... The Incarnation was thus accomplished by uniting humanity with divinity in the person of the Logos.' The explanation ends here. It is hardly enough. Large assumptions about the meaning of the Taittiriya text and the role of the 'I' (*aham*) in Vedantic tradition are left unjustified or unexplored. Once again, Upadhyay makes a promising suggestion that he does not follow up.

He is then prompted, nevertheless, to present to his readers the (Sanskrit) hymn in praise of the Incarnate Logos. The hymn is given in its original Sanskrit, briefly commented upon and translated by

Gispert-Sauch (1972). As Gispert-Sauch says, 'This hymn is perhaps less successful than the *Vande Saccidanandam*, and much less known.'[17] At the end of each stanza there is the refrain 'Conquer, O God (*jaya deva*), Man-God (*nara-hare*)'. We offer our own translation of the hymn:

> [You, who are] the blossoming of the abundance of eternal Knowledge,
> The reflected One, the transcendent form of the Absolute,
> Conquer, O God; Conquer, O God; Conquer, O God, Man-God![18]
> [You, who are] the child of the golden Virgin,
> Ruler of being, delightfully related, yet without relations,
> Conquer, O God etc.[19]
>
> [You, who are] the ornament of the assembly of the learned,
> Destroyer of fear, Scourge of the wicked,
> Conquer, O God etc.[20]
>
> [You, who] remove all kinds of suffering,[21]
> Serving others,. sanctifying by all your doings,[22]
> Conquer, O God etc.

17 Gispert-Sauch goes into the finer points of the rhythm. He also notes perceptively that each of the six stanzas of the hymn sings 'the glories of six stages in the existence and life of Christ': (1) as pre-existing in God; (2) as Incarnate; (3) in his hidden life; (4) in his public life; (5) in his death; and (6) in his glorious and victorious life. It may be of interest to note that when the author was interviewed on Upadhyay in Calcutta for Indian television (Doordarshan, 1994), the programme opened with the background singing of this hymn. It had been put to music by Chitra Bani, a local Communications Centre.

18 *Upacitaciracinmukurita, pratibimbita brahmaparātpararūpa; jaya deva, jaya deva, jaya deva, narahare.* Upadhyay (Up), who provides his own translation, translates *upacita* by 'overflowing' and retains 'Brahman' (as does Gispert-Sauch = GS); *pratibimbita* is glossed as 'mirrored' (G-S:reflexion), and *rūpa* as 'Image' (GS:beauty). The refrain is translated as, 'Victory be to God, the God-man' (GS: Victory to you, Lord, the God-Man).

19 *Kanakakumārībālaka, bhavacālaka, nirguṇaguṇābhirāma; jaya deva* etc. Up: *bhavacālaka:* director of the universe (GS:yet Ruler of the Universe); Up: *nirguṇaguṇābhirāma:* absolute, yet charming with relations (GS:with your qualities enchanting, yet beyond qualities).

20 *Paṇḍitamaṇḍalamaṇḍana, bhayakhaṇḍana, daṇḍitabhaṇḍanabhūta; jaya deva* etc. My translation follows Up except for *daṇḍitabhaṇḍana* (Up: chastiser of the spirit of wickedness; GS, who has 'the Vanquisher of temptation' for *bhayakhaṇḍana*, translates this compound as 'Chastiser of the evil one').

21 So *ādhivyādhivitāḍana.* Up:Dispeller of spiritual and physical infirmities; GS: the Destroyer of all infirmities.

22 *parasevana pāvanalīlākhela*. GS: Love in brotherly service, sanctifying the marvellous works; Up: 'one whose actions and doings are sanctifying' for the second compound.

[You who through] your own words have offered yourself,[23]
Whose life was a sacrifice, who have destroyed the poison of sin,
Conquer, O God etc.

[You who are] the desired one, the beloved, the delight of the heart,
Soothing to our vision, Wondrous destroyer of terrible time(s),
Conquer, O God etc.[24]

The language and the style (especially the refrain) are typical of similar hymns in the Hindu tradition. And while the hymn's Christian connotations are easily intelligible, I venture to say that terminologically they would not jar Hindu ears in the least. Indeed, the words are replete with Hindu resonance (e.g. *brahmaparātpara-*, *nirguṇaguṇābhirāma, bhayakhaṇḍana, kṛtakilbiṣaviṣanāśa, lalitadayita, kālakarāla*). To me this is a more 'Hindu' composition than the other hymn, and certainly deserves to be better known than it is at present.

We may advert to one more item of particular interest in *The Twentieth Century:* Upadhyay's composition of the 'Hail Mary' in Sanskrit. This appeared in the same issue (January 1901) at the end of an article entitled 'The Madonna' ('At the threshold of a new century my heart is intoxicated with a new wine of love for the Madonna, the Spotless Virgin'). Only the Sanskrit is given[25]; there is no translation. Our own translation will show that the Sanskrit is not an exact rendering of the traditional English form: 'Hail Mary (*maryyame*), full of grace (*prasāda*), illumined by the Lord (*virājā virājite*) and blessed among women (*nārīkuladhanye*). Blessed is Jesus (*jiśu*) born (*prasūta*) of your womb. Holy Mary, mother of the child of the Gracious One (*śivasūnuprasivini*), make of us an offering and save us sinners, now and at the end-time (*antakālam*). Amen (*tathāstu*)'. We have already mentioned Upadhyay's much earlier composition of the Lord's Prayer in Sanskrit.

23 Thus *viniveditanijavadana*. This may also be translated as '[You] the Word, who have offered yourself'. Up (curiously): One who has offered up his agony; GS: Lifting yourself up in self-offering. The text continues: *balijīvana kṛtakilbiṣaviṣanāśa; jaya deva*, etc.

24 *Lalitadayitahṛdrañjana, nayanāñjana sudalitakālakarāla; jaya deva* etc. *nayanāñjana*: Up: (soothing) pigment of the eye; GS: ointment of delight to our eyes. *Sudalitakālakarāla*: Up: crusher of fierce death; GS: Victorious crusher of cruel death.

25 *Namas te maryyame, prasādaparipūrṇe. virājā virājite, nārīkuladhanye. tava jaṭharaprasūtaṃ jiśuḥ puṇyabhājanam. maryyame puṇyamayi, śivasūnuprasavini. kuru no nivedanam, pātakijanatāraṇam, sadyaś cāntakālam. tathāstu.*

These Sanskrit compositions are just another indication of an ongoing pioneering attempt by Upadhyay—impelled as he was by love for his faith and ancestral culture—to fuse the two to the best of his ability. As we have seen, the attempt is fraught with problems, both conceptually and linguistically. But it is a passionate attempt, indeed, a brave attempt to make the Christian faith at home in the Hindu context. It is also a highly significant attempt; for never before in modern times had there been so sustained and salient an endeavour to indigenize Christian belief and practice. This endeavour played a crucial role in creating a new climate of exploration, even of experiment, in the process of indigenization. It showed not only how certain things *might* be attempted, but also *that* they might be attempted; it created new room in the breathing space of the Church. And with the passage of time, no one (not even Zaleski) was able to gainsay this.

The new century witnessed fateful turnings in Upadhyay's increasingly anguished life. These led him inexorably along a path of greater frustration as he neared the end of life's journey. They also pointed him in the direction of an overt militancy in the political sphere; after all, the end was only about six years away, and the pace was quickening.

# Chapter 12

# Torch-bearer: Santiniketan and Oxford

It is not well known that it was Brahmabandhab Upadhyay who helped propel Rabindranath Tagore to fame. Upadhyay first publicly noticed Tagore in a serious way in an article entitled 'The world poet of Bengal' in the weekly *Sophia* (September 1, 1900). With uncanny prescience he wrote:

> 'Rabindra is not only a poet of nature and love but he is a witness to the unseen. Revelation apart, Kant, Tennyson and Newman are considered to be three modern witnesses to the invisible world. Poor Bengal has produced another and it is Rabindra Nath.... If ever the Bengali language is studied by foreigners it will be for the sake of Rabindra. He is a world-poet.... He will be ranked amongst those seers who have come to know the essence of beauty through pain and anguish.

Prasanta Kumar Pal, in volume 4 of his *Life of Rabindranath* (*Rabijībanī*, 1988: 292–3) suggests that Tagore sent a cutting of this article to a friend shortly after it was published. If this was the case, Tagore was aware of a notable admirer in Upadhyay.[1]

In any case, it seems that by the first half of 1901 Upadhyay and Tagore had established fairly regular contact. In a letter hand-written in English by Upadhyay to Rabindranath,[2] and dated July 5 of that year, Upadhyay begins: 'My dear Sir, I owe you an apology for not duly acknowledging receipt of your "Naivedya" '. *Naivedya* was a book

1 This does not mean, of course, that Tagore was a regular reader of the *Sophia*, for the article may have been drawn to Tagore's attention by a friend.

2 Preserved in the 'Upadhyay Brahmabandhab' file in the Archives of Rabindra Bhaban, Santiniketan. The letter is addressed from 20/1, Madan Mitra's Lane, Simla P.O., Calcutta.

of poems by Tagore that had recently been published. The opening sentence of the letter intimates that Tagore had sent the work to Upadhyay, possibly with a request for review in his journal. For Upadhyay continues:

> I have roughly analysed it and found in it four divisions: (1) personal, (2) human, (3) national, and (4) transcendental. I have not been able to discover a single theological flaw in the book. Its theism is sound to the core. It is an embodiment of the essence of Bhakti made compatible with transcendence. I am tempted to write, not a critique, but certain reflections which may serve as a key to readers not initiated into the mysteries of the Infinite.

In the July issue (1901) of *The Twentieth Century*, Upadhyay, writing under his nom-de-plume of Narahari Das, published his review of *Naivedya* ('Offering'). It is a substantial and highly appreciative review,[3] in the first part describing this collection of poems as a welcome development of the poet's earlier work.[4]

The content of *Naivedya* is then summarized by Upadhyay under four headings,[5] which are said to correspond to 'four fundamental

3 Reprinted in UBBJ as an Appendix, it runs to 13 pages, pp. 213–25 (inclusive).

4 In an unpublished Note arising out of her research, Linda Woodhead, Lecturer in the Dept. of Religious Studies, University of Lancaster, describes *Naivedya* as follows: '*Naibedya* marks the beginning of a new phase in Rabindranath's literary and intellectual career.... [It] has a more serious tone ... a new sense of purpose.... Like Rammohun's God and like Debendranath's God, the God of *Naibedya* seems to be a universal God ... a God whom India has known and worshipped throughout her history ... God is to be found not outside the world but within it.... God's creative activity runs through everything.... In some respects, the form of theocentric asceticism advocated in *Naibedya* may be compared to the *niskāma karma* advocated by the Gītā (and revived by Bankim).... The God of *Naibedya* is a fiercely moral God ... a God of strength and power, the God of a muscular Hinduism.... He calls those who serve Him not to *jñāna-mārga*, but to *karṃa-mārga*, the path of valiant and noble deeds.... What he requires is truthfulness in word and speech, respect for others, protection of the weak ... [yet] He is a God of love, *bhakti-mārga*.... The links between patriotism and the religion of *Naibedya* are drawn out quite explicitly.... This is Bharat's true God.... It is from Him alone that the gifts of strength, freedom and independence which India so desperately needs will be received ... [yet] the God of *Naibedya* is not a nationalistic God.... *Naibedya* is deeply patriotic, but expresses no longing for political power.'

5 Expressed somewhat differently from the descriptions in the July 5 letter. This July issue of the TC was published very late. There is another hand-written letter in English from Upadhyay to Tagore in the Upadhyay file of Rabindra Bhaban, dated August 8, in which Upadhyay informs Tagore that he has 'great pleasure in sending for your perusal two proof sheets of the "Twentieth Century". They contain a few reflections on your Naivedya.'

ideas' in the work: '(1) Alone to the Alone; (2) God in humanity; (3) God as the moulder of the destinies of nations; (4) the all-inclusive God by himself'. Amid praise for Tagore's literary style, Upadhyay analyses extracts from the poems under each heading. Though 'the All-holy ... lives alone' there are times when it calls 'the spiritually-minded ... human soul alone' glosses Upadhyay; nevertheless, 'to partake of the sufferings of fellow-man is God-like, is to live the life of God on earth. What is innocent suffering but the suffering of God, as it were, in humanity?... Rightly does the poet long to be saved through trouble and turmoil, pain and anguish.... I hope the poet will, in due time, sing more of this sublime theme ... and rouse up the hearts of our people from torpor to the sense of bearing one another's burden.' On the third theme, continues Upadhyay, 'the poet's ideal is to build the national greatness of India on the pure, ancient Hindu foundation purged of its dross.' What is this 'pure, ancient Hindu foundation'? We are not left in much doubt. Earlier in the review Upadhyay had declared that *Naivedya* gave 'expression to the spirit of primitive, universal Theism in a pre-eminently Hindu way'; it is 'religious poetry without being [sectarian] theology.... There is not a single theological blunder in the whole collection. Its theism is sound to the core.... [The poems] are the outpourings of a human heart and, as such, they belong to nature and universal reason.'

Here Tagore, the rising star of literary Bengal, is adduced as supporter and reinforcer of Upadhyay's religio-political vision, that is, that there is in the (principled) human heart (Tagore's[6]) a 'natural' insight into the divine nature and ways, i.e. a propensity to rational theism, which is expressed through the particularities of one's culture. In Tagore's case this is the Hindu culture, and his poetic mastery both displays to good effect and ratifies Hindu culture as a potential natural receptor for the fullest revelation of the divine will, enshrined in the teachings of Catholic Christianity (though this latter aspiration is not stated explicitly, of course). Further, it is a particular aspect of Hindu culture that is best suited to act in this way, viz. Vedanta, and Tagore's poetry intimates this. Upadhyay writes, after quoting an extract supposedly exemplifying the fourth heading noted above: 'Who does not see in [this] sonnet ... the ancient Vedantic aspiration of attaining to *Niralamba-Brahmajnam* (knowledge of God as He exists in Himself)?' Certainly Upadhyay does. So this review, while expressing genuine admiration for the future 'world-poet', depicts him as an

6 Tagore, intimates Upadhyay, is a 'lofty soul ... in personal contact with God's grace.'

unwitting ally of the reviewer's cause. The signs are all unmistakably there, even to the point of using phrases like 'bearing one another's burden', which readers of this book will recognize.[7]

Tagore, however, seemed to have been well pleased with the review. In the Preface to *Car Adhyay*,[8] he wrote: 'Once when Upadhyay was busy editing the monthly journal *Twentieth Century*, he wrote a review in that journal of my newly published work, *Naivedya*. Before that I had not seen such uninhibited praise of my poetry anywhere else. It was on this occasion that I first got to know him *(sei upalakṣe tā̃r saṅge āmār pratham paricay)*.' Pal (1988: 294) queries the last statement. He points out that the *Sophia* article on Tagore (published September 1, 1900) could not have been written without Upadhyay's having actually seen Tagore, and that in the first issue of *Bangadarsan* with Tagore as editor (Baiśākh, i.e. April–May, 1901), Upadhyay published an article whose opening lines were a (substantial) quotation from *Naivedya* that had not been published previously. Only Tagore himself could have provided that, he surmises. So how could Tagore say that his reading of the *Naivedya* review later was the occasion of his and Upadhyay's 'first *paricay*'?

Perhaps this is not a very important issue, but it all depends on what Tagore meant by, and indeed how we interpret, the Bengali word *paricay*. It can mean a first introduction; but it can also be taken to mean the beginning of familiarity with someone. Or perhaps when writing in the early 1930s, Tagore's memory of the strong impression made on him by the *Naivedya* review occluded all remembrance of earlier not very impressionable contacts. We favour the first interpretation. In any case, there is no doubt that in the latter half of 1901, Upadhyay and Tagore entered upon a deepening relationship that, as Pal says, was to affect Tagore profoundly.[9]

With the faithful cooperation of Animananda, Upadhyay had opened a school in the house of his former student and now friend and close collaborator in various matters, Kartik Chandra Nan, at 18

7 Though it is not to our purpose to assess Upadhyay's literary critique of Tagore's work, it is difficult to avoid the comment that Tagore is indeed a 'world-poet' who has been ill served in general by his critics and admirers for want of a sound grasp of his context and language. A proper appraisal of Tagore and his work is still awaited.

8 See Introduction, note 1.

9 *Brahmabāndhaber saṅge jogājoger pratikriyā Rabīndranāther jībane sudūrprasārī hayechila*; ibid. So profoundly, in fact, that Upadhyay became the inspiration for more than one of the characters of Tagore's novels. We shall return to this point later.

Bethune Row in north Calcutta. The school, in a later metamorphosis named the Sarasvata Ayatan ('The Abode of Learning', see chapter 13), was run on 'Aryan' lines.[10] The concept was nothing new. 'Aryan' or 'Vedic' schools of one sort or another, the main purpose of which was to build up a cultural identity in their students on the basis of a study of Sanskrit and conformity to its traditions, were a familiar phenomenon in the country by the late 1880s. The Arya Samaj had given a lead in the Punjab (Jones, 1976, especially chapter 3), and other establishments existed in other parts of the country.[11]

We are told (Bl., p. 93) that six or so students 'of respectable families' (probably, therefore, of Brahmin, Baidya and/or Kayastha stock—and all male, of course) attended to begin with, that they were charged no fees, and that they sat on the ground.[12] In September,[13] the school was moved to a rented building in Simla Bazar Street.

Before the move, and possibly even after it—for Upadhyay seems to have been staying with Kartik Nan—Tagore frequently conversed with Upadhyay at the Nan residence.[14] Where Upadhyay was concerned, Tagore, it seems, had an axe to grind. For, on July 25 (1901) he wrote to his friend, the scientist Jagadishcandra Bose, that he had returned to Calcutta from his estate, Santiniketan[15] (where he wished to open

10. This must have been earlyish in the latter half of 1901. Remarkably, a prospectus survives in the form of a pamphlet, setting out the syllabus for what appears to have been a more established phase of the school. We shall take this up in the next chapter.

11 Some of these institutions professed not to discriminate where caste was concerned (as in the case of the Arya Samaj), whereas others selected pupils only of the higher castes (as in the case of the Vedic School founded in 1884 in Benares by the Bharatvarshiya Arya Dharma Pracharini Sabha).

12 'The paraphernalia that fill the ordinary schools were conspicuous by their absence' (ibid.). Most of the students were the sons of male friends or relatives of Upadhyay; they included Sudhir Chandra, the son of Kartik, and Asok Krishna, the son of Upadhyay's elder brother, Parbaticaran.

13 Soon after the founding says Bl., and 'In September 1901' says *The Sketch*, pt. 1, p. 28.

14 'From Jorasanko, Rabindranath would come, by gharry [horse-drawn carriage] or on foot. "Is Kartik Babu in?" Up the stairs to the first floor he went. There on the floor Upadhyay was squatting in garic garb.... Words were exchanged. They had so many ideals in common.' Animananda writes further on: 'So great was the impression produced by Brahmabandhab on the poet that going home, he ordered tables and chairs out of his room, and returned to the ancient Vedic system. Debendranath [Rabindranath's father] felt quite differently and the European furniture was brought back' (Bl., pp. 93–4).

15 Santiniketan, meaning 'Abode of Peace', was an open tract well endowed with large, shady trees, near Bolepur, about 90 miles (146 km) north-north-east of Calcutta.

an educational establishment along traditional lines) in search of a couple of 'self-denying celibate teachers' (*tyāg-svīkārī brahmacārī adhyāpak*).[16] These without doubt were Upadhyay and Animananda. So, by this time, there had occurred a good meeting of minds between Upadhyay and Tagore at least with respect to educational ideals. The visits to Kartik Nan's house had borne fruit. But Upadhyay and Animananda were running the 'Aryan' school there. The next stage was to negotiate a future for Tagore's proposed school at Santiniketan in conjunction with this one. Tagore had written to Jagadishcandra: 'All the rules [of his intended school] must conform to living with the guru as in ancient times. There musn't be a trace of luxury (*bilāsitā*); everybody, well-off and poor, will have to adopt a strictly celibate way of life (*kaṭhin brahmacarye dīkṣita haite haibe*)'. Can one doubt that in Upadhyay he had found his man?

*The Blade* informs us that 'one fine morning' that year, Kartik Nan, Tagore and Upadhyay went to Santiniketan to inspect the place,[17] and that in December Animananda transferred 'the whole party of children' to Tagore's estate. Thus did the now famous educational experiment of Santiniketan begin. The Santiniketan School was inaugurated on Sunday, December 22, 1901.

In 1933, a rather misguided controversy arose over the origins of the School. The controversy was initiated by a Dr H.C.E. Zacharias, a Christian, who declared in his book *Renascent India* that Rabindranath based his project on the institution already begun by Upadhyay.[18] The other (Hindu) side maintained that the poet had started his ashram school before he knew Upadhyay. Pal mentions some of the details (1990, vol. 5, pp. 61ff).[19] From the evidence at hand, we arrive

16 *Rabijibani*, vol. 5, p. 25.

17 From the evidence adduced by Pal (1990, vol. 5, p. 37), this was in the first half of November.

18 '[Brahmabandhab and Animananda] started in Calcutta a school for high-caste Hindus ... and after a few months were joined there by ... Rabindranath Tagore.... Rabindranath prevailed upon them to transfer their school to a country-seat of his father, near Bolpur; and thus began Santiniketan' (p. 29). In the Introductory, Zacharias describes himself as a western Catholic of Jewish descent, who has 'spent the larger part' of his life in the East and who had become 'an Associate "Servant of India" in that Society founded by [Gopal Krishna] Gokhale' (p. 13). In the section on Upadhyay and Animananda he makes it clear that he had spoken to Animananda about the school at Santiniketan; so he would have been perceived as giving 'the Christian' side of events.

19 Surprisingly, Pal does not refer to evidence from Bl. See also the first Appendix (*Pariśiṣṭa Ka*) of UBBJ, pp. 149–50 (hereafter K). This Appendix is a reprint of an

at the following conclusion: there is no doubt that Tagore already had it in mind to start a school conforming to ancient Hindu ideals before he became closely acquainted with Upadhyay; there is also no doubt that before this acquaintance Upadhyay had begun to implement a similar ideal (the 'Aryan' school). Collaboration was mooted and occurred after Upadhyay and Tagore got to know each other better. This makes sense of Tagore's letter to Jagadish Bose (dated July 25, 1901; see above) and of *The Blade's* testimony (pp. 93ff). More significantly, perhaps, it makes sense of a letter purporting to state the facts of the matter written by Kartik Nan from his house in Calcutta to Tagore, dated August 6, 1933. In somewhat peremptory fashion, Nan writes:

> At about the time of your acquaintance [with Upadhyay], you invited him and us to visit Santiniketan. A few days after this Upadhyay [*Upādhyāy mahāśay*[20]], a relative of mine, myself and my son Sudhir, were your guests at Bolepur for a day or two.[21] At the time there was no Brahmacharya Ashram [Tagore's proposed School] at Santiniketan. When Upadhyay raised the matter of a Brahmacharya Ashram, you said that you too had an exactly similar intention but that it had not been implemented yet. As the result of your joint enthusiasm, then and there plans began to establish such a school.... Upon his return to Calcutta, Upadhyay did not delay to collect pupils—since at the time he had a school in Simla Street; he dissolved that [*seiṭi bhāṅgiyā dilen*[22]], and taking my son Sudhir, my nephew Rajen, his [i.e. Upadhyay's] friend's son Gora, Kala, Nanda and a few more students, Upadhyay and I went to Bolepur. After a day or two, Upadhyay's disciple Rebachand arrived with a few more pupils. You, for your part, made arrangements for 2 or 3 teachers, some more pupils and everything else, and when Rebachand arrived you gave him the responsibility of chief master [*pradhān śikṣak*]. Being in agreement with Upadhyay's proposal, you established the ashram on the basis of *varṇāśrama*.... What I

article entitled 'Rabindranath and Brahmabandhab and the founding of the Bolepur Brahmacarya Bidyalaya' (*Bolpur brahmacarya bidyālay rabīndranāth o brahmabāndhab*) first published in the *Jugantar*, April 16, 1961 (the centenary year of Upadhyay's birth).

20 Throughout this 'deposition', Upadhyay is referred to respectfully as *Upādhyāy mahāśay*.

21 This presumably refers to Bl.'s statement that 'one fine morning' Upadhyay and Kartik visited Santiniketan with Tagore (see above).

22 This may be an overstatement; see our discussion below.

> wish to say is that the Brahmacarya Ashram was founded on your joint efforts. To say that you joined up with Upadhyay's Calcutta school is baseless and to say that Upadhyay joined up with an ashram already established by you is equally incorrect.[23]

This, I believe, is in essence the right conclusion. Tagore was always grateful to Upadhyay for his indispensable collaboration in starting the Santiniketan project.[24] There is some confusion about the extent of the transfer of students from Upadhyay's school which by then was functioning from Simla Bazar Street. *The Blade* says that 'Rewachand [Animananda] took the whole party of children to Bolepur and Santiniketan began' (p. 94). Yet it seems that the school at Simla Bazar Street had not actually been closed down (for, as we shall see later, some students had apparently been sent back to it—or to a hastily reconstituted school?—when dissension broke out in Santiniketan). With the transfer to Bolepur, Upadhyay did not himself move there permanently; it was Rewachand who stayed on with the children at Santiniketan. Upadhyay, one must recall, was at the time of the transfer still tied to Calcutta, editing and defending *The Twentieth Century*

23 Pal, 1990: 62. The whole letter is given in K, pp. 150–2. Tagore replied briefly in a letter dated August 8, in which he acknowledged Kartik Nan's letter and said that his response would be made known in due course (see next note).

24 That it was started as a joint venture seems to be corroborated by Rabindranath himself. In the Rabindra Bhaban Upadhyay file there is a letter written in Bengali by Tagore to Upadhyay in which Rabindranath says: 'If we can involve Manoranjanbabu [i.e. Manoranjan Bandyopadhyay] in *our* school [*āmāder bidyālaye*] I will be particularly happy' (emphasis added). The letter, which lacks a date, is in poor condition and is not preserved in complete form. Years later, in an article published in the *Prabasi* (Āśvin, B.E. 1340, September 1933)—this was the awaited response to Nan's earlier letter—Tagore wrote ambiguously about the matter. He mentions Upadhyay's welcome appreciation of his book, *Naivedya*, and says: 'In connection with our acquaintance in this regard, [Upadhyay] was apprised of my intention [to found a school] and was informed that I had received permission from my father concerning the proposal to establish the school at Santiniketan. There was no need to delay, he said, in implementing my intention. Bringing some of his faithful disciples and students he involved himself in the work of the ashram. At the time, from my side there were Rathindranath and his younger brother Samindranath as students, while [Upadhyay] added a few on his part.... If the main teaching load (*adhikāṃśa bhār*) had not been borne by Upadhyay and Mr Rebachand—whose title is now Animananda—it would have been impossible to carry on the work. The title of 'Gurudev' which Upadhyay gave me at the time is still one I have to bear from the inmates of the ashram .... I have made clear the essentials about the beginning of the Santiniketan school. And with this I acknowledge my unrepayable gratitude to Upadhyay' (see K, p. 155). The semantics in this statement are tortuous on occasion (which I have tried to reflect in the translation), and fail to resolve Kartik Nan's desire to establish the precise sequence of events.

(the last issue of which was dated December 31 of that year, and which must have come out well after that date, in January 1902).[25] Occasionally he would attend meetings of various learned bodies, including the Bangiya Sahitya Parisad (Bengal Literary Society) at which Rabindranath sometimes spoke. He was also contributing to the influential Bengali journal, *Bangadarsan*, which Tagore was editing. When Upadhyay wanted a change he would visit Santiniketan and have impassioned religious discussions with Tagore.[26] While in Calcutta, 'Off and on [Upadhyay] would give a class' there (Bl., p. 95). Whether this was before the Bolepur period or during it (in a re-established Simla Bazar Street set-up) is not clear.

That the Simla Bazar Street School still seems to have been (at least, notionally) in existence even during the Bolepur period we may deduce from a stray comment or two in *The Blade*. Animananda (or his amanuensis, Turmes) says that (probably in the first half of 1902) the bigger boys of the Santiniketan establishment had 'been sent back to Calcutta'—presumably to the parent school.[27] It is not clear why. Then, some months later, it was rumoured that Rewachand, a staunch Catholic, was trying to proselytize the younger children under his

25 This period must have been particularly stressful for Upadhyay. Zaleski's interdiction of the TC had come out in June of that year. By December the journal's demise must have seemed imminent. In a letter in English by Upadhyay to Tagore dated December 5, written from 39 Simla Street, Calcutta (Rabindra Bhaban Archives), Upadhyay says, somewhat cryptically, 'They suspect me, they try to avoid me. However my whole heart is with you and I shall do whatever lies in my power but I shall zealously check my zeal from being demonstrative [sic] lest it prejudices the sacred cause before the eyes of the public.'

26 On this Tagore has written: '[Upadhyay] was my first collaborator in establishing the School at the Santiniketan ashram. In this connection, even today when I think of it, I wonder at all the abstruse points he would clarify during discussions as we often walked along the village paths surrounding the ashram' (*Car Adhyay*, Preface to first edition). As Tagore intimates (see earlier), it was Upadhyay who first called Tagore 'Gurudeb' in connection with the Santiniketan School project; it was an appellation that stuck, and that at times the poet found a heavy burden. The term has resonances that are difficult to translate, but 'Most Sublime Guru' conveys something of the exalted status implied. Ashis Nandy's statement then (1994: 1) that 'Tagore was the first person to call Gandhi a *mahatma*, Gandhi was the first to call Tagore *gurudev*', cannot be correct in this respect.

27 But then who was running this institution, since both Animananda and Upadhyay were otherwise occupied? Upadhyay may have been trying to do both jobs: running the/a reconstituted school and *The Twentieth Century*. The *Sketch* (Pt 1, pp. 30–31) says confusingly, 'In August 1902, eight lads attended a new born school in Simla Street. The ideal that was to be carried out in the romantic scenery of the Bolepur

care in Santiniketan.[28] As a result Upadhyay wrote 'in clear, frank words' to Rewachand from Calcutta. Rewachand felt impugned, and he resigned.[29] 'Thus the second batch of boys returned to Calcutta, and the two institutions of Santiniketan and of Simla Street continued separately. This was in August 1902' (Bl., p. 96). It appears, thus, that the original intake at Santiniketan consisted of pupils from the Simla Bazar Street school and a separate, fresh group, the former returning to Simla Bazar at the rift.[30]

---

School was now to be achieved amidst poverty and suffering in the noisy, dingy streets of Calcutta'. But this source doesn't mention a second return of students from Bolepur.

28 There is no doubt that it was at the behest of Debendranath, Tagore's still dominant father, that Rewachand fell into disfavour, which led to Upadhyay's withdrawal from the Santiniketan project. Debendranath's antipathy to Christianity was long-standing, deep-set and well known. Unlike Upadhyay, who increasingly cloaked his Christian commitment as a private matter, Rewachand made no bones about his Christian faith. Besides, he was permanently on the scene as the master in charge. In a real sense—this emerges from comments in Tagore's letters—the establishing of the Santiniketan Ashram was the realization of a cherished desire of Debendranath's. Debendranath's objections crystallized around an incident involving Rewachand, which both *The Blade* and Pal recount separately. An illustrated Bible had been presented to the Ashram, which attracted the sustained interest of one of the younger pupils. It was felt that in explaining the Bible's content, Rewachand was proselytizing. As we shall see, this matter had dire consequences. Rathindranath, the poet's son, who was one of the original intake in the Ashram, writes that Rewachand 'was an extremely holy man (*sādhuprakṛtir*). He could teach English very well, yet he was in favour of a strict regime. He was a good cricketer, and wished to observe [exact] cricketing rules in every situation. Father didn't like such intransigence' (Pal, 1990 vol. 5, pp. 43–4). Rewachand was not particularly popular with the Tagores. Manoranjan Guha cites telling testimony in this regard. He quotes from a Bengali article entitled 'Rabindranath at Santiniketan' by Jitendralal Bandyopadhyay (*Suprabhat*, Śrāban-Bhādra, B.E. 1316). Jitendralal is quoting Rabindranath: 'The people here [in the environs of Santiniketan] knew that Upadhyay was a Christian and were somewhat upset by it.... Many members of my family were unhappy that the folk round about would get the wrong idea about Santiniketan. Many of the children's guardians too were uneasy that the responsibility for the children was in the hands of a Christian teacher. The matter reached father's ears, and by his instruction and with the approval of the guardians, Upadhyay *mahāśay*'s connection with the school was severed' (p. 40, ftnt). It seems clear that it was Debendranath's objections to Christian involvement at Santiniketan that led to Upadhyay's and Rewachand's withdrawal from the scene.

29 Zacharias writes as follows in his work: 'In 1902 both Brahmabandhav and Animananda had to leave Shantiniketan; the former, because he had too much influence over the Poet; the latter, because he had too much influence over the boys—as Animananda once smilingly explained to me' (1933: 29).

30 Pal (1990, vol. 5, pp. 42–3) echoes our doubt. He gives more than one list of the first intake, all of which include students despatched by Upadhyay. The numbers in

Be that as it may, we have most interesting testimony from Rewachand about the regime at Santiniketan before the break-up. This presumably corresponded to Upadhyay's and Tagore's ideal of running a school on 'Aryan' lines and 'living with the guru as in ancient times', respectively. *The Blade* says (to quote at some length):

> The arrangements in Bolepur were extremely primitive. The ground floor[31] was partitioned into three compartments, one of which served the masters, the second was used as a classroom, and the third one could be used by both. Rewachand was boarding-master, teacher and manager.
>
> The students got up at 4.45, swept, had a swim in the pond, and dressed: the Brahman boys in white silk, the Vaidyas and Kayasthas in red silk, and the Vaishya lads in yellow silk: the various colours representing the various castes. Then they said their individual prayers in Sanskrit, each under a separate tree, had their breakfast which consisted of gram soaked in water and *halwa* [a sweet], and dug the ground for cultivation for about half an hour. The classes opened at 7 a.m. with a prayer in which both the masters and the pupils joined. At ten, class teaching was over, the boys had various indoor games or practised on the harmonium or read story books, each according to his taste. At 11.30, they had their dinner, the Brahmans dining separately. At 12.30 the school reopened. There was recreation for 15 minutes at 3, and the lessons were finished exactly at 4.30. Cricket and football were over by 6.30.
>
> The evening prayers being done, as in the morning, the boys had lessons in music, followed by supper, and exciting games or stories; and when the clock struck 9, all the students were fast asleep (pp. 94–5).

---

these lists range from 5 to 10. In any case, it seems that the original intake was not large. Animananda, in an article for the *Modern Review* (June 1935, quoted in K, p. 157) says: 'In December 1901, the [Simla Street] School's students and a few more gathered by Swamiji [i.e. Upadhyay], and the poet's eldest son, Rathindranath Tagore, made up the first batch of Brahmacaris of the Ashram School at Santiniketan.' This implies that once the Santiniketan institution started there were no students at the Simla Street school, not necessarily that the latter school was formally defunct. K, pp. 157–8, comments on the first intake, giving seven names as the very first batch, and an additional two more after a few days. Zacharias' testimony about the status of the school to which the boys returned is not conclusive. He comments: 'Thereupon [after their withdrawal from Santiniketan] the two Catholic friends founded a new school, once more in Calcutta' (p. 29). But, as we have seen, this leaves a number of questions unanswered, and 'new' here may be more precisely understood as 'reconstituted'.

31 Of a building apparently specially constructed for housing the school.

Here we have a detailed account, from someone closely involved, of the earliest days and ideals of Santiniketan.[32] The divisions among the pupils along caste lines seem disturbing, not least educationally,[33] but Rewachand also writes that they were 'happy, glorious' times.

Upadhyay, as we have noted, was an occasional visitor.[34] He had other things to occupy him in Calcutta, including *The Twentieth Century*. In early 1901, he met up with a Protestant called 'Ananda Babu', and the two decided to keep a house to look after 'the helpless sick and crippled old folk of Calcutta' (Bl., p. 96). They rented a place in Chidam Moodie's Lane in which more than a dozen old people 'were lodged and fed'. The establishment was called the Atur Asrama (the Refuge for the Afflicted). *The Blade* reports that these were times of hardship for both the founders. Food was scarce, and Upadhyay and Ananda Babu had to make great sacrifices. 'Alas, here too the two friends fell out and the poor sick rarely saw the smiling face of the Swami' (Bl., p. 96).

So yet another venture of Upadhyay's could not be followed through by him. This is not a psychological study; yet one is impelled

32 In this connection, Pal (ibid.) quotes from a letter by Tagore written on December 1 to Pramathlal Sen who (together with his elder brother Nandalal) was a member of the Eagle's Nest in 1883 to which Upadhyay also belonged (see chapter 3): 'I have no desire to magically [*mantrabale*] resurrect some ancient dead thing. It's not my business to bring back the past. I want to work for something which though implicit is yet strongly current, that is not dead and which is natural [*prakṛtigata*] to India. The projects we start fail because invariably we blindly try to get along without acknowledging it. We think the present is the current history of some other country, while forgetting that it is not the present for India (*anyadeśer bartamān itihāskei āmrā bartamān kāl baliyā gaṇya kari—bhuliyā jāi tāhā bhāratbarṣer pakṣe bartamān nahe*). Yet to say that it's possible to resurrect India's past but not possible to integrate another country's historical time with India's, and to attempt to implement this, is vain and leads to destruction, not to new life.' Pal goes on to comment that perhaps nowhere else has Tagore explained so pithily his conviction and ideal concerning the Santiniketan School.

33 Though before long all the students were required to wear saffron.

34 Though he made his mark in more ways than one. His stress on 'physical culture' or cultivating a manly image especially for the much-maligned Bengali remained undiminished. In his *On the Edges of Time* (1981, 2nd ed.), Rathindranath Tagore recounts how during one of Upadhyay's visits to Santiniketan, a visiting Punjabi wrestler invited any who cared to respond to wrestle with him. 'Upadhyayji came running in tights and, with loud slaps on the biceps, as is the custom, challenged the Punjabi giant to a fight. And didn't the Bengali intellectual give a good time to the professional wrestler' (p. 51). Such larger-than-life displays by Upadhyay (who was in his early forties at the time) indicate what an impression he could make on those he encountered.

to ask what drove this restless, turbulent, well-meaning man. Animananda says that his inflexible adherence to principle caused these regular partings and that they were not acrimonious. 'He fell out with Ananda Babu over a matter of principles [we are not told why]; he fell out in the same way with P.C. Majumdar, Rabindranath, Aravinda [Ghose], Fr Hegglin, and lastly with me. Yet he never kept a grudge. I begged from him even after we had parted. Though poor as a church-mouse, he gave.... As he dealt with me, he dealt with all others' (Bl., p. 199). Upadhyay had great charm, energy and persuasiveness; his ideals enthralled people, and he inspired a fierce loyalty even in those from whom he parted company. Upadhyay was not at home with himself; torn between consuming passions of a changing age, struggling to locate himself amid the uncertainties of the time, he was a poignant symbol of the new India coming to birth.

We are now well into 1902, nearing the climax of the third period of Upadhyay's life (see chapter 2). It was at this time that Upadhyay resolved once more to visit England. Why did he do so? The motivation is unclear. Here is his own testimony, written some months before his death in 1907 in a short article on Vivekananda, in *Svaraj*, a Bengali weekly he was then editing.[35]

> I had gone to visit the Bolepur ashram for a few days. On my return, no sooner had I alighted at Howrah station, when someone said that Swami Vivekananda had passed away the day before [July 4th]. As soon as I heard this, I felt—I am not exaggerating in the least—as if a knife had pierced my breast. When the intensity of the pain subsided, I thought: 'How will Vivekananda's work continue? Why [I said to myself], he has many worthy, learned fellow-disciples,[36] they will continue it.' Yet even then the thought occurred to me: 'You too, apply yourself to the task to the best of your power; try to fulfill Vivekananda's vow of conquering the foreigner [*phiriṅgijaybrata*]'. I decided at that very moment to visit England.... I would go to England and establish Vedanta. Then I realised who Vivekananda is. One whose strength of inspiration could carry someone as unworthy as myself across the distant sea is no ordinary person. A few days after this, I left Calcutta city with Rs 27 to travel to England.

35 The extract is translated from UBBJ, pp. 75–6, where the article, entitled 'Who is Vivekananda?' (*Vivekānanda ke?*), is excerpted.

36 *Gurubhāi* of Ramakrishna.

There is much poetic licence here. The weekly *Svaraj,* published over four years after Upadhyay set off for Europe, was intended for the educated Bengali constituency, at a time when Upadhyay seemed more keen than ever to play down (at least in public) his Christian commitment and to establish his patriotism. As we shall see, what he said and did during his visit abroad can hardly be described, without further comment, as seeking to 'conquer the foreigner' by 'establishing Vedanta'. Nor, upon hearing of Vivekananda's death, did he promptly board ship and depart for foreign shores. Vivekananda's death may have influenced his thinking, but there is evidence to show that his reasons for visiting England were closely tied with his ongoing, self-appointed mission to bring India to the Catholic faith *through* Vedanta—perhaps a last, desperate effort to go over Zaleski's head and trumpet his cause at the heart of Empire. Four years later, when he adverted to his visit abroad in tendentious circumstances, the Christian motivation for the journey was glossed over.

Thus, before he boarded a ship bound for Genoa, on October 5, 1902 (three months, rather than 'a few days' after Vivekananda's death), he was careful to solicit and obtain an official recommendation (written in Latin) from the Archbishop of Calcutta. Clearly he intended to be active in Catholic circles in England. The text of the recommendation runs as follows: '*Per presentes declaramus Brahmabandhav (Theophilus) Upadhyay, Brachmannum (Brahmin) Calcuttensem, esse virum Catholicum, bonis imbutum moribus, zelo pro conversione concivium suorum flagrantem*' (By means of this statement we declare Brahmabandhav (Theophilus) Upadhyay, a Calcutta Brahmin, to be a Catholic of sound morals, burning with zeal for the conversion of his compatriots).

This shows that even after the controversy surrounding his involvement with *The Twentieth Century,* he had powerful backers in the local hierarchy. In order to obtain this letter patent, had he told the Archbishop that he wished to journey to England, perhaps via Rome, to plead his cause there? We shall never know. It is interesting to note that in the first article he wrote for *The Tablet,*[37] a journal that we have suggested was the official British counterpart of the *Bombay Catholic Examiner,* the text of the Archbishop's official recommendation in Latin precedes Upadhyay's opening statement: 'Since my conversion to the Catholic faith, my mind has been occupied

[37] Published in the January issue of 1903, and adverted to in chapter 11.

with the one sole thought of winning over India to the Holy Catholic Church. I have worked as a layman towards that end, and we are now a small band of converts ready to work in the vineyard of the Lord. My purpose in writing on the present subject is to show to English Catholics what stupendous obstacles stand in the way of India's conversion, and to make certain suggestions towards their removal'. To declare, four years later, that upon hearing of Vivekananda's death he immediately decided to visit England to seek to fulfill Vivekananda's vow of conquering the foreigner by establishing Vedanta, was disingenuous to say the least. Upadhyay was writing somewhat opportunistically at the time.

It would be as well here, on the verge of his journey abroad, to summarize Upadhyay's intellectual position vis-à-vis the role of Vedanta in 'winning over India to the Holy Catholic Church'. This will place his activities in England in clearer focus; in the process we shall be inquiring into the theoretical dimension of his concept of *eknisṭhatā* or Hindu 'one-centredness', discussed in chapter 10.[38] Upadhyay's fullest statement on this topic is an article in Bengali, entitled *Hindujātir Eknisṭhatā* ('The One-centredness of the Hindu Race', hereafter HE) and first published in the *Bangadarsan,* under Tagore's editorship, in 1901 (B.E. Baiśākh (April–May) 1308).[39]

It is this article that begins with the extract from Tagore's *Naivedya* adverted to earlier (before the latter's publication as such), in the manner of a *maṅgalācaraṇa* or benedictory verse. It is an important article—apparently not taken into account by either Väth or Animananda—not only for a grasp of Upadhyay's mature view, but also for an understanding of the development of the concept of *hindutva* or 'Hinduness' in the increasingly strident context of conservative nationalism.

The Hindu's Hinduness, says Upadhyay, is not dependent on a particular religious belief or set of beliefs (*dharmamat*). Hindus have traditionally held all sorts of conflicting beliefs without ceasing to be Hindus (here he includes the Jains but not the Buddhists in the Hindu fold). Nor is it dependent, he continues, on considerations of food and drink, for there is wide diversity among Hindus (here he includes

[38] There, the reader will recall, we examined Upadhyay's understanding of caste and the stages of life (*varṇāśrama dharma*) in their ideal form, which was the practical dimension of *eknisṭhatā*.

[39] An annotated translation of this article by the author appears in *Vidyajyoti,* October 1981. The Bengali version is reprinted as an Appendix in UBBJ, and in Ghosh, 1987.

the Sikhs) in their eating patterns. 'The basis of Hinduness (*hindutva*), its essence, is *varnaśrama dharma* and the one-centredness directing this.' We have already discussed the one-centredness of *varnaśrama dharma* in chapter 10; in this article Upadhyay explains the distinctiveness of one-centredness as a mind-set, a mode of thinking (*hinducinta-pranali*).

> The Hindu's distinctiveness consists in entering *within* [*antare*] an entity, its very ground [*abalambane*], whereas the distinctiveness of the European perspective is to grasp the relationship *between* two things and to see their oneness in terms of this relationship. The mark of the first is one-centredness or interiority [*antardhān*], that of the second multifacetedness [*bahuniṣṭhatā*] or integration [*samadhān*].... The tendency to one-centred thinking, the seeing into the thinghood of a thing, experiencing the ultimate non-difference [*abhedānubhūti*] between agent and effect, the knowledge of the deceptiveness [*māyikatā*] of multiplicity, comprises the Hindu's Hinduness. It has its beginning in the Veda and its consummation (*pariṇati*) in the Vedanta.'

Most of the article is devoted to showing the gradual development of this one-centred, non-dualistic mentality in the history of Hindu thought. Thus, argues Upadhyay, the early portion of the Vedas, contrary to the misinterpretation of western orientalists, is neither polytheistic nor animistic. On the contrary, 'that the Creator [*kartā*] by dint of some wondrous deceptive power [*māyāśakti*] is manifested in the form of the effect, and that though there is difference phenomenally [*byabahāratah*] between cause and effect, ultimately [*paramārthataḥ*] they are non-different—this truth of non-difference—has been sung in all the Vedic hymns.' This unitive insight was developed further in the Samkhya view that all psycho-physical difference, including the multiplicity of natural forces and constituents, is ultimately reducible to one and the same underlying principle of being (*prakṛti*). Nevertheless, since Samkhya posited an irreducible difference between Spirit (*puruṣa*) and Energy (*prakṛti*), 'the oneness of Samkhya is shrouded with the darkness of duality'.

The Viśiṣṭādvaita of Ramanuja improved on the unitive vision of Samkhya, for here 'multiplicity is placed within the oneness of Brahman [*Brahmer ekatār madhyei anekatā nihita*]'. Yet this is not the height of the unitive insight. For, 'if multiplicity is placed within the *essence* [*svarūpe*] of Brahman then oneness' absoluteness [*kebalatā*] or purity is lost'. Further, Brahman must be a changing reality, and this cannot be admitted. Thus, concludes Upadhyay, 'the highest fulfillment of the Hindu's one-centredness has occurred in Shankara's teaching of pure non-duality [*śuddhādvaita*]'. Brahman, who is the absolute and sole principle of existence, is totally undifferentiated and unchanging. The multiplicity, transience and changeability of the world are attributable to *māyā*, the principle of superfluity (*bāhulya*), contingency, and of Brahman's sovereignty. 'This power of *māyā* resides in Brahman but not essentially [*svarūpataḥ*]; it enshrouds Brahman in an adventitious manner (*bāhulyabhābe*). The One has become many, but only phenomenally [*byabahārataḥ*]. It undergoes no [real] transformation or change, yet appears manifold.' In this, the insight of the ancient seers has finally received its culminatory articulation.[40] This is familiar terrain, and we need not dwell on it. From the time that this grasp of one-centredness began to wane both intellectually and practically, continues Upadhyay—that is, from the time Hindus fell away from Advaitic insights and *varṇāśrama dharma*—India's downfall (*adhaḥpatan*) began. Upadhyay concludes on a positive note. In seeking to reinstate their one-centredness Hindus should not neglect European multifacetedness, he advises. On the contrary, (scientific) multifacetedness should be integrated into a basis of Hindu one-centredness; 'then will the Hindu's Hinduness be preserved, increased, and come to fruition'.

We note in passing that over the years Upadhyay consistently attributes Hindu degeneracy to largely self-inflicted cultural and/or moral lapses: in his earlier writings, to belief in rebirth and the reluctance to bear one another's burdens, and later to miscegenation with the 'Sudras' of old, and to succumbing to Buddhist influence, which resulted in a falling away from the distinctive Hindu characteristic of one-centredness. He never argued at any length, as even other 'conservatives' had before him, that such factors as economic exploitation by the British could be significant causes for India's decline.[41]

40 This view implies the acceptance of some theory of evolution, the idea of which was current in India then. The 'evolution' here is largely conceptual, working towards a virtually pre-determined monistic realization. Upadhyay may have been influenced to some extent by Vivekananda here, and perhaps also by western thinkers. See Killingley, 1990 for Vivekananda's position.

41 Amiya Sen (1993: 235) notes, 'even an old-world figure like Sasadhar [Tarkacudamani; 1851–1928] sought to understand India's impoverishment not simply in terms of some infirmity or "moral degradation" of its people, but on account of the systematic siphoning off of the country's resources by what he describes as an "unending cycle of mercantilist exploitation."'

So it was with this understanding of 'Vedanta' (assimilated to Advaita) and of its place in Hindu thought that Upadhyay left for England. One may ask if such a non-dualistic position could be reconciled with the keen theistic dualism that characterized the standard Catholic theologizings of the day, especially if this Vedanta was to be the 'natural (intellectual) platform' (an earlier phrase of Upadhyay's) for the reception of the teachings of the Gospel. The bridge between the two, as we have seen, was Upadhyay's interpretation of the Advaitic concept of *māyā,* and he turns to this in the article referred to in *The Tablet.*

> Hindu thought has reared up a magnificent theism which in its essential conclusions agrees wonderfully with the philosophy of St Thomas. Vedanta, the greatest Hindu philosophy of theism, teaches that the relation of God to the world is an unreal super-imposition.... This unreal super-imposition is called *maya*—a principle of illusion. By it God manifests himself to be the cause of the world without being essentially a Creator. *Maya* is less than being but more than nothing.... The world is, according to Hindu theism ... unreal ... inasmuch as ... the sum total of effects is reduced to nothing when considered in essential relation to the Absolute, who is as he is, whether there be millions of worlds or none at all. The above conclusion of Vedanta is in exact keeping with Catholic philosophy.

'I recently expounded Hindu theism in a lecture at Oxford,' continues Upadhyay in the article. 'The learned Catholic fathers present were of the opinion that the philosophy was Catholic in every way.' But these learned Catholic fathers did not presume to have the knowledge of Vedanta claimed by Fr Hegglin, Upadhyay's former collaborator, now teaching in Bombay. In the last chapter, we saw how strenuously Hegglin attacked this interpretation of *māyā*. But this was the view with which Upadhyay sought to convince his English hearers about the validity of his cause. In his Bengali writings, the Christian in Upadhyay receded out of sight; in his English essays at the time, he announced his intention to convert India to the Catholic faith. The way to reconcile these two positions is to say that appropriate Hindu teaching can act as a natural conceptual basis for receiving the revealed truths of Christianity. But his Hindu readers, at any rate, may be forgiven if they (mis)read Upadhyay as a Hindu returning to the fold, or alternatively, as a go-between with suspect motives. Writing simultaneously for two audiences with quite different expectations, Upadhyay had embarked upon a dangerous enterprise in this phase of his life. It is not surprising that this led to misunderstanding, frustration and a confusion of identities, seemingly even in the man himself. But this is to anticipate the unfolding turn of events.

We have a personal but incomplete account of Upadhyay's visit abroad in a series of letters he wrote for the conservative Bengali weekly, the *Bangabasi*.[42] There are ten letters in all; the first was dated November 13, 1902, the last—the only letter written from Calcutta upon his return—bears the date, September 7 [1903]. The first two letters are entitled, 'Letter from a *Sannyasī* visiting England' (*Bilāt-jātrī sannyāsīr ciṭhi*); the next seven are entitled 'Letter from a *Sannyāsī* staying in England' (*Bilāt-prabāsī sannyāsīr ciṭhi*), and the last is called 'Letter from a *Sannyāsī* [who has] returned from England' (*Bilāt-pherat sannyāsīr ciṭhi*).[43]

The letters are humorous on occasion, and describe not only Upadhyay's activities but also events, scenery and customs encountered during his travels. The style is remarkably crisp and colloquial.[44] This is how the very first letter begins:

42 Most of these letters were written from England. The *Bangabasi*'s founder-editor was Jogendracandra Basu (1854–1905), who started the paper on December 10, 1881. 'Making a humble beginning ... it gradually rose to be the most widely circulated vernacular within Bengal, reaching a record figure of over 20,000 every week by 1889–1890' (A. Sen, 1993: 236). By then the strongly conservative tone of the paper had been set by Indranath Bandyopadhyay (1849–1912), who had joined the *Bangabasi* as a regular contributor in 1883. 'It was he of all the *Bangabasi* writers who attempted to make Hinduism a proud and aggressive religion' (p. 241). The tone of Upadhyay's letters suited this agenda. By 1902–3, the popularity of the *Bangabasi*, which was anti-Congress, seems to have been on the wane, though the paper still commanded wide interest. According to the *Report of Native Newspapers in Bengal* (see Week ending January 3, 1903, and January 2, 1904), the weekly subscription of the *Bangabasi* over 1902–3 held steady at 12,000. It ceased publication in 1949. For information on the *Bangabasi* see A. Sen, 1993: ch. 4, especially pp. 236ff.

43 The ten letters are dated as follows: Nov. 13, 1902; Nov. 20, 1902; Jan. 2, 1903; Jan. 9, 1903; Jan. 16, 1903, March 6, 1903; April 24, 1903; May 5, 1903; June 12, 1903; Sept. 7, 1903. These letters were reprinted in consecutive weeks in the current Bengali journal *Bartaman* (Sunday edition), the first on June 3, 1990, the last on Aug. 12, 1990 (a gap of one week intervening). There is a full summary without further comment (but with one or two significant additions which we shall note) in Simha, Part III, pp. 48–67. The letters are printed *verbatim* in B. Ghosh, 1987:127f. (with some typographical omissions).

44 Quite different, in fact, from Upadhyay's Sanskritized and somewhat sombre Bengali writings for the *Bangadarsan*. The letters created a precedent in style for subsequent popular journalism. Simhà hints as much at the end of his summary: 'Many leading literary experts [*agraṇī sāhityasebī*] of Bengali were captivated by perusing the learning and quality of the letters [Upadhyay] published in the journal *Bangabasi*

> I'm an English-read *sannyasi*. Nowadays, many *sannyasis* visit England, harangue their audiences with religious lectures, and receive much applause. One day, I too fancied receiving English acclaim. I've been much applauded in Calcutta, Bombay and Madras—now I would savour applause from the fairest of hands. Well, you know the *sannyasi* mind—it acts at once upon the whim.
>
> Readers, perhaps you've never set eyes on a *sannyasi* travelling to England. Usually his head's shaved, and so are his moustache and beard. He's got a silk turban and robe, wears English boots, has a cane in the hand and a cheroot in the mouth. There's a Gladstone bag (strap fastened), an English blanket, bedding (rolled up), [a garland of] notes round his neck, and a carrier-bag full of gold coins. My, but doesn't he look grand!
>
> I thought I'd get in on the act—only for lack of funds, the silk didn't materialise, and as for the boots, cheroot, cane, portmanteau and so on, alas, they parted company with me ages ago. All that remained was my knowledge of English. I had a simple wrap round my body and a blanket in my hand. Friends thrust a thick, heavy overcoat upon me. And because they did so, I survived, else I'd have been done for in the English cold.[45]

Considering the author and his readership, it is perhaps not surprising to learn that the letters are highly tendentious. Their gist is to show

---

during his stay 'in England' (p. 67). And Prasanta Gangopadhyay says in his article on Bengali journalistic prose (*Bāṅglāgadya: Sangbādikatā*, 1964: 804–8): 'Rather than expressing his learning, Upadhyay expressed his feelings [*bhāb*]. And these were feelings about his own land [*svadeśī bhāb*]. This lyrical prose Bengali rich in feeling [*bhāb samṛddha*] was a new style in prose.... This language was the colloquial language [*mukher bhāṣā*] of west Bengal' (p. 806).

45 Perhaps a dig here at Swami Vivekananda. The Bengali text follows: *āmi ekjan iṅgreji-paḍā sannyāsī. ājkāl anekānek sannyāsī bilāte giye śāstrer bukni-miśāno-baktṛtā kare khub hāttāli khāy. āmār o ekdin śakh halo je bilāter hāttāli khābo. Kalikātā mumbai o māndājer* [sic] *hāttāli khub keyechi—ekhan dekhi ekbār campakbaraṇ hāter hāttāli keman miṣṭi. sannyāsīr man—jemni kheyāl amni uṭhā. pāṭhak, tomrā bilātgāmī sannyāsīr rūp bodh hay kakhano dekho nāi. sādhāraṇataḥ māthā gõp dāḍi sab muḍāno—reśomer pāgḍi reśomer ālkhāllā, pāye bilātī buṭ, hāte chaḍi mukhe curuṭ; saṅge portmyānto glyādston byāg, styrāp bā̃dhā, bilātī kambal, jaḍāno bichānā, galāy ṭākā, mohar bharā kuriyār byāg. āhā mari, sejeche bhālo. āmi o ai rakam katakṭā ḍhaṅg dharilām: kebal paysār abhābe reśomṭā juṭila nā. ār buṭ curuṭ chaḍi portmyānto ityādi āmār satsaṅga anek din tyāg kareche, hāyre. āmār kebal iṅgreji paḍāi sār. āmār chila: gāye ekkhāni banāt o hāte ekkhāni kambal. bandhubāndhaberā dhare kare ekṭā goddhaḍ moṭa garamkapoḍerer ālkhāllā kare diyechila. diyechila tāi bececchi - nahile bilāter ṭhānḍāy daphā raphā haye jeto.*

that western culture, as represented by the British, is inferior to Hindu culture, and this is highlighted in particular by comparing the brazen behaviour of British women with the more modest ways of their Hindu counterparts. Political comment is conspicuous by its absence. The subtext is that Upadhyay's lectures proclaiming Hindu culture went down well with the discerning among his audiences, and that he has done much in the circumstances to uphold Hindu values and gain proper appreciation for Hinduism's highest philosophy, the Vedanta (Advaita). Let us go into greater detail.

In keeping with his earlier writings, Upadhyay presents an idealized and homogenized version of Hindu culture. Modern western culture, he argues, is based on a strong sense of racial superiority, the lust for power, and a materialistic understanding of the world. Hindu culture is based on selflessness and a unitive understanding of reality. Consequently, the latter is superior to the former, and will endure.

> This belief is progressively taking hold among the Europeans that the white races [*śvetāṅga jāti*] are the best among the human race: that other peoples—fair, dark or black—have been born to serve them. This lust for lordship [*prabhutva*], which is gradually increasing, makes for a demonic mentality [*āsurik bhāb*]... and it is hard to explain how much harm it will do to India if it gets strong.... If India were once again, as of old, established as guru of the world, if students were to come from Europe to India to study her philosophy [*darśan*], reasoning [*nyāy*], traditions [*smṛti*] and literature, then the western world would respect India and that demonic mentality would decrease. For there can be no doubt that even now India is fit to be the guru of the world. Yet India has lost sight of herself....
>
> How can this self-forgetfulness [*ātmabismṛti*] be removed? I thought that if the English become keen to study our wisdom [*śāstrabidyā*], India's self-forgetfulness would depart and the English themselves would benefit. For this reason I journeyed to England. When I arrived I saw that owing to the efforts of scholars who knew Sanskrit like Max Müller and others, respect for India had increased somewhat no doubt, but it would have been better if that had not happened.... For just as experts of things past visit a museum to observe the skeleton of some huge animal and deliberate over how long it survived, so European scholars discuss us. Once we were great, they think; now, however, we have become an object of curiosity in the civilised world. I have tried my best to remove this impression.

> I have shown that the Hindu race is living still.... What is the reason for this? The knowledge of Advaita, as expounded by Vedanta, is the Hindu's sole support and constant ally. The Hindu's yoga, philosophy, traditional rules and teachings and behavioural practices have been nourished by the elixir of Advaita. The Hindu has been saved and has developed by following the selfless dharma that seeks Advaita [*advaitamukhīn niṣkām dharmapālane*] [Letter 10].

Western notions of racist superiority have generated contempt for non-white peoples and their ways.[46] Still, though technologically advanced (because of the lust for power)—'To cut so long a canal [as the Suez Canal] through this desert is a superhuman thing' (Letter 1)—western culture is correspondingly shallow and dehumanized. Its shallowness is betrayed by such things as the pursuit of comfort and order, and the lack of understanding of nature and its role, while its dehumanized character is expressed in increasingly impersonal family and social relationships, especially evident in the relationship between the sexes and the behaviour of women. English life is extremely orderly, no doubt:

> When you see how the shops are done up, you think you've entered a beauty-mart (*ruper bājār*)... the fish and meat shops, the vegetable stalls, the clothes and fancy stores—look where you will, it's as if garlands of flowers are on display.... People moving about in droves, yet not the slightest commotion; thousands of horse-drawn carriages rushing about, but with the precision of machines [*kaler putul*]. The moment a policeman raises his hand, every vehicle stops. There are so many people on London's roads you'd think a fair was in progress. Then there are the trams, omnibuses, private carriages, hire-carriages, bicycles, motor-cars—all moving at speed. Such a multitude, yet neither disorder nor confusion.... And as for comfort, what can I say! Every activity—whether it's eating, fetching, resting, sitting or waiting—has been made so comfortable that you couldn't think how to improve things even in Indra's heaven! [Letter 3].

46 Upadhyay writes frankly about his experiences in England: 'The first day I went out here [Oxford] I faced a big problem. Young boys crying 'Look, Look', ran towards me; men sniggered [*mucke hāse*], while the ladies either started or flashed a tiny smile.... If you're light-skinned and behave very much like one of them, you might get away with it; but if you dress differently—like wearing a silk robe or Indian cap [*tāj*]—then you're in a fix.... After you're introduced to them, the people of this country behave very courteously ... but the moment you express even a slight difference of opinion, then racial terms [*kālo sambhāṣaṇṭā*] such as 'Blackie' and "Nigger" often come out of English mouths' (Letter 3).

But this pursuit of order and ease is a superficial thing,[47] and compares unfavourably with Hindu culture. The English are mechanical: 'For here work goes by the clock.... In winter or summer, whether it's eating, sleeping or working, everything takes place at the same hour' (Letter 7). There is no attention to the appropriateness of the season. Equally superficially, the English, argues Upadhyay in a powerful passage, regard Nature (*prakṛti*) as an object of gratification (*sambhoger bastu*) and so are unable to properly revere the forms and symbols of Nature (*tāder pakṣe rūper pūjā bā pratīk bā upāsanā asambhab*). This only the Hindu is able to do because the Hindu is capable of distinguishing the two modes of beauty: its sweetness or sentiment (*mādhurjya*) and its graciousness (*kalyāṇa/maṅgal*).

Since humans are sensual-minded, the pursuit of sentiment has a divisive effect. It overpowers the graciousness of beauty, elicits selfishness and agitates the senses (*jāhār ākarṣane mādakatā janme indriya biloḍita hay—tāhāi mādhurjya*). Graciousness, on the other hand, is essentially self-giving (*ātmadān-i maṅgal*).

> When fullness overflows and fills the other, subduing desire and transforming sensual pleasure with a pure joy, it is only then that we are privileged to see the inner form of the Gracious One.[48]... The fickle beauty [*capalmādhurī*] of the bedecked, newly-married bride charms her beloved and separates him from the rest of his family, whereas the gracious mother [*kalyāṇmayī mātā*], unadorned and hair dishevelled, is eager only to give; she has no other purpose than to give of herself.... Are there not any number of fruits, flowers, trees and creepers, yet it is the plantain tree that betokens graciousness [*maṅgaler paricāyak*]. No ceremony can be rendered auspicious [*maṅgal*] in the absence of the kindly plantain tree, however many thousands of [fragrant] jasmines may be present. And why? Because there is nothing that gives of itself like the plantain tree. Its leaf serves as an eating-plate; its pith is the ingredient for various dishes, its bark can be used by washermen. And when one observes how its very life is spent in the giving of fruit, one is overcome with amazement [Letter 7].[49]

[47] In Letter 3, Upadhyay gives a detailed and entertaining description of the pleasures of being shaved in a barber's shop.

[48] *Pūrṇatā jakhan upacita hay aparke bharpūr kare, bāsanāke samāhita kare, sambhoger pramodke biśuddhānande pariṇata kare, takhan-i śib-svarūper darśan hay.*

[49] Note in this passage the stereotyping and ambivalence of women's role in the prevailing 'educated' view of Hindu culture. As bride, woman is seductive, divisive and dangerous; as mother, she is selfless and unitive. As mother *and* wife, she occupies an ambivalent status.

Hindu culture recognizes this distinction between sentiment and graciousness in Beauty, not least in the experience of Nature, and hence is able to appreciate Nature for what it is: not something to be only enjoyed as an object of gratification and hence systematically exploited (which is characteristic of western civilization) but as something to be reverenced through form and symbol, to be united with as a partner in life's progress, to be related to as maternal and nourishing. In Letter 5 Upadhyay writes that the English/the West (he assimilates one to the other) strive to conquer Nature for the thrill of conquest itself (*kebal ekṭā jayer ānanda—īśvaratver ātmatuṣṭi*). The Hindu's approach is different: the aim is not to exercise power *by* conquest, to conquer Nature for the sake of conquest, but to conquer the lure of power itself, to conquer Nature with detachment. 'He who by virtue of the surplus or abundance of his authority has transcended want is truly ruler; he is lord, power's master' (*jini svādhikārer prācurja o bāhulya guṇe prayojanke atikram kariyāchen tini-i prabhu, tini-i īśvar, aiśvarjer svāmī*). To this end, Hindu culture advocates engagement with the world, not in a sensual way (*pravṛtti*), but selflessly, through detachment (*niṣkāma-karma/nivṛtti*) in a spirit of oneness (*advaita*).[50]

Again and again, Upadhyay singles out facets of English culture for criticism. True, there is order in English culture and this has its attractive features, but this is a hierarchical order based on the injustice of rampant competitiveness and the oppression of socio-economic status.

> Here there is great wealth [*aiśvarya*] but also a lot of poverty. 30% of the people are poor, that is, they barely manage to keep themselves going. And many among these can't even do that. You won't believe that most of the workers here don't get to eat meat.... They eat meat only on Sundays.... While wealth increases on the one hand, deprivation increases on the other: when competition [*pratijogitā*] is the root of civilisation, this must be the consequence. Here all the unmarried girls work in factories, and they can't make ends meet with their earnings. And it's well known that, because of need, nearly all of them go astray [*duścaritra hay*]. Even then the pressure of competition is so great that it's very difficult to increase their salaries [Letter 7].[51]

50 Perhaps some development has occurred in Upadhyay's thought. Whereas earlier, as noted, in the philosophical writings Nature or *prakṛti* had been desexed and depersonalized, here, it appears, Nature is personalized, though mainly in a stereotyped role of mother. In both cases, however, 'Nature' is hypostatized.

51 This is also a barren form of order. Upadhyay describes the scenery of a walk in Oxford as follows: 'On all sides, everything's clean and neat. It seems as if Nature

Upadhyay was invited to lecture at Ruskin College, Oxford, founded to educate workers (*karmajībīder bidyālay*). He was taken aback at their hostility towards the rich and upper class. The workers were unable to improve their lot amid the pressures of the modern markets; 'so they were hostile towards present society. I told them a bit about our *varṇāśrama dharma*. They were amazed when they heard talk about giving priority to family occupations *[kaulik karma]* without recourse to competitiveness and rivalry [*pratijogitā o pratidvandvitā*], and readily acknowledged that this would bring harmony' (Letter 3).

A robbery was reported at a jeweller's in London: 'robbery, cheating and murder are a regular feature of London' (Letter 6). Upadhyay was invited to lecture on Hindu domestic customs at a women's gathering in Oxford. He spoke about the vows taken by young girls, about Hindu (really Bengali) marriage practices. 'We don't fall in love and then marry; we marry first, and then love. We don't show our respect for women, as you do, by tying their shoelaces or polishing their shoes. We show them proper respect. If my brother's wife becomes a widow, it would be my duty to look after her and her children.... For us, womenfolk are most certainly to be protected.... A gentleman present said that such lectures should be given in every city in England' (Letter 6). Upadhyay didn't approve of the independence women had in England: it led to permissive behaviour. In the Samkhya philosophy it is said, Upadhyay notes, that Nature (*prakṛti*) by unveiling herself helps emancipate the male. But in England, (female) nature is not veiled at all; she displays herself at every turn! Women go around in groups, running and laughing. Husband and wife hold hands, lovers dally arm in arm—why, a chap can't go for a walk in a park without seeing lovers behind every bush! One has to go very carefully in England (Letter 3).

Despite being the centre of attention, Upadhyay lived in financially very straitened circumstances in England. He had left Calcutta for Madras with only Rs 27; in Madras a friend gave him money for the

---

has been carefully tidied up. At first it looks very nice. Then you begin to think that people have tried a little too hard to teach God how to do his job; the natural glow of Nature has been lost. There is so much forest and jungle in our rural areas! Yet in them one can glimpse the abundance of the supreme bliss [*paramānander bāhulya*]: as if Beauty's having a fun-fair [*jena saundaryer melā legeche*], or the Lord's [*śrīnivās*] begun his rituals—everything scattered about! But here it's as if all the flowers, fruit, crops, and vegetation have been carefully measured out' (Letter 4).

journey to Europe. He boarded ship with the minimum of possessions. On board ship he was adopted by some Sindhi merchants bound for various destinations about the Mediterranean; they saw to his food (they had brought a Hindu cook with them). Having left Bombay on October 5 on an Italian ship, Upadhyay reached Naples on November 1 and disembarked there. His ticket was valid till Genoa, but he disembarked at Naples since he wanted to visit Rome. His short stay in Rome is described in Letter 2.[52]

Why did Upadhyay wish to visit Rome? The *Bangabasi* letter gives no reason. Simha (p. 53) hints that Upadhyay wished to see the Pope.[53] With great difficulty he met the 'Pope's Chamberlain'. But the Pope was busy with 'worldly matters *[baiṣayik kārjye]*. He could not give special attention to other subjects [*anya biṣaye*]' says Simha. So Upadhyay left it there, resolving to visit again upon his return from England. What was Upadhyay's apparently non-worldly concern that the Pope could not attend to? His Christian *apologia, The Blade,* is even clearer as to the reason, but diverges regarding the facts. In a letter Upadhyay wrote to Animananda while in Rome, on November 1, he says:

> As soon as I got down from the train I kissed the soil of Rome.... I prayed at the tomb of St Peter, the Rock, the Holder of the Keys, for India, for you all.... While kneeling down at the tomb of St Peter, I thought of the Holy Father, the living St Peter. Oh! how I longed to kneel at his feet and plead for India. I was shown from a distance the window of his apartments. I was tempted to procure an interview ... but I restrained my desire for I felt that the time had not yet come.... I am walking the streets of Rome, free and easy, full of fire for our Holy Faith (Bl., p. 109).

No mention of the Pope's 'Chamberlain', but the reason for meeting the Pope seems clear: to appeal to him for an endorsement of Upadhyay's method for drawing his compatriots to Christ on the basis of the 'natural theism' of (and presumably the traditional caste practices associated with) the Vedanta. Was the time not right because he tried to secure an interview and failed, or did he believe that his

52 At the time he was suffering from a serious pain in his loins which he attributed to exposure on board ship. It began towards the end of his voyage and intensified in Rome. It cleared up in England. It may have been the hernia which was to be instrumental in bringing about his death.

53 Simha adds this to his summary of Letter 2; it is not mentioned in the *Bangabasi* letter.

case would be stronger, upon his return, with letters of recommendation from England? But this talk of 'fire for our Holy Faith' would hardly go down well with the conservative readers (and policy-makers) of the *Bangabasi!* In fact, there is no indication that the writer of the *Bangabasi* letters is a Christian. On the contrary![54] This dual role, privately the Christian, but publicly—at least for Bengal—the apparently Hindu champion of Advaita, Upadhyay maintained throughout his stay abroad.

For the night in Rome, Upadhyay's hotel accommodation was seen to by two Italian gentlemen he had met and charmed in the train from Naples. He reached London on November 4, hoping to be put up free of charge, as might be expected in India in religious houses. In this he was disappointed—things were done differently in England. He arrived in Oxford on the 5th. He had a fever upon his arrival in England, and 'through want of means he could procure neither food nor medicine and found himself on the verge of starvation' (Bl., p. 110). It is here that his letter patent came in handy. He was able to meet Cardinal Vaughan and received help.

Though he visited various places in England, he stayed for the most part in Oxford, perhaps because the then Boden Professor of Sanskrit, A.A. Macdonell, had read some of his pieces in *The Twentieth Century* and invited him to give some lectures. He stayed as a paying guest with a middle-class English family (where he was well received). But he continued to send desperate letters to friends in India, begging for money. In a letter to Nandalal Sen in Calcutta dated January 1, 1903 (he gives his address as care of 'The Librarian, Indian Institute, Oxford'), he writes: 'I cannot live here on less than Rs. 70 a month. I have to pay the landlady 21sh. a week, coal and bath included. That makes Rs 63 a month. I cannot get a cheaper lodge and board.... I am at present hard up.... I shall be glad if you can raise a little money from friends for my expenses here.... It will be a great relief if you can send me something by telegraph' (Bl., pp. 112–3). On one occasion when he lectured he was advised to charge an entrance fee, as was sometimes the custom. But he declined on the grounds that it was un-Hindu to sell knowledge, thus passing up an extra source of income. On another occasion he gave his last shilling to a poor flower-seller telling her that she needed it more than he (Bl., pp. 110–11).

[54] Here and there one can detect a clue with hindsight, as when Upadhyay describes his visit to St Peter's in Letter 2: 'Catholic rites are very similar to those of the Hindus'*(kāsthalikder ācār paddhati anekṭā hinduder saṅge mile)*.

During his stay in England, Upadhyay lectured in various places on diverse topics to different kinds of audiences. Soon after his arrival in Oxford he lectured on 'Hindu thought and western culture', with Professor Macdonell in the chair. This was well received ('Much applause!', Letter 2). Three further lectures were arranged on 'Hindu Theism', 'Hindu Ethics', and 'Hindu Sociology'. The Master of Balliol, the noted philosopher Edward Caird, was to preside. The first two were given with Caird in the chair, but because Caird 'had no time', the third was postponed indefinitely (Letter 6). Upadhyay was also asked to lecture to a women's meeting in Oxford. This is where he spoke about Bengali marriage practices and the kind of respect Hindu women were shown in society (as noted above). He also mentions (Letter 7) that in a lecture in Oxford he spoke about Hindu and western ideas of beauty. The gist of the contrast he drew between the two cultures on this subject has been discussed above. Upadhyay also gave a lecture about *varṇāśrama dharma* and the way it had preserved Hindu culture against all odds. This lecture was so well received, he writes, that a committee of Professors was set up to look into the possibility of teaching Hindu thought at Oxford (Letter 7). But this initiative, which required money for its realization, came to nothing.[55]

In Letter 8 we are told that Upadhyay was prevailed upon to give several lectures apparently to spiritualists, people who believed that a Hindu was able to read other people's minds, see through walls and assume disembodied states. They were oblivious that Hindu tradition could teach them the true nature of devotion or Advaitic knowledge. Women played a leading role in this group. Some of them invited Upadhyay to London at a place called the Sesame Club for dinner. The women had on evening dress, which meant very low-cut gowns with 'half the front and (upper) arms bare'. Upadhyay was horrified; he left as soon as he decently could.

[55] In a letter Upadhyay wrote in English from Oxford ('c/o The Librarian, Indian Institute') to Rabindranath Tagore (dated April 9, 1903, and preserved in the Archives of Rabindra Bhaban at Santiniketan, hereafter OX9), Upadhyay refers to this prospect: 'Dr Stout, Editor of the "Mind" ... advises me to have a committee perfectly independent of the University of Oxford ... Otherwise... there will be many an obstruction in the way proceeding from formalities and conventions.... It is better to institute a lectureship for three years only in the beginning.... The conditions will be: (1) the lecturer must be a Brahman, or a Brahmachari, or a Sannyasi; (2) he must be a vegetarian and a total abstainer; (3) he should not get any pay; and (4) he should be up to the mark in Vedanta as well as in Western systems of philosophy.

Upadhyay also lectured in Cambridge (this seems to have been in early May 1903: Letter 8[56]). He gave three lectures at Trinity College on 'The Nirguna Brahman of the Hindus', 'Hindu Ethics' and 'Hindu Devotionalism'. The well-known philosopher J. McTaggart was in the chair. 'The lectures have resulted in the Professors deliberating as to whether Vedantic thought should be taught in the University alongside western thought.'[57] These deliberations seem to have gone further than in Oxford. *The Blade,* quoting from the *Athenium,* July 11, 1903, notes that the Cambridge Committee consisted of Prof. Rashdall, Mr G. Lowes Dickinson, Dr J. Ellis McTaggart, Dr T. Pielle, Dr W.H.D. Rouse, Prof Sorley and Prof G.F. Stout. In fact the Committee agreed that if Upadhyay raised the capital of £1000 (in Letter 10 Upadhyay mentioned the sum of Rs 9000), and if a suitable Hindu scholar could be found, an appointment would be made for three years in the first instance. This was a considerable achievement of Upadhyay's. We shall return to this matter presently. There were other lectures in the course of his stay in England, of course. He spoke at the North London Theosophical Society at Highbury, and on at least two occasions in Birmingham.[58]

---

The lecturer may receive *daksina* [an offering in cash or kind] from his students.' Expenses would have to be provided, continues Upadhyay, which included the sea passage and board and lodging. Upadhyay calculated that £100 a year (Rs 1500) would see to the board and lodging, and Rs 1500 for passage there and back. 'So Rs 6000 will be required for a three years' lectureship.' He also adds: 'The great obstruction to the carrying out of the scheme will come from the so-called Sanskrit scholars here who do not like at all to have a Hindu as a lecturer. They think too highly of themselves and always speak of Hindu Sanskrit scholars as unhistorical and inaccurate.... Unfortunately they have been hardened in their traditions and they are determined to study Hindu thought and culture as they study the dead civilisations of Babylonia and Assyria.... The Indian Institute here is a game-preserve of retired Anglo-Indians, and it is almost impossible to make it in any way beneficial to India.' This project is not referred to again.

56 *The Blade's* date of March (p. 116) goes against the 'a few days ago' (*alpa din hola*) of Letter 8, dated May 5, 1903.

57 It also resulted in an admirer's giving Upadhyay, unsolicited, a purse of Rs 105 that came in extremely handy. It enabled him to replace some torn clothing which he otherwise could not have afforded to do. 'Now I can go about a little more comfortably' (Letter 8).

58 'I delivered some eight lectures in Birmingham on my second visit. They have created a great sensation. I have addressed the Theosophists, Quakers, Unitarians, the general public, the University, and the Training College for ladies.... The ladies, especially,

No doubt the material for most of these lectures and talks was recycled in one form or another; beyond summaries of varying length, we do not have detailed transcripts of what was said. On occasion there were new ideas—as in the lecture on the appreciation of beauty in Hindu and western tradition—but there was no radical departure from the familiar views Upadhyay had developed in his various publications before his visit to England. The same may be said for his publications in England. We have already noted (see chapters 10 and 11) that he published two articles in *The Tablet* (January 3 and 31, 1903); these re-presented his views on the barrenness of the current Indian Church, on the value of the traditional *varṇāśrama* system, and on the need to understand aright and dialogue with (his interpretation of) the rational theism of Advaita.

In Letter 4 (January 9, 1903) he describes a meeting with the distinguished philosopher, G.F. Stout, then editor of the philosophical journal *Mind*. Upadhyay had recast his Oxford lecture on 'Hindu Theism' in the form of an article entitled 'Freedom of Being', and he took it to Stout for publication in *Mind*. At first Stout was reluctant to accept it; he had enough matter for publication for a full year. But after conversation with Upadhyay he became more amenable. He retained the article, inviting Upadhyay to return. When Upadhyay visited Stout again, the latter expressed appreciation for Upadhyay's views and promised to publish the article. In his letter to Nandalal Sen quoted earlier (Bl., p. 111), Upadhyay writes: 'The January number of "Mind" is shortly expected. My article will be published in the second issue (April) or in the third.' In fact, no article by Upadhyay was published in the journal, nor does Upadhyay refer to

---

have become very enthusiastic. But I am very awkward in my dealings with them. They have great power here over men' (OX9). There is a copy of a handwritten letter in the Rabindra Bhaban Archives from J.H. Muirhead, the editor of the distinguished Muirhead Library of Philosophy series. It is dated 'The University, Birmingham, Feb. 19th, 1903', and is addressed to a Mr Hodgson. It refers probably to Upadhyay's first visit to Birmingham. Professor Muirhead writes: 'You ask me my impression of the effect that the Swami Upadyay's visit seems to me to have had in Birmingham. Considering its shortness and the relatively small number of people he saw I think it was a great success. Everyone who met him was greatly impressed with the singular sincerety of his character and his intellectual ability.... His account of the state of philosophy in India and his own openness of mind as to Western ideas greatly interested all who heard him speak upon this subject.... We hope that if he is in this country later on in the year we may be able to arrange a University audience.' From Upadhyay's remarks in OX9 we may deduce that he did visit Birmingham again and included a talk in the University during his visit.

the matter again. In any event, we can guess what he had to say: his thesis was well rehearsed.[59] He had not gone to England to say new things: he had gone to present a case that was already well developed. Not surprisingly, he had little respect for the way Hindu thought had been received and was being studied and taught in England. As we have seen, Upadhyay was convinced that for the English, Hindu thought was the object either of misunderstanding or of morbid curiosity (that is, it was a spiritualist's paradise) or of antiquarian interest (the past had points of theoretical interest, the present was decadent); it was not a living faith with universal potential, with the resources to renew and transform not only the land of its origin but western civilization as well (not to mention the Christian message) in a new 'federation' between the two cultures.[60]

Upadhyay had returned from England by July 1903, without revisiting Rome or seeking to meet the Pope. *The Blade* says that Leo XIII was celebrating his silver jubilee as Pope and that interviews were very hard to obtain. Perhaps this put Upadhyay off before he even tried.[61] Perhaps his experience in England convinced him that the western mind was too set, too prejudiced against Hindu thought to change at present: a longer softening process was necessary (no doubt by such projects as the prospective teaching post at Cambridge). Or maybe he was just short of money or patience. In any case, Upadhyay came home and wrote his last letter to *Bangabasi* from Calcutta. After rejoicing at touching home soil and enjoying home food again, it reaffirms, in accordance with our review earlier on in this chapter, his view of Advaita being the culmination of Hindu one-centredness, i.e. the intuitive and unitive basis, in contrast to western

59 He gives a brief description in Letter 4: 'In my article I showed that the individual [*jīb*] and the world are unreal [*mithyā*] and that there's no independence of any kind in this realm of illusion [*māyā*]. And I also refuted the view that western philosophy has been able to gainsay the illusory unreality [*māyik alīkatā*] of [this world].' (*āmār prabandhe jīb o jagat je mithyā o māyār rājye jekono svādhīnatā nāi—tāhā-i pratipādita haiyāche. ār pāścātya darśane je māyik alīkatār pratibād āche tāhār-o khaṇḍan karā haiyāche*).

60 'Federation' is a term Upadhyay used in his lecture to the North London Theosophical Society. Federation is born of mutual respect and entails each tradition—Hindu and the western—developing along its own lines but mutually correcting the other (Bl., p. 114).

61 In the first week of July 1903, the aged Pontiff fell ill; his condition deteriorated and he died on July 20 in his 94th year.

preoccupations with plurality, for a Hindu renewal of *varṇāśrama dharma* and constructive dialogue with the west.[62]

What, we may ask in conclusion, did Upadhyay accomplish by his visit to England? And was it a success? We have noted the apparent ambiguity of his motives for going.

The Christian motive was expressed as follows: 'I prayed at the tomb of St Peter, the Rock, the Holder of the Keys—for India, for you all ... (letter to Animananda from Rome, November 1, 1902). Again: 'Since my conversion to the Catholic faith my mind has been occupied with the one sole thought of winning over India to the Holy Catholic Church. I have worked as a layman towards that end, and we are now a small band of converts ready to work in the vineyard of the Lord' (article in *The Tablet*, January 3, 1903).

The Hindu motive: 'It is my belief that India will conquer the world through the power of knowledge. I want us to avenge our defeat by first conquering the sovereign Englishman by the disciplined path of knowledge [*jñānayoga*]' (concluding words of *Bangabasi* Letter 4, January 9, 1903). Again: 'My sole desire is to do whatever is necessary to safeguard the good name of India' (concluding words of *Bangabasi* Letter 6).

We have shown that these aims are not necessarily incompatible where Upadhyay is concerned. But they were signalled by him in an increasingly confusing way. Like St Paul, he wanted to be all things to all, or at least, Christian to his Church and Hindu to his Hindu compatriots. He succeeded in misleading both. He went to England as torch-bearer on several counts. He wanted to convince Catholics that the current evangelizers and their procedures for evangelizing were profoundly flawed; in fact they were counter-productive. It was vital to evangelize India using the unparalleled resources of Hindu

62 It also recounts tongue-in-cheek an amusing encounter in Cambridge with W.T. Stead, the noted editor of the *Review of Reviews*, a well-known journal. Stead had taken to Upadhyay and had invited him to his home. In the course of conversation he informed Upadhyay that he had a 'double' who would emerge from his body and roam at will, engaging in activities unknown to Stead. Stead then left the room to fetch something and returned shortly after. Upadhyay asked if that was Stead himself or his double. Stead said that it was he. 'How can I tell?' demanded Upadhyay. 'I have grey hair and smoke cigars,' answered Stead, 'but my double's hair is not grey, nor does it smoke cigars.' After some more conversation, Upadhyay made a hurried exit. 'And for fear of ghosts I didn't see much of him after that.... Yet he's a friend of our country.'

culture and thought. Hence the *Tablet* articles, and his carefully formulated lectures to certain audiences.[63]

But he also loved his ancestral culture and was jealous of its reputation. He had a burning desire to show it in its best light, and in the process to exhibit his patriotism. To this end it was useful to invoke Vivekananda. Note that his was not a narrowly political aim; Upadhyay did not go to England to berate the British government, to lobby politicians, to collect funds for political causes. Not a whiff of that in any of his activities. This is why he invoked Vivekananda rather than some overtly political figure.

He did not invoke Tagore. Tagore's time had not yet come in the west. But Upadhyay's journey to England was of a piece with his visits to Santiniketan, at least in that his relationship with Tagore at the time must have clarified his thinking and reinforced his broadly nationalistic Hindu ideology. What Tagore's precise influence on Upadhyay was is not at all clear. It will require careful, comparative contextual study to discern that. We know that they were in close touch, even corresponding when Upadhyay was in England. What was the content of those impassioned discussions between them in Calcutta, discussions that first led Tagore to invite Upadhyay to collaborate so significantly with him? It has been said that the influence was mainly one way, from Upadhyay to Tagore, that since Upadhyay seemed to exercise a hold on Tagore he incurred the displeasure of Debendranath, the poet's strong-willed father. But Tagore was a genius too; he also must have contributed to Upadhyay's thought. After all it was Upadhyay who called him 'Gurudeb'. Was it in Tagore's understanding of beauty, of India's destiny among the nations? It would not be right to assume influence where there may be none of significance.[64] Upadhyay had a powerful

63 *The Blade* quotes from two letters by J. Rickaby, the Jesuit theologian, dated 27.1.1908 and 29.11.1922: 'We were very friendly together, and I never discovered in him anything unorthodox. He had small hope of converting Brahmins in any large numbers ... he said that there was a small section of them who were not pantheists, and he thought this section might be Christianised, if Catholic missionaries went the right way about it, which he said they did not do. What the right way would be, I never understood. He was poor and much neglected. It was pitiful to see him shivering in the English winter as he wore his light Indian dress. Why some of our people talk so much against him, I never understood. He always seemed to be a very worthy man and a very able one' (p. 118).

64 However, there can be no doubt, I think, that Upadhyay played a significant role in shaping several of Tagore's literary characters. Though an analysis of this topic is beyond the scope of this book, the influence has been noted by several scholars.

mind too.[65] So here we have Upadhyay as the torch-bearer for Hinduness as well.

There is no doubt that Upadhyay made an impression in England, especially in Oxford and Cambridge, two leading centres of learning at the fountainhead of Empire. Getting the two universities to agree, at least in principle, to sanction the teaching of Hindu thought was a considerable achievement—it was something that Vivekananda did not do. Certainly in the *Bangabasi,* his progress was followed with interest. Upon his return to India, he sought a suitable person to take up the Cambridge appointment. *The Blade* points out that Upadhyay wanted an orthodox Brahmin and says that two notables, Brajendranath Seal and Bipincandra Pal, objected. 'Upadhyay finally agreed to the choice of B.N. Seal, but this time Cambridge did not agree' (p. 119). Simha says that upon his return to India, Upadhyay

---

Thus Ashis Nandy considers three of Tagore's novels, *Gora* (1909), *Ghare-Baire* (1916) and *Car Adhyay* (1934), and concludes, 'In all three political novels, Upadhyay is the model for the hero as well as the "villain"' (1994: 67; see chs. 2 and 3). This is probably true. P Fallon, s.j. (1961) makes the connection with respect to *Gora* and *Car Adhyay.* The Prologue of this book evokes Upadhyay through the words of *Gora*.

65 The dynamics of their exchange of ideas are intriguing and will require careful study, for the intense intellectual relationship between Upadhyay and Tagore during this short period coincided with the development of a conservative phase in Tagore's thought. 'The ... years 1901–1906 are marked by the definite ascendancy of revivalist ideas in Rabindranath's mind.... We are now informed about the essential distinctness of oriental civilisation and its superiority over the European; the traditional samaj [society] is hailed as the real centre of Indian life, not the state; the Hindu past is invoked in poetic language; child-marriage and restrictions on widows are declared to be not unjustified in the context of Hindu society; virtues are discovered in the functional specialisation through caste; and even sati gets an honourable mention .... Rabindranath was to sharply modify this view in his post-1907 essays' (Sumit Sarkar, 1973: 53–4). We have seen that many of these ideas are discussed by Upadhyay in his contributions to the *Bangadarsan,* which was edited by Tagore at the time. It is also clear that Rabindranath read Upadhyay's letters from England with great interest. Manoranjan Guha quotes correspondence from Tagore to this effect. In a letter dated March 10, 1903, Tagore wrote to a friend, from Santiniketan: 'I'm enclosing Upadhyay *mahāśay's* last letter.... The time has come to reveal India as it truly is [*bhāratbarṣer jathārthabhābe ātmaparicay dibār samay asiāche*].' In a letter from Almora (dated July 30, 1903) to the same friend (Mohitcandra Sen), Tagore writes: 'Has Upadhyay *mahāśay* returned? If only he were to visit Almora I would get a good account of his grand tour abroad [*digbijaykāhinī*]' (p. 45).

Rumours and counter-rumours in connection with the controversy mentioned earlier about Tagore's and Upadhyay's influence on each other developed over time after Upadhyay's death, not least within the Santiniketan Ashram culture. Some of these have lived on in various works. Thus Sunil Chandra Sarkar says, 'Brahmabandhav

managed to collect the money but found it more difficult to nominate a suitable person. 'All the newspapers discussed the matter.' Some wanted the Bengali Seal, others the eminent Bombay Sanskritist R.G. Bhandarkar.[66] Upadhyay agreed to Seal and informed Cambridge accordingly (Simha, p. 67). Thus far the reports broadly tally. But the matter didn't go through. Simha gives some cock-and-bull story that the Cambridge Committee first sought the Pope's permission for Seal, but that the Pope did not agree (pp. 67–8). As UBBJ points out (footnote p. 75), the Pope had no jurisdiction in the matter. In any case, the matter was dropped. 'Is it surprising that with all this haggling [Upadhyay's] enthusiasm should have grown cold?' concludes *The Blade* (p. 119)[67]

So Upadhyay had returned home to his beloved Bengal, and was delighted to be back, a fish returned to water.

> By divine grace I have returned to my land.... How constrained I was, living in England! All day long bound up in various ways—fastenings on my feet, around my waist, around my neck—I felt quite choked!...
>
> Upon returning home I longed to eat proper Bengali food ... and through the kindness of my married friends I satisfied all my desires. Oh, how delightful is *sajne caccaḍi*[68]—I sensed then what the bliss of a lovers' reunion must be.

---

Upadhyay, the famous religious reformer, who ... came to join the school as its first principal, sought to make it the training ground of a rigid religious cult. He was relentless in forcing upon everybody his own ideas and ways.... This dogmatic approach went so far that Tagore had even to accept the distinction of castes as a social reality and accede to separate arrangements in the kitchen for Brahmins and lower castes' (see pp. 148–9). Again, in 'Santiniketan and Sriniketan', Uma Dasgupta records that 'Shri Kalipada Ray, a present ashramite ... used to be told by his father, the late Nepal Chandra Ray, Teacher at Santiniketan from 1910 onwards ... that Brahmabandhab had wanted to turn the Santiniketan Ashram into an Anandamath, which Rabindranath would not have. I must add that the late N.C. Ray was not a contemporary of Brahmabandhab Upadhyay' (1975–6: 278 and note 9). And so on. Our own appraisal of the sources leads to the conclusion that such reports, made well after the event, seem tendentiously to favour a particular image of Tagore at the expense of Upadhyay.

66 R.G. Bhandarkar (1837–1925) is described also as an 'educationist and social reformer' in S.P. Sen (ed.), 1974; vol. 1, pp. 165–6. It could be that Bhandarkar's social and political views were too moderate to win Upadhyay's favour.

67 Today both Sanskrit and Hinduism (especially Vedanta) are taught in Cambridge.

68 *Sajne (śāk)* is a bean-like vegetable, *caccaḍi* is a dish prepared from it.

> '*Sajne śāk* says, 'Of all *śāk*s I'm least great,
> I get called upon only in dire straits.'
>
> *Sajne!* Truly you're the friend of those in need! And when I ate *lauḍgā bhāte,* and *kacur śāk,* and *mocār ghanṭa,* and *kaci āmdār ṭak,*[69] I resolved that I would make every effort never to leave Mother Bengal's lap again. But my friends' kindness went much further than *āmdār ṭak*—with *kā̃cāgollās, rasagollās, khīr, pāyes*[70] and so on—with whatever was eatable, suckable, lickable and drinkable, I more than satisfied my palate! Oh you wretched English! I can't sleep for thinking that it's not in your lot to enjoy *rasagollās*! You've admitted that you'll study Hindu thought. But if your benumbed tongues could swim some day in the juice of the choicest *rasagollās*, you'd realise how great and refined the Aryan people are (Letter 10).

But Upadhyay had returned to an uncertain future in the short furious years ahead.

69 Vegetarian fare. The point is that these simple dishes (inexpensive to prepare in Upadhyay's time, though not always so today!), because of their very Bengaliness, can give the greatest satisfaction.

70 Now, in true Bengali fashion, Upadhyay steps up a gear. The vegetarian fare was simple and inexpensive; but the sweets mentioned here, all milk-based, are rich and more costly. Bengali sweets were (and are) regarded as consummating and showing the lavishness of a meal.

# Chapter 13

# A Flashing Sword:
## In Defence of Krishna

It is interesting to note how some of Upadhyay's biographers describe his activities soon after his return from England. After noting that the prospect of the Cambridge lectureship in Hindu studies had to be abandoned, *The Blade* continues the story of the Simla Bazar Street school (still in existence) and Upadhyay's climactic involvement in its fortunes. Simha launches into the absurdity of the Pope's opposition to Upadhyay's choice of B.N. Seal for the Cambridge post (pp. 67–8), while UBBJ, after mentioning this matter (pp. 84–5), stresses Upadhyay's rising nationalistic fervour in the context of the turn of events at the School (pp. 99–100).

We ourselves have called this shortest, final period of Upadhyay's life, 'The Nationalist Phase' (chapter 2). And it is in this period that Upadhyay's nationalism is transformed from an underlying 'cultural nationalism', if you like, to an overtly more political form. Upadhyay returned from England disenchanted with 'western' cultural values and modern thought. It could be argued that he went to England quite prepared to be disenchanted. His tendentious criticism of life in the west began in the very first letter to the *Bangabasi*. By the time he had returned he had built up quite a popular reputation among his Bengali compatriots—who could doubt that it was not premeditated?—as a champion of a Sanskritic (monolithic) traditional Hindu culture. So on his return he had something to live up to. He was now in the public eye, allied to a public cause.

It is in this context that one must follow the turn of events, not least with regard to the long-suffering Simla Bazar Street School. It was still in existence but had not received much active support from Upadhyay. It was now no longer associated with Tagore and Santiniketan. *The Blade* says that in August 1902, shortly before

Upadhyay was to leave for England, it had eight students. Perhaps even before Upadhyay departed for England, the school was moved to 9 Chidam Moodie's Lane, apparently to the very place previously occupied by the now defunct Atur Asrama or Refuge for the Distressed.[1] In any case, Upadhyay embarked on his travels and left the school in the tender care of the faithful Rewachand. 'In course of a year, the number of boys steadily increased from eight to thirty-five.... Most of the grinding work fell on Rewachand. In 1904 the school formally opened and was called the Sarasvat[a] Ayatan or Collegium Sophiae. It comprised boarders as well as day-scholars' (Bl., pp. 119–20).

The name is significant; it discloses the objectives Upadhyay intended for the school. The school was for Hindu boys who were to be trained in traditional Hindu ways (in general terms this conformed with the aim of some of the Indian elite to establish local models of education that would develop an indigenous identity as opposed to the 'deracinating' British system then current; more specifically, the project would embody Upadhyay's own understanding of this identity). 'Traditional' Hindu practices and values were to be tempered, not transformed, by those aspects of western civilization that were 'useful' both negatively and positively, that is, that would show up the depth of Hindu culture on the one hand, and give it a scientific edge on the other. The grand design was to train experts in this tempered Hindu wisdom who would themselves found similar establishments in other parts of India, where discerning westerners could study to their benefit. This is why the school was called 'The Abode of Learning' (*sārasvata āyatana*). Another grand scheme, and alas, another of Upadhyay's ventures that, owing to neglect, eventually ended in failure.

It would be appropriate at this point to consider the prospectus of the Sarasvata Ayatan.[2] Since this document is a relatively rare instance of its kind, and to the best of my knowledge the only copy of the school's prospectus in existence,[3] we now give it in full,

1 *The Blade* says (p. 119), 'The house was once haunted, so the story goes, but the poor of the Refuge had managed to drive out the devil. The boys could thus frequent the house without any apprehension.'

2 This must have been formulated when the school was more established, since the school is given its formal name. *The Sketch* (pt. 1, p. 32) says that in '1905, the Swami published an appeal, *re*, A National College', and proceeds to paraphrase (pp. 32–3) what seems to be another prospectus conceived on similar lines. *The Sketch* concludes: 'The Appeal got no response and the grand idea of a National College remains a paper scheme...'. For the prospectus of the Sarasvata Ayatan, a small document of 8 pages, see the Goethal archives, *Varia* 3, p. 221ff.

3 Not even excerpted, it seems, in any available work on Upadhyay.

translated from the Bengali. Further, it will give us an insight not only into Upadhyay's specific intentions in this regard but also into the kind of thinking that went into the formulation of these composite educational syllabuses.

Saraṣvata Ayatan
Aims [*Uddeśya*]

1. Training in various forms of learning in accordance with dharma.[4]

2. The practice of good conduct. The study of various useful occupations as well as of agriculture, trade and handicrafts for carrying out one's livelihood.[5]

Sections and Stages

There will be three Sections [*bibhāg*] and three corresponding Stages [*krama*] in the Sarasvata Ayatan. The first Section is the Primary School [*pāṭhśālā*]; the second Section is the College of Study [*śikṣālay*], and the third Section is the College of Learning [*bidyālay*]. Appropriate teaching [*anujāyī śikṣā*] will be given in the first Stage in the Primary School, the second Stage in the College of Study and the third Stage in the College of Learning.

1. The First Stage in the Primary School:
   1) Bengali writing and reading [*bāṅgālā likhan o paṭhan*], in particular the *Rāmāyaṇa* and the *Mahābhārata*.[6]
   2) Mathematics [*gaṇita*].
   3) Geography [*bhū-paricay*] and Astronomy [*kha-paricay*].[7]
   4) Study of Society [*samāj-paricay*], especially facts about Bengal and India (*bāṅgālā o bhāratbarṣer itibṛtta*).
   5) Physics [*padārtha-paricay*].
   6) Drawing [*aṅkan-bidyā*].
   7) Handicrafts and Agriculture [*śilpa o kṛṣi*].
   8) Sanskrit language and grammar [*saṃskṛtabhāṣā o byākaran*].

4 *Dharmer anukūl ḅibidha bidyār anuśīlan.*

5 *Sadācārer anuṣṭhān. jībikā nirbbāher upajogī bibidha bṛttir o kṛṣi-bāṇijya śilpa-kalār śikṣā.*

6 i.e., the Bengali *Ramayana* and *Mahabharata;* see chapter 2, note 30.

7 The latter in particular was intended presumably not only for general knowledge but for an appreciation of Hindu religious history and ritual, much of which was based on the lunar calendar.

*Note 1:* Elementary Sanskrit language and grammar is compulsory for Brahmin boys. For other castes the study of Sanskrit is optional [*aparāpar jātir pakṣe saṃskṛtaśikṣā svecchādhīn*], but the study of some arts-subject is compulsory [*kono nā kono kalā-bidyā abaśya śikṣaṇīya*]. For Brahmins handicrafts are optional. Elementary agriculture is compulsory for everyone.

*Note 2:* The first Stage will last for 5 years.

2. The Intermediate *[madhyama]* Stage in the College of Study:

1) Sanskrit and Bengali Literature, in particular the Sanskrit *Rāmāyaṇa* and *Mahābhārata* (selected portions).
2) Grammar: the *Laghukaumudī.*
3) Advanced Geography [*ucca-aṅger bhū-paricay*].
4) Study of Society [*samāj-paricay*].
5) Physics.
6) Arithmetic [*pāṭigaṇita*]; Algebra [*bījgaṇita*]; Geometry [*jyāmiti*]; Trigonometry [*trikonamiti*]; Mensuration (*kṣetrabyabahār*).
7) Logic: the *Bhāṣāpariccheda.*
8) Hindi (optional).
9) English language and literature (optional).
10) Advanced handicrafts or agriculture or estate management [*jamidāri*] and Land-survey [*jarip*] or Banking [*mahājani*].

*Note 1:* English will be taught in the Intermediate Stage to the same standard as English language and literature in the F.A. class of current Colleges.

*Note 2:* Carving [*khodāi*], casting [*ḍhālāi*], dyeing,[8] weaving [*bayan*], electrical expertise [*tāḍit cālanā*] and training in other such skills will be given during this Stage.

*Note 3:* The same rule will apply in this Stage to Brahmins and other groups with respect to the study of Sanskrit and training in various skills, as in the first Stage.

*Note 4:* The Intermediate Stage will last for 7 years.

3. The Final *[carama]* Stage in the College of Learning:

There may be seven branches [*śākhā*] in this stage.

1) Sanskrit and Bengali literature; Hindi and English (optional). Pāṇini: Metre [*chandaḥ*], Tropes [*alaṅkār*], the Principles of language [*bhāṣātattva*] and of grammar [*byākaraṇtattva*].

8 The word following a hyphen after '*raṅg*' is unclear.

2) Study of Society and Economics [*arthanīti*].
3) Philosophy (the Six Systems and European Psychology).[9]
4) Tradition (Practical knowledge).[10]
5) Mathematics and Astronomy [*jyotiṣ*] (Hindu and European).
6) The scientific study of various categories of being [*padārthabijñān*].
7) Medicine [*cikitsāśāstra*].

*Note 1:* Students may elect to study any one of the above-mentioned branches at a time; no other branch may be studied simultaneously. Agriculture is part of scientific study.[11]

*Note 2:* In addition Brahmins must study the Veda [*bed svādhyāy*] and Tradition [*smṛti*].

*Note 3:* The Final Stage will last for 3 years.

General Rules [*sādhāraṇ niyam*]

1. Each student must follow the *dharma* and customs of his own caste (*nija nija barṇer dharma o ācār*).
2. No fees will be accepted in any form. Voluntary contributions from the children's guardians will be welcomed.

Note

1) It is not necessary for all three Sections to exist in every case. Primary Schools, Colleges of Study and Colleges of Learning may exist separately. In some cases any two may exist together. Nor is it necessary for all seven branches to exist in a College of Learning; one or more may be present.

> If any Primary School, College of Learning, or College of Study is established on the model of the Sarasvata Ayatan it may be considered to form part of the Ayatan.

The 'composite' nature of this syllabus is obvious, that is, the attempt to blend Indian and western knowledge and skills. Upadhyay was realistic. He was not opposed to learning from the west, but he did not wish western norms and values to overwhelm indigenous ones, and so the shaping of a patriotic, informed indigenous identity. Note too the attempt to develop a rounded education; at each level there is a balancing of theory and practice, with a stress on occupational

9 *Darśan* (*saddarśan o yuropīya manobijñān*). The term *manobijñān* may have been intended to mean 'psychology' or 'philosophy of mind'.

10 *Smṛti* (*byabahār-bidyā*).

11 *Kṛṣitattva bijñāner antargata*; i.e. is part of no. 6?

training. The syllabus was intended to turn out individuals equipped to lead lives useful to themselves and to society. There is an appreciation too of contact with the land, in the study of agriculture, estate management and so on.

The reader will not have failed to attend too to the emphasis on maintaining caste codes. The document starts with the observation that the education inculcated in the Ayatan will be consonant with *dharma*, and towards the end there is the stricture that 'each student must follow the *dharma* and customs of his own caste'. There is also the requirement for Brahmins to study Sanskrit and in due course the Veda. Finally, we are told that no formal fees will be accepted. This is a long-standing preference of Upadhyay's; he had said on more than one occasion that it is unBrahminical to sell knowledge. In all these observations we may recognize a number of Upadhyay's cherished concerns. The place given to the study of Hindi, a north Indian language, especially in a Bengali context, may surprise. Upadhyay, it may be recalled, had travelled in the north during those troubled early adult years, before he joined the Brahmo Samaj. He would have realized the importance of Hindi as a sort of *lingua franca* for the north. It is striking that he also accepted that it was a potential *national* language when the syllabus was formed, at a time when the national movement in Bengal was shaped by the protest against the impending Partition of the province (see next chapter). This was a proposal that was beginning to be adopted among some of the leading Bengali politicians of the time. Thus Upadhyay was not narrow in his loyalties or thinking as a nationalist. We shall examine his growing political involvement during these years in the next chapter.

It is not clear how strictly this syllabus was implemented in the Ayatan, not least the disclaimer that formal school fees would not be accepted. After Rewachand, who did not work for a salary, left, most of the staff who were taken on were to be paid (Bl., p. 122; see note 12 below). This, of course, did not augur well for the financial situation of the school. The Sarasvata Ayatan ground to a halt in or around 1906. Upadhyay's interest in such 'national' education again comes to the fore during the anti-partition agitation (see chapter 14).

Upon his return from abroad, Upadhyay did not teach regularly in the school; he gave only occasional classes. But in February 1904 he gave instructions that the children were to celebrate the forthcoming festival of Sarasvati, the Goddess of Learning and the patroness, so to speak, of the institution. Rewachand, who was so closely involved with the children, and staunchly, if more conventionally, committed to his Catholic faith, was strongly opposed. Upadhyay argued that though as Christians both he and Rewachand would not take part in the ceremony, the children as Hindus were not only entitled to take part, but were to be encouraged to do so. Besides, Sarasvati could be regarded as a legitimate *symbol* of the divine wisdom and worshipped as such. Those who did not have the fullness of Christian revelation should be encouraged to worship the wisdom of God according to their best lights, and it was precisely this that he asked Rewachand to countenance. The worship should go ahead with the use of Hindu ritual and the familiar image of the goddess; to ease their consciences, Rewachand and Upadhyay would not take part.

This was not good enough for Rewachand. Constantly in touch with the children, he had sought to implement Upadhyay's general ideal but had discouraged them from any semblance of image worship. What Upadhyay was proposing was idolatry in disguise. He would have none of it. The ceremony went ahead, and Rewachand regretfully left the Sarasvata Ayatan.[12] Thus, Upadhyay and Rewachand formally parted company though they remained in touch. A close association of over a decade had finally come to an end.

From one angle, Upadhyay's action over the worship of Sarasvati for his charges appears inconsistent; from another, it may be interpreted as consistent. The reader may recall that in chapter 6 we analysed Upadhyay's view on image worship. As noted there, Upadhyay clearly distinguishes between the Hindu practice of worshipping "idols"—this he pronounces idolatry proper—and the Catholic custom of *honouring* sacred images, analagous to honouring an image of the Queen, for instance.[13] So he has made the distinction

[12] Upadhyay now put the school in the care of Prabodhcandra Simha (who became a biographer) and an orthodox Brahmin pandit, Moksadacaran Samadhyayi. So it was only at this stage it seems that Simha came in close contact with Upadhyay. *The Blade* (pp. 122–3) says that 'more and more teachers had to be enlisted. They were to be paid.... The surroundings were anything but congenial. In 1905 the school was removed to a better locality in Cornwallis Street.... In 1906 it was shifted to Serampore [J.C. Bagal, 1964, gives the local name, 'Srirampur', p. 29].... The number of students, however, gradually went down and the Ayatan died a natural death for the simple reason that Upadhyay was busy with too many things.' (For details of the parting with Rewachand see Bl., pp. 119ff.) It was some time after this that Rewachand started his own school which he called, 'The Boys' Own Home'. It became well known in Calcutta but closed in 1942. The story is told in Turmes' *A Teacher of Genius*, pp. 24 ff.

[13] In Catholic theology, with which Upadhyay was familiar, this was the distinction between that worship due to God alone, called *latria*, and that 'worship', i.e. honour, reverence or homage, permissible to other creatures, called *dulia*.

between only revering and actually worshipping sacred images. He is consistent in saying that every instance of the honour of a sacred image need not be worship proper; in other words, on the face of it, reverence of a Hindu icon in his school *need not* be idolatry. The inconsistency arises when what had been interpreted earlier as idolatry proper is now permitted seemingly on the grounds of (doubtless, non-culpable) ignorance on the part of their wards.

But Upadhyay may simply have reconsidered his position. It is not clear if the children were permitted to proceed with the ceremony apprised of the way their ('more enlightened') superiors interpreted it, or were at least advised to proceed on the basis of regarding the icon as a mere *symbol* of divine wisdom. Whatever they might have been told by Upadhyay, Rewachand, who was less prone to compromise, was unhappy with the decision taken. Since it was he who spent most time with the boys as their teacher and mentor, he would justly have resented Upadhyay's authoritarianism in the matter.[14]

The subtext of the ceremony, of course, was the public image of the school that Upadhyay wished to project, a proper Hindu establishment run on traditional, 'Aryan' lines, where no proselytism was practised by the persons in charge, who happened to be Christians. Perhaps the tension of this situation was unsustainable. Certainly Rewachand could not with integrity countenance it[15]; Upadhyay clearly thought that he himself could and should. It may have been more than just a matter of availability then that Rewachand was replaced by practising Hindus.[16]

14 On the question of icon worship and consistency where Upadhyay was concerned, it could also be argued that Upadhyay was finally reverting to the 'symbolic' view of icon worship espoused by his mentor, the later Keshab (see chapter 3).

15 'Rewachand would banish from the school and from the minds of the children every vestige of an idol, lest there be a possibility of divine honour given to an object of clay' (Bl., p. 121).

16 Some time after this incident, Upadhyay published an article in Bengali entitled, 'The festival of Sri Krishna's birth' (*śrīkṛṣṇer janmotsab*) in his famous Bengali daily, the *Sandhya* (see further), though the exact date is not known. The article is reprinted in Ghosh, 1987: 205ff. In this article, Upadhyay says: 'The forthcoming big festival of Krishna's birth will be celebrated by the revered teachers and student body of the school called the *Saravasta Ayatan*. This institution was established so that our youth may understand that the Hindu race [*hindujāti*] and society are indissolubly bound with the past, that Hindu wisdom, religion [*dharma*] and social norms are intact and noble, and that, sanctified by Krishna's word [*kṛṣṇamantrapūta*], the Hindu race is immortal.'

With Rewachand's departure, and Upadhyay's continuing unwillingness to commit himself wholeheartedly to the running of the school, the Sarasvat Ayatan declined rapidly and, around 1906, eventually closed under the new regime.[17]

We return to 1904. What a contrast between Animananda and Upadhyay! Animananda was steady, focused, self-effacing. Upadhyay had many irons in the fire, toing and froing restlessly, a dramatic actor in the arena of public affairs. In the public eye, he was still the fervent nationalist who was critical of British rule, the conservative religious culturalist who championed Hindu ideals and deplored encroaching westernization. He was to play one last leading part in this role, before his steps turned irrevocably to more overt political involvement.

Some time in July 1904, probably in the first half of that month, Upadhyay delivered an important lecture in Bengali entitled *Śrīkṛṣṇatattva* (which may be translated, 'The essential teaching/truth about the revered Krishna') at the house of 'Raja Benoy Krishna Dey Bahadur of Sovabazar' (Bl., p. 123).[18] As *The Blade* also intimates, the immediate reason for giving the lecture was the alleged attack on Krishna by the Scottish missionary scholar J.N. Farquhar in his *Gita and Gospel,* which had recently been published.[19] Farquhar's argument

[17] See note 12. In fact by 1905 Upadhyay was becoming increasingly involved in the agitation against the partition of Bengal. Binoy Sarkar records: 'In June 1905 ... [two friends and I] made new lodging arrangements together [*natun ek meser byabasthā kari*]. Brahmabandhab was the manager [*karmakartā*]. He was then running a school for boys called the Sarasvata Ayatan. Pandit Moksadacaran Samadhyayi accompanied him' (from H. Mukhopadhyay's *Binoy Sarkarer Baithake,* p. 284, quoted in UBBJ, p. 113).

[18] The lecture has been published in the journal *Sahitya Samhita,* 5, 6 & 7, B.E. 1311 (1904), in Āśvin and Karttik, pp. 321–41 (and reprinted in Ghosh, 1987: 73–96). It is recorded there that the lecture was delivered at the second Special Session of the Sahitya Sabha's fifth anniversary. *The Blade* says that (after the furore created by this lecture) Upadhyay delivered it in English in the Calcutta Albert Hall on Monday, July 25, and that 'several Jesuit Fathers attended' (p. 123). No copy of this English version is available, though a rather lengthy report, as recorded in the daily *Telegraph* of Calcutta of August 1, is quoted in *The Sketch,* Pt. 1, pp. 48–54. It is noteworthy that this report says nothing of Upadhyay's positive and distinctive interpretation of Krishna's relationship with the cowherdesses of Vrindavan, which formed a significant part of the Bengali lecture (see further).

[19] The first edition was published in 1903, the second edition in 1906 (92 pp). On Farquhar (1861–1929) see E. Sharpe, especially 1962 and 1965. In *Faith meets Faith* (1977), Sharpe writes, 'By this time [1903], it was becoming fairly common in some quarters for Indians (and particularly Indian intellectuals) to reject Christianity not because it was untrue, but because it was un-Indian. Farquhar's answer at this time

in this book can be summed up as follows: the *Gita* could not have been Krishna's utterance, 'being in all points the product of an age many centuries later than the time when he lived' (p. 21). The *Gita* rather is to be explained, not as 'a fresh revelation' but as 'the concentrated essence of Hinduism.... In it we see the Hindu people longing for God ... expressing the deepest desires of their religious nature (p. 27).... Rightly read, the Gita is a clear-tongued prophecy of Christ, and the hearts that bow down to the idea of Krishna are really seeking the incarnate Son of God [i.e. Christ]' (p. 73).

If this were true, the *Gita*'s teaching is fulfilled by that of the Gospels, and Krishna's role by that of Christ. In short, according to Farquhar's argument, for a Christian, there is no *continuing* role for *Gita* and Krishna, for they have been superseded. For a Hindu, Farquhar is just pitting *Gita* and Krishna against Gospels and Christ to the advantage of the latter (and inviting a response to this confrontation). But how might a *Hindu-Christian,* or more precisely, a 'Hindu-Catholic', as Upadhyay on occasion famously described himself, meet Farquhar's challenge? Here lies the subtlety of the matter for Upadhyay. It was originally intended that Pandit Mokshadacaran Saṃadhyayi (one of the new managers of the Sarasvata Ayatan) would deliver the counter-attack to Farquhar's thesis. But the Pandit declined and asked Upadhyay to act in his place.

This request was quite remarkable. It speaks volumes not only for Upadhyay's reputation for knowledge, but for the image he had cultivated, presumably still as a Christian, among the circle of observant Hindu Bengali intellectuals. It was agreed among this circle that Upadhyay would answer Farquhar's thesis from a Hindu point of view. This is where the delicacy of his own position as a Hindu-Catholic comes in. It seems that Upadhyay was faced with a dilemma: either rebut Farquhar and abandon your Christian commitment in the process, or let his thesis pass, and relinquish your identity as a Hindu. Indeed, it may well be that many in both camps looked forward to Upadhyay's response as a test of his true loyalties.

As is well known, the way to overcome a dilemma is to slip between its horns. This is what Upadhyay tried to do, though there can be little doubt that the majority of his hearers would not have

---

was simply to stress that the needs of the emergent nation were not only material, but spiritual, and that those needs could be met in and through Christ' (1977: 24). Farquhar went on to develop his influential 'fulfillment theology' in a number of important works over the next two decades.

appreciated the manner of his attempted escape, so subtle does it appear to have been. The exit that Upadhyay sought lay in the theology of his position—more in what he did not say about Christ and Krishna than in what he did say about them. In the process he made a number of other points that were to his purpose.

Upadhyay was not the first, nor the last, in a movement Farquhar describes in an Appendix to his book as the 'neo-Krishna movement'. 'Neo-Krishna literature' (also Farquhar's phrase), which represents this movement, expresses the need for 'a perfect character, such as Christ's, for daily contemplation and imitation. The Neo-Krishna movement endeavours to supply these needs from within Hinduism, offering the *Gita* instead of the Gospels, and Krishna instead of Christ' (p. 86). In the Appendix, Farquhar carefully and helpfully provides a list of such literature, the first of which is Bankimcandra Chatterjee's *Krishnacaritra* (KC). Bankim's substantial work appeared first in the form of essays in his new monthly, the *Pracar,* in 1884. An incomplete edition came out in book form in 1886; the complete revised work appeared in 1892.

The *Krishnacaritra* was undoubtedly a seminal work for the whole of the neo-Krishna movement. It projected Krishna, rather than, say, the deity Rama (Gandhi's preferred character for national aspirations), in the consciousness, especially of Bengali intellectuals involved in various ways in shaping a nascent nationalism, as an exemplar for *human* moral action and wise living *in* the world. This was done sometimes in explicit contrast to the figure of Christ (and occasionally, the Buddha). The KC gave unstoppable impetus to a trend in which, as Farquhar intimates, Krishna became the Hindu's—really, the bhadralok's—own construct as the counterpart to Christ, especially in early religio-nationalist ideology.

The KC was avowedly based on a scholarly, i.e. rationalist, approach to the life of Krishna. In this Bankim adopted the methodology if not the agenda of western Indologists. He is at pains to acknowledge his debt to them as scholars, but also to ridicule their—in his estimation—anti-Hindu presuppositions, which, as paradoxically unscholarly, vitiate the conclusions they anticipate from their research.

> Some European and American scholars have studied Sanskrit. They are engaged in manifesting historical data from ancient Sanskrit works, but can't bear the idea that the dependent and weak Hindu race [*hindujāti*] were once civilised, and that this was an ancient civilisation. So, with few exceptions, they are continually engaged in belittling ancient India's [*bhāratvarṣa*] greatness [*gaurab*]. They

assiduously seek to prove that all that is in the ancient Indian works ... is in fact modern [*ādhunik*], and that everything in the Hindu texts is either completely false or stolen from some other country. One worthy's view is that the *Ramayana* is an imitation of Homer's poetry, another's that the *Bhagavadgita* is but a reflection of the Bible. Hindu astronomy [*jyotiṣ*] has been taken from the Chinese, Greeks [*yavan*] or Chaldeans.... The basis of their method to establish all this is that whatever exists in Indian works to India's advantage is either false or interpolated, while whatever is found opposed to India is true.[20]

Though he personally believes that Krishna is the descent (*abatār*) of God, says Bankim,[21] that is not the presupposition on which he bases his work. On the contrary, in his analyses of the traditional Krishna material, he will accept only those data that stand up to modern criteria of historical scholarship. This will reveal both the historicity and the true human character of Krishna.

Most of India's Hindus and all of Bengal's believe that the Revered Krishna [*śrīkṛṣṇa*] is God's descent [*īśvarer abatār*].... I too believe profoundly that Krishna is the Lord [*bhagabān*] himself.... [But] I do not ask the reader to accept what I believe, and it is not my purpose to establish Krishna's divinity [*īśvaratva*]. In this work I shall discuss only his human character [*mānabcaritra*]... What lord Krishna's true character really is has been described in the Puranas. and epic;[22] to ascertain that, I have discussed the Puranas and the epic to the best of my ability. As a result I have realised that all the reprehensible stories [*pāpopakhyān*] about Krishna current in society are baseless, and that if one excludes all the narratives produced by the story-writers about Krishna, then what remains is extremely pure [*biśuddha*], very holy [*pabitra*], and very great. I have learnt that nowhere else is there a character so endowed with every virtue and so devoid of every sin—neither in the history nor in the literature [*kābya*] of any other country.[23]

Notice that Bankim has 'standardized' belief in Krishna in order to enhance the importance of his subject ('Most of India's Hindus and all of Bengal's believe'). He is concerned only with the human nature of Krishna, and his sources for this are the textual sources that western

20 1.2. p. 410. References to the KC here are taken from *Bankim Racanabali (Sahitya Samagra)*, Tuli-Kalam edition, Calcutta, 1986.

21 Bankim is here in the last, most overtly religious phase, of his personal development.

22 That is, the *Mahabharata*.

23 I.1, p. 407. I have inverted the order of some sentences to establish Bankim's point.

scholars have used for their conclusions about Krishna. In fact Bankim's three main textual sources are primarily the *Mahabharata* (which he reckons contains the oldest Krishna material, see I.2[24]), and then the *Harivamsa* (an extended Appendix to the epic), and the Puranas (chiefly the Vishnu, Bhagavata and Brahmavaivarta Puranas; I.15). However, he has discovered, after his application of scholarly criteria to the material and in sharp contrast to the (biased) judgement of westerners, that the character of Krishna is unparalleled and exemplary—a true model for human virtue. Indeed, he continues, many passages in the texts that seem to throw Krishna in a licentious light have been misunderstood by the general reader. They carry a deep meaning not obvious to the casual or uninformed reader, and can be pondered to one's moral profit.

Though to the best of my knowledge he does not refer to it, there can be no doubt that Upadhyay was familiar with the content of the KC. It was too seminal and germane a text in the religio-political ideology of the times to be ignored[25]. And a great deal of Bankim's argument, though certainly not all of it, was to Upadhyay's purpose. Like Bankim, he focused on Krishna as a potentially national figure. In general he looked to the same textual sources as Bankim; he also was keen to show the exemplary moral character and role of Krishna, and (a methodological sophistication in contrast to earlier days) argued that many well-known but apparently morally dubious escapades of Krishna had deeper and didactic purport than seemed to be the case. But there were significant differences in his interpretation

24 After identifying seven criteria for determining interpolations (e.g. contradictory and inconsistent material) in I.10, he distinguishes three strata in the composition of the epic, the first the oldest and shortest, the last the most recent and voluminous (I.11). Only the first stratum gives authentic data about Krishna; here 'Krishna is not generally seen to be the descent of God or of Vishnu; he himself does not declare his divinity.' He includes the *Bhagavadgita* in the period of the third stratum.

25 Tapan Raychaudhuri comments (1988: 149), 'This work of monumental scholarship [the KC] remains a *tour de force* which had hardly any impact on the reading public. [Bankim's] belief that the superiority of Hinduism was manifest above all in the perfection of its ideal, Krishna, was not shared by many.' This is something of an understatement. What is meant by 'the reading public' here? Rabindranath for one referred to the KC, describing its real hero as the author's nationalism rather than the historical figure of Krishna. As Farquhar's list indicates, by the early 1900s a considerable volume of apologetic literature on Krishna had followed Bankim's work in Bengal, some of which had been written by eminent Bengalis (e.g., Nabincandra Sen, Gaurgobind Ray, Sitanath Tattvabhusan). Farquhar's concern with the *Gita* could be regarded as a kind of response to this, and Upadhyay's lecture as a continuation of the apologetic trend.

of Krishna, which reflected his own particular religious commitment and agenda, as well as the changed socio-political circumstances of his times. It is to Upadhyay's interpretation of Krishna, especially the *Śrīkṛṣṇatattva* lecture (SKT), that we now turn.

In a way, Upadhyay starts his lecture from where Bankim left off. After endorsing an Advaitic or non-dualistic, or Shankarite, interpretation of the Krishna phenomenon (and we shall see how this is applied), he makes two points. First, he universalizes Krishna's avatarhood: 'Two hundred millions of Hindus believe with one heart that Sri Krishna is Vishnu's avatar'; thus is Krishna set up as a potential national figure. Second, on the basis of this declaration, he boldly affirms in contrast to Bankim, that such a person as Krishna, whose way of renunciation (*nibṛttimārg*) proclaimed in the *Gita* has elevated the whole Hindu race (*hindujāti*) to the heights of wisdom and civilization, must indeed be God's avatar. But what does he mean by this?

In answer, Upadhyay first tries to clear up some preliminary objections. To begin with: is Krishna historical? Upadhyay attacks the views not only of western scholars but also of missionaries (*dharmapracārak*) in this respect. In keeping with his earlier position, already discussed, it is clear that those missionaries whom he characterizes as 'sectarian' (*sāmpradāyik*) are meant to be primarily Protestant missionaries; hence his reference to Farquhar's work. The missionaries have realized that 'if instead of lopping off the branches they were to destroy the root, their work of destruction would the more easily be accomplished. Sri Krishna is the living root (*jībanta mūl*) of Hinduness (*hindutva*).' Thus, as in earlier writings, Hinduism has been made a monolithic entity (under the abstract concept of *hindutva*), the sole root of which is Krishna.

In effect, Upadhyay simply asserts that in the light of modern studies it cannot now be doubted that Krishna is historical, and indeed, of good character. The objections that Krishna was not of good character rest on 'unscriptural' (*aśāstrīya*) works about him. There are similar works about Christ, avers Upadhyay, and the missionaries are beginning to appreciate that they can no longer criticize Krishna on such unsound evidence. So now they say that possibly Krishna was a historical individual, but he is not an avatar, and the *Gita* is not his teaching. Rather, in Farquhar's terms, the *Gita* expresses the collective Hindu desire for the coming of the real saviour figure that is God's descent on earth, namely, Christ. We come to the heart of the matter, for 'if it were proved that the *Gita* inculcates worship of

Jesus Christ [*pūjā karā*] and not of Krishna, defeat of the Hindu citadel will most certainly follow.'

Upadhyay's first task is to show that the *Gita* intimates nothing at all about Jesus. Everyone has heard the Christian teaching, he says, that God, having taken on human nature, came down and, offering up his own life, did reparation for the sins of the human race.[26] Farquhar claims, continues Upadhyay, that humans naturally (*svabhābataḥ*) hanker for such a saviour. But this is quite undoctrinal from the Christian point of view. For according to Christian teaching, while humans can naturally desire salvation, they cannot naturally desire the kind of Saviour Christ has been described to be in the statement above. Upadhyay here is harking back to his understanding of Catholic doctrine, according to which the teaching about the incarnation, God's descent among us in human form as Jesus, is not a truth accessible to the *natural* light of reason, but is a revealed truth. Upadhyay's rejection of Farquhar's claim turns on the use of the term 'naturally'—a subtlety bound to be lost on most if not all of his Hindu hearers (it would be beyond most Christians too).

Second, continues Upadhyay, Farquhar's claim intimates that God is constrained to fulfill this natural yearning. But all the Christian theologians maintain that God is not *bound* to save the creature by taking on a human body. If God were so bound, he would be subject to Nature, i.e. to the laws of cause and effect. But God is utterly free; he cannot be constrained to do anything. His saving action lies outside the scope of Nature (*prakṛtir niyamer bāhirbhūta*). Nature (*prakṛti*) cannot impose on God. We can say that this is really an extension of the previous contention, the reverse face, so to speak, of it. After affirming that humans can have no *natural* yearning for a Christ-like saviour figure, Upadhyay now affirms that God's sovereignty can never be subject to finite nature, even if there were such a yearning. But is this what Farquhar, at least, implies? We shall return to this point.

Further, what the *Gita* teaches about Krishna's descent and what Christian theologians teach about Christ's appearance among us (*ābhirbhābtattva*) are quite different. The *Gita* teaches that Krishna descends from period to period to punish wrongdoers, protect the virtuous and establish *dharma* (see *Gita* 4.8). Christianity teaches that God, having assumed human nature, has in this mode given up his life once and for all to atone for sin (*pāper prāyaścitter janya*

26 *Īśvar, mānab prakṛti grahaṇ kariyā, abatīrṇa haiyāchilen o nijer prāṇdān kariyā, mānabjātir pāper prāyaścitta kariyāchen.*

*prāṇdān kariyāchen*). Thus Jesus cannot be said to be an avatar in the way of the *Gita,* and the *Gita,* in turn, says nothing about his saving action at all.

One may think that this attempt at a rebuttal is less than convincing. It contains much rhetoric but little genuine argument. And does Farquhar's claim that there is a natural human yearning for a Christ-like saviour really imply that God is constrained by this yearning? Hardly. Nor is it unanimously held by Christian theologians, certainly, that there can be no natural yearning for God's incarnation. Upadhyay is confusing what is accessible, according to Catholic teaching, to the natural light of reason in the way of religious truth, with certain natural spiritual yearnings that humans may or may not have. Further, though there are clear (and significant) differences between what the *Gita* teaches about the reason for the Krishna avatar, and what Christianity teaches about God's purpose for the world through Christ's coming, as Upadhyay maintains, that does not mean that these teachings are not similar enough to sustain the claim that the Krishna avatar symbolically expresses a yearning for Christian incarnation. To contend that they are not requires more strenuous argumentation.

Upadhyay now takes up some further objections. We may consider the two most important. First, according to Farquhar, Sri Krishna did not promulgate the *Gita,* because the *Gita* was composed much later than the great war that is the scene of its promulgation. So, as the *Gita* cannot be the very words of Sri Krishna, it cannot be his teaching. 'Words fail on hearing Mr Farquhar's reasoning,' laments Upadhyay. The *Gita* is in verse, and there can be no doubt that Krishna and Arjuna, installed in a chariot on the battlefield, did not converse in verse! But this does not mean that the *Gita* does not faithfully convey their discourse, for the composer of the *Gita,* Vyasa, was one in spirit (*ekātmā*) with Sri Krishna, and transformed his words into verse without deviating from their meaning in the slightest. This is the occasion for Upadhyay to eulogize the *Gita* as a '*dharma*-tree' that resolves religious doubts, discords and contradictions by synthesis (*samanbay*) through its unitive largesse (*abhed biśālatāy*); it is a 'recollective' scripture (*smṛti*) in that it 're-collects' the canonical scriptures (*śruti*) integrally and without distortion. The implication is that the canonical scripture (the Veda) and the *Gita* are on a par from the point of view of their teaching authority.

The next objection we shall consider is that, except for 'sectarian Vaishnava works', Krishna is not perceived as an avatar in the ancient classical texts; therefore, belief in his avatarhood was never an ancient or universal belief. Upadhyay turns to 'the Hindu's history' (*hindur itihās*) to counter this view. First he says that about 4500 years ago, the transition to a new world era, the Kali Age, took place. It was at this juncture that Vyasa redacted the Veda into its present form, that the original *Mahabharata*[27] was composed, and that the Kurukshetra war, highlighted in the *Mahabharata,* occurred. Such a tempestuous time calls for the advent of an avatar. And indeed, Krishna appeared on the scene, imparted the *Gita* and played a leading role in the events of the day. Upadhyay offers no sustained reasoning for this; he just pits traditional Hindu claims against the conclusions of western scholars. He then adduces references in various ancient texts—an appended hymn of the Rg Veda, the Chandogya Upanishad, the famous grammarian Panini's magisterial treatise, and the so-called original *Mahabharata* of 24,000 verses—to bolster his claim that Krishna was traditionally worshipped as an avatar. It must be said that none of these references, even in Upadhyay's day, could be regarded as a plausible scholarly basis for this claim. Note, in passing, that the whole tenor of this approach goes against Bankim's thesis in the KC where it is argued that the earliest textual evidence about Krishna, *especially* the 'original *Mahabharata*', simply manifests Krishna's exemplary humanity rather than proclaims him an avatar. But having disposed of preliminary objections to his satisfaction, Upadhyay now takes up the question of Krishna's true nature as an avatar.

This reality must be understood in the context of Advaita, he affirms. 'Being (*vastu*) is one—it cannot be two. The One is manifested as many,' begins Upadhyay. This may be interpreted in a Christian way no doubt, but on the face of it, it is very Hindu talk. Throughout the lecture, Upadhyay is clearly projecting himself as Hindu, if not *a* Hindu. In other words, he is implying that if his words are to be understood in a Christian light, this can be done only on the basis of the appropriate interpretation of their avowed Hindu framework. If Being is one, he continues, where is the scope for, and what is the purpose of, an avatar? The answer is: manifested being, which derives from the One, is diverse and complex; as such it requires order, *dharma,* for its welfare. But, as the *Gita* says (4.6–8), when *dharma*

27 Supposedly comprising 24,000 verses (in contrast to later reckonings of 100,000 verses). Bankim, in the KC, argued strongly for this 'original' *Mahabharata,* on the basis of claims by western scholars.

wanes and disorder or *adharma* is in the ascendant, then the avatar comes to restore *dharma* for the sake of the righteous. This is where Shankara comes in. Following the mind of Krishna, the great Advaitin taught that *dharma* wanes when a disciplined path leading to salvation (*niḥśreyassādhanā*) is absent. And 'the discipline leading to salvation is that discipline by virtue of which all attachments (*bāsanā*) are done away with, and the ties of spiritual unknowing (*abidyā*) are removed.' So, according to Upadhyay, the controlling ethic of right living is the Advaitic ethic of renunciation (*nibṛtti*), in contrast to the ethic of worldly living (*prabṛtti*), of sensual engagement with the world. In this degenerate Kali era, it was to teach this ethic of renunciation by word and example that the Krishna avatar occurred.

The whole of the substantial remaining part of the lecture is an exposition of this view, in terms of the contrast and dialectic between the Sanskritic pair of *nivṛtti* and *pravṛtti,* renunciation and engagement, in their various aspects. After all, it is a celibate renouncer who is speaking, and he will be at pains to show that even those incidents in Krishna's life that seem to depict sensual enjoyment must be interpreted, if one is to understand their true meaning, as expressions of a sublime *nivṛtti*. In adopting this line of interpretation, Upadhyay is following Bankim's hermeneutic.

Human beings, declares Upadhyay, are naturally inclined to gratification (*prabṛttiparāyaṇ*); the desire for sons, wealth and a happy after-life continually leads them on. The only thing that can save them from such corrupting worldliness is *dharma*. 'If only detachment [*nibṛtti*] remained, family life and work [*karma*] would suffer. If, on the other hand, only worldly involvement [*prabṛtti*] remained, unrighteousness and oppression would destroy society. Thus we call *dharma* the balance [*sāmañjasya*] between worldly involvement and detachment, between action and knowledge'.[28] In fact, ideally, knowledge and action are two sides of the same coin. Informed action is necessary—that is the teaching of the *Gita*—but informed action is selfless action (the controlling ethic is still renunciative). If we do not adopt a selfless ethic, or if we seek knowledge away from action in the world, disorder or *adharma* will arise in the vacuum in the form of 'vicious evildoers' (*ghor durbṛtta pāṣaṇḍa-sakal*)' who seek to oppress the virtuous.

28 The notion that virtue (*dharma*) is a harmony or balance of various qualities is also derived from Bankim; see Bankim's *Dharmatattva* ('The Essence of Dharma').

Ordinary mortals cannot provide an adequate exemplar of this ideal synthesis of knowledge and action, because they are under the sway of selfish action (*karma*)[29] and spiritual ignorance (*avidyā*), and are tainted by worldliness. 'The bonds of *avidyā* cannot be severed by *avidyā* itself.' Only someone outside the sway of such action and ignorance can deliver us from their thrall, and act as the exemplar of the ideal synthesis of knowledge and action. This is Krishna the avatar.

> When the whole country is overcome by worldliness [*prabṛtti-parāyaṇatā*], when one and all are oppressed by gross tyranny, when everyone rushes towards the conflicts of division, then the Lord's graciousness takes shape in palpable form,[30] a form which even spiritually blind humans can see, and seeing may attain discerning wisdom; a form through whose influence worldly involvement (*prabṛtti*) and its excesses are subdued, and the human mind becomes capable of following the path of selflessness (*niṣkām*) and renunciation.

As the translation indicates, in the original this passage is in the present tense. Since it sets the scene for the coming of the avatar, in particular the Krishna avatar, semantically the historic present could have been the intention. But the tenor of Upadhyay's whole lecture makes it clear that the present time in his motherland reproduces the context, not for the advent of a new avatar, but for resorting anew to the Krishna avatar as the exemplar that will save his country from its moral malaise. Note that in this lecture Krishna is really a culture-specific *moral* exemplar for Hindus, and that he is primarily an *exemplar* rather than a divine Saviour who will respond to prayer or supplication to accomplish the required ends. This emphasis is not overtly contrary then to what might be expected of a speaker personally and privately committed to Christ—God's Incarnation reconciling the whole world to himself. Though Upadhyay does not

29 Upadhyay uses the term *karma*, literally 'action', continually in the lecture. Occasionally it means 'ritual action', but generally it connotes, according to context, either self-centred action or work, or the opposite of this, selfless action. Its general sense *could* be taken to include the 'karma' that generates rebirth, and that in turn is (metaphysically) stored up by self-centred action which engenders fresh rebirths—a specifically Hindu belief, formally rejected by Christian doctrine. Upadhyay never clears up this perhaps intended ambiguity in the lecture: another example, perhaps, of his cleverly projected Hindu image, which turns as much on what he does not say as on what he does.

30 *Īśavarer anukampā ghanībhūta haiyā 'rūp' dhāraṇ kare.*

use the term, it is clear that Krishna is being proposed here as the exemplary *karmayogī*, the selfless man of action. This is the Krishna of Bankim too. But philosophically, what is the status, we may ask, of the Krishna avatar for Upadhyay? What kind of being is he? This important question is dealt with by Upadhyay next.

First of all, Krishna is a genuine descent of God, as Vishnu, in human shape. As an earlier extract makes clear, he is the Lord's graciousness made visible to us. Upadhyay is not afraid to use Hindu names to describe the divine source of the avatar. On one occasion he says, 'The basic truth [*mūl tattva*] is that Sri Krishna is Vishnu's avatar'; on another occasion he describes Krishna as the descent of Hari's mercy (*harikṛpā*). Here he could be just reporting what Hindus accept as facts, rather than declaring his own belief. Nevertheless, there is further ambiguity in this approach. As divine then in some real sense, Krishna's birth is not subject to the rule of karma and rebirth, which means that he is not under the sway of *avidyā* or rebirth-engendering spiritual ignorance. Thus, as a phenomenon, Krishna is non-natural, i.e. he is *aprākṛta,* not under the thrall of Nature. In traditional Hindu thought, to be under Nature's thrall did not mean that one could not be constituted from natural elements, have a real body and mind, function within natural laws and so on, rather, the essential characteristic of this state was being subject to the cycle of rebirth, as well as to egotism and spiritual ignorance. As a divine avatar, Krishna transcended this state. 'The [Lord's] birth is not subject to karma [*karmabaśe hay nā*]. By his own will he descends in human form [*svecchāy manuṣyarūpe abatīrṇa han*].'

But the Krishna avatar was a real human being with a real human personality.

> When the Godhead mingles with the empirical individual, then the latter can rise to a plane above spiritual ignorance.... Thus God's descent is no less than a true participation in humanity. To say that God has descended in human form is to say that the one who is of universal form has become truly human. He has made himself into the form of a particular individual endowed with senses, intellect and body.... Indeed, if the avatar were only *like* an ordinary individual, then the [Lord's] descent would bear no fruit. The individuality of the avatar is both non-natural and divine. While it duly engages in action, it does not come under action's sway. It is adorned with knowledge and love, yet transcends [the causal nexus of] discipline and achievement.... Yet the avatar is a genuine human

person; he is a [human] person, yet unique, that is, not intrinsically subject to Nature.[31]

This difficult passage is the theological crux of the whole lecture. On it Upadhyay seeks to balance the claims of Krishna as an avatar, on the one hand, by the requirements of his Christian commitment to Christ, the only incarnation of God, on the other. According to traditional Christian teaching, Jesus as the incarnation or 'enfleshing' of God was metaphysically truly human and truly divine. So was Krishna, one might respond, at least according to Upadhyay's depiction of him in this lecture. For orthodox Christianity, further, Jesus, though fully human, was without sin, and indeed incapable of sin. Well, so was Krishna, in Upadhyay's terms. But in traditional Christian doctrine, Jesus was not a *human person.* Theologically, from the point of view of his personhood, Jesus was God the Son, the second Person of the holy Trinity, incarnate in human form. God, in a mode of his infinite being, took on human nature in Jesus, without ceasing to be divine. In Jesus, deity also truly became a human individual (but not a human *person* or agent). Here lies the crucial difference from Krishna in Upadhyay's analysis of the avatar. For Upadhyay, Krishna, though divine in a real sense, and sinless (and above the sway of ignorance and rebirth), was, unlike Jesus, a 'genuine *human person*'. While Jesus was a real human individual, his personhood was that of God the Son who had assumed human nature. In Jesus, according to traditional Christian doctrine, there was one *divine* person and two natures: the divine and the human. Krishna's personhood, on the other hand, in Upadhyay's interpretation, was human.

The reader may be forgiven for thinking that this is a highly subtle distinction, likely to be lost on most of the lecturer's hearers. But from Upadhyay's point of view, a great deal hung on it theologically. It is not to my purpose to explore the theological consequences of this distinction, or indeed to inquire if Upadhyay had said enough to justify the making of it, on the basis of either

31 *Īśvaratva jadi jībatve milita hay, tabei jīb abidyār urddhvadeśe ārohaṇ karite pāre.... sutarāṃ, manuṣyatver bāstabik aṅgīkārke īśvarer abataraṇ kahe. Īśvar, manuṣyarūpe abatīrṇa haiyāchen balile, bujhite haibe je, jini biśvarūp tini bāstabik mānuṣ haiyāchen. Tini āpnāke manobuddhidehasaṃbalita ek biśeṣ byaktirūpe sṛṣṭi kariyāchen ... ābār, jadi abatār kebal prākṛta jīber nyāy han, tāhā haileo abataraṇ niṣphaḷ haibe. abatārer byaktitva aprākṛta o īśvaratvamay. uhā jathārīti karme nijukta hay, karmer baśe āse nā. tāhā jñān o preme bhūṣita, sādhan bā siddhir atīta.... abatār jathārtha mānab puruṣatva. puruṣ kintu aprasiddha arthāt prākṛtatvarahita.*

textual or theological analysis. It sufficed for him to have made it in the way he did, for thereby he could claim that he had not violated either his (and his hearers') Hindu susceptibilities or his Christian commitment. On the face of it, Krishna could function as the moral exemplar for his (Hindu) compatriots, while, behind the scenes, Christ would remain the spiritual Saviour of the world, and of India in particular.[32]

[32] This interpretation is substantiated by the testimony of a Protestant pastor, the Rev B.A. Nag, recorded in Bl. In Nag's words, 'In 1904 [Upadhyay] gave an address on Sree Krishna. I was not present at the meeting but I heard from Brahmo friends and even from a Christian missionary that in this lecture he had completely denied Christ and spoke as if he were a Hindu. The first time I met him after that ... I tackled him ... and his answer was as straightforward as ever before. Indeed he said that he was much grieved that any one who knew him could ever think that he was disloyal to Christ. He said that Sree Krishna was a unique manifestation of rational wisdom and power, but Christ was the Saviour of sinners. Krishna was an *Avatar* but Christ was the Incarnation of God. He always held that the Hindu conception of an Avatar was very different from the Christian conception of Incarnation' (pp. 184–5). No doubt the English version of SKT was given to clear up such misunderstandings; it is not clear if it was successful in this regard. Nevertheless, the author of *The Blade* himself is anxious to establish Upadhyay's orthodoxy (see pp. 128–30). 'Why do you always speak of Krishna and never of Christ?' a disciple had asked Upadhyay. '"But Christ is like the Sun and Krishna ... a juicy ball?" [sic] the master replied there and then' (p. 128).

Further on, *The Blade* continues: 'From an old yellow paper I copy the following lines in the handwriting of Upadhyay.... "If the Universe ceases to exist, Brahma, Vishnu and Maheswar cannot exist [since they are phenomenal manifestations of the supreme Being] and Sree Krishna being the Avatar of Vishnu cannot exist. Now God in Himself manifests Himself in three: God the Father, God the Son, and God the Holy Ghost.... But if this Universe ceases to exist, they exist all the same for they are *Three in One* and *One in Three.* Only Christ as man ceases to exist but Christ as God remains. And this is all the truth. I cannot understand then why there should be any misunderstanding. We should not mix up Christ with Krishna, though they are nothing but of the One God, still we cannot put them in the same category"' (p. 129). The distinction Upadhyay implies here is that of the divine and eternal personhood of Christ in contrast to the human and contingent personhood of Krishna.

In this connection we quote from a letter by Upadhyay to Khemchand who was in Karachi (dated July 6, 1904, from 9, Chidam Moodee's Lane, Calcutta), excerpted in *The Sketch*, Part 2: 'My dear Khemchand, You have done well in writing to me before forming any judgement.... No Hindu theologian believes in the doctrine of incarnation, because the idea is too supra-rational to be believed through the light of reason.... Hindus believe in avatars (descents). European missionaries have made the Hindus confound avatar with incarnation by pitting the latter against the former.... The Krishna as represented by Vaishnava sects is to be denounced. (Bhagavata is a Vaishnava record.) But Krishna of history and philosophy is really an object of

This implied distinction between Christ and Krishna now allows Upadhyay to wax lyrical on the harmonizing exemplary virtues of Krishna—harmonizing, that is, the tension between renunciation and worldly involvement, between *nivṛtti* and *pravṛtti,* as this confronts us in our daily lives. Only Krishna the avatar can do this ideally; but in doing so he has given us (in particular Hindus who can best respond to him) an example and genuine hope amid the tribulations of life, and in striving to imitate Krishna the ordinary mortal can rise to heights of virtue.

Upadhyay now takes recourse to describing incidents from the life of Krishna as portrayed in traditional literature (especially the *Bhagavata Purana*). Though a Kshatriya, Krishna lived the life of a cowherd in Vraja and played with the local cowherd boys, destroying many demonic predators in the surrounding forests; he sported with the *gopī*s or milkmaids in the beautiful setting of Vrindavan, dallying with them in the circular *rāsa*-dance on one memorable occasion under the autumnal full moon. To understand all this, says Upadhyay, we must remember that Krishna was steeped in the spirit of tenderness (*mādhurjya*) and renunciation (*nibṛtti*). These qualities were not acquired by some spiritual discipline (*sādhanā*), in the manner of an ordinary human ascetic. Such individuals, who may be partial avatars (*aṃśābatār*), must still grapple with the bonds of spiritual ignorance (*avidyā*) and the moral frailties that it engenders. Krishna is a full avatar (*pūrṇābatār*), above the sway of *avidyā;* as such, he transcends our congenital moral weaknesses. 'The full expression of worldly involvement devoid of sensuality [*prabṛttir indriyaratibihīn pūrṇabikāś*] is impossible without the descent of him who is sovereign over our delusive world [*māyā*]. It is only when deity [*īśvaratva*] is established in human nature that everyday living [*prabṛtti-sakal*] can overcome carnality [*sthūl bhog*] and come into its own. How wonderful is the

---

unbounded reverence.... Take Krishna's teaching in the Gita. Gita is the cream of Vedanta; it is the highest rational philosophy made practical.... And Krishna's personality was also unique. Think of one guiding the destinies of millions in the war of Kurukshetra.... I must say that I look upon Krishna as a unique manifestation of Divine power and wisdom' (pp. 45–6). Here the belief in the Incarnation of God in Christ is characterized as a 'supra-rational' belief, while the Krishna avatar is the subject of rational belief, and Krishna's teaching of the *Gita* is described as 'the highest rational philosophy made practical'. Further, the Krishna of the Vaishnava sects, including his depiction in the Bhagavata Purana, is allegedly a distortion; however, in the Bengali SKT lecture, Upadhyay spends much time rehabilitating the Krishna of the Bhagavata in rationalist terms.

beauty of the union of the natural and the trans-natural [*prākṛta o aprākṛta*]!'.

So when the 'enraptured milkmaids' (*ātmabismṛta gopījan*) danced with Krishna under the autumnal full moon, there was no sensuality in it, neither on Krishna's side nor on that of his partners. For not only was Krishna an avatar and not susceptible to carnality, but he was also in early youth, and 'to attribute a developed sense experience to someone in early youth [*sukumār śaiśabe*] is both unfair and inappropriate.'[33] The milkmaids too did not participate in the event sensually. The purity of Krishna (and presumably his extreme youth) left no room for carnal thoughts. In fact, the milkmaids were Nature (*prakṛti*[34]) personified. Krishna, the supreme Person (male), danced with his creation, Nature (female)—personified by the milkmaids—on that lyrical night. 'Then were sweet Nature, bathed in moonglow, and the milkmaids, Nature personified and enchanted by Krishna's sweetness, joined in the best of men [viz. Krishna]—renunciation and worldly involvement were synthetised.'[35]

This is the true meaning of the *rāsa*-dance; there is no licence here for carnality. 'Only those whose tendrils of worldly living [*prabṛtti*] are adorned with the Krishna-flower are able to worship Sri Krishna, the fullest enjoyer of the *rāsa*-dance. Alas, how vile a picture of the Krishna-lotus, so completely beyond reproach, have worldly sectaries painted!... Be warned! Without the flowers of renunciation [*nibṛtti*], Krishna cannot be worshipped.'[36]

We may well ask whether this depiction of Krishna in the lecture is of an *effective* moral exemplar, if moral exemplar it is to be. It is not for us to answer this question. The point is that Krishna is set up

33 Upadhyay wants to take no chances here. Two major reasons are adduced to affirm Krishna's innocence: his avatarhood and his youth. Yet they seem to be somewhat incompatible. A full avatar's moral irreproachability should not turn on his youthfulness, while stress on Krishna's undeveloped sensibilities seems to undercut his moral irreproachability.

34 A feminine noun in Sanskrit, and symbolized as female.

35 *Kaumudīsnāta madhurā prakṛti o kṛṣṇamādhurīmugdha prakṛtirūpiṇī gopalalanā puruṣpradhāne milita haila—prabṛttir o nibṛttir samanbay haila.*

36 Bankim adopts a similar interpretation of the *rāsa* dance. In KC, 2.5, he declares that in this event, there was not even a hint of the erotic (*ādiraser nāmgandhao nāi*). For Krishna it was mere enjoyment (*upabhogmātra*), for the milkmaids it was worship of God (*īśvaropāsanā*). It enabled the milkmaids to reach the heights of mystical oneness with Krishna, through the path of devotion, a path particularly suited to women. See also ch. 9 of this Part.

in this rehabilitated image, with the (covert) intention of not being a direct rival to Christ. But as we have intimated, this latter aim was very covert indeed.[37] The SKT lecture may be regarded as an important transition to Upadhyay's more overt political involvement in the remaining few years of his life, and further, as an irrevocable reinforcing of the distinction he was cultivating between his public image as a Hindu and his private commitment as a Catholic. Indeed, towards the end, the privacy of his faith seems to have been attenuated to the point of being submerged by his nationalistic endeavours. One can only appreciate this reconstruction of Krishna by trying to understand Upadhyay's burning desire to show his ancestral religion in its best light, in the face of the vigorous criticisms mounted against it by what he perceived as a supercilious ruling elite seeking inexorably to foist alien values and ways upon his people. Especially active in this regard were Christian missionaries and their western collaborators in scholarly and administrative circles. It was part of Upadhyay's campaign—together with that of other Bengali cultural commentators of his kind—to raise the morale and the self-esteem of his compatriots within a broad nationalist cause. To this end, Upadhyay wrote a number of similar pieces, idealizing Hindu culture, in the last publications of his career.[38]

We shall return to this preoccupation in the next chapter. Here we note that by the SKT lecture the ground had been prepared for the next turn of events. Upadhyay started up, as editor, his daily paper, the *Sandhya,* which soon became one of the most popular and, one must add, chauvinist-populist publications in the Province. The establishment of the *Sandhya* stood at the threshold too of a momentous event in the annals of Bengal: the region's first partition at the hands of its colonial masters. Upadhyay and his paper were to play important roles in the forthcoming agitation. But that is a story for the next chapter.

[37] In his Preface to UBBJ, Bhupendranath Datta records: 'At this time [1907], he [Upadhyay] said to me once in the course of conversation, 'I have never called Jesus an avatar.' This struck me as puzzling for the basis of the Trinitarian Christian faith's Athanasian Creed is belief in Jesus, who *descended* [*jini ... abatīrṇa haiyāchen*; emphasis added] to save mankind, as the Son of God' (see penultimate page of Preface). Datta uses the verb form *abatīrṇa*, cognate with *avatāra*, to describe the Incarnation of the second Person of the Trinity. Clearly any distinction Upadhyay might have intended between 'avatar' and 'Incarnation' was entirely lost on Datta.

[38] The article celebrating Krishna's birth mentioned in note 16 was written in this vein, developing further the idea of Krishna as a national hero and exemplar.

Let us conclude this one by taking stock of our own warrior-*karmayogī*. We are familiar with the way his thinking had developed, but we also have a description of his appearance at about this time. In 1904, Upadhyay had been invited to lecture to the youthful members of the Dawn Society, which had been founded by Satiscandra Mukherjee in 1902 for patriotic ends. One of the members, Binoy Sarkar, writes:

> One day Satishbabu brought Brahmabandhab in as a speaker. He gave a lecture on 'General Training'.... With the help of Hegel's methodology [*tarkapraṇālī*], Brahmabandhab made a comparison between eastern and western culture.... We were told that the westerners valued pleasure [*bhog*] alone ... whereas Hindu culture followed neither pleasure nor renunciation alone. India's eternal ideal was the synthesis [*samanbay*] of renunciation and pleasure. This is where Hegel's 'synthesis' came in....
>
> This was the first time I had seen Upadhyay. A man dressed in saffron; no shoes on his feet. He had the somewhat unkempt look of a holy man [*sadhu*]. About him he wore nothing but a saffron wrap. Through this image I caught sight of a new world.... In my experience Brahmabandhab was the very first modern Bengali sannyasi.... Seeing the way he looked and carried himself I thought, 'Here's someone who's constantly defying the world. A real man [*mānuṣer matan mānuṣ*]'.[39]

Thus primed, Upadhyay now confronted his destiny.

39 From *Binoy Sarkarer Baithake*, 2nd ed., Part 1, Calcutta, 1944, pp. 281–2, quoted in UBBJ, pp. 100–1.

# Chapter 14

# With a Consuming Passion Part I: *Sandhya* and Partition

Though after his return from England in 1903 Upadhyay was associated in one way or another with various nationalistic organizations in the greater Bengal of the time, it seems clear that he himself was not a member of any overtly political society, secret or otherwise. This is an important observation in view of the tenor of his life and writings in these last years. In his book on Upadhyay, Manoranjan Guha records a relevant comment by the radical nationalist, Bhupendranath Datta (Vivekananda's younger brother):

> One day Upadhyay *Maśāy* and Gobindbabu [a boyhood friend of Upadhyay's] said to me on the terrace [of the *Sandhya* office], 'Bhupen, leave the company of [Aurobindo Ghose and the others]. We want to build a revolutionary and secret militant group around you [*tomāy bhitti kare ekṭi baiplabik o gupta sainik dal gaṭhan karte cāi*]. From this I realised that he knew nothing of the secret revolutionary movements that were occurring around Bengal. I know for sure [*āmi dṛḍhabhābe jāni*] that he was not attached to any secret revolutionary society.'[1]

1 Guha (1976: 70). The extract indicates that the matter was not taken any further. In *Two Great Indian Revolutionaries* (Calcutta, 1966, pp. 228–9), Uma Mukherjee writes: 'Under the inspiration of Swami Vivekananda, Hem [Chandra] Ghose organized a society, Mukti Sangha by name, which was wedded to the cult of driving out the British from India by any means whatsoever [p. 228].... The name Mukti Sangha [Association of Freedom] was given to the society at its opening ceremony by Upadhyay Brahmabandhab who visited Dacca in 1902. On that occasion Upadhyay delivered a short speech in Bengali emphasising before the audience that their first duty was to deliver the country from foreign yoke, and that that was their only religion' (p. 229). Notwithstanding his increasingly strident comments on nationalism

From the sources available, a rather curious picture of Upadhyay seems to emerge, after his return from England. It is almost as if two Upadhyays come into view, alternately merging and separating: one struggling to maintain his socio-religious profile of good works as a Hindu-Catholic (the Atur Ashrama, the Sarasvata Ayatan), the other increasingly gaining strength as a militant Hindu nationalist, both culturally and politically. In the public eye at any rate, the second Upadhyay engulfs the first. The first Upadhyay, the Hindu-Catholic, the educator of the young and minister to the afflicted, fades away. We shall see whether this Upadhyay lives on in some way in private till the very end, and whether the two Upadhyays can be reconciled at all.

R.C. Majumdar, the well-known general editor of the multi-volume work, *The History and Culture of the Indian People,* writes in his Foreword to H. and U. Mukherjee's book, *India's Fight for Freedom or the Swadeshi Movement (1905–1906):*[2]

> The emergence of the Swadeshi movement in 1905 ... was a great break with the political traditions of the past. The Indian National Congress from 1885 to 1905 followed what now came to be described

---

at the time, from what we have seen of him this would be a strangely inappropriate piece of advice. There is no transcript of this Bengali speech, and it may be that its contents had been tailored to conform to a particular image of Upadhyay. Whether this report is accurate or not, it does indicate that Upadhyay's anti-British reputation had spread widely already in 1902, irrespective of his Catholic affiliation, and that it was well received in some quarters (on the other hand, the year mentioned in this report may be mistaken). In any case, this does not mean that either then or later Upadhyay was a member of some organization like the Mukti Sangha, but it does suggest that his views were perceived by some as tending towards a form of extremism.

The secret societies (*gupta samiti*) mentioned by Bhupen Datta waxed stronger in the years around the 1905 partition of Bengal, with some numbering thousands of members or supporters. All were not necessarily dedicated to some cult of violence to achieve their ends, at least where the vast majority of their supporters were concerned. Most were engaged 'in many other types of activities—physical and moral training of members; social work during famines, epidemics, and religious festivals ... propagating the swadeshi message ... organizing swadeshi crafts, schools, arbitration courts, and 'palli samajes' [village groups]; and implementing passive resistance through a social boycott of recalcitrants' (Sumit Sarkar, 1973: 71–2; ch. 2 of this work is a slightly larger version of Sarkar, 1965), often with many passages agreeing *verbatim.* See also Heehs, 1993, for further information about some of these societies, especially the most well-known of them all, the Anusilan Samiti.

2 Though tendentious in tone and conclusions, the Mukherjees' book (1958) is a mine of information about the Swadeshi movement and the 1905 partition of Bengal. Its approach also gives an insight into partisan Bengali perceptions of the period.

> as the ... policy of begging, inspired by a genuine belief in the innate sense of justice on the part of the British towards the problems and aspirations of the Indians. The Swadeshi movement, born of the failure of public agitation against the Partition, put the first nail on the coffin of political mendicancy and faith in British justice. This was the genesis of 'extremism' in Indian politics which first wrecked the Congress of Moderates and then renovated it with dynamic force (p. iv).

So by 1904 or 1905, politically we have a division between the 'moderates' and the 'extremists', or as they were contrasted more felicitously in Bengali, the *naram dal* (the Soft Camp) and the *garam dal* (the Hot Camp). The former were represented by such figures as Surendranath Banerjea (still going strong; see chapter 1) and Bhupendranath Basu (anglicized as 'Bose'), the latter by leaders such as Bipincandra Pal, Aurobindo Ghose, and Brahmabandhab Upadhyay.

Before he left for England, a case could be made for saying that Upadhyay still threw in his lot with the moderates. The moderates eschewed violence as a means for their political ends, courted British rule as representative of political fair play and legal justice and, in that belief, sought political freedom (though still under the aegis of British rule in some way) through constitutional agitation. The extremists, as and when they appeared on the scene, veered towards if not actually espoused violence as a political instrument, and sought a clean break from the British, often not only politically but also culturally.

We have quoted enough to show that prior to 1903, Upadhyay was something of a reluctant moderate (with 'extremist' tendencies). The reader may recall his statement, published in the weekly *Sophia* (November 24, 1900), under the title 'Do we love the English?' (and reprinted in the TC, December 31, 1901): 'We look upon the English in the same way as a delicate, helpless, chaste woman looks upon her husband who is alien by race and has won her more by force than by goodness.... She does not love him but clings to him all the same because if deserted by him, she will be a captive of some other gallant bully worse than her present spouse.' Then there is point 9 in his statement defending himself against Zaleski's opposition to the TC, in the *Bombay Catholic Examiner* of August 17, 1901 (quoted in chapter 11): 'I cannot give up my attitude of a constitutional oppositionist to the British Government which must be moved to give us the right of self-government, consistent, of course, with the integrity and supremacy of the British Empire in India.'

In the following year, Upadhyay left for England. There a view aired in the TC that (Advaita) Vedanta was, for all its flaws, a *superior* system of 'natural' human thought to its European (Thomistic) counterpart on which to base revealed Christian truths, was more fully defined and strengthened. In England Upadhyay saw himself, in the role of successor to Vivekananda, as a representative of Vedanta, which he touted as providing guidelines for an outlook and way of life that humanly speaking transcended all others, especially those from Europe. The whole world must sit at the feet of Hindu teachers, he had proclaimed in his letters for the *Bangabasi*. So it is not surprising that when he returned to India he was disposed to join the ranks of the 'extremists', and in due course became one of their leaders. The *Śrīkṛṣṇatattva* lecture of July 1904 consolidated this self-definition culturally, while the looming prospect of the partition of Bengal in 1905 made it overtly political.

The Mukherjees in UBBJ make a pertinent observation in this regard:

> Upadhyay was the incarnate symbol [*mūrta pratīk*] of the Indian longing for self-rule. This self-rule was not limited only to education or economics; the note of national independence [*rāṣṭrik svādhīnatā*] was also very clearly manifest in it. He desired self-rule for India because through self-rule India could once again assume her proud place in the assembly of the world. He believed that there was no hope, no future for a dependent India subject to English Imperial rule. He sought to establish India's sacred striving for self-rule [*svarāj sādhanā*] on a spiritual basis [*ekṭā ādhyātmikatār bhittir upar*]. And the foundation for this spirituality was the Vedanta's immortal message [*mṛtyuhīn bāṇī*]. Here one must note the similarity of Upadhyay's views with the political vision of Bipin Pal and Aurobindo. Bipin Pal clearly described the Swadeshi movement as a spiritual movement. Aurobindo did so too .... Like Bipincandra and Aurobindo, [Upadhyay] also desired total self-rule for India, devoid of any Imperial connection with the British. It is here that they were keenly opposed to the moderate politicians such as Surendranath [pp. 108–10].

December 1904 saw the publication of the daily Bengali paper, the *Sandhya*, with Upadhyay as editor.[3] The paper's office, in due course

[3] 'On Friday evening, December 15, 1904—1st Paus, 1311 Bengali era—the *Sandhya* first appeared' S. Das in 'Bāṇglār nabajāgaraṇer pratyuṣ—Sandhyā', (ii)1961: 198). Das repeats the date in (i)1961: 522. Sumit Sarkar misstates the date as November 1904 (1973: 259).

to become the focal point of various nationalist activities such as meetings and processions, was situated first at 18 Bethune Row, the house of Upadhyay's former student and subsequently collaborator, Kartikcandra Nan; thereafter it moved to 23 Sibnarayan Das Lane.[4] The *Sandhya* became an extremely important publication of the time. Upadhyay's style of writing helped create a new style of popular journalism,[5] while the paper's content played a significant role in priming popular consciousness against western culture, the moderate approach to politics, and the impending partition of Bengal. Pinkish-orange in colour, cheap and easy to procure (it cost one pice[6]), by 1906 it ran to 7000 copies a day.[7] Simha describes the popularity of the paper as follows:

> When reading [the *Sandhya*] shopkeepers, traders, clerks, rent-collectors, teachers and students, labourers and coachmen, would alternately laugh and cry. Landlords, tenants, the poor, the educated, the uneducated, women in the zenana, boys and girls, young and old would either be filled with delight or transported with rage. Everyone was anxious to know, 'When will the *Sandhya* arrive?', 'What's in the *Sandhya* today?' (pp. 84–5).

In Bengali one meaning of '*sandhyā*' is 'evening', and indeed, the paper came out every evening (it was on sale from about 4 p.m.).

4 There is some confusion about the *Sandhya* office address. Sumit Sarkar mentions 193 Cornwallis Street (1973:217). The sources mention both addresses. Sibnarayan Das Lane and Cornwallis Street were in close proximity, and there may have been more than one entrance to the Office.

5 Simha says (p. 84) that it was Upadhyay's intention to reach out to the not-so-educated (*svalpaśikṣita bā ekebārei aśikṣita*) and to rouse them to nationalistic fervour that gave birth to the *Sandhya*, in contrast to the approach to the highly educated (*suśikṣita*) of Bipin Pal and the others. To this end Upadhyay abandoned the ponderous (*gurugambhīr*) language of conventional journalism and, resorting to 'the language of the village, fairy tales, slang and conundrums etc. (*grāmyabhāṣā, rūpkathā, apabhāṣā o heāli prabhṛti dvārā*)', created an innovative language that was highly popular (ibid.). Upadhyay had already started experimenting with this style in his letters for the *Bangabasi*. See chapter 12, note 44.

6 Four pice made one anna, and 16 annas a rupee.

7 C. Fonseca ((ii)1980) notes, referring to the National Archives (Home Dept.), that 'Reporting on the state of the press in 1906, F.C. Daly, Personal Assistant to the I.G.P. records: "Sandhya (circulation 7000)—Exceedingly scurrilous, makes vulgar attacks on Government officers..."' (p. 20). The *Report on Native Newspapers in Bengal* also gives this figure as a constant well into 1907. *The Blade* (p. 167) gives a different figure: 'Day after day some 12,000 copies were sold. Many more were asked for and could not be supplied. Often the advertisements could not be printed for want of time. The articles appeared on one side; the other side was left blank.'

But this sense was incidental to the intended meaning of the term. '*Sandhyā*' also connotes a juncture, including the juncture of any two consecutive ages among the traditional four of Hindu folklore, viz. the Satya or Kṛta age, the Tretā age, the Dvāpara age, and the Kali age. In each age beginning with the Satya, right living or *dharma* progressively declines. At the end of the Kali or most degenerate age, the universe dissolves into the Supreme Being, souls exist in a suspended animation, the universe is then re-generated in its pristine condition under a new Satya age, and the whole cyclic process of slowly declining order starts anew. In this context, the introductory editorial of the paper gave the following explanation of the special sense of '*sandhyā*' intended:

> When bad times occur, people say 'Well, Kali's *sandhyā* ... has begun.' It will be a long time before the darkness dissolves and dawn appears. But there is a scriptural meaning to 'Kali's *sandhyā*' ... Four such *sandhyās* have passed; this is the fifth.
>
> In the first *sandhyā*, Sri Krishna appeared. Lest the individual [*jīb*] drown in the ocean of being, he made a raft available in the form of the *Gita*.... In the second *sandhyā*, the crisis of Buddhism [*bauddhabibhrāṭ*] occurred. The code of the four stages of life [*āśramadharma*] having been broken; society became gravely disordered. The third *sandhyā* saw the rise of Shankaracharya. Having humbled Buddhist arrogance, he raised the victory flag of Hindu *dharma*. In the fourth *sandhyā*, the barbaric foreigners [*mleccha*] have taken control. And they have rendered India completely prostrate.... Perhaps in the fifth *sandhyā* there's chance of some improvement. Yet two hundred years of this fifth *sandhyā* have passed and there has been no sign of that.... What is the remedy?... We are tethered by a long rope. Howsofar we may roam ... we are unable to cut loose from our support: the Hindu has no recourse other than that [support of] the Vedas and Vedanta, the Brahmin caste, and the code of the caste orders [*varṇadharma*]....
>
> Our sole aim through our desire to publish a daily called '*Sandhya*' in this fifth Kali *sandhyā* is no other than to expatiate on this one remedy of ours. The Ruler is an alien [*mleccha*]. To survive, for the sake of our dignity, we must learn an alien language and alien teaching and accept an alien way of life—we have no other recourse.... *Sandhya* will explain what kind of political relationships we should have with our rulers; it will discuss the activities of various peoples [*bhinna bhinna jātir kārjyakalāp*] and give various news of our own country and of other lands. It will also advise on

> how we can increase our own resources by learning foreign strategies. Yet withal in everything, through plain speech, we shall communicate the spirit of the Bengali [*bāṇgālīr prāṇer kathā*]. Whatever you hear, whatever you learn, and whatsoever you do—remain a Hindu and Bengali [*hindu thākio bāṅgālī thākio*].... In all circumstances, if through mind, body and speech, you preserve racial pride [*jātimarjyādā*] as a disciple of the Brahmin [*brāhmaṇer śiṣya haiyā*], no stain will attach to you.... We shall discuss all the following—worship and festivals, art and literature, social and domestic practice etc.—yet in the midst of everything one refrain will ring through—the Veda, the Brahmin and the Code of caste [*bed, brāhmaṇ o barṇadharma*] [Simha: 81–2].

This bold declaration is significant as much for what is openly said as for what is glossed over. The context of the declaration is wholly and aggressively nationalistic, in favour of Brahmin hegemony on the one hand, and to the exclusion of any mention of Christian commitment or sympathy on the part of the editor on the other. The insistence on Brahminic (cultural) hegemony in what was specifically intended to be a paper for mass readership is striking. There is no attempt to accommodate Indian Muslims, Christians or Buddhists (on the contrary, the advent of the Buddha is described as a disaster). As we shall see, the tone of the *Sandhya* was acerbic in the extreme, and in many instances offensive to its political and cultural targets. Yet, as Simha's description intimates, it was highly popular among its wide readership. Clearly, notwithstanding his excesses of style, Upadhyay struck a chord at the time. His journalistic technique had come into its own.

To return to Upadhyay's insistence on Brahminic hegemony. Even in personal dealings, matters of caste and ritual purity had become a sticking point. In his Preface to Bolai Debsarma's book on Upadhyay, Bhupendranath Datta[8] recounts two incidents:

> One day I was walking along Cornwallis Street. At the corner of Sibnarayan Das Street Upadhyay called to me from the second floor [of a building]. When I went up, he said: 'Can you get hold of a few well-born [*kulīn*] Kayastha boys to take on the distribution [*egenci*] of the *Sandhya*? Those with corrupt ancestry [*paca maulik*] won't do.' I would get upset at such show of Brahminical bigotry [*brāhmaṇya gōḍāmite*]'.

8 Bhupen Datta also contributed an important Introduction to UBBJ.

He continues:

> At the time, the radical group would meet in the evenings [*garam daler āḍḍā basto sandhyāy*] in a room of the Field Academy. Bipin Pal, C.R. Das, Upadhyay, Aurobindo, Subodh Mallik and others would be present. Naren Seth and I would also go there. Once Upadhyayji felt thirsty and the servant brought some water. Upadhyay got annoyed and said, 'Why in this glass? Those who've been abroad [*bilāt pherotrā*] drink from that glass.'[9] At this, Kumarkrishna Datta (the attorney) said, 'And what would you yourself do in England?' I realized then that Upadhyay's Brahminic bigotry had not abated.

One interpretation of such behaviour—which could be extended to the similarly uncompromising tone of his writing in the *Sandhya*—would be that Upadhyay needed to establish credentials of patriotic orthodoxy among the political radicals with whom he kept company, *precisely* because he had not publicly repudiated his personal Christian commitment. *They* didn't need to make such a show; Upadhyay probably felt that he did in order to be accepted and to feel that he belonged with them (and with his Hindu compatriots in the political context of the time).[10] Nevertheless, this strikes us (as it struck some of his companions, many of whom were not themselves Brahmins) as an objectionable trait.

But if one considers the larger picture, a further, not incompatible, interpretation becomes possible. It is well documented[11] that 'extremist' politics at the time, of which Upadhyay had become a prominent leader, was closely associated ideologically with Hindu revivalism. It was itself being given a strong religious Hindu colouring. The sacred cause of freedom was just that—*sacred*—and a religious commitment was called for to implement it. For many of the extremists who championed that cause, this was not the time to initiate a democratizing critique of their ancestral faith. Rather, it was by taking one's stand upon that faith—warts and all—that in the heat of the

9 Upadhyay would have meant by this that he himself would incur ritual pollution if he drank from a glass polluted by those who had returned from abroad.

10 From time to time one comes across reports that Upadhyay's display of patriotic feeling was not trusted by some, that they suspected him of being a kind of fifth columnist on behalf of his Christian faith with a view to 'converting' those who had been taken in by his so-called patriotism. No doubt Upadhyay was aware of this suspicion, and this may well have prompted an even more forceful reaction to the contrary.

11 See, e.g., Sumit Sarkar, 1965: 148, and Heehs, 1997.

moment one could establish a sense of solidarity and purpose with the greatest number and in the shortest possible time for the task in hand. Since in fact Brahminic hegemony was a prime characteristic of normative Hindu tradition, at best one should argue for a reversion to a 'pure' Brahminism—an idealized Brahminism, if you like—to rally popular support. According to this ideal, caste divisions and practices should be unitive not discriminatory (some interpreted this as the original ideal of caste), giving the individuals and sections of (Hindu) society a clear order of relationships and objectives within a larger whole.[12] How outcastes and non-Hindus fitted into this picture

[12] This explains a journalistic characteristic of Upadhyay's, his refusal to criticize publicly aspects of Hinduism that he might privately have found wanting. There is plenty of evidence for this. Manoranjan Guha quotes Bipin Pal's testimony on Upadhyay's notion of reform. Upadhyay was not opposed to social reform, said Pal. He was opposed to reform taking place piecemeal on the basis of western norms. For on this basis Hindu society's identity (*svādeśikatā*) would be destroyed. Upadhyay is said to have argued as follows: 'The influence of this foreign force must first be checked. To begin with, our own country's society and people must be made self-reliant [*ātmastha*]. Let them first come to their senses [*jāguk*]. Let them come to terms with themselves. Then of their own accord they will hammer into shape their character [*prakṛti*] and, as the need arises, their society' (op.cit., p. 58).

Upadhyay, says Guha, regarded his country with the eyes of a devoted son so that he might say of her: 'I know that my mother is not beautiful in every feature, yet she is my mother, and at this I well up with emotion' (*āmi jāni āmār mā sarbāṅgasundarī nahen, kintu tini āmār mā, tātei āmār prāṇ bhare oṭhe*; p. 56). Upadhyay gave further expression to this sentiment when, according to Bolai Debsarma (1961:86–7), he would say, 'One must love one's country as in the words of Nidubabu's little song: "I know nothing but you"—not on the basis of conditions or by critical analysis. That love must be simply, "I know nothing but you". It's not love's way to say, "This much is okay, but that won't do". What I regard as good, I regard as good in every way' (*deśke bhālobāsite haile nidhubābur ṭappāy jeman āche 'tomā bai ār jāni ne' temni kariyā bhālobāsite haibe. bācbicār nahe biruddha buddhir biśleṣaṇ nahe—se bhālobāsā ekebāre 'tomā bai ār jāni ne'. etaṭuku bhālo, etaṭuku manda, ihā premer rīti nahe. je āmār bhālo, tāhār sabṭukui·bhālo* ).

Upadhyay wrote in a note dated January 3, 1906, to Nanda Sen, who seems to have been away on a family visit in rural Bengal: 'I've received your card. I was glad to hear that you arrived safely. Now that you're taking a break, come back after a good tour of the place. Look at the ponds, the tanks [*dīghi*], the rivers, the woods and fields in a spirit of love. Love comes if you show love. [*pukur dīghi nadī ban kṣeta—bhālobāsār sahit dekhio. bhālobāsile bhālobāsā paoyā jāy*]. You've heard that Bengal's soil is not soil but the Mother [*śuniyācho ta bāṅglār māṭi—māṭi nay—kintu mā-ṭi*: this is a pun on the word '*māṭi*']. And try and mingle with the poor. We Calcuttans say 'I salute the Mother' [*āmrā kalikātār loke bande mātaram bali*, but we don't know what our beloved Mother Bengal [*mā baṅgalakṣmī*] really is. Those who do not love our land, who have no respect for our land's history and culture, have no self-respect [*ātmamarjyādā*] either, and without this all else is vain' (see facsimile of Upadhyay's handwritten note in UBBJ, p. 196).

tended not to be clearly defined.[13] Upadhyay, the Brahmin, was conforming to and reinforcing this trend, and the earlier writings we have studied, especially in Bengali, on caste and the rehabilitation of Hinduism, fit neatly into a developing personal articulation of this pattern.[14] Thus already by the turn of the century Upadhyay was heading for the extremist camp.

The Bengali sources say that for about a year after Upadhyay's return from abroad, after the *Sandhya* had started, from about mid-1905 to mid-1906, he and Satiscandra Mukherji, the founder of the Dawn Society, worked in the closest collaboration with the partition agitation in view (they were staying together with three of Satiscandra's students in the same house, with Upadhyay acting as mess manager; see UBBJ: 113–4).[15] Binoy Sarkar, one of Satiscandra's students in this arrangement (see chapter 13, note 17), records:

> The address was a big house on Cornwallis Street.... One had to enter by Sibnarayan Das' Lane.... We lived on the second floor.[16] From our room we could see an open space [or field, *māṭh*] and Cornwallis street to the west, and to the south the field again and the Metropolitan College.
>
> Many things concerning the Bengal agitation [*baṅga-biplob*] took place on this field facing us. We could see everything from our room. There was no need to be present at the assemblies on the field. Yet much of what occurred in these assemblies was prepared in advance in the rooms of our residence and on the first floor. This is because Satishbabu and Upadhyay were in constant confabulation

13 As Sarkar notes (1965: 149), from this 'the later theory of Muslim Separatism and Pakistan is just one more step.'

14 There were other prominent thinkers, not all Brahmins, who defended an idealised caste system during these volatile years. We have noted that Tagore himself passed through a 'conservative' phase in which he endorsed 'functional specialisation through caste' (see chapter 12, note 64), while an editorial (17.9.1907) of the revolutionary *Bande Mataram*, a paper not particularly associated with Brahmins, 'after hailing the labour movement went on to praise the caste system in its ideal form for having "had the true socialistic aim of keeping awake in every class of the society a sense of duty to it". Shorn of its abuses, caste could serve as the basis for a purified democracy and socialism' (Sumit Sarkar, 1965: 148).

15 Thereafter Upadhyay moved to the *Sandhya* office at Sibnarayan Das Lane in the proximity of Cornwallis Street, though he frequented Kartik Nan's house in Bethune Row as well.

16 This may have been the very place from which Upadhyay hailed Bhupen Datta in the extract mentioned above.

> about various activities of the Swadeshi movement. You could say that ... we spent weeks, rather months, in the 'Green Room' of the Bengal-agitation.... At the time our spiritual mentors were Satishbabu and Upadhyay.[17]

We must now say a few words about the agitation against the proposed partition of Bengal, and the part Upadhyay and the *Sandhya* played in it. So far we have referred to the broad division between the moderates and the extremists. But this distinction can be refined further in the context of the partition agitation. For this we turn to Sumit Sarkar: 'A fourfold classification ... begins to emerge—[1, the] moderates; [2] the trend towards self-development without inviting an immediate political clash (which I have decided to call 'constructive swadeshi' for want of a better name); [3] political extremism using 'extended boycott' or passive resistance in addition to selfhelp efforts; and [4] terrorism' (1973: 33; see also Sarkar 1965: 11–12). As Sarkar himself notes, these are not watertight divisions; in individuals and groups features of two or more of these trends often coexisted, merged, alternated or developed successively, at least for a time. Thus they represent emphases under helpful headings rather than mutually exclusive options.

As noted above, the moderates sought self-rule in some larger colonial framework (two of their leading representatives, according to Sarkar, being Surendranath Banerjea and Bhupendranath Bose); the 'constructive swadeshi' current was 'quieter [than the third group] and sometimes rather non-political in its tone, [and] emphasized patient efforts at self-development, ignoring rather than launching an immediate attack on foreign rule' (1965: 23)—Satiscandra Mukherji being named as prominent in this regard.[18] The extremists 'tried to turn the boycott into a campaign of full-scale passive resistance, and set its sights on immediate independence rather than partial reforms or slow self-regeneration' (p. 23). While this group sought mass

[17] UBBJ, pp. 113–4.

[18] 'The message of self-help in industry and education was being spread by Satischandra Mukherji through his journal *Dawn* (started in 1897) and his Dawn Society (1902–1907) [p. 31].... Though personally a friend of political Extremists like Aurobindo [and we may add, Upadhyay], his journal *Dawn* concentrated on constructive themes, and the sketch of basic principles published in the *Dawn* of March 1907 as a kind of swan-song for the Dawn Society emphasised self-help in industry, education, justice, and rural life to the exclusion of a direct political clash with the foreign government' (1965: 34).

appeal, the terrorist group 'came to rely almost entirely on the heroism of an elite' (p. 140) dedicated not to 'passive resistance' but to the use of violence or armed force to bring about their ends. For more information on the early phases of terrorism, see Heehs (1993). Prominent leaders among the extremists included Bipin Pal, Aurobindo Ghose, Aswinikumar Datta and Upadhyay. In fact, if we accept Sarkar's classification, Upadhyay would fall into the extremist group with a tendency to border, at least ideologically in some of his last writings, on 'terrorism'.[19]

The partition agitation had not really begun when Upadhyay returned from England in July 1903. Partition of Bengal had been mooted internally in British Indian Government circles well before 1903. By the middle of 1903, Lord Curzon the Viceroy had privately approved the idea. The proposal to partition Bengal was made public, after a lengthy period of rumour and counter-rumour, in a letter dated December 3,1903, by H.H. Risely, Secretary to the Government of India.[20] It was after this that the momentum developed, mainly in Bengal, to fight the proposal. The reasons given for partition included the following: administrative expediency (greater Bengal was said to be too large and too populous); the liberation of the eastern areas from the stifling domination of Calcutta (the capital of the new eastern province was to be Dhaka); giving access to the sea for Assam Province as a measure to increase its economic development; and giving the more populous Muslims of the eastern areas a base for the development of their self-identity. Bengali objections included the following: partition would increase taxes and complicate administration; modern communications did not necessitate the need for partition as an administrative measure; a cultural, social and political divisiveness would be established between Hindu and Muslim; the importance of Calcutta would be weakened; and the solidarity and nationalist aspirations of the Bengali people would be gravely undermined.

As the Bengali politicians of all shades realized very well, the main reason the British administration wished to dismember Bengal was to weaken Bengali solidarity and rising nationalism. Sarkar quotes from private notes by Risely (written on February 7, 1904, and

[19] In his Preface to the first edition of *Car Adhyay*, Tagore remarks: 'It was in this paper [*Sandhya*] that the beginning of the terrorist way [*bibhīṣikā-panthār sūcanā*] was hinted at for the first time.'

[20] The sequence of events is given in H. and U. Mukherjee, 1958, and Sumit Sarkar, 1973: ch. 1.

December 6, 1904) to this effect: 'Loss of national unity—This is the Congress point. Bengal united is a power; Bengal divided will pull in several different ways. That is perfectly true and is one of the great merits of the scheme.... One of our main objects is to split up and thereby weaken a solid body of opponents to our rule' (1965: 19).[21] An influential number among the British administration believed that after an initial storm of protest, Bengali opposition would die down, and the break-up of the region would be established. Things didn't quite turn out that way. On the one hand, partition was realized to be unworkable by the administration and was eventually undone in 1911[22]; on the other hand, the partition agitation as a popular movement never really got off the ground in Bengal, the Hindu-Muslim divide was consolidated, and in time Bengal ceased to be at the forefront of the agitation for independence. It was Gandhi who later gave a populist dimension to the freedom movement in India as a key figure among another group of nationalist leaders.

Though only a tiny portion of the *Sandhyas* published from 1904 to 1907 (the year of Upadhyay's death) is available for our purposes, the development of the paper to some extent can be followed in the *Report on Native Papers in Bengal* [hereafter *Report*], a Government review of the time. In Part I the *Report* published extracts officially translated into English from the original[23] under various headings (e.g. 'Foreign Politics', 'Home Administration' including Education, Local Self-Government, Railways, and 'General'). It is interesting to note that after a flurry of protests from mid-December 1903 in the various Bengali papers reviewed in the *Report* (including, to give them their *Report* names, the *Bangabasi, Basumati, Hitavadi, Sanjivani, Charu Mihir,* and *Sri Sri Visnupriya o Ananda Bazar Patrika*), against the first partition proposal announced earlier that month, activity on this front, at least from the viewpoint of the *Report,* gradually died down. Thus the *Dacca Gazette* of August 8, 1904 'takes the opponents of the partition proposal to task for discontinuing all agitation over the question, and exhorts them to be up and doing' (*Report* for week ending August 13). The tenor of the opposition to the British

[21] This was Curzon's view already in June 1903; see Argov, 1967: 103.

[22] As is well known, there was another, more terrible and permanent Partition a generation or so later with the creation of east and west Pakistan. For a Muslim view see Ahmed, 1997.

[23] The shorter Part II quoted extracts from English papers, including the *Indian Mirror, Amrita Bazar Patrika, Bengalee* and *Hindoo Patriot.*

Government hitherto is well captured in an early extract taken from the *Sri Sri Vishnu Priya o Ananda Bazar Patrika*[24] (issue of December 30, 1903; see *Report* for week ending January 9): 'Uprightness is an ingrained virtue of Englishmen, and it is because the Indian people believe it that they are about to bring their objections to the [proposal] ... to the notice of Lord Curzon [the Viceroy]'—in other words, the 'moderate' response.

The Calcutta weekly, the *Sanjivani* (circulation about 3000), which played a particularly persistent role in the anti-partition agitation, in its issue of November 3, 1904, 'appeals to the leaders of the Bengali community to bestir themselves ... and set on foot a *fresh* and vigorous agitation against the proposed dismemberment of Bengal' (*Report* for week ending November 12, emphasis added). It was in December 1904, the reader will recall, that the *Sandhya* commenced publication. However, the *Sandhya* first comes to the attention of the *Report* in the latter's coverage for the week ending January 14, 1905, and then apparently not in an overtly political context (i.e. the reference appears under the heading, 'Miscellaneous'). An article in the January 11 issue of *Sandhya*, entitled 'What do Englishmen take us for?', is quoted. After referring to the resolution of the Indian National Congress to send a deputation to England to represent Indian grievances and aspirations for greater self-rule to the British public, the *Sandhya* is recorded as saying, 'But the British public will never take up our cause.' The writer of this article is clearly Upadhyay, for Upadhyay's experiences of his visit to England are described:

> The British public generally have a notion that we are steeped in ignorance and prejudice, that we are illiterate and half-civilised, and that we ill-treat our women.... As soon as an Indian ventures out in the streets, the sound of 'darkie, darkie' greets his ears. All passers-by smile at him as if he was some curious animal.... We must show that as Hindus we belong to a higher race. To this end we must ... demonstrate that we hold sway over men's minds by our superior knowledge and civilisation.

So the appeal to sweet reason will not do, because the British public (and still more, their politicians) do not respect Hindu culture and abilities.

Henceforth, the *Sandhya* appears regularly in the *Report*, week after week under various headings. These appearances are invariably

24 A weekly from Calcutta, listed as having 1000 subscriptions per week.

hostile to the colonial administration, and to westerners and their ways.[25] Though other Bengali papers are recorded as continuing to oppose the partition proposal, the *Sandhya* is first referred to in this connection only in the week ending February 11. An article of February 3 is quoted as saying that 'the people of Bengal should not sit quiet. The sooner they can convince the English authorities of the mischievousness and unreasonableness of the proposal, the better will it be for them.'

By early July 1905 it was generally known that the British Government had formally approved the partition of Bengal; details of the final scheme (hitherto planned in secret without any Bengali consultation) were intimated from July 7, the full facts being known in a Government Resolution released from Simla (and dated July 19). When published on July 20, this information created outrage in Bengal, Bengali politicians of all shades feeling, in the words of Surendranath Banerjea, 'insulted, humiliated and tricked'.[26] With the *Sanjivani* in the vanguard, a new phase of the Bengali opposition to partition began, i.e., the boycotting of mainly British goods in favour of the purchase of indigenous products. Thus the Swadeshi movement formally began. Though this phase of the agitation was endorsed by leaders both moderate and more extremist (including some Muslims), for the more radical Bengali politicians the call to boycott foreign goods was but the economic cutting edge of a growing wholesale cultural turning away from the British.[27]

The *Sandhya* was in the forefront of this trend. In an article on March 9 (*Report*, week ending March 11) the *Sandhya* could still say,

25 'Lord Curzon has created a mess in everything that he has set his hand to' (article of January 21, 1905, under 'Foreign Politics' in *Report* for week ending January 28; again in an excerpt of February 16 decrying Curzon for insinuating in a Convocation Speech to the University of Calcutta that Indians had a lower standard of veracity than that of the West: 'What a rash, foul-tongued man!'); under 'The Victoria Memorial Hall', the *Sandhya* of February 12, 1905 is reported as saying, 'A large number of busts, statues and paintings have been collected for the Victoria Memorial Hall; the collection, however, consisting mostly of the likenesses of Englishmen, the Hall will contain rows of English cats who killed native mice'; on the colonial regime: 'If a dog enters into one's kitchen, the cooking-pot has to be rejected and the animal has to be turned out as well. The door is the place for the dog; he is to stand there to warn the householder' (*Report*, week ending January 12, 1907).

26 See H. and U. Mukherjee, 1958:34ff.

27 Sarkar gives figures from the *Annual Reports on the Maritime Trade of Bengal* to show that, in economic terms, 'the whole impact [of the boycott] appears to have been marginal' (1965: 151; see also 1973: 137f.). There was neither a general mobilization of the ordinary worker or peasant nor a viable infrastructure in place for the production of indigenous goods. The boycott's real effect was political and cultural.

'[We] wish to be partners with the English in the work of governing our country under the imperial suzerainty of Britain'. But in what appears to be a watershed article entitled 'Men of Words' of July 18 (*Report*, week ending July 29), it now castigates the moderate leaders of the Bengali community as follows: 'Give up the holding of meetings, cease to be mere men of words ... *and keep yourselves aloof*, and then will the Englishman appreciate your strength. If instead of that you simply lick his feet and whine, you will only continue to receive kicks from his boots' (emphasis added). From here on the *Sandhya* keeps up a relentless pressure to boycott not only English goods, but especially the English.

A marked feature of the anti-partition agitation in greater Bengal, including the Swadeshi protest, was the growing participation of the student body from schools and colleges. Matters came to a head towards the end of October 1905 with the publication in the local press of two letters written by Government officials—the so-called Carlyle Circular and the Pedlar Letter[28]—singling out students for disciplinary action for involvement in anti-partition protests.[29] This gave rise to renewed calls for establishing a system of 'national education' for the young. It was really a Hindu initiative, the intention being to provide an education that would equip one to cope with the challenges of a modernizing world without becoming culturally alienated. As we have seen, the idea itself was not new: various steps had been taken to establish a system of indigenous education, of which the Santiniketan experiment and the Sarasvata Ayatan were two examples, for a number of years. The *Sandhya* now added a strident voice to the call to create a national University for Bengal. On October 31 it expostulated (*Report*, week ending November 4): 'What audacity to say that if schoolboys join in the Swadeshi agitation their names should be sent to the police.... If you want to make a real protest, you must be prepared to forego the education imparted by Englishmen. Let the native Fellows of the University [of Calcutta] come out of the *golamkhana* (slave house) of *Goldighi* (College Square)[30] and establish a University of their own, and let the native colleges and schools join this new University' (see also week ending

[28] R.W. Carlyle was Officiating Chief Secretary to the Government of Bengal, and A. Pedlar was Director of Public Instruction, Bengal.

[29] Several similar government directives seeking to restrain students from participating in the anti-partition movement were to follow.

[30] These are the translator's parentheses.

November 18). The attempt to establish national education on a large scale, as a rival to the existing westernized system, was not a success. Such indigenous institutions as were set up were largely of symbolic rather than utilitarian value in public consciousness; most parents, with a realistic eye to the future of their children, continued to support the westernized system.[31] Upadhyay, however, through his involvement in the well-publicized projects of Santiniketan and the Sarasvata Ayatan, and subsequently in the pages of *Sandhya*, played a salient part in the bhadralok attempt to add a new focus to Bengali patriotism, which was the real contribution of the 'national education' movement.[32]

In 1906 Upadhyay's participation in the burgeoning national movement intensified on several fronts. It may be hard to believe that there could be an appreciable increase in the *intensity* of his life, yet this is the term that comes to mind to describe these last two years. His antipathy towards the colonial regime and western ways became extreme, often descending to offensiveness in the pages of *Sandhya*. We have already noted some examples, but perhaps the *locus classicus* for his vituperative style and dismissive attitude is to be found in an article entitled 'The Etymology of the Word *Phiriṅgi*'

31 Among other efforts, a Bengal National College was inaugurated in August 1906, of which Aurobindo Ghose was the first principal. Heehs (1993: 92) comments: 'But the College proved to be a disappointment. Most members of the National Council of Education [set up in March] were reluctant to do anything to offend the government.... Under such stewardship 'national' education became little better than a second-rate copy of the British variety. Whatever its merits, it no longer could be considered a part of the national movement as a whole.'

32 *The Blade* provides the gist of a 'paper on National Education' read by Upadhyay on the occasion of the visit of B.G. Tilak and other Maharashtrians to Calcutta to celebrate the Shivaji festival in June 1906 (pp. 152ff.: 'night after night [Tilak] sat with Upadhyay and listened with rapt attention'). Upadhyay speaks of the College as an 'Ayatana' consisting of three divisions, primary and general (10 years), special (4 years) and advanced (4 or more years). The syllabus bears a marked resemblance to that devised for the Sarasvata Ayatan (see chapter 13), but there are differences: e.g. compulsory study of Hindi 'as the *lingua franca* of the country' would be included, in the 'general' stage elementary French or German would be taught (in addition to English), and in the special division 'Natural Theology' (Hindu and European) finds a place. Other features include no fees, and the exclusion of married students and 'boys of low caste, and of families who have broken away from the pale of caste' (p. 154). These recommendations, however, were not implemented. Note the idealism of not asking for fees, the broadness in insisting on the teaching of Hindi, and the narrowness of the exclusions.

(*phiriṅgi śabder vyutpatti*), published in the *Sandhya* on November 23.[33]

> A new English daily called *Empire* has appeared. In this paper it is said that the English are referred to contemptuously as *phiriṅgi*[34] in the *Sandhya*. So today we will say something about the meaning of the word *phiriṅgi*....
>
> First, take *phi*: those who want a 'fee' (viz. money) for everything are *phiriṅgis*. They would even bill their parents for feeding them, i.e. require a fee of them. If someone seduces their wife [*bhraṣṭā kare*] they demand a fee from her to write a bill of divorce. So the word 'fee' [*phi*] lies at the very root of their name. Now ... consider *phiri*: there are no other hawkers [*phirioālā*] to match them. It's not just that they go about peddling things [*saodā phiri kariyā beḍāy*]; they'll take a fee off you and continue peddling. And if you don't pay the fee or do business with them, they'll send you all the way to hell and back.
>
> Next consider *phiṅgi:* nowhere in the world are there shrikes [*phiṅgi bā phiṅge*] quite like them; they pester everyone. At every turn they'll extort a fee; they'll even enter your home and forcibly do business [*phiri karā*] with you. Then they turn into shrikes [*phiṅgi-phiṅge haiyā*] and like some shameless hussy [*dhiṅgir mata*] they'll go after you and make your life miserable. You may be a rum bird [*paṅkhī*] yourself, but if the *phiriṅgi* shrikes go after you they won't leave you till they finish you off.
>
> The proper term in Hindusthani is *phiraṅgi*. *Phi* has been seen to, as has *phiri* and *phiṅgi*. What remains is *raṅgī*.
>
> To begin with, their colour [*raṅg*] is wishy-washy white—they're almost colourless, like pot-covered [*ṭab-cāpā*] grass.[35] So how can they be said to have colour [*raṅgī*]? Well, why do people call the pomegranate [*bedānā*] 'seedless' [*be-dānā*] when it is full of seeds? They can be said to have colour in the same way, even though they're colourless....
>
> They also have great fun [*raṅg*] with women - that's why they're syphilis-prone [*phiraṅgi*]. Even when it's freezing their womenfolk expose their necks, chests and arms and gather in mixed company to gossip, sing and play music. Oh yes, they're colourful [*raṅgī*]!

33 And reprinted in Das, (i)1961 (and also in B. Ghosh, 1987: 97ff. Das gives the more accurate account). Upadhyay indicates that this is not meant to be a scholarly derivation of the term.

34 Foreigner, outsider of western extraction.

35 i.e. like grass lacking exposure to the sun.

> They'll fawn over [*pā dharā*] their own wives and the wives and daughters of others in helping them alight from a carriage, but they won't look after their own aunts, sisters and sisters-in-law. Has anyone ever seen such antics [*raṅg*]?
>
> But when one sees their final antic [*śeṣ raṅg*] one just can't control one's mirth. Their wisdom extends no further than smokey machinery—yet they've set themselves up as teacher [*guru*] of the philosophically acute [*sūkṣma-darśī*] Aryan race! Such a perverse antic [*raṅg*] has never occurred before! In this way there's *phi, phiri, phiṅgi-phiṅge,* and finally *raṅg,* inside *phiriṅgi.* O Phiringi! truly, you're a pest unto death [*tor bālāi niye mari*]!

Besides demonstrating Upadhyay's almost obsessive love for word-play, this piece expresses the heightened disdain he felt for the British.[36] But it struck a chord—this is why the *Sandhya* continued to be as popular as ever. As early as November 25, 1905, the *Nava Jug* of Calcutta is reported as saying, 'A number of so-called Bengali patriots are at present leading the people in a wrong direction in the matter of the *swadeshi* movement, and the editor of the *Sandhya* newspaper, Pandit Brahma Bandhab Upadhyaya, is one of them. This man is doing great harm to the country by his vulgar and uncontrolled writings.... The true leaders of the people should try to check him, or his misconduct will draw official displeasure on the entire Native Press. Of course, the *Sandhya* has no influence among respectable people.' (*Report,* week ending December 2).

The *Nava Jug* had misread the situation. Not only was the *Sandhya* playing a key role in broadening the appeal of the anti-partition agitation by its populist tone—a fact that the so-called true leaders of the people must have noted with quiet satisfaction—but its 'vulgar writings' may have been just what respectable people needed to let their hair down in expressing resentment for the way the British had peremptorily partitioned their land without the least consultation. Without necessarily intending to be one, the *Sandhya* was a sort of safety valve in a highly volatile situation. Besides, the moderates and the extremists, Upadhyay included, on the whole got on well with each other; there was quite a clubbable atmosphere among this elite group.[37]

[36] Perhaps the racism he encountered during his visit to England exacerbated this.

[37] As evidenced by an incident recounted in *The Blade* by Bipinbehari Dasgupta, a former editor of the *Bande Mataram*. Bipinbehari tells how on the morning of

Upadhyay's antipathy towards British rule and western ways began to peak in the second half of 1906. Earlier that year, the *Sandhya* seems to eschew violence. In an article of February 14 (see *Report* for week ending February 17), the *Sandhya* says:

> Europe is civilized, but the last arbiter there is still the sword. This method of arbitration has lately been brought to bear on us here in this country also ... by the free use of *lathis* [staves].... As for those [Indians] who make claims on the European, pleading principles of equality, who hold meetings, make stirring speeches, and then draft petitions to the Europeans, we regard them as objects of pity. There is another party, very weak in numbers, who advocate the use of force to meet force.... The ideas of this party we regard as mistaken. We are not in favour of calling up and awakening the brute strength which every society possesses.... That is exactly what the European wants. He wants to ... awaken us, and then to give us such a belabouring that we shall fall into our last sleep. But we are wholly averse to awaken these brutal instincts.... For thousands of years, Hindu society has been engaged in gathering strength of quite a higher sort ... and this is the strength ... which now lies dormant that we would awaken and stimulate.

Though the use of physical violence is repudiated in favour of spiritual strength and resilience, one detects an ambivalent note in this regard—almost a hint that if Indians could 'belabour' the British back and survive, perhaps they should consider it.

In mid-April of 1906 Upadhyay was involved in a major fracas that took Bengal by storm, the Provincial Conference of the National Congress party in Barisal, a coastal town of the upper Gangetic delta in the heart of the eastern wing of the partitioned province. Barisal town and district, largely under the leadership of Aswinikumar Dutt, had acquired a reputation for resistance to partition. The Conference

---

April 8, 1907, Upadhyay hired a steamer to take a party of volunteers along the Ganges to Bankimcandra Chatterjee's 'native village' of Kantalpara to observe the anniversary of the author's death. The steamer passed by the house of Surendranath Banerjea, the doyen of the moderates, who had been joined by Bipinbehari to celebrate the sacred thread ceremony of Surendranath's son. Bipinbehari takes up the story: 'I had enjoyed a hearty meal when a steamer came near and shouts of *Bande Mataram* from the passengers could be heard. We realised it was the steamer hired by the Sandhya Office.... Surendranath beckoned to them. He requested all to get down to his place. They agreed and squatted down on the lawn near the bank of the river and enjoyed a grand breakfast.... I had to sit down and breakfast a second time' (pp. 139–40).

had been scheduled for April 14–15; many delegates began to arrive on the 13th. The problem arose when it was decided that the delegates would march to the Conference venue on the 14th chanting *bande mātaram*—the Bengali equivalent of the Sanskrit *vande mātaram*: I salute the Mother. The chant, as we have seen in chapter 8, was derived from Bankimcandra's patriotic novel *Anandamath.* By the time of the Conference, *bande mātaram* had already become a defiant slogan linked with anti-partition and anti-British sentiments; accordingly, the British authorities had ruled that the use of the slogan would be severely limited during the procession to the Conference venue. The scene was set for confrontation.

What occurred during the march is not wholly clear. But the police *lathi*-charged a section of the delegates (some of whom wore *bande mātaram* badges). There was some bloodshed, a famous arrest (Surendranath Banerjea was apprehended), subsequent disruption of the Conference and Bengali outrage, not least in the Bengal press for days afterwards. Upadhyay had been present at Barisal, and 'gave a stirring address' (Bl., p. 149), but he was nowhere to be seen during the *lathi*-charge. Had he escaped? UBBJ informs us (p. 117) that a supporter of the moderate Surendranath published a telling cartoon in the *Hitavadi* depicting Bipin Pal, Upadhyay and other extremists fleeing ignominiously from the police during the *lathi*-charge. *The Blade* provides an explanation: 'The truth had to come out. He had not been in the procession at all; he was suffering from diarrhoea. Had he to go afterwards and single-handed challenge the police?' (p. 150).

Still the *Sandhya* seemed to hold back. In response to the Barisal incident, the paper says (April 23; *Report* for week ending April 28): 'We do not counsel the return of *lathi*s for *lathi*s. The revenge which is possible to be taken consistently with the observance of the laws of the Feringhi is the course which it now behoves all Bengalis to adopt. We can easily give up all kinds of contact with the Feringhi. This is what we should now do.'[38] Yet on October 29 (*Report,* week ending November 10), the *Sandhya* says with almost startling venom with reference to an alleged police attack on locals in Mymensingh in eastern Bengal: 'What is wanted now is a band of *lathials*[39] in

[38] The *Sandhya* of May 7 (*Report,* week ending May 19) specifies four ways of boycott: giving up foreign products, giving up foreign ways of life and thought, cutting off all social and unnecessary occupational contact with the foreigner, and ostracizing those Indians who do not observe the former modes of boycott.

[39] A tough, often hired and unscrupulous, who fights with a staff (*lāṭhi*).

every town and in every village. They will wield *lathi* for *lathi* when unlawful oppression is committed, either by police or by any other party.... The [local] lads must henceforth be taught less of grammar and something of *gundaism* [strong-arm tactics]. Life and honour come first and your grammar next.' The *Sandhya* has stepped up a gear; the continuous reviling of the 'Phiringi' and his ways and the call for a complete boycott of the Phiringi and the setting up of indigenous educational, juridical and other institutions continue, but there is a new note of violence that recurs from time to time: 'If the Feringhi ... forcibly violates our *swadeshi* and wishes to keep us the sons of slaves, then force will arise in return for force' (January 8, 1907; *Report,* week ending January12); 'As to how we are to protect ourselves from the *feringhi*'s firearms, we can rely on Kali Mayi's boma (bomb).[40] We have repeatedly asserted that the explosion of this bomb is sure to overcome rifle-shots.... There should be two to five hundred bombs in each village' (May 18, 1907; *Report,* week ending May 25). With regard to the British authorities, the situation had indeed become explosive for the editor of the *Sandhya;* in the tense atmosphere of the time, Upadhyay was perilously close to a charge of sedition.

What had given rise to this acuity in the state of affairs? The effect may have been cumulative. UBBJ rightly comments that the radical difference that existed politically between the moderates and extremists gradually became clearer and clearer after the Barisal incident (p. 117); for many, that incident became a litmus test of viable political strategy. The difference between the two camps came to a head in the wheeling and dealing between them to define the Resolutions for adoption at the National Congress' general meeting in Calcutta at the end of December 1906. Significantly and revealingly for current trends in Bengal politics, the radicals succeeded in getting Resolutions favouring the boycott and Swadeshi movements and the ideals of national education and self-rule through. These concerns were now on the national agenda and fanned the flames of Bengal extremism. Upadhyay, closely in touch with these events and the radical leaders, espoused the extremist cause with increasing vehemence in the *Sandhya,* so much so that he bordered on the advocacy of terrorism.

He was now firmly in the sights of government retribution. He had already had a brush with the law when as editor of the *Sandhya*

40 A handmade explosive named after Kali, the Goddess of destruction.

he was convicted on December 4, 1905, in the Calcutta Police Court 'for having omitted to notify the change of the place of publication [of the *Sandhya*] within three days' (Bl., p. 148). The presiding judge was the Chief Presidency Magistrate, D.H. Kingsford (who plays a significant role later in our story). Upadhyay was arrested again towards the end of the first week of September 1906 on a charge of defaming a Mr Robert Malcolm, manager of a silk factory in the Rajshahi district. Coverage in the *Report* indicates that in both instances an undue show of force by the authorities occurred. Clearly, Upadhyay had become a salient object of government displeasure.

Here we must consider a further sequence of events. Not long after mid-1905, two anonymous Bengali pamphlets entitled *Sonar Bangla* (Golden Bengal), and published from Calcutta, circulated in their thousands around greater Bengal. The first was produced in mid-July, the second appeared at the end of the first week of August. These publications bore a marked resemblance in style and content, were directed largely at the young, especially high school students, and generally advocated in rousing terms the use of (under-cover) violence if necessary against the British in the cause of patriotism.[41] By the last quarter of the year, the British authorities were well aware of the *Sonar Bangla* publications (including the original pamphlets), but besides monitoring the situation seemed not to take action. Almost a year later, in September 1906,[42] a section of the Anglo-Indian press (notably *The Englishman* of Calcutta) claimed that a secret revolutionary society called *Sonar Bangla* and based in Chinsurah was operating in parts of Bengal; in support it published a translation of one of the pamphlets. Before long the matter had become an issue, and the authorities reacted accordingly. The Calcutta police appointed a special officer to study the case; from November 2, 1906, to January 17, 1907, six special reports were compiled with special reference to two pamphlets in the possession of the police and written in 1905 (at least one of which was one of the first two pamphlets that started the *Sonar Bangla* affair). The reports opined, on the basis of an analysis of vocabulary and style, that the pamphlets had been written by the same hand and that the author was Upadhyay, the editor of *Sandhya*. It was also stated that in producing the pamphlets Upadhyay had been assisted by a former sub-inspector of police, a certain Jyotilal

41 Before long a number of other pamphlets/leaflets and poems also entitled *Sonar Bangla* made their appearance.

42 The sequence of events is analysed in UBBJ, Appendix *Kha*, pp. 165ff.

Mukhopadhyay, who bore a grudge against the British and who worked for a Calcutta weekly called the *Pratijna.* The Reports concluded by mooting the prosecution for sedition of Upadhyay and others.

After consideration at the highest levels, it was decided not to prosecute, largely on two grounds: (1) The pamphlets, though probably seditious, had been written about a year and a half earlier; the matter was now 'cold', and since conviction was by no means assured, the prosecution was not worth the agitation among the Bengali public that would certainly ensue. (2) Since the person perceived as a ringleader of the extremists, Bipincandra Pal, seemed not to be implicated, he would continue to remain at large (the authorities were particularly interested in him). Besides, it was pointed out, it was not going to be difficult to apprehend Upadhyay since 'If we want to prosecute, I believe there is hardly a week in which the *Sandhya* does not publish some article which would justify our doing so' (UBBJ, p. 177).

I am far from convinced that Upadhyay authored either of the pamphlets scrutinized by the reports, notwithstanding the official analysis of vocabulary and style (this does not mean he may not have been implicated in some way). One of the pamphlets is quoted in UBBJ (pp. 167–9), and despite the use of certain words like *phiriṅgi,* there are insufficient grounds to conclude that its author was Upadhyay. Upadhyay's style and vocabulary in the *Sandhya* may well have been similar (UBBJ says that the reports contained comparative lists of words), but we cannot conclude on this basis alone that he wrote either or any of the *Sonar Bangla* pamphlets. *Phiriṅgi* in particular was a derogatory term associated with his style, but not exclusively so. Besides, if the *Report on Native Papers in Bengal* is a more or less accurate record, then, as we have seen, the *Sandhya* started advocating a more aggressive response to the British only in latish 1906, well after the pamphlets were written. Moreover, as UBBJ itself points out (pp. 178–9), close associates of Upadhyay (including the manager of the *Sandhya*) were not convinced that he had written the pamphlets.

But whether Upadhyay was actually the author is not really the point. The point is that so far as the British authorities were concerned he may well have written the pamphlets, and that by earlyish 1907 his history as a troublemaker was coming to a head. From the British point of view the case was mounting against him, and it would not be long before the authorities started looking for a chance to bring him to book.

# Chapter 15

# With a Consuming Passion Part II: End of a Journey and Assessment

We are approaching the end of Upadhyay's life, and the momentum was building up alarmingly. He was overtly and almost wholly involved in politics now: in *Sandhya,* in the anti-partition and Swadeshi agitation, and in the national education movement. He continued to take further commitments upon himself. In June 1906 he had played a leading part in organizing the Shivaji festival in Calcutta. Shivaji was the seventeenth century Maratha leader who successfully challenged Muslim might in the Deccan and consequently became a folk hero. The well-known nationalist, Bal Gangadhar Tilak (1856–1920), also a Maratha, had from the mid-1890s organized annual Shivaji festivals in Maharashtra, with a view to popularize Shivaji as a national patriot. Calcutta had followed suit and from the early 1900s held annual Shivaji festivals.

In 1906 the Calcutta organizers decided to hold an exhibition of indigenous goods (*svadeśī melā*) in conjunction with the festival (which was to run officially from June 4 to 8). Tilak (whose political views aligned him with the extremists) and other Maharashtrian leaders were to be present. Upadhyay argued for 'a booth with a large picture of Sivaji at the feet of Durga' (Bl., p. 150) among the exhibition stalls. After a bitter wrangle with other organizers (including Bipin Pal), Upadhyay's view prevailed on the grounds that this distinctive form of goddess symbolism would help popularize what Tilak described as a 'political festival', in Bengal.[1] Upadhyay also undertook to oversee the

[1] This only goes to show that in many eyes the extremist stance was strongly coloured by Hindu religious symbolism. The idea of the Shivaji festival as a 'national' phenomenon was not in tune generally with Muslim sentiment, in spite of efforts

menu for a grand banquet with numerous guests held in honour of the Maratha visitors (remember he had acted as mess-manager while staying for about a year with Satiscandra and the latter's pupils in the house on Cornwallis Street). There are ecstatic reports about the menu for the banquet; it was a real *tour de force* of Bengali cuisine.[2]

On March 10, 1907, the first issue of a new Bengali weekly 'in folio, comprising from 12–14 pages' (Bl., p. 154), entitled *Svaraj*, with Upadhyay as editor, was published. Twelve numbers appeared in all, says *The Blade* from March to July. In contrast to the *Sandhya*, the *Svaraj* was aimed at a higher-brow readership. If the *Sandhya* gave Upadhyay the opportunity to be earthy in style and content, making use of homely imagery and expression (picked up, as Simha points out (see chapter 2), from the rustic experiences of his boyhood days), the *Svaraj* allowed him to indulge his talent for impressive description and sophisticated analysis. There is some magnificent writing by Upadhyay in *Svaraj*: popular religious and social festivals, aspects of the anti-partition movement and other subjects[3] are analysed with erudition and not a little wit against the pervasive backdrop of overt or covert patriotic ideals. Thus the festival of *Snān-jātrā*, in which an image of the Lord Krishna as ruler of the world (*jagannātha*) is ceremonially bathed,[4] becomes an occasion for the now unperceptive Bengali to wake up and experience the Lord's pervasiveness in nature.

---

on the part of Hindu leaders to explain Shivaji as opposed not to Islam and Muslims but to oppressive rule from wherever it might come. Thus the *Mihir-o-Sudhakar* of July 31, 1903 (a Calcutta Muslim weekly; subscription 1000 copies) says: 'The festival in honour of Shivaji, the founder of that band of robbers known as the *bargis* ... has just been held with great *eclat*. Brother Hindu ... you reserve all your honours for a robber-chief'. The Calcutta weekly, *Pratijna*, on the other hand (August 5), exclaims: 'Among the patriots born in India ... Sivaji is, as it were, the lustrous central gem.... The murders committed by him cease to be such when the noble end which prompted them is taken into consideration.... Sivaji is the last independent Hindu king, India's last patriotic hero' (*Report*, week ending August 8). The Muslim *Soltan* of June 8, 1906 commented thus on the holding of the recent Shivaji festival in Calcutta: 'The man who advocates the holding of such a festival cannot help stigmatising the Musalman rule in India as tyrannical.... The exploits of Sivaji may justly be compared with those of Chenghiz Khan.' (*Report*, week ending June 16). A telling difference of view.

2 Some 50–60 dishes were served (Bl., p. 152).

3 Which included the autobiographical account of the youthful Upadhyay's attempt to 'deliver' India (*Āmār Bhārat Uddhār*) quoted in chapter 2. *The Blade* (pp.154–9) gives a summary of the contents of *Svaraj*.

4 Celebrated during the period of the full-moon in the month of Jyaiṣṭha (May–June).

The blissful, all-powerful, transcendent One doesn't need a bath! 'Yet, so captive to love is he, that to fulfill the heart's desire of the devotee, he himself becomes small' (*māyāmay. śrī-hari etai premer baś je bhakter manobāñcā pūrṇa karibār janya nijei choṭo han*). *This* is true lordship. Note, this is also in tune with Christian thinking.

Again, continues Upadhyay, cannot the Bengali see that, in the same required spirit of service, Nature itself, as it were, regularly bathes the Lord. 'The sky is purple with dark clouds, the horizon is becoming dark, a great display is visible on all sides. Suddenly there's a fearful roll of thunder here, a flash of lightning there! In contrast to this grand display, how insignificant the canopy, the drumming and row of lights of your own ceremony! See what a great bath this is! The rain has poured down in torrents, the sun-scorched earth is now refreshed—all life can relax again.... Can you not understand that he who is Being itself has taken recourse to bewitching, welcoming nature, and is enjoying his bath?'[5] The Lord has united with Nature to accomplish his purpose; the Bengali too must put aside all division, and adopt a spirit of magnanimity. There is nothing here that an empathetic Christian could not write—at least by today's standards in some dialogic circles. Upadhyay may have been ahead of his time, but the indications are that he continued to interpret Hinduism to his compatriots in a way that he thought was not incompatible with his adopted faith. But where was this faith in the turgid whirlpool of politics that he was now immersed in? Let us not anticipate.

Above we have given only an example, taken from an ostensibly cultural piece of writing.[6] The article is a pleasure to read, replete with imagery and religious symbolism, and hard to translate adequately (at least for this translator). What we would call today the 'mission statement' of *Svaraj* is given in an editorial in the first issue.

5 *Ākāś ghananīradnīl—dinmaṇḍal śyāmāyamān—caturdike ghor ghaṭā. kakhano bā bajrer bhairab rol kakhano bā bijlīr hāsi. tomār candrātap ḍhakḍhol ālokmālā ei gambhīr śobhār kāche kī tuccha! ār dekho kī birāṭ snān! dardar kariyā muṣaldhāre barṣā nāmila. ātaptāpita basundharā snigdha haila—biśvaprāṇ juḍāila.... tumi ki bujhite pāritecho nā je svayaṃ satsvarūp māyāmayī śyāmā prakṛtike abalamban kariyā snānbilās karitechen.* (see Ghosh, p. 211).

6 *Snān-jātrā* was originally reprinted in *Pāl-Pārbban*, which has been reprinted anew in Ghosh, 1987. For a reference to its source see Bagal, 1964: 61. Bagal also points out (p. 41) that a bi-weekly (*ardha-sāptāhik*) called '*Karālī*' was published. 'In it articles from *Sandhyā* were reprinted. It was for those who were not able to read the *Sandhyā* regularly'. I have not been able to find dates for this publication.

> 'In correct speech it is *svarājya,* but colloquially we say *svarāj....* Existing by one's own power or greatness [*mahimā*] is *svarāj. Svarāj* is based on greatness, dignity [*mahimā*]. Greatness is not charm [*madhurimā*]... nor is it vastness [*biśālatā*]. Then what is it? The completeness which brings about synthesis in difference and conflict, the nobility which accomplishes harmony in great discord, is the essence of greatness, *mahimā.* You will be able to understand this spirit if you consider the following example:
>
> If you want to see greatness in bodily form then come to the Himalayas. Those lordly mountains which you behold are a store of immortality as well as a repository of death. The bosom of that immense mass of stone is forever refreshed by the cool flow of rivers that carry immortality ... and great trees that have the property of regenerating the dead derive nourishment from that expanse of stone. Yet deadly flowers also bloom in that impregnable snowy range, huge serpents emit their venom, and deadly forest creatures exist there. That lofty northern region is the recourse of ascetics and hermits, as well as the domain of fell hunters and predators....
>
> What unmanageable contrast, what awesome differences ... what tremendous disharmony!... But if you view things from the perspective of yoga rather than of divisiveness [*biyogdṛṣṭi barjan kariyā jadi jogdṛṣṭite dekho*][7] ... then you will see that the [Himalayas'] constancy subsumes all the transience of the tempests of time, that their sublimity harmonizes every contrast, their fullness founds non-difference amidst the plurality of difference.... Were you to take your stand on the yogic greatness of the Himalayas, you would be glad to accept all their differences and discrepancies ... every disharmony would in fact immerse you in boundless delight! This is why the Himalayas are called the abode of yoga [*jogālay*].... Where there is yogic mastery over separation and union, there supreme greatness (*mahimā*) exists.'

Hindu society (*hindu samāj*), continues Upadhyay, is as great as the Himalayas. In spite of the depredations of the Buddhists and various sectarian and foreign groups over the centuries, in essence it continues unmoving, unshaken, undying (*acal aṭal amar*). Only a yogic gaze can perceive this; a divisive view will but see the external divisions. The foreigners have imposed upon us, says Upadhyay, only a divisive perspective, and we use it to try and make sense of our culture. As a

7 One well-known etymology of *yoga* derives the word from a root connoting a joining together, an integrating (*yuj, yunakti/yuṅkte*).

result we have forgotten our ever-present greatness (*sarbamay mahimā*), and take the imperfections of our 'Mother'—the culture that has nurtured us—out of all proportion. 'The child of the mother loves the whole reality of the mother ... accepts it as such, without analysing what's good or bad' (*māyer santān samagra mātṛbastuke bhālobāse—bhālo baliyā bāse—aṅgīkār kare—dośguṇer samālocanā kare nā*). 'What a catastrophe! We have lost the yogic perspective and been overcome by difference and conflict. We have fallen from our greatness; we have lapsed from *svarāj*' (*sarbanāś haiyāche. jogdṛṣṭi hārāiyā bheddvandve āmrā abhibhūta haiyāchi—nija mahimā haite bicyut haiyāchi—svarājbhraṣṭa haiyāchi*). The aim of *Svaraj*, the publication, will be to try and restore this longstanding though now obscured Hindu greatness and dignity by calling to mind the significance of accomplishments of the past and of current institutions and practices. In that light, Hindu society and Hindu culture will be perceived for what it truly is and should be—a fullness, a wholeness, a unity. 'We will dissolve every opposition in the bosom of non-difference—and we shall live in our own greatness.'

For this to happen Hindu society must set itself apart from western ways and nourish its own customs and culture. If this is done the yogic perspective will return and the Aryan greatness (*ārjamahimā*) will once again become manifest. The *Svaraj* journal will do all it can to help bring this about. Thus the aim of *Svaraj* was to instructively boost morale in keeping with Upadhyay's ongoing appreciation of non-dual or Advaitic insights. Upadhyay concludes by saying that though he is dedicated to this goal, he has very little resources of any kind—from wealth to knowledge—to fall back on. 'Our sole recourse is the grace of the Mother and the favour of the Mother's children.'[8]

The reader will not have failed to notice Upadhyay's references to 'the Mother'. Similar references occur especially in the later portions of the *Sandhya*. To what exactly does 'Mother' refer? The seminal influence here was Bankim's *Anandamath*, of course. For Bankim, the Mother was the motherland, India, as focused in and through Bengal and Bengali ways and history, and as symbolized by the mother goddess, especially Durga (and her terrible form of Kali). Indians, especially Hindus, and in particular Bengalis, were the offspring, the children (*santān*) of this mother. This concept of 'mother' coincided

8 I have translated from the first editorial reprinted in UBBJ, pp. 188–93. Also see Ghosh, 1987: 50–5.

with Upadhyay's, though not exclusively so. It was not uncommon for Bengali nationalists, especially the radical-minded, to adopt this understanding of 'mother'.[9] This intermingling of political and religious imagery and symbolism rendered the cause of nationalism sacred—understood thus it had a distinctive potency for Bengalis—and called for dedication and sacrifice, even unto death.

The religious side of Upadhyay's conception of 'Mother' is graphically portrayed in a short article entitled 'Mother Kali of the Dance' (*mā nṛtyakālī*), and published possibly in the *Sandhya.*[10] It is a stirring piece and captures the mood of Goddess symbolism in Bengal at the time. Here it is in full:

> 'Tomorrow, Thursday, is Mahālaya.[11] Tomorrow the darkness of the new moon will cover heaven and earth. Mother Kālī of the dance herself will hold Jayā and Bijayā[12] by the hand and dance frenziedly [*tāṇḍab nāc*] with her witches, sorceresses and she-ghouls. Tāl and Betāl[13] will roar out to the rhythm and Śiva the Terrible [*kālbhairab*] will sound the destruction of the world on his kettle-drum. Come, let us dance too with the dancing Kālī. Let us watch how Mother's garland of human heads swings to and fro, how Mother's flashing scimitar emits lightning in the gloom.
>
> Bengali, you love your darling dark Mother, and seek refuge behind the hem of her loin-cloth. But tomorrow on Mahālaya you will have to worship Mother Kālī of the dance. Behold her attire and drink the nectar of her red liquor, but don't lose control; you must dance wine-intoxicated with Mother. Look, look! Mother's dark tresses are flying about and every glimmer of light has been blotted out; earth and sky reel under her thumping feet.
>
> Bengali! Today abandon your gentle disposition and take on a fierce demeanour. Drunk with beholding the form of your beloved Mother, sound the rhythm of destruction's dance with Tāl and Betāl. Dancing Mother Kālī's reddened feet must be worshipped with red flowers. Where will you get red flowers? Mother's feet are red, and red your

9 In his Preface to UBBJ, Bhupen Dutta gives an account of various contexts in which the goddess was invoked in Bengal during these times.

10 The exact source is not clear, and I cannot find a date for it.

11 The day of the new moon before the great festival of the Goddess Durga in Bengal. Kali is a fearful form of Durga.

12 *Jayā* and *Bijayā* (names signifying victory) are female attendants of Durga/Kali.

13 Two demons; reference to them suggests both the rhythm (*tāl*) and frenzy (*betāl*) of Kali's dance, usually accompanied by the kettle-drum.

devoted blood: mix red with red—you are to shed much blood together.

The time to shelter behind the hem of Mother's loin-cloth has passed. Be inflamed—you must sound Time's drum and dance the dance of destruction with Mother Kālī. Awake, awake! Madden yourselves! Tomorrow is Mahālaya!'

The style and tone suggest that this was published in the *Sandhya,* probably in 1906 (September–October). Note that Kali here is not the sensual mother figure popularized by the sage, Ramakrishna; though protective of her devotees, she is bloodthirsty and terrible, a suitable symbol for the radical politics of the time. The latent call to violence though is not far below the surface. This piece echoes the insistent tone of the *Sandhya* to 'awaken' the culturally uncomprehending and politically apathetic Bengali.

Now we may ask, can—may—a Christian write like this? To compound these questions, we quote from Upadhyay's current writings on a developing icon of Bengali consciousness: Ramakrishna Paramahamsa.[14]

God [*debatā*], Guru, Companion, Friend, Luminous One [*basu*]—our All [*sarbbasva*]—now that you have come do you once more, O divine One (*debatā*), guide us, installed in the chariot of our heart's great longing, just as in another age you descended to this human realm in the guise of Krishna [*pārthasārathi*]. Then by your immortal words we shall be rejuvenated, and encouraged by you once again we shall foregather on the field of dharma, on this field of India.... O man-god in Brahmin-form (*he brāhmaṇ-rūpī nara-debatā*), drive forward the chariot of our society [*samāj-rath*] today....

Who will protect us if you do not? You are the saviour of the fallen [*patiter saṃrakṣaṇ-kārī*]—the strength of the weak. Man-god in the shape of holy Ramakrishna, since you have come down to us through mercy, free your beloved land of India from the ravages of the foreigner [*mleccha-durgati*].... We long to banish that unclean shadow [*malin chāyā*] whence the house of our society has been rendered untouchable[15].... You are divine [*debatā tumi*], powerful—give us

14 The article, entitled *Naradebatā* (the term is a Karmadhāraya Tatpuruṣa compound which may be translated as 'man-god', possibly 'god-man'), was first published in *Svaraj* (I am unable to confirm the date); it was reprinted in the *Masik Basumati,* B.E. Phālgun 1354 (C.E. 1947), p. 505.

15 This evokes a long-standing rule of untouchability by which even the shadow of an outcaste polluted a ritually pure Hindu.

> such power by which we can purify the basis of self-rule [*svārājya-pratiṣṭhā*] in the form of our society.... Deep in our hearts have we[16] felt your coming. Almighty One [*sarbbaiśvarjyamay*], though you have come in the form of a destitute, ascetic Brahmin, we[17] were able to understand who you are from the serene glance of your eyes. Though you appeared illiterate, we knew you to be the Guardian of the Vedas himself!... You are Ramakrishna, for are you not Rama and Krishna in one?
>
> Rise up, rise up Bengali! Rise up, sweet Mother Bengal [*mā baṅgalakṣmi*].... Rise up, village deities.... Let us all gather today and offer our reverence [*śraddhā nibedan kari*] to this wondrous man-god in the form of Ramakrishna, for he is the very one who in a former age freed us from evil.

If one were so minded, a most intricate and tendentious theological web could be woven around this passage. One could argue that there is nothing unChristian about these words, that Upadhyay could write as he did about Ramakrishna without abandoning his Christian allegiance. All he has done in this extract is identify Ramakrishna's person and mission with that of Krishna of old. And just as the Krishna of his *Śrīkṛṣṇatattva* lecture can be regarded as a unique and timely *human* manifestation of the divine presence among us, so can Ramakrishna's appearance in modern times according to this interpretation. God has not forgotten his beloved Hindu people; he reappears to give them guidance and succour.

But what about the use of such terms as *nara-debatā* ('man-god', or even 'god-man'), 'saviour of the fallen', 'almighty' and so on? From the point of view of a benign Christian interpretation, this is in tune with the psychology of Indian praise; in traditional literature such language may well be addressed to royal figures or great sages, while theologically they may be interpreted as saying that as a unique human manifestation or vehicle of the divine presence, Ramakrishna is indeed not God in person (only Christ could be so), but God's personal representative among us. He is a unique human being in whom the power of God manifests uniquely, just as Krishna was (see chapter 13). In this extended sense, he is Krishna (and Rama) come among us again, the 'presence of God in our midst', our inspirer, our saviour, guardian of the Veda, a guru, a luminous one, a god-

16 Or possibly, 'I'.

17 Or possibly, 'I'.

man/man-god, the result of a gracious God uniquely adopting and manifesting in a human representative. He is not the divine person itself incarnated in human nature—as Christ was. Understood in context—in the context of Upadhyay's private understanding of the distinction between 'incarnation' and *avatāra*, there is no sliding away from his Christian commitment. In a good cause, not so much now the cause of showing the compatibility of Christian faith with Hindu natural theology, but the cause of boosting the morale of a dispirited people and rallying them for political purposes, Upadhyay is showing the maximum reverence a Christian can show to a Hindu religious figure in Hindu idiom.

Similarly for Kali. She is but a potent symbol for the Bengali, of the times and circumstances. She is a valid expression of God's protective wrath against apathy and oppression: through Kali God manifests his maternal, protective love especially of the Bengalis (for whom she is a distinctive divine symbol) but also of the motherland, against the depredations of the foreigner, and seeks to arouse his children from an apathy that is destroying their self-respect. Violence and scathing and harsh words are in extreme circumstances justified; when the patient is in danger of death only strong medicine will do.[18]

Perhaps. But could public scrutiny appreciate the carefully honed subtlety of the distinction between public and private in the editor of *Sandhya* and *Svaraj*? Hardly. Did Upadhyay make public pronouncements at the time, about his Christian allegiance? No. Was he not guilty of dissembling then, of allowing observers to naturally assume from his words that he had abandoned his adopted faith? The issue is certainly not straightforward,[19] but he chose to follow a different course of action from that of his famous patriot uncle Kalicaran, whose

18 Prabhat Basu (1948) writes: 'As to why [Upadhyay] used strong language, he argued as follows: 'Why is our language ... [in *Sandhyā*] so strong?... Normally we [Bengalis] do not write so harshly. But when one has to show anger, to raise a hue and cry, then gentle words won't do. The country's disease is rather severe, so one has to slap the patient after giving him the medicine!... There's apathy, insensibility on all sides in the land.... Let me give another example. Suppose foul slime has arisen at the bottom of a pond, and people are catching typhoid by drinking the water. That slime must be shifted. When this is done the water will become turbid. When they see this happening our genteel folk [*sabhya bāburā*] turn up their noses. But they're not in the least concerned, don't care that people are dying. They don't understand that after the stirring when the water settles the pond will be clear and healthy.' No source is given for this quotation of Upadhyay's.

19 A number of Upadhyay's personal acquaintances, e.g. Tagore, were able to perceive that according to his own lights Upadhyay remained a Christian, or at least a Hindu-Christian of some kind, even if they were not able readily to understand the intricacies

Christian allegiance though by no means trumpeted, remained unambiguous. In support of our interpretation we shall note in due course how Upadhyay in these last days continued to observe Christian rituals, though not on a regular basis, and acknowledged his Christian faith, though only in private circumstances.

The author of *The Blade* reports that already sometime in June 1901, well before he left for England, Upadhyay said, 'We must make *Prayascitta,* must eat a little cow-dung' (Bl., p. 159). *Prāyaścitta* is Sanskrit for 'expiation' due for an infringement of *dharma*. As is usually the case with regard to regulatory principles in Hinduism, there are different traditional authoritative views as to the role, extent and content of particular forms of *prāyaścitta.* Cow-dung in traditional Hindu practice is regarded as a ritually purifying agent,[20] and its token ingestion is not infrequently part of the expiatory process. So what did Upadhyay understand by saying that he needed to do *prāyaścitta?*

There is a revealing article entitled 'Social Penance' that Upadhyay wrote for the *Twentieth Century* (July 31, 1901). 'What is *prayascitta* or social penance according to Hindu lawgivers?' he asks.

> It is making the unclean clean, the impure pure, by imposing upon guilty persons certain social chastisements. Society cannot arrogate to itself the power of removing *moral* defilements, but it has every right to punish *social* violations.... If a Hindu enters into any social alliance with aliens [foreigners] calculated to injure the integrity of his race, society has every right to impose corrective chastisements on such a truant.... Interdining or intermarrying or such other acts which lead to social defilement by the admission of uncongenial, extraneous elements should come under the cognisance of the tribunal of the community.... The most potent safeguard against racial impurity and social vitiation is to place those who interdine and intermarry with non-Hindu races under ban. And the ban should be withdrawn only on the condition of their submitting to certain expiatory ordinances. By social expiation is not meant internal purification but the performance of a humiliating act prescribed by the injured society as a public confession of sorrow for the guilty attempt of breaking social integrity.

---

of this allegiance (cf. Tagore's description of Upadhyay as a 'Roman Catholic ascetic *yet* a Vedantin' at the beginning of the Introduction to this book); however, other acquaintances thought that he had returned to the Hindu fold.

20 For further information on this function and an associated originative myth, see Leslie, 1989: 60–62.

Notice the clear distinction drawn here between social and moral infringement, and Upadhyay's identification in this context of *prāyaścitta* with expiation for *social* transgression. Expiation for sin or moral wrongdoing is solely a matter for the individual concerned and God; society has a role to play in laying down expiatory rites for the infringement of *social* rules. In other words, it is very clear that by *prāyaścitta* Upadhyay understood expiation for transgression not of moral *dharma*, but of *samāj* or social *dharma*. His chief examples of this are interdining and/or intermarrying with the foreigner.

In August 1907, two months or so before he was to die, Upadhyay underwent a ceremony of *prāyaścitta*. Many knew that he had become a Christian. It was likely that he had consorted with foreigners in this connection, and everyone knew that he had travelled abroad and 'interdined' there. It would be an important symbolic act of solidarity with his compatriots if the now high-profile and virulently patriotic Brahmin editor of *Sandhya* performed a public act of expiation for violating traditional caste rules. After all, he was continually holding up the role of the Brahmin for bringing about *svarāj* in the new India to be, and recommending a return to traditional values and loyalties. Surely as a prophetic Brahmin he should lead by example.

This was the rationale underlying Upadhyay's act of *prāyaścitta*. *The Blade* gives an inconsistent account of how Upadhyay was perceived to have performed the expiatory act by a number of people involved (pp. 162–7).[21] It is not to the point to try and iron out the inconsistencies. The issue turns on whether Upadhyay intended to abandon his personal Christian faith in the process, or just perform an act of *social* expiation while continuing to believe as a Christian. From the evidence recounted concerning what Upadhyay understood *prāyaścitta* to be, I do not think there is much doubt as to what Upadhyay intended by the ceremony. He was not abandoning his Christian faith; he was doing the requisite penance in order to be formally readmitted to Hindu society.[22]

[21] Based on a number of interviews undertaken in 1925. One interviewee was Pandit Pancanan Tarkaratna of Bhatpara, on the basis of whose written injunction the *prāyaścitta* was conducted by another priest.

[22] In spite of a confusing account, Tarkaratna (see previous note) is clear that Upadhyay had no intention of abandoning his personal Christian faith, but wished to do penance for 'violating the duties of a Brahmin' (Bl., p. 165). Simha also says, though somewhat ambiguously, that by undergoing *prāyaścitta* Upadhyay did not become opposed to the Christian faith (*tabe je tini khṛṣṭīyadharmabidveṣī hailen tāhā nahe;* p. 99).

However, what he was perceived to do in the public eye—and what he did not attempt to do to clear up any general misunderstanding—is another matter. Most people thought that he had ceased to be a Christian, and that he was formally ratifying the tenor of his writings by *religiously* rejoining the Hindu fold. Upadhyay seemed to say nothing publicly to counter this impression, and here again he may be regarded as less than forthright, but he was being rushed along on a tidal wave of patriotic sentiment and adulation largely of his own making; to require clarificatory declarations that would run counter to this headlong current is easier said than done; his credibility was at stake.

*The Blade* reports that already in 1897, on a visit to Calcutta, Upadhyay wanted a 'dispensation for not attending' Church services. Animananda continues, 'Early in 1904 he did not approve of my letting an Orthodox Brahman know that we were both Catholics. Hindus as a rule, he thought, have such an extravagant notion of Christianity. Until this notion has been corrected, it is better not to mention the matter. His intimate friends among Hindus knew it, of course, and did not mind' (p. 180). In fact, upon his return from England in July 1903, Upadhyay was almost wholly in the company of Hindus, developing his campaign for Hindu patriotic ideals. Nevertheless, he had not abandoned his faith in Christ, and according to his own lights practised it openly but privately. *The Blade* gives a catalogue of these instances: 'Kartik's wife had died on a Wednesday. Every Wednesday Upadhyay would say the usual Catholic prayers in Sanskrit, leading the family worship before a picture of the *Ecce Homo* that had been woven by the dear departed' (p. 180). 'Christmas Day, December 1904, he celebrated the feast of the nativity of Jesus Christ in the suburbs of Calcutta' (p. 181). 'During the Lent of 1905, I found him, kneeling at the railings of the Cathedral Church to receive the holy sign of the Cross with ashes blessed for the occasion' (p. 181).

Yet his faith became increasingly a private affair from 1906, though not entirely. While he rarely, if ever, went to Mass, it seems he did on occasion observe other rituals among those who would not misunderstand. 'In February 1907, on a solemn occasion, he said among others the following prayers: (1) The Lord's prayer in Sanskrit, (2) A Canticle in praise of the Holy Trinity, (3) A Hymn on Jesus Christ' (Bl., p. 182). A Protestant friend, the Rev. Bimalananda Nag, asked him in February–March 1907 to write a review of some lectures given in Calcutta by a Dr Cuthbert Hall. Though Upadhyay seems not to have completed the review, he read the lectures, and, claims

Nag, was given a new impetus to return to his earlier religious way of life. He had grown dull, he said, because he thought no one sympathised with him in his conception that Vedantic Theism was to be the basis of Indian Christianity, but in Dr Cuthbert Hall he found a kindred spirit. He added: 'I have entangled myself too much in political affairs, but as I read Dr Cuthbert Hall's lectures, I seriously thought if I should not give up all these entanglements and begin to preach the religion of Christ as I was doing before' (Bl. pp. 185–6). He had not given up his allegiance to Christ.[23]

Upadhyay seems to have been torn, as he was approaching the end of his life, between his personal religion and his politics. Perhaps this casts light on a famous interview he had with Rabindranath Tagore some time before his death. Tagore records the meeting, which took place after a long period of having lost touch personally with Upadhyay, in the Preface to the first edition of *Car Adhyay*.

> During those days of blind madness (*andha unmattatār dine*) [as the partition agitation escalated], one day as I sat alone in my third-floor room in Jorasanko, Upadhyay suddenly arrived. During conversation we spoke a bit of our earlier discussions [when we were together at Santiniketan]. When we had finished conversing, Upadhyay rose to take his leave. He reached the door and turned to look at me. He said, 'Rabibabu, I have fallen grievously' (*rabibābu, āmār khub patan hayeche*). After he said this, he did not wait; he just left. I understood clearly then that he had come just to say these heart-rending words. By then the net of his activities had closed tightly around him; there was no chance of escape.

The report of this episode generated much controversy (Tagore was accused of maligning Upadhyay the radical patriot through the depiction of some of his characters), and was omitted in subsequent editions of the publication. But perhaps we can understand better the personal turmoil Upadhyay was going through. Once again, Tagore's closing words seem to capture a piercing insight into Upadhyay's state of mind at the time.

Upadhyay kept up an exhausting daily routine. He would be in the *Sandhya* office, sitting cross-legged on the floor in front of a wooden desk, by 5.30 a.m. As chief writer for the paper, he wrote steadily till noon, then handed over the manuscript to the compositors. He would then walk from Sibnarayan Das Lane along Simla Street to

23 During the Christmas season of 1906 he wrote a letter to Animananda and concluded, 'Yours affectionately in Christ' (see Bl., pp. 187–8).

Kartik's house in Bethune Row. Bl. says that there he would pray, read, and think. At about 5.30 p.m. friends and others would arrive, and discussions would continue till the early hours. But by 5.30 a.m. he would be at work on the day's *Sandhya* again (p. 149).[24]

The time had now come for a hostile administration to curb the activities of the radicals. 'In 1906 and 1907 the governments of Punjab and Bombay had instituted cases [for sedition] against newspapers in those provinces. Now it was the turn of Bengal' (Heehs, 1993: 99). The *Jugantar, Sandhya* and *Bande Mataram* were singled out. Notices warning the three editors to desist from inflammatory writing were sent out on June 7, 1907; the papers continued regardless. The authorities acted first against the *soi-disant* editor of *Jugantar,* Bhupen Datta. Bhupen Datta was convicted, and on July 24 was sentenced by Chief Presidency Magistrate, D.H. Kingsford, to one year's rigorous imprisonment. Next in line was *Bande Mataram;* eventually (since there was no obvious editor of the publication) Aurobindo Ghose was arrested and tried but was acquitted (Bipin Pal who refused to testify against him was found guilty of contempt of court and sentenced to six months' imprisonment).[25]

On August 7, the *Sandhya* office was searched but only material relating to the publication of *Jugantar* was found. Upadhyay, forewarned that the police were coming, had cleared the decks of his own papers, which 'were burned in Nimtolla Ghat Street in a timber godown [warehouse].... the letters of Rabindranath to Upadhyay perished in that bonfire' (Bl., p. 168). When three well-wishers, one of them a Deputy Magistrate and relative, came about three weeks later to offer government aid if he toned down his writings, Upadhyay refused point blank. On August 30, the *Sandhya* office was searched and the manager, Saradacaran Sen, being the only person then present, was arrested. Summons were also issued against Upadhyay and the printer of the paper, Haricaran Das.

On September 3 Upadhyay and Haricaran were arrested at the *Sandhya* office in Sibnarayan Das Lane and taken to Jorasanko police station. They were then released on bail (as Saradacaran had been

24 There was a round of other activities too. As Sumit Sarkar points out, 'The *Sandhya* office ... became a great meeting place. A Railwaymen's Union was started on 27 July [1906] at a meeting held in this office.'(1973: 217), and 'the puja-cum-boycott meeting at Kalighat on 9th August 1907 was addressed by Pal, Shamsundar Chakrabarti and Upadhyay' (p. 312). This exemplifies a high-visibility programme.

25 Details are given in Heehs, 1993: 99ff.

before them). The hearing was fixed for September 9, but since the *Bande Mataram* case was in progress at the time, no progress could be made. This case came to an end on September 23; it was then that the court turned its attention to *Sandhya.*

The *Sandhya* case was based chiefly on three articles: (1) *Ekhan theke gechi premer dāye* ('Now love has us in a fix'; August 13); (2) *Chidiśaner huḍum duḍum, phiringir ākkel guḍum* ('When he hears the boom of sedition the Firingi gets in a tizz'; August 20); and (3) *Bockā sakal niye jācchen Śrībrndāban* ('They're taking all our stuff to holy Vrndavan'; August 23).[26] *The Blade* gives a transcript of the official translation of the first article, and summarizes the other two. We quote from the transcript:

> We have said over and over again that we are not Svadeshi only so far as salt and sugar are concerned.... Our aim is that India may be free, that the stranger may be driven from our homes, that the continuity of the learning, the civilisation and the system of the Rishis may be preserved....
>
> First free the Mother from her bondage, then seek your own deliverance.... Heaven we do not want. Deliverance we seek not. O Mother! let us be born again and again in India till your chains fall off.... O Feringhi, here I am with my neck outstretched: offer it up as a sacrifice. You will see, I shall again be born in the land of Bengal and shall cause much more serious confusion.... We have heard the voice telling us that the period of India's suffering is about to close, that the day of her deliverance is near at hand.... Your overweening pride is due to your possessing a few cannon and guns.... [But] we have all the advantages of the ancient greatness of India on our side.... If you are wise, you should help towards the attainment of deliverance [of] India. Otherwise, come, let us descend into the arena of war. We hereby summon you to battle.... The sons of the Mother are preparing themselves. All the arms, fiery [*agneya*], watery [*varuna*], airy [*vayabya*]—in her vaults are being polished.... Are we afraid of your cannon and guns? Arm, brothers, arm! The day of deliverance is near (Bl., pp. 170–1).

A poor translation, but the echoes of Bankim's *Anandamath* still ring clear. Some bravado here, but hardly worth the trouble of a sedition trial. The gist of the second article is as follows: 'What is all this fuss about Sedition? A dog has entered your kitchen and put his

26 As *The Blade* (p. 172) and UBBJ (p. 142) point out, other articles got a mention. UBBJ goes into details.

nose into your pot. You raise your stick and drive him out. He snarls at you.... Even so does the Feringhi. Fear not ... he will not bite. He is looking for a way to get out' (Bl., p. 171). The third article slights the 'Feringhi' again for being arrogant; the British who have come abroad are insignificant in their own land, but they dare to lord it over the Indians in India. The Britisher is nothing more than a beggar: 'Put that beggar on a horse, head to tail, and parade him about the streets' (ibid.). Crude, but not particularly martial. Nevertheless, as we have noted earlier, the authorities were out to silence Upadhyay, and they needed some ammunition.

And Kingsford, the presiding magistrate, was hardly disposed to be in the least sympathetic. It could not have escaped his notice that on several occasions he had been described, to say the least, unflatteringly in the *Sandhya.* For example, on February 17, 1906, the *Sandhya* had declared that in his court one felt more in the presence of an executioner than a judge; on July 10, 1907, the *Sandhya* said that his face seemed to be made of marble, so unrelenting did it appear; on August 30 that year, he was called a 'butcher of a magistrate'. *The Blade* adds a choice description or two by Upadhyay, e.g. *pājīr pājī,* an utter scoundrel.

The trial began sensationally. On September 23, 1907, Upadhyay's counsel, Cittaranjan Das, read the following statement on behalf of his client[27]:

> I accept the entire responsibility of the publication, management and conduct of the newspaper Sandhya and I say that I am the writer of the article, *Ekhan theke gechi premer dai* [sic] which appeared in the Sandhya of the 13th August 1907, being one of the articles forming the subject matter of this prosecution. But I do not want to take any part in this trial because I do not believe that in carrying out my humble share of the God-appointed mission of Svaraj, I am in any way accountable to the alien people who happen to rule over us and whose interest is and must necessarily be in the way of [i.e. opposed to] our true national development.

The *Bande Mataram* of the following day declared: 'Never in the history of seditious trial in India has a statement so bold, so straightforward

27 UBBJ intimates that it was Upadhyay who read this statement ('firmly', *dṛḍhakanṭhe;* p. 138); however, since *The Blade's* testimony (pp. 169ff.) seems to be based on an eyewitness account, I have followed it as the more reliable. Das eventually gave up his brief during the trial, apparently as a delaying tactic, and another lawyer had to be found.

and so dignified been filed' (UBBJ, p. 140). In fact, courageous and selfless though he was, by not cooperating with the court Upadhyay was following in the footsteps of some of the accused involved in the *Jugantar* and *Bande Mataram* trials.

As the hearing continued, Upadhyay stood for hours on end in the dock.[28] During the trial, Upadhyay did not wear his usual saffron robes; he did not wish to be accorded any special privilege. Dressed in simple white *swadeshi* clothes, he once more wore the sacred thread proudly. He was entitled to do so now that he had performed *prāyaścitta*. The gruelling hours standing in the dock took their toll. The old hernia complaint (recall his acute discomfort during his journey to England in 1902) reasserted itself. Though in increasing pain, he did not ask for the support of a chair. Eventually he could continue no longer and on Monday, October 21, arrived for treatment at the Campbell Hospital (now the Nilratan Sircar Hospital).

Upadhyay was operated on for hernia the next day. His entry in the hospital register against 'caste', reads 'Brahmin' (Bl., p. 173). 'Three times he was asked to state his religion, but he refused to comply with the request' (ibid.). If he thought it was a straightforward issue of his having become a Hindu again, there was nothing to prevent him from entering 'Hindu' in the register. The operation, we are told, was a success, and Upadhyay began to make good progress. The case was postponed to November 18, pending his recovery.[29] Friends and well-wishers visited him in hospital. On Wednesday October 23, when a friend, Sadhu Vasvani, came to see him, Upadhyay said 'in the course of [a] conversation ... looking back at the ups and downs of his chequered career... "Wonderful have been the vicissitudes of my life; wonderful has been my faith"' (Bl., p. 174). On Thursday and Friday he continued to do well, though on Saturday the 26th a friend noticed signs of anxiety and depression, for Upadhyay had heard of the re-arrest of Saradacaran and Haricaran; he was particularly close to the young Saradacaran and concerned for his welfare.[30] He was visited by 'fifty gentlemen ... read the newspapers and discussed the articles to be put in the Sandhya' (p. 174). From 4 p.m. he began to feel a pain in his neck; the discomfort gradually increased till at

28 *The Blade* says 'from 10 to 4' (p. 173).

29 In the meantime, on or about October 24, the manager and printer of the *Sandhya* were re-arrested on a new charge of sedition; this time they were not granted bail.

30 This sequence of events, based on an eyewitness report, is given in *The Blade*, pp. 173ff.

8 o'clock a spasm occurred: Upadhyay was suffering from a form of tetanus commonly called lockjaw.

How he got this fell disease is not clear; he did not eat the hospital food. In accordance with caste rules, his food would be brought from 'a Brahmin's house' (Bl., p. 174). Perhaps the food, or some aspect of his treatment, carried the infection. After 8 p.m. the spasms became more frequent and grew worse ('every twelve or fifteen minutes'). 'When oppressed with pain, the patient exclaimed "O Thakur"' (Bl., p. 175). *Thākur* is often used by Bengalis as a friendly expression for God (rather as Christians might say 'The/Our Lord' when referring to Christ). *The Blade* recounts evidence for Upadhyay's regular use of this term in reference to Christ, as when he conducted the weekly Wednesday devotions in Kartik Nan's house. There can be no doubt that by *Ṭhākur* in these dire moments Upadhyay was referring to Christ as his divine Lord.

The few remaining hours saw a speedy and most painful onset of the disease. Medical relief was sought by those attending him and crude attempts were made to pour a few drops of milk or water into the exhausted patient's clenched mouth. 'Altogether more than thirty spasms occurred. The hands closed; the jaw was locked; he made fearful faces. This lasted for about two minutes and the spasm left him. He remained in a coma-like state.... Upadhyay felt suffocated' (Bl., pp. 175–6).

At about 8 o'clock on the Sunday morning his surgeon, Dr Mrigendralal Mitter, reappeared (he had last attended shortly after midnight). Upadhyay asked to be relieved of the pain; Dr Mitter agreed, and after consulting briefly with a group of eight other doctors in another room, made an attempt to treat him.

> As the medicine could not be introduced through the mouth, they tried with a catheter tube. In trying to force the jaws open a couple of front teeth got broken. His face and hands became covered with blood. This brought on another spasm. They said they would use chloroform. He replied that he wanted to die fully conscious. They proceeded in spite of his desire. Barely two or three minutes passed and Dr Kedar Das, M.D. exclaimed 'Stop!' They laid him on the ground and tried artificial respiration for some eight minutes. A galvanic battery was applied. But all in vain. His great spirit had left the body. It was about 8.30 a.m. on Sunday, October 27th, 1907. Upadhyay was in his 47th year (Bl., p. 176).

It was only about a week from the time of his entering the hospital till his death, and barely 16 hours from the apparent onset of the disease till its grim conclusion.

Did Upadhyay die a Christian? If to die as a Christian entails personally acknowledging Christ to the end as one's divine saviour, then he seems to have died a Christian. But if part of dying a Christian means that one must be recognized in the public forum to have lived ritually as a Christian before death, then it is doubtful if Upadhyay died a Christian. Did he die a Hindu? If self-ascription has a bearing on one's answer, then he did, since he famously described himself in considered terms both as a 'Hindu-Catholic' and a Hindu, and never repudiated this description. Certainly, for reasons already given, so far as the general public was concerned he died a Hindu. I have added these comments because for some people applying religious labels to dead individuals is an important matter, as it seems to be in the case of Upadhyay. Perhaps he died as he lived: as a Hindu and a Christian according to his own distinctive lights. That by his life and death he has raised such an issue for serious debate can be one of his most rewarding legacies. How narrow must our religious labels be? How open to hyphenated religious identities should we become? What is the scope for religious dialogue in a religio-culturally divisive world?[31]

Whether Upadhyay died as a Christian or not, he was not buried as one. The news of his death spread rapidly, and crowds of people began to gather at the hospital. The hospital authorities, increasingly nervous at the mounting excitement, required the body to be removed. At about 1 p.m. as the body was being carried out of the hospital, the Jesuit parish priest arrived, but neither he nor Animananda was allowed to claim the body. There was no proof, said Upadhyay's Hindu friends, that the deceased had died a Catholic; the body now belonged to the people. The body was placed on the roadside under a tree while further preparations were made. Upadhyay was then carried in procession by friends and relatives towards the *Sandhya* office, the flower-bedecked bier stopping on occasion along the way,[32] and the numbers joining the procession mounting.

At the *Sandhya* office it was announced that the procession to the cremation ground would start at 4 p.m. About five thousand people

[31] The author has discussed these questions at some length in his Dasturzada Dr Jal Pavry Memorial Lecture and Seminars given in the University of Oxford in May 1997; these are being prepared for publication.

[32] One such stop was in front of the building of the Sadharan Samaj so that the Sadharanists could pay their respects.

had gathered by the time it started. One must remember that through the *Sandhya* Upadhyay spoke to the common man and woman, and at this hour of farewell, it was especially they who responded. The procession, chanting *bande mātaram,* wound its way from Sibnarayan Das Lane, along Cornwallis Street, Beadon Street and Nimtolla Ghat Street to the cremation ground, having passed Bethune Row—so familiar to Upadhyay—on the way. The cremation ground was reached at about 5.30 p.m. Some patriotic songs were sung and a number of poignant speeches made. Since Upadhyay had no offspring of his own, the funeral pyre was lit by a nephew. The flames were fed by streams of *ghi* and quantities of sandalwood. Songs continued to be sung and people came up to the pyre to pay their respects till well into the night. Thus were Upadhyay's mortal remains reduced to ashes.

What did this remarkable revolutionary, this forgotten colossus, achieve by his life and death? A number of condolence meetings and widespread coverage in the Bengal press, both vernacular and English, marked his passing. The usual silly rumours and fancies did their rounds: he was poisoned; he committed suicide to thwart the British; he chose the hour and manner of his death to avoid imprisonment and humiliation by the authorities (in either case it might well have occurred to him to die in less traumatic circumstances). But after the fuss, save for sporadic newspaper and journal articles especially in the early decades, he was largely forgotten by an era that loved to pigeon-hole and was ill equipped to come to terms with the enigmatic elusiveness of the man. Almost every side in the polarized religious, social, and political culture of the times could wonder of him: 'One of us or one of them?'—and either bemused, or with the failing bravado of imposed certainties, may well have found it more convenient to draw a veil over his memory.

But perhaps the time has come, in a world more sensitive to human frailties and ambiguities, to recover and reassess Upadhyay. He was and could still be of immense consequence in a number of areas. In modern times, in the context of interreligious relations, he did more by thought and deed than perhaps any other Indian Christian to raise key issues for debate. Is there a legitimate method by which one may engage in religio-cultural discussion? Across cultural and religious divides is there a 'natural platform', to use Upadhyay's expression, on the basis of which, first, cross-cultural religious understanding and then, the transaction of cognitive content, is possible? Some incommensurabilists say there is not, but others say there is common ground.[33] It was Upadhyay more than any other Indian Christian in British India, I believe, who notably made it an issue by his numerous theological writings. It was the appropriate climate, almost single-handedly created by him in Catholic circles, that subsequently encouraged such sustained publications as the Jesuit *Light of the East* to take the matter further.

For Upadhyay, reflection was not enough. His very appearance, soon after his conversion, saffron-robed and becrossed, was a living challenge to the alienating modes of Christian behaviour, practice and teaching that had taken root in the land. The Jabalpur monastery was a practical extension of his thinking and way of life; the experiment fizzled out for want of appropriate support, but reappeared decades later—and there was express acknowledgement of Upadhyay's influence in the re-creation—in the Shantivanam ashram in south India. Today, Indian Christian ashrams are a commonplace.

Though Upadhyay's theological conclusions are controversial—I have argued that they are largely neo-Thomism in Sanskritic disguise—not only is their methodology, as noted, thought-provoking ('If cross-cultural dialogue is possible, how exactly is it viable in context: by way of linguistic correspondence, bridging metaphor(s), *praxis* rather than *theoria*, or what?'), but their message raises key questions of the patriotic aspirations of the convert. Specifically, is Christianity as believed and practised in its multifarious forms in India (or in any traditionally 'alien' environment) perceived by the majority to be an indigenous phenomenon, furthering the common weal? Certainly it should be, if native Christians are to play their rightful part in shaping the destiny of their nation. To consider Upadhyay is not only to be unable to evade this crucial question, but is also to be impelled to seek some practical response. The consuming passion of his life was to be not simply a Christian, but a *patriotic* Christian for *all* to eventually appreciate and emulate.

But Upadhyay's theological contributions do not end here. Many even of his dialogic Christian writings, notwithstanding their Thomistic derivation, are genuinely stimulating if not inspiring. Among these his Sanskrit hymn, *Vande Saccidānandam,* occupies a special place. Nevertheless, a further question must be raised. Were not Upadhyay's dialogic preoccupations theologically elitist? On the Hindu side, he concerned himself exclusively with the Hinduism of the elite; indeed, he showed scant understanding of and respect for the religious

33 The author has argued for the possibility of such dialogue. See his 'Philosophy and World Religions', in Davies, 1998.

aspirations and heritage of dalit Christians, viz. those who come from 'oppressed' castes and classes. It must be noted that most Christians in India today are of dalit derivation. Again, this issue is not a straightforward one. The solution is not to discount Sanskritic Hinduism in the ongoing dialogue with Christianity in India. This would be to neglect immensely rich, deep, and even pervasive theological insights; it would be another form of cultural extremism. All significant religio-cultural heritages of India must be embraced, in different ways in different contexts, in the Christian synthesis of an indigenized faith. But the solution is also not to denigrate or overlook the heritages of large constituencies of less-advantaged Christians. No doubt, Upadhyay functioned in times when Christian Churches were less prone to affirm 'a preferential option for the poor'. This must be taken into account. Nevertheless, even in Upadhyay's time, both Catholic and Protestant Churches laid plenty of emphasis on the need to pay special attention to the poor and disadvantaged. In his consuming passion to reach out to and identify with his (bhadralok) compatriots, Upadhyay seemed not to be sensitive enough to this emphasis.

But, as we have seen, later in life he also wrote powerfully and instructively on Hindu religious ideas for a Hindu readership. Though his elevation of (his interpretation of Advaitic) Vedanta and Krishna as common bases for pan-Hindu religious belief and solidarity may have been elitist and impractical, Hindus themselves have acknowledged the many fine insights he expressed on Hindu religious concepts, symbols and practices. It is good that a collection of some of these pieces has been published (Ghosh, 1987). A fuller anthology should be prepared and given wider publicity.[34] No doubt by generally disdaining those who were culturally or religiously non-Hindu in these writings (especially the Muslims and the British), Upadhyay expressed some objectionable sentiments; nevertheless, he was a keen observer and brilliant communicator, and in his popular publications, especially for the *Sandhya* and *Bangabasi*, he is credited with propagating a fresh journalistic style that must have had an inestimable literary impact on his contemporaries and future generations.[35]

34 A substantial number of Upadhyay's available articles have been translated into English by the author for vol. 2 of the anthology of Upadhyay's works, edited by G. Gispert-Sauch and the author, for the Library of Indian Christian Theology, and published by The United Theological College, Bangalore (forthcoming).

35 Recall too Upadhyay's formative role in establishing the *Jote* in Sind; the journal continued as an influential trendsetter for style and content for many years

We must not forget here the influence he had on perhaps the greatest Bengali savant of the twentieth century, Rabindranath Tagore. Upadhyay's indigenizing ideals played a pioneering role in establishing not only Tagore's school at Santiniketan (not to mention the Sarasvata Ayatan), but also other institutions with comparable goals, for example, Animananda's Boys' Own Home, which received effusive praise in subsequent years for its educational work not only from the British authorities but also from Tagore himself. As we have noted, Upadhyay played a significant didactic part in Tagore's creative writing by appearing in more than one character in his novels.

Upadhyay's impact on the national movement in Bengal, directly and indirectly, especially after his return from England, was incalculable. Even before leaving for England, his articles in the *Bangadarsan* under Tagore's editorship were significant. Besides providing subtle (and controversial) analyses of Hindu society and thought, these articles contributed to the standardization of Hinduism in the understanding of Bengali intellectuals through Upadhyay's construct of *hindutva*, which, as we have seen, consisted of two facets: *varṇāśrama dharma,* and the Hindu's intuitive approach of one-centredness. Caste was idealized and rehabilitated; *hindutva* intellectually became an exclusivistic synthetizing process, a form of penetrative intuition into the underlying core reality of a thing. The advantage of this form of analysis is to confer a simple, unitive clarity to the object analysed on the basis of which a sense of solidarity among its appropriators is generated; the disadvantage is that as a construct it may not reflect the more multifarious reality 'on the ground', and is likely to alienate or marginalize those who do not fall under its purview.

Through the *Sandhya,* Upadhyay almost single-handedly popularized the Bengal nationalist movement in the context of the 1905 partition agitation among the newly-formed (Hindu) urban 'middle-class'.[36] A significant proportion of the readership was

---

subsequently. Though an attempt was made to continue the *Sandhya* after Upadhyay's death, the paper folded in 1908.

36 Among the bhadralok or more westernized elite the *Bande Mataram* played a similar though less widespread popularizing role (many readers of the *Bande Mataram* would also have read the *Sandhya,* of course); here too, it should be noted, Upadhyay made a significant contribution. He played a leading role in getting the newly started *Bande Mataram* off the ground (see testimony of Hemendra Prasad Ghose, one of the first journalists of the paper, as given in *The Bengalee* of 26.10.1924; Bl. p. 192).

certainly not of the elite; they belonged to what some would call the *petite bourgeoisie.*[37] Through its popularizing impact, the *Sandhya* had a standardizing effect, not only linguistically, but also socially and politically. In spite of its vituperative style, its non-elitist idiom also generated self-esteem among its readership and by injecting a religious tone with special reference to Goddess symbolism into political discourse, helped create a sense of Hindu solidarity.[38] More research needs to be done on these features of the *Sandhya*'s impact.

Last but not least, one must take note of Upadhyay's powerful *charisma.* Such a contentious man, yet so persuasive of apparently improbable dreams and ideas, and such a purveyor of profound and lasting loyalties! It was his deep spirituality, earnestness and intensity of commitment that won people over, and led them to look for extenuating circumstances in the face of his excesses. As India and the world look to the future through the turbulent past of its nationalist history and post-independence years, may Brahmabandhab Upadhyay, 'friend of God' and 'teacher' of the people, stand out as a salient marker—religiously, socially and politically—of battles still to be fought and victories yet to be won.

[37] Sumit Sarkar describes them as 'the Hindu lower middle class' (1973: 259).

[38] Though the *Sandhya* occasionally issued calls for Hindu-Muslim unity to oppose and boycott the British, its general tone and message were overwhelmingly pro-Hindu. Note, however, that 'after the winter of 1906–7, [the Muslim] Liakat Husain broke sharply with the moderates—he was now to be found addressing meetings jointly with Pal and Brahmabandhab Upadhyay, and put up for a time at the *Sandhya* offices' (Sumit Sarkar, 1973: 434). So there were exceptions.

# References

## Upadhyay's Works (including articles, and journals started by him)


*The Harmony*, monthly, 1890.

'A short treatise on the existence of God' (tract), Victoria Press, Karachi, 1893.

'The Infinite and the finite' (tract), 1896(?), 3rd ed., 1918.

*Sophia*, monthly, Karachi and Calcutta, 1894–99.

*Jote*, started 1896.

*Sophia*, weekly, Calcutta, 1900.

*The Twentieth Century*, monthly, Calcutta, 1901–2.

*Panchadasi: A Literal English Translation with Original Texts and a Commentary in English*, by B. Upadhyay, R.C. Ghosh, Kaiser Machine Press, 48 Grey Street, Calcutta, 1902.

'Christianity in India' in two parts, *The Tablet*, Jan. 3, 31, 1903.

*Sandhya*, started 1904.

*Svaraj*, weekly, Calcutta, 1907.

*Karali*, bi-weekly, Calcutta (dates not available).

*Amar Bharat Uddhar*, Prabarttak Publishing House, Candannagar, B.E. 1331.


Collections of Upadhyay's writings:

## English (with translations)


*The Writings of Brahmabandhab Upadhyay, Vol. I (Including a Résumé of His Life and Thought)*, ed. J. Lipner and G. Gispert-Sauch, s.j., The United Theological College, Bangalore, 1991; Vol. 2 (which includes translations from the Bengali), in press.

## Bengali

*Samaj*, Burman Publishing House, Calcutta, n.d. (75 pp.): contains various articles.

*Pal-Parbban*, Prabarttak Publishing House, Chandannagar, n.d. (40 pp.): contains various articles.

*Brahmabandhab Upadhyayer Racana Samgraha*, ed. Baridbaran Ghosh, publ. Samiran Chaudhuri, College Street Publications Pvt Ltd., Calcutta, 1987 (228 pp. +): contains various articles (including all those in *Samaj* and *Pal-Parbban*) and the letters to *Bangabasi*.

## Manuscripts/Archives

*An Indian Nation-Builder: Brahmabandhab Upadhyay (1861–1907)*, by B. Animananda (Rewachand Gyanchand), Goethal's Library Archive, St Xavier's College, Calcutta.

*Light of the East*, ed. G. Dandoy, s.j., in collaboration with P. Johanns, s.j., Calcutta, 1922–46, Goethal's Library Archive, St Xavier's College, Calcutta.

*Father Louis Lacombe, s.j.*, The Catholic Truth Society of India, Trichinopoly, 1930.

*Upadhyay File*, Archives of Rabindra Bhaban, Santiniketan, West Bengal.

*Varia*, in 5 volumes, Goethal's Library Archive, St Xavier's College, Calcutta.

## Early Journals consulted (other than those edited by Upadhyay)

*Arya Messenger*, Lahore, 1894–.

*Bangadarsan*, New Series, Calcutta, 1901–.

*The Bombay Catholic Examiner*, Bombay, 1896–.

*The Calcutta Review*, 1844.

*The Concord* (monthly), Calcutta, January–June, 1887.

*The Friend of India*, Serampore, 1824.

*Theistic Quarterly Review*, Calcutta, 1879.

*The Theistic Review and Interpreter*, Simla, 1881–.

## General

Abhishiktananda, Swami (aka Dom Henri le Saux): (editor and part-author), *Swami Parama Arubi Anandam (Fr J. Monchanin), 1895–1957: A Memorial*. Saccidananda Ashram, 1959.

———, (co-author with Abbé Jules Monchanin), *A Benedictine Ashram.* Times Press Ltd., Douglas, Isle of Man, 1964 (rev. ed.).

———, (co-author with Abbé Jules Monchanin), *Saccidananda: a Christian Approach to Advaitic Experience.* ISPCK, Delhi, 1974.

Advaita Ashrama, *The Life of Swami Vivekananda.* Almora, 1960 ed.

———, *Life of Sri Ramakrishna.* Calcutta, 1928 (2nd ed.) and 1971 (9th impression).

Ahmed, Akbar, *Jinnah, Pakistan and Islamic Identity: The Search for Saladin,* Routledge, London, 1997.

Aleaz, K.P., 'The Theological Writings of Brahmabandhav Upadhyay Re-examined', *Indian Journal of Theology,* April–June 1979.

———, *The Gospel of Indian Culture.* Punthi Pustak, Calcutta, 1994.

———, *Jesus in Neo-Vedanta: A Meeting of Hinduism and Christianity,* Kant Publications, Delhi, 1995.

Ali, M.M., *The Bengali Reaction to Christian Missionary Activities, 1833–57.* Mehrub Publications, Mehrub, Chittagong, 1965.

Animananda, B., *Swami Upadhyay Brahmabandhav: A sketch in two parts.* Publ. by the author, Calcutta, 1908.

———, 'Swami Upadhyay Brahmabandhav', in *The New Review,* 1 (Jan–June), 1935, ed. M. Ledrus s.j. Published by C.A. Parkhurst for Macmillan & Co., Ltd., Calcutta.

———, 'How I found Christ', in *Light of the East,* ed. G. Dandoy s.j., June, 1935.

———, *The Blade: Life and Work of Brahmabandhab Upadhyay.* Roy and Son, Calcutta, n.d. [1946].

Aquinas, Thomas, *Summa Theologiae,* Blackfriars edition.

Argov, D., *Moderates and Extremists in the Indian Nationalist Movement, 1883–1920 with special reference to Surendranath Banerjea and Lajpat Rai.* Asia Publishing House, London, 1967.

Bagal, Jogescandra, *Brahmabāndhab Upādhyāy.* Published by Sri Sanatkumar Gupta, Bangiya Sahitya Parisat, Calcutta, B.E. 1371 (C.E. 1964).

Banerjea, Krishnamohan, 'The Kulin Brahmins of Bengal', *Calcutta Review,* 2 (3), 1844.

———, *Dialogues on the Hindu Philosophy comprising the Nyaya, the Sankhya, the Vedant, to which is added a discussion of the Authority of the Vedas* (1st ed. 1861), 2nd ed. The Christian Literature Society for India, London and Madras, 1903.

Banerjea, Surendranath, *A Nation in Making*. Oxford University Press, Calcutta, 1925 and 1963.

———, *Speeches and Writings of Hon. Surendranath Banerjea (Selected by himself)*. Natesan & Co., Madras, n.d.

Banerjee, Sumanta, *The Parlour and the Streets*. Seagull Books, Calcutta, 1989.

Banerji, G.C., *Keshab Chandra and Ramkrishna*. Published by the author (?), Allahabad, 1931.

Barber, B.R., *Kali Charan Banurji: Brahmin, Christian, Saint*. The Christian Literature Society for India, London, Madras and Colombo, 1912.

Basu, Prabhat, 'Biplober Dīkṣāguru Brahmabāndhab Upādhyāy', in *Jugāntar Sāmayik*, B.E. 23 Phālgun, 1354 (C.E. 7 March, 1948).

Basu, T., P. Datta, S. Sarkar, T. Sarkar and S. Sen, *Khaki Shorts and Saffron Flags: A Critique of the Hindu Right*. Orient Longman, Hyderabad, 1993.

Bayly, C.A., *Indian Society and the Making of the British Empire*, II.1, in *The New Cambridge History of India*. Cambridge University Press, 1988.

Bayly, Susan, 'Hindu modernizers and the public arena: Indigenous critiques of caste in Colonial India', in C.W. Radice (ed.). Oxford University Press, 1998.

Bharadwaja, Chiranjiva. See Sarasvati, Dayananda

Borthwick, M., *The Changing Role of Women in Bengal 1849–1905*. Princeton University Press, 1984.

Boyd, R.H.S., *India and the Latin Captivity of the Church: the Cultural Context of the Gospel*. Cambridge University Press, 1974.

Breckenridge, C. A., and P. van der Veer (eds), *Orientalism and the Postcolonial Predicament: Perspectives on South Asia*. University of Pennsylvania Press, 1993.

Broomfield, J.H., *Elite Conflict in a Plural Society: Twentieth-century Bengal*. University of California Press, Berkeley and Los Angeles, 1968.

Cannon, G. and K. Brine (eds), *Objects of Inquiry: The Life, Contributions, and Influences of Sir William Jones (1746–1794)*. New York University Press, New York and London, 1995.

Census of India, 1901, vol. VII, *Calcutta, Town and Suburbs, Part III*, Bengal Secretariat Press, Calcutta, 1902.

Chatterjee, Bankimcandra, *Kṛṣṇacaritra* in *Baṅkimcandrer Granthābalī*, Part II. Published by Upendranath Mukhopadhyay, Calcutta, B.E. 1316 (C.E. 1909).

Chaudhuri, Sukanta (ed.), *Calcutta: The Living City (Vol. 1: The Past)*. Oxford University Press, Calcutta, 1990.

Colaco, P.A., *Select Writings of the Most Reverend Dr Leo Meurin, s.j. with a Biographical Sketch of His Life*. Examiner Press, Bombay, 1891.

Crawford, S Cromwell, *Ram Mohan Roy: Social, Political, and Religious Reform in 19th Century India*. Paragon House Publishers, New York, 1987.

Damen, F.L., *Crisis and Religious Renewal in the Brahmo Samaj (1860–1884): A Documentary Study of the Emergence of the 'New Dispensation' under Keshab Chandra Sen*. Katholieke Universiteit Leuven, Leuven, 1983.

Das, Sajanikanta, (i) 'Phiriṅgibhay-hārī Brahmabāndhab', in *Śanibārer Ciṭhi*, B.E. Āśvin 1368 (C.E. October 1961).

———, (ii) 'Bāṅglār nabajāgaraṇer pratyuṣ—Sandhyā', in *Biśvabhāratī Patrikā*, 18.2, B.E. Kārtik-Pauṣ, 1368.

Dasgupta, Uma, 'Santiniketan and Sriniketan', in *Visvabharata Quarterly*, vol. 41, (1–4), May 1975 to April 1976, pp. 270–325.

Day, Lal Behari, *Govinda Samanta or the History of a Bengal Raiyat*, vol. I. Macmillan & Co., London, 1874.

Davies, B. (ed), *Philosophy of Religion: A Guide to the Subject*. Geoffrey Chapman, London, 1998.

Debsarma, Bolai, *Brahmabāndhab Upādhyāy*. Prabartak Publishers, Calcutta, B.E. 1368 (C.E. 1961).

de Melo, Carlos Merces, *The Recruitment and Formation of the Native Clergy in India (16th–19th century): An Historico-Canonical Study*, Thesis defended at the Gregorian University, Rome, for the Doctorate in Canon Law, 1954. Published by Agencia Geral do Ultramar Divisao de Publicacoes e Biblioteca, Portugal, 1955.

de Steenhault, Y., 'Fr Vath on Upadhyay Brahmabandhav', in *Indian Theological Studies*, 30 (3), September 1993.

Deussen, P., *System of the Vedanta* (originally in German, entitled *Das System des Vedanta*, F.A. Brockhaus, Leipzig, 1883), first translated into English in 1912.

Dharwadker, Vinay, 'Orientalism and the Study of Indian Literatures', in Breckenridge and van der Veer (eds), 1993.

di Bruno, Joseph Faa, *Catholic Belief or A Short and Simple Exposition of Catholic Doctrine*. Burns & Oates, London and New York, 1884 (5th ed.).

Duff, Alexander, *India, and India Missions.* Published by John Johnstone, Edinburgh, 1839.

Fallon, Pierre, 'Brahmabāndhab Upādhyāy', in *Viśvabhāratī Patrikā,* 18.2, B.E. Kārtik-Pauṣ, 1368 (C.E. 1961).

Farquhar, J.N., *Gita and Gospel* (1st ed. 1903), 2nd ed. Published by CLS, London, Madras and Colombo, 1906.

Fonseca, C., (i) 'A Prophet Disowned: Swami Upadhyaya Brahmabandhav', in *Vidyajyoti: Journal of Theological Reflection,* April 1980.

———, (ii) 'Upadhyaya Brahmabandhav: The Political Years', in *Indian Church History Review,* XIV, (1), 1980.

Forsyth, Capt. J., *The Highlands of Central India: Notes on their Forests and Wild Tribes, Natural History and Sports.* London, Chapman & Hall Ltd., 1919 ed.

Gangopadhyay, Prasanta, 'Bāṅglāgadya: Saṅgbādikatā', in *Bhāratbarṣa,* Agrahāyaṇ, B.E. 1371 (C.E. 1964).

Ghosh, J.C., *Bengali Literature.* Oxford University Press, London, 1948.

Gispert-Sauch, G. 'The Sanskrit hymns of Brahmabandhav Upadhyay', in *Religion and Society,* xix, 1972.

Gordon, Leonard A., *Bengal: The Nationalist Movement 1876–1940.* Columbia University Press, New York and London, 1974.

Government of India (Occasional Reports No.6): *Educational Buildings in India,* Calcutta, 1911.

Gough, A.E., *The Philosophy of the Upanishads and Ancient Indian Metaphysics,* 2nd ed. Kegan Paul, Trench, Trubner and Co. Ltd., London, 1891.

Guha, Manoranjan, *Brahmabāndhab Upādhyāy.* Published by Sri Sadhana Bhattacarya, Siksa Niketan, Bardhaman, B.E. 1383 (C.E. 1976).

Gupta, Samita, 'Theory and practice of town planning in Calcutta, 1817 to 1912: An Appraisal', in *The Indian Economic and Social History Review,* 30 (1) 1993, pp. 29ff.

Hawley, J.S. and Wulff, D.M. (eds), *The Divine Consort: Radha and the Goddesses of India.* Motilal Banarsidass (Ind. ed.), Delhi, 1984.

Heehs, Peter, *The Bomb in Bengal: The Rise of Revolutionary Terrorism in India 1900–1910.* Oxford University Press, Delhi, 1993.

———, 'Bengali Religious Nationalism and Communalism', in *International Journal of Hindu Studies,* 1.1, 1997.

Heiler, F., *The Gospel of Sadhu Sundar Singh.* Abridged trans. by O. Wyon, Indian Society for Promoting Christian Knowledge, Delhi, and Christian Institute for Sikh Studies, Batala; New Delhi, 1989.

Hull, E.R., *Bombay Mission–History with a special study of the Padroado Question* (2 vols). Examiner Press, Bombay, n.d.

Jackson, Carl T., *The Oriental Religions and American Thought: Nineteenth Century Explorations.* Greenwood Press, Westport, Connecticut and London, UK, 1981.

Jarrett-Kerr, M., *Patterns of Christian Acceptance: Individual Response to the Missionary Impact.* Oxford University Press, London, 1972.

Jitatmananda, Swami, 'Brahmabandhav Upadhyay and Swami Vivekananda', in *Prabuddha Bharata,* May 1981.

Jones, Kenneth W., *Arya Dharm: Hindu Consciousness in 19th Century Punjab.* University of California Press, 1976. .

Jordens, J.T.F., *Dayananda Sarasvati. His Life and Ideas.* Oxford University Press, Delhi, 1978.

Kaviraj, Sudipta., *The Unhappy Consciousness: Bankimchandra Chattopadhyay and the Formation of Nationalist Discourse in India.* Oxford University Press, Delhi, 1995.

Killingley, D.H., *Rammohan Roy's interpretation of the Vedanta.* Ph.D. thesis, University of London, 1977.

———, '*Yoga-Sutra* IV, 2–3 and Vivekananda's Interpretation of Evolution', in *Journal of Indian Philosophy,* vol. 18, 1990.

Kling, B.B., *The Blue Mutiny. The Indigo Disturbances in Bengal, 1859–1862.* University of Pennsylvania Press, Philadelphia, 1966.

———, 'Economic Foundations of the Bengal Renaissance', in Rachel Van M. Baumer (ed.), *Aspects of Bengali History and Society,* University Press of Hawaii, 1975.

Kopf, David, *British Orientalism and the Bengal Renaissance: The Dynamics of Indian Modernization, 1773–1835.* University of California Press, Berkeley and Los Angeles, 1969.

———, *The Brahmo Samaj and the Shaping of the Modern Indian Mind.* Princeton University Press, 1979.

———, 'The Historiography of British Orientalism, 1772–1992', in Cannon, and Brine (eds), 1995.

Lavaranne C., *Swami Brahmabandhab Upadhyay (1861–1907): Theologie chretienne et pensee du Vedanta.* Ph.D. thesis, Universite de Provence, 1992.

le Saux, Henri, See under Abhishiktananda, Swami.

Leslie, I. Julia, *The Perfect Wife: The Orthodox Hindu Woman according to the Strīdharmapaddhati of Tryambakayajvan.* Oxford University Press, Delhi, 1989.

Lipner, J., 'The One-Centredness of the Hindu Race', annotated trans. of B. Upadhyay's *Hindujātir Eknisthatā,* in *Vidyajyoti: Journal of Theological Reflection,* Delhi, October 1981.

———, 'A modern Indian Christian Response', in H.G. Coward (ed.), *Modern Indian Responses to Religious Pluralism.* State University of New York Press, 1987.

———, 'On Woman and Salvation in Hinduism: Paradoxes of Ambivalence', in N. Smart and S. Thakur (eds), 1993.

———, *Hindus: Their Religious Beliefs and Practices.* Routledge, London, 1994 (paperback 1998).

———, 'Ancient Banyan: An Inquiry into the Meaning of "Hinduness"', in *Religious Studies,* 32, March 1996.

———, 'Philosophy and World Religions', in B. Davies (ed.), 1998.

Littledale, R.F., *Plain Reasons against Joining the Church of Rome.* SPCK, London, 1881–2.

Lopez, Donald S. jr. (ed.), *Religions of India in Practice.* Princeton University Press, 1995.

'M': *Śrī Śrī Rāmkrṣṇakathāmṛta.* Published by Sri A.K. Gupta, 17th ed., Calcutta, B.E. 1356.

McDermott, Rachel F., 'Bengali Songs to Kali', in Donald S. Lopez, jr. (ed.), *Religions of India in Practice.* Princeton University Press, 1995.

Majumdar, R.C. (ed.), *The History and Culture of the Indian People,* vol. 10, *British Paramountcy and Indian Renaissance,* Part II. Bharatiya Vidya Bhavan, Bombay, 1965.

Manning, H.E., *The Internal Mission of the Holy Ghost.* Burns & Oates, London, 1875.

Marshall, P.J., *The British Discovery of Hinduism in the Eighteenth Century.* Cambridge University Press, 1970.

———, *Bengal: The British Bridgehead. Eastern India, 1740–1820,* II.2 in *The New Cambridge History of India.* Cambridge University Press, 1987.

Marshman, Joshua, 'Reply to Rammohun Roy's finai appeal against the atonement and the Deity of Christ,' in *The Friend of India,* Serampore, 1824.

Mitra, P.K., 'The Derozian Revolt: Rationalist Dissent and Orthodox Reaction in Nineteenth-Century Bengal', in *The Journal of the Institute of Bangladesh Studies*, Institute of Bangladesh Studies, Rajshahi University, vol. XI, 1988.

Monchanin, J. and H. le Saux, *A Benedictine Ashram*. Times Press, Douglas, Isle of Man, 1964 (rev. ed.).

Morris, Donald R., *The Washing of the Spears: A History of the Rise of the Zulu Nation under Shaka and Its Fall in the Zulu War of 1879*. Jonathan Cape Ltd., 1965.

Morris, James, *Heaven's Command: An Imperial Progress*. Faber & Faber, London, 1973.

Mukherjee, H. and U. (see Mukhopadhyay).

Mukherjee, Nilmani, *A Bengal Zamindar: Jaykrishna Mukherjee of Uttarpara and His Times, 1808–1888*. Firma K.L. Mukhopadhyay, Calcutta, 1975.

Mukherjee S.N., *Sir William Jones: A Study in Eighteenth-century British Attitudes to India*. Cambridge University Press, 1968.

Mukhopadhyay, Haridas, *Binoy Sarkārer Baiṭhake*. Cakrabarti, Cyatarji & Company Ltd., Calcutta, 1942.

Mukhopadhyay, Uma and Haridas, *India's Fight for Freedom or the Swadeshi Movement (1905–1906)*. Firma K.L. Mukhopadhyay, Calcutta, 1958.

———, *Upādhyāy Brahmabāndhab o bhāratīya jātīyatābād*. Firma K.L. Mukhopadhyay, Calcutta, 1961.

Nandy, Ashis, *At the Edge of Psychology: Essays in Politics and Culture*. Oxford University Press, Delhi, 1980.

———, *The Intimate Enemy: Loss and Recovery of Self under Colonialism*. Oxford University Press, Oxford and New Delhi, 1983.

———, *The Illegitimacy of Nationalism: Rabindranath Tagore and the Politics of Self*. Oxford University Press, Delhi, 1994.

Neill, Stephen, *A History of Christianity in India, 1707–1858*. Cambridge University Press, 1985.

Neuner, J., s.j. and J. Dupuis, s.j. (eds), *The Christian Faith in the Doctrinal Documents of the Catholic Church*, rev. ed. Collins Liturgical Publications, London, 1983.

Nistarini Devi, *Sekele Kathā*, in *Āptakathā* (vol. 2), ed. by N. Jana, M. Jana and K. Sanyal. Ananya Prakasan, Calcutta, 1982.

Olivelle, P., *The Āśrama System: the History and Hermeneutics of a Religious Institution.* Oxford University Press, 1993.

Pal, Prasanta K., *Rabijībanī,* vols 1ff. Ananda Publishers Ltd., Calcutta, 1982–.

Peterson, Peter, *Hymns from the Rigveda edited with Sayana's Commentary, Notes and a Translation.* Bombay Sanskrit Series, No. XXXVI, Government Central Book Depot, 1888.

Philip, T.V., *Krishna Mohan Banerjea: Christian Apologist.* The Christian Literature Society, Madras, 1982.

Pollock, S., 'Deep Orientalism? Notes on Sanskrit and Power Beyond the Raj', in Breckenridge. C.A. and van der Veer (eds), 1993.

Potts, E. Daniel, *British Baptist Missionaries in India, 1793–1837.* Cambridge University Press, 1967.

Radice, C.W. (ed.), *Swami Vivekananda and the Modernization of Hinduism.* Oxford University Press, Delhi, 1998.

Raychaudhuri, T., *Europe Reconsidered: Perceptions of the West in Nineteenth Century Bengal.* Oxford University Press, Delhi, 1988.

Reichenbach, B., *The Law of Karma: A Philosophical Study.* Macmillan, London, 1990.

Report of the Council of Education, Bengal Presidency, for 1851–52.

*Report of Native Newspapers in Bengal,* 1903–

Roy, Manisha, *Bengali Women.* University of Chicago Press, Chicago and London, 1975.

Roy, Rammohan, *The Precepts of Jesus, the Guide to Peace and Happiness extracted from the Books of the New Testament ascribed to the four Evangelists to which are added the First, Second and Final Appeal to the Christian Public in reply to the Observations of Dr. Marshman of Serampore.* London Unitarian Society, 1834 (2nd ed.).

Said, E., *Orientalism.* Penguin, 1985.

Sarasvati, Dayanand, *Satyarth Prakas; Light of Truth or An English Translation of the Satyarth Prakash,* by Dr Chiranjiva Bharadwaja. Sarvadeshik Arya Pratinidhi Sabha, New Delhi, 1975 ed.

Sarkar, Sumit, 'Trends in Bengal's Swadeshi Movement (1903–1908),' in *Bengal, Past and Present,* Journal of the Calcutta Historical Society, vol. 84, Jan.–June 1965.

———, *The Swadeshi Movement in Bengal (1903–1908).* People's Publishing House, New Delhi, 1973.

———, 'Calcutta and the "Bengal Renaissance"', in Sukanta Chaudhuri (ed.), 1990.

Sarkar, S.C., 'Derozio and Young Bengal', in Atulchandra Gupta (ed.), *Studies in the Bengal Renaissance.* National Council of Education, Jadavpur, 1958.

———, *Tagore's Educational Philosophy and Experiment.* Visva Bharati, Santiniketan, 1961.

Scott, David C., *Keshub Chunder Sen.* The Christian Literature Society, Madras, 1979.

Seal, Anil, *The Emergence of Indian Nationalism: Competition and Collaboration in the Later Nineteenth Century.* Cambridge University Press, 1970.

Sen, Amiya P., *Hindu Revivalism in Bengal, 1872–1905: Some Essays in Interpretation.* Oxford University Press, Delhi, 1993.

Sen Dineshchandra, *The Bengali Ramayanas.* University of Calcutta, Calcutta, 1920.

Sen, S.P. (ed.), *Dictionary of National Biography,* vols.1ff. Institute of Historical Studies, Calcutta, 1974.

Seth, Mesrovb Jacob, *Armenians in India from the earliest times to the present day.* Published by the author, Calcutta, 1937.

Sharpe, E.J., *J.N. Farquhar: A Memoir.* YMCA, Calcutta, 1962.

———, *Not to Destroy but to Fulfil: The Contribution of J.N. Farquhar to Protestant Missionary Thought in India before 1914.* Swedish Institute of Missionary Research, Uppsala (Studia Missionalia Upsaliensia V), 1965.

———, *Faith Meets Faith.* SCM Press Ltd., 1977.

Simha, Prabodhcandra, *Upādhyāy Brahmabāndhab.* Published by Sri Amarendranath Cattopadhyay, Calcutta, n.d.

Smart, N. and S. Thakur (eds), *Ethical and Political Dilemmas of Modern India.* Macmillan, London, 1993.

Stanley, Brian, *The History of the Baptist Missionary Society: 1792–1992.* T. & T. Clark, Edinburgh, 1992.

Stokes, E., *The English Utilitarians and India.* The Clarendon Press, Oxford, 1959.

Stuart, James, *Swami Abhishiktananda: His Life Told through his letters.* ISPCK, Delhi, 1989.

Swahananda, Swami, *The Pañcadaśī of Śrī Vidyāraṇya Swāmī*, English translation. Sri Ramakrishna Math, Madras, 1980, 3rd ed.

Tagore, Rabindranath, *Cār Adhyāy*. Published by Sri Kisorimohan Satra, Bisvabharati Granthalay, Santiniketan, B.E. 1341 (C.E. 1934).

Tagore, Rathindranath, *On the Edges of Time*. Visva Bharati, Calcutta, 1981 (2nd ed.).

Thibaut, G., *The Vedānta Sūtras of Bādarāyaṇa with the Commentary by Śaṅkara* (translated by George Thibaut), Part I, *Sacred Books of the East*. Ed. Max Müller, vol. 34. Clarendon Press, Oxford, 1890.

Trautmann, Thomas R., *Aryans and British India*. University of California Press, 1997.

Trevelyan, Sir George O., *The Life and Letters of Lord Macaulay*. Longmans, Green & Co., London, 1901.

Turmes, P., *A Teacher of Genius: B. Animananda*. Xavier Publications, Calcutta, 1963.

———, 'The Founder of Jote', in *Jote* (Special Golden Jubilee Number, 1896–1946).

Vandana, Sister, *Gurus, Ashrams and Christians*. Darton, Longman & Todd, London, 1978.

Väth, Alfons, *Im Kampfe mit der Zauberwelt des Hinduismus: Upadhyay Brahmabandhav und das Problem der Überwindung des höheren Hinduismus durch das Christentum*. Ferd. Dummlers Verlag, Berlin & Bonn, 1928.

Vetticatil, Jose, 'Brahmabandhav Upadhyaya: A Hindu-Christian', *Jeevadhara*, July 1987.

Watzlawik, J., s.v.d., *Leo XIII and the New Scholasticism*. San Carlos Publications, The University of San Carlos, Cebu City, Philippines, 1966.

Wessinger, Catherine L., *Annie Besant and Progressive Messianism (1847–1933)*. The Edwin Mellen Press, Lewiston/Queenston, 1988.

Zacharias, H.C.E., *Renascent India: From Rammohan Roy to Mohandas Gandhi*. George Allen & Unwin Ltd., London, 1933.

Zaleski, L.M., *Epistolae ad Missionarios*. Mangalore, 1915.

# Index